NORTHWEST BEST PLACES

Restaurants, Lodgings, and Touring
in Oregon, Washington, and British Columbia

David Brewster
Stephanie Irving

Sasquatch Books
Seattle

Library of Congress Catalog Card Number LC88-655110

Contributors: Angela Allen, Carol Brown, Kim Carlson, Corbet Clark, David Cowan, Anne Depue, Sheri Doyle, Susan English, Richard Fencsak, Helen Gould, Sue Frause, Joan Gregory, Jan Halliday, Eve Johnson, Lauren Kessler, Ann Mellor Katzenbach, Lane Morgan, Tim Pawsey, Dave Preston, Kathryn Robinson, Kate Roosevelt, David Sarasohn, Jane Steinberg, Marilyn and Fred Tausend, Brooks Tish, Cleve Twitchell, Kasey Wilson, Kathy Witkowsky, Stephen Wong.

Assistant Editor: Emily Hall
Copy Editor: Don Roberts
Proofreader: Marianne Moon
Factchecker: Kate Ffolliott
Cover Design and Maps: Karen Schober
Interior Design: Lynne Faulk
Typesetting: Seattle Weekly

The *Best Places* guidebooks have been published continuously since 1975. Evaluations are based on numerous reports from locals and traveling inspectors. Final judgments are made by the editors. Our inspectors never identify themselves (except over the phone) and never take free meals or other favors. Readers are advised that places listed in previous editions may have closed or changed management or may no longer be recommended by this series. The editors welcome information conveyed by users of this book as long as they have no financial connection with the establishment concerned. A report form is provided at the end of the book. Contact us at the address below for a catalog of our regional books.

Sasquatch Books
1008 Western Avenue, Suite 300
Seattle, Washington 98104
(206) 467-4300

CONTENTS

Introduction

Northwest Best Places was born on a dare some twenty years ago. The dare was that there were enough quality restaurants in the Northwest to make a 300-page book. I had only an inkling that this might be true, stemming from my experience editing a monthly newsletter for restaurant fanciers in the Northwest called "A Gourmet's Notebook." After a couple of years, when I had maybe a third of a book in hand, Dan Levant of Madrona Publishers called to ask if I could round up more places, adding lodgings and a few travelers' notes to the recipe. It meant wandering into towns I had never heard of before, and then writing the first food-lover's guide to this region.

Sounded like fun, so off I went. I had one guide, and one epiphany, in mind. Years before, my wife and I had been touring England, eating abominably, when we came across the English guidebook *The Good Food Guide.* The book's intrepid band of reviewers had managed the impossible: finding excellent places for dining and lodging in the culinary wasteland of the English countryside. This little book made all the difference to our trip. I gratefully remembered its detailed descriptions of meals, which table to insist on, and why the tomato soup no longer impressed one of the volunteer inspectors. I had the model, I had the dare, and I had the curiosity about my adopted region of the country.

It was glorious fun researching the first *Best Places.* By asking the folks who lived in remote Northwest towns where they ate and where to find honest and friendly lodging, I began to experience firsthand the remarkable hospitality of the Northwest, then as now relatively unjaded from a surfeit of visitors. I glimpsed the incredible variety of landscape, foodstuffs, and traditions packed into this hot/cold, dry/wet, mountainous/maritime region. I saw how solid customs of craftsmanship, honest provisions, and respect for nature's bounty were fashioning a distinctive, country-based brand of cooking and tourism. I was on a Western gold rush, finding hidden nuggets almost every other day.

Dan Levant's publishing gamble worked. *Best Places* revealed a bounty under our noses, and sold very well. The nicest compliment I ever got came from a woman who told me that, while home with the flu, she actually read the book cover to cover and thereby learned that it was not just a guidebook but an exploration of the values and history of the Northwest. Other gratifying moments came when restaurants, discovered by the entire region thanks to the book, reported that they could now stay alive and keep their standards higher than a purely local clientele could support. Hundreds told me, with touching gratitude, that *Best Places*, like that English guidebook for us in 1967, had simply made their vacation.

Much has changed in these two decades, of course, particularly in the big cities. Northwest cuisine, adapted from California and pan-Asian cooking, has come and somewhat faded. Bed and breakfasts, virtually unknown except in places like Ashland and Victoria in earlier days, have spread like mushrooms. Service has gotten more manipulative and hard-eyed. Smallish hotels have enjoyed a renaissance. Cross-country skiing has extended the typically short season of country tourism, enabling remote places to invest more optimistically in their facilities. Something like a Northwest romantic tradition has been created around country and island getaways. A book that began as a dare threatens to become a lifestyle.

Mostly, though, I am struck by how much that was enduring and distinctive in that first gathering of gold remains that way. Most places are still a good value. Greetings are still normally and disarmingly genuine, from people who take real interest in folks passing through. Franchises still have trouble catching on out here, since people want non-generic, individually accented experiences. Without a real cuisine of our own, we celebrate the whole world's cooking. And always, the true accent of our Northwest experience shines through: it feels best when establishments draw closest to nature—in view, in setting, in ingredients.

By now, hundreds of reviewers have roamed these roads, finding and re-inspecting our Best Places. It's exhausting work. Frustrating, too, since we must keep our distance and anonymity among people we'd love to thank and befriend. But for all of us, it remains a loving labor—a privilege, never a chore.

—*David Brewster*

ABOUT THE *BEST PLACES* GUIDES

Sasquatch Books' *Best Places* series is unique in that the guidebooks are written by and for locals, and are therefore also coveted by visitors. Our books are designed for Northwesterners who enjoy exploring the bounty of this region, who like out-of-the-way places of high character and individualism, and who take the time to seek out such places. Paradoxically, those very characteristics make the *Best Places* guides ideal for tourists, too. The best places in the region are the ones that denizens favor: independently owned places of good value, touched with local history, run by lively individualists, and graced with natural beauty.

What makes our guidebooks different? Our knowledgeable reviewers both re-evaluate the old favorites and seek out new discoveries. All visits are anonymous; we accept no free meals, accommodations, or other complimentary services. This allows us to be tough and candid about places that have rested too long on their laurels and frees us to delight in new places whose efforts have paid off. Our forthright reviews rate establishments on a scale of zero to four and describe the true strengths, foibles, and unique characteristics of each.

Here is the new 20th anniversary edition of *Northwest Best Places*, the grandfather of all regional guides, thoroughly researched and including hundreds of new finds. This wealth of honest reviews and frank reports will arm travelers with the information they need: where to go and when, what to order, which rooms to request (and which to avoid). And for the first time ever, we're betting on your satisfaction with a money-back guarantee (for more information, see the back page).

How to Use This Book

Reviews are listed alphabetically within each star rating. We rate establishments based on value, performance measured against goals, uniqueness, and professionalism of service. Our evaluations are based on numerous reports from local and traveling inspectors. Final judgments are made by the editors. Our inspectors never identify themselves (except over the phone) and never accept free meals or other favors.

(no stars) Worth knowing about if nearby

★ A good place

★★ Excellent; some wonderful qualities

★★★ Distinguished; many outstanding features

★★★★ The very best in the region

[*unrated*] New or undergoing major changes

 A new symbol created for this edition to congratulate those establishments that were in David Brewster's original edition of *Northwest Best Places*

ᕑ Wheelchair-accessible facilities

Price Range Prices are based on high-season rates. Prices throughout the British Columbia section are in Canadian dollars.

$$$ Expensive (more than $80 for dinner for two; more than $90 for lodgings for two)

$$ Moderate (between expensive and inexpensive)

$ Inexpensive (less than $30 for dinner for two; less than $60 for lodgings for two)

Checks and Credit Cards Most establishments that accept checks also require a major credit card for identification. American Express is abbreviated as AE, Diners Club as DC, Discover as DIS, MasterCard as MC, and VISA as V. In British Columbia there are two more cards that are often used: Enroute (abbreviated as E) and a Japanese credit card known as JCB.

Maps and Directions Each section in this book begins with a regional map that shows the towns being covered. Throughout the book are town maps, and basic directions are provided with each entry. Whenever possible, call ahead to confirm hours and location.

Reader Reports At the end of the book is a report form. We receive hundreds of these reports from readers suggesting new finds or agreeing or disagreeing with our assessments. They greatly help in our evaluations. We encourage you to respond.

Index All restaurants, lodgings, and town names and some tourist attractions are listed alphabetically at the back of the book.

OREGON

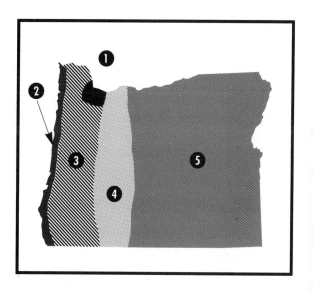

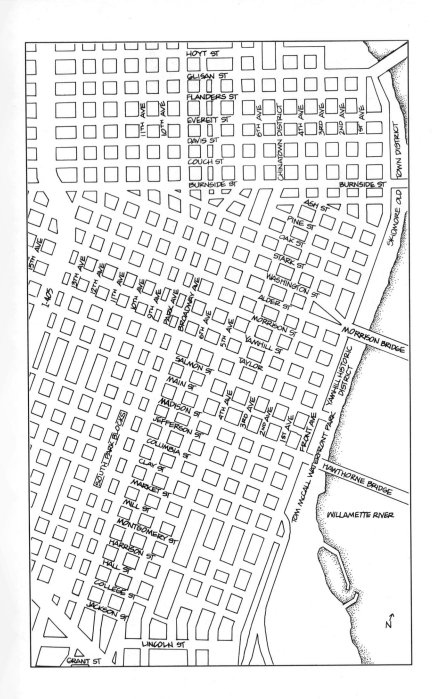

Portland and Environs

Including outlying areas: Forest Grove, Beaverton, and Tigard to the west, Lake Oswego to the south, Milwaukie to the southeast, and Gresham to the east.

PORTLAND

For decades, Portlanders worked hard to make the Rose City a great place to live, and by almost every measure they've succeeded. With its plethora of parks, its charming downtown core, its splendid westside riverfront, and its proximity to so many of Oregon's finest diversions, Portland is a gem. Now the secret's out, and Portlanders are bracing for dramatic population growth. Still, there's every reason to think that this city can hold on to those ideals that have made it great.

It's easy to see what makes Portland such a sought-after place. During the past few years, it has acquired a nationally noted light-rail service, which soon will be greatly expanded; a small jewel of a downtown performing arts center (with a resident company from the Oregon Shakespeare Festival); a downtown shopping complex starring Saks Fifth Avenue; a major convention center; and stunning new digs for its science museum, Oregon Museum of Science and Industry. The downtown riverfront development on the west side has become so popular that visionaries have since moved to match it on the east bank by attempting to relocate Interstate 5.

Portlanders insist that their city must not become a place only for networking or catching planes to other places, but

must remain a city for living. What they prize about their town
is not its per capita income but its rivers, its neighborhoods, its
waterfront festivals, its microbreweries, and its Trailblazers.
Like any city, Portland has its flaws but, better than most, it's
able to meet them head on.

Below is a glimpse of Portland (followed by reviews of its
top restaurants and lodgings); for a more comprehensive city
guide, see our series companion, *Portland Best Places*.

THE ARTS

Music. Nothing has ever done so much for this city's aural
offerings as the Arlene Schnitzer Concert Hall. Portlanders
pack the place 52 weeks a year. Besides the essential house
"given"—the Oregon Symphony Orchestra, under conductor
James DePreist—the "Schnitz" has expanded Portland's musical agenda significantly; (503) 248-4496. Chamber Music
Northwest presents a five-week-long summer festival spanning
four centuries of music; (503) 223-3202.

Theater. Neighboring Schnitzer Hall is the Center for
Performing Arts, which contains two performance spaces. Its
full-time resident company, the Oregon Shakespeare Festival
Portland, is a northern offshoot of the acclaimed festival in Ashland. OSF's season runs the gamut from Chekov to August Wilson to the Bard himself. You can always be assured of work by
Shakespeare with productions by Tygres Heart, (503) 222-9220,
housed in the same facility. The Portland Repertory Theater,
(503) 224-4491, puts on dependable productions in a theater
just off Front Street. Musicals of any caliber land at the Portland Civic (home of the Portland Opera).

Visual Arts. The Portland art scene continues to grow.
Gallery walks on the first Thursday of every month have encouraged the expansion of that community: The Portland Art
Museum, Augen, Blue Sky, Quartersaw, Blackfish, Elizabeth
Leach, Jamison/Thomas, Pulliam Deffenbaugh Nugent, and
Laura Russo are among the hot showcases of both local and national work. The city is popping with public art, too; just start
watching for it. Pioneer Courthouse Square is a good place to
begin any search.

Dance. The Oregon Ballet Theater enlists youth and daring to serve the needs of Portland's ballet fans; (503) 227-6867.
Nancy Matchek's Contemporary Dance Season at Portland
State University brings in the hottest out-of-town dance action,
(503) 725-3131, and probably the most creative productions are
performed by Oslund and Company, (503) 236-3265.

Literature. Besides Powell's, the superpower of used (and
new) bookstores, Portland has a flock of other strong hard-
cover contenders, including Conant and Conant, for academic
titles; the Catbird Seat, in the center of the city; Annie Bloom's

Books, especially for Judaica; and Murder by the Book, which is to mysteries what Powell's is to everything else. Any of these, or a local church or college, might on any day be presenting readings by local or visiting writers. Portland Arts and Lectures produces a series of lectures by nationally known literary figures, and although tickets are scarce, you might get lucky; (503) 241-0543.

Architecture. Portland's downtown skyline has become dramatically sophisticated in recent years. In March 1991, the American Institute of Architecture presented its most prestigious National Honor Award to Zimmer Gunsul Frasca's (ZGF) Convention Center, with its distinctive illuminated twin towers. Other outstanding buildings include Pietro Belluschi's glass-box Equitable Building, Michael Graves' controversial post-modern Portland Building, Will Martin's swank, complexly designed Pioneer Courthouse Square, A.E. Doyle's spectacularly ornate Old US Bank Building, ZGF's KOIN Center and its blue-reflective One Financial Center, and the city's most recent architectural entry, Broome, Oringdulth, O'Toole, Rudolf, Boles and Associates' 1000 Broadway, distinguished by its copper-colored glass and white illuminated dome.

OTHER THINGS TO DO

Nightlife. Although the jazz scene has diminished in recent years—the result of fewer venues that regularly offer jazz—there are still many goings-on each night. Check local newspapers' calendar listings (*Willamette Week* is out each Wednesday; the *Oregonian*'s entertainment section is in Friday's paper). The Portland Art Museum is an unusual hot spot; its After Hours gigs are each Wednesday evening. Rock fans get their best licks at Key Largo, LaLuna, and the Roseland. Music on or past the edge—and followers of the same—can be found at Satyricon or the X-Ray Cafe, both in Old Town.

Sports. The town's only big-league action is the Portland Trailblazers basketball team. While they usually manage to make the playoffs, the Blazers have a penchant for fizzling in the finals; (503) 234-9291. The Winter Hawks, member of the Western Hockey League, hit the ice 72 times a season in Memorial Coliseum; (503) 238-6366. Individual sports thrive: runners have access to over 50 manicured miles of trail in the 5,000-acre Forest Park complex; rowers are guaranteed miles of flat water on the Willamette; and bicyclists use more than 100 miles of off-street paved bike path in the greater Portland area.

Parks and Gardens. Besides the sprawling and primitive Forest Park, there are nearly 150 other parks in the city. The Hoyt Arboretum, close to the Washington Park Zoo, has the most impressive collection of native and exotic flora, as well as the best-kept trails. More formalized grounds are the International

Rose Test Garden, the Japanese Gardens, and the Crystal Springs Rhododendron Gardens. The World Forestry Center Building, also next to the zoo, has ongoing displays worth checking. And the largest memorial of its kind in the nation, the Vietnam Veterans' Living Memorial, is an inspiring outdoor cathedral commemorating the Oregon victims of that conflict; call Washington Park for more information, (503) 796-5274.

Shopping. Crafts and renaissance-style goods can be found weekends at Saturday Market under the Burnside Bridge; upscale specialty shops and eateries are found at Pioneer Place, the Water Tower at John's Landing, and Lloyd Center. Northwest Portland's 23rd Avenue and SE Hawthorne Boulevard between 35th and 45th feature great neighborhood merchants; NE Broadway and Multnomah (in Southwest Portland) are up-and-comers in the neighborhood shopping scene. Antiques are found in Sellwood, in the city's southeast corner.

Transportation. The city's public transportation system, Tri-Met, runs throughout the metropolitan area and is free in the downtown core area. The light-rail system, MAX, is a speedy conduit to the east side, going as far as Gresham. Once a day, Amtrak heads north, south, and east. Plans are under way for a west-moving rail line, which should be completed in the next few years. The airport (PDX) is a $20 cab ride (or less than half that on shuttle buses from major hotels). Parking meters must be fed even on Saturdays in Portland.

RESTAURANTS

Genoa ★★★★ Portland's love affair with Genoa shows no sign of fading after more than two decades. The restaurant is nestled in a Southeast Portland residential neighborhood not normally associated with extravagance (passersby gawk as a limousine waits for three hours to whisk away a dinner party), but understated elegance is what you expect behind these four walls. High on indulgences but low on light, Genoa is best known for its exquisite Northern Italian dinners served over the course of an entire evening. Four longtime employees took over the restaurant a while back, but besides that switch—unnoticeable to most patrons—little has changed in recent years.

An evening here goes something like this: an appetizer (maybe fresh asparagus with a garlicky mayonnaise and a whisper slice of prosciutto) arrives soon after you sit down. Then through the next few hours come, perhaps, a saffron-inflected fish soup, ribbons of pasta with morels, a well-dressed salad, your entrée (maybe pheasant scented with grappa, lemon, and rosemary, or prized Copper River king salmon cooked in a reduction of leeks and shallots and topped with plump caramelized onions and pancetta), your dessert (the showstopper is the boccone dolce, a layering of meringue, chocolate, berries, and whipped cream), and finally, passed around the table, a plate of perfectly ripened fruit. Not all of the seven courses will be spectacular, but a couple will certainly be, and the rest will be very good. You can count on the well-informed waiters to keep the evening moving along with seasoned professionalism—and seemingly little effort. In the end, there is scarcely room for anything more but conversation, and there's a well-cushioned parlor beyond the dining room for that. An abridged version of the dinner is served at 5:30pm and 6pm for those who don't have all night. ■ *NE 29th and Belmont; (503) 238-1464; 2832 SE Belmont St, Portland; $$$; wine only; AE, DC, MC, V; checks OK; dinner Mon-Sat. &*

The Heathman Restaurant and Bar ★★★★ Greg Higgins has now consolidated his sole command of the kitchen here, and the Heathman's position atop the Pacific Northwest food chain is even more entrenched. Salmon, venison, and Muscovy duck decorate the menu, gilded with local wild mushrooms or hazelnuts along with—in the roundest definition of Pacific Rim—Thai and Sichuan flavors plus ancho chiles and other inspirations of the Southwest. You might also find yourself facing a pungent Brazilian black bean stew, but the kitchen goes particularly deeply into local resources: a green salad here can offer shades of green you've never noticed before. Sommelier John Poston, fortuitously returned from New York, pours from Portland's largest Oregon wine list.

Breakfast is served in an elegant setting, with great attention to taste and detail. King salmon hash is an impressive justification of a Multnomah morning. Eggs Benedict takes on a Northwest flavor, with smoked salmon replacing the ham; cornmeal cakes with fresh blueberry compote take griddle food to new heights. The bar, a rich, glinting affair of marble and brass, features tapas and a fine selection of Portland's best microbrews, and the library—with fireplace and grand piano—reinvents afternoon tea. ■ *Salmon and SW Broadway; (503) 241-4100; 1009 SW Broadway, Portland; $$$; full bar; AE, DC, MC, V; checks OK; breakfast, lunch, dinner every day. &*

 L'Auberge ★★★★ Some people date the final triumph of what Julia Child calls the food police to the recent day when L'Auberge began offering à la carte dinners. For 20 years, after all, this restaurant had promoted a classic three-hour, six-course meal, from pâté to patisserie; now the place is open to (shudder) nibblers. But there's no real reason to panic. The dinners—and the shrimp quenelles, and the filet mignon with onion marmalade, and the poached lemon cheesecake—are still available and are still among the most satisfying and artistic in town. And on some occasions—such as a theater evening or the night of a really good "Cheers" rerun—you too might try to make a meal of just an ethereal vichyssoise and tender duck pieces in a blackberry demiglace. Just don't let it become a habit.

And then there's the L'Auberge bar. This softly lit den of elegant rusticity and upscale hipness has a well-stoked hearth in winter, a homey outdoor dining deck in summer, and, in all seasons, a witty, personable staff. The bar is easily the most relaxing and attractive retreat in town. Changing every two weeks, June Reznikoff's bar menu is replete with great finds, such as pork medallions in chipotle pepper sauce and a salad of wild edible greens cultivated on a farm in southern Oregon. Sunday night means classic movies, terrific ribs, and what can only be called haute cuisine cheeseburgers. ■ *26th and Vaughn; (503) 223-3302; 2601 NW Vaughn St, Portland; $$$; full bar; AE, DC, DIS, MC, V; local checks only; dinner every day; Sunday, bar menu only.* &

Zefiro ★★★★ Zefiro blew into town a few years ago and swept Rose City restaurant-goers off their sensibly shod feet. It's not for everyone (it's anything but intimate, for instance), but Portlanders who love it love it with an enthusiasm that's usually reserved for the likes of the Trailblazers or Packy the elephant. Since the day it opened, the quality of the often changing menu has been highly consistent, the servers are among the most polished and informed in town, and the humming, gold-tinged atmosphere is as vibrant as a sunny day. (No wonder people flock here.) The three owners strive for perfection in every aspect of their operation, and their efforts have gotten them attention in places like *Gourmet* and *The Atlantic*. But even without the national media hype, Zefiro stands apart as the most intriguing restaurant in town.

The menu offers unusual takes on grilled fish and pastas, with influences ranging from Morocco to Italy to Thailand. The signatures include a creamy, inviting risotto with different ingredients based on season and whim; a crisp, well-dressed caesar salad for two; and chewy, intoxicating bread. The desserts are understated and divine—the chocolate and vanilla pots de crème remind one of the artistic power of black and white. Zefiro's bar area—a good bet if a reservation is not to be had—has the same particle-board-gone-fashionable interior as the dining room. ■ *Corner of NW 21st and Glisan; (503) 226-3394; 500 NW 21st, Portland; $$$; full bar; AE, DC, MC, V; local checks only; lunch Mon-Fri, dinner Mon-Sat (closed late Jan-early Feb).* &

Atwater's ★★★ After more than a year in charge of Portland's highest-altitude eatery, chef Mark Gould's hands seem even more seasoned. Arriving from Chicago, Gould took rapidly to Northwestern and Pacific ingredients, with impressive self-introductions such as grilled ahi tuna in a sesame crust in hot oil, and cured salmon with shiitake "chopsticks" in egg-roll wrappings. The menu changes every season, but continues its reliance on Northwest seafood, game, and wild mushrooms, and Gould seems quite intrigued by Asian connections. You can easily spend a lot of money here—especially if you get lost in the thick, leatherbound wine list. But the three-course dinner for $26 is a bargain, and you can also explore a five-course weekly dinner with specially selected wines. The all-you-can-eat Sunday brunch buffet has been a particular hit, tables groaning with a vast assortment of traditional and contemporary items, chefs whipping up omelets, and only a few steam-table perennials. The 30th-story space itself is worth a visit: there's an etched-glass wine cellar in the middle of the peachtone dining room and hundreds of miles of Oregon and Washington stretching out beyond the windows. ■ *Off Burnside on 5th; (503) 275-3600; 111 SW 5th Ave, Portland; $$$; full bar; AE, DC, DIS, MC, V; no checks; dinner every day, brunch Sun.* &

Briggs and Crampton ★★★ OK, you've heard this before—or seen it in *People* or on "Good Morning America" or in *The Wall Street Journal*—but let's go through it once again. Briggs and Crampton has just one table, serving one lunch for two, four days a week. The process sounds like a tax audit procedure: you phone at the beginning of the first business day of the quarter, and you can book a date sometime in the next quarter—if you connect before 9:30am. Even the price, now at $75 for two (before wine or tip), hasn't slowed the phones. But when you call for a reservation, don't ask what's for lunch; they won't have a clue. Every day's new menu is built around what's local and fresh that day. One day that meant chilled prawn and buttermilk soup, wild green salad, blackberry sorbet, grilled spring chinook with red pepper and garlic butter and roast garlic pudding, coffee and walnut bread, and dense chocolate torte. Nancy Briggs and Juanita Crampton's restaurant acts as a playground for their true passion—catering. ■ *Montgomery Park between Thurman and Vaughn; (503) 223-8690; 1902 NW 24th Ave, Portland; $$$; beer and wine; MC, V; checks OK; lunch Tues-Fri (by appointment only).*

Cafe des Amis ★★★ If Cafe des Amis offered nothing but the three upscale pillars of its menu —a filet mignon in port garlic sauce that could convert a vegetarian, salmon in sorrel, and duck in a zippy blackberry sauce that could put oranges out of work—it would still have a strong claim to a place among Portland's best. But the restaurant has recently returned to its down-home French cafe roots, so the upscale entrées share menu space with reasonably priced soups and hearty stews, such as an $8 spring lamb stew and a $10.50 cioppino. All options are promising; chef Dennis Baker's ways with soups suggest he may be the missing Campbell Kid. Add a salad with toasted walnuts, a basket of terrific oven-fresh French rolls, and one of the many bottles of good wine, and you have the makings of a light but satisfying meal. The dessert tray always merits serious consideration—seriously consider any fruit tart—and you can rely on the serving staff to assess the day's offerings candidly. ▪ *Corner of 20th and NW Kearney; (503) 295-6487; 1987 NW Kearney St, Portland; $$; full bar; AE, MC, V; checks OK; dinner Mon-Sat.* ⌖

Esparza's Tex-Mex ★★★ Esparza's is now even more crowded since winning the *Oregonian*'s Restaurant of the Year last year. Lots more people waiting out by the jukebox stocked with thousands of classic rock and country singles. People staring at the thickly displayed decorations—cowboy movie posters and puppets, in a style that might be called 1950s Texas Soda Fountain Goes Crazy—and most important, studying the specials list. Is Esparza's tonight offering the Gene Autry or the Annie Oakley, the smoked tongue or the calf's brain tacos? If Joe Esparza had brought to Portland nothing but his smoked brisket, it alone would make him a welcome arrival. Instead, he's overthrown all of the area's ideas about Tex-Mex, bringing freshness and clarity to everything from smoked chicken in mole sauce to the basic tacos and enchiladas, which turn out not to be basic at all. Everything gets a lot of help from dazzling, utterly fresh tortillas, which have the body and aroma of a Mexican crumpet. Portions are vast; prices aren't. So far, however, it must be said that Esparza's ideas on interior design have not spread. ▪ *Burnside and SE 28th; (503) 234-7909; 2725 SE Ankeny, Portland; $$; full bar; MC, V; no checks; lunch, dinner Tues-Sat.*

Indigine ★★★ Beloved by many, Indigine is low-key in the best sense of the expression, but don't make the mistake of walking in off the street without a reservation. Portlanders who are serious about food fill up this intimate wooden nest on Division, where impressive multicourse dinners are to be had for less than $20. The chief ingredient here is owner/chef Millie Howe, whose maverick style and obsession with quality guarantee that nothing here will be routine or prepackaged. Saturdays are reserved for a blowout East Indian feast that starts with something unexpected, perhaps mango mousse and homemade goat cheese in phyllo. There's a choice of entrées, typically a searing rabbit vindaloo, lamb curry, seafood curry, or a collection of vegetarian options. Howe's stunning chutneys are served on the side. You can get East Indian food during the week, too; the other offerings have Latin American, European, or Pacific Northwest overtones: roast chicken stuffed beneath its skin with wild, garlicky pesto, or roast pork smothered with spicy pinto beans. There are usually a half dozen dessert offerings, including a boccone dolce that will send you away purring. ■ *In Hawthorne neighborhood; (503) 238-1470; 3725 SE Division St, Portland; $$; beer and wine; MC, V; checks OK; dinner Tues-Sat.* &

La Mirabelle ★★★ Since Robert Kincaid journeyed up from the Bay Area to open the jewel-box-size La Mirabelle, he has operated on a policy of uncompromising classic French cuisine. Kincaid is not one for nouvelle or Northwest deviationism; he believes in cassoulet and cream sauces and tuxedoed waiters who say "Bonjour." More important, he makes it all work and recently has made one small accommodation; his prices have gotten slightly lower. Starting with a dazzlingly flaky onion tart, through duck with blackcurrant sauce or rack of lamb to tarte Tatin or gâteau de mousse au chocolat, the food is likely to be consistently impressive. It is also, in line with haute classicism, likely to be consistently rich, but it is all so pretty to look at that you might not even notice. In two tiny dining rooms, the tables are barely a croissant's distance apart, but when you call for a reservation—essential, and with some notice—request the front room. ■ *Between Jefferson and Salmon; (503) 223-7113; 1126 SW 18th Ave, Portland; $$$; beer and wine; MC, V; checks OK; dinner Wed-Sat.*

McCormick & Schmick's Seafood Restaurant ★★★ The interstate McCormick & Schmick's restaurant empire, of which this place is the eponymous flagship, grows regularly; recent additions have included huge new outposts in Los Angeles and San Francisco. Overseeing the multiple menus is Bill King, former executive chef here, and the kitchen he left behind is still a firm foundation. McCormick & Schmick's has outstripped its big brother Jake's—with which it shares a daily, 30-item fresh list—in consistency and imagination. It does consistently interesting things with sturgeon, yellowfin tuna, and, when the season is right, Dungeness crab. But it also has its own specialties, such as grilled smoked salmon—the alder smoke can be smelled two MAX stops away—and impressive selections of fresh oysters. All of it can be started—or finished—with a dose from the restaurant's unique single-malt Scotch list. ■ *Oak and 1st; (503) 224-7522; 235 SW 1st Ave, Portland; $$; full bar; AE, DC, DIS, MC, V; checks OK; lunch Mon-Fri, dinner every day.* &

Pazzo Ristorante ★★★ It hasn't taken long for this classy uptown eatery to win the affection of Portlanders and the attention of more out-of-towners than just those staying at the Hotel Vintage Plaza next door. Chef David Machado runs a consistently interesting kitchen. Upstairs, the busy brick dining room is one option; you can also eat in the bar, with garlic and whatnot hanging overhead. The most romantic choice, on Thursday, Friday, and Saturday nights, is the fragrant wine cellar downstairs. Highlights of the menu include fish grilled over wood fires, designer pizzas, unusual pastas including a suave seafood risotto, and the day's specials, recited in reverent detail at tableside. This is a kitchen with confidence—an upscale pork chop, jeweled with currants, arrives with garlicky, ricotta-smoothed mashed potatoes. To start, the grilled radicchio with goat cheese is a gem, and throughout the meal you can dip the house breads in opulent extra-virgin olive oil. Semifreddo—chocolate cake, mocha mousse, and something like magic—is worth saving space for. Count on the service to be forthright and attentive. ▪ *Downtown, corner of Broadway and Washington; (503) 228-1515; 627 SW Washington St, Portland; $$; full bar; AE, DC, DIS, MC, V; checks OK; breakfast, lunch, dinner every day.* ♿

Ron Paul Charcuterie ★★★ With the imminent opening of a third branch, Ron Paul has Portland nearly covered—good news for the cultlike following the place attracts. His room-to-move-about restaurant over in Portland's exploding NE Broadway area followed the smashing success of the longtime cafe and catering headquarters on NW 23rd Avenue. Now Ron Paul on Macadam Boulevard will bring its assorted charcuterie to the John's Landing area. There's a new chef, Mark Bernetich, over from the Heathman, who has fine-tuned an already impressive menu, adding specials such as wild mushroom ravioli carbonara dotted with chunks of the house pancetta and a caesar salad that rivals any in town. Dinner is served with a basket of delicious specialty breads; don't overlook the rich, dark walnut wheat. Ultra-chocolatey Black Angus cookies and a strawberry tart are fine choices from a dessert menu of more than two dozen possibilities. Quality control here is an obvious priority: the kitchen cures the salmon, smokes the sausages, and mixes the pâtés. If there's a complaint, it would be that the service is not always on a par with the food. ▪ *1441 NE Broadway and 15th; (503) 284-5347.* ♿ ▪ *Everett St and NW 23rd; (503) 223-2121; 2310 NW Everett St, Portland; $$; beer and wine; MC, V; checks OK; breakfast Sat-Sun, lunch, dinner every day.* ♿

Westmoreland Bistro ★★★ When hotshot Seattle chef Caprial Pence (Fullers) and her husband, John, wanted to get off the fast track, they landed in Portland's Westmoreland neighborhood—and the track there is now a good deal faster. After more than a year, word has gotten out, and the creativity that once concentrated on dinners has now spread to lunches. The blackboard menu changes constantly, but it consistently offers upscale inspiration and storefront prices. Start with smoked tomato salsa bruschetta, and then look for something like the braised rabbit with saffron, or a deft noodle dish called Hot-as-Hell Chicken—which is. Wines are available from the sizable retail wine supply, and a $2 corkage fee gets any bottle from the shelf to your table. Desserts are serious, and while a projected bakery is now on hold while the chefs embark on a cable TV project, there's no reason to think the imagination is going to give out. ■ *Across from U.S. Bank; (503) 236-6457; 7015 SW Milwaukie Ave, Portland; $$; beer and wine; MC, V; checks OK; lunch, dinner Tues-Sat.*

Yen Ha West ■ Yen Ha East ★★ Bach Tuyet is widely considered the top Vietnamese chef in Portland, even working out of a building that still looks like a Mexican restaurant. From sticky rice to rice stick, Tuyet does remarkable things, especially with chicken and seafood, and occasionally with something as unVietnamese as venison. That's not meant to omit the beef classic, bo nuong vi. For this amazing do-it-yourself dish, you plunge slivers of marinated beef into a pool of hot oil on a stove placed on your table. Once cooked to taste, the beef is wrapped with assorted fresh greens and mint in a pliable, edible rice skin. A frisky anchovy sauce is the finishing touch, bringing out all of the succulent package's exotic flavor. Try the barbecued chicken or the best spring rolls around. The menu is enormous, so you might just suggest that Tuyet order for you.

Ever since Duck Van Tran inherited the original Yen Ha from his celebrated culinary cousin, he's steadily expanded the menu. The service and execution are not quite up to Tuyet's standards—but they're still better than most Vietnamese operations. Try the Lau seafood—multiple marine materials in a hot-and-sour broth over noodles, the succulent salt-fried Dungeness crab in tangy sauce, or the hot pot with seafood, vegetables, and Asian exotica. ■ *West Portland on SW Canyon Rd; (503) 292-0616; 8640 SW Canyon Rd, Portland; $$; full bar; MC, V; no checks; lunch, dinner every day.* &. ■ *Near Sandy and NE 67th Ave; (503) 287-3698; 6820 NE Sandy Blvd, Portland; $; beer and wine; MC, V; checks OK; lunch, dinner every day.* &.

Al Amir ★★ After years of successful operation, Al Amir has not only become the most prominent Middle Eastern restaurant in Portland, but redecoration is even beginning to overcome the episcopal aura of Bishop's House. Middle Eastern decor and rugs have made the place a more fitting home for dishes such as pungent kabobs; kharouf muammar, a huge pile of moist, faintly sweet lamb chunks; and dujaj musahab, a charcoal-grilled chicken breast in lemon and olive oil. New variations, generally successful, appear on the menu from time to time, and holding everything together are pools of creamy, nutty-flavored hummus. Soups are deep and rich, the baklava sticks with you. Service can be a bit casual and vague—diners might want to bring something suitable for waving—but the food is strong, consistent, and reasonably priced. ■ *Between*

*2nd and 3rd, downtown; (503) 274-0010; 223 SW Stark St,
Portland; $$; full bar; AE, MC, V; local checks only; lunch
Mon-Fri, dinner every day. &*

Alexis ★★ You want intimacy, or you want action? You want
a hearty meal, or you want just to nibble on some of the best
calamari in town? This spacious, white-walled Greek eatery sat-
isfies several longings at once. There's never a dearth of ac-
tivity, from lawyers' conventions to Old World folk dancing to
Aurelia, the region's hottest Middle Eastern dancer. The little
taverna, tucked away on the first floor, is an easy place to linger
over a glass of retsina and a plate of olives. And the food in the
dining rooms—upstairs or down—is worth hanging around
for: it's authentic and of consistently high quality. It's easy to
find the makings of a meal in the appetizers, but you might
want to try the bronzed oregano chicken dinner, full of robust
flavors. Plan to dip into everything with the sensational house
bread, which, along with some of the menu items, is available
in Portland food stores. Members of the Alexis Bakouros fam-
ily and their loyal staff patrol the premises with professional-
ism. This is a place to come back to—whatever you're in the
mood for. ■ *Between 2nd and 3rd on Burnside; (503) 224-
8577; 215 W Burnside, Portland; $$; full bar; AE, DC, DIS,
MC, V; checks OK; lunch Mon-Fri, dinner every day. &*

B. Moloch/The Heathman Bakery and Pub ★★ This is one of
the few places in town where everyone—from budget-minded
PSU students to frazzled tourists to boisterous toddlers to
wheeling lawyers—can lunch comfortably in the same attractive, high-ceilinged, window-walled room. It is also one of the
few places where you stand in line to order, pay $12.95 for a
special (although there are many items priced considerably
less than that), and then hope a table is ready before your entrée is. One of the big attractions is a 25-ton wood-burning brick
oven, embellished with a copper hood and old Dutch tiles,
where some of the city's best pizzas and breads are born. A pepperoni pizza, dotted with rounds of homemade pepperoni, is a
tribute to the classic pie; the pizza with bay shrimp, roasted red
peppers, and feta is a Northwest spin on the classic pie.
Salmon, peppered ham, and sun-dried tomatoes are cured in a
cold-smoker in back of the massive baking furnace, and the
smell mingles with the pungent aromas from the Widmer microbrew pub that sits beyond the restaurant. Breakfasts are a
little slower paced. ■ *At the north end of the South Park Blocks;
(503) 227-5700; 901 SW Salmon St, Portland; $$; beer and
wine; AE, DC, DIS, MC, V; checks OK; breakfast, lunch, din-
ner every day. &*

Bangkok Kitchen ★★ Don't hesitate, just go in. Outstanding
food makes up for the dearth of decor and the less-than-opu-
lent setting. The authentic Thai offerings and the wacky good

humor of owner/chef Srichan Miller and her family usually have the place jammed. They come for the heat treatment—the array of searing house soups, peanut sauces, and salads of fresh shrimp and lime. One of the popular specials is a whole fried fish covered in a feverish chile paste and deeply sautéed peppers, all decorated with basil leaves and other artful trimmings. If you want good food at decent prices—and are in no particular hurry—this is the ticket. ▪ *Corner of Belmont and 26th; (503) 236-7349; 2534 SE Belmont St, Portland; $; beer and wine; no credit cards; local checks only; lunch Tues-Fri, dinner Tues-Sat.*

Basta's ★★ Some think happy hour is this trattoria's finest hour. We think it may be lunch, when fragrant loaves of bread the size of bed pillows are stacked two by two on the cooler near the front door, and the proprietor comes around to chat about the day's specials. Pasta is not the strongest attraction here, but try the risotto—one day mingling beautifully with bits of spinach, chicken, and fresh herbs. You'll usually do well, too, with the entrées such as lamb stew or specials such as an herby grilled salmon. Prices are low enough for you to take some risks, and when you get to a dessert such as the espresso chocolate mousse—actually more of a pot de crème—any misjudgments you may have made earlier won't matter so much. The owners have done a terrific job of rehabilitating a former fast-food place; there's even a new patio that has no playground equipment. ▪ *At 21st and Glisan; (503) 274-1572; 410 NW 21st Ave, Portland; $$; full bar; MC, V; checks OK; lunch Mon-Sat, dinner every day.* &

Berbati ★★ Although competition among Greek restaurants is stiff in Berbati's neighborhood, this spirited Aegean eatery shines, in part because of the warm welcome you'll receive by members of the Papaioannou family and their cadre of amiable servers. The food holds it own, too, with careful preparation and brilliant, robust flavors. Ladle a mass of garlicky tzatziki onto the house's warm, crusty whole-wheat bread; among the other stars are a moist lemon oregano chicken and inviting tender octopus. There's an unexpectedly strong wine list and dessert tray for a Greek restaurant, and the cheesecake is nothing like feta. On arty First Thursdays, the place is packed with gallery-goers; on weekends there's live music in the bar. ▪ *1 block south of Burnside on 2nd; (503) 226-2122; 19 SW 2nd Ave, Portland; $$; full bar; AE, DC, DIS, MC, V; local checks only; lunch Tues-Fri, dinner Tues-Sun.*

BJ's Brazilian Restaurant ★★ Portland's first Brazilian restaurant offers reasonably good, moderately priced versions of specialties such as bacalhoada (dried codfish) and feijoada (a black bean and pork stew). Chicken dishes, such as one baked in dark beer and red palm oil—we're a long way from Kentucky

Fried—are also admirable, along with appetizers of small, deepfried meat pies called pastels. In the low-key storefront atmosphere, decorated with little more than a poster on the wall, everything comes with rice, a grain dish called farofa, and a mixture of chopped cilantro and red pepper that can and should be spooned on everything in sight. Even with a huge bottle of an intense dark Brazilian beer called Xin Gu, you haven't spent $40 for two. ■ *A half block off Bybee on Milwaukie; (503) 236-9629; 7019 SE Milwaukie Ave, Portland; $$; beer and wine; MC, V; checks OK; lunch, dinner Mon-Sat.* &

Brasserie Montmartre ★★ Right in the middle of downtown, Brasserie Montmartre is a number of different restaurants, many of them fairly unique for Portland. It's one of the very few places around that literally feature dining and dancing, with a serious menu and lively jazz. In the early morning hours—until 2am weekdays, 3am weekends—it's not only one of the few places open, but it probably offers more choices than all other open places put together. And no other restaurant in Portland has a strolling magician—who's hardly ever asked to disappear. Nobody would call it one of the most exciting kitchens in Portland, but it's reliable and often interesting; check out the linguine with pesto and scallops or the salmon with lingonberry sauce, or the roast lamb sandwich at lunch. There are some decent desserts: try the chocolate gâteau with almonds and currants. The scene can be livelier than the checkered floor. ■ *Between Alder and Morrison; (503) 224-5552; 626 SW Park Ave, Portland; $$; full bar; AE, DC, MC, V; checks OK; lunch Mon-Fri, dinner every day, brunch Sat-Sun.* &

Bread and Ink Cafe ★★ You can find the legendary Bread and Ink baguette in grocery stores these days, but you'll have to drop by the restaurant itself for any of its other signature items: the city's best homemade blintzes, a nearly perfect house salad, and raved-about burgers in which the condiments—mayo, mustard, ketchup—are made right on the premises. Blackboard specials venture successfully into neo-American, Mediterranean, and Mexican specialties, and there's a sublime Italian cassata for dessert. For breakfast there are delicious, billowing omelets, assorted homemade breads, and great coffee. Not surprisingly, there's a large and loyal clientele, many of whom come by on Sunday for the four-course Jewish-style brunch. The atmosphere is cool—linoleum flooring, emerald green cushioned chairs, and wide windows to the scene on Hawthorne—but the service can be also. ■ *2 miles east of downtown; (503) 239-4756; 3610 SE Hawthorne Blvd, Portland; $$; beer and wine; DIS, MC, V; checks OK; breakfast, lunch, dinner Mon-Sat, brunch Sun.* &

Bush Garden ★★ Other places boast of imagination in sushi creation; the sushi chefs at Bush Garden seem to be making it up as they go along. Look carefully at the specials and marvel at items not found elsewhere: Alaska roll with crab and smoked salmon; spicy shrimp maki; pungent hamachi hand rolls with scallion. Demand translations of everything; it's awful to learn of something particularly dazzling only after watching the Japanese businessman in the next seat consume it. Take nothing for granted; even something as straightforward as albacore tuna might appear with a dash of garlic paste and scallion garnish. Regular Japanese fare is offered in multiple tatami rooms; however, some of those entrées have been thoroughly stripped of authentic character. Others, such as tea on rice and jellyfish salad, are so authentic they can only be meant for the Japanese business crowd. You figure it out, but have some sushi while you do. ▪ *9th and Morrison near Nordstrom; (503) 226-7181; 900 SW Morrison St, Portland; $$; full bar; AE, DC, MC, V; no checks; lunch Mon-Fri, dinner every day.* ⅋

Cajun Cafe and Bistro ★★

Under new chef Mary McConnel, the Cajun Cafe continues along its tasty and successful Cajun path—even though the craze has effectively returned to Louisiana. (The disappearance of most of the other Cajun options in town must help.) The blackened and bronzed seafood specialties have never lost their color, the Cajun martinis can still clean your palate like a 100 proof sorbet, and the rest of the menu is now more consistent and reliable. The Cajun Cafe is also a restaurant given to frequent visiting chefs and special menus, from Mardi Gras to Caribbean excursions and pasta weeks, that help keep things interesting. One dining room has spun off to create a Middle Eastern fast-food place, and the space that remains tends to fill up a little more densely than before. ▪ *Corner of 21st and NW Lovejoy; (503) 227-0227; 2074 NW Lovejoy St, Portland; $$; full bar; AE, DC, DIS, MC, V; checks OK; lunch Mon-Fri, dinner every day.* ⅋

Campbell's Bar-B-Que ★★

Bring your appetite—you won't want to skip dessert—and come when you're not in a hurry, because there will probably be a steady line out the door of this small, plain house on the eastern fringe of the county. Campbell's serves some of Portland's best barbecue, and word has gotten out. Four different sauces invigorate a range of meats, from turkey to beef to pork. Try the smoky brown sugar on the pork ribs and you'll never be able to face a bottle of Lea and Perrins again. To go along with the meat there's coleslaw, pinto beans, potato salad, and pillowy white rolls or dense corn bread. Did we mention dessert? Sweet potato pie and luscious peach cobbler are just two. The service—mostly by people named Campbell—is on a par with the food. ▪ *Powell St exit off I-205, corner 85th and Powell; (503) 777-9795; 8701 SE Powell, Portland; $; no alcohol; MC, V; checks OK; lunch Tues-Fri, dinner Tues-Sat.* ⅋

Casa U-Betcha ★★ These urbane cantinas are just the place to take (or find) a first date: you can always fill up the better part of an evening gaping at Casa's in-yo'-face interior design. In any case, Casa on NE Broadway led an explosion of eateries along that busy arterial, and if you come to revel in the scene—without too many expectations about the food—you'll probably have a grand time. A mosaically laid tile path leads the eye and the foot into a dining room that's as loud aurally as it is visually. Here the Southwestern menu is open to influences from Japan to Brazil—intriguing but not always consistent. Sante Fe rolls, for instance—a take on sushi complete with wasabe-guacamole—are an acquired taste (one that we haven't yet acquired), but the crisp chimichangas filled with duck confit give new life to a Mexi standby. The original, smaller Casa up on NW 21st is still a vivid outpost of Northwest nightlife, and the atmosphere here is nothing to nod off about either. ▪ *Between Hoyt and Irving; (503) 227-3887; 612 NW 21st Ave, Portland.* & ▪ *NE Broadway and 17th; (503) 282-4554; 1700 NE Broadway; $$; full bar; AE, MC, V; no checks; lunch Mon-Fri, dinner every day.* &

Celilo (The Governor Hotel) ★★ After years of 30 stories in the air at Atwater's, it seemed to take chef George Poston a little while to find his footing on level ground. Early reports of Celilo (in an old Portland hotel remodeled by the Salishan empire) were of some kitchen inconsistency and dining room disorganization. Months later, Poston's skill and commitment to regional and Pacific Rim ingredients were starting to straighten things out. Led by its signature dish of salmon three ways—grilled, smoked, and in parchment—the menu has stabilized. The Governor has quickly become a popular place for private parties, and its expansive buffet Sunday brunch extends from smoked scallops to buffalo sausage to blintzes with brambleberry sauce. The dining room itself is a comfortable success, although it stretches from elevated banquettes in the front to what looks like a soda fountain in the back. ▪ *Downtown at Alder and SW 10th; (503) 224-3400; 611 SW 10th Ave, Portland; $$$; full bar; AE, DC, DIS, MC, V; checks OK; breakfast, lunch, dinner every day.* &

Chen's Dynasty ▪ Chen's Dynasty West ★★ Low lighting and warm colors give this popular place a special intimacy, belying the notion that Chinese restaurants must look like Fu Manchu sets and setting one to wondering how many people here are lunching with their paramours. The 12-page menu includes such rarities for these parts as sweet and pungent fish with honey-roasted pine nuts, squid cut to look like clusters of flowers and perfumed with Sichuan peppercorns, and pheasant Hunan-style, but the kitchen can also produce clunkers.

At Chen's Dynasty West in Beaverton, you're greeted with giant papier-mâché fish hanging from the ceiling, and a menu swimming with seafood, including 28 different shrimp dishes. Shanghai Harbor Crab, a whole Dungeness in a hoisin sauce flecked with ginger and scallions, shows off this place at its best. Chiang siu (whole crispy fish) and scallops in a nest, Hunan-style, demonstrate how effectively Northwestern seafood and Far Eastern inspiration can blend. Be warned: you're going to pay more than you might expect for Chinese food, and when Chen himself is not in the kitchen, standards dip toward the waterline. ■ *Between Broadway and SW 6th; (503) 248-9491; 622 SW Washington St, Portland; $$; full bar; AE, DIS, MC, V; no checks; lunch, dinner every day.* ■ *Near Scholl's Ferry Rd; (503) 292-4898; 6750 SW Beaverton Hillsdale Hwy, Beaverton; $$; full bar; AE, DC, DIS, MC, V; no checks; lunch, dinner every day.*

Esplanade at RiverPlace (RiverPlace Hotel) ★★

At press time, Esplanade was once again facing a new chef and a new format, another try at coming up with a menu to match the marina that sits just outside the elegant eatery's huge picture windows. After years of aiming at the top-of-the-gold-card crowd, Esplanade had already reconsidered itself into more of a bistro identity, with nothing over $20 and most entrées under $15. Now the reported goal is to head further into a bistro mode at lunch, and maybe into a bit more price downsizing at dinner as well. So far, a few Esplanade specialties such as the deeply rich lobster bisque and the artfully constructed salads, including Esplanade greens with a warm Brie dressing, have survived all overhauls. With luck, the new direction of the kitchen should help the restaurant's permanent strengths—a lovely room, a wide-angle view of the Willamette, and a formality of service that can convince you that something special is going on—which are now available at considerably less cost. The admirable and elaborate sit-down brunch probably won't be washed away either. ■ *City Center exit off I-5; Harbor Way off Front; (503) 295-6166; 1510 SW Harbor Way, Portland; $$; full bar; AE, DC, DIS, MC, V; checks OK; breakfast, dinner every day, lunch Mon-Fri, brunch Sun.* &

Fong Chong ★★

Part of the fun of this dim sum parlor, which shares an address with one of the busiest Chinese markets in the city, is that you can try anything once; dishes are inexpensive enough for you to discard the occasional one that fails to please. Bring your adventurous spirit from 10:30am to 3pm daily, when young waiters scurry from table to table, hawking their handmade morsels—an array of steamed buns and savory dumplings—on miniature saucers; then order simply by pointing at what looks interesting. At night, Fong Chong is transformed into a quiet Cantonese eatery, with average food

and a few surprises. ■ *Everett and NW 4th; (503) 220-0235;
301 NW 4th Ave, Portland; $; full bar; no credit cards; checks
OK; lunch, dinner every day.*

Fuji ★★ You wouldn't pick either this address or this exterior
for Portland's top sushi bar, but Fujio Handa is widely considered the sharpest blade in town. There are those who eat here
once a week just to challenge his resourcefulness. Handa regularly departs from old-school rules of sushi making to whip up
creative concoctions (incorporating Western ingredients) that
would make natives of Tokyo blush—and ask for more. The
sharp black-and-white geometric decor has flair, though the
regular menu is really worth the trip, too. One unfortunate recent cut of Handa's knife was to slice off lunch, but dinner starts
early—or you could have a very Happy Hour. ■ *South of SE
Powell on 28th; (503) 233-0577; 2878 SE Gladstone St, Portland; $; beer and wine; MC, V; no checks; dinner Tues-Sat.* &

Jake's Famous Crawfish ★★ Jake's storms into its second century concentrating on the same things it did
right during the first one: fresh seafood, an expansive bar
scene, a strong interest in Oregon wines, and softly professional service that puts it all together. Of course, you can't
reach landmark status without some changes: asterisks on the
menu now mark the dishes that appear in *Jake's Seafood Cookbook*. The length of its daily fresh list keeps this brass and mahogany landmark at the top of Portland's seafood restaurant
list. Fresh crawfish are available May through September, but
every night's list—usually about two dozen items long—will include some surprises, from New Zealand green-lipped mussels
to Idaho catfish to Alaska white salmon. Items on the extensive
menu, which is re-created daily, can be inconsistent. But when
the restaurant is hot (the bouillabaisse, packed with fish and
fennel, for example), it's hot. The ultra-rich truffle cake leads
the desserts, but the peach-and-pear crisp has loyal supporters.
■ *Stark and SW 12th; (503) 226-1419; 401 SW 12th Ave,
Portland; $$; full bar; AE, DC, DIS, MC, V; checks OK; lunch
Mon-Fri, dinner every day.* &

(badge: 20 YEARS)

Jarra's Ethiopian Restaurant ★★ Neither those four-alarm
Texas chilis nor those palate-flogging peppers from Thailand
pack the wallop of this kitchen's wat stews. Made of chicken,
lamb, or beef, they are deep red, oily, and packed with pepper
after-kicks. Full dinners come with assorted stewed meats and
vegetables, all permeated with vibrant spices and mounded on
enjera—the spongy Ethiopian bread that doubles as plate and
fork. This is the area's unequaled heat champ. Be sure to take
time to chat with the friendly owners, Petros Jarra and Ainalem
Sultessa, who will explain the origins of the food, give you an
Abyssinian history lesson, and debate Ethiopian politics. Take
it all in with plenty of cold beer, the logical beverage with this

cuisine. The downstairs cafe is open for lunch; at dinnertime, venture upstairs to the attractive dining room, hung with Ethiopian posters and artwork. ■ *14th and Hawthorne; (503) 230-8990; 1435 SE Hawthorne Blvd, Portland; $; beer and wine; MC, V; checks OK; lunch Tues-Fri, dinner Tues-Sat.* ♿

Java Bistro ★★ Java Bistro is simply among the prettiest restaurants around, with striking colors and Javanese artwork. You could begin your meal with the basics, the multidish rijstaffel or some of the pungent soups or satays. Something you won't run into in every Borneo bistro is the salmon satay, half a pound of fresh fish on a skewer, with a crisp, spicy edge to it. Along with peanut and chile sauces, there is a heavy emphasis on deep frying, and you might try the Ngo Hiang, bits of pork elevated to a higher destiny. Cruise on through all sauces provided, but watch your speed; some of the spicier ones can put your tongue into overdrive. ■ *On Terwilliger near Taylor's Ferry; (503) 452-1360; 8601 SW Terwilliger Blvd, Portland; $$; beer and wine; MC, V; no checks; dinner Tues-Sat.* ♿

Kashmir ★★ It may not be the most literal setting, but there is something appropriate about an Indian restaurant in a Victorian house, and the soothing mood here enhances the fiery entrées. When things are running well—musicians are sitting barefoot in the middle of the dining room, and the lamb korma is blazing away—the feeling of contentment can overpower any alcohol, which is fortunate, because the place doesn't offer any. The lights are low and the air is colored with the tinkling, rambling-creek sounds of the East. Five-course dinners, around $20, are generously portioned with crispy vegetable samosas with hot dip, a tangy cucumber and tomato salad alert with cilantro, a feather-light poppadum, two chewy Frisbees of chapati, raita (yogurt with cucumbers, tomatoes, and spices), basmati rice, an entrée of terrific lamb biryani or chicken liver curry, and a rice pudding. Close the meal with a milky tea spiced with cardamom. ■*NE 17th and Couch; (503) 238-3934; 1705 NE Couch St, Portland; $$; no alcohol; AE, MC, V; checks OK; dinner Tues-Sat.*

L'Etoile ★★ If traditional French cuisine is dying, word hasn't gotten to L'Etoile, which may be why a lot of Portland eaters are getting there. An imaginative but classic menu, which never stints on richness, combines with a deep-pile Continental atmosphere to produce one of Portland's most intriguing new restaurants. Elaborate, deftly wrought dishes, such as rack of lamb in an herb crust with a poached garlic sauce, veal with three mustards, and a goat cheese and leek tart, are subtle and satisfying, and desserts such as chocolate torte with truffle sauce or an artistic plate of cookies can be addictive. Austerity is not a theme here, but the effect is worth it. Some dishes can be inconsistent, but the place is likely to get better. Garden

▼

▲

seating is available from Memorial Day to Labor Day. ▪ *NE Fremont and 46th; (503) 281-4869; 4627 NE Fremont St, Portland; $$$; beer and wine; MC, V; local checks only; dinner Wed-Sat.*

London Grill (Benson Hotel) ★★ Recently, *Glamour* magazine called the London Grill one of the six most romantic restaurants in the United States. Without knowing just how the editors conducted the play-offs, we do know there are considerable elements of romance here: dramatic tableside cooking, including endearing crêpes suzette; a rich, plush ambience; multiple choices of champagne, part of a 600-bottle wine list that's Portland's largest; and, of course, hundreds of bedrooms just over your head. After a considerable overhaul, part of the change in ownership of the Benson itself, the London Grill has emerged much as it was before. The tableside cooking carts still glide across the room, the ingredients are still of high quality, and the strains of the harpist still wash over the deep, comfortable armchairs at each table; however, the menu is still bigger on ceremony than on imagination or consistency. In many cases, both innovation and flavoring seem to be restrained. On what has become a considerably faster restaurant track, the London Grill moves at a slow—but still very comfortable—pace. ▪ *SW Broadway at Oak St; (503) 295-4110; 309 SW Broadway, Portland; $$$; full bar; AE, DC, DIS, MC, V; checks OK; breakfast, lunch, dinner every day, brunch Sun.* ᕕ

Murata ★★ Tucked into the ground floor of an office building resembling a black glass doorstop, Murata seems an unlikely location for Portland's best Japanese restaurant. But it can take you to places no other eating establishment in town is likely to, although some nerve might be required on your part. There is serious authenticity in the seafood dishes and sushi here—especially in the untranslated specials. From simpler offerings such as whole steamed Dungeness crab with ginger vinegar dipping sauce to an impressive, silken version of kasu cod or to huge, multiperson nabes (seafood stews), Murata produces some dazzling options. It's also one of the few places in Portland where you can order (in advance) the elaborate Japanese multicourse banquet kaiseki, starting at $35 a person and running as high as you want. The unusual elements of the banquet—fish roe in a carved mandarin orange basket, soup with hand-gathered pine mushrooms—represent the elaborate dishes offered daily. ▪ *Downtown between 2nd and 3rd; (503) 227-0080; 200 SW Market, Portland; $$; beer and wine; AE, MC, V; no checks; lunch Mon-Fri, dinner Mon-Sat.*

Opus Too ★★ You know the nouvellization of America is complete when Opus' menu starts including ingredients such as grilled green beans, smoked pears, and morels. But the core at Opus Two is still fish and fire: a half-dozen fresh options daily, tossed onto the mesquite-fueled flames and slathered with any of the restaurant's eight sauces, from béarnaise to beurre rouge. Hunks of red meat are also traditional, but the menu is inching in some subtler directions. The decor is urban cool—tile floor, dark wood booths, and a long swivel-chair bar overlooking the open kitchen and grills. The exuberant environment is complemented by a respectable wine list, some fine desserts, and piles of hefty fettuccine. A terrific sourdough bread is part of the deal. ■ *Couch and 2nd, Old Town district; (503) 222-6077; 33 NW 2nd Ave, Portland; $$; full bar; AE, DC, DIS, MC, V; local checks only; lunch Mon-Sat, dinner every day.* &

Panini ★★ Bring one good friend—or a couple of good magazines—to this tiny jewel of a bistro. It's a sensational place to hang out, although with three or more in your party you begin to feel the squeeze. There are waffles and scones in the morning, and a mini-trattoria's worth of pastas for later in the day, including a great pre-movie bargain: for $7.50 you get a well-dressed salad, chewy Italian bread, and a plate of pasta—maybe penne in a creamy sauce with sausage and mushrooms. But the heart of the place is the dish it's named for: petite sandwiches such as Brie and mushrooms on a just-baked roll or smoked chicken on focaccia. The panini, of course, would have to be extraordinary to stand up next to Linda Faes' desserts: sinuous tiramisu, miniature melting lemon tarts, and something called chocolate salame that we're not even going to try to describe—but would be happy to eat any time at all. ■ *9th and Morrison, across from the Galleria; (503) 224-6001; 620 SW 9th Ave, Portland; $; beer and wine; no credit cards; checks OK; breakfast, lunch, early dinner Mon-Sat (closes at 5pm on Sat).*

Papa Haydn ★★ Glittering, lively Papa overflows with diners who know that in the end they'll get their just desserts. The dinner menu is strikingly imaginative and ambitious for a spot that once offered sandwiches mostly so that people wouldn't feel guilty about just going there for the sweets. Still the best-known aspect of the two Papas remains such indulgences as the Autumn Meringue—layers of chocolate mousse and baked meringue festooned with chocolate leaves—or the boccone dolce, a mountain of whipped cream, meringue, chocolate, and fresh berries. There are also subtler temptations, including a shocking purple blackberry ice and dense shortbread cookies. The northwest location has decent wine and beer lists and a full bar. The clientele there tends toward the upscale, while the original southeast branch owes more to the cerebral Reed College crowd, but both have lines running out the door. ■ *In Sellwood district, between Bybee and Holgate; (503) 232-9440;*

▼
Portland
Restaurants
▲

*5829 SE Milwaukie Ave, Portland; $$; beer and wine; AE,
MC, V; local checks only; lunch, dinner Tues-Sat, brunch Sun.
&. ▪ Irving and NW 23rd; (503) 228-7317; 701 NW 23rd Ave,
Portland; $$; full bar; AE, MC, V; local checks only; lunch, din-
ner Tues-Sat, brunch Sun. &.*

Portofino ★★ The center of Portland's antique trade, Sellwood
knows craftmanship when it sees it, and it has snuggled up to
Portofino. Although you know that no restaurant is a one-man
show, watching Carlo Rostagni swoop through the storefront
dining room—welcoming arrivals, whipping up a tableside zabaglione, and warmly commenting on the food or anything
else—you can believe that everything here, including the
customers, is the product of his energy. Rostagni has almost
departed restaurant land and headed for trattoria territory—
dramatic cooking, outside seating in good weather, moderate
prices. The most exciting dishes are the ones Rostagni prepares tableside by himself, such as gamberi al Sambucca, huge
prawns sautéed in garlic and shallots and perched on toast
points; or steak Diane. Off the cart, head for the agnolotti in
walnut sauce, and welcome to Mr. Rostagni's neighborhood.
▪ *On 13th near Tacoma; (503) 234-8259; 8075 SE 13th Ave,
Portland; $$; beer and wine; MC, V; local checks; lunch Tues-
Fri, dinner Tues-Sat.*

The Ringside ★★ After decades while the world changed
around it, Portland's premier porterhouse palace carries on like
a place that never heard of cholesterol. For texture, color, fla-
vor, and character, the steaks here are everything you could
want from a hunk of steer. The degree of cooking is as ordered
and deviations are few. Still, it's the plump but light, slightly
salty onion rings, made with Walla Walla sweets, that single-
handedly made the Ringside famous—an order is essential.
The menu includes some ocean fare; other house specialties in-
clude crackling fried chicken and nicely charred burgers. Ap-
petizers and salads are limited, although the marinated herring
deserves attention; the desserts do not. You can have French
fries or cottage cheese with your entrée, but the baked potato
is best. It has a crisp skin and a firm, piping-hot interior beg-
ging for sour cream and chives. The dignified black-jacketed
and bow-tied waiters are eminently professional. ▪ *2 blocks west
of Civic Stadium; (503) 223-1513; 2165 W Burnside, Portland;
$$; full bar; AE, MC, V; checks OK; dinner every day. &.*

Shakers ★★ A wide counter runs up one side of Shakers, a
line of booths down the other, and chairs and small tables take
up what space is left. It sounds like a lot of options, but chances
are that when it comes to seating in this narrow storefront,
you'll have to take what you can get—especially if it's mid-
morning on a Saturday. Portlanders line up for Jeani Subot-
nick's eye-opening breakfasts, with swollen omelets and thick

challah French toast. Serious effort goes into the corned beef hash, and the substantial blueberry pancakes are perfectly cooked. On the side, or filling up your meal by themselves, are some of Portland's most calculatedly crumbly scones, and if you can't get in for breakfast, a mean Texas chili looms over lunch. Dozens of salt and pepper shaker sets provide this place its name; they contribute to a retro cafe atmosphere that makes almost anyone feel right at home. ▪ *NW Glisan and 12th; (503) 221-0011; 1212 NW Glisan St, Portland; $; wine and beer; no credit cards; checks OK; breakfast, lunch Mon-Sat.*

Sumida's ★★ Try going in and asking for something unusual, and you'll discover something intriguing: Etsuo Sumida is nothing less than the patron saint of Portland's sushi scene. He started well before most of the other sushi shops in town, and the betting is that he'll outlast them. Just watching this master's virtuoso knifework is an experience: he's the Toshiro Mifune of seafood carving. Everything in this cozy neighborhood eatery is impeccably fresh, from tuna to uni with quail eggs. Sumida is also an expert at sushi rice preparation: proper vinegared rice must be sticky enough inside to hold fish, avocado, and such, but easy to handle on the outside. This difficult balance is something of a litmus test for true sushi chefs, rare in the Northwest. Most of the grilled seafood is reliable here, if your taste for the raw is limited, and familiar items like tempura and teriyaki chicken are well executed. ▪ *NE Sandy and 67th; (503) 287-9162; 6744 NE Sandy Blvd, Portland; $$; beer and wine; MC, V; checks OK; dinner Wed-Sun.*

Portland

Restaurants

▲

Tak Kee Seafood Restaurant ★★ After a few years, Tak Kee is now entrenched as one of the landmarks of Chinatown, a district that for years seemed as unchangeable as the Great Wall. Tak Kee treats seafood with care and respect, and before ordering, diners can inspect live lobsters, crab, and geoducks in front-room tanks. (Why anyone would want to inspect a live geoduck is another question.) The crabs, with ginger and green onion, top the popularity list, and you can see why. Tak Kee can operate smoothly on land as well—try the barbecued duck won ton soup—but with alternatives such as pepper-and-salt shrimp in shells and seafood in a ceramic pot, you may never find out. ▪ *Just off Burnside on 4th Ave; (503) 229-1888; 28 NW 4th Ave, Portland; $$; full bar; MC, V; no checks; lunch, dinner every day.* &

Thanh Thao ▪ Thanh Thao II ★★ Anchoring the east end of the bustling shopping district on Hawthorne Boulevard is this busy diner, where the barbecued pork noodles could turn anyone into a regular. The friendly Nguyen family can tell you everything you need to know about the Vietnamese or Thai food. A bowl of vegetable curry (crisp broccoli, snow peas, and sprouts in a creamy curry broth with fresh pineapple and cilantro) warms the body. You'll find some ordinary dishes here (like cashew chicken), but all are generous. Try the muc xao thap camp (squid sautéed with pineapple, tomato, mushroom, and celery) or the dau hu chua ngot (sweet-and-sour tofu) for a delicately steamed and sauced dinner. A second branch is a bit farther to the southeast. ■ *Off 39th in Hawthorne district; (503) 238-6232; 4005 SE Hawthorne Blvd, Portland; $; beer and wine; MC, V; checks OK; lunch, dinner Wed-Mon.* ■ *On Powell off 82nd; (503) 775-0306; 8355 SE Powell Blvd, Portland; $; beer and wine; AE, MC, V; checks OK; lunch, dinner every day.*

Vat & Tonsure ★★ A sense of European tradition pervades this place like pipe smoke—they even close the restaurant during the month of August—and perhaps that's why it has one of the most devoted followings in town. For a large slice of the musical and artistic world in Portland—and also a few lawyers—the Vat combines coffeehouse conversation with solid food and an impressive wine list. The high-backed wooden booths on the upper and lower decks of this split-level eatery are filled with serious discussion to a background of opera. Rose-Marie Barbeau handles the kitchen, turning out some fine stuffed Cornish gamehens, Guinness stew, and lamb chops. ■ *1 block west of Broadway between Yamhill and Taylor; (503) 227-1845; 822 SW Park Ave, Portland; $; beer and wine; no credit cards; checks OK; lunch, dinner Mon-Sat.* &

Zell's: An American Cafe ★★ Now *this* is breakfast: smoked sturgeon omelet, spring chinook salmon and scrambled eggs, huckleberry pancakes, home-baked scones and two jams. The powerful coffee and fresh-squeezed orange juice are the kinds of touches that make getting up in the morning worthwhile. Finally, if you can't resist recklessly sweet things in the morning, try the German pancakes with apples. This establishment boasts one of the few soda fountains around that isn't a campy imitation of the originals: Zell's is a converted '50s drugstore whose owners wisely spared the fountain counter from the remodeler's saw. Zell's is stunningly accommodating to kids, but the typical wait for a table may complicate things. ■ *13 blocks up from Morrison Bridge; (503) 239-0196; 1300 SE Morrison St, Portland; $; beer and wine; AE, MC, V; checks OK; breakfast, lunch every day.* &

Doris' Cafe ★ Success has sent Jewel Thomas seven blocks from his original down-home location to a cool, attractive new space right off Martin Luther King Boulevard, with hardwood floors, whitewashed walls, and high ceilings hung with blue banners. The hinged oil drums turned into barbecue grills are no longer the main decoration, but you can still smell the smoke well down the block. You'll recognize the heartening barbecue itself, tender ribs (or chicken or prime rib) in a sauce more sweet than angry. If you've sworn off barbecue, the fried chicken is lovely, fresh, and gently complex, and the list of specials seems to have grown longer. The buttery pound cake and the mousselike sweet potato pie should not be missed. And in the new atmosphere, Doris' may become less a take-out place and more a linger-on spot. ■ *North end of town, near Kirby exit off I-5 northbound; (503) 287-9249; 325 NE Russell, Portland; $; no alcohol; AE, MC, V; local checks only; lunch, dinner Mon-Sat.* ᕒ

Hunan ★ Visit Hunan if you want to get acquainted with some of the more fervid aspects of Chinese cooking, at a more reasonable cost than some of Portland's Peking palaces. Despite an occasional misfire, it's one of the most consistently on-target Chinese eateries in town. Among the standouts: Hunan beef, Lake T'ung T'ing Shrimp, and minced Sichuan chicken wrapped in pancakes. The restaurant's versions of the spicy standards—General Tsao's chicken, twice-cooked pork, chicken in tangy sauce—are pungent and massively popular. Service comes in one mode: fast and impersonal. ■ *Between Washington and Alder on SW Broadway; (503) 224-8063; 515 SW Broadway, Portland; $$; full bar; MC, V; local checks only; lunch, dinner Mon-Sat.*

Portland

Restaurants

Kornblatt's ★ Mornings, Kornblatt's sells bushels of bagels, probably Portland's closest approximation to circular success, in a dozen different varieties—including some that even serious bagel mavens have never noshed. Lunchtime, it provides a reasonably classic approximation of a pastrami—or corned beef or tongue or heartwarming chicken liver—on rye, and the menu even offers a low-fat Russian dressing. But lately, it's been extending itself in the evenings, with entrées such as brisket, roast chicken, and stuffed cabbage. Anyone can—and lots of people do—have the pastrami or bagels at any time, and the menu now includes some more varied smoked fish plates. Kornblatt's expanding range of Jewish specialties may not be perfect—just the best for about a thousand miles. ■ *On NW 23rd near Glisan; (503) 242-0055; 628 NW 23rd Ave, Portland; $; beer and wine; MC, V; checks OK; breakfast, lunch, dinner every day.* ᕒ

Marrakesh ★ Go seeking something unusual, and you'll find interest enough in the atmosphere and drama of the presentation; the five-course Moroccan dinners themselves, though unusual, are sometimes uneven. Your meal will begin with the customary finger-washing ceremony and end with the sprinkling of rose water over your hands. In between, you sit on cushions (not chairs) along a tapestried wall and eat without the benefit of utensils. The first course is harira Marrakshia, the cumin-and-coriander lentil soup of North Africa and the

Middle East, and dinner continues through a Moroccan eggplant salad and a bastela royale (chicken pie). You select your entrée—but choose carefully; some are too sweet, and others are uninspired. Try the lamb with eggplant or the braised hare in a rich cumin and paprika sauce. Or visit with a large group and order the mechoui, Morocco's famous roast lamb (three days' notice required). ▪ *NW 23rd and W Burnside; (503) 248-9442; 121 NW 23rd Ave, Portland; $$; beer and wine; AE, MC, V; checks OK; dinner Tues-Sun.*

The Original Pancake House ★ The name says it all. This landmark operation does its sourdough flapjacks from scratch, nearly 20 species of them—from wine-spiked cherry to wheat germ to a behemoth apple variety with sticky cinnamon glaze. A good bet is the ultrathin, egg-rich Dutch baby, dusted with powdered sugar and served with fresh lemon (essential to its overall flavor). Drawbacks are a painfully long wait for seating (bring a copy of *War and Peace* if you're thinking of weekend breakfast), a 90-decibel interior, and the town's weakest coffee. Once you're seated, the service is rushed and aloof. ▪ *Barbur Blvd exit of I-5 south, SW 24th and Barbur; (503) 246-9007; 8600 SW Barbur Blvd, Portland; $; no alcohol; no credit cards; checks OK; breakfast, lunch Wed-Sun.*

Plainfield's Mayur ★ Everybody needs a hobby, and for an Indian restaurant, Plainfield's Mayur has come up with an unusual one: a serious wine list. The list is now substantial enough to win recognition from the *Wine Spectator*, and fits neatly into the idea that this is not your basic curry cafe. The feeling is confirmed by the inside formality—bone china, crystal, candles, and linen-covered tables—and by an occasional Occidental dish such as lobster (although it does appear in an impressive Indian brown sauce). The style is basically Mogul, with an emphasis on subtle flavors and aromatic spices. Portions are small and tariffs a bit steeper than one usually expects for this cuisine. For starters, bypass the traditional offerings for something unusual, such as tomato coconut soup. The tandoori dishes—roasted prawns in tandoori jhinga, for one—are outstanding. ▪ *1 block west of Civic Stadium; (503) 223-2995; 852 SW 21st Ave, Portland; $$; full bar; AE, DIS, MC, V; checks OK; dinner every day.* ᕫ

Salty's on the Columbia ★ One of the real strengths here is the Columbia, rolling on just below the outdoor deck and outside the picture windows. It's a good idea to take the hint and order something that came out of the water as near here as possible. Stay close to the grilled fresh fish, with unusual sauces and salsas, and maybe sample an oyster or two to start with. Especially on warm, clear evenings, remember to call for a reservation early; the restaurant is usually jammed, both the dining room downstairs and the upper deck lounge, for the view as well as the food. ■ *Marine Dr exit from I-5; (503) 288-4444; 3839 NE Marine Dr, Portland; $$; full bar; AE, DC, DIS, MC, V; checks OK; lunch Mon-Sat, dinner every day, brunch Sun.*

Perlina *[unrated]* For a while it looked as if Perlina was on its way to stardom; however, that was three chefs ago. Just as we went to press, Eugene Bingham took over the kitchen with a mission to move away from Italian and more toward the challenges of Northwest cuisine. At last reports, the regular menu has some intriguing options—perhaps the fettuccine al limone—and the specials are usually tempting, but at times disappointing. No one will be disappointed by the appointments; the owners have done a sensational job of refurbishing a building that has housed too many failed restaurants. We just hope that soon the kitchen will match the composure of the dining room and that Bingham keeps the marionberry ice on the dessert menu. ■ *Corner of NW Glisan and 14th; (503) 221-1150; 1425 NW Glisan St, Portland; $$; full bar; AE, MC, V; checks OK; lunch Mon-Fri, dinner every day.* &

LODGINGS

The Benson ★★★★ Lumber tycoon Simon Benson built the Benson Hotel in 1912, giving orders to spare no expense. The creation was a noble 13-story affair of brick and marble, with a palatial lobby featuring a stamped-tin ceiling, mammoth chandeliers, stately columns, a generous fireplace, and surrounding panels of carved Circassian walnut imported from Russia. For decades this was the only classy lodging in town; then competition eventually brought an end to the Benson's exclusive status. A major renovation a couple of years ago by WestCoast Hotels was a gallant attempt to return it to its original stature. The marbled elegance of the lobby and lounge have been restored, and the rooms are slightly bigger (bath and all). Enough of an improvement to win the attention of both President Clinton and Madonna. Heathman, watch out. There are two pricey restaurants in the hotel, the London Grill (with a stunning wine cellar; see review in this section) and Trader Vic's. ■ *SW Broadway at Washington; (503) 228-2000 or toll-free (800) 426-0670; 422 SW Broadway, Portland, OR 97205; $$$; AE, DC, DIS, MC, V; checks OK.*

The Heathman Hotel ★★★★ A host of intimate luxury hotels have opened in Portland over the last few years, but the Heathman retains its favored status—and it's clear why: tea every afternoon, an exquisite bar, elegant rooms, and one of Portland's finer restaurants. The Heathman is a historic landmark, restored about a decade ago (the generous use of Burmese teak paneling inside reflects the owner, timber magnate

Wallace Stevenson). Guest rooms are small but tasteful, furnished with leather-and-rattan chairs, marble-topped bathroom pieces with brass fittings, chintz window shades, celadon lamps, and original prints and paintings, and colored in soft green, rose, and cream. Among the amenities are complimentary movies, European soaps, bathrobes, a nightly turndown service, a new third-floor exercise room with windows overlooking Broadway and Salmon, and an excellent restaurant (see review in this section). One of the Heathman's nicer qualities is the service; employees are low-key (a highly valued quality in Oregon) but meticulously attentive, so guests feel well taken care of but not fussed over. Rooms facing away from Broadway are best, since the hotel is on downtown Portland's busiest street. Rooms start at $155 (double). ■ *SW Broadway at Salmon; (503) 241-4100 or toll-free (800) 551-0011; 1009 SW Broadway, Portland, OR 97205; $$$; AE, DC, DIS, MC, V; checks OK.*

Governor Hotel ★★★ Downtown Portland is home to a short but impressive list of small luxury hotels—most that have been brought back to life through renovation just this decade. The newest of these is the 100-room Governor, a grand establishment housed in two buildings. The former Seward Hotel (1909) and the Italian Renaissance Princeton Building (1923) were renovated in a $16 million effort by the Salishan empire, and the nicest thing about the refurbishment is that instead of relinquishing the history of these two remarkable buildings, it plays it up. The Governor's lobby is a clubby room filled with deep couches, gleaming mahogany, and careful tile work. A sepia-toned mural of scenes from the Lewis and Clark journey decorates one wall. Upstairs, the rooms are decorated in cool Northwest earth tones: sage, honey beiges, and rusts, with classic upholstered chairs or couches and actual usable desks. Whirlpool tubs and large windows are signature items in most rooms, and several suites feature fireplaces, discreet wet bars, and balconies. The off-center downtown location (across from the Galleria) is more convenient than scenic, although some of the suites in the Princeton building have rooftop balconies with views to the east. The list of amenities is long: access to the Princeton Athletic Club (in the west wing) and the business center, and full concierge service. The hotel's restaurant, Celilo, serves Northwest cuisine edged with flair from the Pacific Rim (see review). ■ *SW 10th and Alder; (503) 224-3400 or (800) 554-3456; 611 SW 10th Ave, Portland, OR 97205; $$$; AE, DC, MC, V; checks OK.*

Heron Haus B&B ★★★ It's located in the exclusive Northwest Hills overlooking Portland, and you won't find more luxurious lodging. Built in 1904 for a local cranberry baron, Heron Haus maintains many of its original touches, including parquet flooring on the main level. Updated amenities, however, are no less pleasant: one of the five rooms has an elevated spa offering a view of the city below, and each room has its own bath (one with a turn-of-the-century seven-nozzle shower). This is a spacious operation for a B&B, 7,500 square feet. There's a living room with modern furniture, a handsome, well-stocked library, a TV room, an enclosed sun room, and an outside pool. A very comfortable spot, especially for the business traveler: there are phones in every room, and downstairs you'll find a fax machine and a work area. If you're visiting in late summer, you'll get in on the harvest from a miniature orchard of pear, apple, and cherry trees. It's also two blocks from the city's most popular shopping district. ■ *NW 25th and Johnson; (503) 274-1846; 2545 NW Westover Rd, Portland, OR 97210; $$$; MC, V; checks OK.*

Hotel Vintage Plaza ★★★ The attentive bellhops (some of the best in town) who don't let you lift a thing, the complimentary Oregon wines and classical piano in the early evening, and the crackling fire regularly stoked by the doorman are the subtle touches that attract well-heeled travelers to this relatively new hotel. Each room is individually decorated with cherry-wood furnishings and rich colors. The bi-level suites are indeed stunning, but for the money we prefer the starlight rooms with greenhouse-style windows, perfect for city stargazing. All rooms come with complimentary shoe shine, nightly turndown service, morning coffee and sweets in the lobby, and the newspaper delivered to your door. Bill Kimpton of San Francisco's Kimco Hotels saved this 1894 hotel from being converted into office space—and we're thrilled he did.

Pazzo Ristorante on the main floor serves excellent Northern Italian cuisine (see the review in this section). On Thursdays, Fridays, and Saturdays, be sure to request a table in the enchanting wine cellar. ■ *SW Broadway at Washington; (503) 228-1212 or toll free (800) 243-0555; 422 SW Broadway, Portland, OR 97205; $$$; AE, DC, DIS, MC, V; checks OK.*

RiverPlace Hotel ★★★ Although it is no longer an Alexis hotel (WestCoast Hotels took over the management in August 1992), the elegant RiverPlace remains one of the best places to stay in the city. Situated in Portland's showcase riverfront district, it features 10 chic condominiums, 74 rooms, specialty shops, two restaurants (one, The Patio, is open summers only), scenic jogging paths, and an upscale bar. Inside are plush furnishings, postmodern colors, televisions concealed in armoires, smashing views of the river, and a lively night scene. The best rooms face the Willamette or look north across park lawns to the downtown cityscape (though there's no guarantee of a river-view room). A paved path, extending along the riverfront from the hotel's front door to downtown, is popular with guests. Use of the adjacent RiverPlace Athletic Club facilities is an extra $8. The restaurant, Esplanade, is good for more than the view (see review); stroll down to the Pilsner Room at the other end of the RiverPlace complex if you want more casual fare. ■ *Harbor Way off Front Ave; (503) 228-3233 or toll-free (800) 426-0670; 1510 SW Harbor Way, Portland, OR 97201; $$$; AE, DC, MC, V; checks OK.* &

Portland Guest House ★★
What the PGH lacks in grandeur, it makes up for in simplicity and class—and location: it's in the bustling NE Broadway neighborhood, just up the street from a handful of the city's better restaurants, and not far from the Oregon Convention Center. Since owner Susan Gisvold doesn't live here, she runs it like a small hotel; she's usually around just long enough to advise you on Portland doings and bake a batch of cookies. The rest of the time, guests have full run of the parlor, dining room, and—dare she?—the fully stocked fridge. In the morning, Susan drops in to prepare a fine breakfast of fresh fruit, scones, and maybe even a basil omelet. Each room has its own phone and clock, items that, we're finding, are not standard in many B&Bs. Several of the suites (including two new ones that weren't yet completed at press time) are suitable for families (with a queen and twin beds). When the weather's warm, the garden's the spot. ■ *NE Broadway and 15th; (503) 282-1402; 1720 NE 15th Ave, Portland, OR 97212; $$; AE, DC, MC, V; checks OK.*

Portland's White House ★★
Another local timber baron, Robert F. Lytle, built to last what is now a popular B&B—constructed of solid Honduras mahogany. From the outside it's an imposing white mansion with all the trappings of Brahmin taste: fountain, carriage house, and a grand circular driveway. Inside are six roomy units, exquisite Oriental rugs, and other elegant appointments. The Canopy Room has its own balcony and a large canopied bed. Another room, equally romantic, has a vintage brass bed and delicate lace curtains. All rooms have private baths. Teatime is quiet time—unless your visit coincides with a wedding (for which they're consistently booked). ■ *Coliseum exit from I-5, head east to NE 22nd; (503) 287-7131; 1914 NE 22nd Ave, Portland, OR 97212; $$$; MC, V; checks OK.*

Sheraton Airport Hotel ★★
For the traveling businessperson, the airport's Sheraton tops the list. For one thing, it's located—literally—on the airport grounds (Fed Ex planes load up next door, and arrival and departure times are broadcast at the main entrance). Inside, amenities abound: everything from meeting rooms and a complete, complimentary business center (IBM computer, printer, fax machine, and secretarial services) to an indoor swimming pool, sauna, and workout room. Details down to hair dryers in the women's room (we didn't

check the men's) are covered here. The executive suites consider the personal needs of the businessperson, with extra touches such as two phones, sitting areas, and pullout makeup mirrors in the bathrooms. We only wish they would give the hotel a quarter turn: Mount Hood stands tall to the east, but you'd never know it from the airport-facing rooms. ■ *On Airport Way just before the terminal; (503) 281-2500, toll-free (800) 325-3535; 8235 NE Airport Way, Portland, OR 97220; $$$; AE, DC, DIS, MC, V; checks OK.* &

 Mallory Motor Hotel ★ This place is an older establishment in every sense—from the massive pieces of ornate wooden lobby furniture to the clientele to the senior staff. It's also one of the best bargains in town—starting at $50 for a double, with vast suites for $85—and it's no secret, so you'll want to book far in advance. While rooms are spacious, they bear no resemblance to the hotel's more elaborate entrance. On the other hand, this is one of the few areas bordering downtown Portland that is genuinely quiet. Parking is easy to find (Mallory has two lots across the street), and several of the rooms have good views of the city or the west hills. The bar, a kind of bizarre hybrid of '50s dark-plushy and '60s eccentric-cutesy, is not the major attraction here. The irritating Muzak in every corner of the ground floor is a drawback. The flaws fade, however, next to simple, charming touches such as the small, lace-trimmed pillow with needle, thread, and buttons left in your room and the almost motherly service. ■ *Corner of SW 15th and Yamhill; (503) 223-6311 or toll-free (800) 228-8657; 729 SW 15th Ave, Portland, OR 97205; $; AE, DC, DIS, MC, V; checks OK.* &

Marriott Residence Inn/Lloyd Center ★ This new hotel near the Lloyd Center Cinema has 168 rooms, each with a full kitchen and most with wood-burning fireplaces (it's geared toward longer stays of four to seven days). Extras include a continental breakfast (bagels, muffins, cereal, and fruits) served in the lobby. There isn't much of a view and no restaurant, but the rooms are bigger than those at other standard hotels. There are a couple of Jacuzzis for guest use and a heated outdoor pool; an extra $4 gains you access to the Lloyd Center Athletic Club seven blocks away. ■ *2 blocks east of Lloyd Center on Multnomah; (503) 288-1400; 176 NE Multnomah, Portland, OR 97232; $$$; AE, DC, DIS, MC, V; checks OK.* &

Red Lion at Lloyd Center ★ Its daunting size (a map in the lobby directs you to the three restaurants) and proximity to Lloyd Center, Memorial Coliseum, and the new Convention Center make this corporate hotel a good choice for eastside conventions or seminars. With 476 guest rooms, it's Oregon's second-largest hotel (the Marriott is slightly bigger), with a number of well-organized meeting rooms, an outdoor pool, a workout room, and a courtesy airport van. Reserve a west-facing room above the fifth floor for a view of Mount Hood. ■ *Lloyd Center/Weidler exit from I-5; (503) 281-6111 or (800) 547-8010; 1000 NE Multnomah St, Portland, OR 97232; $$$; AE, DC, DIS, MC, V; checks OK. &*

FOREST GROVE

Pacific University is probably why most people come here, and the towering firs on the small campus do justice to the town's name. But there's also quite a collection of local wineries now, making the area worth exploring, perhaps on your way to the ocean. South of town on Highway 47 is the huge new **Montinore Vineyards,** (503) 359-5012, which has a fancy tasting room, and wines that are improving with each vintage. In nearby Gaston, **Elk Cove Vineyards,** (503) 985-7760, has a spectacular site for a tasting room perched on a forested ridge, and **Kramer Vineyards,** (503) 662-4545, is a tiny place in the woods with tasty pinot noir and excellent raspberry wine. West of Forest Grove on Highway 8, on the site of a historic Oregon winery, **Laurel Ridge Winery,** (503) 359-5436, specializes in sparkling wines and also makes good sauvignon blanc. **Shafer Vineyards,** (503) 357-6604, has produced some fine, ageable chardonnays, and **Tualatin Vineyards,** (503) 357-5005, produces exquisite chardonnay, as well as a tasty Müller Thurgau. Finally, just outside of town you can sample sake from **Momokawe Sake,** (503) 357-7056, a Japanese producer building a new Oregon brewery.

RESTAURANTS

El Torero ★ You may have a tough time getting past the terrific, light, crisp chips, but if you do, you'll probably end up devouring all your excellent homemade-tasting refritos. For the main course, stick with the specialty beef items—the massive serving of carnitas de res is super. The decor is college hangout, but the service is very friendly and the English (authentically) limited. ■ *Just off Highway 8 on Main; (503) 359-8471; 2009 Main, Forest Grove; $; MC,V; checks OK; lunch, dinner every day. &*

BEAVERTON

RESTAURANTS

Swagat Indian Cuisine ★★ Swagat has quickly risen to the top of the list of Portland-area Indian restaurants, not only because its food is skillfully cooked and, well, darned cheap, but also because its menu offers uncommon and terrific Southern Indian dishes. The Andhra masala dosa is an enormous, thin crêpe, folded around a heaping spoonful of vegetable curry.

Served with a vivid lentil soup, this is an appetizer that could make a meal. The pakoras are crisp, succulent vegetable fritters; eggplant is best. If you're the type who enjoys setting your mouth afire, the chicken vindaloo should do the job: a red stew heated by the flame of many chiles, it's a dish that will either leave you begging for mercy or begging for more. Check at the door any reservations you have about the tract house setting of Swagat; once you start eating, the food will transport you halfway around the world. ▪ *Canyon Road exit of Highway 217; (503) 626-3000; 4325 SW 109th Ave, Beaverton; $; beer and wine; AE, DIS, MC, V; checks OK; lunch and dinner every day.*

LODGINGS

Greenwood Inn ★ A recent refurbishing here incorporates the works of area artists, and has given the modern, 253-room Greenwood Inn new aesthetic appeal. Before that, the draw to this motel and convention complex was its location for businesspeople—just off Highway 217, the freeway connecting the Sunset Highway with the teeming suburbs of Beaverton and Tigard. A few of the suites have Jacuzzis and kitchens, some are set aside for guests with pets, but the nicest rooms are those that have been redone in the last year. One unusual feature for a motel is room service; place an order the night before with the wake-up operator. Inside the Pavillion Bar and Grill, lights are soft, and service treads the delicate line between chummy and concerned. The food's absolutely okay without being remarkable. ▪ *Hwy 217 and Allen Blvd; (503) 643-7444; 10700 SW Allen Blvd, Beaverton, OR 97005; $$; AE, DC, DIS, MC, V; checks OK.*

TIGARD

LODGINGS

Embassy Suites Hotel ★ The Embassy is urban-moderno, right down to its location, adjacent to the sprawling Washington Square shopping complex in Tigard, about 15 minutes' driving time from Portland. The only feature that recommends this monolithic structure is its quick access to Oregon's "Silicon Forest" business district of Beaverton and Tigard. A major new wing has added 110 more rooms, an elaborate ballroom, and a swanky conference center. Complimentaries include full breakfast, athletic club use (five minutes away by complimentary limo), and shopping-mall limo service. Restaurant and lounge are the usual Denny's-gone-velvet found in all hotels of this genre. Double occupancy begins at $132. ▪ *Off Hwy 217, follow signs to Washington Square; (503) 644-4000; 9000 SW Washington Square Rd, Tigard, OR 97223; $$$; AE, DC, DIS, MC, V; checks OK.* &

LAKE OSWEGO

RESTAURANTS

Riccardo's ★★ The food here is overshadowed by the Italian wine list—well on its way to becoming two volumes—although a new chef has begun to liven things up. You'll do best to stray from the regular menu and order from the list of specials, which might include a tender veal chop topped with wild mushrooms. The raviolis—whose fillings change each night—are also worth a taste. A fountain tinkles in the expansive outdoor dining area, and across the parking lot is Riccardo's new wine shop, where you can buy all the Italian bottlings that you don't get to at dinner. ■ *Lake Grove; (503) 636-4104; 16035 SW Boones Ferry Rd, Lake Oswego; $$; beer and wine; AE, DC, MC, V; checks OK; lunch Mon-Fri, dinner Mon-Sat. &*

Thai Villa ★★ Hidden away in a corner of a municipal parking lot next to the Lake Oswego fire station is a Thai restaurant with few matches but a lot of fire. Thai Villa specializes in a wide range of seafood dishes and in pungent soups served swirling in a moat around a pillar of flame. The spicing is up to you, but the highest level of heat is called "volcano," and they're not kidding. The chef is also handy with basil, garlic, and subtle hints of sweetness, and the prices are reasonable, especially on a cost-per-tingle basis. Hit the King's Favorite Chile—the king knows his stuff—or the accurately named Seafood World. ■ *Downtown Lake Oswego; (503) 635-6164; 340 N 1st St, Lake Oswego; $; beer and wine; MC, V; no checks; lunch Mon-Fri, dinner every day.*

MILWAUKIE

RESTAURANTS

Thai Restaurant ★★ In an unpromising setting in an unpromising location, Thai Restaurant very quietly produces some of the most exciting Thai food in Portland. When you connect with Emerald Pork, with spinach and peanut sauce, or Panang Nuea, beef in a blast of fiery red curry, you may lose complete contact with your location in an old fast-food place on a street populated largely with new fast-food places. But by then you've already been through the unusual vibrant barbecued pork and a sizzling salad of grilled shrimp with chile and lemon grass. Nobody's set off Gladstone like this since Disraeli. ■ *Milwaukie; (503) 786-0410; 14211 SE McLoughlin Blvd, Milwaukie; $; MC, V; no checks; lunch Tues-Fri, dinner Tues-Sun. &*

Buster's Smokehouse Texas-Style Bar-Be-Que ★ One deep whiff as you come in tells you all you need to know about Buster's, where huge wood-smoke ovens leave their mark on both the meat and the atmosphere. Brisket, chicken, beef and pork ribs, and links all pass through the cooker and come out estimably pink and juicy. The pungent barbecue sauce helps considerably, and beer is the beverage of choice. Accompaniments are simple: fries, slaw, barbecue beans, and, for the daredevil, stuffed jalapeño peppers. Pecan pie is a solid finish. Equal emphasis on barbecue essentials at both the original Milwaukie location and the Gresham branch. The new Buster's in Tigard features a mesquite broiler, for those of fainter disposition. ■ *2 miles north of I-205, take Oregon City exit; (503) 652-1076; 17883 SE McLoughlin Blvd, Milwaukie. ċ ■ From I-84 East, take Wood Village exit; in Hood Center shopping mall; (503) 667-4811; 1355 E Burnside, Gresham. ċ ■ Near the Tigard exit off I-5 southbound; (503) 452-8384; 11419 SW Pacific Hwy, Tigard; $; beer and wine; MC, V; local checks only; lunch, dinner every day.*

GRESHAM

RESTAURANTS

Roland's ★★ The road through Germany, Sweden, Australia, Brazil, and San Francisco doesn't usually end in Gresham, but Roland Blasi's did, and all of east Multnomah County is grateful. A mile from the MAX line, Blasi has produced a splendid continental restaurant—continental not in the sense of the 38th version of veal Oskar, but in surefooted and imaginative menu choices drawn from all over Western Europe. Try the Pasta Angelo with an unusually subtle Italian sausage, and hope that the specials include the poached salmon with two sauces. Torta di formaggio is actually cheesecake, but this version can call itself anything it wants to. ■ *Off Powell (Hwy 26); 2 blocks from downtown Gresham; (503) 665-7215; 155 SE Vista, Gresham; $$; beer and wine; MC, V; local checks OK; dinner Tues-Sat. ċ*

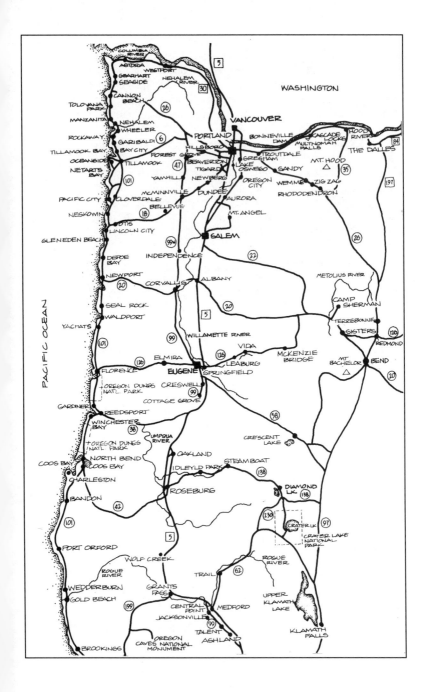

Oregon Coast

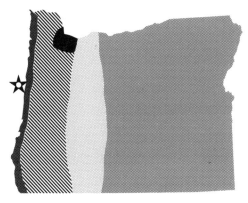

*From Astoria (at the mouth of the Columbia River),
a southward route down the coast.*

ASTORIA

This fishing town (and former salmon-canning capital) was founded in 1811 and lays claim as the first permanent American settlement west of the Rockies. Today, the well-maintained **Victorian homes** lining the harbor hillside at Franklin, Grand, and Irving avenues provide glimpses of that era. Now Astoria is a museum without walls, an unstirred mixture of the old and new that finds common ground along the bustling waterfront—once the locale for canneries and river steamers, now an active port of oceangoing vessels and fishing boats. Salmon- and bottom-fishing trips leave from the West End mooring basin, just west of the large interstate bridge.

The **Columbia River Maritime Museum**, 1792 Marine Drive, (503) 325-2323, is the finest of its kind in the Northwest. Restored small craft are displayed in the Great Hall; seven thematic galleries depict different aspects of the region's maritime heritage. The Lightship *Columbia*, the last of its kind on the Pacific coast, is moored outside (a tour is included).

Fort Clatsop National Memorial, six miles southwest of Astoria off Highway 101, (503) 861-2471, recreates Lewis and Clark's 1805-1806 winter encampment. Besides the audiovisuals and exhibits in the visitors center, there are living history displays (firing black-powder musket, making candles) in the summer.

Captain George Flavel House/Heritage Museum. Both of these museums are run by the Clatsop County Historical

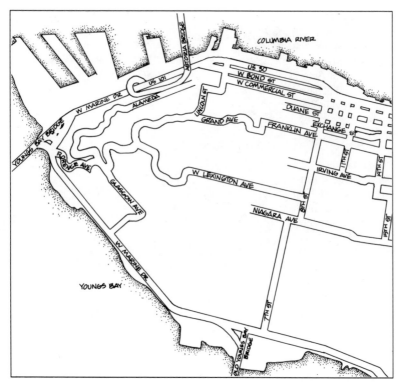

Astoria

Society and feature local historical displays. The Flavel House, named after a prominent 19th-century businessman and Columbia River bar pilot, is the city's finest example of ornate Queen Anne architecture; 8th and Duane streets, (503) 325-2563. The restored Heritage Museum is eight blocks away at 1618 Exchange Street; (503) 325-2203.

The **Astoria Column** sits atop the city's highest point, Coxcomb Hill, and offers a breathtaking panorama of the Columbia River estuary, the Pacific, and beyond. Well worth the 160-step climb. To get there, drive to the top of 16th Street and follow the signs.

Sixth Street River Park has an always-open, covered observation tower providing the best vantage point to view river commerce, observe bar and river pilots boarding tankers and freighters, and watch seals and sea lions looking for a free lunch. Another public viewing pier is located at 14th Street.

Josephson's Smokehouse, 106 Marine Drive, (503) 325-2190, prepares superb alder-smoked salmon, tuna, and sturgeon, while the **Astoria Coffee Co.**, 1154 Commercial Street, (503) 325-7173, serves the best joe in town. Ask owners Peg Davis and Rick Murray about in-town events. **Ricciardi**

Gallery, 108 10th Street, (503) 325-5450, offers an attractive selection of regional art. Espresso, juices, and desserts are available up front.

Fort Stevens State Park, off Highway 101, 20 minutes northwest of Astoria, (503) 861-1671, is a 3,500-acre outdoor wonderland of paved bike paths, forest trails, a freshwater lake, and uncrowded beaches—including the permanent resting spot of the hulk of the *Peter Iredale*, wrecked in 1906. There are also 604 campsites, making Fort Stevens Oregon's largest publicly owned campground. Within the park, the **South Jetty lookout tower**, perched at Oregon's northwesternmost point, is a supreme storm-watching spot. It also marks the start of the Oregon Coast Trail, which traverses sandy beaches and forested headlands all the way to the California border.

Approximately 48 eagles feed and roost at **Twilight Eagle Sanctuary**, eight miles east of Astoria (off Highway 30 on Burnside Road). The **Jewell elk refuge** is an area of rolling meadows, at times populated by hundreds of elk; 26 miles east of town on Highway 202, (503) 755-2264.

RESTAURANTS

Columbian Cafe ★★ The Columbian keeps getting more publicity (and therefore more crowded), but this small vegetarian, nonsmoking cafe continues to be Astoria's best bet for good grub. Be prepared for long waits, cramped quarters, erratic hours, uneven service, an eccentric chef, and great food—delicately crafted crêpes, sumptuous soups, black bean burritos, and perhaps the finest seafood and pasta dishes on the Oregon Coast. Dinner specials change daily (as do noontime soups), sauces are superb, and "hot" means fiery. If you're feeling frisky, order the Chef's Mercy, an eclectic combination of the day's best (and freshest) ingredients. Virtually everything on the menu is handcrafted by chef Uriah Hulsey, a real character. Sit at the counter, and he'll probably engage you in stimulating conversation and offer up-to-the-minute tidbits on local happenings. ■ *Corner of 11th St and Marine Dr; (503) 325-2233; 1114 Marine Dr, Astoria; $; beer and wine; no credit cards; checks OK; breakfast, lunch Mon-Sat, dinner Wed-Sat.* &

Cafe Uniontown The latest incarnation of a restaurant that has gone through several, the Uniontown is now the spot for decent food, good service, and pleasant ambience. You probably won't be overwhelmed here by anything (except perhaps the portions), but if you're looking for halibut or salmon (in season, and correctly cooked), this is the place to go. Specials also show promise: a recent pasta plate included salmon (big chunks, not flecks), asparagus, tomatoes, mushrooms, and avocado in a light cream sauce. The two dining rooms are nicely furnished with rich wood paneling, and the new lounge, although smoky, is a visual delight. ■ *Under the interstate bridge on Marine Dr;*

(503) 325-8708; 218 W Marine Dr, Astoria; $$; full bar; AE, MC, V; checks OK; lunch, dinner Tues-Sat.

The Ship Inn An Astoria waterfront institution, this congenial and crowded eatery is operated by English expatriates Jill and Fenton Stokeld. Your best bet here is the halibut fish 'n' chips, although other varieties are available. All fish is double-dipped in a delicately seasoned batter and cooked moist in fresh oil, while all the chips are made from large potato slices. Somehow, neither is greasy. Wash your meal down with a pint of Watney's or Labatt's, both on tap. Ask for a window table, where you can watch bar and river pilots get on and off ocean-going vessels in the river channel just a hundred yards away. No reservations are accepted, but a hospitable (if smoky) bar up front affords a cozy waiting area. ■ *On the west end of town, on the waterfront at the foot of 2nd St; (503) 325-0033; 1 2nd St, Astoria; $$; full bar; MC, V; checks OK; lunch, dinner every day.* &

LODGINGS

Franklin Street Station ★★ In a town where B&Bs are blooming everywhere, Jim and Renee Caldwell's eight-year-old establishment continues to be the best. The location, two blocks from downtown on a rather ordinary street, could be better, but almost everything else is done with style and eloquence. A local shipbuilder constructed the house at the turn of the century for his son; lavish woodwork attests to dad's fondness for local forest products. The interior is exquisitely appointed with Victorian furnishings; frilly drapes (sewn by Renee and her mom) frame the windows. There are now six guest rooms (two are suites that sleep up to four persons), all with private baths. Three rooms open onto river views, and two have outside decks. An attic room, the Captain's Quarters, has the best view, its own living room, and a host of amenities. ■ *Between 11th and 12th on Franklin; (503) 325-4314 or (800) 448-1098; 1140 Franklin St, Astoria, OR 97103; $$; MC, V; checks OK.*

Astoria Inn Bed and Breakfast ★ No doubt about it, this 1890s Victorian farmhouse is the best *situated* B&B in town, located above the city with a sweeping view of the Columbia. The grounds are meticulously landscaped, just steps away from trails leading up into the woods—very green and alive, very Astoria. There are three handsomely furnished rooms (all with private baths), an out-of-the-wind verandah, and a cozy library. Relax and watch the Columbia's many moods. Full breakfast is served; children (but no pets) are welcome. ■ *Irving Ave and 34th St; (503) 325-8153; 3391 Irving Ave, Astoria, OR 97103; $$; DIS, MC, V; checks OK.*

Crest Motel ★ This tidy, well-maintained lodging is situated on a forested bluff overlooking the Columbia River, the best

▼

Astoria

Restaurants

▲

motel view in town. It's at the east edge of Astoria (two miles
from downtown), back from the highway and therefore quiet—
except, of course, for the sound of foghorns, which on winter
evenings can be heard bellowing up the hillside from the ship
traffic below. In the large backyard, you can recline in lawn chairs
and enjoy a bird's-eye view of the in- and out-going tankers and
freighters, or unwind in a gazebo-enclosed whirlpool. All 40
nicely furnished rooms come equipped with coffeepots; pets
are welcome and one section is nonsmoking. ■ *2 miles east of
downtown; (503) 325-3141; 5366 Leif Erikson Dr, Astoria,
OR 97103; $$; AE, DC, DIS, MC, V; checks OK.*

GEARHART

Surely, Gearhart is the town with the most (and the best) ex-
amples of "Oregon Coast" architecture, with an assortment of
beachfront weathered-wood homes in shades of gray and white.
Fashionable Portlanders put their summer cottages here—
some of which are substantial dwellings—when the coast
was first "discovered." Unlike other coastal towns, Gearhart is
mostly residential. Razor-clam digging is popular, and many
gas stations rent shovels. The wide beach is backed by lovely
dunes. Gearhart Golf Course, opened in 1892, is the second-
oldest course in the West—a 6,089-yard layout with sandy soil
that dries quickly; open to the public, (503) 738-3538.

RESTAURANTS

Pacific Way Bakery and Cafe An airy and impeccably clean
establishment, with hardwood floors, lots of windows, mini-
malist (but hip) service, cool sounds, and hot espresso. And
Pacific Way is the only restaurant in downtown (such as it is)
Gearhart. It continues to thrive on a mix of suspender-and-
clam-shovel locals and out-of-town "gearheads," the BMW-
and-summer-beachfront-home crowd. They come to hang out,
hobnob, and sample the best cinnamon rolls, French apple
turnovers, pecan buns, cheesecake, and breads the North
Coast has to offer. Lunch fare is also good, including the Greek
sandwich, a lusty affair with gobs of salami, olives, mozzarella,
and feta on French bread. ■ *Downtown Gearhart, corner of Cot-
tage and Pacific Way; (503) 738-0245; 601 Pacific Way,
Gearhart; $; beer and wine; MC, V; checks OK; breakfast,
lunch Wed-Sun.*

SEASIDE

One hundred years ago, affluent Portland beach-goers rode
Columbia River steamers to Astoria, then hopped a stagecoach
to Seaside, the Oregon Coast's first resort town. Seemingly the

place has become more crowded every year since (knotty summer traffic is second only to Lincoln City). The crowds mill along Broadway, eyeing the entertainment parlors, the taffy concession, and the bumper cars, then emerge at the Prom, the two-mile-long cement "boardwalk" that's ideal for strolling.

Fishing. Surf fishing is popular, particularly at the south end of town in the cove area. Steelhead and salmon can be taken (in season) from the Necanicum River, which flows through town. Occasional minus tides provide good razor clamming along the wide, flat beach.

Hiking. The trailhead for the six-mile hike over Tillamook Head begins at the end of Sunset Boulevard at the town's south end. The ruggedly spectacular trail ends in Ecola State Park near Cannon Beach.

Recreation. Sunset Empire Park and Recreation District, headquartered at Sunset Pool, 1140 E Broadway, (503) 738-3311, promotes various activities from biathlons to lap swims to seasonal outdoor concerts.

Art. The Weary Fox Gallery in Sand Dollar Square on Broadway, (503) 738-3363, features Northwest arts and crafts. Quatat Marine Park, downtown on the Necanicum River, is a relaxing picnic spot where there are free concerts in the summer.

RESTAURANTS

Dooger's Where do you eat in a town full of taffy concessions, hot dog stands, and bumper cars? Frankly, there aren't many choices, but your best bet is Dooger's, for decent seafood and chowder—as the line outside on weekends (and sometimes during the week) will attest. Inside, it's clean, smokeless, and unkitschy, and the service is friendly. This is a good place to bring the family, and there are plenty of nonfish options for the kids. Stick with the simpler offerings and the local catch.

There's another, larger Dooger's in Cannon Beach; 1371 S Hemlock, (503) 436-2225. ■ *Broadway and Franklin; (503) 738-3773; 505 Broadway, Seaside; $$; beer and wine; MC, V; local checks only; lunch, dinner every day.*

Vista Sea Cafe It may be frenzied outside at Seaside's busiest intersection, but inside there's a pleasant, nonsmoking respite. There are five wooden booths, a couple of tables, lots of plants, and some pretty fair pizzas. Choose from tons of toppings, including some unorthodox cheeses (Montrachet, Oregon blue), to create your mouthwatering pie—slightly light on the sauce (request more), but piled on a hefty, chewy crust. We've also enjoyed the Greek pasta salad and Italian sodas mixed with real cream. ■ *On the corner of Broadway and Columbia; (503) 738-8108; 150 Broadway, Seaside; $; beer and wine; MC, V; local checks only; lunch, dinner every day.*

The Boarding House★ Fir tongue-and-groove walls, beamed ceilings, and wood paneling recall traditional boardinghouse decor at this turn-of-the-century Victorian. The house fronts Seaside's busy Holladay Drive, but the backyard slopes gently to the Necanicum River—convenient and close to the beach. All six guest rooms have private baths and a wicker-and-wood beachy feeling. There's also a miniature Victorian cottage that sleeps up to six people. Full breakfasts included. ■ *N Holladay and 3rd at 208 N Holladay Dr; (503) 738-9055; PO Box 573, Seaside, OR 97138; $$; MC, V; checks OK.*

Beachwood Bed and Breakfast Beachwood, just a block east of the beach, is nicely ensconced in a quiet residential neighborhood, nestled in among coastal pines, an easy walk from downtown. The 1900 Craftsman-style lodging was originally known as Kinni-kinnic Lodge (after the local Indian term for the leafy ground cover that was dried and used as a smoking mixture). All three guest rooms have private baths, and one, the Astor room, is outfitted with an unusual sleigh-shaped bed and comfy window seat with a peek of the Pacific. The first-floor Holladay suite has a frilly canopy bed, a gas fireplace, and Jacuzzi. No children or pets. ■ *Beach Dr and Ave G; (503) 738-9585; 671 Beach Dr, Seaside, OR 97138; $$; MC, V; checks OK; (closed mid-Nov to mid-Feb).*

Cannon Beach

Shilo Inn We tend to be wary of glitzy establishments that hog the shoreline, but this one has a good reputation. The setting, of course, is superb; the lobby is stylish and mirrored (perhaps too dazzling for some tastes); the prices are stratospheric. But all the amenities expected in a resort hotel are here: indoor pool, steam room, sauna, workout room, and therapy pool. The choicest rooms face the ocean and are further graced with fireplaces, kitchens, and private patios. The Shilo frequently hosts conventions, so it's not the place to get away from the hubbub of urban life. The restaurant is overpriced and does not maintain the overall quality of the rest of the place. ■ *N Prom and Broadway at Seaside's turnaround; (503) 738-9571 or (800) 222-2244; 30 N Prom, Seaside, OR 97138; $$$; AE, DC, DIS, MC, V; checks OK.* &

CANNON BEACH

Cannon Beach is the Carmel of the Northwest, an artsy community with a hip ambience and strict building codes that ensure only aesthetically pleasing structures are built, usually of cedar and weathered wood. Still, the town is tourist-oriented, and during the summer (and many winter weekends as well), it explodes with visitors who come to browse the galleries and crafts shops or rub shoulders with coastal intelligentsia on crowded Hemlock Street. The main draw continues to be the wide, inviting beach, among the prettiest anywhere; the stretch south from Tolovana Park is the least crowded.

Haystack Rock, one of the world's largest coastal monoliths, dominates the long, sandy stretch. At low tide you can observe rich marine life in the tidal pools.

Ecola State Park (on the town's north end) has fabulous views, quiet picnic areas, and fantastic hiking trails. Head up the trail from Indian Beach and catch a glimpse of the former Tillamook Rock Light Station, a lighthouse built offshore more than 100 years ago and abandoned in 1957. Today it's a columbarium (where cremated remains are stored) named Eternity at Sea. No camping along the trail, except for campsites atop Tillamook Head.

Haystack Program in the Arts, offered through Portland State University, conducts music, art, and writing workshops; (503) 725-8500. **Coaster Theater** hosts good summer plays and year-round entertainment; 108 N Hemlock, (503) 436-1242.

Galleries abound in the area, all on Hemlock Street, the main drag. Three especially good ones are the White Bird, 251 N Hemlock, (503) 436-2681, which has a variety of arts and crafts; the Haystack Gallery, 183 N Hemlock, (503) 436-2547, with a wide range of prints and photography; and Jeffrey Hull Watercolors in Sandpiper Square, 178 N Hemlock, (503) 436-2600, a collection of delicately brushed seascapes.

Other shops of interest include Osburn's Ice Creamery & Deli, 240 N Hemlock, (503) 436-2234; Cannon Beach Bakery, 144 N Hemlock, (503) 436-2592, with one of the few remaining brick oil-fired hearth ovens on the West Coast; Cannon Beach Book Company, 132 N Hemlock, (503) 436-1301, with a surprisingly extensive selection and an owner who encourages browsing; and El Mundo Ltd. Clothing for Women, 215 N Hemlock, (503) 436-1572, and El Mundo for Men, 231 N Hemlock, (503) 436-1002, both specializing in natural-fiber clothing in youthful styles. Bill's Tavern (188 N Hemlock; (503) 436-2202) is a hot spot for music and gab.

RESTAURANTS

Cafe de la Mer ★★★ The original quality, high-end eatery on the North Coast, this upscale cafe has won a considerable following among Willamette Valley visitors and the moneyed old guard with vacation homes in Tolovana Park and Gearhart. Husband-and-wife owners Ron Schiffman and Pat Noonan have transformed a post-'60s coffeehouse into a fine dining establishment. There has been some remodeling, the pretentious atmosphere has mellowed (thanks to some well-chosen staff), and the food continues to shine. Seafood, simply and perfectly prepared, is the cafe's raison d'être, manifest in appetizers of steamed clams and mussels, an interesting crab legs Dijon, and a scallop ceviche with just the right amount of lime and cilantro. Entrées can be as unorthodox as scallops and shrimp sautéed with filberts or as traditional as a lusty bouillabaisse. Salmon, oysters tarragon, and (in a gesture to carnivores) rack of lamb—it's all good, at times outstanding. Desserts can be ethereal. You pay dearly here for the various epicurean delights, and the kitchen follows the dictum of "small portions of good things." ■ *Hemlock and Dawes; (503) 436-1179; 1287 S Hemlock St, Cannon Beach; $$$; beer and wine; AE, MC, V; local checks only; dinner Wed-Sun (days vary in winter).*

The Bistro ★★ You may have difficulty finding the Bistro, tucked away among other shops on a back walkway apart from the Cannon Beach bustle. But once inside, you'll appreciate the intimate, removed setting at this, perhaps the least pretentious, fine dining establishment on the North Coast. Matt and Anita Dueber know where to procure the finest local ingredients (from their greenhouse next door, for instance) and every four-course dinner is substantial, tasty, and reasonably priced. You may start with an antipasto plate of salami, provolone, peppers, and lightly dressed vegetables, and then move on to a delicate Greek lemon soup, then a simple salad. From the entrées you'll choose from the usual shellfish dishes, or fresh halibut, or a tomatoey fish stew (a cioppino, really) with every kind of seafood on the menu thrown in, and there are meat dishes for the non-fishivores among you—chicken stuffed with mushrooms and spinach pesto, for example. We've heard reports of unprofessional service, but have only encountered the opposite. Matt Dueber frequently comes out of the kitchen to make sure all's well. ■ *Opposite Spruce in downtown Cannon Beach; (503) 436-2661; 263 N Hemlock, Cannon Beach; $$; full bar; MC, V; no checks; dinner every day (days vary in winter).*

Lazy Susan Cafe ★ Very Oregon. Definitely Cannon Beach. Everyone in town seems to gather at this airy, sunny, double-deck restaurant in a courtyard opposite the Coaster Theater. The nonsmoking interior is bright with natural wood, plants hanging from the balcony, and local art on the walls. Breakfast is the best time here, when you can order omelets, oatmeal, waffles topped with fresh fruit and yogurt, and excellent coffee to prolong your stay. Eggs—sided with home fries—are correctly cooked. Lunch includes quiche and some interesting sandwiches, such as turkey exotica, made with curried mayonnaise and a chutney garnish. Expect long waits on sunny weekends. ■ *Coaster Square; (503) 436-2816; 126 N Hemlock, Cannon Beach; $; beer and wine; no credit cards; local checks only; breakfast, lunch Wed-Mon (days vary in winter).*

Midtown Cafe ★ *Just* bigger than a hole in the wall, this is a homey, cheery, Cannon Beachy kind of place. There are a few tables, weird windup toys and ceramic animals all over the

▼

▲

place, and right under your nose—the day's baked goods and desserts. Everything's made from scratch using organic fixings whenever possible, the portions are good-size, and the prices reasonable. No wonder, then, that it's usually crowded. Most of the patrons seem to know each other and know, at breakfast, 'bout the fresh bagels, frittatas, eggs, nitrate-free bacon, and tofeta (a scramble of tofu, feta, onions, and spices). Lunch is an adventure of burritos, salads, sandwiches, and smoothies; when it's available, order the special Jamaican stew, a grab bag of fish and exotic condiments. ■ *6 blocks south of downtown; (503) 436-1016; 1235 S Hemlock, Cannon Beach; $; beer and wine; no credit cards; no checks; breakfast, lunch Wed-Sun (closed Jan).* ⅋

LODGINGS

The Argonauta Inn ★ In downtown Cannon Beach, between bustling Hemlock Street and the beach, there is a confusing number of lodging options. The Argonauta, not really an inn but rather a cluster of five well-situated residences, is the best of the bunch. All units come equipped with comfy beds, pleasant furnishings, fireplaces, and color TVs. All but one have a complete kitchen. The lower Lighthouse, a cozy retreat for two, is the best deal. The Beach House, while expensive, is more like a miniature lodge (with a river-rock fireplace, a spacious living room, two sun porches, three bedrooms, and two baths). Two suites within the Beach House, perfect for couples, are available at select times during the year. ■ *Corner of 2nd and Larch; (503) 436-2601; 188 W 2nd, PO Box 3, Cannon Beach, OR 97110; $$; MC, V; checks OK.*

Cannon Beach Hotel Originally a boardinghouse, the Cannon Beach Hotel is a tidy, nine-room operation with a decidedly European flavor. There's a small, pleasant lobby with a fireplace, and books and magazines strewn about. The rooms are reasonable (especially compared to the pricey motels nearby), and vary from a nicely decorated, one-bed arrangement to a one-bedroom suite with a gas fireplace, spa, and ocean view. All rooms include a "light" breakfast. No pets are allowed, and the interior is a no-smoking zone. The adjacent restaurant (called J.P.'s at Cannon Beach) also has a nice feel, with large windows, striking woodwork, and friendly service—a good option. ■ *Corner of Gower and S Hemlock; (503) 436-1392; 1116 S Hemlock, PO Box 943, Cannon Beach, OR 97110; $$; MC, V; checks OK.*

▼

▲

TOLOVANA PARK

Nestled on Cannon Beach's south side, Tolovana Park is laid back and less crowded, and possesses a residential character. Leave your car at the Tolovana Park Wayside (with parking and restrooms) and stroll an uncluttered beach, especially in the off season. At low tide you can walk all the way to the Arch Cape, some five miles south, where you can pick up the Oregon Coast Trail. (But be careful, the incoming tide might block your return.)

LODGINGS

Sea Sprite Motel This cute, always popular, ocean-front motel is a good getaway choice for couples or the family (but no pets). Each of the six small but homey units includes a kitchen and color TV. Most have woodstoves. There's a washer and dryer on the premises, and firewood, beach towels, and blankets are provided. A two-bedroom cottage enjoys great views and can sleep eight, although there have been complaints about less-than-satisfactory service. If the Sea Sprite is full, ask about the Hearthstone Inn (nonsmoking), located in Cannon Beach and under the same ownership. ▪ *At Nebesna and Oceanfront; (503) 436-2266; PO Box 66, Tolovana Park, OR 97145; $$; MC, V; checks OK.*

Stephanie Inn [*unrated*] It's new, it's gorgeous, and its elegance of a New England country inn distinguishes the Stephanie Inn on the Oregon Coast. The oceanfront location is not isolated, but there's a definite sense of privacy here. Inside, the emphasis is on pampered and purposeful service. All of the 46 rooms include gas fireplaces, Jacuzzis, VCRs, and stunning furnishings; however, the deck rooms on the second and third floors are best. A full complimentary breakfast is served in the dining room or in your room. Come evening, Northwest wines are profiled in the library. Watch the ocean, play the piano, or cozy up to the fireplace in the hotel's Chart Room. Prix-fixe dinners are available to guests on a daily basis. ▪ *On the beach, at 2740 S Pacific, Tolovana Park; (503) 436-2221 or (800) 633-3466; PO Box 219, Cannon Beach, OR 97110; $$$; AE, DC, DIS, MC, V; checks OK.* &

Manzanita

MANZANITA

Resting mostly on a sandy peninsula with undulating dunes covered in beach grass, shore pine, and Scotch broom, Manzanita is a lazy but growing community gaining popularity as a coastal getaway for in-the-know urbanites. The adjacent beach and nearby Nehalem Bay have become windsurfing hot spots, and **Nehalem Bay State Park**, just south of town, offers hiking and bike trails, as well as miles of little-used beaches. Overlooking it all sits nearby Neahkahnie Mountain with a steep, switchbacked trail leading to the 1,600-foot summit, the best viewpoint on Oregon's North Coast.

Just north of town, **Oswald West State Park** has one of the finest campgrounds on any coast in the world. You walk a half-mile from the parking lot (where wheelbarrows are available to carry your gear) to tent sites among old-growth trees; the ocean, with a massive cove and tidepools, is just beyond. Surfing, kayaking, and sunbathing are favorite summer activities. No reservations, as the walk deters the crowds that would otherwise come. Be sure to secure all your valuables out of sight, or take them with you. Call (503) 731-3411 for advance word on availability.

RESTAURANTS

Jarboe's ★★★ Jarboe's is in a snug (eight tables), remodeled cottage, where the mood is set to mellow and the food is set to sublime. Menus, which change every day, are the work of Danish-born owner and chef Klaus Monberg, and show off his evident imagination and feel for food. A recent crawfish bisque with juicy scallops, for example, challenged the vocabulary to describe its texture—beyond velvety, beyond smooth —and its nectarlike taste. Even a simple salad of radishes, endive, filberts, and sun-dried tomatoes becomes more than the sum of its parts. Entrées run to mesquite-broiled meat, fowl, and seafood, and with Monberg working the grill, a simple fresh ingredient (snapper, perhaps, or skewers of scallops and oysters) takes on a new texture and flavor. Sauces, like the soups, are light and flavorful. Desserts are delicate, understated concoctions such as poached pear with crème Anglaise or simple, almond-crusted chocolate cake. ■ *Laneda and Carmel; (503) 368-5113; 137 Laneda Ave, Manzanita; $$$; beer and wine; MC, V; local checks only; dinner Thurs-Mon (Thurs-Sun in winter).*

Blue Sky Cafe ★★ Comfortable, but not too casual; elegant, unpretentious; reliable, but untraditional (as you'll know right away by the salt and pepper shakers). Seasonal offerings here include such culture-crossing appetizers as delicate sushi served with potted Montrachet and entrées such as spicy Sichuan chicken (stir-fried in peanut sauce with coconut, curry, and cilantro) and roasted Poblano chiles (stuffed with mass quantities of goat cheese and sided with sautéed bananas, black beans, salsas, tortillas, polenta, and who knows what else). Baked salmon and smoked salmon pasta are more down-to-earth, and are just fine. It's a tropical delight of colors and tastes. An extensive wine list has an all-Oregon reserve pinot noir section. ■ *Laneda and 2nd; (503) 368-5712; 154 Laneda Ave, Manzanita; $$; full bar; MC, V; local checks only; dinner Wed-Sun.* ᕀ

Cassandra's ★ Beachy and hip—airy deck, good magazine selection, and waitresses who surf—Cassandra's purveys the best pizza around. Owner Fawn de Turk assembles ample pies with interesting names and good ingredients (artichoke hearts, feta cheese, lots of olive oil). Four can feast on a large primavera, a savory affair built on a base of olive oil, garlic, and herbs with mushrooms, green peppers, red onions, and tomatoes, then heaped with provolone, Romano, and mozzarella. Fawn knows that the heart of a good pizza is good crust, gobs of cheese, and a zesty sauce. You'll wait a bit for it. ■ *Laneda and 4th; (503) 368-5593; 411 Laneda Ave, Manzanita; $; beer and wine; no credit cards; checks OK; dinner every day (days vary in winter).*

LODGINGS

The Inn at Manzanita ★★ One block off the beach, occupying a multilevel, woodsy setting similar to a Japanese garden, the Inn at Manzanita is a quiet, tranquil retreat. You fall asleep with the roar of the surf in your ears and awake to the sound of chirping birds. Inside, each of the eight spacious, nonsmoking units is finished in pine or cedar, with panels of stained glass here and there. All units have a fireplace or wood-burning stove, a good-sized spa, a wet bar with fridge, a view deck, and a TV with VCR. Some units have skylights. And the luxury doesn't stop there. Friendly but unobtrusive innkeepers Larry and Linda Martin attend to the little things: fresh flowers on the table; bathrobes hanging in your room (which is meticulously clean); a stack of wood for your evening fire; and a daily paper at your door. All in all, a subdued, romantic getaway. Leave the kids and the pets at home. ■ *One block from the beach at 67 Laneda; (503) 368-6754; PO Box 243, Manzanita, OR 97130; $$$; MC, V; checks OK.*

Garibaldi/
Bay City

Restaurants

▲

GARIBALDI/BAY CITY

The Tillamook Bay front is one of the homes for the summer salmon fleet, and there are several establishments that sell fresh seafood. **Miller Seafood**, right on Highway 101, is easiest to find. Call (503) 322-0355 to find out what's fresh. **Smith's Pacific Shrimp Co.** is located at 608 Commercial Dr; (503) 322-3316. If you'd rather catch it yourself, head for **Siggi-G Ocean Charters** in Garibaldi; 611 Commercial, (503) 322-3285.

Artspace in Bay City, located in a converted meat market, features avant-garde art and a limited-hours restaurant with good chow; on Highway 101 and Fifth, (503) 377-2782.

RESTAURANTS

Downie's Cafe A neighborhood eatery patronized almost entirely by locals, Downie's is right off the set of the '60s television show "Mayberry R.F.D." Might be the town's police chief in the booth behind you, so watch your manners. Clean, tidy, unpretentious, and small (one lit cigarette, unfortunately, fills the room), Downie's offers down-home service and food. Clam chowder is good—a rich, creamy potion of potatoes, celery, and thick chunks of clam. Although the hand-hewn chips are greasy, the fish fried in a light batter is not. Pies are yummy too. ■ *5th and C streets; (503)377-2220; 9320 5th St, Bay City; $; no alcohol; no credit cards; local checks only; breakfast, lunch every day, dinner Mon-Sat.* ⅄

TILLAMOOK

A broad, flat expanse of bottomland created by the confluence of three rivers (Tillamook, Trask, and Wilson), Tillamook is best known as dairy country. On the north end of town along Highway 101 sits the home of Tillamook cheese, the **Tillamook County Creamery Association** plant and visitors center; 4175 Highway 101 N, (503) 842-4481. The tour is self-guided and, frankly, there's not that much to see. But the parking lot is always crowded. A better choice for browsing is the **Blue Heron Cheese Company**, about one mile south on 101. Less kitschy and better stocked than the Tillamook Creamery, Blue Heron offers a variety of cheeses and other made-in-Oregon munchies, and has a wine-tasting room for Northwest wines; 2001 Blue Heron Drive, (503) 842-8281.

OCEANSIDE

A tiny seaside resort that defines "quaint," Oceanside lies eight miles west of Tillamook along the 22-mile **Three Capes Scenic Drive**, one of Oregon's most beautiful stretches of coastline. The narrow, winding road skirts the outline of Tillamook Bay, climbs over Cape Mears (where you can walk up to, and inside, the Cape Mears lighthouse), then traverses the shores of Netarts Bay. **Cape Lookout State Park**, another jewel in Oregon's park system, offers 250 campsites, along with headland-hugging trails and a huge stretch of little-used beach; (503) 842-3182. Continuing south, the scenic drive scales Cape Lookout, the westernmost headland on the North Oregon coast. The trail from the parking lot at the cape's summit (also part of the state park) meanders through primeval forests of stately cedar, Western hemlock, and Sitka spruce. Spectacular ocean vistas fill the lower side of the drive. Find your way to the top of **Mount Maxwell** for a stunning vantage point of the ocean and migrating gray whales. Back at sea level lies a desertlike landscape of thousands of acres of sandy dunes, a favorite area for off-road recreational vehicles (which are required to stay in designated areas). The road to Pacific City and the route's third cape, Kiwanda, runs through lush, green dairy country.

RESTAURANTS

Roseanna's Oceanside Cafe ★ The sole restaurant in picturesque, pint-size Oceanside (well, except for the tavern across the street), Roseanna's feels like a funky fern bar—lots of plants, a piano, an overdone pink-and-mauve motif with a ubiquitous signature parrot, all packed into an old converted grocery store with wooden floors. After a day spent windsurfing in Netarts Bay or hang gliding off Maxwell Mountain, there's nothing better than a bowl of tasty clam chowder, a wedge of crab or shrimp quiche, or a plate of grilled oysters. Desserts score high points, especially an oven-warmed Toll House pie topped with Tillamook ice cream. Service is laid back but efficient. Dining room views of the ocean and nearby Three Arch Rocks make meals more memorable. ■ *On the main drag through Oceanside; (503) 842-7351; 1490 Pacific St, Oceanside; $$; beer and wine; MC, V; no checks; breakfast, lunch, dinner every day (closed Mon in winter).* &

LODGINGS

House on the Hill Bring your binoculars. The setting here, on a bluff overlooking Three Arch Rocks (a bird, seal, and sea lion sanctuary) and the blue Pacific, is unbeatable. The house is actually four buildings, home to sixteen units and a honeymoon suite. The Rock Room, with telescopes to spy on the wildlife and scan the horizon for whales, is open to all guests. The trapezoidal architecture is unusual at best, and the furnishings nothing special, but the gorgeous views make up for any shortcomings. Choose a unit with a kitchen and stock up on groceries from Tillamook, since local pickings are pretty slim. Kids are fine here. ■ *Maxwell Mountain Rd at Maxwell Point; (503) 842-6030; PO Box 187, Oceanside, OR 97134; $$; MC, V; no checks.*

CLOVERDALE

LODGINGS

Hudson House Bed & Breakfast ★★ Perched on a bluff in the middle of nowhere, the picturesque Hudson House, built in 1906 and on the Historic Register, evokes memories of a country weekend at Grandma's house. The entire restored Victorian farmhouse is dedicated to the guests; your hosts, the amicable Kulju family, reside next door. The four guest rooms (each with private bath) are decorated in an early-century country style and overlook forested hillsides surrounding the pastoral Nestucca River valley, home to contented Holsteins, Herefords, and Jerseys. Breakfasts are exceptional, including unusual treats such as British bangers (sausages), Dutch pancakes, and homemade Wholly Cow cereal. No children, smoking, or pets. ■ *2½ miles south of Cloverdale and east of Pacific City; (503) 392-3533; 37700 Hwy 101 S, Cloverdale, OR 97112; $$; MC, V; checks OK.* &

PACIFIC CITY

Pacific City is where the dory fleet (Oregon's classic fishing boats) is launched from trailers in the south lee of Cape Kiwanda. Up above, hang gliders swoop off the slopes of the cape and land on the sandy expanses below. The region's second Haystack Rock (Cannon Beach has the other) sits a half mile offshore. **Robert Straub State Park** is situated at the south end of town and occupies most of the Nestucca beach sandspit. **Fishing** enthusiasts flock to Pacific City—the Nestucca and Little Nestucca rivers are known as two of the finest salmon and steelhead streams in the state.

RESTAURANTS

Grateful Bread Bakery It's about time someone opened a decent bakery in these parts, and in this case someone is transplanted New Yorkers Laura and Gary Seide. These extroverted owners purvey robust breads, muffins, and a scrumptious array of sweets—carrot cake and gargantuan cinnamon rolls, to name a few—in a cheerful, beachy setting. Try the crusty French (all dough, no air) and herb garlic. There are breakfast and lunch menus listing some very cheesy New York-style pizza, veggie lasagne, and a few hearty soups. Enjoy your coffee and cake out on the deck. ■ *On the Pacific City loop road; (503) 965-7337; 34805 Brooten Rd, Pacific City; $; no alcohol; MC, V; checks OK; breakfast, lunch every day (closed Jan).* ⅋

Riverhouse Restaurant You might see a great blue heron perched on a log on the Nestucca River, which flows idly to the sea right outside the window. The Riverhouse is a cozy, calming stop, 3 miles off Highway 101, and far removed from the typical tourist trappings. It's small—10 or so tables—with hanging plants and a piano in the corner for local musicians who perform on weekends. Everything's homemade: soup might be chunky fresh vegetable or French onion, the deluxe hamburgers are consistently good, and this is definitely an apple-pie sort of place (theirs is especially tasty). ■ *¼ mile north of the stoplight on Brooten Rd; (503) 965-6722; 34450 Brooten Rd, Pacific City; $$; full bar; MC, V; checks OK; lunch, dinner every day (days vary in winter).* ⅋

NESKOWIN

A diminutive, mostly residential community lying in the lee of Cascade Head, a steeply sloped and forested promontory, Neskowin affords the final port of refuge before the touristy "20 miracle miles" (as the stretch from Lincoln City to Newport used to be called). The beach here is narrower but less crowded than other locales. Proposal Rock, an offshore island, is reachable at very low tides. **Cascade Head** has miles of little-used hiking trails that traverse rain forests and meadows, then skirt rocky cliffs. They begin at a marked trailhead about two miles south (visible from Highway 101). The old Neskowin Road, a narrow route that winds through horse farms and old-growth forests, is an enchanting side trip.

The **Sitka Center for Art and Ecology** operates on the south side of Cascade Head and offers summer classes on many subjects, plus numerous talks and exhibits; (503) 994-5485.

LODGINGS

The Chelan ★ This attractive white-and-blue adobe structure encompasses nine condominium units, all with lovely ocean views. Even though there are private homes nearby, this place feels like a getaway retreat. There's a manicured front lawn, lush gardens, and a secluded atmosphere. Each condo has a well-equipped kitchen, a large living room with picture window, and a brick fireplace. Most have two bedrooms. Ground-floor units have a private entrance to a small backyard, with the ocean just beyond. Upstairs accommodations (off-limits to children) enjoy private balconies. ▪ *Off Salem Blvd at 48750 Breakers Blvd; (503) 392-3270; PO Box 732, Neskowin, OR 97149; $$$; MC, V; checks OK.*

Pacific Sands Literally a stone's throw from breaking waves, this well-maintained resort condo-motel with an average, bland exterior, enjoys a spectacular setting. Only 10 of the condos are for rent; each has a fireplace, kitchen, and more than enough room to stretch out and get comfortable. Opt for a beachfront unit (if available), and step out to miles of untrampled sand and primitive Cascade Head a short distance to the south. ▪ *Breakers Blvd and Amity at 48250 Breakers Blvd; (503) 392-3101; PO Box 356, Neskowin, OR 97149; $$; MC, V; checks OK.*

OTIS

RESTAURANTS

Otis Cafe ★ The Otis Cafe is simply *thriving*. It does all those things small-town eateries all over America used to do, only better—honest, no-frills food at old-fashioned prices. Everyone appreciates this basic ethic, and on summer weekends they line up outside for it. Inside, contented diners nosh on beefy burgers, thick 'n' chunky soups, filling breakfasts (including plate-sized portions of hashbrowns with melted cheese), and huge malts and milk shakes. Dinner specials run along the lines of fish, pork chops, and chicken-fried steak. The buttery black bread is also sold to go, in case you can't get enough of it while you're there; other baked items, especially the pies, are delish. ▪ *Otis Junction; (503) 994-2813; Hwy 18, Otis; $; beer* and wine; DIS, MC, V; checks OK; breakfast, lunch every day, dinner Thurs-Sun.

LINCOLN CITY

September-'til-spring used to be the ideal time to visit the coast and escape the summer hordes. Now some areas of coastline, such as the super-congested stretch between Lincoln City and Newport, have no off season. Every weekend is crowded, and traffic can be the pits (local officials, along with the Oregon Department of Transportation, are searching for solutions, but so far, none have emerged). Whether you come for summer sun or winter storm (or whale) watching, be prepared to move slowly through these parts.

Barnacle Bill's seafood store, 2174 NE Hwy 101, (503) 994-3022, is well known (and open daily) for fresh and smoked fish: salmon, sturgeon, albacore tuna, black cod, crab, and shrimp. On the north end of town, **Lighthouse Brewpub**, 4157 N Highway 101, (503) 994-7238, handcrafts some alluring ales. Right in the midst of all the hubbub, **Cafe Roma**, 1437 NW Highway 101, (503) 994-6616, offers coffee drinks and exotic Italian sodas.

▼

Otis

Restaurants

▲

RESTAURANTS

The Bay House ★★★ Shoreside restaurants with spectacular views can often get away with serving overpriced, mediocre food. Happily, this is not the case at the Bay House, located on the banks of Siletz Bay, just out of reach of the glitzy Lincoln City tourist trade. It has been remodeled by new owners Leslie and Dennis Dressel, but the traditional feel remains—helped along by lots of richly finished wood and brass—as does the stunning view of the bay. Since the Dressels have also retained chef William Purdy, the food remains stellar too. The seasonal menu is as imaginative, if not more so, as ever. Appetizers such as chicken satay now appear, as does smoked salmon with vodka crème fraîche. Entrées are similarly intriguing (curried yogurt chicken with banana-coconut accoutrements, grilled catch-of-the-day served with shiitake mushrooms and a blue-cheese potato pancake), and the more traditional dishes (creamy onion soup with tiny shrimp, fresh halibut, rack of lamb) are reliable and still special. Desserts, fittingly, are exquisite. Time your reservations with sunset and experience Siletz Bay's daily light show at dusk—like the food, a treat worth savoring. ■ *5911 SW Hwy 101, on the south edge of town; (503) 996-3222; Lincoln City; $$$; full bar; AE, DIS, MC, V; checks OK; dinner every day (Wed-Sun in winter).* &

Road's End Dory Cove Appreciative crowds continue to flock to this place, rain or shine, especially since the menu has expanded. Hearty Americana, Oregon Coast-style, is the theme here: lots of seafood, steak, tasty chowder, and 20-plus kinds of burgers (including a half-pound monster). Dessert centers around homemade pie à la mode, which is no problem for us. Road's End Wayside, a small state park, is right next door and offers good beach access and decent clamming (tide tables available inside the restaurant). ■ *Next to state park; (503) 994-5180; 5819 N Logan Rd, Lincoln City; $; beer and wine; MC, V; checks OK; lunch, dinner every day.* &

LODGINGS

Palmer House ★ Palmer House is a perfect alternative to Lincoln City's glitzy beachfront lodgings. It's still close to the beach (less than a quarter-mile away), but situated in a woodsy setting. The house, originally John Gray's (the developer of the Salishan, a few miles south down the road), is built in the Northwest regional style with three bright, airy guest rooms (all with private bath). The Azalea Room has an ocean view and fireplace; the Agate features a large skylight over the bed. A memorable three-course breakfast may offer omelets, crêpes, handmade sausage, breads, scones, marmalade, and lots of fresh fruit. No smoking, children, or pets. ■ *On Inlet, ¼ mile north of the D River Wayside; (503) 994-7932; 646 NW Inlet, Lincoln City, OR 97367; $$$; MC, V; checks OK.*

GLENEDEN BEACH

RESTAURANTS

Chez Jeannette ★★★ Windows with flower boxes, white-washed brick walls, and an intimate woodsy setting (as well as two fireplaces, usually blazing away in winter) give this establishment the appearance of a French country inn. And although the clientele is upscale, the feel here is less formal and more comfortable than, say, the Salishan a half-mile away. The food is French, traditionally so: butter and cream are used in abundance, most entrées are carefully sauced. And, bucking the seafood tradition seen up and down the coast, veal, rack of lamb, duckling, and filet mignon make appearances on the menu (with quail, or even venison, showing up occasionally as specials), though Chez Jeannette is by no means a slouch when it comes to seafood, as Umpqua oysters, mussels in sumptuous cream sauce (*naturellement*), and poached salmon with aioli will attest. Vegetables arrive in imaginative combinations—carrots and mangos, cabbage with walnuts and onions—and desserts carry the cholesterol count into the stratosphere. ■ *¼ mile south of Salishan Lodge; (503) 764-3434; 7150 Old Hwy 101, Glenden Beach; $$$; full bar; AE, MC, V; checks OK; dinner every day (Tues-Sat in winter).* &

Salishan Lodge ★★ Salishan, the first and perhaps the biggest resort on the Oregon Coast, can seem stuffy, and there's certainly a sense of exclusivity, but the place *is* special. Sprawled over a thousand acres, Salishan includes 205 guest rooms, arranged in eightplex units nicely dispersed over the lush, green landscape. There's an 18-hole (par 72) golf course, plus driving range, pro shop, and resident PGA professional. You can swim in an indoor pool, work out in the sizable fitness center, sweat in a sauna, or jog on the trails winding through the 750-acre forest. Kids (and you'll see them here since Salishan is geared to families as well as couples) have their own game room and play area. The focal point is a huge lodge with restaurants, a nightclub, a library, meeting rooms, and a gift shop. There's lots of attractively exposed wood and stone. The guest units are spacious and tastefully furnished but not extravagant, with brick fireplaces, view balconies, splashes of regional art, and individual covered carports. Distances within Salishan are considerable, so specify where you'd like to stay depending on what you want to be near (for example: Spruce, Fairway, Chieftain House South, and Sunset Suite overlook the links; Tennis House is near the courts; and the Blue Heron and Tide units have the best views of Siletz Bay and the ocean). The beach is a good half mile away.

▼

Gleneden Beach

Lodgings

▲

The main dining room in the lodge was once the premier gourmet destination on the coast. Under the skillful direction of executive chef Rob Pounding, the kitchen can still purvey top-notch cuisine; however, the quality of meals can vary. You might encounter a glorious salmon or halibut entrée, or be disappointed by a dry and tasteless paella. Service can be pretentious and overindulgent, and prices are sky-high. The voluminous wine list represents a cellar stocked with 20,000 bottles. Ask wine steward Phil de Vito for his advice. ■ *Hwy 101 in Gleneden Beach; (503) 764-3600 or (800) 452-2300; PO Box 118, Gleneden Beach, OR 97388; $$$; AE, DC, DIS, MC, V; checks OK; breakfast, lunch, dinner every day.*

DEPOE BAY

Once a charming coastal community, Depoe Bay is today mostly an extension of Lincoln City's strip development. Fortunately, some of the original town, including its tiny harbor, remains intact. Depoe Bay bills itself as a **whale-watching** mecca, and during the gray whale migratory season (December through April), the leviathans may cruise within hailing distance of the headlands. **Deep Sea Trollers** is one of several operations offering whale-watching cruises; (503) 765-2248.

Channel House ★ Intimate seaside inns (generally larger than B&Bs) with great settings and gracious service are the latest news in the Northwest, and the Channel House was among the first. Spectacularly situated on a cliff overlooking the ocean and Depoe Bay Channel (literally right above the water), this place has 12 rooms, all with private baths and ocean views. They're truly special accommodations (if rather spendy, starting at $115), each outfitted with private deck, gas fireplace, spa, and in the morning, a breakfast that's aimed to satisfy anyone's hunger. Be sure to bring your binoculars, especially during whale-watching season. ■ *35 Ellingson St, at the end of the street; (503) 765-2140 or (800) 447-2140; PO Box 56, Depoe Bay, OR 97341; $$$; MC, V; checks OK.*

Inn at Otter Crest ★ This inn is really a rambling destination resort perched on 100 acres at Cape Foulweather. It's lushly landscaped with evergreens, coastal shrubs, and every color of rhododendron imaginable. Breathtaking views abound, and an isolated low-tide beach awaits at sea level, 50 or so feet below. However, paradise it is not, exactly. For starters, Cape Foulweather is aptly named, as fog often enshrouds the headland even though sunny skies may prevail just north and south. The resort hosts many conventions, which can be intrusive. And it's so large (more than 280 rooms and suites) that a personal touch can sometimes be lacking (so large, in fact, that you leave your car a short distance away and hop a shuttle van to your room). Still, most of the rooms open onto marvelous views, and many have fireplaces and full kitchens. All in all, a nice but expensive ($99-$248) alternative to beachfront motel life. The on-premises restaurant, the Flying Dutchman, is nothing special. ■ *Otter Crest Loop, two miles south of Depoe Bay; (503) 765-2111 or (800) 452-2101; PO Box 50, Otter Rock, OR 97369; $$$; AE, DC, DIS, MC, V; no checks.* ♿

20 YEARS

▼

Newport

▲

NEWPORT

The most popular tourist destination on the Oregon Coast, Newport exhibits a mix of tasteful development (the Performing Arts Center, for example) with unending shopping center sprawl. Veer off Highway 101's commercial chaos and seek out the real Newport.

The bayfront is a working waterfront going full tilt, where fishing boats of all types—trollers, trawlers, shrimpers, and crabbers—berth year-round. A number of **charters** operate from here. They'll provide bait and tackle, clean and fillet your catch, and even smoke or can it for you. Many charter operators have initiated whale-watching excursions, in addition to their half- and full-day fishing trips. Sea Gull Charters, 343 SW Bay Boulevard, (503) 265-7441, and Newport Sport Fishing, 1000 SE Bay Boulevard, (503) 265-7558, are two operators.

Afterward, quench your thirst with a microbrew at **Roque Ale Brewpub**, 748 SW Bay Boulevard (503) 265-2537. For a bird's-eye perspective of boats, bay, and ocean, take a drive through **Yaquina Beach State Park**, which wraps around the south end of town. **Oceanic Arts Center**, 444 SW Bay Boulevard, (503) 265-5963, and the **Wood Gallery**, 818 SW Bay Boulevard, (503) 265-6843, both on the bay front, are galleries worth visiting. The former offers mostly jewelry, paintings, pottery, and sculpture; the latter, functional sculpture, woodwork, pottery, and weaving. The Nye Beach area, on the ocean side of Highway 101, houses a potpourri of neo-professionals, tourists, writers, artists, and fishermen.

On the south side of the Yaquina Bay Bridge, Oregon State University's **Hatfield Marine Science Center** offers displays, a facsimile tidepool, and a full range of free nature walks, field trips (including whale watching), and films, especially during the summer Seatauqua program; 2030 S Marine Science Drive, (503) 867-0100. Nearby, the pride of Newport, the **Oregon Coast Aquarium**, features furry, finny, and feathery creatures cavorting in re-created tidepools, cliffs, and caves. The exhibits are first-class; 2820 SE Ferry Slip Road, (503) 867-3474. A drive out the South Jetty Road affords sea-level views of harbor traffic. A couple of miles farther south is the area's best, and most extensive, camping site, **South Beach State Park**; (503) 867-4715.

RESTAURANTS

The Whale's Tale ★★ In tourist-oriented Newport, where mediocre restaurants come and go, the Whale's Tale has been purveying the best food in town inside the bay front's hippest setting for many a year. Customers are a zesty mix of fishermen, aging hippies, Newport yuppies, and adventuresome tourists who've forsaken Mo's (just down the block). Breakfasts are outstanding, with fresh jalapeño omelets, scrumptious poppyseed pancakes, and home-fried potatoes with onions and green chiles smothered in cheese. The coffee will getcha goin'. Lunches include good-sized sandwiches, sumptuous, well-seasoned soups, and a lusty cioppino. A plate of grilled Yaquina oysters is a dinnertime favorite, along with lasagne, German sausage and sauerkraut, and excellent black bread. Save room for the signature mousse-in-a-bag dessert. Summer weekends sometimes feature live music, and the mood inside "the Whale" can be boisterous. ■ *At SW Bay and Fall; (503) 265-8660; 452 SW Bay Blvd, Newport; $$; beer and wine; AE, DC, DIS, MC, V; checks OK; breakfast, lunch, dinner every day.*

Canyon Way Restaurant and Bookstore ★ Canyon Way is as much an emporium as an eatery, with a bookstore, gift shop, deli, and a restaurant on the premises. You could easily get sidetracked on the way to your table, or decide to forgo a sit-down meal in favor of the many take-out munchies available. If you stay, you'll find a pleasingly diverse menu loaded with seafood and fresh pasta plates. A Cajun turkey sandwich, grilled lingcod 'n chips, and Dungeness crab cakes with angel-hair onion rings, along with a variety of salads, are good noon-time options. For dinner, there's a different baked oyster preparation daily, and choices as diverse as chicken curry (with a splash of tropical flavors and textures) and prawns Provençal. Desserts are made daily. On sunny days, request an outdoor table overlooking the bay. ■ *At the bottom of Herbert off Hwy 101; (503) 265-8319; 1216 SW Canyon Way, Newport; $$; full bar; AE, DIS, MC, V; local checks only; lunch Mon-Sat, dinner every day (Tues-Sat in winter); bookstore and deli open every day.* ⅋

LODGINGS

Sylvia Beach Hotel ★★★ Owners Goody Cable (of Portland's Rimsky-Korsakoffee House) and Sally Ford have dedicated their bluff-top hotel to bookworms and their literary heroes and heroines. They gave several like-minded friends the task of decorating each of the 20 rooms, and the results are rich in whimsy and fresh, distinct personality. Most luxurious are the three "classics" (Mark Twain, Agatha Christie, and Colette). The Agatha Christie suite, for instance, is decorated in a lush green English chintz, with a tiled fireplace, a large deck facing out over the sea cliff below, and—best of all—clues from the writer's many murders: men's shoes poking out from beneath a curtain, notes on the walnut secretary, bottles labeled "poison" in the medicine cabinet. The "best sellers" (views) and the "novels" (non-views) are quite small, not as impressive (some even look a bit tattered), but they are equally imaginative. A mechanized pendulum swings over the Edgar Allan Poe bed, the Cat in the Hat smirks on the wall of the Dr. Seuss room. There aren't any reading chairs in the best sellers or novel rooms, but upstairs, books and comfortable chairs abound in the library. Hot wine is served nightly at 10pm. Breakfast (open to nonguests by reservation) is included in the price of the room. Prepare for a stay sans phones, TVs, and stress.

Dinners in the hotel's Tables of Content restaurant, located downstairs and just above the beach, are prix-fixe affairs, open to the public on a reservation-only basis. The main attraction here is the company; the food gets secondary billing. Meals are eight or so "chapters" long, and courses (with plentiful portions) are brought to your table family-style, making dinner more like a picnic than a gourmet meal. But the stories told here are what you'll remember. ■ *West on NW 3rd off Hwy 101, 6 blocks to NW Cliff; (503) 265-5428; 267 NW Cliff, Newport, OR 97365; $$; AE, MC, V; checks OK.* &

Ocean House ★★ If you haven't been here in a while, you'll be surprised. The place has been remodeled and apartments have been added; needless to say, it's bigger, and perhaps not quite as cozy. But your hosts, Bob and Bette Garrard, are still the epitome of congeniality. And the setting remains picture-perfect, overlooking the surf at Agate Beach, with Yaquina Head and its lighthouse towering nearby. The four guest rooms are neither elegant nor luxurious, but are comfortable and well appointed. There's a small library with cushy chairs and a roaring fireplace in the winter. Bob's paintings decorate the walls. Outside, you can relax and sunbathe protected from the summer northwest wind (but not from the neighbors) in the sheltered backyard and garden. A short trail (with some steep steps) leads to the beach below. Full breakfasts complement the Garrards' hospitality. ■ *Just off Hwy 101 N in Agate Beach; (503) 265-6158 or (800) 56BANDB; 4920 NW Woody Way, Newport, OR 97365; $$; MC, V; checks OK.*

SEAL ROCK

RESTAURANTS

Yuzen ★ You may think you're hallucinating. A Japanese restaurant residing in a Bavarian-styled building, located in Seal Rock, a blink of a town with a wild West, chainsaw-art kind of motif? No, Yuzen is for real. Certainly it purveys the coast's finest Japanese cuisine. Even if uncooked fish isn't your idea of a delectable morsel, you'll enjoy the mildly flavored (unless you use the accompanying green Japanese horseradish) tuna, salmon, and prawn served in the sushi sampler appetizer. Of course, you can try everything from a miniature maki (tuna) cucumber roll, to tamago (egg) and sushi pizza at the sushi bar. Dinners include a decent miso soup and a small salad. Sushiyaki is splendid, as are the tempura dishes such as Ten Don (five prawns tempura on a bowl of rice). There's even a wafu steak, a traditional Japanese grilled New York steak with veggies. You'll also find sake here, as well as ginger and matsucha (green-tea flavored) ice cream. Service can be painfully slow. ■ *8 miles south of Newport on Hwy 101; (503) 563-4766; Seal Rock; $$; beer and wine; MC, V; checks OK; lunch, dinner Tues-Sun.*

WALDPORT

Not all coastal towns are touristy. Small, quiet, unpretentious Waldport is situated on the wide Alsea River estuary, where

Highway 101 makes a big bend to accommodate its sandy shore. There's good clamming and crabbing in the bay, and equipment can be rented at the dock in the Old Town section, on the water just east of the highway.

LODGINGS

Cliff House Bed and Breakfast ★★★ A whimsical retreat. A romantic fantasy come true. A dream weekend. The Cliff House is all of these things and more, thanks to the unyielding efforts of owners Gabriella Duvall and D.J. Novgrad. The house is exactly where it claims to be—perched on a cliff atop what must surely be one of the Oregon Coast's most prized parcels. The ocean vistas are endless. Seals and salmon-hungry sea lions frequent the mouth of the Alsea River, and migrating whales pass across the watery panorama of the Pacific. Seemingly every nook and cranny in the house enjoys an ocean or bay view. There are now four guest rooms, all enjoying super-comfy beds, chandeliers, cedar-lined baths, and balconies. The Morning Star room is furnished with a wood stove and two skylights; the second-story Alsea has a refrigerator and a private entrance. The luxurious Bridal Suite enjoys a tufted velvet sleigh bed with canopy, an ocean-front mirrored bath with Jacuzzi, and a shower for two. Out back, there's an ocean-view deck with Jacuzzi, a hammock for two, and a game of croquet. Breakfasts are elaborate and first-rate. Gabriella and D.J. will give you as little or as much attention as you want...and they always seem to know how much. ■ *1 block west of Hwy 101 on Adahi Rd; (503) 563-2506; PO Box 436, Waldport, OR 97394; $$$; MC, V; checks OK.*

Cape Cod Cottages ★ Between Waldport and Yachats, the beach becomes narrower and less used. Cape Cod Cottages, sitting on a low-lying bank just off Highway 101, occupy 300 feet of this ocean frontage. There are nine spic-and-span and cozy one- and two-bedroom units. All come with completely equipped kitchens, fireplaces (with wood provided), decks, and picture windows overlooking the ocean. Some even have garages. All in all, a nice, out-of-the-way place that allows kids. ■ *2½ miles south of Waldport, on Hwy 101; (503) 563-2106; 4150 SW Pacific Coast Hwy, Waldport, OR 97394; $$; MC, V; checks OK.*

Edgewater Cottages ★ Lots of honeymooners land here, and the place is usually booked from the beginning of the tourist season. The seven units are varied and rustic-looking, with lots of wood paneling and a beachy feel throughout. The cute, pint-size Wheel House (a steal at $35) and Crow's Nest are strictly two-person affairs, while the Beachcomber can accommodate as many as 15 guests. Every cottage has an ocean view, a fireplace (firewood provided), an equipped kitchen, and a sun deck.

There's only one phone on the premises, but other necessities, such as corkscrews, popcorn poppers, and food processors, are available to borrow. Kids and well-behaved dogs are fine (but pets cost extra). There are minimum stay requirements. ■ *2½ miles south of Waldport, on Hwy 101; (503) 563-2240; 3978 SW Pacific Coast Hwy, Waldport, OR 97394; $$; no credit cards; checks OK.*

YACHATS

Yachats (pronounced ya-hots) is a small community straddling the picturesque Yachats River on the basaltic marine terrace tucked between mountains and sea. In fact, Yachats means "at the foot of the mountain." Tidepools brimming with sea life dot the rocky shoreline, overlooked by dramatic headlands that provide excellent ocean-viewing vistas (and whale watching in season). Between April and October, sea-run smelt (savory sardinelike fish) are harvested in the coast's sandy coves.

Cape Perpetua. A spectacularly located visitors center offers films and dioramas to orient you to the surrounding natural formations, and you'll want to step out on the viewing deck to take in the breathtaking Pacific panorama (also visible from inside the center). Hiking trails (maps are available at the center) fan out in all directions. The Auto Tour Viewpoint Road begins three miles south of Yachats on Highway 101; (503) 547-3289.

RESTAURANTS

La Serre ★ The fine dining choice in Yachats, La Serre ("the greenhouse") is the best restaurant in the culinary poverty zone between Newport and Coos Bay (and locals know it—it's usually crowded). The main dining area, which is nonsmoking, has an airy, open-beamed ceiling with skylights overhead and the largest collection of plants this side of Cape Perpetua's rain forest. The aroma of garlic and saffron drifts down from the open kitchen. Seafood, cooked correctly as befits a seaside town, is a good bet, be it catch-of-the-day Pacific whitefish, Umpqua oysters, zesty cioppino, or salmon (when available); the kitchen attends to vegetarians with made-to-order vegetarian plates. A large fireplace highlights a lounge and smoking area where live acoustic music is featured on most weekends. Unfortunately, it's amplified throughout the restaurant. ■ *2nd and Beach, downtown Yachats; (503) 547-3420; Yachats; $$; full bar; AE, MC, V; checks OK; dinner every day, breakfast Sun (closed Tues, Oct-June).*

New Morning Coffeehouse ★ A cross-section of Yachats society attends the New Morning: tourists, hip locals in Gore-Tex and faded jeans, and Eugene weekenders. With hanging plants, handmade quilts, the right reading material, and a cathedral ceiling with built-in loft—well, this place oozes the right stuff, and the kitchen ain't bad either. Muffins, Danishes, pies, can cakes (such as carrot and coffee) are superb; the rest of the breakfast menu is somewhat limited and may only offer a couple of omelets, served with potatoes and a homemade scone. Savory soups and black bean chili are typical luncheon fare. There's a good selection of coffees, occasional live music, and a homey wood stove for cold winter days—everything a soul needs on a stormy day on the Oregon Coast. ■ *At Hwy 101 and 4th St; (503) 547-3848; 373 Hwy 101 N, Yachats; $; beer and wine; no credit cards; checks OK; breakfast, lunch Wed-Sun.*

LODGINGS

Sea Quest Bed & Breakfast ★★ If there's a better situated B&B on the coast of Oregon (except, perhaps, for the Ziggurat next door), we haven't found it. At Sea Quest you spend the night in a luxurious, estatelike structure located on a sandy, beach-grassed bluff right above the ocean and nearby Ten Mile Creek. All five guest rooms have private baths *plus* their own hot, bubbling spa. They also enjoy plush queen-size beds, private entrances, and (of course) an ocean view. A large living room provides wood-burning stove, comfy couches, and miles of Pacific vistas. The building is encircled by an outside deck, site of many of Elaine Ireland's healthy and hearty breakfasts. Two-night minimum stay on weekends. ■ *6½ miles south of Yachats on west side of Hwy 101 (between mile markers 171 and 172); (503) 547-3782; 95354 Hwy 101, Yachats, OR 97498; $$$; MC, V; checks OK.*

Ziggurat ★★ This stunning glass-and-wood four-story structure takes its name from the ancient Sumerian word for "terraced pyramid." Owners Mary Lou Cavendish and Irv Tebor will gladly discuss its architectural fine points; you'll probably be too busy enjoying the scintillating views from all 40 windows to do much listening. There are two guest rooms downstairs, both with private baths. The east suite boasts a sauna, while the west suite has a round, glass-block shower and a magnificent view. Upstairs, at the apex of the pyramid, there's a guest room with open-air decks. Guests share the 2,000-square-foot living and reading rooms, complete with fridge, books, and games. Storm watching and ocean gazing are enhanced from glass-enclosed decks. ■ *6½ miles south of Yachats on west side of Hwy 101 at 95330 Hwy 101; (503) 547-3925; PO Box 757, Yachats, OR 97498; $$; no credit cards; checks OK.*

The Adobe Resort ★ Nicely ensconced in a private, parklike setting, the Adobe fans out around the edge of a basalt-bumpy shore. At high tide, waves crash onto the rocks below while their thunder echoes into the rooms. The original rooms—with knotty pine woodwork, beamed ceilings, fireplaces, and ocean views—are quite popular; the two newer wings have more amenities, but only some have fireplaces and face the ocean (and they're more expensive). There's a six-person Jacuzzi and a sauna for all. Children are welcome, but pets are allowed only in the original building. The restaurant is overpriced, yet rates a notch above the usual mediocre oceanfront fare. Relax in the lounge for panoramic ocean views, or try the upstairs loft for a quiet drink or snack. ■ *In downtown Yachats at 1555 Hwy 101; (503) 547-3141; PO Box 219, Yachats, OR 97498; $$; AE, DC, DIS, MC, V; local checks only; breakfast, lunch Mon-Sat, dinner every day, brunch Sun.*

Burd's Nest Inn Bed and Breakfast ★ This is one distinctive roost, perched halfway up a hillside and enjoying a big bird's-eye view of the Pacific. As you head up the narrow driveway, you'll notice the multicolored tile roof right away, as well as all manner of paraphernalia deliberately strewn about. This half-century-old home has a cluttered but comfortable look, especially inside, where antiques, unusual toys, and knickknacks compete for wall and table space. The Nest sports three guest rooms (all with views of the ocean), only two of which are rented at once. Proprietors Big Burd and Joni Bicksler, escapees from Southern California, lend an animated, friendly ambience and specialize in big Mexican breakfasts. They're often dressed as colorfully as the roof. ■ *East side of Hwy 101, just before the bridge; (503) 547-3683; 664 Yachats River Rd, Yachats, OR 97498; $$; MC, V; no checks.*

Oregon House You can't see Oregon House from the highway, and therein lies its charm. It's definitely private, out of the wind, away from the hustle and bustle, and a very reasonable stay to boot (rates begin at less than $50). An interesting complex of five buildings in a woodsy setting houses 10 lodging units, each different in its own way. Some have skylights, some have fireplaces; in some you'll step out on the balcony to enjoy the ocean view, in others you'll relax in a wicker rocking chair or a big brass bed. All have private baths and kitchen facilities and all but the Creek Side have a view of the ocean. Take the cliffside trail down to the uncrowded beach. Kids are fine, but pets (aside from the resident cats, goats, and chickens) and smoking inside are taboo. A good choice for groups and touring cyclists. ■ *8 miles south of Yachats on the west side of Hwy 101; (503) 547-3329; 94288 Hwy 101, Yachats, OR 97498; $$; DC, DIS, MC, V; checks OK.* &

FLORENCE

Florence is intersected by the deep, green Siuslaw River and surrounded by the beauty of the Oregon Dunes National

Recreation Area, several large freshwater lakes, and, in May, bright pink and red rhododendron flowers. The geography here, and for 50 miles south, is devoid of the trademark rugged Oregon Coast headlands. Instead, expansive sand dunes, some of them hundreds of feet high, dominate the landscape. Although it draws plenty of tourists, **Old Town** is authentic enough to interest the locals, who hang out at the **Old Town Coffee Company**, 1269 Bay Street, (503) 997-7300, and the **Harbor House Seafood Cafe**, 1368 Bay Street, (503) 997-6816. Also on Bay Street, a public fishing pier and park is a nice place to get close to the river.

Oregon Dunes National Recreation Area (see Reedsport for headquarters info). Orient yourself to this intriguing ecosystem by exploring the South Jetty Road just south of town, or the Oregon Dunes Overlook, another 11 miles south on Highway 101. The dunes, which reach 600 feet high, hide lakes with excellent swimming potential and mysterious tree islands.

Heceta Head Lighthouse and former light-keeper's home, 12 miles north, offer marvelous photographic opportunities. The (supposedly) haunted but truly lovely house can be reserved for weddings or other gatherings; (503) 747-4501, extension 2558. At **Sea Lion Caves** you can descend 21 stories to a peephole in a natural cave swarming with hundreds of sea lions—11 miles north of town at 91560 Highway 101, (503) 547-3111. **Darlingtonia Botanical Wayside** is a bog five miles north of town featuring insect-eating plants called cobra lilies. Their unusual burgundy flowers bloom in May.

RESTAURANTS

Blue Hen Cafe ★ Just try to suppress a cackle when you notice the glass, ceramic, and plastic chickens—blue, naturally—everywhere. What's important, though, is that the place is friendly, the prices are reasonable, the food is tasty, and there's lots of it. As you might expect, chicken (mostly fried) dominates the menu, although pasta and burgers also make a showing. Dinners are well attended with extras (soup, bread, veggies, and mashed potatoes), and you'd be hard pressed to finish off an entire "four-clack" special. Try a glass of cherry juice with your meal. Pies are good, too. ■ *On Hwy 101 in the north part of town; (503) 997-3907; 1675 Hwy 101 N, Florence; $; beer and wine; DIS, MC, V; local checks only; breakfast, lunch, dinner every day.*

LODGINGS

Johnson House Bed & Breakfast ★★ We can't recommend *any* hotels in Florence, so we're thankful for the wit, curiosity, and lofty aesthetic standards Jayne and Ron Fraese bring to their perennially popular B&B. Reflecting their interests (he's a political science prof, she's an English teacher), the library is strong on local history, natural history, politics, and collections of essays, letters, cartoons, and poetry. There are six guest rooms (three with private baths), one of which is a cute garden cottage outside, furnished in a way not out of keeping with the 100-year-old house. Breakfasts, which include fresh garden fruit and produce (grown out back) and home-baked bread, are among the best on the coast. In addition, two cabins are spectacularly situated 10 miles north—Moonset, a two-person octagonal structure facing Lily Lake, and Coast House, a remodeled artist's shack clinging to a cliff. Calling them breathtaking would be an understatement. Both of the cabins include all the amenities and breakfast, and require minimum stays. ■ *One block north of the river at 216 Maple St; (503) 997-8000; PO Box 1892, Florence, OR 97439; $$ (cabins $$$); MC, V; checks OK.* &

Edwin K Bed & Breakfast ★ Built in 1914 in the Craftsman style by one of Florence's founders, the Edwin K is set in a quiet residential neighborhood beyond the bustle of Old Town. Ivory wall-to-wall carpeting contrasts nicely with aged and swarthy Douglas fir woodwork; furnishings are elegant (perhaps too much so). All four guest rooms are fitted with antiques—perhaps a huge mirrored dresser, a claw-footed tub, a massive four-poster bed. On the more modern side, a spacious double shower graces one bath, a whirlpool tub another. Breakfast is served in the formal dining room, another shrine to the woodcrafter's art. Sterling silver servers, fine linens, and crystal are in abundance. ■ *On the west edge of Old Town, across the street from the river at 1155 Bay St; (503) 997-8360 or toll free (800) -8EDWINK; PO Box 2687, Florence, OR 97439; $$; MC, V; checks OK.*

REEDSPORT AND WINCHESTER BAY

Reedsport is a port town on the Umpqua River a few miles inland, while Winchester Bay is at the river's mouth. Headquarters of the **Oregon Dunes National Recreation Area** are located in Reedsport at the intersection of Highway 101 and Route 38; (503) 271-3611.

The former Antarctic research vessel *Hero* is moored on the Reedsport riverfront and is open to the public. Adjacent is the Umpqua Discovery Center Museum, due to open in July '93. The **Dean Creek Elk Reserve**, where wild elk graze on protected land, is four miles east of town on Route 38.

The **Umpqua Lighthouse** (not open to the public) and Coastal Visitor Center are perched atop a headland overlooking Winchester Bay and the river mouth. Follow the signs to Umpqua Lighthouse State Park.

RESTAURANTS

The Brass Rail A visual oasis in an otherwise frumpy downtown. On looks alone, the Brass Rail's interior is a must-see. It's a mini-maze of rooms chock full of stunning antique furniture, stained glass, and skylights. A garden courtyard accommodates outdoor eating in temperate weather, and there's a truly nonsmoking section. The food—mostly the stick-to-your-ribs kind of thing (deli lunches, burgers, prime rib, pasta dinners)—isn't extraordinary, but is solid at all three meals. Avoid the attempts at culinary cuteness and order something your mom might have made. ■ *Hwy 101 at the south end of downtown; (503) 756-2121; 2072 Sherman Ave, North Bend; $; beer and wine; AE, DIS, MC, V; checks OK; breakfast Sat-Sun, lunch Mon-Sat, dinner Fri-Sat.*

LODGINGS

Highlands Bed & Breakfast ★ It's the secluded woodsy setting and the view of the Coast Range and Coos Bay that lure people to these six acres of highlands. Then there's the comfortable 2,000-square-foot lower level of Marilyn and Jim Dow's contemporary cedar home. A commodious living room with a soapstone stove and wraparound windows are at your disposal, as well as a private solarium deck with a spa. Both bedrooms have private baths and use of the kitchen. If you want to try your hand at crabbing, the Dows will loan you their crab ring and cook whatever good creatures you net. Children under 10 and pets are not allowed. ■ *Please call for directions; (503) 756-0300; 608 Ridge Rd, North Bend, OR 97459; $$; MC, V; checks OK.*

▼

Coos Bay

▲

COOS BAY

The south bay's port city and formerly the world's foremost wood-products exporter, Coos Bay has been undercut by a sagging timber industry and the political struggle to control the Northwest's forests. But this Scandinavian/German town is still the Oregon Coast's largest city and the largest natural harbor between San Francisco and Seattle. And it's currently making the painfully slow transition from an economy based on natural resources to one that's service-based, helped along by the growing number of tourists.

The Coos Art Museum, 235 Anderson, (503) 267-3901, offers many exhibits of big-city quality. **Playwrights' American Conservatory Theater** stages nine productions a year, as well as classes, 226 S Broadway, (503) 269-2501. **Southwestern Oregon Community College**, 1988 Newmark, (503) 888-2525, schedules art shows and musical performances. The **Oregon Coast Music Festival** happens in July—call (503) 267-0928. **Gourmet Coastal Coffees Co.** is a good place for espresso, pastries, and local chit-chat, 273 Curtis, (503) 267-5004.

RESTAURANTS

Blue Heron Bistro ★★ *Voila*, a real bistro with European flair in the heart of Coos Bay. Airy atmosphere, indoor and outdoor tables (overlooking bustling sidewalk traffic), and an innovative menu, priced reasonably. Owner Wim de Vriend keeps people coming back at all times of day. For waffles, breakfast parfaits (yogurt, fruit, and muesli), stuffed croissants, and good strong jolts of joe in the morning. For an array of salads and sandwiches (such as blackened snapper on a toasted onion roll with green chiles), lasagne, or a German sausage plate at lunch. For handcrafted pasta (ravioli with spinach and three cheeses) or continent-hopping cuisine (chicken in peanut sauce with Indonesian fried rice) for dinner. If pan-fried salmon in dill mustard sauce appears on the specials sheet, order it. Desserts are delectable—particularly the coast's finest apple pie. ▪ *Hwy 101 and Commercial; (503) 267-3933; 100 W Commercial, Coos Bay; $$; beer and wine; MC, V; local checks only; breakfast, lunch, dinner every day.* ও

Kum-Yon's ★ On the southern end of Coos Bay, in a fast-food ghetto, Kum-Yon's has transformed a nondescript eatery into a showcase of South Korean cuisine. Some Japanese (sushi, sashimi) and Chinese (eggflower soup, fried rice, chow mein) dishes are offered, but to discover what really makes this place special, you'll have to venture into the unknown. Try spicy hot chap-chae (transparent noodles pan-fried with veggies and beef) or bulgoki (thinly sliced sirloin marinated in honey and spices). Or you can leave yourself in the kitchen's hands and order the sushi special. Good chow at low prices means lots of customers, so get there early on weekends. ▪ *On the south end of the main drag; (503) 269-2662; 835 S Broadway, Coos Bay; $; beer and wine; MC, V; local checks only; lunch, dinner every day.* ও

LODGINGS

Coos Bay Manor Bed & Breakfast Inn ★ Head up the hill away from the commercial glitz of Highway 101 and you'll discover nicely restored homes among deciduous and coniferous trees and flowering shrubs. The Coos Bay Manor is such a place, on a quiet residential street with a bird's-eye waterfront panorama. The view is even more stunning from the upstairs balcony patio where Patricia Williams serves breakfast on mellow summer mornings. If the sun doesn't make an appearance, there's plenty of room to roam inside her Colonial-style manor. Between three and five guest rooms are available (depending on the time of year), all distinctively decorated (the cattle baron's room is decked out with bear and coyote rugs) and sporting comfortable feather beds. Only one bathroom is private. Mannerly dogs (who tolerate cats) are welcome, but children are not. ▪ *On S 5th, 4 blocks above the waterfront; (503) 269-1224; 955 S 5th St, Coos Bay, OR 97420; $$; MC, V; checks OK.*

CHARLESTON

Charleston's docks moor the bay's commercial fishing fleet. Fresh fish is inexpensive, the pace is slow, and there's lots to do.

Oregon Institute of Marine Biology is the University of Oregon's respected research station; (503) 888-2581. The **South Slough National Estuarine Research Reserve** (a paddler's paradise) has an interpretive center, info, and free maps; 4 miles south of Charleston, (503) 888-5558. Visit **Chuck's Seafood**, 5055 Boat Basin Drive, (503) 888-5525, for fish and **Qualman Oyster Farms**, 4898 Crown Point Road, (503) 888-3145, for oysters.

To the west, **Sunset Bay State Park** has year-round camping and a bowl-shaped, protected cove to dip your feet in; (503) 888-4902. Nearby **Shore Acres State Park** has a colorful botanical gardens complex with native and exotic plants and flowers, and an enclosed shelter for storm and whale watching; (503) 888-3732. Just south, **Cape Arago State Park** overlooks the Oregon Islands National Wildlife Refuge, home to birds, seals, and sea lions. The Oregon Coast Trail winds through all three parks.

Bandon

RESTAURANTS

Portside ★ It's kinda dark and cavernous inside, so the first thing you notice are the lighted glass tanks containing live crabs and lobsters, a good sign that the kitchen is concerned with fresh ingredients. From your table you watch fishing gear being repaired and vessels coming and going, since you're right at the Charleston Boat Basin. Naturally, utterly fresh fish, simply prepared, is the house specialty. Steamed Dungeness crab, grilled Empire clams, and sautéed calamari are good choices, and on Fridays there's a sumptuous Chinese seafood buffet that includes everything but the anchor. ▪ *Just over the Charleston bridge, in the midst of the boat basin; (503) 888-5544; 8001 Kingfisher Rd, Charleston; $$; full bar; AE, DC, MC, V; local checks only; lunch, dinner every day.*

BANDON

Some locals believe Bandon sits on a "ley line," an underground crystalline structure that is reputed to be the focus of powerful cosmic energies. Certainly there's magic here: this little community at the mouth of the Coquille River bustles. North of town is the **Coquille River Lighthouse**, accessible through **Bullards Beach State Park**. The south jetty has the best beach access: **Coquille Point** at the end of 11th Street or the **Face Rock Viewpoint** on Beach Loop Road.

In town, sample the famous cheddar cheeses (especially the squeaky cheese curds) at **Bandon Cheese** at 680 Second, (503) 347-2456. For another treat, try the *New York Times*-touted handmade candies (fudge, creams, and taffy) at **Cranberry Sweets**, (503) 347-9475, First and Chicago. Bandon's cranberry bogs make it one of the nation's largest producers. Call (503) 347-9616 or (503) 347-3230 for a tour (May through November). **Old Town** features **Harbor Hall**, which books ballet to blues, (503) 347-4404. There are also **Second Street Gallery** and other fine crafts shops and at least 11 food purveyors.

RESTAURANTS

Sea Star Bistro ★★ The Sea Star began years ago as a friendly hostel. In time, it grew to include more private accommodations, and a small bistro. Today, Dave and Monica Jennings' guest house is also home to one of Bandon's better restaurants. The theme is healthy, low-fat cuisine that's good enough to create cravings. Try the black bean burger, with beans, cheese, sesame, pumpkin, and sunflower seeds, plus green chiles and cumin. Seafood burritos and tofu veggie stir-fry also are popular. And the soup of the moment is always a treat. The place is small (no smoking). There's a newspaper/magazine rack to help pass the time when the kitchen slows down.

The Guest House ($60 for two) with natural wood interior, skylights, and harbor-view deck, offers a comparatively lavish alternative to the hostel next door. The less formal neighbor (connected to the guest house by a courtyard) offers small men's and women's dorms ($9 per person), private rooms for couples and families, a common room, kitchen, secluded courtyard, and sun decks. ■ *Take 2nd St off Hwy 101 into Old Town; (503) 347-9632; 375 2nd St, Bandon; $$; beer and wine; MC, V; local checks only; breakfast, lunch every day, dinner Thurs-Sun.*

Andrea's ★ Andrea Gatov's eclectic South Coast restaurant continues to be very popular, in part because it doubles as the unofficial information hub of Bandon. Breakfasts are filling. Substantial sandwiches on homemade whole-grain breads, soups, and pizza by the slice round out the lunch menu. For dinner, Andrea draws on many traditions, from Cajun to Russian. She's strong on seafood cooked any of six different ways, from blackened to fat-free. Her lamb is homegrown. And on Friday nights, locals descend on the place for pizza. Sunday brunch may bring seafood hash or apple-cranberry blintzes,

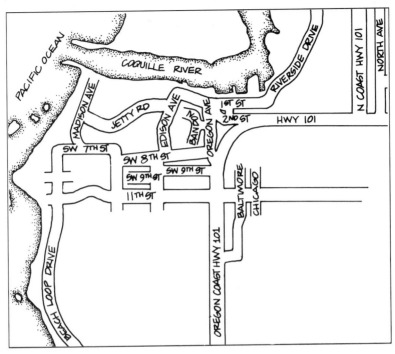

Bandon

and Bandon's best cup of coffee. ■ *1 block east of ocean; (503) 347-3022; 160 Baltimore, Bandon; $$; beer and wine; no credit cards; checks OK; breakfast, lunch Mon-Sat, dinner every day (Fri-Sat only during winter), brunch Sun.*

Bandon Boatworks ★ A local favorite, the Boatworks takes advantage of its two-story location near the south jetty on the Coquille River to provide fine dining with an equally fine view. If the restaurant is packed, wait anyway for a table upstairs; it's a shame to miss the sunset on the river and ocean. Dinner selections include baked butterflied shrimp served in a light and tangy mustard sauce, and fresh oysters roasted in anisette. The decent salad bar includes warm loaves of sweet, if crumbly, cranberry bread (cranberries are an important local crop). For lunch, the sautéed calamari is especially good. On Sundays the Boatworks features an above-average Mexican menu. Service is excellent. ■ *Follow River Rd out to the jetty; (503) 347-2111; S Jetty Rd, Bandon; $$; beer and wine; AE, DIS, MC, V; checks OK; lunch, dinner Tues-Sun (closed January).*

Harp's ★ Don't look for unusual background music. The name is derived from the presence of chef/owner Michael Harpster. Do look for some wonderful halibut with hot pistachio sauce, worth the trip to this intimate Old Town bistro. The house pasta comes with scampi and a sauce of hot pepper and lemon. And the filet mignon is marinated in garlic and teriyaki. The salmon poached with capers in vermouth can be dry, and there's no rice, just a baked potato. But Harpster does a good job with his house sweet onion soup made with beef broth and cognac. Salads feature organically grown greens when he can get them. Your chair leans sideways a bit because of the old floors in the building. No smoking. ■ *Half a block east of ocean; (503) 347-9057; 130 Chicago St, Bandon; $$; beer and wine; AE, MC, V; checks OK; dinner Tues-Sat (every day in summer).*

LODGINGS

Lighthouse Bed & Breakfast ★★ Spacious and appealing, this contemporary has windows opening toward the Coquille River, its lighthouse, and the ocean. Nonsmoking guests can watch fishing boats, seals, and seabirds nearby or stroll into Old Town. Hosts Linda and Bruce Sisson serve local organically grown strawberries for the morning's meal of French toast. The Sissons offer four rooms year-round, all with private baths: two view the ocean, the others look at the river and the town. Three rooms with queen beds run about $80, depending on the season; the fourth, the Green House Room—with king bed, fireplace, whirlpool tub, and TV—runs about $100 in the high season. ■ *First St at 650 Jetty Rd; (503) 347-9316; PO Box 24, Bandon, OR 97411; $$; MC, V; checks OK.*

Inn at Face Rock ★ This elegant resort is just across the road from the beach. Choose from one-bedroom to two-bedroom two-bath suites with kitchens, queen hideabeds, fireplace, and balconies. Many rooms have views (except newer units in back). Prices vary as dramatically as the weather ($49-$109). The rooms are large, comfortable, and very attractive. There are four nonsmoking king units. The Jacuzzi is exclusive to guests; the nine-hole golf course, restaurant, and bar are not. The golf pros can give you a lesson in coping with the often irritating winds. You can find better dining elsewhere. ■ *2 miles south of Bandon, right turn at Seabird Lane; (503) 347-9441 or toll-free (800) 638-3092; 3225 Beach Loop Rd, Bandon, OR 97411; $$; AE, DC, DIS, MC, V; checks OK.* &

Windermere Motel ★ Many guests wouldn't change a thing about this quintessential family motel. Where else can you find wonderfully battered oceanside cottages with kitchenettes and room for kids to run, all at moderate rates? For years it was nothing fancy, even a little run-down, but recently the place has been extensively remodeled. The rooms are clustered in units of three or four. The best are those with sleeping lofts, but all rooms have truly magnificent ocean views and access to an uncrowded beach. A big sign says "No Pets", and they mean it. ■ *1½ miles south of Bandon, west on Seabird; (503) 347-3710;*

PORT ORFORD

It's got history (the oldest townsite on the Oregon coast), location (prime views and beaches with summer wind protection), mild climate, natural resources, and talented residents. Sheep ranching, fishing, sea-urchin harvesting, and cranberries dominate. Several surprises await. **Cape Blanco State Park**, 6 miles north of town, is the westernmost point in Oregon, with empty beaches, a scenic lighthouse, and the nearby historic **Hughes House**, built in 1898; the **Elk** and **Sixes** rivers are prime fishing streams. Check out the once-thriving **Lakeport**, now a ghost town, on Floras Lake Road a little farther north, near Langlois.

RESTAURANTS

CB's Bistro (Sixes River Hotel) ★ Chef/owner Christophe Baudry went from Ashland's Mark Antony Hotel to the Whale Cove restaurant in Port Orford. When the rent got too high, he moved 6 miles north to this turn-of-the-century farmhouse, once part of a sheep ranch. It's now a French restaurant with four guest rooms (which come with breakfast). Ginger Dijon vinaigrette and some great sourdough launch the meal. Our fresh salmon with beurre blanc was tasty but would have been better with fewer bones. Christophe also does a fine tortellini and prawns dish, as well as roasted rabbit, Thai chicken, jambalaya, and lamb chops. Presentation, with elegant vegetables and fresh herbs, is superior. The wine list, posted on a blackboard, is heavily French and a bit spendy. The intimate dining room seats only about a dozen people, so reservations are a must here. ■ *Turn east off Hwy 101 onto Sixes River Rd at town of Sixes, watch for driveway ¼ mile on right; toll-free (800) 828-5161; Sixes; $$; full bar; MC, V; dinner Tues-Sun.*

Port Orford

Lodgings

Truculent Oyster Restaurant and Peg Leg Saloon Enter the dark nautical interior of the Truculent Oyster through the Peg Leg Saloon. The fresh oyster shooters, homemade soups (clam chowder, split pea with ham), weekend prime rib, and mild Mexican entrées are the strong points of the eclectic menu. The slow-broiled chinook salmon (seasonal) can be outstanding. Portions are sizable, service prompt, and coffee miserable. The bar can be noisy. ■ *At the south end of town; (503) 332-9461; 236 6th St, Port Orford; $$; full bar; AE, MC, V; local checks only; lunch, dinner every day.*

LODGINGS

Floras Lake House Bed & Breakfast ★ If the hot summer sun beckons you to cool swims in a freshwater lake, choose Floras.

This modern two-story house offers four spacious rooms, each with private bath and access to a deck, two with fireplaces. The two most elegant are the North Room with its garden decor and the South Room with four-poster king bed. You can see Floras Lake and the ocean beyond from all rooms. Hosts Will and Liz Brady serve a continental breakfast with homemade muffins and sticky bun cake, plus espresso. The area is pleasantly isolated. Hiking and biking trails abound, and Floras Lake is great for windsurfers (and you might just have the beach to yourself). No smoking. ■ *From Hwy 101, turn W on Floras Lake Rd, 9 mi N of Port Orford, and follow signs to Boice Cope Park; (503) 348-2573; 92870 Boice Cope Rd, Langlois, OR 97450; $$$; MC, V; checks OK.*

Home by the Sea Bed & Breakfast ★ The ocean view is one of southern Oregon's best, and you can see it from both guest rooms in this modest, homey B&B that sits atop a bluff near Battle Rock. Hosts Alan and Brenda Mitchell offer two rooms, both with myrtlewood queens. Both have private baths, although in the case of the smaller Coral Room, it's across the hall. Guests have the run of a large dining/living room area, also with ocean view. Alan is the chef, and quiche, waffles, omelets, and fresh strawberries are mainstays. No smoking. ■ *1 block west of Hwy 101 at 444 Jackson St; (503) 332-2855; PO Box 606-B, Port Orford, OR 97465; $$; MC, V; checks OK.*

Castaway by the Sea This bluff-top 14-unit, two-story motel sits on history: ancient Indian artifacts, plus the former sites of both Fort Orford, the oldest military installation on the Oregon coast, and the Castaway Lodge, once frequented by Jack London. The two three-bedroom units have kitchenettes and glassed-in sun decks with harbor and ocean views ($40-$90). Avoid the dank older section under the office, except in a pinch. It's an easy stroll to the beach, harbor, or shops. Look for off-season specials. ■ *Between Ocean and Harbor drives on W 5th; (503) 332-4502; PO Box 844, Port Orford, OR 97465; $$; MC, V; local checks only.*

GOLD BEACH

This is famous as the town at the ocean end of the Rogue River, a favorite with Zane Grey, and one of the dozen Wild and Scenic rivers in the United States. It's also a supply town for hikers heading into the remote Kalmiopsis Wilderness Area.

Fishing. The river is famous for steelhead and salmon. You might want to visit some of the lodges favored by fisherfolk to pick up tips, or rent clam shovels and fishing gear at the **Rogue Outdoor Store**, 560 N Ellensburg, (503) 247-7142.

Jet boat trips. Guides will discuss the area's natural history and stop to observe wildlife on these thrilling trips from 64 to 104 miles up the Rogue River. You'll even get a hearty lunch or dinner, with local sweet corn and tomatoes, at one of the inns along the way (extra charge). One caution: prepare for sun exposure, as most of these boats are open. Call **Jerry's Rogue Jets**, Port of Gold Beach, PO Box 1011, Gold Beach, OR 97444, (503) 247-7601 for information or toll-free (800) 451-3645 for reservations; **Mail Boat Hydro-Jets**, PO Box 1165-G, Gold Beach, OR 97444, (503) 247-7033 for information or toll-free (800) 458-3511 for reservations. Better yet, a call to **Rogue River Reservations**, (503) 247-6504 or (800) 525-2161, can gain information on or arrange bookings on just about any Rogue River outing, jet boat trip, or overnight stay in the wilderness.

Whitewater trips. Traffic on the all-too-popular Wild and Scenic part of the Rogue is controlled. People interested in unsupervised trips must sign up for a lottery—the first six weeks in the new year—with the U.S. Forest Service; (503) 479-3735.

Hiking. Trails cut deep into the Kalmiopsis Wilderness or the Siskiyou National Forest, or follow the Rogue River. A jet boat can drop you off to explore part or all of the 40-mile-long Rogue River Trail along the river's north bank. Spring is the best time for a trek, before 90-degree heat makes the rockface trail intolerable. Stay at any or all of seven remote lodges, where—for prices ranging from $55 to $180 per night—you end your day with a shower and dinner, and begin with breakfast and sack lunch for the next day. (Reservations are a must.)

In the Agness area the lodges are **Cougar Lane Lodge**, 04219 Agness Road, Agness, OR 97406, (503) 247-7233; **Lucas Pioneer Ranch**, 03904 Cougar Lane (PO Box 37), Agness, OR 97406, (503) 247-7443; and **Singing Springs Ranch**, 34501 Agness-Illahee Road (PO Box 68), Agness, OR 97406, (503) 247-6162.

In the Rogue River Wilderness, contact **Clay Hill Lodge** and **Wild River Lodge**, PO Box 18, Agness, OR 97406, (503) 247-6215; **Half Moon Bar Lodge**, 719 NW Third Street, Grants Pass, OR 97526; (503) 476-4002; or the crown jewel, the **Paradise Bar Lodge**, PO Box 456, Gold Beach, OR 97444, (503) 247-6022 or toll-free (800) 525-2161. For information about trails, contact the Gold Beach Ranger District, 1225 S Ellensburg, Gold Beach, OR 97444, (503) 247-6651.

RESTAURANTS

The Captain's Table ★ This is Gold Beach's old favorite, though the seafood's inconsistently prepared. On our recent visit, however, the fresh lingcod and salmon were just right. The corn-fed beef from Kansas City is meat you can't often get this far west. One nice touch: the salad is served family style and you can help yourself to as much as you want. The dining area is moderately small, furnished with antiques, and can get smoky from the popular bar. Both dining room and bar have nice ocean views. The staff is courteous, enthusiastic (if a bit hovering), and speedy. ■ *Hwy 101, south end of town; (503) 247-6308; 1295 S Ellensburg Ave, Gold Beach; $$; full bar; MC, V; local checks only; dinner every day.*

Nor'Wester ★ From the windows of the Nor'Wester you may watch fishermen delivering your meal: local sole, snapper, halibut, lingcod, and salmon. Most seafood is served simply: broiled or sautéed, perhaps sprinkled with some almonds. You can also find a decent steak, or chicken with Dijon or orange glaze. Dinners feature both soup and salad, served simultaneously. Try a spinach salad, the classic with bacon and chopped egg. ■ *On the waterfront; (503) 247-2333; Port of Gold Beach, Gold Beach; $$; full bar; AE, MC, V; checks OK; dinner every day.*

LODGINGS

Tu Tu Tun Lodge ★★★ The lodge is one of the loveliest on the coast, though you are seven miles inland from the ocean. Tall, mist-cloudy trees line the north shore of the Rogue River. The building is handsomely designed, with such niceties as private porches overlooking the river, racks to hold fishing gear, and stylish, rustic decor throughout. There are 16 units in the two-story main building and two larger, noisier kitchen suites in the lodge. In the apple orchard is a lovely garden house (sleeps six) with all the amenities, including two baths, kitchen, deck, and old stone fireplace. You can swim in the heated lap pool, use the four-hole pitch-and-putt course, play horseshoes, relax around the mammoth rock fireplace, or hike. Many people come to fish for the chinook salmon and steelhead, of course.

Three meals a day are served in the lodge or on the patio, family style, from lazy Susans. The prix-fixe dinner begins with hors d'oeuvres in the bar. Your own fish might be the entrée, or perhaps chicken breasts with a champagne sauce, or prime rib, along with freshly made soup, salad, bread, and dessert. Only the two river suites and garden house are available in winter (restaurant open high season May through October only). Fido's welcome spring and fall: $3 charge. ■ *Follow the Rogue River from the bridge up the north bank for 7 miles; (503) 247-6664; 96550 North Bank Rogue, Gold Beach, OR 97444; $$$; full bar; MC, V; checks OK.*

Inn at Nesika Beach Bed & Breakfast ★★ This three-story Victorian home built in 1992 is spacious and grand, and on the ocean too. It has quickly caught on with southern Oregonians as a romantic destination. Guests have the run of a living room and parlor, where wine is served in the evening, plus formal dining room for breakfast. Three of the four oversize bedrooms enjoy ocean views and fireplaces, and all have Jacuzzi tubs.

Owner Ann Arsenault serves a breakfast that may include crêpes, scones, fresh asparagus, and homemade muffins. No smoking. ■ *West off Hwy 101 on Nesika Rd 5 miles north of Gold Beach; (503) 247-6434; 33026 Nesika Rd, Gold Beach, OR 97444; $$; no credit cards; checks OK.*

Gold Beach Resort ★ If you want a fairly fancy motel room with a good ocean view, this is probably your best bet in Gold Beach. During the summer season the 39 units range from $79 for a standard room to $105 and up for a condo with fireplace and kitchen. Most are quite spacious. It's an easy walk to the beach. There's an indoor swimming pool and Jacuzzi, and hosts Pravin and Mridula Patel serve a complimentary continental breakfast in the lobby for early risers, May through September. ■ *Hwy 101, near south end of town; (503) 247-7066 or (800) 541-0947; 1330 S Ellensburg Ave, Gold Beach, OR 97444; $$; AE, DC, DIS, MC, V; checks OK.* ᕕ

Jot's Resort ★ The manicured grounds of this lovely resort spread out on the north bank of the Rogue River near the historic Rogue River Bridge; the lights (and the traffic) of Gold Beach are just across the river. The 140 rooms are spacious, tastefully decorated, and well furnished (many with refrigerators), but try for one of the newer ones. Summer rates range from about $80 for a standard room to $165 for a two-bedroom condo accommodating six. There's an indoor pool, spa, and weight room. Rent a bike (or a boat!) to explore the riverfront. Rogue River jet boats and guided fishing trips leave right from the resort's docks. An unexpected fishing trip? The lodge rents necessary gear. The adjacent Rod 'N' Reel Restaurant serves fairly standard meals, but a fine spinach salad comes with dinner. ■ *At the Rogue River Bridge, at 94630 Waterfront Loop; (503) 247-6676 or toll-free (800) 367-5687; PO Box J, Gold Beach, OR 97444; $$; AE, DC, DIS, MC, V; checks OK.* ᕕ

▼

Brookings

▲

BROOKINGS

Brookings sits in Oregon's "banana belt," just 6 miles north of the California line: it enjoys the state's mildest winter temperatures. In addition, the town is bookended by breathtaking beauty. To the northwest are the **Samuel H. Boardman** and **Harris Beach state parks**. To the east are the verdant Siskiyou Mountains, deeply cut by the Chetco and Winchuck rivers. Brookings also boasts the safest harbor on the Oregon Coast—and therefore a busy port.

Azalea State Park just east of 101. Fragrant Western azaleas bloom in May, alongside wild strawberries, fruit trees, and violets; you can picnic amid all this splendor on hand-hewn myrtlewood tables. Myrtlewood, which grows here and in Palestine, can be seen in groves in Loeb Park, 8 miles east of town on North Bank Chetco River Road, or carved up into far too many souvenir knickknacks.

Outdoor activities. Fishing is usually good here: a small fleet operates at the south end of town. And there's access from Brookings to trails into the Kalmiopsis Wilderness Area and the Siskiyou National Forest. The Redwood Nature Trail winds through one of the few remaining groves of coastal redwoods in Oregon.

RESTAURANTS

Caffe Fredde ★ This relative newcomer has taken Brookings by storm. Locals and visitors from the Rogue Valley descend on this place (as well as the adjacent Italian restaurant Basil, which shares a common kitchen) for fresh seafood with interesting sauces, like salmon with artichoke tartar and baked cod with sorrel mayo. The baked prawns come with crab and tri-mustard cream, the chicken with apples and Swiss. The house black bean soup with crème fraîche is notable, as is a kind of creamy caesar salad. Presentation is artistic, with sliced vegetables and Parmesan potatoes. You can wash it down with some good Oregon wines and microbrews. Caffe Fredde and Basil can be busy on weekends, and the single kitchen is sometimes overwhelmed, resulting in slow service. Still, this nonsmoking establishment is Brookings' best. ■ *In Northgate Center, west side of Hwy 101 midway through town; (503) 469-3733; 1025 Chetco Ave, Brookings; $$; beer and wine; MC, V; local checks only; lunch Mon-Fri, dinner every day.* &

Hog Wild Cafe ★ This boutiquey restaurant has gone a bit wild on the pig theme, what with pig dolls, pig cups, and a sign that reads "Please don't hog the bathroom." You'll find jambalaya, veggie lasagne, and Cajun meat loaf on the regular menu, plus a good many blackboard items, such as a veggie frittata or prime rib sandwich. The chicken Garibaldi is a soupy tureen of chicken and vegetables in a wine sauce. The pasta salad can be a bit oily, but the barbecued beans are first-rate. ■ *West side of Hwy 101, mile south of Brookings-Harbor bridge; (503) 469-8869; 16158 Hwy 101 S, Harbor; $; beer and wine; MC, V; local checks only; breakfast, lunch every day.*

Rubio's ★ The salsa is outstanding; you can buy bottles of it here and elsewhere in Brookings. But the restaurant itself is the only place you can get Rubio's incredible chiles rellenos and chile verde. And—wow—the seafood à la Rubio combines fresh lingcod, scallops, and prawns in a butter, garlic, wine, and jalapeño sauce. Avoid the greasy entomatada. There are 13 tables inside and 5 on the patio and a drive-thru for take-out orders. ■ *At the north end of town; (503) 469-4919; 1136 Chetco Ave, Brookings; $$; beer and wine; AE, DIS, MC, V; local checks only; lunch, dinner Tues-Sat.* &

LODGINGS

Chetco River Inn ★★ Expect a culture shock: the fishing retreat sits on 35 acres of a peninsula wrapped by the turquoise Chetco River, 17 miles east of Brookings (pavement ends after 14 miles) and 6 miles from a phone. There's a radiophone operator, but forget private conversations. The lovely deep green marble floors are a purposefully practical choice for muddy fishermen's boots. Three rooms have private baths (a fourth shares) and a view of river or forest, but the place is not so remote that you can't read by safety propane lights and watch TV via satellite (there's even a VCR). The large, open main floor offers views of the river, myrtlewood groves, and wildlife. Porch overhangs and clerestory windows keep the building cool in summer; solid construction and a wood stove provide winter warmth. Innkeeper Sandra Brugger serves a fisherman-size breakfast that may include Italian frittata with fresh vegetables, homemade biscuits, or Dutch baby pancakes. She will provide early-riser breakfast service, pack a deluxe sack lunch, or serve an exemplary five-course dinner on request. All told, this is getting away from it all in fishing style. No smoking indoors. ■ *Follow North Bank Rd 16 miles, left after South Fork Bridge, take second guest driveway on left; (503) 469-8128 (radiophone), toll-free (800) 327-2688 (Pelican Bay Travel); 21202 High Prairie Rd, Brookings, OR 97415; $$; MC, V; checks OK.*

Holmes Sea Cove Bed & Breakfast ★ If you want an ocean view coupled with B&B ambience in Brookings, this is it. Jack and Lorene Holmes offer two guest rooms on the lower level of their cozy home north of town. But try for the guest cottage that has privacy, a living room nook, and refrigerator (no kitchen). The home sits on a waterfront bluff, with a trail that winds its way down to the ocean, also a private park with picnic tables. Lorene brings a continental breakfast to your room, with fruit, juice, breads, and coffee or herbal tea. No smoking. ■ *Take Hwy 101 north to Dawson Rd, left to Holmes Dr; (503) 469-3025; 17350 Holmes Dr, Brookings, OR 97415; $$; MC, V; checks OK.*

Beachfront Inn Sure, it's only a Best Western, but if you want an ocean-front motel room in Brookings, this is the closest you can get. The three-story structure opened in 1990 with 39 rooms. A second building, added a year later, doubled that number, including a suite with a two-person Jacuzzi. Some have kitchens. Nothing special, but the view and beach access are pluses. ■ *On Lower Harbor Rd, south of the Port of Brookings; (503) 469-7779 or toll-free (800) 468-4081; PO Box 2729, Brookings, OR 97415; $$; AE, DC, DIS, MC, V; checks OK.* &

Willamette Valley and Southern Oregon

North to south roughly along the I-5 corridor from Yamhill and Washington counties in the north to the Rogue River Valley in southern Oregon.

AURORA

In 1856, Dr. William Keil brought a group of Pennsylvania Germans to establish a communal settlement. Called the Harmonites, the commune faded away after the death of its founder, but the town is a well-preserved, turn-of-the-century village on the National Register of Historic Places. Most people come to comb through the myriad antique stores that now occupy the many clapboard and Victorian houses along the highway. The **Old Aurora Colony Museum** offers tours that recount the communal history of the town; (503) 678-5754.

RESTAURANTS

Chez Moustache ★ The name of this tavern turned restaurant comes from a Frenchman who migrated up from California. Joel and Barbara Miller now run the place, seating the guests at oilcloth-covered tables in a series of small rooms and verandahs. They spend nothing on advertising, preferring to put money into fresh ingredients. Three-course dinners begin with a soup, followed by a salad with a marvelous (and secret) vinaigrette. The main course—depending on the season and on what's fresh and available—might be a fillet florentine David, served on a bed of spinach with fresh bay shrimp and béarnaise sauce. The best desserts consist of fresh fruit. ■ *Corner of Hwy 99E and Main St; (503) 678-1866; 21527 Hwy 99E, Aurora; $$; full bar; MC, V; checks OK; dinner Tues-Sat.* ↺

WILLAMETTE VALLEY WINERIES

The Oregon wine country now stretches from Portland all the way south (more or less along the I-5 corridor) to the California border. But the greatest concentration of wineries is in Yamhill County, mostly between Newberg and McMinnville. Here, among rolling oak-covered hills, are increasing numbers of vineyards and enough wineries to keep the touring wine lover tipsy for a week.

The good news is that this is not yet Napa Valley. Although summer weekends can be quite busy, many wineries are small family operations well off the beaten track, and visitors are still rare enough that they receive hearty welcomes. The downside is that some wineries have limited hours, and a few are not open to visitors at all. The best advice is to arm yourself with a map (it's easy to get lost on the back roads) and the winery guide from the **Oregon Winegrowers Association**, 200 NW Front Avenue, Suite 400, Portland OR 97209, (503) 228-8337, or any member winery. In fine weather take along a picnic lunch: many wineries have tables outside, some sell chilled wine and picnic supplies.

Driving south on Highway 99W, you will first hit **Veritas Vineyards**, (503) 538-1470, makers of excellent chardonnay, and **Rex Hill Vineyards**, (503) 538-0666, a decidedly upscale winery with a splendid tasting room and outstanding (if pricey) pinot noir. In the hills west of Newberg is **Autumn Wind Vineyard**, (503) 538-6931, a small new place beginning to turn out fine pinot noir.

In Dundee, you will find the **Elk Cove** tasting room, (503) 538-0911, where you can have a light lunch and taste not only the fine rieslings and pinot noirs of Elk Cove but also the wines of **Adelsheim Vineyard**, an industry pioneer in Oregon and one of its leading quality producers. You can't miss the tasting room of **Argyle**, (503) 538-8520, which is producing some of the best sparkling wines in the region. Behind Dundee are **Cameron Winery**, (503) 538-0336 (open only by appointment), with its lovely view and stylish wines, and **Lange Winery**, (503) 538-6476, where you can try an interesting pinot gris, the hot new white wine in Oregon. Nearby are two much larger wineries: **Knudsen Erath Winery**, (503) 538-3318, one of the oldest and largest in the state (nearby Crabtree Park makes a nice midday stop), with a full lineup of wines in a variety of price and quality categories (one of the best values in pinot noir), and **Sokol Blosser Winery**, (503) 864-2282, another large producer with a most handsome tasting room. Just south, outside Lafayette (home of a Trappist monastery, Our Lady of Guadeloupe), **Chateau Benoit**, (503) 864-3666, sits right on the crest of a ridge, with spacious visitor facilities. They specialize in Müller Thurgau (a great picnic wine), sauvignon blanc, and sparkling wine.

Near the railway tracks in the heart of McMinnville are another couple of wineries worth a visit: **Arterberry Winery**, (503) 472-1587, which has come to be one of the best producers of pinot noir in the state and also makes sparkling wine, and **Panther Creek Winery**, (503) 472-8080 (open only by appointment), a maker of fine, full-bodied pinot noir. Continue south of town on Highway 18 toward the ocean and you will pass **Yamhill Valley Vineyards**, (503) 843-3100, a lovely winery which makes pinot noir and is set among old oaks that provide good shade for lunch on a hot day. Just a bit farther along is the **Oregon Wine Tasting Room**, (503) 843-3787, which stocks a huge variety of wines for sale and always has an interesting assortment to taste, including wines from places such as top-notch producer **Eyrie Vineyards**, which are not open to the public on a regular basis. If you take 99W out of town, you will drive past the Eola Hills, home to another half-dozen or so wineries, including **Amity Vineyards**, (503) 835-2362, a small rustic winery that consistently produces excellent pinot noir, gewürztraminer, and dry riesling. Continuing south you will see signs for **Bethel Heights Vineyard**, (503) 581-2262, another winery high on a hill (one of the oldest vineyard sites in the area), which makes tasty chenin blanc and fine pinot noir in several price ranges, and **Eola Hills Winery**, (503) 623-2405, in Rickreall, which makes good cabernet sauvignon, a rarity for the Willamette Valley.

In a small valley near Highway 99W yet farther south are two neighboring wineries, both very small and definitely off the beaten track. **Airlie Winery**, (503) 838-6013, makes excellent Müller Thurgau and has well-priced wines (take some extra time and visit the birds at their pond). **Serendipity Cellars**, (503) 838-4284, makes some unusual wines, including Marechal Foch, a very good (and rare) red. **Tyee Wine Cellars**, (503) 753-8754, south of Corvallis, makes excellent whites, especially pinot gris and gewürztraminer. Right in Monroe is **Broadley Vineyards**, (503) 847-5934, a storefront winery that's not much to look at but has some powerful pinots. In the hills to the west is picturesque **Alpine Vineyards**, (503) 424-5851, about the only winery in the Willamette Valley to make good cabernet consistently (as well as a fine riesling).

Don't overlook the wineries in the **Tualatin Valley** that lie in the suburbs just west of Portland. Beaverton's **Ponzi Vineyards**, (503) 628-1227, is an excellent close-in destination which produces powerful pinot noir, elegant chardonnay, and fine pinot gris and dry riesling (an outstanding lineup). **Cooper Mountain Vineyards**, (503) 649-0027, has a beautiful hilltop site and makes tasty pinot gris and promising chardonnay. South of Hillsboro, **Oak Knoll Winery**, (503) 648-8198, in an old dairy barn, maintains an Oregon tradition of fruit wines (these are very good), but also produces fine, fruity pinot noir and a variety of other wines at good prices.

NEWBERG

RESTAURANTS

Ixtapa ★ After the long string of fast-food places along 99W, this little restaurant right in town is a refreshing change. You'll be given a hearty welcome as you're ushered into this narrow but colorful and lively place. The service really hustles: you won't get much time to peruse the long menu. Some will like their Mexican food a little spicier, but most will appreciate the freshness and lightness of the dishes. Grilled chicken is very tasty, there's lots of tomatoes and guacamole. And the beans, the real test of a Mexican place, are just right. ■ *On Hwy 99W northbound, in town; (503) 538-5956; 307 E 1st St, Newberg; $; full bar; MC, V; checks OK; lunch, dinner every day.* &

▼

**Willamette
Valley
Wineries**

▲

LODGINGS

The Partridge Farm ★★ Yes, they do raise partridges and other exotic and not-so-exotic birds, and the eggs you have for breakfast will be fresh. Innkeeper Nancy Gehrts also helps run the Red Hills Cafe in Dundee and has a special interest in fresh, local ingredients for breakfast—fruit, vegetables, and herbs are likely to be right out of the extensive garden. The thoroughly remodeled farmhouse is just off the highway, but the broad lawn and garden in back will help you feel way out in the country. Rooms are furnished in dark antiques: upstairs there are three rooms, which share a bath, but two of them have in-room sinks. The east bedroom is a little larger. A separate parlor downstairs has a TV. The inn is owned by the folks at Rex Hill Vineyards (about a mile away); romantics can arrange a soar in the winery's hot-air balloon. ■ *Just off Hwy 99W, north of Newberg; (503) 538-2050; 4300 E Portland Rd, Newberg, OR 97132; $$; MC, V; checks OK.* &

Springbrook Hazelnut Farm ★★ Informal Oregonians will be surprised to step into the colorful elegance of this landmark farmhouse. Owner Ellen McClure is an artist, and it shows. The large, paneled dining room with elegant table and chairs will make you feel as if you're in some Italian palazzo. The B&B guest wing upstairs is spacious, with two shared bathrooms furnished in green wicker, and there's a library and a TV room devoted to guests. The carriage house out back beyond the pond has a perfect little apartment: well-stocked kitchen (guests can prepare their own breakfast from fixings in the fridge), master bedroom, large bath with old-fashioned, deep tub, and a living room with a hideabed ($125 a night with two-night minimum on weekends). Guests explore the 60-acre filbert orchard, take a swim in the pool, or play tennis on the private court. No children or pets. ■ *Just off Hwy 99W, north of Newberg; (503) 538-4606; 30295 N Hwy 99W, Newberg, OR 97132; $$$; no credit cards; checks OK.*

Spring Creek Llama Ranch ★ When they began taking their new baby on backpacking trips, Dave and Melinda Van Bossuyt discovered that llamas make great pack animals. The Van Bossuyts have been aficionados ever since. Their llamas are gentle and eager for visitors (especially at mealtime) and provide fine diversion for children 3 years and up. This large, airy, modern house has two guest rooms, and the openness of the ranch is best for those who like to be social, but its proximity to the trails in the woods, Newberg, and Highway 99W is a plus. ■ *2 miles east of Newberg, please call ahead for specific directions; (503) 538-5717; 14700 NE Spring Creek Ln, Newberg, OR 97132; $$; no credit cards; checks OK.*

DUNDEE

RESTAURANTS

Red Hills Cafe ★★ Used to be, this was a friendly place to get a burger or homemade sandwich and some fresh pie for lunch. It's still friendly and still informally presided over by longtime owner Alice Halstead, but recently, thanks to partner and chef Nancy Gehrts, there has been some serious cooking going on at dinner. The chalkboard menu emphasizes what's fresh. An appetizer of pear-Brie was perhaps a little too delicately flavored, but the green salad was right-out-of-the-garden crisp and lightly dusted with fresh Parmesan and filberts. Sole wrapped around fresh asparagus with hollandaise is cooked with a light hand. Pork tenderloin with lively flavors of mushroom, fennel, and bacon is an exquisite combination. For dessert there's a tangy rhubarb crisp with crème fraîche. Wine lovers will appreciate being able to pick out their own bottle from the well-priced retail shelf and have it with dinner for a $3 corkage fee. It's enlightening to discover such delight in a tiny cinderblock building dressed up only with fresh flowers on each table. ■ *On Hwy 99W; (503) 538-8224; 976 Hwy 99W, Dundee; $$; beer and wine; no credit cards; checks OK; lunch Tues-Sun, dinner Fri-Sat.*

Tina's ★★ Tiny Dundee now has two noteworthy restaurants. Owners Tina Landfried and husband, David Bergen, have done the best they can with this small, squat building by the side of the road: a vest-pocket herb-and-salad garden outside, plain white walls inside. As for the food, there's a spirit of innovation and creativity rarely found in these parts. The half-dozen entrée choices are on the chalkboard: try rabbit risotto or grilled pork tenderloin in port-garlic sauce, or Thai chicken. The salmon Troigros is plump and delicate, with a rich reduced sauce of vermouth, crème fraîche, shallots, and sorrel. Soup might be a flavorful cream of cucumber with dill and cilantro, and the green salad is simple and absolutely fresh. The details are right, such as the best green beans you'll find outside France. Wines by the glass offer a good selection of local picks, all reasonably priced. Our one caveat is erratic service, sometimes painfully slow. ■ *On Hwy 99W; (503) 538-8880; 760 Hwy 99W, Dundee; $$; beer and wine; no credit cards; checks OK; lunch Tues-Fri, dinner Tues-Sun.* &

LODGINGS

Wine Country Farm ★ Drive up through the Red Hills of Dundee (the soil really is red), just past the unmarked entrance to Domaine Drouhin, France's outpost in wine country (no visitors). Vineyards all around will remind you that you're in the very heart of wine country, and from the hilltop you can watch clouds (or Oregon's trademark rain squalls) drift across the valley below. Guests are invited to take breakfast in warm weather on the deck or sun porch of this restored 1910 white stucco house. Upstairs, two of the four eclectically furnished bedrooms have spectacular views. Owner Joan Davenport raises Arabian horses and can take you on a buggy ride. For breakfast she might serve you home-baked goodies with her own pinot noir jelly. Relax and let her fuss over you. ■ *From Hwy 99W southbound, turn right onto McDougall just past Sokol Blosser Winery, then right again to Breyman Orchard Rd; (503) 864-3446; 6855 Breyman Orchards Rd, Dayton, OR 97114; $$; no credit cards; checks OK.*

▼
Dundee

Restaurants

▲

YAMHILL

LODGINGS

Flying M Ranch ★★ This place has become a local institution and has gotten a bit upscale. The lodge (completely rebuilt after the original burned down some time back) has a Western-style lounge (with bar made from six-ton logs) and a restaurant that serves the standards but has also been experimenting recently with more exotic fare. But the terrific setting is what draws people: literally at the end of the road in the Coast Range—there's nothing around but mountains and forest. Ponds for swimming and fishing, and miles of trails for hiking or horseback riding (you can actually follow trails all the way to the coast) should keep anyone busy. The motel rooms are pretty ordinary; savvy visitors rent one of the cabins (one of which has 10 beds)—they have their own kitchens and are plenty rustic, with no phones or TVs. Prices range from $50-$150. And for a really large group (up to 20) you might check out the small lodge on Trask Mountain (highest peak in the Coast Range)—you can rent the whole thing: rates are negotiable. You can also camp along the little creek. You can even fly in—there's an airstrip. For a fee, local cowboys can take you trail riding on one of the Flying M's horses and maybe even grill you a steak on the way. ■ *10 miles west of Yamhill: follow the little red flying M's; (503) 662-3222; 23029 NW Flying M Rd, Yamhill, OR 97148; $$; AE, DC, DIS, MC, V; checks OK.*

MCMINNVILLE

Serious wine lovers can OD on great wine and food while hobnobbing with wine celebrities (including some of France's hot young winemakers) at the three-day **International Pinot Noir Celebration** in late July on the gracious old Linfield College campus; call (503) 472-8964 for information.

RESTAURANTS

Lavender's Blue, a Tea Room ★★★ Farming town McMinnville may seem an unlikely location, but Montanan Terese Blanding has created an oasis of quiet elegance in a pleasant family neighborhood close to downtown. The sprawling old house is surrounded by a tidy garden, with attention paid to detail: soothing blues and beautiful floral patterns; books for reading piled on each table; soft music in the background; menus done in calligraphy; linen, china, and silver at each place. Even small children act subdued in the restful atmosphere. The wonderful house specialty tea includes lavender and lemon peel; black or herb teas are served along with excellent scones and shortbread; a small savory dish such as marinated asparagus or hot, creamy artichoke puffs, and a sweet dessert can make a satisfying supper at $10. An ideal place to recover from a day's wine-tasting, but also worth its own trip from Portland. Reservations only. ■ *1 block east of Hwy 99W on Cowls; (503) 472-4594; 535 N Cowls, McMinnville; $; no alcohol; no credit cards; checks OK; afternoon tea Wed-Sat.*

Nick's Italian Cafe ★★★ Nick's has been going strong for 16 years, and while the spirit of innovation may have weakened a bit, the cooking is still consistently outstanding. The setting is completely unpretentious: a former luncheonette that still has the original counter and stools. Owner Nick Peirano has created a friendly, relaxed atmosphere in which to eat marvelous, untrendy Northern Italian food. The fixed-price five-course meal always includes a second-course tureen of Nick's grandmother's heavenly, rich, garlicky minestrone, followed by a fresh, simply dressed green salad and chewy, dense French bread. Seasonal antipasto might include shellfish in winter or prosciutto and melon in summer. The fourth course is always pasta, always homemade, and always delicious (perhaps ravioli stuffed with spinach or hazelnuts and cheese). Entrées might include a simple, perfectly grilled shark or sirloin steak with capers. Homemade pastries make up the dessert list, including Italian specialties created by Nick's mother, but you may not have room. The famous wine list, the best in the Valley, has over 100 Oregon wines, including a number of older vintages unobtainable elsewhere, and—hallelujah!—they're all priced very reasonably. ■ *Off Hwy 99W, across from the movie theater; (503) 434-4471; 521 E 3rd St, McMinnville; $$; beer and wine; no credit cards; checks OK; dinner Tues-Sun.*

Kame ★ McMinnvilleites aren't used to getting their change counted out in Japanese, but for food this good and this inexpensive, they don't seem to mind one bit. A tiny storefront place with white walls, plain wooden tables and chairs, a few artfully placed decorations, and simple Japanese food served graciously. Owner Mieko Nordin learned to cook family style from her mother. A basic (and satisfying) meal might include tasty miso soup, a small salad of pickled cabbage, and chicken or pork with vegetables on a bed of steaming rice. Tempura and teriyaki for dinner, too. ■ *At Evans and 3rd; (503) 434-4326; 228 N Evans, McMinnville; $; beer and wine; MC, V; local checks only; lunch Tues-Fri, dinner Tues-Sat.*

LODGINGS

Youngberg Hill Farm ★★★ A more spectacular setting would be hard to devise. At the crest of a 650-foot hill, the view stretches 180 degrees from an exquisite, small pastoral valley to the hills of the wine country and across to Mount Hood and the Cascades. It's so pleasant that even in the dead of winter, guests want to take their coffee and sit out on the wraparound porch. Eve and Norman Barnett (who also run a sheep ranch and a vineyard on this 700 acres) take an obvious delight in their surroundings and clearly enjoy pampering their guests. The house has the design and feel of an old country house. The five spacious bedrooms are furnished in dark colors and heavy wooden furniture, and each has its own bathroom and spectacular views. The sitting room downstairs has a wood stove (TV in the basement) and everything is air-conditioned. There's a conference room that accommodates 20. Older children and babies are welcome. Outside are miles of old logging roads for walking through the woods, which are also open to guests who would like to hunt during the season. A daily menu in the foyer announces the breakfast selections, which might include puffed pancakes, smoked ham, and fresh fruit. The Barnetts are good sources of information on the area's wineries—they have their favorite wines in their own wine cellar. ■ *Old Sheridan Hwy to Peavine Rd and left on Youngberg Hill Rd; (503) 472-2727; 10660 Youngberg Hill Rd, McMinnville, OR 97128; $$; MC, V; checks OK.* ♿

Steiger House ★★ Decks wrap around the chalet-style house at a couple of levels, offering plenty of opportunities to sip coffee outside and enjoy the large woodsy backyard. Five rooms (three downstairs, two up) all have private baths, and there's a conference room available. The house has a comfortable, Northwest feel, with lots of light. Owner Doris Steiger is a weaver who sells woolen goods in a small guest shop. Breakfasts include Doris' homemade granola. Children over 10 are welcome. ■ *From 99W turn east on Cowls at the hospital; (503) 472-0821 or (800) 445-7744; 360 Wilson St, McMinnville, OR 97128; $$; MC, V; checks OK.*

Safari Motor Inn ★ Just off Highway 99W as it enters McMinnville, this unassuming motor lodge doesn't offer anything fancy, but it's ideally located for visitors who shy away from the B&B scene, and the prices can't be beat. The Safari offers relatively new, perfectly quiet rooms with wonderfully comfortable beds. The former motel pool is now pushing up daisies, but if you want to cool off on a hot afternoon, head a quarter mile south on 99W to McMinnville's modern Aquatic Center. Here you can frolic in a large pool for a couple of bucks. A small exercise facility with Jacuzzi is available. No pets, please. ■ *19th St and Hwy 99W; (503) 472-5187; 345 N Hwy 99W, McMinnville, OR 97128; $; AE, DC, MC, V; no checks.* ♿

BELLEVUE/SHERIDAN

Bellevue (a little bump on the road) is the site of three fine establishments, all under one roof. The **Oregon Wine Tasting Room**, (503) 843-3787, offers tastes of the best bottlings from two dozen Oregon wineries. **The Lawrence Gallery**, (503) 843-3633, is an excellent showcase of fine regional talent in all media. Upstairs is **Augustine's**.

RESTAURANTS

Augustine's ★★ With assured, knowledgeable service and fresh ingredients carefully and imaginatively prepared, Augustine's continues to be a bright spot for dining in the Willamette Valley. The clean, open space has scenic views out both sides: farmland on one side and down into the Lawrence Gallery on the other. You could start your meal with a smoked seafood platter (salmon, mussels, halibut, and cream cheese) or some of the excellent creamy clam chowder. Soup or green salad (veggies and greens come from a local organic farm) is included with the entrée. For the main course, there are pasta dishes, filet mignon, and lamb chops, but seasonal seafood is the real focus of owner/chef Jeff Quatraro. A huge poached salmon fillet is served with a simple herb butter. A special of fresh sturgeon is tender and delicious. The legendary hazelnut cheesecake is rich, light, and not too sweet; citrus tart (orange, lemon, and grapefruit curd) is tangy and refreshing. The all-Oregon wine list is reasonably priced and changes quarterly. ■ *Hwy 18, 7 miles west of McMinnville; (503) 843-3225; 19706 Hwy 18, Bellevue; $$; full bar; DIS, MC, V; checks OK; lunch Wed-Mon, dinner Wed-Sun.*

LODGINGS

Sheridan Country Inn There's not much in Sheridan (besides the state prison), but you're not far from either the wine country or the ocean. This old house is now an inn with 10 rooms, six in the funky but spacious mansion and four in the outside duplexes. The rooms (starting at $50) are large and comfortable and look out on the surrounding acre of grounds. Some rooms come with refrigerator and microwave, all have private bath and TV. Room 7 ($125) is a huge suite with private Jacuzzi. The inn is a friendly place and kids are welcome, making it a nice alternative to a motel. ■ *1 mile west of Bridge St on Hwy 18 (business loop); (503) 843-3151; 1330 W Main, Sheridan, OR 97378; $$; AE, DC, MC, V; checks OK.* &

MOUNT ANGEL

A recent earthquake has closed the historic church at **Mount Angel Abbey**, a hundred-year-old Benedictine seminary. But the campus is still worth a visit, for its beautiful setting atop a butte sacred to the Indians, as well as for the architecture (the library is a gem by the internationally celebrated Finnish architect Alvar Aalto). For hours, call (503) 845-3030. Bach lovers descend on the place in July for the Bach Festival.

SALEM

Except for the state capitol and office buildings, it has the look and feel of a small town. The 1938 capitol has an art deco cum grandiose classical look and is worth a visit, though the recent earthquake shook loose the statue on top of the dome and engineers are still trying to decide what to do with it. Attractive parks flank the building, and just behind is the campus of **Willamette University**, the oldest in the West. The campus is a happy blend of old and new brick buildings, with a small stream, Mill Creek, nicely incorporated into the landscape. A pleasant place to stroll, and plant lovers should visit the small, well cared for botanic gardens on the east side of the campus.

Across the road from Willamette University is **Historic Mission Mill Village**, 1313 Mill Street SE, (503) 585-7012, an impressive 42-acre cluster of restored buildings from the 1800s: a woolen mill, a parsonage, a Presbyterian church, and several homes. The mill, which drew its power from Mill Creek, now houses a museum that literally makes the sounds of the factory come alive. The Jason Lee House, dating from 1841, is the oldest remaining frame house in the Northwest; regular tours of the premises run from 10am to 4:30pm, Tuesday-Saturday. Picnic along the stream and feed the ducks, if you like. The Salem Visitor Information Center is part of the complex, as are several shops selling handcrafted clothing, gifts, and antiques.

Bush House, 600 Mission Street SE, (503) 363-4714, is a Victorian home built in 1877 by pioneer newspaper publisher Asahel Bush. It sits in a large park complete with conservatory, rose gardens, hiking paths, and barn turned art gallery. Tours available.

Gilbert House Children's Museum, (503) 371-3631, on the downtown riverfront between the bridges has a variety of hands-on learning activities for young children. Children will also appreciate **Enchanted Forest**, (503) 371-4242, a nicely wooded storybook park with space for picnicking, just off I-5 south of town.

Salem is off the beaten winery track, but **Willamette Valley Vineyards**, (503) 588-9463, a big investor-owned winery, is just off I-5 south of town and commands a spectacular view of the countryside; **Evesham Wood Vineyard**, (503) 371-8478, in West Salem, a tiny winery making some top-notch wines receives visitors by appointment; and **St. Innocent Winery**, (503) 378-1526, is not far from downtown.

Salem

Restaurants

Old-fashioned ferries, operated by cable, still cross the Willamette River in a few places and offer a fun alternative to bridges, if you've got some extra time. Two run in the Salem area: the Wheatland ferry, just north of town in Keizer (follow Highway 219 north from downtown, and turn off on Wheatland Road) and the Buena Vista (from I-5 take exit #243 and follow Talbot Road west). They run every day (except during storms or high water) and cost very little.

RESTAURANTS

Alessandro's Park Plaza ★★ Pretty formal for Salem: you may feel out of place if you don't dress up. This lovely urban oasis overlooks Mill Creek Park just next to the downtown business district. Owner Alessandro Fasani calls it Roman; most diners would call it upscale Italian, with just-short-of-pretentious service and a menu that emphasizes elegant pasta and seafood dishes. The hearty bouillabaisse is laced with saffron and studded with shellfish and chunks of tomato. In addition to the regular menu, a multicourse dinner is offered daily; the staff asks only if there's a particular dish you don't like, and they surprise you with the rest: three appetizers (maybe smoked salmon over linguine), an entrée such as veal Marsala, and an elaborate dessert. ■ *Trade and High sts; (503) 370-9951; 325 High St SE, Salem; $$; full bar; AE, MC, V; checks OK; lunch Mon-Fri, dinner Mon-Sat.* &

DaVinci's ★ If you think of this as an upscale pizza place, you'll be surprised by its ambitions. Individual pizzas come with an interesting assortment of toppings, and there are different homemade whole-wheat pastas each day. An appetizer of thin, light bread covered with garlic and herbs is simple and flavorful. The ravioli might be cheese and artichoke covered with a sauce of scallops and tomatoes and herbs—rich and flavorful, but too many disjointed flavors. Eggplant on top of polenta, covered with a tangy tomato sauce is simple and more successful. Wine by the glass comes dear: you're better off making a selection of one of the well-priced wines from the extensive list. The brick and dark wood building opens into two stories inside—try not to sit near the stairs unless you enjoy the bustle. A very popular place. Prices on pizzas are fine; others tend to sneak too high for Salem. ■ *On High St near Ferry; (503) 399-1413; 180 High St, Salem; $$; full bar; AE, MC, V; checks OK; lunch Mon-Fri, dinner every day.* &

La Margarita ★ Definitely one of the livelier spots in downtown. The unassuming front opens to a colorfully decorated, two-storied interior, with lots of mirrors to make it look bigger than it is and music to keep it hopping. The staff hops, too—this place is busy. The menu has all the usuals, but the specialty is mesquite grilling, especially the tender and lightly cooked beef and chicken. Sauces are subtle, too, with the emphasis on eating healthy. Margaritas are mammoth. ■ *Near corner of Ferry and High sts; (503) 362-8861; 545 Ferry St SE, Salem; $; full bar; AE, MC, V; checks OK; lunch, dinner every day.* &

McGrath's Publick Fish House ★ This sharp-looking restaurant might be just a knockoff of more famous Seattle and Portland fish houses, but in restaurant-poor Salem it has a fresh feel. Good prices and special attention to children should keep families happy. Crowds pack this glass-fronted, multitiered building. The menu's diverse, but you should order the seafood off the daily fresh sheet. The blackened oyster appetizer is almost a meal in itself—plump oysters, plenty spicy. Mesquite-broiled salmon and the trout are cooked perfectly though sauces tend to be uninteresting. No complaints on the tangy marionberry cobbler, except perhaps that there's too much of it. The young service lacks real expertise but is cheerful and eager. ■ *Chemeketa and High sts; (503) 362-0736; 350 Chemeketa, Salem; $$; full bar; AE, DC, DIS, MC, V; checks OK; breakfast, lunch, dinner every day.* &

Morton's Bistro Northwest ★ Clever design puts the diner *below* roadway level, looking out on an attractive courtyard backed by an ivy-covered wall. The interior is intimate, with dark wood beams and soft lighting. The menu is probably one of the most ambitious in Salem—predominantly Northwest cuisine with hints of French and Oriental influences—but the prevailing theme is calories and cream sauce. A slightly overdone veal with Calvados is drenched with a rich sauce of apples, onions, and mushrooms. The tortellini stuffed with pumpkin is a great idea—but, again, too heavy. Add to that a soup such as cream of asparagus (lots of asparagus, lots of cream) and a dessert such as chocolate mousse, and you may be hard pressed to make it back up the stairs. Instead, choose wisely and you'll find there's serious intent here. The service is expert and pleasant, and the wine list features a good selection of Northwest wines at responsible prices. ■ *Across the Marion St bridge from downtown; (503) 585-1113; 1128 Edgewater, West Salem; $$; full bar; MC, V; checks OK; dinner Tues-Sat.* ♿

Off Center Cafe A throwback to the '60s, the Off Center Cafe features a genuine soda fountain, demure classical music or rock 'n' roll (depending on the chef's mood), a clientele ranging from aging hippies to professors grading papers to bankers in three-piece suits, and intriguing food: scrambled tofu for breakfast, black Cuban beans and rice at lunch, fresh halibut with lime at dinner, and fruit pies all day long. It's not a fancy place, but one that offers "real food" and prides itself on serving its customers well. Many have their own special concoctions listed on the menu: try Ed's Cooler, a mixture of ice cream, mocha, and Pepsi. Mmmmm. ■ *17th and Center NE; (503) 363-9245; 1741 Center NE, Salem; $; no alcohol; no credit cards; checks OK; breakfast Tues-Fri and all day Sat-Sun, lunch Tues-Fri, dinner Thurs-Sat.* ♿

LODGINGS

Phoenix Inn ★ A spanking new place that is the best in town for the business traveler. Spacious rooms in muted colors all have small refrigerators and microwaves; some have their own Jacuzzis. Conference rooms, fax, and copy services are available; there's a small pool, Jacuzzi, and fitness room to relax in; and if you want you can load up on the complimentary buffet breakfast in the morning. Staff is helpful, rates are reasonable, and kids stay free. ■ *From I-5, exit 252, west on Kuebler to Commercial; (800) 445-4498; 4370 Commercial St SE, Salem, OR 97302; $$; AE, DC, DIS, MC, V; checks OK.* ♿

Hampshire House Bed and Breakfast This unpretentious Craftsman-style bungalow sits across the street from the sumptuous (and controversial) state Archives Building in a handsome, tree-lined neighborhood just north of the Capitol. The

▼
Salem
Lodgings
▲

two upstairs rooms are small and sparely furnished, so ask for the front room, with white wicker furniture. The shared bathroom is spacious and sunny, with an old-fashioned bathtub. It's an informal place: host Audie Hampshire is a critical-care nurse and enjoys the chance to chat with healthy folks. Husband Mike is the breakfast chef and produces hearty, English-style meals. It's a lot like staying with your neighbors. ■ *D St off Summer; (503) 370-7181; 975 D St NE, Salem OR 97301; $; DIS, MC, V; checks OK.*

INDEPENDENCE

As long as anyone can remember, **Taylor's Fountain and Gift**, on the corner of Main and Monmouth, has been serving up old-fashioned sodas, burgers, and breakfasts. Marge Taylor, her daughter, and two granddaughters run the place and haven't changed it much in its 49 years.

RESTAURANTS

Amador's ★★ Here's a little gem: just north of the restored main part of town, tucked into a fading strip mall, it produces some of the most honest Mexican fare around. Brothers Manuel and Antonio Amador do the cooking while their families (down to the youngest children) wait on the customers. Nothing elaborate in the way of decor: a whitewashed space, a few Mexican fans, paper flowers. But you know it's going to be good as soon as the first basket of chips arrives (thick, crunchy, homemade) along with a fresh salsa; you can taste the corn and tomatoes. Everything from tacos to enchiladas is exquisitely fresh, piping hot, and lavishly garnished with sour cream, avocado, fresh tomatoes, and green onions. ■ *Hoffman Rd and Main St; (503) 838-0170; 870 N Main St, Independence; $; full bar; MC, V; checks OK; lunch, dinner Mon-Sun.* ♿

ALBANY

Don't be discouraged by the pulp mill next to the freeway; Albany is really quite a pleasant stop. With its broad, quiet streets, neat houses, and slow pace, it nicely represents the small-town Oregon of an earlier era. Once an important transportation hub in the Willamette Valley, the town has been passed by and left with an unequaled selection of historic homes and buildings in a wide variety of styles, many of them lovingly restored.

Historic buildings. A self-guided tour displays 13 distinct architectural styles in the 50-block, 368-building Monteith Historic District alone. Then there are the Hackleman District (28 blocks, 210 buildings) and downtown (9½ blocks, 80 buildings). Many of the buildings are open for inspection on annual tours—the last Saturday in July and the Sunday evening before Christmas Eve. A guide is available from the Albany Chamber of Commerce, 435 W First Avenue, (503) 926-1517, or the Albany Convention and Visitors' Center, (503) 928-0911.

Covered bridges. The covered bridges that were so characteristic of this area are disappearing. From 450 their number has dwindled to less than 50, but that's still more than in any state west of the Mississippi. Most of the remaining ones are in the Willamette Valley counties of Lane, Linn, and Lincoln. Local preservationists are fighting to save the remaining bridges. Best starting points for easy-to-follow circuits of the bridges are Albany, Eugene, and Cottage Grove; in addition, many handsome bridges dot the woods of the Oregon Coast Range. Six of these bridges lie within an eight-mile radius of Scio, northeast of Albany; for a map, contact the Visitors' Center.

RESTAURANTS

Novak's Hungarian Paprikas ★★ Refugees from Hungary and extremely warm hosts, Joseph and Matilda Novak run this place with help from their family (so your waitress will help you pronounce the Hungarian dishes). The homemade sausages are mild and delicately spiced, the stuffed cabbage is oozing with flavor, and the sides of tangy spiced cabbage are to kill for (though surprisingly the signature chicken paprika is bland). The huge servings come with lots of vegetables and potatoes, and small prices. Don't forget dessert: the pastry chef is full-time and the dessert menu is longer than the main one. The simple poppyseed torte is terrific, and they just get more elaborate from there. ■ *Take exit 233 toward town; (503) 967-9488; 2835 Santiam Hwy SE, Albany; $; no alcohol; MC, V; checks OK; lunch Sun-Fri, dinner every day.* &

CORVALLIS

The town is dominated by **Oregon State University**, which gives it a more cosmopolitan flavor than most towns of its size. The campus is typical of other Northwest megaversities, with a gracious core of old buildings in several styles, magnificent giant trees, and lots of open space, surrounded by a maze of modern boxlike classroom and residential buildings of little character. Sports are big here, especially basketball and gymnastics, but the basement of Gill Coliseum also houses the **Horner Museum**, which has a wonderfully eclectic, rather dilapidated collection that relates the history of Oregon's development, from native Americans to the Oregon Trail to economic growth. A grand place for kids, with lots of nooks and crannies and large artifacts from yesteryear; (503) 737-2951. **Corvallis Art Center**, 700 SW Madison, (503) 754-1551, located in a renovated 1889 Episcopal Church off Central Park, displays local crafts and hosts weekly lunchtime concerts.

Corvallis is ideal for biking and running; most streets include a wide bike lane, and routes follow both the Willamette and Mary's rivers. Avery Park, 15th Street and US 20, offers a maze of wooded trails as well as prime picnic sites and a rose garden. Tree lovers may also enjoy OSU's 40-acre **Peavy Arboretum**, 8 miles north of town on Highway 99W—it has hiking trails and picnic facilities.

RESTAURANTS

The Gables ★★ No dispute among the locals: this is still the place to eat in town when you want fine, formal dining. The cooking is very consistent (though the menu's uninspired). A homey atmosphere—with dark wood furnishings, low beams, fireplace—and a courteous staff combine to make this a very comfortable place. The menu features tried-and-true American fare: prime rib, lamb chops, teriyaki chicken, and seafood. Dinners are huge and come with all the trimmings: sourdough bread, relish tray, salad or chicken bisque, veggies, rice or potato. The prime rib has the reputation as the best in town, and the seafood sauté is a generous crock of prawns, scallops, salmon, and halibut in a delicate lemon-butter-wine sauce. A heaping bowlful of homemade garlic croutons comes to your table for soup and salad. The wine cellar is available for special occasions. ▪ *Follow Harrison to 9th; (503) 752-3364; 1121 NW 9th St, Corvallis; $$; full bar; AE, DC, DIS, MC, V; checks OK; dinner every day.* ⅋

▼

Corvallis

▲

Nearly Normal's ★ You gotta love a place with an official bird (the flamingo) and an official motto ("When the going gets weird, the weird turn pro"). The aging hippies who run the place advertise their food as "gonzo cuisine": vegetarian food, organically grown, but prepared with originality and panache. There's lots of Mexican on the menu, plus a few Middle Eastern items and excellent veggie burgers. Try the falafel, a hearty mix of spicy garbanzo patties packed into pita with fresh veggies and a cool yogurt sauce, or the Acapulco sunburger, with avocado and salsa. Fresh fruit drinks are great. This place can get crowded, and you bus your own dishes. Live music Wednesday, Thursday, and Saturday nights in summer, but no smoking ever. ▪ *Near the corner of Monroe and 15th; (503) 753-0791; 109 NW 15th St, Corvallis; $; beer and wine; no credit cards; checks OK; breakfast, lunch, dinner Mon-Sat, brunch Sun.*

La Estrellita A little star on the outskirts of Corvallis where the choices off the large Mexican menu are cooked in the style of the Jalisco region. The food may seem mild to those who like their Mexican hot and spicy, but the chips are fresh and crisp, the salsa is tangy, and the enormous servings are full of fresh vegetables. The friendly and lightning-fast service softens somewhat the uncomfortable hard bench backs in the booths, and the list of Mexican brews is as long as you're likely to find in these parts. Success has meant expansion, and there are now three others like it, all in the Salem-Keizer area. Children welcomed here, and there are lots of them. ■ *In the Timberhill shopping center at Walnut and King blvds; (503) 754-0514; 2309 NW King Blvd, Corvallis; $; full bar; AE, MC, V; checks OK; lunch, dinner every day.* &

LODGINGS

Hanson Country Inn ★★ You're just a few minutes from town, but you'll feel you're in the country as you drive up to this wood-and-brick 1928 farmhouse. Formerly a prosperous poultry-breeding ranch, it's now, thanks to an extensive renovation by former San Franciscan Patricia Covey, a registered historic home. The gleaming living room (with piano and fireplace), sun room, and library are often used for weddings. Step outside into a formal lawn and garden. Upstairs are four guest rooms, luxuriously wallpapered and linened. The best suite has a four-poster bed, private bath, and a study. After breakfasting on crêpes with blackberries or fresh frittata, explore the grounds and original egg house. Bring the kids but not the dog. ■ *Five minutes west of town off West Hills at 35th; (503) 752-2919; 795 SW Hanson St, Corvallis, OR 97333; $$; AE, DC, DIS, MC, V; checks OK.*

Madison Inn ★ The wife of host Richard Down grew up in this imposing Tudor-style house, which also housed a college fraternity for some years, and the rooms upstairs are named after the family's children. Furnished with antique beds and woolen patchwork quilts, the rooms have a rustic, cozy feel. Request the Kathryn room on the top floor for a cathedral ceiling and the best view of the park across the street, or the Matt and Mike room for a private entry and private bath. (There's also a small guest cottage next door for longer-term rental.) Downstairs there are lots of nooks and crannies for lounging, and in the big dining room you can enjoy Dutch babies with blueberry topping, homemade scones, or quiche for breakfast. Very convenient to the University, but because it's on a cul-de-sac, rather quiet as well. ■ *Corner of 7th and Madison, near the University; (503) 757-1274; 660 Madison Ave, Corvallis, OR 97333; $$; AE, DIS, MC, V; checks OK.*

Elmira

Lodgings

ELMIRA

LODGINGS

McGillivray's Log Home Bed and Breakfast ★ This spacious log home on five wooded acres makes a lovely, pastoral retreat for urbanites and a fine introduction to the beauties of Western Oregon for out-of-staters. The two large guest rooms (one with a king-size bed and two twins—perfect for families) both have private baths. A hearty breakfast is prepared on the wood cookstove with antique griddle, and there are fresh Northwest berries in season. ■ *14 miles west of Eugene off Hwy 126; (503) 935-3564; 88680 Evers Rd, Elmira, OR 97437; $$; MC, V; checks OK.* &

EUGENE

Although it's the state's second-largest city, Eugene is still very much Portland's sleepy sister to the south. There's no skyline here—unless you count the grain elevator (well, okay, there's a 12-story Hilton, too). A Eugenean's idea of a traffic jam is when it takes more than five minutes to traverse downtown. There's always parking; people smile at you on the street and, even in its urban heart, Eugene is more treed than paved.

Still, this overgrown town has a sophisticated indigenous culture, from its own symphony (conducted by the justifiably celebrated Marin Alsop), to homegrown ballet, opera, and theater companies. There are more speakers and events (courtesy of the University of Oregon, the state's flagship institution) than one could possibly ever attend. There are good bookstores (don't miss the new **Book Bin**, Eugene's answer to Powell's), the requisite number of coffeehouses (including the newest entry into the world of caffeine, **Java Joe's**, out Willamette Street), trendy brew pubs (try **Steelhead** in Station Square), two serious chocolatiers (**Euphoria** and **Fenton & Lee**) and enough local color—from persevering hippies to backcountry loggers—to make life interesting.

Whatever else you do in Eugene, here are the musts: a hike up **Spencer's Butte**, just south of town, for a spectacular view of the town, valley, and its two rivers; a morning at **Saturday Market**, the state's oldest outdoor crafts fair; an afternoon shopping and eating your way through the **Fifth Street Public Market**; an evening at the **Hult Center for the Performing Arts**. In early July, don't miss the area's oldest and wildest countercultural celebration, the **Oregon Country Fair**.

Hult Center for the Performing Arts is the city's world-class concert facility, with two architecturally striking halls. The 24-hour concert line is (503) 342-5746.

University of Oregon features a lovely art museum with a permanent collection of Orientalia, a new natural history museum, several historic landmark buildings, and a wide variety of speakers and events.

Wistech, a small but nicely conceived hands-on science and technology museum (with accompanying laser light-show planetarium) is the place to take kids on rainy afternoons; open Wednesday through Sunday noon-5pm, 2300 Centennial Boulevard, (503) 484-9027.

Saturday Market, a thriving open-air crafts and food fair, is the ultimate Eugene experience. Unique crafts sold by the artisans themselves, continental noshing, eclectic music, and inspired people-watching; open April through December on High Street at Broadway.

Fifth Street Public Market has undergone a facelift, with an airier, more spacious (and more upscale) crafts area. But the rest of this lovely place, with its three levels of shops surrounding a pretty brick courtyard, remains the same. The Market houses the city's best bakery, Metropol.

Eugene

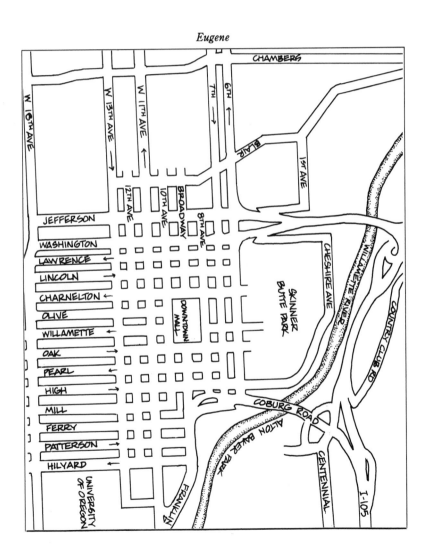

Outdoors. The two rivers that run through town, the Willamette and the McKenzie, provide opportunities for canoeists and rafters, both first-timers and whitewater enthusiasts. Hikers will find miles of forest trails just outside the city limits. Runners will love the city's several groomed, packed running trails.

Parks. Run along the banks of the Willamette through Alton Baker Park on the 6.3-kilometer groomed Prefontaine Trail. Women will feel safer on the sloughside 1.6-kilometer circuit that borders Amazon Park, site of spirited outdoor concerts in the summer. Hendricks Park, the city's oldest, features an outstanding 10-acre rhododendron garden (best blooms in May and early June). Skinner's Butte Park, which skirts the Willamette, includes a lovely rose garden, several playgrounds, picnic areas, and a 12-mile bike/running path. Spencer's Butte, just south of town, offers sweeping urban and pastoral views to those who hike up the two relatively easy trails to the top.

RESTAURANTS

Chanterelle ★★★ Understated, sophisticated, and unfailingly wonderful, Chef Rolf Schmidt's intimate restaurant offers the very freshest of every season, cooked with respect and restrained imagination. The small menu with its delicate basil scallops and richly sauced tournedos of beef is supplemented by a wide selection of chef's specials. In the spring, there's chinook and local lamb. In the winter, Rolf's deeply satisfying onion soup will warm the inner you. In between there's sturgeon, ahi, New Zealand venison, even antelope—whatever is fresh and appeals to the chef's sense of adventure. Rolf does it all alone in a kitchen the size of a walk-in closet—and comes out smiling and only slightly disheveled at the end of the evening to greet his loyal patrons. A respectable wine list and extraordinary desserts; try the chocolate silk pie. ▪ *Across the street from Fifth St Public Market; (503) 484-4065; 207 E 5th, Eugene; $$; full bar; AE, MC, V; checks OK; dinner Tues-Sat.* ⅊

Excelsior Cafe ★★ The bad news is that Stephanie Pearl, the woman who single-handedly brought culinary culture to Eugene, has sold the Excelsior after almost 20 years. The good news is that new owner Maurizio Paparo is not jumping in with big changes. He'd have a revolt on his hands if he did, so cherished is this Eugene institution. The menu is moving ever so slightly away from French cuisine, in favor of more international selections, but all the "Ex's" standbys are here, from the exquisite pear, butterleaf lettuce, blue cheese, and hazelnut salad, through the perfectly grilled swordfish, and on to the Frangelico cheesecake. Fortunately, the new owner is just as committed to quality and freshness as was the old owner. The elegant but informal restaurant and its small, bustling bar are favorites with the university crowd. ▪ *Across from Sacred Heart*

▼

Eugene

▲

Hospital; (503) 342-6963; 754 E 13th, Eugene; $$; full bar; AE, MC, V; checks OK; lunch Mon-Fri, dinner every day, brunch Sun.

Grapevine ★★ This urbane bistro located on the slowly reviving pedestrian mall is a welcome addition to downtown. Opened by a first-time restaurateur and his Chez Panisse-trained chef, Grapevine specializes in cuisine of the sun. Mediterranean dishes such as the penne pasta with grilled eggplant, sun-dried tomatoes, pine nuts, and pesto are Italy captured gloriously in a bowl. The paella, made with a creamy risotto, is a colorful combination of chorizo, chicken, clams, and bell peppers. Grapevine offers more than 50 regional and international wines by the glass, half-glass, and "tastes." All this plus lovely desserts (orange Madeira carrot cake, ricotta cannoli) and friendly, unpretentious service. ■ *On the east end of the downtown mall; (503) 686-5622; 30 E Broadway, Eugene; $$; beer and wine; MC, V; checks OK; lunch, dinner every day, brunch Sat-Sun.*

Zenon Cafe ★★ Urbane, noisy, crowded—and always interesting—this is the place upscale locals go when they want to pretend they don't live in Eugene, Oregon. Zenon's formidable, ever-changing international menu ranges from blackened catfish to Thai green curried beef, from Greek lamb meatballs to fettuccine with morel, shiitake, and agaricus mushrooms. On any given night, the cuisines of a dozen countries might be represented, and how the large kitchen staff keeps it all straight is the ongoing miracle of Zenon. A good selection of regional wines by the glass is available. And do leave room for dessert (not difficult, since entrée portions are small), for Zenon's are among the city's very best. The outdoor seating in mild weather is delightful. ■ *Corner of Broadway and Pearl; (503) 343-3005; 898 Pearl St, Eugene; $$; beer and wine; MC, V; checks OK; breakfast, lunch, dinner every day.* ৬

Ambrosia ★ The pizza is wonderful here: small, crisp pies topped with rich plum tomato sauce and your choice of trendy ingredients (sun-dried tomatoes, artichoke hearts, roasted eggplant) and baked in a huge, wood-burning oven. But Ambrosia is much more than a designer pizzeria. Pasta comes in all shapes and varieties, from angel hair noodles topped with grilled, marinated vegetables to zucchini and fennel lasagne. Fresh fish specials might include a grilled halibut in tomato caper butter or Chilean sea bass finished in dry wine and topped with Dungeness crab and toasted almonds. Gelato provides the finishing touch. ■ *Corner of Broadway and Pearl; (503) 342-4141; 174 E Broadway, Eugene; $; full bar; MC, V; checks OK; lunch Mon-Sat, dinner every day.* ৬

Baja Cafe ★ With its zany decor—watermelon piñatas, spinning globes, a 7-foot mounted swordfish, and lots of turquoise, this informal eatery is a downtown favorite. If you're looking for real Mexican food, don't come here. But if homemade chips with blue-cheese dip, shark tacos, and black beans with a sprinkling of Parmesan sounds good, Baja is your kind of place. The chicken fajitas are wonderful. With its fast counter service, flexible kids' menu, and naturally exuberant atmosphere, this is a great place to eat if you have a young family. ■ *Pearl between Broadway and 8th; (503) 683-8606; 860 Pearl, Eugene; $; beer and wine; MC, V; checks OK; lunch, dinner Mon-Sat.* ♿

Cafe Navarro ★ Like the world beat music that plays on the sound system, Jorge Navarro's new restaurant is a rich cross-cultural experience, with dishes ranging from Africa and Spain to Cuba and the Caribbean. Cafe Navarro is a simple, casual place with friendly service, sizable portions, reasonable prices, and wonderful, inventive offerings. Navarro freely combines cuisines, often arriving at extraordinary results such as his south-of-the-border interpretation of Italian cioppino, made here with cilantro, chiles, and roasted tomatoes. Try the spiced snapper in tamarind-coconut or the shredded pork with red beans, plantains, and salsa. There are no bad choices. For lunch, Navarro's version of arroz con pollo, with seared chicken chunks, red peppers, capers, and cilantro, is a good bet. For breakfast, the hands-down favorite is ginger waffles with mango syrup. ■ *At the foot of Willamette St; (503) 344-0943; 454 Willamette St, Eugene; $; beer; MC, V; checks OK; lunch Tues-Fri, dinner Tues-Sat, brunch Sat-Sun.* ♿

Chez Ray's ★ It's the quintessential Eugene eatery: an unprepossessing venture catering to an eclectic clientele (where suit and hirsute mix freely), with an unpretentious but inventive menu (marionberry chicken, rosemary snapper), all presided over by the former road chef for the Grateful Dead. The eponymous Ray Sewell, resplendent in tie-dye, serves up hearty breakfasts (try the simple but delectable eggs and sautéed veggies), satisfying lunches (choose the locally famous salmon burger), and commendable, ever-changing dinners. ■ *2 blks southwest of U of O campus; (503) 342-8596; 1473 E 19th, Eugene; $; beer and wine; MC, V; local checks OK; breakfast, lunch, and dinner every day.* ♿

Mekala's ★ This pretty Thai restaurant with its light-filled dining area overlooking the Fifth Street Public Market courtyard (outside seating, weather permitting) features a six-page menu with more than a dozen fiery curries and two dozen vegetarian dishes. Chef/owner Payung Van Slyke is an inventive cook who shows sensitivity to a wide range of palates and will spice up or cool down most dishes. The magnificent angel wings (deboned chicken wings stuffed with ground pork, glass noodles, and bean sprouts) are a must appetizer. For a light dinner, try the

Thai noodle salad, soft noodles mixed with crunchy sprouts and studded with chicken and cashews. Interested in waking up your taste buds? Try the homoke souffle (shrimp, scallops, and fish in a curry and coconut sauce with fresh lime leaves, green pepper, and cabbage). A glass of Thai iced tea goes nicely. End the meal with a dish of velvety homemade coconut ice cream. ■ *In the 5th St Public Market Building; (503) 342-4872; 296 E 5th St, Eugene; $; beer and wine; MC, V; checks OK; lunch, dinner every day.* ⅙

Napoli ★ Pasta of all sorts is good here, from fusilli with chicken and artichoke hearts to cheese-filled spinach tortellini in pesto sauce. Designer pizza is available by the slice or pie, but carbo-loading locals prefer the "white pizza"—focaccia—Italian dough drizzled with olive oil, garlic, and Parmesan. Possibly the best item on the menu is the simplest: insalata mista, a huge bowl of fresh seasonal greens, artichoke hearts, and roasted bell peppers served with chianti vinaigrette. If you feast on the salad, you might allow yourself a slice of the sinful tiramisu for dessert, a chocolate sponge cake soaked in rum, layered with Italian cream cheese, and topped with shaved bittersweet chocolate. ■ *Across from Sacred Heart Hospital; (503) 485-4552; 686 E 13th, Eugene; $; beer and wine; MC, V; checks OK; breakfast, lunch, dinner Mon-Sat.* ⅙

Oregon Electric Station ★ So your father's in town and to him dinner means prime rib and baked potato—but you're of the yellowfin-tuna-in-roasted-pepper-butter persuasion? Don't despair. The Electric Station narrows the culinary generation gap. While there is nothing spectacular about the diverse menu—no great risks taken—there are also few failures. The seafood is never overcooked; the steak is invariably juicy. You eat in converted railroad cars parked behind the lovely brick station that gives the restaurant its name. The station building itself, a significant piece of historical architecture with its 30-foot ceilings, arched windows, and extraordinary light fixtures, houses the city's prettiest bar. Live jazz on weekends in a separate (but not pretty) room off the station. ■ *2 blocks north of the Hult Center; (503) 485-4444; 27 E 5th, Eugene; $; full bar; DIS, MC, V; local checks OK; dinner Mon-Sun, brunch Sun.* ⅙

Hilda's Latin American Restaurant Tucked away in a downwardly mobile westside neighborhood and housed in a middling 1930s bungalow, Hilda's, with its exotic menu of Latin American dishes, comes as a lovely surprise. Here you'll find the cuisines of Brazil, Peru, Argentina, Chile, Guatemala, and Venezuela represented by a pleasing diversity of meat, seafood, and vegetarian offerings. ■ *Take W 6th to Blair; (503) 343-4322; 400 Blair Blvd, Eugene; $; beer and wine; MC, V; checks OK; dinner Mon-Sat.*

Jamie's Take the kids to Jamie's, where they (and you) can eat terrific burgers (11 varieties), inspired onion rings, the best grilled chicken sandwich in town and real—yes, real—milk shakes. Kids can play on the red Vespa and sidecar while you listen to tunes from the '50s jukebox and await your order. There's a second Jamie's in Eugene at 2445 Hilyard Street, (503) 342-2206, a third in Corvallis, and a fourth in Portland. ■ *Near Hilyard and 24th; (503) 342-2206; 2445 Hilyard St, Eugene; $; no alcohol; AE, MC, V; checks OK; lunch, dinner every day.* &

West Brothers Bar-B-Que Another sign that Eugene's downtown pedestrian mall is coming back to life is the opening of this spirited barbecue eatery. It's not Texas, but the dry-rubbed baby back ribs give a good imitation. The North Carolina pork shoulder, Kansas City beef ribs, Louisiana links, and Oregon chicken come tender and tasty with three sauces—hot, sweet, and regular. Black beans, smoked barbecue beans, and a good poppy-seeded coleslaw are the sides of choice. If you're not in the mood for barbecue, check out the back of the menu. There you'll find unusual choices that serve as a reminder that one of the West brothers used to be a chef at Zenon: jalapeño noodles with mussels, clams, and shrimp, critter potpie, and smoked hominy and black-eyed peas. A number of Northwest microbrewery beers will help wash it all down. ■ *Northwest corner of the downtown mall; (503) 345-8489; 844 Olive St, Eugene; $; beer and wine; MC, V; checks OK; lunch, dinner every day.* &

▼

Eugene

Restaurants

▲

LODGINGS

Campus Cottage ★★ Eugene's premier bed and breakfast is classy, cozy, comfortable, and convenient. The three guest rooms, all with private baths, are beautifully furnished with antiques. One of the rooms is very private, with its own entrance and bay windows overlooking a pretty garden and deck. Innkeeper Ursula Bates, the doyenne of the Eugene B&B scene, does everything right, from the crisp linen on the beds to the crock full of warm-from-the-oven chocolate chip cookies (cold milk in the guest fridge, of course). Her full breakfasts are both delicious and elegantly served. ■ *1 block south of the U of O on E 19th; (503) 342-5346; 1136 E 19th Ave, Eugene, OR 97403; $$$; no credit cards; checks OK.*

Maryellen's Guest House ★★ This airy Northwest contemporary tucked into a wooded hillside is just three minutes from the University of Oregon campus. Quiet and unharried, Maryellen's has only two rooms, each of them tastefully decorated and private, each with its own well-appointed bath (one has a double shower and Roman soaking tub). The rooms open onto their own private decks, but it is the main house's deck, recently expanded, that is the real drawing card, with its lovely pool and all-weather hot tub screened by dense greenery and a natural cedar fence. Innkeeper Maryellen Larson is the perfect hostess: friendly, accommodating, knowledgeable, and respectful of your privacy. Oh, yes—she's a terrific breakfast chef too. Guests are raving about her old-fashioned bread pudding with warm berry sauce. No smoking in the house. ■ *East side of Hendricks Park; (503) 342-7375; 1583 Fircrest, Eugene, OR 97403; $$; AE, MC, V; checks OK.*

Valley River Inn ★★ Don't be put off by the Inn's neighbor, a regional shopping mall with acres of parking lots. The Inn looks to itself and to the Willamette River, which it hugs, for its ambience. With pretty inner courtyards, lovely plantings, and an inviting pool area, this sprawling complex effectively creates a world of its own. The rooms are oversize and well decorated, with the best ones facing the river. The restaurant is forgettable, but the outdoor dining area hard by the river is a wonderful place to enjoy drinks and hors d'oeuvres. ■ *Exit 194B off I-5 to 105 (west) to Exit 3; (503) 687-0123; 1000 Valley River Way, Eugene, OR 97401; $$$; AE, DC, MC, V; checks OK.* ﬢ

Duckworth's Bed and Breakfast ★ This English Tudor home just blocks from the University of Oregon campus features three pretty rooms (only one with a private bath) with antique furnishings, lace curtains, window seats, fresh flowers, and their own VCRs. Downstairs there's a 600-movie video library, an overstuffed sofa in front of the fireplace, and perhaps just a few more knickknacks than necessary. Innkeeper Peggy Ward serves lovely three-course breakfasts and plies summer guests with iced tea in the English garden out back. ■ *2 blocks south of the university on 19th; (503) 686-2451; 987 E 19th, Eugene, OR 97403; $$; no credit cards; checks OK.*

Eugene Hilton ★ If it's a convenient downtown location you're after, the Hilton fits the bill. It's across a brick courtyard from the Hult Center for the Performing Arts, a block from the downtown mall, two blocks from the thriving Market district, and easy strolling distance to a half-dozen good restaurants. The rooms are comfortable and predictable, with nice city views from south-facing rooms and quieter butte views from the north. Amenities include a (very small) indoor pool along with a sauna, Jacuzzi, and game room. Breakfasts can be included in the price; the lobby bar is lively, but don't plan to eat at either of the hotel's two lackluster restaurants. ■ *Exit 194B off I-5, then Exit 1 to city center; (503) 342-2000; 66 E 6th Ave, Eugene, OR 97401; $$$; AE, DC, DIS, MC, V; checks OK.* ﬢ

New Oregon Motel The free sports center and this Best Western's location just across from the University of Oregon elevate this place from strip motel status. The 128 rooms are a cut above motel standards. The sports facility includes an indoor pool, Jacuzzi, two saunas, and two racquetball courts. ■ *Across from the university; (503) 683-3669; 1655 Franklin Blvd, Eugene, OR 97403; $$; AE, DC, MC, V; checks OK.* &

SPRINGFIELD

RESTAURANTS

Kuraya's ★ Although its location is off the beaten path, Kuraya's remains a popular spot with local Thai-food lovers. The casual atmosphere, friendly service, and large, inventive menu keep people coming back. So do the seafood basket—shrimp and scallops in a hot, coconutty sauce—and the Bangkok prawns, charcoal-broiled and served with a crabmeat-and-peanut dipping sauce. ■ *Market and Mohawk; (503) 746-2951; 1410 Mohawk Blvd, Springfield; $; beer and wine; MC, V; checks OK; lunch Mon-Sat, dinner every day.* &

Spring Garden ★ This resolutely uncharming spot on Springfield's decaying Main Street serves some of the best Chinese food south of Portland. Although you dine on Naugahyde banquettes with a panoramic view of a Goodwill Industries outlet, you can feast on truly inspired sizzling rice soup, egg rolls that are simultaneously crunchy and eggy, and a variety of fresh, flavorful entrées. The David Tofu, silky bean curd and pork (or no for vegetarians) in a deep, rich sauce, is a delight. Seafood lovers should make a beeline for the stuffed garlic prawns or the pan-fried shrimp, two of the best items on the menu. Ignore those around you who order the combination plates and deep-fried items. ■ *Downtown Springfield; (503) 747-0338; 215 Main St, Springfield; $; full bar; AE, MC, V; local checks only; lunch, dinner every day.*

LEABURG

LODGINGS

Marjon Bed and Breakfast ★ Thirty minutes east of Eugene, just off the road that threads its way through the Oregon Cascades, sits Marjorie Haas' immaculate contemporary home. If your idea of heaven is two private acres by the banks of the pristine McKenzie, dotted with 2,000 azaleas and 7,000 rhododendrons, then pull into Marjon. The junior room ($80 a night) is a nice-size bedroom with bath (including fishbowl shower) across the hall. The master suite ($100) has a 7-by-12-foot bed, an adjoining bath with sunken tub and a view of the Japanese garden. Breakfasts are five-course affairs served with seasonal flair. ■ *3 miles east of Leaburg on McKenzie Hwy, turn at Leaburg Dam Rd (milepost 24), ignore the dead-end signs; (503) 896-3145; 44975 Leaburg Dam Rd, Leaburg, OR 97489; $$$; no credit cards; checks OK.*

OAKLAND

RESTAURANTS

Tolly's ★ Oakland is one of Oregon's older towns, dating back to 1851. Tolly's is a special-occasion place for locals; still, it's a bit of an oddity. Downstairs there's an old-fashioned ice cream parlor, candy counter, and antique gift shop. Upstairs the Tollefsons get a bit more serious. One elegant room, with high wingback chairs and candlelight, is reserved for couples only, and is nonsmoking. At last report, the Tollefsons had the restaurant (but not the adjacent antique store) up for sale. So menu and chefs may continue to change. On our last visit, the chicken with mushrooms, sherry, and artichoke hearts was respectable, served with fettuccine and fresh asparagus. And for the bread course: nothing but croissants. But the only soup served any day of the week was an average clam chowder. The wine list is the region's longest, at 128 labels. ■ *Exit 138 off I-5 to middle of Oakland; (503) 459-3796; 115 Locust St, Oakland; $$; full bar; AE, MC, V; checks OK; lunch, dinner every day.*

STEAMBOAT

LODGINGS

▼

Roseburg

▲

Steamboat Inn ★ On the banks of a fly-only fishing stream is the plain-seeming lodge run for many years by Jim and Sharon Van Loan. Linked by a long verandah paralleling the North Umpqua River are eight small guest cabins; rooms have knotty-pine walls, a bath, and just enough space. In the woods are five secluded cottages with living rooms and kitchens. Latest additions are two riverside suites. Prices begin at $85 for a stream-view double and climb to $195 for a suite. Remarkably good family-style dinners are served in the main building each night a half hour after dark, by reservation only ($30 per person, including premium Oregon wines). That's just enough time to prepare your fishing stories. The meals are elegant multi-course feasts, and (with advance notice) chef Sharon can design one around your special tastes or diet. A dinner might include cheese-stuffed mushrooms, tossed greens with fresh blackberries, leg of lamb, trout and scallops served with rice, and dessert. ■ *38 miles east of Roseburg on Hwy 138; (503) 498-2411; Mail: Steamboat Inn, Steamboat, OR 97447-9703; $$$; MC, V; checks OK; breakfast, lunch, dinner every day.*

ROSEBURG

The Roseburg area now has seven wineries, five of which are open for tours and tastings most of the year: **Callahan Ridge**, 340 Busenbark Lane, (503) 673-7901; **Girardet Wine Cellars**,

895 Reston Road, (503) 679-7252; **Henry Winery**, 687 Hubbard Creek Road, Umpqua, (503) 459-5120; **HillCrest Vineyards**, 240 Vineyard Lane, (503) 673-3709, and **La Garza**, 491 Winery Lane, (503) 679-9654. La Garza also has a tasting room restaurant, first in the region, serving lunch Wednesday through Sunday and dinner by reservation.

Douglas County Museum imaginatively displays logging, fur-trapping, and pioneer items in one of the handsomest contemporary structures you'll find. It's free and open Tuesday through Sunday; off I-5 at the fairgrounds, exit 123, (503) 440-4507.

K&R's Drive Inn dishes out huge scoops of Umpqua ice cream. One scoop is really two; two scoops are actually four. Located 20 miles north of Roseburg, at the Rice Hill exit off I-5; the parking lot is full from before noon till after dark, all year-round.

RESTAURANTS

Cafe Espresso It's a smart, sunny cafe with black-and-white tiled floor, red-and-white-checked tablecloths, and Roseburg's best espresso bar. They have good coffee and croissants at breakfast, and Italian sodas, soups, salads, and hot croissant sandwiches for lunch. Daily specials range from beef stroganoff to quiche to lasagne. Low prices and weekday-only hours confirm our hunch that the locals want to keep this place all to themselves. No smoking. ▪ *Corner of Douglas and Jackson; (503) 672-1859; 368 SE Jackson St, Roseburg; $; no alcohol; no credit cards; checks OK; breakfast, lunch Mon-Fri.*

AZALEA

RESTAURANTS

Heaven on Earth Heaven this is not, but it's at least partway there. Six-inch-diameter cinnamon rolls weigh in at a pound or more. It's all very quaint; they serve water in canning jars. Food is basic (roast beef, chicken-fried steak) and the soups superior, notably the split pea. The apple butter is homemade. Owner Christine Jackson likes to chat with guests, who are usually frequent travelers of I-5. ▪ *Exit 86 off I-5; (503) 837-3596; 703 Quines Creek Rd, Azalea; $$; no alcohol; MC, V; local checks only; breakfast, lunch, dinner every day.*

WOLF CREEK

LODGINGS

Wolf Creek Tavern ★ An old 1850s stagecoach stop, this inn was purchased by the state and restored in 1979. There are eight guest rooms, seven that rent for about $55. All have private baths. Downstairs there's an attractive parlor and a dining room open to the public for all meals, including Sunday brunch.

The menu changes from time to time, but the fare, while standard, is usually hearty and inexpensive. It's open year-round (except sometimes in early January). Children are okay; pets are okay with payment of a deposit. ■ *Exit 76 off I-5 at 100 Railroad Ave; (503) 866-2474; PO Box 97, Wolf Creek, OR 97497; $$; DIS, MC, V; no checks.* ⅄

GRANTS PASS

The Rogue is one of Oregon's most beautiful rivers, chiseled into the coastal mountains from here to Gold Beach, protected by the million-acre Siskiyou National Forest, flecked with abandoned gold-mining sites, and inhabited by splendid steelhead and roaming Californians. Two companies offer jet boat tours. **Hellgate Excursions**, (503) 479-7204, departs from the Riverside Inn in Grants Pass. **Jet Boat River Excursions**, (503) 582-0800, leaves from the city of Rogue River, 8 miles upstream. One guide service that conducts wild and daring whitewater trips is **Orange Torpedo Trips**, (503) 479-5061. Or you can hike the Rogue, a very hot trip in the summer.

RESTAURANTS

Hamilton House ★ Chef/owner Doug Hamilton grew up in this house when it was his parents' home, hidden in the trees east of town. Now it is sandwiched between Fred Meyer and Wal-Mart, but Hamilton has remodeled the structure so that it serves as a handsome dinner house yet retains some of the old charm. On a recent visit the salmon beurre blanc was moist and exquisite, and the creamy Jamaican jerk chicken over angel hair pasta so rich we took half of it home. There's a daily fresh sheet often likely to feature lingcod, snapper, and halibut, plus all the usual steaks. Grants Pass is noted for inexpensive dining, and Hamilton House fits the mold. Two can get by for $25 in many cases. Hamilton recently added periodic dinner theater productions. ■ *South Grants Pass exit off I-5, 3 blocks to Terry Ln, left 1 block; (503) 479-3938; 344 NE Terry Ln, Grants Pass; $; full bar; AE, DC, DIS, MC, V; local checks only; dinner every day.* ⅄

Pongsri's ★ Thai restaurants now abound in southern Oregon, but Don and Pongsri Von Essen were here first, and locals still consider their place the best. You don't need to dress up or bring much money. Still, you can choose from more than 75 selections. Hot and spicy dishes such as massamam (beef curry with peanuts and potatoes, onions, and coconut milk) are marked on the menu with an asterisk. Order a two-asterisk dish like pla kung—spicy shrimp salad—and be prepared for an adventure. ■ *North Grants Pass exit off I-5, continue 1 mile; (503) 479-1345; 1571 NE 6th St, Grants Pass; $; beer and wine; MC, V; local checks only; lunch, dinner Tues-Sun.* ⅄

Paradise Ranch Inn ★★ Paradise, once a working dude ranch, is now a full-service resort, right in the heart of the verdant Rogue River Valley. Activities abound: fishing for trout or bass, swimming in a heated pool, boating on a 3-acre lake, playing tennis on two lighted courts, riding bicycles or hiking along miles of trails, relaxing in a hot tub. Three holes of an eventual 18-hole golf course have opened. With all this planned action, you might expect a sprawling modern resort, but Paradise Ranch Inn defies that image: there are only 17 large Early American-style guest rooms. Best are those that overlook one of the three ponds. The emphasis is on peace and quiet: no TVs or phones in rooms (but good message takers in the office). The four-bedroom Sunset House on the back 40 is a good choice for a couple of families or small groups. Dinner explores the likes of tarragon pork, chicken paprika, fresh pasta, and fresh fish; the restaurant is open to nonguests. The menu changes from time to time, and so do the chefs; but all in all, this is a divine getaway. ■ *Hugo or Merlin exit off I-5, west to Monument Dr; (503) 479-4333; 7000-D Monument Dr, Grants Pass, OR 97526; $$$; full bar; MC, V; checks OK; breakfast, dinner Wed-Sun (every day in summer).* &

Riverbanks Inn ★★ It's on the Rogue, so you'd expect a fine river ambience. You might not expect parklike surroundings with an Oriental garden, a teahouse for meditation, and a therapeutic massage room (Myrtle Franklin, who opened this gorgeous B&B in 1988, is a licensed therapist). The rooms are quite exotic: Caribbean Dream Suite with plantation canopy queen bed draped with Mombasa netting; Rain Forest room wetted with a bar, Jacuzzi, and two private patios; Casablanca furnished with Peruvian carved furniture and tribal carpets. All units have private baths; most have VCRs with a movie selection that corresponds to the room's motif. The emphasis here is on fun and imagination. For breakfast, Franklin often prepares Christmas hash—sausage, red potatoes, and vegetables—or sheepherder's-bread French toast. Smoking is permitted outside only. No pets. ■ *8 miles south of town on Hwy 199, then right on Riverbanks Rd for another 8; (503) 479-1118; 8401 Riverbanks Rd, Grants Pass, OR 97527; $$$; MC, V; checks OK.*

Lawnridge House ★ This restored historic (1909) home turned B&B permits easy access to Ashland (45 minutes) or Jacksonville (30 minutes). The place has two suites, each with private bath. One is designed for families; the other has a king-size curtained canopy bed. Breakfasts are Northwest hearty: baked salmon, crab cakes, croissants, and quiche. Innkeeper/chef Barbara Head makes an effort to accommodate special dietary requests, so speak up. ■ *Savage and Lawnridge; (503) 476-8518; 1304 NW Lawnridge, Grants Pass, OR 97526; $$; no credit cards; checks OK.*

JACKSONVILLE

The town started with a boom when gold was discovered in Rich Gulch in 1851. Then the railroad bypassed it, and the tidy little city struggled to avoid becoming a ghost town. Much of the 19th-century city has been restored; Jacksonville now boasts 85 historic homes and buildings open to the public. The strip of authentic Gold Rush-era shops, hotels, and saloons along California Street has become a popular stage set for films, including *The Great Northfield, Minnesota Raid* and the TV movie *Inherit the Wind.* Jacksonville is renowned for antique shops.

Britt Festival, an outdoor music and arts series, runs from late June through September on the hillside field where Peter Britt, a famous local photographer and horticulturist, used to have his home. Listeners gather on benches or flop onto blankets on the grass to enjoy open-stage performances of jazz, bluegrass, folk, country, classical music, musical theater, and dance. Quality of performances varies, but the series has big-name artists from the various categories, and listening to the music under a twinkling night sky makes for a memorable evening. Begun in 1963, the festival now draws some 50,000 viewers through the summer. For tickets and information, call the Britt Festival office, (503) 773-6077 or toll-free (800) 882-7488.

Jacksonville

Restaurants

Jacksonville Museum, housed in the stately 1883 courthouse, follows the history of the railroad in the Rogue Valley with plenty of photos and artifacts. Another section displays works of Peter Britt. The adjacent children's museum lets kids walk through various miniaturized pioneer settings (jail, tepee, schoolhouse) and features a collection of the cartoons and memorabilia of Pinto Colvig, the Jacksonville kid who became Bozo the Clown and the voice of Disney's Pluto, Goofy, and three of the Seven Dwarfs; (503) 773-6536.

Valley View Winery, the area's oldest, is at Ruch, five miles west of here; (503) 899-8468. The winery maintains a second tasting room in town, at the rear of the Village Gallery, 130 W California Street, (503) 899-1001.

RESTAURANTS

Jacksonville Inn ★★★ Ask a native to name the area's best, and the answer will often be the Jacksonville Inn. The staff is considerate, and the antique-furnished dining room, housed in the original 1863 building, is elegant and intimate. Executive chef Diane Menzie expertly creates the full realm of continental cuisine: steak, seafood, pasta, plus health-minded low-cholesterol fare and an expanded variety of vegetarian entrées. Dinners can be ordered as a leisurely seven-course feast or à la carte (or save money by ordering from the bistro menu in the lounge). A la carte is substantial enough. The petrale sole is a favorite, as are the veal piccata and baked polenta with tomatoes, garlic, cheese, and pesto. Desserts are lovely European creations. The place is full of locals during weekday lunch. Jerry Evans exhibits one of the best-stocked wine cellars in Oregon, with more than 600 domestic and imported labels on hand.

Upstairs, eight refurbished rooms are decorated with 19th-century details: antique four-poster beds, patchwork quilts, and original brickwork on the walls. Modern amenities include private bathrooms and air conditioning (a boon in the 100-degree summer swelter). The rooms, especially the sought-after corner room, are a bit noisy—street sounds easily penetrate the walls. Guests enjoy a full breakfast. Reserve rooms in advance, especially during the Britt Festival. ■ *On California St, the town's main thoroughfare; (503) 899-1900; 175 E California St, Jacksonville; $$; full bar; AE, DC, DIS, MC, V; checks OK; lunch Tues-Sat, dinner every day, brunch Sun.*

Bella Union ★★ This restaurant, in the original century-old Bella Union Saloon (half of which was constructed when *The Great Northfield, Minnesota Raid* (1969) was filmed in Jacksonville), has grown into a first-rate dinner house with everything from pizza and pasta to elegant dinners to picnic baskets for the summertime Britt Music Festival. The place usually has a good fresh sheet with choices such as Cajun-style swordfish with black bean sauce and salsa, petrale sole with pesto, lingcod, flounder, and steamed mussels, as well as oyster-mushroom fettuccine. The garden out back is pleasant in warm weather. Proprietor Jerry Hayes is a wine fancier and pours 35 labels by the glass as well as by the bottle. ■ *On California St; (503) 899-1770; 170 W California St, Jacksonville; $$; full bar; AE, DIS, MC, V; checks OK; lunch, dinner every day.* &

LODGINGS

Old Stage Inn ★★★ This is Jacksonville's classiest B&B: a century-old farmhouse renovated by Hugh and Carla Jones and opened in 1990. There's an extensive library, a parlor, and a formal sitting room with a rare 1865 Hallett & Comston square parlor grand piano. The two rooms with king-size beds (one of them wheelchair-accessible) have their own baths, while two rooms with queen-size beds share a magnificent bath. In her kitchen, the size of a living room in most normal homes, Carla creates breakfasts of homemade breads, poached pears with raspberry purée, and entrées such as croissants stuffed with mushrooms, cheese, and fresh herbs. She also provides afternoon refreshments. ■ *Take Oregon St just beyond Livingston*

Rd to 883 Old Stage Rd; (503) 899-1776, or toll-free (800) US-STAGE; PO Box 579, Jacksonville, OR 97530; $$$; MC, V; checks OK. &

McCully House Inn ★ One of the first six homes in the city, McCully House was built in 1861 for Jacksonville's first doctor, and later housed the first girls' school. It's elegant inside, with hardwood floors, fresh paint, lace curtains, and lovely antiques. The three guest rooms have private baths, and the McCully Room flaunts a fireplace, a claw-footed pedestal tub, and the original black-walnut furnishings that traveled 'round the Horn with J.W. McCully. The inn's restaurant has reopened with a new chef, William Prahl, and early reports are promising. At McCully House you're likely to find interesting combinations such as citrus-soy grilled halibut with ginger, tamari, Asian vegetables, and a cup of konbu, or grilled fillet of beef with sun-dried tomato butter, peppercorns, and roasted red potatoes. It's open late nights after the Britt Festival—sit outside and cool off with a fruit taco (a sweet toss of fruit inside a taco-shaped pastry capped with mint and whipped cream). ■ *Follow the signs from I-5 to 5th and E California; (503) 899-1942; 240 E California St, Jacksonville, OR 97530; $$; full bar; MC, V; checks OK; lunch, dinner every day, brunch Sun.* &

SHADY COVE/TRAIL

RESTAURANTS

Bel Di's ★★ Ray and Joan Novosad took over this riverside country dinner house a couple of years ago and have maintained the quality that makes it a special place. The dining room has a grand view of the Rogue River. The full dinner is served with elegance, but you're out in the boonies and don't need to dress up. The overall ambience, the attentive service, and the fine soups and salad dressing are more special than many of the entrées, but try the scampi or the Louisiana stuffed prawns. ■ *North side of Shady Cove's bridge, first drive after BP station; (503) 878-2010; 21900 Hwy 62, Shady Cove; $$; full bar; MC, V; checks OK; dinner Tues-Sun.* &

Rogue River Lodge ★ The oldest dinner house in Jackson County has been owned by ex-Navy man Ken Meirstin for two decades now. The walls are decorated with his collection of ship paintings. Dory, his wife, supervises the cooking here and maintains a high standard of consistent quality with a somewhat predictable menu: steaks, scampi, teriyaki chicken, and prime rib (on weekends). The view of the Rogue isn't as good as at Bel Di's down the road, but the locals like the ambience, food, and piano bar. ■ *25 miles from Medford on Hwy 62; (503) 878-2555; 24904 Hwy 62, Trail; $$; full bar; AE, MC, V; checks OK; dinner every day (closed Tues in winter).*

MEDFORD

Southern Oregon's largest city may not win any contests with nearby towns for prettiness, but it is the center of things in this part of the world. The city is well known across the nation, due to the marketing efforts of Harry and David's, the mail-order giant known for its pears, other fruit, and condiments.

Harry and David's Original Country Store, Highway 99 south of town, offers "seconds" from gift packs and numerous other items, as well as tours of the complex, which is also the home of **Jackson & Perkins**, the world's largest rose growers. The firm ships from Medford, although most of the flowers are grown in California, (503) 776-2277.

The Grub Street Grill, the Rogue Valley's best pub, serves up Irish stout as well as Northwest microbrews, 35 N Central Avenue, (503) 779-2635. Around the corner is **CK Tiffin's**, a lunchtime cafeteria that's become a mecca for fans of vegetarian and low-fat cuisine, 226 E Main Street, (503) 779-0480. Locals also like the lunches at **Samovar**, a new Russian cafe nearby, 101 E Main Street, (503) 779-4967.

River rafting on a nearby stretch of the Rogue, between Gold Hill and the city of Rogue River, is safe for beginners. You can rent a raft at River Trips in Gold Hill, (503) 855-7238, or try one of the shop's Rogue Drifters, a large sack filled with Styrofoam balls.

▼

Medford

▲

The Oregon Vortex at the House of Mystery, between Medford and Grants Pass, is a "whirlpool of force" that causes some people to experience strange phenomena such as an inability to stand erect and apparent changes in the laws of perspective; 18 miles northwest of Medford on Sardine Creek Road, Gold Hill, (503) 855-1543. Closed in winter.

RESTAURANTS

Genessee Place ★ Chef/owner Michael Issacson moved from a job with Hilton to this charming former residence, originally built circa 1910. At first it was only a luncheon establishment, and the lure of quiche, potpies, and cheese bread still keeps the place packed at lunchtime. But Issacson's dinners are catching on with the locals: homemade canneloni with ground chicken and cheese in a Pernod-infused tomato sauce, tournedos with red-pepper herb butter, a good Cobb salad, and a palette of stir-fries. The baguette comes with "holy oil," olive oil in which Italian spices have been marinated for three weeks. In a town not noted for its food, Genessee is an oasis. ■ *2 blocks east of I-5, between Main and Jackson sts; (503) 772-5581; 203 Genessee St., Medford; $$; full bar; MC, V; local checks only; lunch, dinner Mon-Sat.* ⅙

Hungry Woodsman ★ Bob LaFontaine, owner of a Medford hardware store, tired of the rowdy nightclub next door, bought it nearly two decades ago, tore it down, and erected the Hungry Woodsman. The building is a testimonial to the forest products industry. Old saws, photos, and other logging memorabilia adorn the walls. The menu is pretty basic: steak, prime rib, shrimp, crab, lobster. You're probably best off with a steak or an English cut of prime rib; crab tends to be too pricey here. Locals like the Woodsman, as they call it. Few patrons dress up; the waiters wear jeans. ▪ *Just down from the Rogue Valley Mall; (503) 772-2050; 2001 N Pacific Hwy, Medford; $$; full bar; AE, MC, V; no checks; lunch Mon-Fri, dinner every day.*

LODGINGS

Under the Greenwood Tree ★★ Its name refers to a popular Elizabethan song that appears in *As You Like It.* And it certainly is: green lawns, 300-year-old trees, and a 10-acre farm with an orchard, riding ring, beautiful rose gardens and gazebo, and antique farm buildings. The 1862 home has four guest rooms, each with private bath. Innkeeper Renate Ellam, a Cordon Bleu chef, goes all out. Guests who arrive by 4:30pm receive British-style afternoon tea, and her elaborate three-course breakfasts may include dishes such as vanilla-poached pears with Chantilly cream or strawberry blintzes with eggs-and-yogurt filling and strawberry preserves. ▪ *Exit 27 off I-5, Barnett #27 to Stewart, left on Hull, right on Bellinger; (503) 776-0000; 3045 Bellinger Ln, Medford, OR 97501; $$$; MC, V; checks OK.*

Red Lion Inn ★ It's only a Red Lion, smack in the middle of Motel Row. But it's the best of its kind. Some units overlook a small creek, which in turn overlooks I-5. A better strategy is to get a room facing the small inner courtyard with garden and pool. The restaurant has its ups and downs, but nothing keeps locals from their favorite brunch. ▪ *Right off I-5, look for the signs; (503) 779-5811; 200 N Riverside Ave, Medford, OR 97501; $$; AE, DC, DIS, MC, V; checks OK.* &

Talent

Restaurants

RESTAURANTS

Arbor House ★★ The exterior, though it has been recently enhanced by a Japanese garden, is still modest enough to fool you. Aging granola types consider this place a find, as it remains surprisingly congenial—one of the most comfortable restaurants in the Rogue Valley, with both indoor and outdoor dining. The menu ranges the world—vegetarian plates, curries, sauerbraten, jambalaya, enchiladas, eggplant Parmigiana, fresh seafoods, and good old American steak. Try the chicken tandoori with light curry and a wealth of vegetables. No smoking indoors. ▪ *Talent Ave to the RR tracks, west on Wagner; (503) 535-6817; 103 W Wagner St, Talent; $$; beer and wine;*

no credit cards; checks OK; dinner Tues-Sat in summer, Wed-Sat in winter.

New Sammy's Cowboy Bistro ★★ Proprietors Vernon and Charleen Rollins do no advertising, rely entirely on word of mouth (they didn't even want us to include them here). There's no sign other than a flashing light at night. And the outside looks barely a cut above a shack. Inside, though, is as charming a dinner house as you're likely to find in southern Oregon. There are just six tables; reservations are a must, and you may have to wait a couple of weeks to get in. The French-inspired menu usually lists just a handful of entrées—salmon, veal stew, a beef dish (the New York steak was perfectly cooked). The wine list is extensive: 40 choices from Oregon, California, and French wineries. No smoking. ▪ *Halfway between Talent and Ashland on Hwy 99 (Pacific Hwy); (503) 535-2779; 2210 S Pacific Hwy, Talent; $$; wine only; no credit cards; checks OK; dinner Thurs-Sun.*

Chata ★ The name (pronounced HAH-tah) means "cottage" in Polish, but the restaurant is neither small nor strictly Polish. The eastern- and central-European menu features dishes such as *bigos*, Polish hunter's stew, and *mamaliga de aur* ("bread of gold")—Romanian cornmeal cakes sprinkled with cheese and served in a sauce of mushrooms, cream, and wine. Owners Jozef and Eileen Slowikowski have the smooth service and splendid consistency in the food down to a practiced art. The bad news is: they want to retire. As long as the Slowikowskis are the owners, choose the Yugoslav *juvec*, with layers of pork roast and vegetables swimming in tomato sauce, or the equally fine Polish hunter-style chicken with ham and wine sauce. The wine list presents Oregon labels side by side with white riesling from Yugoslavia, among others from that region. And, of course, there's Polish vodka and Serbian plum brandy. ▪ *Talent exit off I-5, watch for signs; (503) 535-2575; 1212 S Pacific Hwy, Talent; $$; full bar; MC, V; checks OK; dinner every day (sometimes closed in January).*

ASHLAND

The remarkable success of the Oregon Shakespeare Festival, now over 50 years old, has transformed this sleepy town into one with, per capita, the best tourist amenities in the region. The Festival now draws a total audience of some 350,000 through the nine-month season, filling its theaters to an extraordinary 97 percent capacity. Visitors pour into this town of 17,000, spawning fine shops, restaurants, and bed-and-breakfast places as they do. Amazingly, the town still has its soul: for the most part, it seems a happy little college town, set amid lovely ranch country, that just happens to house one of the largest theater companies in the land. And people still walk downtown at night.

The Festival mounts plays in three theaters. In the outdoor Elizabethan Theater, which seats 1,200, appear the famous and authentic nighttime productions of Shakespeare (three different plays) each summer. The outdoor theater has recently been remodeled to improve acoustics. Stretching from February to October, the season for the two indoor theaters includes comedies, contemporary fare, and some experimental works. Visit the Exhibit Center, where you can clown around in costumes from plays past. There are also lectures and concerts at noon, excellent backstage tours each morning, Renaissance music and dance nightly in the courtyard—plus all the nearby daytime attractions of river rafting, picnicking, and historical touring. The best way to get information and tickets (last-minute seats in summer are rare) is through a comprehensive agency: Southern Oregon Reservation Center, (503) 488-1011, (800) 547-8052; PO Box 477, Ashland, OR 97520. Festival box office is (503) 482-4331.

Ashland is home to a growing number of smaller theater groups, whose productions are often called **Off Shakespeare** or **Off Bardway**. They are worth checking into. Festival actors often join in these small companies, giving audiences a chance to see Shakespearean actors having a bit of fun and going out on a theatrical limb. Oregon Cabaret Theater presents musicals and comedies through much of the year, with dinners, hors d'oeuvres, and desserts for theater patrons, First and Hargadine streets, (503) 488-2902. Others include Actors' Theater of Ashland, now in both Ashland and nearby Talent, (503) 482-9659, and Studio X, (503) 488-2011, and Ashland Community Theater, (503) 482-0361, both in the old Ashland Armory on Oak Street.

Touring. The Rogue River Recreation Area has fine swimming for the sizzling summer days, as does the lovely Applegate River. Twenty-two scenic miles up Dead Indian Memorial Road is Howard Prairie Lake Resort, where you can camp, park your trailer, shower, rent a boat, and fish; (503) 482-1979.

Mount Ashland Ski Area, (503) 482-2897, 18 miles south of town, offers 22 runs for all classes of skiers, Thanksgiving to April. It's going strong since a 1992 fund drive raised $1.7 million to buy it from an out-of-town owner who had threatened permanent closure.

Lithia Park. Designed by the creator of San Francisco's Golden Gate Park, Ashland's central park runs for 100 acres behind the outdoor theater, providing a lovely mix of duck ponds, Japanese gardens, grassy lawns, playgrounds, groomed or dirt trails for hikes and jogging, and the pungent mineral water that gave the park its name. Great for picnicking, especially after stocking up at nearby Greenleaf Deli, 49 N Main, (503) 482-2808.

Ashland

Manna from Heaven Bakery is a distinguished Old World bakery famous for elaborate breads and pastries, plus good coffee. Definitely worth a visit for breakfast; 358 E Main Street, (503) 482-5831.

Mark Antony Hotel. This downtown landmark is of some historic interest. Lately, ownership has stabilized and food service has improved notably in the last couple of years; 212 E Main Street, (503) 482-1721.

Weisinger Ashland Winery, Ashland Vineyards, and **Rogue Brewery & Public House** offer opportunities to sample Ashland products. The Weisinger winery is snuggled in a Bavarian-style building; the gift shop offers jams, jellies, sauces, and, of course, their wines for sale; Highway 99 just outside Ashland, (503) 488-5989. Ashland Vineyards is near the Highway 66 exit from I-5. Turn north onto E Main Street and follow signs; (503) 488-0088. Wash down a sandwich or a pizza with a Golden Ale at the Rogue Brewery, located at 31-B Water Street —a good place to unwind after a day of theater; (503) 488-5061.

RESTAURANTS

Chateaulin ★★★ Less than a block from the theaters you'll find a romantic cafe reminiscent of New York's upper West Side; the dark wood-and-brick dining rooms (primarily nonsmoking) are accented with copper kettles hung from the ceiling and displays of vintage wine bottles. During the Shakespeare season, the place bustles with before- and after-theater crowds gathered for the fine French cuisine or for drinks at the bar. House specialties are pâtés and veal dishes, but seafood is also impressive: the delicate butterflied shrimp in a subtle sauce of sherry, cream, tomato, and brandy were delicious. Chef David Taub and co-owner Michael Donovan change the menu seasonally, and several daily specials feature seasonal entrées prepared with classic French flair. The cafe menu is a favorite of the after-show crowd: baked goat cheese marinated in olive oil on featherweight squares of toast, an outrageous onion soup. Service is polished and smooth even during the rush of theater crowds. The owners also have a shop next door with rare and gourmet foods and fine wines. ■ *Down the walkway from Angus Bowmer Theater; (503) 482-2264; 50 E Main, Ashland; $$; full bar; AE, DC, MC, V; local checks only; dinner every day.*

Monet ★★ The waiters in berets and the reproductions of guess-who on the walls might seem a bit pretentious in this town, but Pierre and Dale Verger have created a French restaurant that has become the talk of Ashland (and even a mention in Portland). Before opening this gentrified French restaurant in a gracious house, Pierre Verger had restaurants in Montreal, New York state, and the San Francisco Bay Area. Favorite dishes include spirales de sole aux ciboulettes, fillet of sole wrapped around salmon and served in a sauce of chives, spinach, and chervil, accompanied by zucchini, puff potatoes, purée of carrots, and fresh herbs. We also admire the fillet of salmon and salmon mousse steamed in spinach and presented with a shallot-and-white-wine sauce. Verger goes out of his way to make interesting vegetarian choices, such as sautéed artichoke hearts with sun-dried tomatoes, olives, mushrooms, garlic, shallots, feta, and Parmesan, or eggplant bathed in tomato, herbs, and Swiss on a bed of creamy spaetzle. The wine list goes on and on. Try for outdoor dining in summer. ■ *Half a block from Main St; (503) 482-1339; 36 S Second St, Ashland; $$; full bar; MC, V; checks OK; lunch, dinner every day (closed Sun-Tues in winter).* ₺

Primavera ★★ Even if you find the bold red, blue, and orange decor a bit much, wait for the appetizers—they're among the best in southern Oregon. Pasta with capers, raisins, and shrimp along with tomatoes and browned onions is a meal in itself. Spring rolls filled with duck and served with a raspberry catsup will forever alter your feelings about both duck and catsup.

Ashland

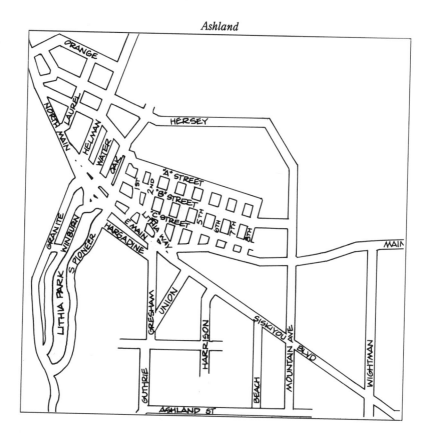

Entrées usually include chicken, seafood, and a vegetarian choice or two. None approaches the inspiration or execution of the appetizers, but they are still very good and—like the halibut with mustard and fennel with a tomato coulis—capture intense, clean flavors. Desserts, like everything else, are made on the premises. A thoughtfully selected wine list complements the food. The garden is a gorgeous place for a midsummer's night dinner. ■ *Below Oregon Cabaret Theater; (503) 488-1994; 241 Hargadine, Ashland; $$; full bar; MC, V; checks OK; dinner Wed-Mon (Thurs-Sun in winter).* &

The Winchester Country Inn ★★ Pay a visit to the Winchester when you feel like being pampered. You sit amid crisp country furnishings on the slightly sunken ground floor of this century-old Queen Anne-style home and look out on tiers of neatly snipped garden outside. The staff attends to your every need. The menu covers an ambitious range of entrées, from Vietnamese marinated broiled teng dah beef to lamb or salmon du jour, as well as a less expensive bistro section with smoked salmon ravioli, mini beef Wellingtons, and polenta aubergine. Owners Michael and Laurie Gibb are locally famous for the Dickens Feasts they present each December. The inn is now smoke-free.

In addition to being one of Ashland's finer restaurants, the Winchester provides seven antique-furnished guest rooms upstairs. Guests are treated to full breakfasts. ■ *Half a block from Main St; (503) 488-1113; 35 S 2nd St, Ashland; $$; full bar; MC, V; checks OK; dinner every day, brunch Sun (closed Mon in winter).*

Green Springs Inn ★ Here's an escape from the tourist crowds of Ashland—a cozy, rustic spot dishing up Italian specialties in the midst of the splendid hills. The restaurant doubles as a neighborhood convenience store. The 35-minute drive through the red-soil hills, jutting cliffs, and thick evergreens is worth the trip in itself, especially if you want to hike or cross-country ski along the Pacific Crest Trail that runs ¼ mile from the restaurant. The hearty soups, sandwiches, and 12 different pasta dishes make this a welcome stopping point. Our black bean soup was a generous dish, rich and lightly garlicked—perfect when lapped up with sweet, just-baked brown bread. Also try the mushroom fettuccine. ■ *17½ miles east of Ashland; (503) 482-0614; 11470 Hwy 66, Ashland; $$; beer and wine; AE, DIS, MC, V; no checks; breakfast, lunch, dinner every day.* &

Il Giardino ★ Order the risotto when you place your reservation—it's as close to Italy as you'll get without a plane ticket. It's not on the menu and it's time-consuming to make, but Franco Minniti and Maurizio Contartese love to cook and are anxious to please. Both are recent immigrants and know just enough English to be dangerously charming. If Minniti and

Contartese don't win your heart, their capellini con pomidoro and basilico (angel-hair pasta with tomato and basil) will. The carpaccio is a flawless antipasto, and the black ravioli with salmon, tarragon, and cream sauce is one of Il Giardino's most popular entrées. On a recent visit the ravioli shells stuffed with ground veal and topped with carrot sauce sounded strange but had wonderful flavor. The place is intimate and can seem crowded. ■ *1½ blocks from Shakespeare Festival; (503) 488-0816; #5 Granite St, Ashland; $$; beer and wine; MC, V; local checks only; dinner Tues-Sun (every day in summer).*

LODGINGS

Chanticleer Bed & Breakfast Inn ★★★ One of Ashland's original B&Bs, Chanticleer has a new owner, Pebby Kuan, but is still a preferred destination. The home has an uncluttered country charm, with an open-hearth fireplace in the spacious sitting room and carefully chosen antiques throughout, plus the plush extras of fresh-cut flowers, imported soaps and lotions in the rooms, and scripts of all the plays running at the Shakespeare Festival. In the morning, a lavish breakfast is served in the dining room or (on request) brought to your room for breakfast in bed. It's a setting that promises to rejuvenate your soul and your romance. There are six rooms. Chanticleer is four blocks from the theaters, but surprisingly quiet. Make reservations early. No smoking. ■ *2 blocks from the library off Main St; (503) 482-1919; 120 Gresham St, Ashland, OR 97520; $$$; MC, V; checks OK.*

Ashland

Lodgings

Mount Ashland Inn ★★★ Wind your way up Mt. Ashland Road and you discover a huge, custom-made two-story log cabin. This is the dream home of Jerry and Elaine Shanafelt, who designed and built the lodge in 1987, using some 275 cedar trees cut from their 160-acre property in the Siskiyous. The magnificent inn is more posh inside than you'd expect from a log house: golden aromatic-cedar logs, high beamed ceilings, large windows, and a huge stone fireplace. Examples of Jerry's handiwork are seen throughout the house: stained-glass windows, a spiral cedar staircase with madrona railing. Guests sleep in handcrafted beds covered with elaborate patchwork quilts, and each of the five units has a private bath. Try for the newer Sky Lakes suite with a two-person whirlpool bathtub, king-size bed, wet bar, private entrance, and a sitting room, plus a view of Mt. McLoughlin. Be prepared for snow (November to April). No smoking. ■ *Follow signs to Mt. Ashland Ski Area; (503) 482-8707; 550 Mt Ashland Rd, Ashland, OR 97520; $$$; MC, V; checks OK.*

Romeo Inn ★★★ This imposing Cape Cod home has four plush guest rooms and two suites decorated in contemporary and antique furnishings. The spacious rooms all have king-size beds—covered with hand-stitched Amish quilts—phones, and private baths; the Stratford Suite is a separate structure with its own bedroom, bath, and kitchen; it features a vaulted ceiling with skylight, a marble-tiled fireplace, and a raised whirlpool bathtub for two. Owners Bruce and Margaret Halverson give up their own quarters (in summer only) to create the second suite, the Cambridge, with fireplace, patio, and private entrance. There's a baby grand piano off the living room, and the heated pool and hot tub on the large back deck are open year-round. No smoking, please.

The generous breakfast of baked fruit, specialty main course such as eggs rarebit (chosen from 40 possibilities), and fresh baked goods reportedly satisfies through dinnertime. The Halversons keep a computerized record of what they served you last time, so regular clientele never get the same meal twice. Clever. ■ *Idaho and Holly; (503) 488-0884; 295 Idaho St, Ashland, OR 97520; $$$; MC, V; checks OK.*

Country Willows ★★ Set on 5 acres of farmland six minutes from downtown Ashland, this rebuilt 1896 country home offers peace and quiet and a lovely view of the hills. Bill and Barbara Huntley offer five rooms and two suites, with air conditioning and private baths, plus a swimming pool and a newly built hot tub on the large back deck. The best room is, well, in the barn: it has a two-person soaking tub, fireplace, and private deck. Breakfast is presented on a pretty sun porch. The mushroom quiche and homemade jams are notable. The grounds outside offer running and hiking trails; and the owners keep a small flock of ducks, a gaggle of geese, a herd of horses on the property, and even a couple of goats. No smoking, please. ■ *4 blocks south on Clay St from Siskiyou Blvd; (503) 488-1590; 1313 Clay St, Ashland, OR 97520; $$$; MC, V; checks OK.*

Fox House Inn ★★ Jim and Jacqueline Sims remodeled an early Victorian home to create this two-bedroom inn that offers guests the utmost privacy, perfect for families or two couples traveling together. The rooms (no smoking) are furnished with brass beds with half-canopies and private baths with claw-footed tubs. The Garden Room downstairs, highlighted with stained and etched glasswork, opens into an enclosed flower garden. Annabel's Suite upstairs is well suited for a romantic getaway: guests have the entire second story, with private sitting room and dressing room, and a lavish satin-and-lace bedroom. Breakfast, of course, and an outdoor hot tub. ■ *2nd and B off Main; (503) 488-1055; 269 B St, Ashland, OR 97520; $$$; no credit cards; checks OK.*

Arden Forest Inn ★ Walking distance from Shakespeare, this remodeled folk (but not folksy) farmhouse is a refreshing change of pace from the antique motif that abounds in bed and breakfasts. The light and airy living room and each of the four guest rooms are decorated with lovely examples of host/artist Audrey Sochor's vividly hued paintings. Host/Shakespeare teacher Art Sochor's extensive theater library is available for guests' perusal, and the longtime theater buff welcomes chats with his show-bound guests. The hosts have made the common room and three of the bedrooms wheelchair-accessible. The two carriage-house rooms offer optimum privacy, and all rooms have private baths and air conditioning. Children are welcome; smoking is not. ■ *On Hersey at Laurel; (503) 488-1496; 261 Hersey St, Ashland, OR 97520; $$; AE, MC, V; checks OK.* &

Cowslip's Belle ★ Unintentionally named after a song in *A Midsummer Night's Dream*, the home has a cheery charm, with its swing chair on the front porch, vintage furniture, and fresh flowers inside. There are two lovely bedrooms in the main house, a 1913 Craftsman bungalow, two more in a romantic carriage house in the back, with extra privacy, one of them a suite. A main attraction is proximity to the theaters, downtown, and Lithia Park, three to four blocks away. ■ *3 blocks north of the theaters on Main; (503) 488-2901 or toll-free (800) 888-6819; 159 N Main St, Ashland, OR 97520; $$; MC, V; checks OK.*

Morical House ★ This large farmhouse dates back to the 1880s. Its proximity to busy Main Street somewhat takes away from its ambience, but owners Patricia and Peter Dahl have worked hard to soundproof the five bedrooms and provide backyard views into the fields and mountains beyond. The rooms are furnished with antiques, handmade quilts, and family heirlooms. The attractive grounds include a putting green and a place to play croquet. Breakfasts are substantial. As with most B&Bs, smoking is permitted outside only. Children over 12 are welcome; pets are not. ■ *Exit 19 from I-5, turn left onto Hwy 99; (503) 482-2254; 668 N Main St, Ashland, OR 97520; $$$; MC, V; checks OK.*

Woods House ★ This 1908 Craftsman, once the home of a doctor, boasts a beautiful setting out back, with a half-acre of terraced English gardens. Out front is the busy boulevard and traffic, so try for one of the Carriage House units in the rear. All six guest rooms have private baths. A big plus is that you can walk the four blocks to the theaters. Lester and Francoise Roddy are gracious hosts and serve a nifty spinach cheese egg bake, in the garden when weather cooperates. ■ *4 blocks north of the theaters on Main; (503) 488-1598 or toll-free (800) 435-8260; 333 N Main St, Ashland, OR 97520; $$$; MC, V; checks OK.*

Windmill's Ashland Hills Inn For those who prefer motels to B&Bs, this is the best Ashland has to offer, with 159 rooms, several elegant suites, a pool, and tennis courts. The food is not

▼

Ashland

Lodgings

▲

bad; locals like the Sunday brunch. The banquet area, Ashland's largest, plays host to everything from wine tastings to formal balls. ■ *Hwy 66 exit from I-5; (503) 482-8310 or toll-free (800) 547-4747; 2525 Ashland St, Ashland, OR 97520; $$; AE, DC, DIS, MC, V; checks OK.*

CAVE JUNCTION

Though the tight quarters can get awfully packed with tourists, the **Oregon Caves National Monument** is a group of intriguing formations of marble and limestone. Tours leave periodically each day year-round. They are a bit strenuous, and the caves are a chilly 41 degrees. Children under six are allowed if they meet the height requirement. However, babysitting service is available. Arrive early during summertime, or you may have a long wait; (503) 592-3400.

LODGINGS

Oregon Caves Chateau ★ This fine old wooden lodge is set amid tall trees and a deep canyon. Doors don't always close properly, but the place is restful. The sound of falling water from numerous nearby mountain streams will help lull you to sleep. Views are splendid, the public rooms have the requisite massive fireplaces, and the down-home cooking in the dining room is quite good. The wine list features lots of local bottlings. There are 22 rooms—nothing fancy, but clean. ■ *Route 46, 20 miles east of Cave Junction, follow signs; (503) 592-3400; PO Box 128, Cave Junction, OR 97523; $$; MC, V; checks OK (open June-Sept).*

▼

Cave Junction

Lodgings

▲

Oregon Cascades

The Columbia River Gorge—Troutdale to The Dalles—
followed by two easterly Cascade crossings: Sandy to Mount
Hood in the north, McKenzie Bridge to Bend midstate.
Finally, a southward progression through the heart
of the mountains to Klamath Falls.

COLUMBIA RIVER GORGE

The wild Columbia has been dammed into near lakehood, but its fjordlike majesty is part magnificent waterfalls, part dramatic cliffs and rock formations cut by the country's second-largest river, and part wind tunnel. Watch for the colorful fleet of board sailors who have made this stretch of the river world-renowned.

Most of the traffic is out on I-84, which leaves the old **Columbia Gorge Scenic Highway** (Route 30) for take-your-time wanderers. This 22-mile detour traverses the waterfall-riddled stretch from Troutdale to Ainsworth Park. Popular viewpoints and attractions are as follows: **Crown Point**, 725 feet above the river, features an art deco-style vista house. Below, at Rooster Rock State Park, one of the attractions is a nude bathing beach. **Larch Mountain**, 14 miles upriver from Crown Point, is even more spectacular than the more famous overlooks. **Multnomah Falls** ranks second highest in the country, at 620 feet (in two big steps). **Multnomah Falls Lodge**, at the foot of the falls, was designed in 1925 by Albert E. Doyle, of Benson Hotel fame, in a rustic stone and timber style. Now a National Historic Landmark, the lodge houses a popular naturalists' and visitors' center; (503) 695-2376. It has a restaurant that is a good stop for breakfast, but dinners are unremarkable (better just to go for dessert). **Oneonta Gorge** is a narrow, dramatic cleft through which a slippery half-mile trail winds to secluded Oneonta Falls. **Bonneville Dam**, the first federal dam on the Columbia, offers tours of the dam, the fish ladders (seen through underwater viewing windows), and the navigational locks; (503) 374-8820. You can tour the Bonneville Fish Hatchery (next to the dam) year round; however, the best time is in September and November when the chinook are spawning; (503) 374-8393.

The old highway disappears briefly at Hood River; it picks up again between Mosier and The Dalles, where the forests give way to grasslands and the clouds vanish. Wildflowers abound from February to May.

TROUTDALE

RESTAURANTS

Shirley's Troutdale Cafe ★ After cooking 18 years on the Oregon coast, Shirley Welton swam upstream and landed in Troutdale; the decor and the menu of her corner cafe still recall the beach. Portions are huge—omelets are as big as a plate, and spuds and toast are served on a separate platter with homemade jam. Shirley cooks the way we used to eat, with butter, cream, and Tillamook cheese. Both crab sandwiches and seafood-stuffed quiches are pleasingly drenched in hollandaise sauce; clam chowder is thickened with whipped cream. Dinners are all seafood (changes daily) and they're more than most people can eat. Needless to say, many Portlanders like to bike here on Marine Drive path along the Columbia River (and work off breakfast, or dinner, on the way home). ■ *Troutdale exit off I-84; (503) 666-7913; 202 E Columbia River Hwy, Troutdale; $; full bar; MC, V; checks OK; breakfast, lunch every day, dinner Tues-Sun.*

Tad's Chicken 'n' Dumplings ★ A down-home country restaurant, 20 miles east of Portland as you head up the Columbia Gorge, this decades-old Oregon institution is popular with kids, bargain-hungry families, tourists—and fanciers of chicken. You can make quite an evening of it: a drink on the back deck, dinner at a window table where you can watch the sunset, a family-style meal (you should know what to order), topped off with ice cream or homemade pie. The place is usually packed, so call ahead to get on the waiting list, particularly for Sunday dinner. ■ *Exit 18 off I-84; (503) 666-5337; 943 SE Crown Point, Troutdale; $$; full bar; AE, MC, V; checks OK; dinner every day.*

LODGING

McMenamins Edgefield ★ Over the last decade, the McMenamin brothers have enlivened Portland-area neighborhoods

with 27 Euro-style pubs, many of them in resurrected buildings. Now they've found the ultimate project—Edgefield
Manor, a former county poor farm where residents worked and
lived together in a self-sufficient community. The M brothers
bought the estate in 1990 and moved a brewery into the spacious old cannery, a winery into the infirmary's first floor, and
planted a garden and a three-acre pinot gris vineyard. The old
power station is now a lively pub and movie theater (with eight
bed-and-breakfast rooms upstairs), and the administrator's
house, an old Craftsman-style bungalow, has six bed-and-breakfast rooms as well. The main lodge, in the four-story brick manor,
just opened with 45 guest rooms, wide verandahs, a huge ballroom, and the Black Rabbit dining room and bar. All rooms
($35 to $95) are outfitted with beer glasses and a canning jar
to carry brew back to your room. Guests are loaned terrycloth
robes to make the trek to the shared baths on each wing
(which isn't as bad as it sounds). ■ *Wood Village Exit off I-84,
south to Halsey, turn left, drive ½ mile to Edgefield sign;
(503) 669-8610; 2126 SW Halsey, Troutdale, OR 97060; $$,
MC, V, checks OK.*

CASCADE LOCKS

Before the dams, the riverboats often foundered on nasty
rapids here. Locks smoothed things out; their remains are the
centerpiece of the town's Marina Park. A fine little museum at
the **Bridge of the Gods** explains the legend of the rapids.
There are also the Port of Cascade Locks Visitor Center, a sail-
board launch, and oodles of picnic spots. The **Sternwheeler**
Columbia Gorge revives the Columbia's riverboat past; there
are three trips daily and extra lunch, brunch, and dinner
cruises, mid-June through the end of September, with stops at
Bonneville Dam and Stevenson Landing; (503) 374-8427.

LODGINGS

Scandian Motor Lodge ★ Norway wandered west and
landed here. The large rooms are woodsy, with bright
Scandinavian colors and tiled baths (one with a sauna).
Try for an upstairs room near the office for the best river views.
Even in these, the rates are quite reasonable. Very clean and not
too much *Uff da!* There are several nonsmoking rooms. Reserve
early for summer months. ■ *Wa-Na-Pa St in town; (503) 374-
8417; PO Box 217, Cascade Locks, OR 97014; $; AE, DC,
MC, V; no checks.*

HOOD RIVER

Fruit orchards are everywhere. Hood River is ideally located on
the climatic cusp between the wetter west side and the drier

east side of the Cascades, alongside the mighty Columbia, so it gets the sun *and* enough moisture (about 31 inches annually) to keep the creeks flowing and the orchards bearing. Thirty miles to the south, 11,245-foot Mount Hood supervises; however, from the town itself, the views are of Washington's Mount Adams, the Columbia, and its ubiquitous sailboarders. In town, you're as likely to see orchard workers as boardheads, 2-inch steaks as espresso. Restaurants, inns, and shops are constantly opening (and closing) in flux with the high and low seasons.

Visitors come to hike, fish, climb, and ski on Mount Hood and Mount Adams. In between is the Columbia River. And on it are the boardheads who can't get enough of the famous winds that blow in at that ideal opposite-to-the-current direction. At least 27 local businesses cater to the sailboard crowd; several offer lessons and rentals, and all will tell you where the winds are on any given day. The **West Jetty** and **Columbia Gorge Sailpark/Marina** are favorites. The latter also features a fitness course, a marina, and a cafe.

As locals strongly attest, there was life in Hood River before board sailors descended. Native American artifacts are on

Hood River

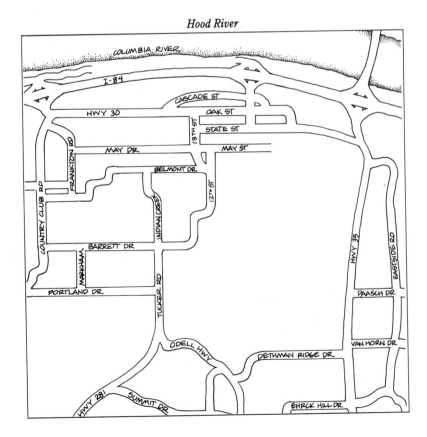

exhibit in the **Hood River County Museum**; (503) 386-6772, open 10am-4pm Wednesday through Saturday, 10am-5pm Sunday, April through October, or when flags are flying. The town's Visitor Information Center adjoins, though it's sometimes closed on winter weekends; (503) 386-2000 or (800) 366-3530. Orchards and vineyards are the valley's other economic mainstays. The wonderful small-town **Blossom Festival** (mid-April) celebrates the flower-to-fruit cycle. From Highway 35 you can catch the vista of the orchards fanning out from the north slopes of **Mount Hood Scenic Railroad**. The Fruit Blossom Special departs the quaint Hood River depot April through December. You can buy the fruit bounty at **The Fruit Tree**, 4030 Westcliff Drive, (503) 386-6688, near the Columbia Gorge Hotel, or at **River Bend Country Store**, 2363 Tucker Road, (503) 386-8766, or toll-free (800) 755-7568; the latter specializes in organically grown produce. Or visit the tasting rooms of the **Three Rivers Winery**, 275 Country Club Road, (503) 386-5453, or the **Hood River Vineyards**, 4693 Westwood Drive, (503) 386-3772, known for its pear and raspberry dessert wines. Beer aficionados will head for the **WhiteCap BrewPub**, 506 Columbia Street, (503) 386-2247, for handcrafted Full Sail ales and light meals. The outdoor deck (live music on weekends) provides a fitting place for tired board sailors to unwind while keeping the river in sight.

For a breath-taker, head half a mile south of town on Highway 35 to **Panorama Point**. Or go east on I-84, exit at Mosier, and climb to the **Rowena Crest Viewpoint** on old Highway 30; the grandstand Columbia River view is complemented by a wildflower show in the Tom McCall Preserve, maintained by the Nature Conservancy. **The Coffee Spot**, Oak Street and First, (503) 386-1772, is a good spot to pick up sandwiches for a picnic.

RESTAURANTS

Peter B's ★★   Peter B's is the happy metamorphosis of one of the few charming houses left that's not a bed and breakfast. Peter Bollinger's place is gracious and very good. Chef Nan Bains ventures broadly, but fish is her thing. There's an ahi with black beans and saffron rice, a really garlicky fettuccine alfredo, and a hot and spicy New Orleans-style seafood gumbo served over rice. Specials daily. On one visit it took two convicted chocoholics to finish the chocolate truffle cake with raspberry sauce. ■ *13th and B sts; (503) 386-2111; 1302 13th St, Hood River; $$; full bar; MC, V; checks OK; dinner every day.*

The Mesquitery ★   The mesquite grill takes center stage here. It's housed in a glass-enclosed frame surrounded by booths and small tables. So it's barbecue—not super-hot, but A-okay. There are baby back ribs, a chicken combo, pollo vaquero (grilled chicken to roll in tortillas with pico de gallo), and fish, including recent specials: tender, moist halibut in a spicy tomatillo sauce or topped with orange-basil butter. Fill up with soup or salad, a roll, and two of eight side dishes, from coleslaw to barbecued baked beans to fettuccine pesto. The apple crisp à la mode is dandy; so are the service and the bill. A good, nonsmoking place to bring the kids. ■ *12th and B sts; (503)386-2002; 1219 12th St, Hood River; $; beer and wine; MC, V; checks OK; lunch Mon-Fri, dinner Mon-Sat.*

Stonehedge Inn ★ Beyond the funky markers and up a rutted gravel drive to this turn-of-the-century summer estate, owner Jean Harmon makes you instantly at home. She'll get the kids looking through her stereopticon viewer and tell the history behind each decoration as she leads you to a table in the fire-warmed and dark wood-paneled main room, the garden-viewing porch room, the homey library, or the intimate bar. The food has been better in the past, but tender steaks might come buried under whole, fresh morel mushrooms, and the seafood arrives fresh and cooked right (although we found a halibut special rather surprising—a slab of pepperjack cheese melted on top with a dollop of unripened pineapple salsa). The famous stuffed potato seemed to be right out of Betty Crocker's kitchen, and the appetizers, salad, and vegetables on the plate all looked the same. Still, sincere service and general high quality keep this on our list. ■ *Exit 62 off I-84; (503) 386-3940; 3405 Cascade Dr, Hood River; $$; full bar; AE, DC, MC, V; checks OK; dinner Wed-Sun.*

Purple Rocks Art Bar and Cafe Despite its name (a self-evident boarder's term), we like this cafe where art takes the form of sketchbooks filled with patrons' doodles. Housed in a cute little cottage on Hood River's main street, this local hangout offers the best $2 multigrain walnut pancakes ever. With the exception of turkey and tuna, this is vegetarian fare with a somewhat limited menu (sprout and cottage cheese sandwich, lasagne, quiches, and black bean burritos). Still, we just *like* it— from the blue-enameled wood stove to the views out paned-glass windows and the kids sitting at their own kid-size table. ■ *West on Oak from downtown; (503) 386-6061; 606 Oak St, Hood River; $; MC, V; local checks only; breakfast, lunch every day (summer: dinner Thurs-Sat).*

LODGINGS

Hood River Hotel ★★ A careful 1989 restoration revived this hostelry's past as a turn-of-the-century country hotel. Thirty-two rooms, including nine one-bedroom kitchen suites (some with fireplaces and whirlpool baths) come with four-poster, sleigh, and brass beds, pedestal sinks, and plenty of cheerful floral chintz. Since it's in the center of town, there's some noise from the street, the railroad, and I-84. A small downstairs dining room serves reasonably priced breakfasts, lunches, and dinners that are strong on Italian specialties and local fruit and fish. Enjoy your espresso or after-dinner drink in front of the lobby fireplace or at an outside table. A casual place, with live jazz, blues, or country music on weekends. ■ *Oak and 1st; (503) 386-1900; 102 Oak St, Hood River, OR 97031; $$; full bar; AE, DC, DIS, MC, V; checks OK; breakfast, lunch, dinner every day.*

Lakecliff Estate ★★ Everyone's favorite Hood River bed and breakfast, Lakecliff Estate delivers fine hospitality in outstanding surroundings. The forest green home, just a short jog off I-84, is sheltered by woods to create quiet seclusion with an astonishing view of the Columbia River. Built in 1908 by architect Albert E. Doyle (who also designed Multnomah Falls Lodge and the Benson Hotel in Portland) as a summer estate for a Portland businessman, Lakecliff now is listed on the National Register of Historic Places. It features five fireplaces of locally quarried stone, a large and inviting living room, a cheerful sun porch, and an elegant dining room where breakfast is served. Some rooms have fireplaces and private bathrooms, others have views. Owners Bruce and Judy Thesanga are friendly and fun. Guests often linger over their oatmeal with sautéed nectarines or Dutch babies with fruit sauce while watching windsurfers below. ■ *Exit 62 off I-84, ½ mile west of Hood River at 3820 Westcliff Dr; (503) 386-7000; PO Box 1220, Hood River, OR 97031; $$; no credit cards; checks OK.*

State Street Inn ★★ Mac and Amy Lee fled aerospace careers to live in Hood River. Now Amy's a systems engineer and Mac runs the B&B. He does it right. The place, an impeccable and well-crafted 1932 English Tudor, is ideally located on a quiet street that's still close to everything. The queen beds are comfy. Four nonsmoking rooms share three baths; the decor of each reflects the character of the states where the Lees used to live. The Chesapeake-inspired Maryland Room and the bright and colorful California Room are the largest, with views of Mount Adams. Almost everyone gathers around the fire or in the game room at night and meets again for breakfast (wholewheat waffles or lemony cream cheese filled crêpes with fresh fruit) in a dining room in which they sit eye-to-eye with Mount Adams. ■ *Near the corner of State and 10th; (503) 386-1899; 1005 State St, Hood River, OR 97031; $$; MC, V; checks OK.*

Columbia Gorge Hotel ★ Lumber baron Simon Benson capped his successful completion of the Columbia Gorge Scenic Highway when he built his luxury hotel in 1921 and brought in his famous chef, Henry Thiele. Instantly the hotel became a favorite of honeymooners and tourists. The old dear (restored a number of times) can't compete with the luxury of 1990 hotels, but it does have some pluses: a stunning structure, with a private window on Wah-Gwin-Gwin Falls of the Columbia River, and a colorful past, which included visits by Rudolph Valentino. The public rooms are large and elegant. Each guest room has its own color scheme and its own small bath with a basket of scented soap and bath oils. On the down side, the rooms are too small for the big price and maintenance is not always on top of it (we've witnessed cracked sinks and broken fireplace screens). But the price does include turn-down service, a newspaper in the morning, and an insultingly large breakfast. Aim for a gorge-side room; they're quieter and have the best views. The best deals (and the most fun) are packages: murder mystery weekends; seven-course winemaker dinners; and bed, breakfast, and private lessons with a premier windsurfer, fly-fishing in the mountains, or eco-tours of the Gorge. ■ *Exit 62 off I-84; (503) 386-5566, toll-free (800) 345-1921; 4000 Westcliff Dr, Hood River, OR 97031; $$$; AE, DC, DIS, MC, V; no checks; lunch Mon-Fri, dinner every day.*

Vagabond Lodge ★ So close to the Columbia Gorge Hotel it could almost be another wing. It's got the identical view as (some say better than) CGH; the rooms are twice the size and a fraction of the price. The front building is nothing but a nondescript unit. The surprise is in back. Ask for a room in the riverfront building. If there are four of you, get a suite with a fireplace and separate bedroom (it'll cost you less than the smallest room at CGH). ■ *Exit 62 off I-84; (503) 386-2992; 4070 Westcliff Dr, Hood River, OR 97031; $; MC, V; checks OK.*

THE DALLES

The Dalles is *the* historical stop along this stretch. For centuries, this area was the meeting place for native Americans. In the 1840s, it was the official end of the Oregon Trail. Later it served as the only military fort in the Northwest and the county seat of Wasco County, then a 130,000-square-mile vastness that spread from the Cascades to the Rockies. Gold miners loaded up here. Thomas Condon, Oregon's father of geology, got his start amid local basalts.

Signs of all this remain—the native American petroglyphs, the 1850 surgeon's house from the old Fort Dalles (now a museum at 15th and Garrison streets), the east side's "houses of entertainment," and nicely maintained examples of Colonial, gothic revival, Italianate, and American renaissance architecture. Take a tour by car or on foot; maps are available at The Dalles Convention and Visitor Bureau, 901 E Second Street, (800) 255-3385 or (503) 296-6616.

Uphill from downtown are irrigated cherry orchards; Wasco County is the largest producer in the country and celebrates its

Cherry Festival in mid-April. Spreading far to the east are the grainfields and grasslands of drier Eastern Oregon. Annual precipitation is no more than 15 inches; trees thin out quickly, and rocks protrude more visibly. Most of the year the ground is golden, except for the wildflowers in spring.

RESTAURANTS

Baldwin Saloon ★ The Baldwin Saloon, built in 1876, has been a steamboat navigational office, a warehouse, coffin storage site, employment office, and saddle shop, and now it's been restored back to its original use as a restaurant and bar. It's nicely done—stripped to the original brick, with fir floors, wooden booths, light streaming in the windows, a cherrywood bar, and large old Hudson school-style paintings of the Gorge hanging on the walls. Piano, cello, and violins (on tape) are a nice break from the country western you might expect. But the food is what impressed us most: fresh oysters on the half shell, smoked salmon mousse, and chicken liver pâté served with homemade bread and fresh vegetables, thick sandwiches, and filet mignon. Pick up a history of the place with your menu, and try the walnut tart—carameled walnuts encased in sweet dough and topped with chocolate ganache. ▪ *At 1st and Court St; (503) 296-5666; PO Box 1239, The Dalles; $; full bar; MC, V; checks OK; lunch, dinner Mon-Sat.*

Ole's Supper Club ★ Ole's isn't glamorous. In fact, it's in the industrial west end of The Dalles. But locals like it this way. The consistent quality of the food and the commitment to good wine make it notable—in spite of the fact that it looks like a double-wide mobile home. The house special turns out to be one of the best cuts of prime rib we've tasted. Everything is included: delicious homemade soup, a standard salad, an individual loaf of hot homemade bread, and a potato, rice, or a vegetable. Although the restaurant has established its reputation on beef, it also features chicken, seafood, and lamb. When fresh razor clams are available, it treats them well. The wine list bears mentioning because the bar is one of the few in Oregon that doubles as a wine shop, and it is known regionally for a wide selection. ▪ *Exit 84 off I-84, go west 1 mile; (503) 296-6708; 2620 W 2nd St, The Dalles; $$; full bar; MC, V; checks OK; dinner Tues-Sat.*

LODGINGS

Williams House Inn ★★ A manicured three-acre arboretum surrounds this classic 1899 Queen Anne house. It has been in the Williams family for more than 60 years and is now on the National Register of Historic Places and run as a bed and breakfast by Don and Barbara Williams. Nicaraguan mahogany decorates the walls, and Oriental rugs cover the floor of the large living room that contains a piano, a bass fiddle, and a fireplace.

Two of the three rooms have their own balconies. We especially like the downstairs Elizabeth Suite with its separate bedroom, writing desk, hideabed, and private bath with marble-topped washbasin and a six-foot-long claw-footed tub. The Williamses serve a fine breakfast of fresh or canned local fruits, including cherries from their own orchard, home-roasted granola, muffins, fresh-ground coffees, and eggs. Don Williams happily shares his love and encyclopedic knowledge of the area's rich history, which includes his own. ■ *Corner of Trevett and 6th; (503) 296-2889; 608 W 6th St, The Dalles, OR 97058; $$; AE, MC, V; checks OK.*

MOUNT HOOD

At 11,245 feet, Hood may not be the highest in the chain of volcanoes in the Cascades, but it *is* one of the best-developed. The Timberline Day Lodge Wy'East, at the 6,000-foot level, has plenty of facilities to equip the mountaineer, hiker, or skier. Chair lifts take you to the Palmer Snowfield, up in the glaciers, where you can ski in the middle of summer. The lower parts are ablaze with rhododendrons (peaking in June) and wildflowers (peaking in July); all are easily reachable from trails that spread out from Timberline Lodge. One of the best trails leads 4½ miles west from Timberline Lodge to flower-studded Paradise Park. Like Rainier, the mountain is girt by a long trail (called Timberline Trail), a 40-mile circuit of the entire peak that traverses snowfields as well as ancient forests.

Mid-May to mid-July is the prime time for climbing Mount Hood, a peak that looks easier than it is, since the last 1,500 feet involve very steep snow climbing. Timberline Mountain Guides, in the Timberline Lodge, equip and conduct climbers to the summit; (503) 636-7704.

RESTAURANTS

Mount Hood Brewing Company The theme is universal—trout fishing and beer—in this knotty-pine brewpub, where you can watch the brewmasters at work. Try an oatmeal stout or unfiltered Gypsy with a hearty Brewmaster pizza loaded with capers, cream cheese, and smoked salmon, or design your own from an impressive list of toppings that include fontina, feta, Gorgonzola, and smoked cheddar cheeses, Andouille sausage, pesto, and walnuts. Excellent burgers, beer-battered vegetables, and smoked-salmon ravioli are on the menu too, all fine (although the caesar that comes with them isn't a true caesar). While you're sipping, try to guess what kind of fly the trout is biting over the bar. ■ *Take the Government Camp loop off Highway 26; (503) 272-3724; 87304 E Government Camp Loop, Government Camp; beer and wine; $; AE, DIS, MC, V; checks OK; lunch, dinner every day.*

Timberline Lodge ★★ Built in 1937 as a WPA project, Timberline Lodge is a wonderland of American crafts—carved stone, worked metal, massive beams with adze marks plain to see, rugged fireplaces everywhere, and a huge, octagonal lobby that is an inspiring centerpiece for the steep-roofed hotel. In 1975 an organization called Friends of Timberline was formed to supervise and finance the restoration of the magnificent craftsmanship. Since then, many of the upholsteries, draperies, rugs, and bedspreads in the public and guest rooms have been re-created in their original patterns—in some cases with the help of the original craftspeople.

Fortunately, much of the ski traffic is diverted from the historic lodge to the Wy'East Day Lodge. So visits here can be quite special. There are bunk rooms for $52, but it's worth it to book a room with a fireplace for $140. The resort is known for its year-round downhill skiing, but come also for cross-country skiing and other wintertime activities. During the summer, Timberline offers great hiking, picnicking, chair-lift rides, and guided nature tours (the staff is a great source for suggestions). There's also a sauna and heated pool. The lobby's best for lounging (as the rooms are quite small); desk nooks upstairs are *the* postcard-writing spots.

As for the restaurant, fish is Leif Eric Benson's strong point. The food in the Ram's Head Lounge is not quite as good, but do take time for a drink while looking into the heart of the mountain. Fast food is available in the Wy'East Lodge. ■ *60 miles due east of Portland off Hwy 26; (503) 272-3311, toll-free (800) 547-1406 outside Oregon; Timberline Ski Area, OR 97028; $$; AE, MC, V; checks OK; breakfast, lunch, dinner every day.*

▼

Zig Zag

Restaurants

▲

ZIG ZAG

RESTAURANTS

Salazar's ★ All three dining rooms are filled with the fruits of owner/chef Al Salazar's 30-odd years of collecting: antique lamps, tapestries, stained glass, ornate carving knives, a huge collection of doorknobs, and so on. The effect is as disconcerting as it is fascinating. The cuisine is equally eclectic and somewhat uneven: blackened cod, Oriental duck, lamb shanks, Swiss steak. The wine list is adequate. Our advice is to order a tender steak, dine in the upstairs loft for the view (particularly if there's a snowscape), and be sure to enjoy the doorknob collection. ■ *Hwy 26, 1 mile east of Zig Zag; (503) 622-3775; 71545 E Hwy 26, Rhododendron; $$; full bar; AE, DC, DIS, MC, V; checks OK; dinner every day.*

LODGINGS

Mountain Shadows Bed and Breakfast ★ It's definitely off the beaten path—on a rutted gravel road that passes through a clearcut under power lines and ends with a spectacular view of Mount Hood. There are three large guest rooms—one with a private bath—in this handcrafted log house. Cathy and Paul Townsend genuinely like preparing your full breakfast; in summer they'll serve it on the deck with Mount Hood almost in your lap. And maybe you'll also see elk, river otters, and deer. Extensive hiking trails abound. Kids are welcome, but no smoking in the rooms. ■ *3 miles north of Zig Zag off east Lolo Pass Rd; (503) 622-4746; PO Box 147, Welches, OR, 97067; $$; no credit cards; checks OK.*

WEMME (AKA WELCHES)

This pretty little town is known as Wemme on maps, but Welches at the post office because so many Welches have settled here.

RESTAURANTS

Chalet Swiss ★★ Open the door and walk into Oregon's version of Switzerland—a world of peasant dresses, cowbells, and hand-carved wooden furniture. And consistently excellent food. Owner/chef Kurt Mezger prepares classics with élan: Bündnerfleisch (paper-thin slices of beef salt-cured in alpine air); traditional fondues; raclette (cheese broiled on potatoes and served with pickles and onions); a superb salmon bisque; greens dressed with lemon, garlic, and herbs; and fresh vegetables cooked just right. Try the Zurcher Geschnizteltes (veal in cream sauce with mushrooms) or the trout amandine. You may be tempted to take an order of the homemade spaetzle (noodles) with you. It's all filling and delightful fare, and we actually managed to save room for tiramisu and fresh strawberries. Chalet Swiss seats only 75, so make reservations a day before. ■ *Hwy 26 and E Welches Rd; (503) 622-3600; 24371 E Welches Rd, Welches; $$; full bar; AE, MC, V; checks OK; dinner Wed-Sun.*

LODGINGS

The Resort at the Mountain ★★ At the right time of the year, you can ski one day and play golf the next. Proximity to Mount Hood and their 27-hole golf course makes the Resort at the Mountain a good choice for the sportive traveler. The 157 rooms are large and quiet (but management should remember to turn on your room's heat *before* the guests arrive); each has a deck or patio and a view of the pool, forest, or, yes, freeways. Most have a sports-gear closet (a necessity here) and many have fireplaces (though the third duraflame log will cost you extra). And, as if the mountain, the golf course, and nearby rivers didn't offer enough recreational options, there are six tennis courts, an outdoor heated pool and Jacuzzi, a fitness center, mountain-bike rentals, hikes, horseshoes, golf lessons, volleyball, badminton, croquet, and basketball. Of course, it's also a very popular conference center. Rates run anywhere from $99 for a regular resort room to $185 for a two-bedroom suite. The food is acceptable, but pricey for such unexciting fare. ■ ½ mile south of Hwy 26 on E Welches Rd; (800) 669-7000 or (503) 622-3101; 68010 E Fairway Ave, Welches, OR 97067; $$$; AE, DC, DIS, MC, V; checks OK; breakfast, lunch, dinner every day, brunch Sun.

Old Welches Inn ★ Judi and Ted Mondun have reopened what was the first summer inn on Mount Hood (1890). A hundred years later it's still perfectly placed: French windows give views of the Resort at the Mountain's 27-hole golf course, the mountains that ring the valley, and a yard filled with wildflowers that stretches down to the Salmon River. The three upstairs rooms are small and share two full baths, but all are attractive and have views. Relax by the fire, read in the sun room, and pat good old Rocky the dog (your own dog is welcome with Rocky's approval). Larger groups may prefer to rent the adjacent and comfy no-frills two-bedroom cabin with fireplace, kitchen, and views. Kids over 12 welcome. ■ 1 mile south of Hwy 26 on E Welches Rd; (503) 622-3754; 26401 E Welches Rd, Welches, OR 97067; $; AE, MC, V; checks OK.

SANDY

A pleasant town on the way to Mount Hood, Sandy (named for the nearby river) offers a white-steepled church, quaint shops, a weekend country market, ski rentals, and big fruit stands purveying the local fruits, vegetables, wines, juices, and filberts. In short—a nice stop en route to the mountains.

The **Oregon Candy Farm** features Bavarian truffles (90 cents each) along with hand-dipped chocolates, caramels, barks, chocolate-covered prunes, apricot-walnut jellies, and on and on. Kids can watch the candymakers in action. It's 5½ miles east of Sandy on Highway 26; (503) 668-5066.

Oral Hull Park is designed for the blind, with splashing water and plants to smell or touch; it is a moving experience even for the sighted; (503) 668-6195.

RESTAURANTS

The Elusive Trout Pub A giant marlin guards the entryway and wagonwheel chandeliers hang over the tables; neon cats and an old wooden canoe hanging upside down from the ceiling complete the look. As you might have guessed, the theme in Sandy's popular pub is fish and fishing; the personal collection of trout flies, fish toys, and other fishy stuff has been gathered and donated by patrons over the years. The menu reflects the slang of one who lived in hip-waders until he spawned the idea for the pub: the Keeper, Bucktail Caddis, Eastern Brookie, Red Sider, and German Brown—all names for better than average sandwiches. A large selection of brews is on draft, and you can try the ale sampler, six five-ounce glasses for $5. ■ *At Hoffman Ave and Proctor Blvd; (503) 668-7884; 3933 Proctor Blvd, Sandy; $; beer and wine; MC, V; local checks only; lunch, dinner Tues-Sun.*

MCKENZIE RIVER

The highway through this river valley is the most beautiful of all the Cascade crossings. Following Highway 126 from Eugene, you pass through farm country alongside the green water of the McKenzie River. Soon there are lovely campgrounds, waterfalls and amazingly transparent lakes. At Foley Springs, catch Highway 242 for the pass (opens about July 1 each year). This is volcanic country, with vast 2,000-year-old lava beds.

    McKenzie River runs. Long celebrated for trout fishing, the McKenzie has become known for river-runs in rafts or the famous McKenzie River boats, rakish dories with upturned bows and sterns. **Dave Helfrich River Outfitter** in Vida conducts springtime day trips on the river and also arranges for fly-fishing expeditions in drift boats; (503) 896-3786.

MCKENZIE BRIDGE

Tokatee Golf Course, 3 miles west of McKenzie Bridge, is commonly rated one of the five finest in the Northwest: lots of trees, rolling terrain, and distracting views of the scenery; (503) 822-3220.

RESTAURANTS

Log Cabin Inn The fundamentals of home cooking and clean, comfortable lodging are enshrined here in eight newly re-modeled cabins on the water. Dinners are popular and offer a range as broad as wild boar, buffalo, venison, and quail, as well as the more traditional prime rib. Folks come from miles around to top it all off with marionberry cobbler. ■ *50 miles east of I-5 on Hwy 126; (503) 822-3432; 56483 McKenzie Hwy, McKenzie Bridge; $$; full bar; DIS, MC, V; local checks only; brunch Sun, lunch Mon-Sat, dinner every day (hours vary in winter).*

LODGINGS

Holiday Farm ★ First-time visitors to Holiday Farm wouldn't know at first glance that the resort encloses 90 acres and a hidden lake or three. They would find a main house (an old stagecoach stop), pleasant dining in the restaurant, and some amiable riverside cottages with knockout views of the McKenzie. Open April through November, all of the cabins feature decks and bright windows. Some are older green and white (with a rebuilt porch here and there); others are cedar-sided and more contemporary. Big and Little Rainbow is a large and modern unit that can be joined for a larger group (two families).

The restaurant, open to tourists passing through, makes a very pleasant dining stop on a porch overhanging the river. Hot and cold sandwiches, fresh salmon for lunch; pasta, steaks, seafood, and game for dinner. ■ *3 miles west of McKenzie Bridge on McKenzie River Dr; (503) 822-3715; 54455 McKenzie River Dr, Blue River, OR 97413; $$$; full bar; no credit cards; checks OK; breakfast, lunch, dinner every day.*

CAMP SHERMAN

LODGINGS

House on the Metolius ★★ This private fly-fishing resort, open all year now (and it's still hard to get into and impossible to drop by), is set in 200 acres of gorgeous scenery, with the Metolius River nearby. The cabins are lovely, fully equipped with fireplace, kitchenette, and king, double, or twin beds. Reservations needed at least a week in advance. Well-behaved pets are okay. Don't forget your fly rod. ■ *Forest Service Rd 1420, 2 miles north of Camp Sherman; (503) 595-6620; PO Box 601, Camp Sherman, OR 97730; $$$; MC, V; checks OK.*

Camp Sherman

Lodgings

Lake Creek Lodge ★ The resort has been here for over 60 years, popular with families who want a knotty-pine cabin from which to enjoy the fishing, the tiny pond, and the hearty food at the lodge. Best choice is a lodge house, a cheerful, open-ceilinged home with two or three bedrooms, one or two baths, possibly a fireplace, a complete kitchen, living room, and screened porch; less expensive are the two-bedroom cottages, which have no kitchens. The cabins are spread around the grassy grounds dotted with pines, overlooking the small lake made from a dammed stream. Facilities are extensive: tennis (two courts), fishing, hiking and biking, and children's activities. The lodge serves excellent breakfasts and dinners, and if it's not too busy with guests, it is also open for outsiders by reservation. You bring your own wine. ■ *4 miles north of Hwy 20 at Camp Sherman turnoff; (503) 595-6331; Star Route, Sisters, OR 97759; $$$; no credit cards; checks OK; breakfast, dinner every day (restaurant open summers only).*

Metolius River Resort ★ Not to be confused with the lower-priced, circa 1923 Metolius River Lodges across the bridge (worn and well loved, like the Velveteen Rabbit, by generations of guests), this new lodging is a nesting of 12 identical elegant wood-shake cabins with large decks and river-rock fireplaces, built last year on the west bank of the Metolius. All cabins have river views, master bedrooms and lofts, furnished kitchens—and French doors leading to large decks overlooking the river. Because the cabins are privately owned, interiors differ; we especially liked numbers 8, 2, and 10 with natural ponderosa pine interiors; and number 1, spiffed up in country floral. All cabins are smoke and pet free. Don't want to cook? We've heard good reports on the resort's Kokanee Cafe (open May through October). ■ *Camp Sherman, 5 miles north of Highway 20; (503) 595-6281; Box 1210, Camp Sherman, OR 97730; $$; MC, V; checks OK.*

SISTERS

Named after the three mountain peaks that dominate the horizon (Faith, Hope, and Charity), this little community is becoming a bit of a mecca for tired urban types looking for a taste of cowboy escapism. On a clear day (and there are about 250 of them a year), Sisters is exquisitely beautiful. Surrounded by mountains, trout streams, and pine and cedar forests, this little town is beginning to capitalize on the influx of winter skiers and summer camping and fishing enthusiasts.

There's mixed sentiment about the pseudo-Western storefronts that are thematically organizing the town's commerce, but then again, Sisters does host 56,000 visitors for each of four shows during its annual June rodeo. In the early 1970s Sisters developed the Western theme that by the '90s has grown more sophisticated and even slightly New-Aged. The town, built on about 30 feet of pumice dust spewed over centuries from the nearby volcanoes, has added numerous mini-mall shopping clusters with courtyards and sidewalks to eliminate blowing dust. There are several large art galleries, a knowledgeable mountain supply store and excellent fly-fishing shop, and even a store for freshly roasted coffee beans. Although the population of the town itself is only about 820, more than 7,500 live in the surrounding area on mini-ranches.

RESTAURANTS

Hotel Sisters Restaurant and Bronco Billy's Saloon ★ The social centerpiece of Western-theme Sisters, this bar and eatery serves up Western-style ranch cooking, with good burgers and some Mexican fare served by a friendly and diligent waitstaff. Seafood is fresh (deliveries thrice weekly from Salem), the filet mignon grilled perfectly, the chicken and ribs succulent. For a couple of bucks more, they'll split your single dinner into servings for two. Owners John Keenan, Bill Reed, and John Tehan have succeeded in turning old friendships into a going business consortium, re-creating the look of a first-class hotel, circa 1900. The old upstairs hotel rooms are now private dining rooms, and historical photos enhance the pleasant dining decor downstairs. Drop-ins often eat in the saloon or on good days take a drink on the deck. ▪ *Cascade and Fir sts; (503) 549-RIBS; 101 Cascade St, Sisters; $$; full bar; MC, V; local checks only; lunch, dinner every day (in winter, lunch Sat-Sun only, dinner every day).*

Papandrea's Pizza ★ Oregonians love this place. The original link in a small chain of pizzerias, Papandrea's has built a quality reputation on fresh dough, homemade sauce, real cheese, and fresh vegetables. Because of all this freshness, the place does seem to abide by its disclaimer sign—"We will not sacrifice quality for speed, so expect to wait a little longer." Actually, you wait quite a bit longer for the original thick-crust pies, but there's a You-Bake line for take-out. Pasta and sandwiches too. ▪ *East end of town; (503) 549-6081; E Cascade Hwy, Sisters; $; beer and wine; MC, V; local checks only; lunch, dinner every day.*

LODGINGS

Black Butte Ranch ★★★ With 1,800 acres, this vacation and recreation wonderland remains the darling of Northwest resorts. Rimmed by the Three Sisters mountains, scented by a plain of ponderosa pines, and expertly developed by the Brooks Scanlon Company, these rental condos and private homes draw families year-round to swim, ski, fish, golf, bike, boat, ride horses (summer only), and play tennis. The best way to make a reservation is to state the size of your party and whether or not you want a home (most are quite large and contemporary) or simply a good-sized bed and bath (in the latter case, the lodge condominiums will suffice, although some are dark and dated, with too much orange Formica and brown furniture). The main lodge is a handsome but not overwhelming building that serves as dining headquarters. Tables at the Restaurant at the Lodge are tiered so that everyone can appreciate the meadow panorama beyond. Food is straightforward and hearty, and servings are generous. ▪ *Hwy 20, 8 miles west of Sisters; (503) 595-6211; PO Box 8000, Black Butte Ranch, OR 97759; $$$; AE, DIS, MC, V; checks OK; breakfast, lunch, dinner every day (closed Mon-Tues from Jan-Apr).*

BEND

Bend was a quiet, undiscovered high-desert paradise until a push in the 1960s to develop recreation and tourism potential tamed Bachelor Butte into an alpine playground. Then came the golf courses, the airstrip, the bike trails, the river-rafting companies, the hikers, the tennis players, the rockhounds, and the skiers. Bend's popularity and population (currently 50,000) have been on a steady increase ever since, propelling it into serious destination status. The main thoroughfare, 5 miles of strip development, bypasses the town center, which thrives just to the west between two one-way streets, Wall and Bond. Part of the charm of the town comes from the blinding blue sky and the sage-scented air. The other part of its appeal is due to its proximity to the following attractions.

Mount Bachelor Ski Area (22 miles southwest). Bachelor Butte, known to skiers as Mount Bachelor, now has six high-speed lifts, which makes a total of 10 lifts feeding skiers onto 3,100 vertical feet of dry and groomed skiing. The Skier's Palate serves excellent lunches of grilled pistachio oysters or a hot sandwich of Dungeness crab and bay shrimp (and the best margarita around). The 9,060-foot elevation at the summit makes for late-season skiing (open until July 4th). High-season amenities include ski school, racing, day care, rentals, an entire Nordic program and trails, and better-than-average ski food at six different lodges. Call (800) 829-2442 or the ski report at (503) 382-7888.

The High Desert Museum (59800 S Highway 97, Bend, OR 97702) is an outstanding nonprofit center for natural and cultural history, located 6 miles south of Bend, that includes live-animal educational presentations. Inside, the new expanded center is a walk through 100 years of history, featuring excellent dioramas from native American times through the 1890s. A new "Desertarium" exhibits desert animals including live owls, lizards, and Lahontan cutthroat trout. Twenty acres of natural trails and outdoor exhibits offer replicas of covered wagons, a sheepherder's camp, a settlers' cabin, and an old sawmill, and support three resident river otters, porcupines, and raptors (otter and birds-of-prey presentations daily). Open every day from 9am to 5pm; call (503) 382-4754.

Pilot Butte (just east of town). This cinder cone with a road to the top is a good first stop, offering a knockout panorama of the city and the mountains beyond.

Lava River Caves (12 miles south of Bend on Highway 97). Tours of the lava caves include a mile-long lava tube. As you descend into the dark and surprisingly eerie depths, you'll need a warm sweater. **Lava Lands Visitor Center**, atop a high butte formed by a volcanic fissure, is a lookout point with accompanying geology lessons about the "moonscape" panorama caused by central Oregon's volcanic history. Call (503) 593-2421; open mid-March to the end of October.

Pine Mountain Observatory, 30 miles southeast of Bend on Highway 20, (503) 382-8331, is the University of Oregon's astronomy research facility. One of its three telescopes is the largest in the Northwest.

Deschutes Historical Center (corner of NW Idaho and Wall) features regional history and interesting pioneer paraphernalia, but keeps limited hours. Call (503) 389-1813 (open Wed-Sat, 1pm to 4:30pm).

Cascade Lakes Highway/Century Drive. This 100-mile tour needs several hours and a picnic lunch for full appreciation; there are a number of lakes along the way. Begin in Bend along the Deschutes, using the National Forest Service's booklet "Cascade Lakes Discovery Tour."

Smith Rock State Park. Twenty-two miles north of Bend in Terrebonne, some of the finest rock climbers gather to test their skills on the red rock cliffs.

The **Crooked River Dinner Train** ambles up the 38-mile Crooked River Valley between Redmond and Prineville with excursions and white-tablecloth dinner service during the summers, champagne-brunch train on Sundays year-round, and special events throughout the year (murder mysteries, wine-tastings, and holiday celebrations). Call (800) 872-8542 for dates.

Bend

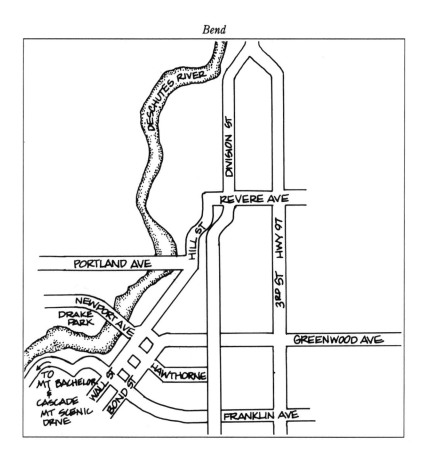

Pine Tavern Restaurant ★★ Buttonhole three out of four Bend citizens on the street and tell them you're ready for a fancy night out, with good food, service, atmosphere, and a decent value for your dollar. The recommendation time and time again will be the Pine Tavern. Under the ownership of Bert Bender, Joe Cenarrussa, and Brad and Theresa Hollenbeck, this establishment—and 50 years of history make it truly established—has regained its reputation for quality. Consider window-shopping at the Brooks Street Mercantile next door or Periwinkle in the alley while you wait for a table (yes, even with reservations). Request a table by the window in the main dining room and marvel at the tree growing through the floor. The menu runs about $10 to $16 for various beef entrées, but a lighter dinner menu offers smaller cuts of steak and petite portions of veal. The prime rib petite cut is ample even for a hungry diner, but prime rib is the forte of the restaurant and few can resist the larger cut. ■ *Foot of Oregon Ave downtown at Mirror Pond; (503) 382-5581; 967 NW Brooks, Bend; $$; full bar; AE, DC, MC, V; checks OK; lunch Mon-Sat, dinner every day.*

Scanlon's ★★ Scanlon's adjoins the Athletic Club of Bend, but aside from an aerobic instructor's distant bark and the slightest whiff of chlorine that may greet you at the front door, you'd never know it. Once you're ensconced in a cozy white-tablecloth booth, your mind will be on the food—meals start right away with a complimentary caper-loaded caponata and sweet homemade breads (Tuscan and focaccia) with virgin olive oil and balsamic vinegar for dipping. Dinners may be dressed up or dressed down: verdure pizza made with caramelized onions and grilled eggplant, sea scallops in creamy port wine sauce with green peppercorns and orange. Fresh fish is chef Maureen Schlerf's specialty and it's perfectly prepared. Meats are grilled on cherry wood. The wine list is thoughtful. ■ *Just off Century Dr on the way to Mt Bachelor; (503) 382-8769; 61615 Mt Bachelor Dr, Bend; $$; full bar; MC, V; local checks only; lunch, dinner Tues-Sat.*

Le Bistro ★ Owner Axel Hoch remains at the helm in the kitchen, and his wife, Salli, handles the front at this French specialty restaurant. Don't be put off by the austere old church facade; inside, the sidewalk-cafe decor warms things up, as does the superlative waitstaff. Yes, it's expensive and pretentious, but it's tough to fault the food, which you can watch being prepared in the open kitchen. Although Hoch's sauces (nantua, béarnaise, pepper-cream) are ever present on the seafood entrées, we prefer the simpler preparations of lamb and chateaubriand. A hearty beef bourguignon and braised lamb shanks finished with herbs and red wine warm up an evening too.

Don't miss the lounge downstairs; it's a good place to sample from an appetizer menu or to take your after-dinner coffee. ■ *1 block off Greenwood on Hwy 97; (503) 389-7274; 1203 NE 3rd St, Bend; $$; full bar; AE, DC, MC, V; local checks only; dinner Tues-Sat.*

Pescatore ★ Brad Haun's restaurant is nowhere close to the water, but Pescatore (it means "fisherman") is proud of its Italian renditions of seafood (many of them heart-healthy, too). A lusty penne pescatore is a mixture of clams, mussels, calamari, shrimp, and salmon in a spicy marinara served atop penne; capellini vegetali tangles fresh vegetables in angel-hair pasta. Pollo all'aglio e rosemarino is a simple, fragrant grilled chicken breast with garlic and rosemary. Every entrée comes with a salad or soup. Desserts—hazelnut white chocolate mousse, four-layered chocolate contessa, and panne de ganache—are not heart-healthy, for which we are grateful. Piano jazz on weekends. Rosy lights, rosy dining room, rosy service. ■ *Minnesota at Gasoline Alley; (503) 389-6276; 119 NW Minnesota, Bend; $$; full bar; AE, MC, V; checks OK; dinner every day.*

Westside Bakery and Cafe ★ Once just a bakery in the corner of the building, the ever-popular Westside has taken over the entire building (at last count there were four rooms). You can still get good coffee and wholesome baked goods to go, but most choose to stay for the huevos rancheros, croissant scramble, blueberry pancakes, or homemade granola for breakfast. Lunches consist of turkey, ham, or pastrami piled high on thick slabs of homemade bread, generous salads, and pasta dishes. The staff (and prices) are some of the friendliest in town. ■ *Past Drake Park to the other side of the river on Galveston; (503) 382-3426; 1005 NW Galveston, Bend; $; beer; AE, DIS, MC, V; local checks only; breakfast, lunch every day.*

Bend

Restaurants

Deschutes Brewery & Public House A very social spot, whether you're a local or not. The place was designed by Portland city folk, with urbanites in mind: exposed rafters and dark wood wainscoting. The beer is dark, too: a rich Black Butte Porter, a hoppy Cascade Golden Ale, a robust Bachelor Bitter and, for nondrinkers, a tasty, not-too-sweet *rootbier* or peppery ginger ale. There's also a special seasonal beer—Great American Beer Festival winners such as Mirror Pond Pale Ale, August's Wychick Wheat Ale, or the malty Christmas Jubel. The kitchen has created light gourmet bar food for midday (French onion soup, black bean chili, and homemade sausages with sauerkraut) that has been attracting lunching professionals, and a full dinner menu. Many locals are proud to see Bend on a beer-bottle label; but they can also bring in a sealable bottle and get brew to go for 10 cents an ounce. ■ *Corner of Bond and Greenwood; (503) 382-9242; 1044 NW Bond St, Bend; $; beer and wine; MC, V; local checks only; lunch, dinner every day.*

LODGINGS

Sunriver Lodge ★★★ More than a resort, Sunriver is an organized community with its own post office, realty offices, grocery store, and 1,000 or so full-time residents. The unincorporated town now sprawls over 3,300 acres, and its own paved runway for private air commuting does a brisk business. Nevertheless, its specialty is big-time escapist vacationing, and this resort has all the facilities to keep families, couples, or groups of friends busy all week long, year-round. Summer months offer golf (two 18-hole courses), tennis (22 courts), rafting, canoeing, fishing, swimming (two pools, seven hot tubs), biking (25 miles of paved trails), and horseback riding. In winter the resort is home base for skiing, both Nordic and alpine, ice skating, snowmobiling, and indoor racquetball. For the best bargain, deal through the lodge reservation service and request one of the large and contemporary homes (these often have luxuries like Jacuzzis, barbecues, and decks) and split expenses with another family. If you want access to the pool and hot tub facility, be sure to request a house that has a pass. Bedrooms and suites in the lodge village run from $84 to $155. Even the minimal bedroom units have a small deck and fireplace and come with exclusive privileges, including the use of two bicycles and free or discounted recreation depending on season.

Lodge dining includes the Meadows, a much-acclaimed showplace for dinner and Sunday brunch, and the Provision Company for breakfast, lunch, and light suppers. Off premises are Chen's Garden Chinese Restaurant and the popular Mexican menu at spacious Casa de Ricardo. We like to catch the inexpensive breakfast down at the Trout House, too. ■ _Off Hwy 97, 15 miles south of Bend; (503) 593-1221 or (800) 547-3922; PO Box 3609, Sunriver, OR 97707; $$$; full bar; AE, DC, DIS, MC, V; checks OK; breakfast, lunch, dinner every day._

Inn of the Seventh Mountain ★★ The Inn offers the closest accommodations to Mount Bachelor and is especially popular with families, no doubt due to the vast menu of activities built into the multicondominium facility. In the winter it has the biggest (though not full-size) ice rink around, one coed sauna large and hot enough to accommodate a group of about 15 guests, three bubbling hot tubs, and two heated swimming pools. In the summer the pools are the centerpiece of activity—there's a whole layout complete with water slide and wading pool. The Inn does a terrific job of social planning and offers fabulous off-season rates. An activities roster for the week gives the rundown on tennis, riding, biking, skating, rafting, snowmobiling, skiing, aerobics, frisbee, golf—you name it. The rooms are beginning to show their age in decor and wear, and you'll want to avoid buildings 18 and 19; they are the least scenic and the most removed from the center.

There is plenty of good eating at the resort. The Poppy Seed Cafe puts on a plentiful and tasty breakfast. Barron's, a deli/hamburger joint, is fine for those who prefer less formal surroundings. El Crab Catcher Restaurant and Lounge remains a local favorite for stepping out. We like the après-ski Warren Miller films in the lounge. ■ *18575 Century Dr, 7 miles west of Bend; (503) 382-8711 or toll-free in Oregon (800) 452-6810; PO Box 1207, Bend, OR 97709; $$$; full bar; AE, DC, DIS, MC, V; checks OK.*

Mount Bachelor Village ★★

You don't want a social chairman, you can live without an adjacent dining room, and you rarely need a hot-tub soak after 11pm? Then Mount Bachelor Village may be your style. What this development has over some of its more famous neighbor resorts is spacious rooms (there are no studios—all accommodations have one-bedroom, one-bedroom/loft, or two-bedroom floor plans). Every unit has a completely furnished kitchen, wood-burning fireplace, and private deck. We like the newer units, where the color scheme is modern and light and where the soundproofing helps mute the thud of ski boots in the morning. The views aren't particularly breathtaking (some units look out to the busy mountain road). There are 110 units to choose from, with prices starting at $60 a night without cooking facilities, $84 to $260 for condo units. Two outdoor Jacuzzis, seasonal outdoor pool, six tennis courts and a 2.2-mile nature trail round out the amenities. ■ *Toward Mount Bachelor on Century Dr; (503) 389-5900, toll-free (800) 452-9846 in Oregon; 19717 Mt Bachelor Dr, Bend, OR 97702; $$$; AE, MC, V; checks OK.*

The Riverhouse ★★

The Riverhouse has become an institution in Bend for comfortable stays at more reasonable rates than the out-of-town recreation resorts offer. It's really a glorified motel, and a river runs through it. Amenities are still abundant: indoor and outdoor swimming pools, saunas, whirlpools, exercise room, and indoor Jacuzzi; 19-hole golf course with driving range, tennis courts, walkable shopping, and adjacent restaurants. The Deschutes creates welcome white noise as it rushes over rocks and under the connector bridge. Request a room with a view of the river and away from the yahoos in the hot tub.

This is where you'll find Tito's, serving Mexican cuisine, and the Riverhouse Dining Room, respected for its continental cuisine (with some tableside preparations). The après-ski lounge rocks with contemporary bands six nights a week (country western on Sundays), so avoid nearby rooms unless you plan to dance all night. ■ *On Hwy 97 in Bend; (503) 389-3111, toll-free (800) 547-3928; 3075 N Hwy 97, Bend, OR 97701; $$; full bar; AE, DC, DIS, MC, V; local checks only; breakfast, lunch, dinner every day.*

Rock Springs Guest Ranch ★★ The emphasis here is very much on family vacations, but only July through Labor Day (the rest of the year it functions as a top-notch conference center). Counselors take care of the kids in special programs all day while adults hit the trail, laze in the pool, play tennis, or meet for hors d'oeuvres every evening on the deck. The cabins are quite nice—comfy knotty-pine duplexes with fireplaces. Only 50 guests stay at the ranch at one time, so it's easy to get to know everyone, particularly since all eat together in the lodge. The setting, amid ponderosa pines and junipers alongside a small lake, is secluded and lovely.

The main activity here is riding, with nine wranglers and a stable of 68 horses. Summer season is booked by the week only, starting at $1,175 per person (kids for less, children under 2 free), which includes virtually everything with your room (meals for guests only, snacks, riding, trapshooting, game tables, spa, and special events). Tennis courts are lit, there's a free-form whirlpool with 15-foot waterfall over volcanic boulders, a sand volleyball court under the tall pines, and fishing in the ranch pond. Note the special financial arrangements (such as reduced-price meals and accommodations) for baby-sitters brought for young children. Also open to families on major three-day holidays. ■ *On Hwy 20, 7 miles from Bend and 20 miles from Sisters; (503) 382-1957; 64201 Tyler Rd, Bend, OR 97701; $$; AE, DC, MC, V; checks OK.*

▼

Bend

Lodgings

▲

Entrada Lodge ★ Whether you're a weary traveler or just an avid skier looking for a firm mattress, a dependable shower, a clean room, and decent TV reception, you'll get that and more here. The "more" is a covered outdoor hot tub that cooks all season long, closer proximity to the mountain than town lodgings provide, a spa room, hot chocolate and snacks from 4 to 6pm by the office fireplace, and free continental breakfast. Friendly owner Brett Evert works hard to personalize this 79-room ranch-style Best Western motel. Pets are allowed—for $5 a night and with some restrictions. The price is thrifty, and the proximity to the mountain is a plus. Brett also owns another Best Western in town, The Woodstone Inn, 721 NE Third St, Bend, OR 97701, (503) 382-1515. ■ *3 miles from Bend on Century Dr; (503) 382-4080; 19221 Century Dr, Bend, OR 97702; $$; AE, DC, MC, V; no checks.*

Lara House Bed and Breakfast ★ One of Bend's largest and oldest (1910) homes, Lara House is a bright and homey bed and breakfast. The main room is perfect for small-group socializing—with a large stone fireplace and sunny adjacent solarium that looks out over the large yard onto the river parkway. A large breakfast is served at small tables on the sun porch as well as at the community oak table. Each of the four guest rooms upstairs has a queen-size bed, cheery wallpaper, and its own shower and vanity sink. Two rooms have private bathrooms—one on the main floor and a two-room suite on the third floor. The spa tub has been moved to the deck, and bicycles are available for guests. ■ *Louisiana and Congress; (503) 388-4064; 640 NW Congress, Bend, OR 97701; $$; AE, DIS, MC, V; checks OK.*

ELK LAKE

LODGINGS

Elk Lake Resort ★ Elk Lake is a small mountain lake about 30 miles west of Bend on the edge of the Three Sisters Wilderness Area. This remote lodge—reached by snow-cat or 10 miles of cross-country skiing in the winter—consists of a dozen self-contained cabins, most with fireplace, kitchen, bathroom, and sleeping quarters for two to eight people. It's nothing grand, but the place is much favored by Bend dwellers (a good recommendation) and the scenery is wonderful. There is a dining room with standard American grub; reservations required. Getting a reservation can prove almost as tough as getting here, since there's only a radiophone (you'll probably have to inquire by mail) and the place is often booked up to a year in advance. ■ *Century Dr, Elk Lake; radiophone YP7 3954; PO Box 789, Bend, OR 97709; $$; MC, V; no checks.*

MOUNT BAILEY

Mount Bailey Alpine Ski Tours offers a true backcountry skiing experience, with snow-cats instead of helicopters to take you to the top of this 8,363-foot ancient volcano, and experienced guides who stress safety. Diamond Lake Resort, (503) 793-3333, headquarters the guide service. When the snow melts, the operation turns to mountain-bike tours.

WESTFIR

This former logging town flanks the North Fork of the Middle Fork of the Willamette River, excellent for fishing for rainbow trout. The **Aufderheide National Scenic Byway** winds east out of Westfir into the heart of the Cascades, meandering along the river, and is popular with bicyclists, although heavy snowfall closes the route from November until early April.

LODGINGS

Westfir Lodge ★ Westfir Lodge has long anchored the tiny community of Westfir; however, for many years it housed the former lumber company offices. Gerry Chamberlain and Ken Symons converted the two-story building into a very pleasant inn. The bedrooms ring the first floor and in the center is a living area, kitchen, and formal dining room where guests are served a full English breakfast (English bangers and fried potatoes, eggs, broiled tomato topped with cheese, and scones). Across the river and beyond the old Westfir mill site, 28 trains (daily) whistle and speed through town. So, best to get the rooms on the north side of the lodge which don't have the river view but do muffle the sound better. Cottage gardens outside and a plethora of antiques throughout the lodge lend a country English ambience. In good weather, guests can enjoy the morning sun with coffee and breakfast on the patio amid the pink hedge roses, daisies, and poppies. The longest covered bridge in Oregon—the 180-foot Office Bridge (1944)—is just across the road. ▪ *3 miles east of Hwy 58 near Oakridge; (503) 782-3103; 47365 1st St, Westfir, OR, 97492; $$; no credit cards; checks OK.*

ODELL LAKE

LODGINGS

Odell Lake Lodge and Resort This resort on the shore of Odell Lake is ideal for the outdoorsperson. The surrounding geography beckons the fisher, the hiker, and the skier in all of us. The lake's a bit alpine for much swimming; instead cast about for the Mackinaw trout, rainbow, or kokanee. (Most sports equipment, from fishing rods to snowshoes, is for rent here.) In cool weather, the small library is the perfect place to sink into an overstuffed chair and read in front of the fireplace. The lakeview restaurant is open only seasonally Wednesdays though Sundays. As you might expect the rainbow trout is very fresh.

As for accommodations, request a lakeside room. Room 3, specifically. It's a corner suite warmed with knotty-pine paneling and views of lake and stream. If you'd rather a cabin, the few additional dollars required to get a lakeside one are well spent. All are clean and offer kitchen and bedding essentials (wood stoves too). The new cabin 10 is the best (and the only handicapped-accessible one), well lit by large windows all around, with the living room and one bedroom overlooking the lake. Or try cabins 6 or 7. Cabin 12 sleeps a friendly crowd of 16. The second-tier cabins are significantly smaller (no view, too). Pets OK in cabins only; minimum stays during peak season. ▪ *Take E Odell Lake exit off Hwy 58, 30 miles east of Oakridge; (503) 433-2540; PO Box 72, Crescent Lake, OR 97425; $ (lodge rooms), $$ (cabins); DIS, MC, V; checks OK.* ⅃

CRATER LAKE

Some 6,500 years ago, 15,000-foot Mount Mazama became the Mount St. Helens of its day, blew up, and left behind a deep crater that is now filled with Crater Lake. The area is extraordinary: the impossibly blue lake, the eerie volcanic formations, the vast geological wonderland. The visitors center, at the park headquarters, (503) 594-2211, offers a theater, an information desk, and a good interpretive exhibit. Visitors to Crater Lake should plan to camp, since the lodge is being remodeled (scheduled to open in 1995); Mazama campground is a good place. Be sure to take the two-hour boat ride from Cleetwood Cove out to Wizard Island and around the lake. There are dozens of trails and climbs to magnificent lookouts. In the winter, when the crowds finally thin out, only the south and west entrance roads are kept open.

Even though the lodge is temporarily closed, you can get a decent meal at the Watchman dining room on the second floor above the Rim Village cafeteria. The place serves dishes such as chicken Jerusalem, and shrimp and cashew stir-fry, as well as southern Oregon wines and microbrews.

KLAMATH FALLS

This city of 17,000 people, the largest for 70 miles, is so isolated that it once led a movement to secede from Oregon and become the state of Jefferson. Now the residents happily welcome tourists, bird-watchers, and sportspersons from both Oregon and California (just 25 miles south).

Klamath Falls

Restaurants

Favell Museum of Western Art is a true Western museum, with arrowheads, native American artifacts, and the works of more than 200 Western artists; 125 W Main Street, (503) 882-9996.

The **Klamath County Museum** exhibits the volcanic geology of the region, native American artifacts from all over Oregon, and relics from the Modoc wars; 1451 Main Street, (503) 883-4208.

Baldwin Hotel Museum, in an old (1906) hotel, retains many fixtures of the era; 31 Main Street, June through September, (503) 883-4207.

Ross Ragland Theater, a onetime art deco movie theater, now presents stage plays, concerts, and the like, an impressive 130 nights a year; (503) 884-0651.

Upper Klamath Lake, 143 square miles, is the largest lake in Oregon; it's fine for fishing and serves as the nesting grounds for many birds, including white pelicans. The Williamson River, which flows into the lake, yields plenty of trout.

RESTAURANTS

Chez Nous ★ The name may be French, but Achim and Arlette Bassler serve more of a continental menu in the graceful older home on the south side of town. It's a favorite with locals, who go there for dishes like tournedos gourmet Chez Nous, with artichoke bottoms, scampi, and béarnaise atop the fillets. You get béarnaise with the salmon and halibut, too. The veal marsala comes on a bed of spinach. And they do chateaubriand or giant lobster for two. Otherwise, it's pretty standard, but nicely done. ■ *Follow 6th St south, a few blocks past Altamont; (503) 883-8719; 3927 S 6th St, Klamath Falls; $$; full bar; AE, DC, DIS, MC, V; local checks only; dinner Tues-Sun.*

Fiorella's ★ Residents of Klamath Falls appreciate the Northern Italian fare at Fiorella and Renato Durighello's restaurant. On a recent visit we had fine scalloppine Marsala and the house special, pastitsio, both of which came with soup, salad (in summer, fresh from their own garden), and garlic bread. The pasta is homemade and delicious. Reservations welcome. ■ *S 6th St to Simmers; (503) 882-1878; 6139 Simmers Ave, Klamath Falls; $$; full bar; MC, V; local checks only; dinner Tues-Sat.*

LODGINGS

Thompson's Bed and Breakfast by the Lake ★ Mary and Bill Pohll offer four bedrooms on a separate level with private entrance. Two have private baths, the other two share. Sunsets over the Cascade Range provide a backdrop to the spectacular view of Upper Klamath Lake. Deer are frequent visitors to the backyard. Bring your binoculars for bird-watching. Bald eagles roost in the backyard. Mary can cook virtually anything for breakfast, but apple pancakes and French toast are her specialty. This was the first B&B in town, launched when Mary's last name was Thompson. Others have come and gone, but this is still the best. ■ *Call for directions; (503) 882-7938; 1420 Wild Plum Court, Klamath Falls, OR 97601; $$; no credit cards; checks OK.*

▼

LAKEVIEW

At an elevation of nearly 4,300 feet, Lakeview also calls itself "Oregon's Tallest Town." It's better known for its geyser, Old Perpetual—which doesn't exactly rival Yellowstone's Old Faithful, but it's Oregon's only geyser. It's located in a pond at **Hunter's Hot Springs**, a 47-acre property dotted by hot-springs pools, on the west side of Highway 395 about 2 miles north of town. The geyser goes off once every 30 seconds or so, shooting 75 feet into the air for 3 to 5 seconds. It's been erupting regularly for some 60 years, apparently unleashed by someone trying to drill a well. **Hunter's Hot Springs resort**, built in the 1920s, now includes an Italian restaurant and a 33-unit motel, with 12 new rooms added in the early 1990s; (503) 947-2127.

Abert Lake, 20 miles north of Lakeview, is a stark, shallow body of water over which looms **Abert Rim**, a massive fault scarp. One of the highest exposed geologic faults in North America, the rim towers 2,000 feet above the lake.

LODGINGS

Aspen Ridge Resort ★ This resort is a complex of log homes which appear like a mirage in the high meadow of south central Oregon, and reminds one somewhat of an early-day miniature Sunriver. The resort sits on 160 acres, once part of 14,000-acre Fishhole Creek Ranch. The log homes sleep six ($120); or stay in one of the four bedrooms in the main lodge for less. Most come here to be outside, go mountain biking, or ride horseback...but there is a tennis court for those who prefer to stick around the ranch. If you don't like beef, you don't fit in here. The resort is adjacent to a working cattle and buffalo ranch which provides a view and influences the restaurant's menu. Best meal bargain is the $24 (for two) steak dinner, barbecued on the back porch. ■ *18 miles SE of Bly on Fishhole Creek Rd; (503) 884-8685; PO Box 2, Bly, OR 97622; $$; full bar; no credit cards; checks OK; breakfast, lunch, dinner every day (closed March).*

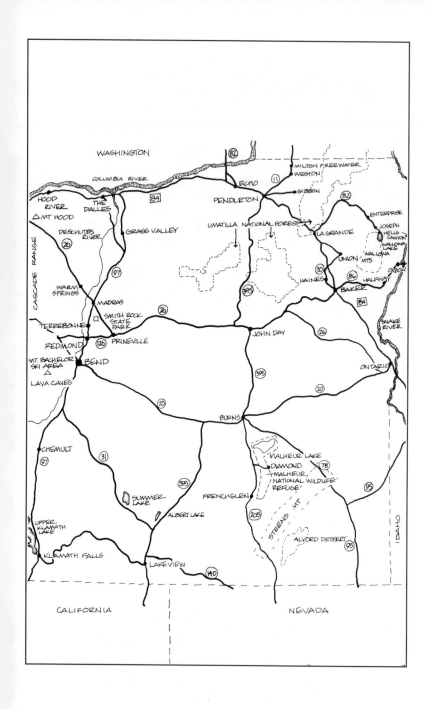

Eastern Oregon

Two major routes: eastward midstate from Warm Springs to John Day, and southeastward along I-84 from Pendleton to the Idaho border (with a diversion into the Wallowas), turning in-state again to Burns and Frenchglen.

GRASS VALLEY

RESTAURANTS

Holmestead Wheat and barley farmers, ranchers, and Bend-bound truckers and travelers have one thing in common: an affection for Carol Grout's homemade cinnamon rolls. When Grout sold her cafe last year, the new owners didn't change a thing—the rolls, the malted milk shakes, meaty cheeseburgers, or fresh-cut fries. All road trips deserve a stop like this.
■ *Easy to find; (503) 333-2255; Highway 97, Grass Valley; $; no alcohol; no credit cards; checks OK; breakfast, lunch, dinner every day.*

WARM SPRINGS

For most highway cowboys, Warm Springs is just a small bend in the road at the bottom of a pine-studded rimrock canyon on Highway 26. In 1993, however, **The Museum at Warm Springs**, (503) 553-3331, opened on the bank of the Shitike Creek, and what a museum it is. Built by the three native American tribes (Wasco, Paiute, and Warm Springs) who live on the barren 644,000-acre reservation, the museum houses a permanent collection that includes prized heirlooms, protected by tribal families for generations, on view to the public for the first time. The best of the architecturally magnificent museum is a ceremonial

Wasco wedding: tule-mat lodge, wickiup and plankhouse, song chamber, and drums accompanying rhythmic hoop dancing.

LODGINGS

Kah-Nee-Ta Resort ★★ The Confederated Tribes of Warm Springs Reservation some years ago built this posh resort, complete with a large, arrowhead-shaped hotel, a vast mineral-springs pool, tepees and cottages for rent, and such amenities as golf, tennis, riding, river rafting, and fancy restaurants. The Indian fry-bread and the bird-in-clay dish are the crowd-pleasers, but the flavors are uninspired. Even so, Kah-Nee-Ta is an unusual experience, with excellent service. You might stay in a roomy tepee (the lodge rooms are usually small) for instance, gathering the family around the fire pit in the evening. During the day, ride into the desert countryside, splash in the pool, or watch native American dances. ■ *11 miles north of Warm Springs on Hwy 3; (503) 553-1112 or toll-free (800) 831-0100; PO Box K, Warm Springs, OR 97761; $$$; AE, DC, MC, V; checks OK.*

REDMOND

RESTAURANTS

Paradise Grille ★ Eric Laslow, former chef of Bend's Cyrano's, opened his own restaurant in Redmond's historic 1918 brick bank building one year ago. Inside is a surprise—Southwestern adobe curved walls, warm colors, and ponderosa pine archways. Curly willow branches arch over the windows. Hungry highway travelers can find a simple meal of mesquite-grilled chicken or steak here, or more complex and delectable fare such as tequila prawns, whiskey fennel sausage, and smoked pork sauté topped with grilled polenta. Condiments swing to Santa Fe tastes: corn chile relish, mesquite salsa, and pineapple jalapeño jelly. Eric's signature: monthly five-course wine-and-food-paired dinners. ■ *At Deschutes and 6th; (503) 548-0844; 404 SW 6th St, Redmond; $$; full bar; MC, V; checks OK; lunch Tues-Fri, dinner Tues-Sun.*

LODGINGS

Inn at Eagle's Crest ★★ Sisters has Black Butte, Bend has Sunriver, and Redmond has Eagle's Crest. The private homes at this full resort rim the 18-hole golf course, and visitors choose one of the 75 rooms in the hotel (the best ones have a golf course-facing deck) or a condominium. The condos are the better deal, especially if you come with four to eight people. They've got kitchens and access to the recreation center (not available to those who stay in the main building) with its indoor tennis, squash, and racquetball courts, workout room, masseuse, tanning salon, heated outdoor pool, and tennis courts; miles of biking and jogging trails; an equestrian center; and playfields. The food at the resort's formal Canyon Club is predictable for such a clubby atmosphere, with rancher-size portions. Service can be slow. The three-tiered deck outside provides a good view. ■ *5 miles west of Redmond on Hwy 126, turn south on Cline Falls Rd; (503) 923-2453 or toll-free (800) MUCH-SUN; PO Box 1215, Redmond, OR 97756; $$; full bar; AE, MC, V; checks OK; breakfast, lunch, dinner every day.*

JOHN DAY

You are in the midst of dry cattle country in an area loaded with history: John Day is just off the old Oregon Trail, and the whole region was full of gold (during the height of the Gold Rush in 1862, $26 million in gold was mined in the neighboring town of Canyon City).

Kam Wah Chung Museum, next to the city park, was the stone-walled home of two Chinese herbal doctors at the turn of the century. A tour makes for an interesting glimpse of the Chinese settlement in the West: opium-stained walls, Chinese shrines, and herbal medicines are on display, as well as a small general store. Open May-October.

John Day Fossil Beds Monument lies 40 to 120 miles west, in three distinct groupings: the banded Painted Hills, extremely ancient fossils, and fascinating geological layers; 420 W Main Street, (503) 575-0721 for maps and brochures.

Dayville

Lodgings

▲

DAYVILLE

LODGINGS

Fish House Inn Mike and Denise Smith escaped San Diego with two young children for considerably smaller Dayville (population 214). They settled into a century-old house built by Dayville's first liquor store owner. Denise has turned the tiny original liquor store into a dance studio for local children; Mike remodeled a small cottage in the back into two private guest rooms. There are three more rooms in the main house as well ($35 to $45), all decorated with stuff gleaned from farm sales (old rakes, ice tongs, and horseshoes), things Piscean (old rods, reels, and creels among them), and baskets Denise wove from river willows. In warm weather a bountiful breakfast (with the best coffee in 4,528 mostly empty square miles) is served in the garden. ■ *On Highway 26 west of John Day at 110 Franklin Ave; (503) 987-2124; PO Box 143, Dayville, OR 97825; $; no credit cards, checks OK.*

If you've found a place that you think is a best place, send in the report form at the back of this book. If you're unhappy with one of the places, let us know why. We depend on reader input.

I

165

PENDLETON

In these parts, the name of this town is synonymous with the Wild West. Each September the Pendleton Round-up rolls around—a big event since 1910 that features a dandy rodeo; call toll-free (800) 524-2984 for tickets and information. **Hamley's and Company** has been selling Western clothing, boots, hats, tack items, and custom-made saddles since 1883. It's a kind of shrine, the L.L. Bean of the West; 30 SE Court Street, (503) 276-2321.

Pendleton Woolen Mills gives tours Monday through Friday and sells woolen yardage and imperfect blankets at reduced prices; 1307 SE Court Place, (503) 276-6911. Pendleton Underground Tours provides a 90-minute walk through Pendleton's history—most of it underground—to view the remains of businesses that date back to the turn of the century: bordellos, opium dens, and Chinese jails. Reservations are necessary and should be made at least 24 hours in advance. Price is $10 per adult; 37 SW Emigrant Avenue, (503) 276-0730.

RESTAURANTS

Raphael's Restaurant and Lounge ★ In the historic Roy Raley House, across from the landmark Clock Tower, the Hoffmans continue the charming and somewhat eccentric approach to food which they mastered at the former Skyroom. Visit the authentic native American fine art gallery (Raphael Hoffman is a member of the Nez Percé tribe) while waiting for your table. Her husband Robert, the chef, is not Indian—but some of the dishes show a native American touch. Emphasis is more on flavor than presentation. Indian salmon wrapped in spinach and smothered with wild huckleberries appears too dark until the pink of the salmon breaks through with the first fork cut; the flavor is incredible. An applewood-smoked prime rib is the most popular beef entrée; many of the patrons are crazy about it. Wild game such as alligator, rattlesnake, and elk is featured during the hunter's months of September, October, and November. The wine list features a good selection of moderately priced Northwest wine. Varietal wines are sold by the 8-ounce glass. ■ *Court and Dorion; (503) 276-8500; 233 SE 4th, Pendleton; $$; full bar; MC, V; checks OK; lunch Tues-Fri, dinner Tues-Sat.* ₺

LODGINGS

Swift Station Inn Bed and Breakfast ★ Ken and Lorry Schippers both work full time for the state of Oregon, but the love of their labor on weekends and evenings has turned one of Pendleton's white elephants into its classiest lodgings. The ground-floor Victorian Room (our favorite) and the Summer Room have private baths. A large hot tub in the backyard melts away the driving fatigue (and you do a lot of it in these parts).

Breakfasts are large, and the Schippers are so anxious to please you'll probably leave feeling guilty for not finishing what's on your plate. Well-behaved, courteous children are welcome. Rates are higher during September due to the Round-up. ■ *Exit 210 off I-84, north on state hwy into town, north on 9th St 3 blocks to Byers; (503) 276-3739; 602 SE Byers, Pendleton, OR 97801; $$; MC, V; checks OK.*

Indian Hills Motor Inn A little to the south of Pendleton is the Red Lion's Indian Hills Motor Inn, the most lavish motel in town. Amenities include heated pool, lounge, dining room, and coffee shop. There are outsized, gaudy Western bas-reliefs in the reception areas. The view from your balcony over the low mountains and tilled fields of Eastern Oregon can be inspiring—more so than the food, which ranges from indifferent to passable. Sunday morning brunch is the best meal of the week. Well-behaved pets okay. ■ *Exit 210 off I-84 at 304 SE Nye Ave;(503) 276-6111; PO Box 1556, Pendleton, OR 97801; $$; AE, DC, DIS, MC, V; checks OK.* &

Working Girl Hotel (Bed and Breakfast) This refurbished historic building was once one of central Oregon's popular bordellos. If you love high ceilings (18 feet), huge windows, and lots of exposed brick, you will appreciate this Working Girl. Each of the five rooms is decorated with pieces from a different era and named after the owner and her siblings. The most romantic choice is the Pamela, with two rooms and Oriental rugs. Breakfast is simple but adequate help-yourself continental. Women and men have separate baths. No children under 12. ■ *Next to the Underground Tour office at 17 SW Emigrant; (503) 276-4767; 505 NW Destain, Pendleton, OR 07801; $$; MC, V; checks OK.*

Echo

Restaurants

ECHO

RESTAURANTS

The Echo Hotel Restaurant and Lounge ★ The Echo's cedar-shake interior is filled with a bar, a split-level dining area, and three blackjack tables. Co-proprietor Susan Sperr greets every guest. This former rabbit cannery and historic hotel (there are hopes of reopening the upstairs as a bed and breakfast) serves up generous portions of 16-ounce prime ribs and ranch-wagon specials. This once primarily whiskey-and-rib place is getting more and more attention for its seafood and Northwest wine by Pendletonites who flock here on weekends. ■ *20 miles west of Pendleton on US 84; (503) 376-8354; 110 Main St, Echo; $; full bar; DIS, MC, V; local checks only; breakfast, lunch, dinner every day.* &

Inspectors for the Best Places series accept no free meals or accommodations; the book has no sponsors or advertisers.

WESTON

RESTAURANTS

Tollgate Mountain Chalet Walla Walla folks often drive 50 miles south through the lovely, waving wheat fields to this rustic eating place in the Blue Mountain forest. Locals order the chili, or the prime-rib sandwich on homemade bread, a hamburger, a Reuben sandwich, or a reasonable steak; the pies are homemade and different every day. It makes a particularly good spot for breakfast before a day of hiking or mushroom hunting. ■ *16 miles E of Weston on Tollgate Mtn Hwy; (503) 566-2123; Weston; $; full bar; MC, V; local checks only; breakfast, lunch, and dinner Tues-Sun.*

MILTON-FREEWATER

RESTAURANTS

The Oasis This isn't a copy of a 1920s Western roadhouse, it's the real thing—and it hasn't ever changed: linoleum floors and lots of chrome. Eat in the bar and eavesdrop on the cowboys swapping stories. Although not every dish on the menu is a culinary triumph, the steaks are uniformly reliable and gigantic. Prime rib is good. On Sundays, chicken and dumplings is served family style, all you can eat, for about $7 per person—and a fine meal it is. A breakfast platter of biscuits and gravy goes for just over $2. Students from Walla Walla are fascinated with this place. ■ *Old Milton-Freewater Hwy and State Line Rd; (503) 938-4776; Milton-Freewater; $; full bar; MC, V; local checks only; breakfast, lunch, dinner Tues-Sun.* &

LODGINGS

Bar-M Guest Ranch ★ The Bar-M is a 2,500-acre down-home dude ranch with few of the frills associated with more spendy ranches. The relaxed atmosphere and loosely scheduled activities make it ideal for families looking for a low-key vacation. The wranglers lead two trail rides each day plus an overnight into the stunning Blue Mountains. Accommodations include two cabins and eight guest rooms on the second floor of the 1864 ranch house. Additional accommodations are available in the Homestead, a large building with four two-bedroom, single-bath suites. Meals, included in the package, feature homemade raspberry jam and breads. In the evening the adults tend to congregate on the wide front porch or the nearby spring-fed pool. The last day of each week includes an in-the-saddle competition plus an evening square dance in a lovely log barn. Minimum stay is six days from June through mid-September ■ *8 miles east of Gibbon on Umatilla River Rd; (503) 566-3381; Rt 1, Box 263, Adams, OR 97810; $$; no credit cards; checks OK.*

RESTAURANTS

Golden Harvest Chinese and American Restaurant ★ In 1989, Albert and Monita So (from China and Hong Kong respectively), opened their restaurant in Union. Success in that unlikely place financed the move (and expansion) to La Grande. Now waits for tables in the newly redecorated spacious dining room can be up to 15 minutes, even on weeknights. The sauces lost a little of their authority in the move but not enough to send us away. The Sichuan dishes are still our favorites. Most dishes here are ordered on a heat scale of one to five, but be aware that five almost raises blisters. ■ *1 block northeast of Adams on Greenwood; (503) 963-3288; 214 Greenwood St, La Grande; $; full bar; MC, V; local checks OK; lunch, dinner every day.* &

Mamacita's ★ House specials such as the Full Meal Steal for less than $3 at lunch are usually the best things coming out of the kitchen, typically two chicken soft tacos with beans and rice. Food is not overly spiced and not as fat-laden as Mexican food often is. Local college students provide most of the helpful service. Wine margaritas and an adobe-colored wall adorned with bright splotches of Mexicana round out the experience. ■ *On Depot near Adams; (503) 963-6223; 110 Depot St, La Grande; $; beer and wine; no credit cards; checks OK; lunch Tues-Fri, dinner Tues-Sun.* &

LODGINGS

Stange Manor Bed and Breakfast ★★★ This restored timber baron's house on the hill behind town returns an elegance to this once-booming town. A sweeping staircase leads up to the four bedrooms. The master suite is, of course, the best—and biggest—accommodation, but even if you opt for the former maid's quarters, you won't have to lift a finger. The owners, Marjorie and Pat McClure, have given personal attention to an already nurturing environment. Cookies—madeleines, perhaps—with tea await you at afternoon checkin. Breakfasts vary, but favorites include plenty of fresh fruit, German pancakes, and French toast, always served on china and crystal. ■ *Corner of Spring and Walnut; (503) 963-2400; 1612 Walnut St, La Grande, OR 97850; $$; MC, V; checks OK.*

Joseph

JOSEPH

This is the fabled land of the Wallowas, ancestral home of Chief Joseph, from which he fled with a band of Nez Percé warriors to his last stand near the Canadian border. Although Chief Joseph's remains are interred far from his beloved "land of the winding water," he saw to it that his father, Old Chief Joseph, would be buried here, in an Indian burial ground on the north shore of Wallowa Lake. The town itself is becoming something of an art colony. David Manuel, State of Oregon official sculptor for the Oregon Trail Celebration, has just opened the **Manuel Museum and Studio** on Main Street, (503) 432-7235. **Valley Bronze of Oregon** has built a foundry and a showroom in Joseph. Tours are offered on weekdays. Phone (503) 432-7551 for information.

Wallowa Lake State Park, on the edge of the **Wallowa Whitman National Forest** and **Eagle Cap Wilderness**, is perhaps the only state park in the country where locals still lament the fact that there are "never enough people." An Alpenfest with music, dancing, and Bavarian feasts happens every September, but the peak season is still midsummer, when the pristine lake and its shores are abuzz with go-carts, sailboats, and windsurfers. In winter the attraction is miles and miles of unpeopled cross-country trails throughout the lovely Wallowa highlands.

Wallowa Lake Tramway takes you by a steep ascent in a four-passenger gondola to the top of 8,200-foot Mount Howard, with spectacular overlooks and two miles of hiking trails. Summer only; PO Box 1261, La Grande, OR 97850, (503) 432-5331.

Joseph

Hell's Canyon, 35 miles east of Joseph, is the continent's deepest gorge, an awesome trench cut by the Snake River through sheer lava walls. The best view is from Hat Point near Imnaha, though McGraw Lookout is more accessible if you don't have four-wheel drive. Maps of the region's roads and trails, and information on conditions, are available at the Wallowa Valley Ranger District in Joseph, (503) 426-4978.

Hurricane Creek Llamas. You explore the lake-laden Eagle Cap Wilderness with a naturalist, while smiling llamas lug your gear. Hikes vary in length; hearty country meals are included (May to September). Call in advance, (503) 432-4455.

Wallowa Alpine Huts. Experienced backcountry ski guides offer 3- to 5-day powder-bound tours for skiers seeking the best of the Wallowa winterland. You stay in spartan tents and dine in a yurt; (208) 882-1955.

RESTAURANTS

Vali's Alpine Deli and Restaurant ★ Don't let its "deli" status mislead; a dinner at Vali's usually requires reservations. The food here is Hungarian-German (and so is the decor) interspersed with a few authentic renditions from other cuisines. Paprika chicken and dumplings is not to be missed when offered. Wiener schnitzel is also exceptional. At breakfast, Maggie Vali's homemade doughnuts are local legend, but don't show up hungry—the morning meal ends there. In the summer, sausage and cheese are available to take out for picnics. A new enclosed deck adds a nice touch to the dining experience. ▪ *5 miles south of Joseph on Hwy 82 near Wallowa Lake State Park; (503) 432-5691; 59811 Wallowa Lake Hwy (Hwy 82), Joseph; $; full bar; no credit cards; checks OK; breakfast, dinner Tues-Sun (winters Sat-Sun).*

LODGINGS

Chandlers—Bed, Bread, and Trail Inn ★ Cedar shingles, multiangled roof lines, and cushiony wall-to-wall carpets make this bed and breakfast resemble an alpine ski lodge—in the middle of Joseph. A log staircase climbs from the comfortable living room to a loft where five simple bedrooms share three baths, a sitting room, and a workable kitchenette. The mountains almost climb into room number 1. The substantial breakfast and knowledgeable hosts make this a wonderful stopover for area explorers. No pets, children under 12, or smoking. ▪ *700 S Main St; (503) 432-9765 or (800) 452-3781; PO Box 639, Joseph, OR 97846; $; MC, V; checks OK.*

Wallowa Lake Lodge ★ The rooms in this historic lodge are very small (especially the $50 ones), and you must promise not to smoke. You'll do best if you reserve one of the originally restored rooms with a lake view. If you plan to stay longer, the rustic pine cabins on the lake, with a living room, fireplace, and a kitchen, allow for a bit more flexibility. Even if the rooms *were* spacious, we'd spend most of the evening in front of the magnificent stone fireplace in the knotty pine lobby, and the days on the lake or in the mountains. A new deck is a splendid addition. Winters are painfully slow, especially in the dining room. ▪ *Near Wallowa Lake State Park; (503) 432-9821; 60060 Wallowa Lake Hwy, Joseph, OR 97846; $$; beer and wine; DIS, MC, V; checks OK; breakfast, dinner every day (dinner Fri-Sat winter).*

HAINES

RESTAURANTS

Haines Steak House ★ There's no mistaking that you're in cattle country, pilgrim. Most of the vehicles surrounding this ever-busy spot are of four-wheel-drive breed and many of the men wear their cowboy hats while eating. Cowbells add to the ranchlike bedlam about every five minutes to announce a birthday or anniversary. We particularly like the log cabin-type booths and the singletree curtains. Stay with the beef; it's well selected, cut, and cooked. Next to beef, the hashbrowns are the best thing on the menu. ▪ *On old Hwy 30, a short detour from I-84, exit 285 (eastbound) or exit 306 (westbound); (503) 856-3639; Haines; $$; full bar; AE, DIS, MC, V; checks OK; dinner Wed-Mon.*

UNION

LODGINGS

Queen Ann Inn Bed and Breakfast If the immaculately kept grounds at the edge of town and the picture-perfect 1894 Victorian don't draw you in, then the smells from the kitchen and the warmth of your hostess, Blanche Kohler, surely will. It has four oak and ceramic-tiled fireplaces, and fancy moldings and gingerbread trim to spare. Three guest rooms are on the second floor and a fourth takes up the third floor. At press time, only one bath, on the second floor, served all rooms, although a bath on the third floor is planned. No smoking and no pets. Well-behaved children over 12 are welcome. ■ *On 5th; (503) 562-5566; 782 N 5th St, Union, OR 97883; $$; no credit cards; checks OK.*

BAKER CITY

Baker's restful city park, old-time main street, and mature shade trees may give it a Midwest flavor, but the backdrop is decidedly Northwest. Located in the valley between the Wallowas and the Elkhorns, Baker makes a good base camp for forays into the nearby mountain Gold Rush towns. The newly opened **Oregon Trail Interpretive Center**, 4 miles east of I-84 on Hwy 86, is worth the detour. The multimedia walk-through brings the Oregon Trail experience to life. The animals look so real that you might be struck by the lack of normal animal sounds and odors. Open every day except Christmas and New Year's Day. Admission is free; donations accepted.

The **Elkhorn Mountains**, west of Baker, contain most of the old mining towns, which you can tour on a 100-mile loop from Baker (some on unpaved roads).

Ghost towns. There's a restored narrow-gauge steam train at Sumpter that operates between Memorial Day and Labor Day. The deserted towns of Granite, Bourne, Bonanza, and Whitney are well worth visiting.

Anthony Lakes Ski Area, 20 miles west of North Powder, has good powder snow, a chair lift, and cross-country trails; (503) 856-3277.

LODGINGS

À demain Bed & Breakfast ★ Stuffed French toast is not on the menu every morning, but when it is, you will understand why we would stay here just for the breakfast. The lovely old home is in one of Baker's quiet neighborhoods. The upstairs suite, our favorite, is comprised of two bedrooms that accommodate two couples traveling together (or a small family). And the price is reasonable enough to rent the suite for one. Hostess Kristi Flanagan is quite fond of down comforters and pillows.

■ *Corner of 4th and Valley sts; (503) 523-2509; 1790 4th St, Baker City, OR 97814; $$; no credit cards; checks OK.*

Best Western Sunridge Inn A sprawling Best Western, it is better than the average motel, with 124 comfortable, spacious, air-conditioned rooms and an attractive pine finish. In the hot summer, you'll appreciate the grassy courtyard/pool area (summers only). Come winter, move indoors to the 18-foot whirlpool. ■ *Off City Center exit; (503) 523-6444; 1 Sunridge Lane, Baker, OR 97814; $; AE, DC, DIS, MC, V; checks OK.*

HALFWAY

Once just a midway stop between two bustling mining towns, Halfway is now the quiet centerpiece of Pine Valley—stashed between the fruitful southern slopes of the Wallowa Mountains and the steep cliffs of Hell's Canyon.

Hell's Canyon, the continent's deepest gorge, begins at Oxbow Dam, 16 miles east of Halfway. For spectacular views of the Snake River, drive from Oxbow to Joseph (take Highway 86 to Forest Road #39; summers only). Maps of the region's roads and trails are available from the Forest Service, just outside Halfway, (503) 742-7511.

The folks at **Wallowa Llamas** lead 3- to 8-day trips along the edge of Hells Canyon or into the pristine Eagle Cap Wilderness high in the Wallowas, while their friendly sure-footed beasts lug your gear and plenty of food; for a brochure or information call (503) 742-4930.

▼

Halfway

Lodgings

▲

For those who would rather experience the raging river up close, **Hell's Canyon Adventures** in Oxbow arranges jet boat tours or combination excursions leaving from Hells Canyon Dam; call (503) 785-3352.

RESTAURANTS

Amador's of Halfway Sally Hollins' restaurant, in a former church in Halfway, is a welcome addition to this corner of Oregon. The menu's simple (a couple of entrées—stuffed tomato with tuna salad and pickled asparagus, fettuccine alfredo—and a number of deli sandwiches). Always a nice alternative to the heavily beefed menus found elsewhere in the high desert. The homemade desserts lay heavy on the chocolate, but we don't mind that a bit. ■ *Located in the Olde Church Building; (503) 742-2025; 166 N Main St, Halfway; $; no alcohol; no credit cards, checks OK; breakfast, lunch Tues-Sat, dinner Tues, Fri.*

LODGINGS

Clear Creek Farm ★ Once you find this somewhat quirky paradise, you'll know why Mary Ann Hamley and 373 other residents of Halfway have carefully chosen this fertile valley as home. There are four homey bedrooms in the farmhouse, but during summer families and small groups bunk up in either of the two board-and-batten cabins. It's delightfully campish, with bathrooms in a separate building. There are several small ponds for swimming, a field of lavender, fragrant herb garden, and 500 peach trees. When the snow falls, getting up the driveway can be treacherous, but the cross-country skiing is unbeatable. Billowing Dutch babies, luscious peaches (seasonal), and fresh-squeezed grapefruit juice await you in the morning. Bring your friends; group rates are cheaper. ■ *Call ahead for directions; (503) 742-2238; Rt 1, Box 138, Halfway, OR 97834; $$; DIS, MC, V; checks OK.* ♿

ONTARIO

RESTAURANTS

Casa Jaramillo This Mexican cantina gives cool respite from the hot eastern Oregon desert. Expanded and remodeled, it has a tropical atmosphere perfect for families. For the past 25 years, John Jaramillo and his family have been turning out authentic Mexican fare. Try the enchiladas rancheros, with fresh crunchy onions and a chile verde sauce that delivers. Great guacamole. ■ *2 blocks south of Idaho Ave; (503) 889-9258; 157 SE 2nd St, Ontario; $; full bar; AE, MC, V; checks OK; lunch, dinner Tues-Sun.*

LODGINGS

Howard Johnson's ★ It keeps changing its affiliation and has been remodeled twice in the past five years, but it continues to be Ontario's finest. All 97 rooms have been completely refurbished. Handicapped and nonsmoking rooms are available. Well-mannered pets are okay. There is a heated outdoor pool for summertime relaxing. No charge for children 18 and under. ■ *Off I-84 in Ontario;(503) 889-8621; 1249 Tapadera Ave, Ontario, OR 97914; $$; AE, DC, DIS, MC, V; checks OK.* ♿

BURNS

The town of Burns, once the center of impressive cattle kingdoms ruled by legendary figures Pete French and William Hanley, is a welcome oasis in this desolate high-desert country. The look of the land, formed by 10 million years of volcanic activity, was branded on the American consciousness in a few decades by the thousands of Western movies filmed in the area.

Malheur National Wildlife Refuge, 37 miles south on Route 205, is one of the country's major bird refuges—184,000 acres of verdant marshland and lakes. It is an important stop for migrating waterfowl in spring and fall, and the summer breeding grounds for magnificent sandhill cranes, trumpeter swans, and many other birds; (503) 493-2612.

RESTAURANTS

Pine Room Cafe ★ The Oltman family now operates this pleasant cafe, and they've kept the same faithful clientele once fed by the Kinders for 30 years. Careful preparations and interesting recipes are the reason: the chicken livers in brandy and wine sauce are different and popular, and the Oltmans still refuse to give out the secret ingredients of their German potato-dumpling soup, a local favorite. They also make their own bread and cut their own steaks in the kitchen. ▪ *On Monroe and Egan; (503) 573-6631; 543 W Monroe St, Burns; $$; full bar; MC, V; local checks only; dinner Tues-Sat.* ᕫ

LODGINGS

Best Western Ponderosa With 52 rooms, this is the preferred place to stay in Burns. It's blessed with a swimming pool to cool you off after a hot day's drive. What more? Pets are okay. ▪ *Hwy 20; (503) 573-2047; 577 W Monroe, Burns, OR 97720; $; AE, DC, DIS, MC, V; no checks.* ᕫ

DIAMOND

LODGINGS

Diamond Hotel Except for the new paint on the Diamond Hotel (and a couple of trucks parked out front) you might mistake Diamond for a ghost town. Its six residents keep the looming ghosts at bay. In 1991, Judy and Jerry Santillie, formerly of the Frenchglen Hotel, remodeled this building and opened it to those exploring Malheur territory. It now quintuples as hotel, general store, deli, post office and—late in the afternoon—local watering hole. The five small bedrooms upstairs share two baths and a sitting area on both floors. The Santillies have lived in the area for seven years and are filled with high-desert stories. Judy used to be a ranch cook (there's always meat, potatoes, vegetables, salad, bread). A platter of tenderloin comes with slabs for every taste from well-done to "so rare that a good vet could get it back up on its feet." Desserts (perhaps a marionberry cobbler with ice cream or Judy's Guadalupe River Bottom Cake) are double, no triple, the size you need them to be—and that's okay with us. ▪ *12 miles east of Hwy 205; (503) 493-1898; Box 10, Diamond, OR 97722; $; beer and wine; MC, V; checks OK; breakfast, dinner every day for hotel guests only.*

FRENCHGLEN

The flooding around Harney Lake kept tourists away from this beautiful little town (population 15) a few years back, but now, happily, the highway is above water and tourists are once again stopping in while touring Malheur (see Burns introduction) or to spy Steens Mountain, Frenchglen's biggest tourist attraction. It rises gently from the west to an elevation of 9,670 feet, then drops sharply to the Alvord Desert in the east. A dirt road goes all the way to the ridge top (summers only), and another skirts this massive escarpment (an adventurous day trip by the vast borax wastelands of the once Alvord Lake, numerous hot springs, and fishing lakes near the northeastern end of the route). Neither route is recommended if there's been much precipitation. Geologically, Steens forms the world's largest block fault, created by volcanic lava flows and glacial action.

LODGINGS

Frenchglen Hotel ★ A small, white frame building that dates back to 1916 has eight small, plain bedrooms upstairs with shared baths, renting for about $40 a night; room 2 is the largest, nicest, and the only one with a view of Steens. Nothing's very square or level here, and that's part of the charm. Downstairs are a large screened-in verandah and the dining room. The current manager, John Ross, will cook up good, simple meals for guests and drop-by visitors. Ranch-style dinner is one seating only (6:30pm sharp) and reservations are a must. But if you miss dinner, John won't let you go hungry (this is ranch country and there's usually leftovers). ▪ *60 miles south of Burns; (503) 493-2825; General Delivery, Frenchglen, OR 97736; $; beer and wine; MC, V; checks OK; breakfast, lunch, dinner every day (closed mid-Nov through mid-Feb).*

WASHINGTON

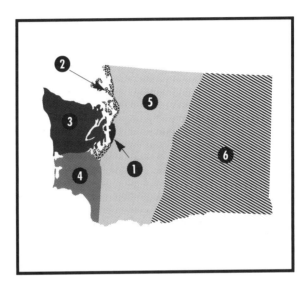

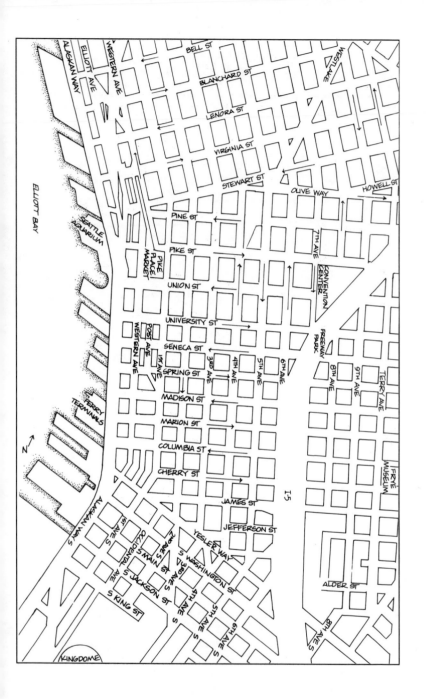

Seattle and Environs

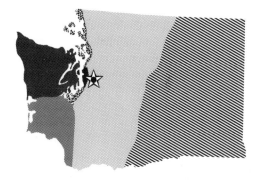

Including Edmonds and Bothell to the north; Woodinville, Redmond, Kirkland, Bellevue, Mercer Island, and Issaquah to the east; Bainbridge Island to the west; and Tukwila, Burien, Des Moines, and Kent to the south.

SEATTLE

In the past few years, the entire nation turned its eyes on this far corner of the United States. National polls voted it the best city for just about everything, housing prices were still competitive, hit TV series were filmed in nearby towns, and it was one of the few places in the country left unscathed by the recession. With all this attention (and the resulting immigrants from all over the country) the Emerald City has lost a little of its sparkle—traffic is getting more congested, the skyline is cluttered with major new buildings, and layoffs at Boeing suggest that the national financial woes are catching up with us.

Still, the city is a nothing less than a gem, with its striking views of Puget Sound and the Olympic Mountains to the west, the Cascades to the east, and Mount Rainier looming south. The up side of this rapid growth and international sophistication is outstanding restaurants, thriving cultural organizations, fine sports, and fabulous citywide festivals. The Seattle area supports such abundance because it has a highly educated population dedicated to making it work, a surplus of singles, lots of young families (determined to make it a kids' place), and a climate as temperate in weather as it is tolerant in politics. Add to this one of the largest universities in the West, and you can see why the populace has a striving, bettering cast of mind.

THE ARTS

Music. Seattle Opera has entered the big leagues with productions of often stunning brilliance. The Seattle Symphony, under conductor Gerard Schwartz, maintains a high level of consistency and artistic acclaim. Chamber music has become a local passion, with the Seattle Chamber Music Festival (at bucolic Lakeside School) taking center stage during the summer; the Early Music Guild, the Northwest Chamber Orchestra, the Ladies Musical Club, and the International Chamber Music Series at Meany Hall round out the winter and spring seasons. Summer's popular Seattle International Music Festival (formerly the Santa Fe Chamber Music Festival) is expanding its repertoire to include orchestral and vocal performances.

Theater. This is the city's strongest cultural card, with a dozen professional theaters and twice as many small groups producing a good deal of quality work. The Seattle Repertory Theatre mounts classics and contemporary fare with the highest production values (October through May). A Contemporary Theatre (ACT) excels at modern drama in an intimate space (May through November); the Empty Space, in new Fremont digs, has a national reputation for new works, crazy comedies, and classics (October through July); Intiman is the place for classics and some more adventurous works (May through December); the Group Theatre (now housed in Seattle Center) is the city's only theater with a strong ethnic approach; and finally, LOFT (League of Fringe Theaters) maintains a telephone hotline providing up-to-date information on what's happening across the fast-moving fringe scene.

Dance. Pacific Northwest Ballet has evolved into a company of national stature; its regular season mixes Balanchine masterworks with new pieces, and at Christmas is a breathtaking *Nutcracker* with sets by Maurice Sendak. World Dance and On the Boards present touring companies.

Visual Arts. The new Seattle Art Museum, designed by Robert Venturi, is by now an established part of the downtown skyline, with Jonathan Borofsky's *Hammering Man* towering beside it. The downtown building on University Street between First and Second avenues houses the museum's permanent collections, and the Volunteer Park branch is closed for remodeling. The Henry Art Gallery at UW mounts thoughtful and challenging shows. The main art galleries—and it's a very good scene—are found predominantly in the Pioneer Square area; gallery openings are the first Thursday of every month.

There are more than 1,000 works of art on public display in the city (due in part to a city ordinance calling for 1 percent of capital improvement funds to be spent on public art); for a free map to these places, call the Seattle Arts Commission, (206)684-7171.

OTHER THINGS TO DO

Nightlife. There are clubs all over town, but Seattle's music scene is centered around two neighborhoods: Pioneer Square offers various acts, from jazz to rock 'n' roll, and Ballard brings in the blues, as well as traditional and new folk music. The jazz scene is often very good, especially at Dimitriou's Jazz Alley, one of the West Coast's nicest jazz clubs. There are good coffeehouses on Captitol Hill and in the University District; the alternative music scene is found in clubs primarily in the Denny Regrade.

Exhibits. The Woodland Park Zoo is a world leader in naturalistic displays, particularly the uncannily open African savannah and the exotic Asian elephant forest. The Museum of Flight, south of the city, is notable for its sophisticated design and impressive collection. Pacific Science Center, with a planetarium and revolving displays on all sorts of subjects, graces Seattle Center, the legacy of the 1962 World's Fair; there is a decent aquarium on the waterfront; and at the Hiram M. Chittenden Locks in Ballard, where ships are lifted to Lake Washington, salmon climb the ladders on their way to spawn.

Parks. Seattle's horticultural climate is among the finest in the world—damp and mild all year—so the parks are spectacular and numerous. The Washington Park Arboretum, with 5,500 species of plants and gentle pathways amid azaleas, is the loveliest; Discovery Park, with grassy meadows and steep sea cliffs, is the wildest; Green Lake, with its 2.8-mile running-walking-skating track, is by far the most active. Freeway Park, built over I-5 downtown, is the most urban.

Sports. The town is football-mad, which means there are hardly any tickets (test your concierge's powers). The UW Huskies, usually contenders, play in one of the land's most beautiful stadiums, with arrival by boat a local custom; the Seahawks lift the roof off the drab Kingdome. The SuperSonics are playing great basketball in the Coliseum; the UW women's basketball team is very strong; and Seattle's baseball team, the Mariners, is on an upswing in the ill-suited Dome.

Shopping. The downtown area has designer-name stores, plus some excellent full-line department stores, and Westlake Center, a glossy mall smack in the middle of the downtown congestion, across from Nordstrom's headquarters store. Of the specialty shopping areas, we favor the Pike Place Market (for foodstuffs), Capitol Hill (for funky clothes and furnishings), the U District (for books), and Pioneer Square (for fine arts and crafts).

Transportation. The Metro bus is free in downtown's commercial core; otherwise the fare is 85 cents within the city ($1.10 during peak hours) and $1.10 if you cross the city line ($1.60 peak). Another common commute is on Washington State ferries, which cross Puget Sound to various destinations frequently. Riding the ferries also happens to be one of the most enjoyable ways to view the city's skyline.

RESTAURANTS

Dahlia Lounge ★★★★ The Dahlia Lounge has become, for many locals and out-of-towners, synonymous with the Seattle food scene. Many of us learned about Northwest foods from kitchen maverick Tom Douglas, and grew accustomed to his bold juxtaposition of cultures within a meal, indeed within a plate. His greatest strength remains in marrying the substance and satisfaction of home cooking with a world-ranging artfulness so clever the very plate seems to be winking. To wit: charred sashimi-grade tuna served with pasta puttanesca. Hoisin barbecued salmon with fried rice. Homemade gnocchi with arugula. Roast duck with green peppercorn sauce and butternut squash risotto. In Douglas' world, the fun with food never seems to end. Any problems (a rarity) are artfully righted by the ever-gracious waitstaff (Douglas manages to find the city's most intelligent waiters). The Dahlia's scenic appeal lies in a stylish landscape of vermilion and gold and brocade (and papier-mâché fish lamps between the booths)—and the stylish landscape on your plate. Don't hesitate to finish your meal with the ethereal pear tart, and chat with Douglas if he comes by. ■ *4th Ave between Stewart and Virginia; (206) 682-4142; 1904 4th Ave, Seattle; $$; full bar; AE, DC, DIS, MC, V; checks OK; lunch Mon-Fri, dinner every day.* &

Fullers (Seattle Sheraton Hotel and Towers) ★★★★ After more than a year behind the line, chef Monique Andree Barbeau has won back Fullers' fourth star. Her execution is exacting, the service top-notch and unobtrusive, and the portions surprisingly substantial. A complimentary crab-topped crostini comes moments after you're seated. For appetizers try Fullers' cured salmon with vinaigrette wild greens sandwiched between two thin, unsweetened pancakes. Or the seared, herbed sweetbreads crusted with a light sourdough covering. The appetizers and soups are both substantial enough to satisfy before dinner, but don't pass on delightful soup purées such as the cumin-infused sweet potato or the earthy wild mushroom. Throughout the meal, Barbeau displays her ability to achieve subtle combinations of sometimes very strong flavors, as in an ample serving of the most tender pork loin (devoid of any fat) touched with a superb and subtle sauce of apple brandy and blue cheese, or grilled sea scallops floating in a tangy green sea of puréed sorrel and matched with a stack of lemon fettuccine. It's nice to see a meal so well thought-out without being precious. ■ *Between Pike and Union on 6th; (206) 447-5544; 1400 6th Ave, Seattle; $$$; full bar; AE, MC, V; checks OK; lunch Mon-Fri, dinner Mon-Sat.* &

Adriatica ★★★ In an old house perched high above Lake Union is one of Seattle's most civilized dining rooms. Up two challenging flights of stairs, you will find owner and host Jim Malevitsis on hand most nights to welcome guests to their table in one of the small, elegant rooms that comprise the main eating area. Adriatica's gifted chef Nancy Flume partners her grilled herbed lamb and pork dishes with chunks of ruby red beets and silky cooked greens, and she does a turn on a simple pork and spinach sausage by serving it on a bed of braised lentils. If physically up to it, you can climb one more flight of stairs to the more casual attic bar which is an ideal spot for a pretheater meal of appetizers—a baked sweet onion intriguingly stuffed with angel-hair pasta in a truly sensational onion sauce, or hauntingly spicy prawns. And at Adriatica, only a fool would skip dessert—in fact, it's best to look at the dessert menu when you first sit down and order the rest of the meal around the sweet, whether an intricately layered pear tart or the airy chocolate espresso soufflé. Excellent wine list. ■ *Corner of Aloha and Dexter; (206) 285-5000; 1107 Dexter Ave N, Seattle; $$$; full bar; AE, DC, MC, V; checks OK; dinner every day.*

Al Boccalino ★★★ The rustic Al Boccalino is equally as good for a business get-together, a special celebration, or a meaningful dinner for two. Intoxicating drifts of herbs and garlic greet you when you enter the old brick building just off Pioneer Square. Its chic mottled mustard and raw-brick walls are accented with dark wood and stained glass; a skewed shape to the two rooms creates the desired atmosphere of intimacy and intrigue. It could be a noisy restaurant, but because the crowd here values conversation, courtesy prevails. The menu continues to feature the best of southern Italian cuisine with an expanded focus on Italy's other regions. Superb Ellensburg lamb is usually on the menu, simply prepared with tomato sauce, and aromatic with basil and brandy. The kitchen really shines with fish; one of the finest dishes imaginable is salmon strewn with sliced red onions and mushrooms and finished with fragrant dry vermouth. The local passion for pasta is addressed in several soul-satisfying ways, and risotti are excellent—risotto alla pescatora is a steaming helping flavored with a virtual ocean of tiny squid, prawns, clams, and scallops infused with tomato-basil sauce. The assorted antipasti are displayed as in restaurants in Mediterranean coastal towns. Desserts do not match the quality of the other courses; instead spend a bit more on

▼

wine. Unfortunately, at times Al Boccalino operates a touch below expectation, and sometimes there is that clubby feeling that gives all but the regulars a sense of being left out. ▪ *At Yesler and Alaskan Way; (206) 622-7688; 1 Yesler Way, Seattle; $$$; beer and wine; DC, MC, V; checks OK; dinner every day.*

Campagne (Inn at the Market) ★★★ White linen tablecloths, tiny vases of flowers and wall space dedicated to wine bottles help set the mood for country French in a very urban setting at Campagne. Located in a courtyard of Pike Place Market, the restaurant's inspiration comes from the southern reaches of France, where one lives to eat with the greatest gusto. Owner Peter Lewis surely hopes that you will do the same here. Searching for the pulse of Southwestern French cuisine, Campagne offers a deliciously rich cassoulet, one of the most typical dishes from that region. Other nightly specials reflect the day's catch, the season's offerings, and Chef Murphy's soothing inspirations. There are so many successes here, most worth the dear price you will pay. The wine list includes selections from the cellars of importer/wine guru Kermit Lynch. In homage to the night-owl French, Campagne has a wonderful late-night menu available in the bar every day until midnight. Here you will find true bistro fare (omelets, pan bagna—a crisp roasted eggplant and goat cheese sandwich—with crisscross frites, and steamed mussels). Guests at the Inn at the Market get room-service dinner from Campagne. Lucky them. ▪ *At the Inn at the Market, between Stewart and Pine on Post Alley; (206) 728-2800; 86 Pine St, Seattle; $$$; full bar; AE, DC, MC, V; no checks; lunch Mon-Sat (summers only), dinner every day (all year).* රු

Chez Shea ★★★ Chez Shea really is one of Seattle's gems at the same time it's a secret. You might walk through the Market a hundred times and not know Chez Shea is perched just above, looking out over the Sound. Climb the stairs of the Sanitary Building and, like going through the looking glass, you're in another world when you pass through the door. Dinner at Chez Shea is a prix-fixe affair, with four courses carefully chosen by Sandy Shea and realized by chef Martha McGinnis to reflect the bounty of the market stalls below (upon request, vegetarian offerings can be provided). Two- and three-course meals, which are $25 and $30 respectively, are also available. An autumn meal might begin with a roasted onion soup, smooth as silk, followed by a pumpkin risotto sprinkled with toasted pumpkin seeds and nut-brown butter. The main course could be loin of pork stuffed with wild mushrooms and hazelnuts in a sublime cider-sage sauce. Or roasted poussin (baby chicken) nestled in cranberry Yorkshire pudding with inspiring reduction sauce. Attention is paid to detail, down to the steamed baby bok choy, wonderful roasted potatoes, and a purée of celery root, parsnip, and pear. ■ *Across from the clock in Pike Place Market; (206) 467-9990; Corner Market Building, Suite 34, Seattle; $$$; beer and wine; AE, MC, V; checks OK; dinner Tues-Sun.*

Georgian Room (Four Seasons Olympic Hotel) ★★★

A pretentious space with high ceilings, huge chandeliers, and all the accoutrements of formal dining. Chef Kerry Sear has turned a meal at the Georgian Room into an elegant, innovative, and very unexpected evening: you may be surprised by a poached scallop in pear relish or crab mounded on an apple blini and moistened with tart apple cider sauce—food and *objets d'art*. A succulent tenderloin comes crowned with cherry and yellow pear tomatoes and a roasted Spanish onion. The moist Mount Baker venison is served with a vegetable onion stew. But the best way to sample Sear's talents is the three- to four-course chef's menu, complemented at each course by carefully selected wines by the glass. The chocolate mousse pyramid at dessert is a monument to the cacao bean. Private parties can reserve in the Georgette Petite room. ■ *In the Four Seasons Hotel at 4th and University; (206) 621-7889; 411 University Street, Seattle; $$$; full bar; AE, DC, MC, V; no checks; breakfast every day, lunch Mon-Sat, dinner Mon-Sat, brunch Sun.* &

Il Bistro ★★★

Through the years, Il Bistro has been a special place, a cherished refuge down a narrow cobblestone street in Pike Place Market. The intimate rooms with their low ceilings, rounded arches, and whitewashed walls are a perfect background to enjoying food, wine, and friends. The lower-level bar is a favorite spot to linger over an aperitif or share a convivial late-night supper. Owners Tom Martino and Dale Abrams have restored Il Bistro's reputation for excellent food, in no small part because of chef Dino D'Aquila, the son of the restaurant's first chef. There are always interesting-sounding specials at Il Bistro, but this is a place where many patrons know what to order before they leave home. Those having a love affair with pasta know they are going to carry on their long-term relationship with the thin ribbons of silky linguine, simply cloaked in olive oil, garlic, and wild mushrooms. Others have a sensory remembrance of the calamari saltate, tiny, tender squid in a garlicky white wine sauce. Il Bistro consistently serves one of the best racks of lamb in Seattle, and the wine selection, by the glass or bottle, is well chosen to complement the food. There is a small and excellent selection of desserts, but the pecan pie continues to be the choice of most regulars. The food deserves time; unfortunately, the service sometimes takes the leisure thing a bit too far. ■ *Just below Read All About It in Pike Place Market; (206) 682-3049; 93-A Pike St, #206, Seattle; $$$; full bar; AE, DC, MC, V; no checks; lunch Tues-Sat, dinner every day.*

Il Terrazzo Carmine ★★★ Be prepared to spend an entire evening at Il Terrazzo, for dining at Carmine Smeraldo's restaurant is an event. Not only will it take you awhile to graze through the wonderful antipasti—laid out for perusal in the entry—but watching Seattle's rich and famous dine at tables with a background of dramatic heavy European draperies provides entertainment too. You are likely to be dining cheek by jowl with politicians, famous (at least locally) attorneys, and prestigious old-money types. But that's not the biggest attraction at this comfortable restaurant. Deciding among the several unusual pastas is a feat, but it's the reduced sauces on the mostly meat entrées here that get greatest applause. Carmine's sauces have your nostrils quivering before you even taste them, and once you do, you know that his fairly young chefs have acquired the secrets of the great Italians. The wine list is extensive and includes some prime Tuscan reds found only in tiny hill villages. Prices are high, so it's not unusual to see diners sharing the unique antipasti and a couple of glasses of wine, and calling it dinner.

A more ambitious menu characterizes Smeraldo's Trattoria Carmine, 3130 E Madison Street, (206) 323-7990; so far dishes are competent but don't soar to greatness. Risotto with seafood was fine, as was duck ravioli in mushroom sauce (though salty). The place emits a polished sheen, but tables feel cramped on crowded evenings. ■ *1st and King; (206) 467-7797; 411 1st Ave S, Seattle; $$$; full bar; AE, DC, MC, V; checks OK; lunch Mon-Fri, dinner Mon-Sat.* ⅋

Italia ★★★ Italia seems to be the perfect match for chef David Lantz (formerly of Eugene, Oregon's esteemed Cafe Central), who knows how to bring out the true flavors of fresh foods. One of the most satisfying appetizers in town is his creamy polenta with a simple ragout of wild mushrooms. You'll see a similar stir of these earthy delights on tagliarini (this time with a caramelized shallot twist) and be perfectly content to eat it again. Pan-roasted duck is lightly sauced in its own reduction touched with the juice from a honey-baked pear; the salmon comes quickly pan-fried to perfection in browned butter, shallots, and thyme. And Lantz proves pumpkin is not just for November with an utterly smooth mound of pumpkin risotto studded with feta and an occasional crunch of pumpkin seeds. For dessert, the lemon-poppyseed cheesecake with a raspberry coulis appears to burst with flavors all at once. At lunch, Italia has an excellent pizza with a crackerlike crust that lets the tomato sauce and cheese take over, as well as pasta salad and other foods of that ilk. At night, the lights dim and the focus is on more serious food at very reasonable prices. On warm

The facts in this book were correct at press time, but places close, chefs depart, hours change. It's best to call ahead.

evenings, sit at the sidewalk tables and watch the horse carriages roll by. ▪ *Between Madison and Spring on Western; (206) 623-1917; 1010 Western Ave, Seattle; $$; beer and wine; AE, DC, MC, V; local checks only; lunch, dinner Mon-Sat.* ♿

Labuznik ★★★ While other chefs have followed fads and experimented with showy Mediterranean, Japanese, and nouvelle influences, Peter Cipra has stuck steadfastly by the stolid meat-and-potatoes traditions of his native Czechoslovakia. It's no surprise Cipra, concentrating on a near-changeless menu, has found the very best meats and paired them with simple preparations to parade their virtues. Diners who've known Labuznik since its inception 16 years ago have found service to be as exact and professional as ever (if tinged with hauteur). Others are pleased Cipra has relaxed his rules a bit (the limit of three entrée selections per table is sometimes waived). We admire the confidence of a chef who dares ignore color in presentation (and who never tires of carrots and spinach); the monochromatism (in both food and decor) is at once elegant and comforting. Perfection is attained in the garlic-, Dijon-, and pepper-encrusted Ellensburg lamb (you are encouraged to pick up the savory ribs with your fingers). Another flawless choice is the chateaubriand (not on the regular menu, but often a special) stuffed with mushrooms, green onions, and prosciutto, and draped with both a béarnaise sauce and a smooth vegetable-and-Madeira-based glaze. But, for the first time in a long time, small glitches hold back that fourth star. Sometimes the meats are unevenly roasted, soups can be oversalted, and salads can seem perfunctory. Perhaps Cipra's time-tested menu is getting timeworn or perhaps the Seattle dining field has matured so that Labuznik is not the glowing exception it once was. Then suddenly flaws are forgiven when a sublime side of shiitake mushrooms touched with béarnaise arrives tableside. Labuznik's wine list is an intelligent selection of some of the world's top-rated bottlings (with prices to match). The cafe in front is a bargain, relatively speaking. Skip dessert—you've already tasted the best of Cipra's talents. ▪ *On 1st between Stewart and Virginia; (206) 441-8899; 1924 1st Ave, Seattle; $$$; full bar; AE, DC, DIS, MC, V; no checks; dinner Tues-Sat.* ♿

Le Gourmand ★★★ This unprepossessing, not-quite-Ballard storefront doesn't quite fit one's image of what a lovely upscale restaurant should be, but lovely it is. Owners Robin Sanders and Bruce Naftaly have created a calm, intimate dining space, simply appointed to show off the fine French/Northwestern fare. Seasonal mushrooms, blossoms, and fish arrive daily from Naftaly's carefully chosen list of local suppliers, all to be generously embellished with his forte, sauces. Dinner here is comprised of appetizer, entrée (which carries the price of the meal), and salad (in true European style, the salad follows the

Seattle

Restaurants

▲

main course); every dish is carefully considered as to season, taste, and presentation—the entrée arrives alone, center stage, on its plate, with vegetables served in a separate dish. Depending on the time of year, you might enjoy earthy nettle soup at the beginning of your meal, or delicate leek and onion tarts crowned with juniper berries. In the main course, flounder is set off perfectly with tangy parsley butter, tender venison may be complemented by a dark elderberry and pinot noir stock, or rack of lamb may be served with homemade mustard. Finish with a wild-greens salad feathered with calendulas, nasturtiums, and rose petals. Service can be slow here, but you shouldn't be in a hurry anyway. ■ *At the corner of Market and 6th; (206) 784-3463; 425 Market St, Seattle; $$$; beer and wine; AE, MC, V; checks OK; dinner Wed-Sat.*

Nikko (Westin Hotel) ★★★ When Nikko occupied a small, slightly shabby space in the International District, it was a word-of-mouth kind of place with lots of regulars; now it's rooted in a big, easy-to-find, intensely decorated, multi-roomed space in the Westin Hotel. No matter—Nikko is in many ways the pinnacle of Japanese food in Seattle. Hiroichi Shiroyama, now the executive chef, is for the most part bearing out Nikko's culinary reputation.

Sushi, prepared behind the lively and congenial sushi bar, is impeccable. For many patrons, this is the only place to sit, and most start by asking, "What's fresh today?" It may be thin, sweet slices of flounder, fresh uni in season, or a handroll made from maguro (tuna) and yamano (mountain potato), topped with a cheerful, tiny quail egg. The less adventurous, ordering off the sushi menu, will still do well with such prizes as a salmon-skin roll and a sour-plum roll with shiso leaf, a fragrant, zen morsel. Perennial favorites in the main restaurant include black cod marinated in sake lees and then broiled to flaky perfection, or crisp soft-shelled crab. One of the most satisfying rainy-day dishes is the much-maligned sukiyaki, a soulful one-pot meal cooked at your table, or perhaps a plate of grilled thises and thats from the robata bar. Faults here are few—laughable salads (clearly a Western concession), service that's slightly below par—and pleasures are many. ■ *In the Westin Hotel at 5th and Westlake; (206) 322-4641; 1900 Fifth Ave, Seattle; $$$; full bar; AE, DC, MC, V; checks OK; lunch Mon-Fri, dinner every day.* &

Place Pigalle ★★★ Place Pigalle offers up an invigorating menu and a changing view of Puget Sound and the Olympics, perfectly framed by an old-fashioned bank of windows. Its range of intriguing dishes combines the freshness of Pike Place Market ingredients with recipes inspired by the Pacific Rim countries, India, and other regions, all filtered through the imagination of executive chef Will McNamara and the young kitchen crew who enjoy coming up with new dishes to tantalize their regular customers. The joy is that most of these innovations work well. If you can get a table by the window, a leisurely lunch is the pleasantest meal. A panoply of local crab, scallops, and prawns, plus oysters and mussels, star in the Thai seafood stew with a broth subtly enhanced with coconut milk and cilantro. A pairing of pumpkin and parsnip in a thick soup takes naturally to a curry chutney of apples. Quickly seared sea scallops are layered between crisp pappadum with red bell pepper and julienned vegetables. And don't neglect Pigalle's first-course tarts, such as the colorful pepper and mushroom one, nestled with cheese in a puff-pastry shell and just sprinkled with a tingling chile chipotle vinaigrette. For dessert, the apricot tart is a longtime favorite. On sunny days, a small crowded skyway is used by those anxious to catch every daylight ray, but the inside tables have the advantage of being in the sightline of your waitperson. The service can be inconsistent, though pleasant. ■ *81 Pike St; (206) 624-1756; Pike Place Market, Seattle; $$$; full bar; MC, V; no checks; lunch, dinner Mon-Sat.*

Ponti Seafood Grill ★★★ Tucked almost under the Fremont Bridge, Ponti has been wooing Seattle's seafood crowd with inventive yet sound preparations of the local (and not so local) harvest. It's a very sleek operation, done up in green and black and white, a place where even in Seattle most people dress up. This is the kind of place that knows the value of restraint coupled with invention: just a few shimmering slices of black pepper tuna carpaccio drizzled with soy vinaigrette before a meal. We regularly order from the specials list, and are treated with such delights as mild, meaty monkfish swimming in crayfish sauce (and sided with the most airy eggplant fritters) or tomatoey Brazilian lobster stew, earthy (with Thai essences of coconut milk and peanuts) and challenging (with a petite dollop of cilantro pesto). It's as though someone in the kitchen (in this case, Alvin Binuya) knows just how far he can go. Non-seafood entrées are treated judiciously, not as second thoughts: braised Ellensburg lamb or silky, cheesy ravioli. Service in the past has been slow and scattered, but on recent visits seemed to be improving. Eat canalside on warm evenings. ■ *Behind the Bleitz Funeral Home; (206) 284-3000; 3014 3rd Ave N, Seattle; $$$; full bar; AE, DC, MC, V; local checks only; lunch, dinner every day, brunch Sun.*

Ray's Boathouse ★★★ The peerless, unabashedly romantic vistas that one enjoys from Ray's deserve a scrupulous attention to fresh seafood to go with them— and Ray's rises to the occasion. It's a rare pick—one favored by tourists and locals alike—where the food is superior and the service still efficient and helpful (and very knowledgeable about fish). In fact, Ray's is a good place to educate yourself about seafood—about different kinds of oysters, perhaps—and what wines go well with them. In composing your meal, concentrate on the fresh items that Ray's has proven it can do: grilled rockfish splashed with white wine, capers, and lemon; meaty, slightly oily smoked black cod; scallop sauté; and several kinds of salmon (no overcooking at Ray's). The superb wine list is organized by country and varietal, with a page devoted to splits.

If the reservation wait for the dining room proves weeks long (and it well may), try the moderately priced upstairs cafe. Here the food seems more casual—fried versions of fish, sandwiches, and the like—and walk-ins are often successful. ■ *60th NW and Seaview; (206) 789-3770; 6049 Seaview Ave NW, Seattle; $$$; full bar; AE, DC, MC, V; checks OK; lunch Mon-Fri, dinner every day, lunch Sat-Sun in the cafe.* ঌ

Rover's ★★★ Chef Thierry Rautureau has created a neighborhood restaurant that reaches beyond the boundaries of any neighborhood. The semiformal setting offers quiet intimacy, and the simultaneously unobtrusive and attentive service puts you at ease. Great for a three-hour meal—never rushed (though some would prefer a more dimly lit ambience). Dinners are marvelously sauced, classically French-inspired treatments of not strictly Northwest fare. Rautureau's forte is seafood, and he's adept at finding the best quality ingredients. It may feel a tad fussy and expensive, but portions are served with a generous hand. The outstanding Columbia River sturgeon is served on a bed of ocean salad (seaweed, agar, Japanese mushrooms, sesame, rice vinegar, and white sesame seed) and complemented by a rich, fresh black truffle sauce. Rautureau's version of tiramisu is infused with a sweet hint of goat cheese. Wines are carefully chosen from the Northwest and France, with many half-bottles available (a good way to match different wines with each course). Or try a five-course feast: the *menu dégustation*, Rautureau's masterpiece for a fixed price (vegetarian versions available). Wonderful on a summer night when you can linger over your meal in the enclosed garden courtyard. ■ *1½ blocks from the Arboretum at 28th and Madison; (206) 325-7442; 2808 E Madison St, Seattle; $$$; beer and wine; AE, DC, MC, V; checks OK; dinner Tues-Sat.*

Saleh al Lago ★★★ Some think Saleh Joudeh, a Syrian who studied medicine in the central Italian city of Perugia, puts out some of the best Italian food in Seattle. There's little to fault here. Service is completely competent and politely distant. Wineglasses are filled immediately when emptied. And the food, if your arteries can handle it, is simply wonderful. Recently, he's scaled down a few of his pasta dishes to appetizer status, giving diners the chance to try, for example, his sumptuous ravioli al burro nero (pasta stuffed with ricotta and spinach, with rich brown garlic sauce) without committing themselves to a full dinner of it. Risotto, a dish that's extremely difficult (and time consuming) to make is done to chewy perfection in any number of ways, perhaps with a rich red sauce and bits of filet mignon, or arugula and Gorgonzola. Or try the veal medallions, either sautéed with mushrooms or in a dense, delicate quattro formaggi. You may feel transported back in time, especially as you see Joudeh go from table to table, shaking hands and greeting friends in the way of the old-boy restaurant. ■ *On the east side of Green Lake; (206) 524-4044; 6804 E Green Lake Way N, Seattle; $$$; full bar; AE, MC, V; local checks only; lunch Mon-Fri, dinner Mon-Sat.* &

Szmania's ★★★ This restaurant's sleek contemporary style initially looked out of sync with the folksy family-style village of Magnolia, but a few years and many loyal patrons later, Szmania has become a respected neighbor. In fact, some cite Ludger and Julie Szmania's restaurant as being the primary catalyst behind the recent gentrification of the block—if not the village itself. Ludger has proven that the Pacific Rim is not the only cuisine whose influence melds well with Northwest ingredients. Portions are large (even the appetizers seem generous). One starter consisted of walnut Gorgonzola ravioli with a nutty basil cream sauce. The honest salads are large, judiciously dressed, and on certain nights free with your entrée (Ludger's even been bottling his own dressing). Ludger successfully pulls off stunts such as minted mashed potatoes that work wonderfully, especially when accompanied by grilled beef tenderloin with roasted-garlic sauce, or roasted pheasant with a dark cherry sauce and spaetzle very smooth and cheesy yet just crunchy on top, a variation on sauerkraut on the side, and some veggies. The standby dessert is the three little pots de crème (raspberry, Kahlua, and vanilla), but if the citrus white chocolate cheesecake is anywhere near the menu, order it. ■ *34th Ave W and McGraw; (206) 284-7305; 3321 W McGraw St, Seattle; $$; full bar; MC, V; checks OK; lunch Mon-Sat, dinner every day.* &

Union Bay Cafe ★★★ Part local hangout, part destination restaurant, this comfortable Laurelhurst storefront offers seasonal fare in a low-key setting. Chef/owner Mark Manley is likely to leave his open kitchen to wander among the linen-topped tables, welcoming guests and discussing dishes. The ever-changing menu is small and trenchant; performance never wavers. Usually there's a calamari, a crostini, and some sort of grilled vegetable on the starter list. On a recent visit we began with a plate of steamed mussels, slyly sweetened with mango, and a serving of marvelously delicate handmade bell pepper pasta stuffed richly with smoked chicken and cheeses. To follow: exquisitely grilled pork tenderloin in a sage and Madeira

▼
▲

sauce, with a plate of canneloni yielding pecans here, Gorgonzola there. Fresh fish and seasonal produce are well respected in this kitchen; the menu has vegetarian options at every meal; a reasonable wine list offers first-rate choices by the glass. For dessert—anything, from the bread pudding to the dense chocolate mocha mousse. The bill is the final (unexpected) pleasure—a delectable splurge for just $60. ▪ *2 blocks east of University Village; (206) 527-8364; 3505 NE 45th St, Seattle; $$; beer and wine; AE, DC, DIS, MC, V; checks OK; dinner Tues-Sun.*

Wild Ginger ★★★ The passionate eater will revel in Wild Ginger's classic Sichuan rendition of fragrant crispy duck. With chopsticks, pull off some spicy skin and meat, dip one end in the plum sauce or seasoned salt, enclose it in a warm fold of steamed bread, and then bite in. A sensuous delight. Chinese food is only a part of the eclectic culinary experience to be shared at Wild Ginger. Just as the restaurants and markets of Bangkok, Singapore, Saigon, and Djakarta offer a wide range of multiethnic foods, so does this restaurant bring together some of the best dishes from these Southeast Asian cities. At the polished mahogany satay bar, you order from a wide array of sizzling, skewered selections: simple seared slices of sweet onion and Chinese eggplant, or large gingery coconut sweet prawns. This eating station blends together with the booths, tables, and regular bar into one room that always seems filled with people. There are succulent Singapore-style stir-fried crab, fresh from live tanks, and now redolent with ginger, garlic, and spicy black beans; mildly hot, slightly sweet beef curry from Thailand; and an Indonesian lamb curry. Here at Wild Ginger are the soft, crunchy, and slippery textures and the hot, sour, sweet, and salty flavors of Southeast Asia, all to be combined and eaten in friendly family-style with a bowl of rice. ▪ *1 block east of the waterfront on the corner of Western and Union; (206) 623-4450; 1400 Western Ave, Seattle; $$; full bar; AE, DC, MC, V; checks OK; lunch Mon-Sat, dinner every day.* ఉ

Arrowhead Cafe ★★ Inside this arrowhead of a building is one of the freshest spots around: an upbeat come-as-you-are restaurant/bar serving tantalizing morsels of the Southwest. It isn't perfect—the Navajo fry-bread can be greasy, the margaritas weak—but it's full of an irresistible, imaginative spirit. Fruit is used here in all sorts of unusual ways, from a Saturday breakfast side of mild apple sausage to a surprisingly good watermelon salad drizzled with raspberry purée and walnut oil and sprinkled with black pepper and red onions. (In winter, it's pears and onions.) The menu proceeds through a litany of fish (one recently sampled was blacktip shark with spicy fruit salsa), chicken (stuffed with goat cheese, perhaps, or served with a chile-corn sauce), salads (a nice selection), and standards, including cheeseburgers. Brunch at the Arrowhead is wonderful, with warm light refracting off butter-colored walls and a plate full of chorizo scramble before you. Service is tireless and ebullient. ■ *On Westlake across from Franco's Hidden Harbor; (206) 283-8768; 1515 Westlake Ave N, Seattle; $$; full bar; MC, V; checks OK; lunch every day, dinner Tue-Sat, brunch Sat-Sun.* &

Asuka ★★ In Jun Miwa's downtown location, you'll find superior sushi, private tatami rooms, and a skyline view of the city. Classic Japanese dishes are augmented by more unusual lobster arrangements. Provided you have ordered a day in advance you can be served omakase, a multicourse "chef's choice" dinner. The food is very subtle and quite good, though the prices are particularly high. The decor is especially beautiful, with the private, rice paper-paneled dining rooms prefabricated in Japan. It makes an elegant place for consummating business deals in the Japanese manner. Service is best midweek. In summer, sit outside in the pretty courtyard. ■ *2nd and Madison;(206) 682-8050; 1000 2nd Ave, Seattle; $$$; full bar; AE, MC, V; no checks; lunch, dinner Mon-Fri.* &

Ayutthaya ★★ This Capitol Hill fave attracts a mixed clientele: couples in their finery, young families, and savvy businesspeople. Soft pastel colors and clean, smooth lines create a calming antidote to the fiery food, which is prepared carefully and authentically by the Fuangaromya family (members of which also own Thai Restaurant on lower Queen Anne). It's good to make reservations, since there's little waiting room. The showy seafood is excellent—perhaps a sizzling platter of shrimp spiked with basil, chile, and garlic that's a show in itself. With the exception of the fried noodles (too sweet), everything is good: Naked Bathing Rama; a Thai meat-and-potato dish called massaman beef in a toned-down curry sauce; exceptionally delicate grilled chicken in coconut milk. Local businesspeople are catching on to the best lunch deal in town, so arrive early to avoid crowds. Service is patient and sweet, and the only thing smoking here is the food. ■ *1 block west of Broadway at Harvard and Pike; (206) 324-8833; 727 E Pike St, Seattle; $; beer and wine; AE, MC, V; no checks; lunch Mon-Fri, dinner Mon-Sat.*

Botticelli Cafe ★★ This very polished, very Italian four-table aperitif bar is a place to linger over one of Seattle's finest espressos or irresistible panini—delectable sandwiches assembled with such fine ingredients as artichoke hearts, fontina cheese, and sweet red peppers on grilled focaccia bread, drizzled with good olive oil. If you so much as peek in the door, you might be coaxed in by Angelo Belgrano and expected to stay awhile. Even if he's not there, the excellent sandwiches are enough of a draw. Expect exceptional quality and freshness. Espresso, fresh fruit ices, and Italian mineral waters for sipping. ■ *Corner*

of 1st and Stewart; (206) 441-9235; 101 Stewart St, Seattle; $; no alcohol; no credit cards; checks OK; breakfast, lunch Mon-Sat. &

Brad's Swingside Cafe ★★ In its most recent guise, the tiny Swingside in funky Fremont is an amiable place where Brad Inserra (along with Bryant Bader in the kitchen) dreams in colors Italian with playful accents. Some dishes, while labeled North African or Cajun, owe as much in inspiration to Sicily or to world-beat cuisine: chunks of Ellensburg lamb in Moroccan stew, gumbo filé over basmati rice, a voluptuous kitchen sink of a Mediterranean shellfish stew vibrant with sage and red pepper, served over linguine. And bagna cauda, the classic hot bath of olive oil, butter, and anchovies in which raw and blanched vegetables are cooked and snatched out piping hot. There's a tangible mix of fun and real cooking here—the Swingside's not a place for the grand occasions of life, but for that night, any night, when you're hungry and crave something satisfying. ■ *Across from the Buckaroo Tavern at 43rd and Fremont; (206) 633-4057; 4212 Fremont N, Seattle; $$; beer and wine; MC, V; local checks OK; brunch Sat-Sun, dinner Tues-Sat.*

Cafe Flora ★★ Cafe Flora, the new vegetarian mecca in Madison Valley, emerged out of a whole slew of broad cultural drifts: the new multiculturalism, a mystical fascination with the American Southwest, an emphasis on responsible global stewardship, and a fervid righteousness about health. And it seems to have caught on. Rustic country-style pâté is not as ordinary as it sounds, but is made of seitan (a wheat-gluten substitute for meat), pistachios, bourbon, roasted garlic, herbs, and currants, and served with sautéed cabbage, brussels sprouts, and cranberry sauce, and nary a goose liver in sight. The problem here is resisting the temptation to try everything—regulars work their way systematically through the menu. Enchiladas—not quite what you expect—are filled with crimini mushrooms, leeks, smoked mozzarella, and a variety of winter squash; and the curried cauliflower is served with basmati rice, pear-ginger chutney, and black-pepper dumplings (nondairy, of course). It's food that appeals to vegetarians and carnivores alike. Recent desserts—especially lemon mousse—have been spectacular. ■ *28th and Madison; (206) 325-9100; 2901 E Madison, Seattle; $$; no alcohol; MC, V; checks OK; lunch Tues-Fri, dinner Tues-Sat, brunch Sat-Sun.* &

Cafe Lago ★★ Montlake's rustic Italian cafe with its flaming brick oven is reminiscent of trattorias that dot the hills of Tuscany. The menu is small but changes every three days, and all the ingredients are fresh; even the pasta is handmade. The pizzas are original and some, such as the Pizza Caprino (goat cheese, red onion, garlic, and herbs), win raves. As do the ravioli stuffed with spinach, raisins, and walnuts in a Roquefort and mascarpone sauce, and one of the best antipasti plates in the city. Ever since Carla Leonardi and Jordi Viladas doubled the size of their well-intentioned restaurant, we've received mixed reviews. Some say the extra space has taken the pressure off the employees (and you don't have to feel guilty lingering just a little longer). Others complain that the place has lost a little of its spark, especially where service is concerned. But the brick oven is warm, the neighborhood welcoming, and the energy that goes into the menu admirable. We just love Lago, but we're holding on to that third star until service gets its act together.

- *On 24th Ave E, 6 blocks south of Hwy 520; (206) 329-8005; 2305 24th E, Seattle; $$; wine and beer; AE, MC, V; checks OK; dinner Tues-Sun.* &

Chau's Chinese Restaurant ★★ The decor here isn't much to speak of, but some insist that Yick Chau serves up the best Cantonese seafood this side of the Far East, taking advantage of the Northwest's abundant selection of undersea edibles. Friendly and knowledgeable staff help you wade through the menu, perhaps suggesting instead that you order the specials—a good idea. This may result in asparagus tossed with sea scallops, garlic, black mushrooms, and carrots in sesame-soy sauce (tender yet crunchy, scallops not overcooked) or a deliciously fruity but not sweet mango chicken. Geoduck with ginger-soy-scallion dipping sauce can be wonderful. Chau's grinds its own curry—commendable—but stay away from beef dishes, as they're often overcooked, fatty, or grisly. Chau's is amenable to large groups: a 10-course seafood banquet can cost as little as $15 per person (in a room that accommodates up to 80 people). It's near the Kingdome, so parking can be a hassle on a game night. Open late. *4th and Jackson; (206) 621-0006; 310 4th Ave S, Seattle; $; beer and wine; MC, V; no checks; lunch Mon-Fri, dinner every day.* &

El Puerco Lloron ★★ This place transports you back to that cafe in Tijuana, the one with the screaming hot pink and aquamarine walls and the bent, scarred "Cerveza Superior" tables. Remember the wailing jukebox and the cut-tin lamps and the woman quietly making corn tortillas by the door? It's all here. Belly up to the cafeteria line, put in your order (dishes run a paltry $4-$5), and fight for a table—in clement weather those outdoor ones are as hard to get as parking spots. One eater's favorite is the taquitos plate, three excellent masa corn tortillas rolled around a filling and served with rice, beans, and a scallion. And the chiles rellenos, so often bungled by American chefs, are fresh and bright with flavor. At the end of the counter you pick up fresh lemonade or a Mexican beer. This is also where you add the fire to your gently spiced dishes—a zippy carrot-and-pepper pickle or a lethal red tomato salsa. *On the Pike Place Market Hillclimb; (206) 624-0541; 1501 Western*

Ave, Seattle; $; beer and wine; AE, MC, V; no checks; lunch, dinner every day.

Hunt Club (Sorrento Hotel) ★★ The Hunt Club, along with Fullers and the Georgian Room, remains in the bold forefront of good, even excellent, hotel dining. This restaurant, warmed with burnished mahogany paneling and deep red bricks, is still pleasant, especially on a rainy Seattle evening. New executive chef Christine Keff is a worthy successor to the much-lauded Barbara Figueroa and sports an excellent restaurant pedigree of her own. Our early visits suggest that she is certainly capable, if sometimes hesitant with seasonings. Tiny unexpected treats, such as bite-size crostini spread with nut-rich Romesco, arrive gratis before the appetizers. You may start your meal with crab cakes, the city's creamy best, or a silken cold-cured halibut with the slightest essence of juniper and gin. Some of Keff's pairings are welcomely bold, as in a lovely chunk of foie gras surrounded by creamed lentils (when was the last time you saw lentils in a fine restaurant?). Keff's menu features hunterly meats and robust fishes—fillet of beef, Muscovy duck, tuna, Portuguese fisherman's stew—but not all of them shine in the final execution (though you can't go wrong with rack of lamb, whatever its guise). While we've enjoyed many of her creations, a recent sturgeon roulades appetizer was pretty but tasteless, an entrée of grilled pheasant with risotto was perfectly cooked but drastically undersauced. Service is stellar, the food is good, but until Keff settles in a bit, we'll withhold the third star.

After dinner, savvy patrons retire to the lobby bar for coffee and dessert—fascinating, innovative homemade ices or something indulgently creamy from pastry chef (with our favorite pastry-chef name) Steven Whippo. ■ *Madison and Terry; (206) 343-6156; 900 Madison St, Seattle; $$$; full bar; AE, DC, MC, V; checks OK; breakfast, lunch, tea, dinner every day, brunch Sat-Sun.* &

Huong Binh ★★ Lately there seems to be a new Vietnamese restaurant opening every week. This tidy one, on the busy commercial corner of 12th and Jackson, was booming (both in take-out and eat-in) from the day it opened. It's that good. We've had feasts here, huge brimming tables-full, for under $20. One such: banh beo (steamed rice cake topped with brilliant orange ground shrimp), cha hue (a pâtélike steamed pork roll), bahn hoi chao tom (grilled shrimp on sugar cane—hint to novices: you eat the shrimp, then suck the cane), and a couple of dishes starring pork and shrimp skewers with rice. Shrimp isn't their forte—it's often tough—but pork is particularly nicely done: tender, pounded thin, and marinated in garlic and lemon grass. Best, these grilled dishes come in traditional Vietnamese fashion with an accompanying fragrant garden of herbs, to allow

▼
Seattle

Restaurants

▲

you to spice your food to your liking. No matter if you're unfamiliar: Huong Binh's owners are genuinely interested in making you feel at home with their cuisine. They're also genuinely tolerant of children. ■ *At S Jackson and 12th; (206) 720-4907; 1207 S Jackson St, Seattle; $; beer and wine; no credit cards; checks OK; lunch every day.* &

I Love Sushi ★★ The name of the restaurant belongs on a bumper sticker, but head chef Tadashi Sato has created a pair of premier sushi bars on either side of Lake Washington. Both feature bustling, high-energy sushi bars with exquisitely fresh fish. There are traditional (and more expensive) Japanese dishes, such as sea urchin, fermented bean paste, and crunchy coated herring, but this is the place to coax non-sushi eaters into giving it a bite. Sato-san will start them off with a California roll that sneaks in crab and smelt eggs along with avocado and cucumber. Then he might graduate them to a terrific spicy tuna roll, the "I Love Roll," with eel, shrimp, and flying-fish eggs, or the artful "Spider Roll," which comes with the legs of soft-shell crabs sticking out from the top like synchronized swimmers. Hot dishes are also excellent, including flame-broiled fish cheeks, and chawan mushi, a steamed custard egg soup that is the ultimate in Japanese comfort food. If you stick around until 10:30pm, the karaoke bar starts up. There's not much of a nonsmoking section at the Lake Union restaurant. ■ *On the Yale St Landing off Fairview; (206) 625-9604; 1001 Fairview Ave N, Seattle; $$$; full bar; AE, MC, V; no checks; lunch Mon-Sat, dinner every day.* ■ *NE 8th St and 118th Ave NE; 11818 NE 8th St, Bellevue; (206) 454-5706; $$; V, MC; no checks; full bar; lunch Mon-Sat, dinner Mon-Sun.* &

India Cuisine ★★ Your mouth will water just reading the menu, and the food delivers. Start with a mixed appetizer platter—a little of this and a little of that, including a generous sampling of deep-fried, battered veggies. It comes with a colorful trio of chutneys that tingle the taste buds—sprightly mint-coriander, spicy cumin-carrot, and a heavy sweet tamarind. Then try seekh kebab, beef minced with ginger, garlic, and green chiles, molded on a sword half a man tall and seared in a clay tandoor, or okra masala—tender, slippery okra chunks in a gingered tomato sauce. Sop up the sauces with pillows of fragrant, parslied nan glistening with butter. Go for lunch—you'll eat well for under $4 if you skip the meat. ■ *N 45th and Wallingford Ave; (206) 632-5307; 1718 N 45th St, Seattle; $; full bar; MC, DC; checks OK; lunch Mon-Sat, dinner every day.*

Kaspar's ★★ Kaspar Donier, who came to Seattle a few years ago from Vancouver's Four Seasons, is an imaginative coupler of classic international cooking styles with fresh Northwest ingredients, and the best of the results can be astonishing. We've had marvelous Northwest mushrooms, set off in a sampler with creamy risotto and piquant peanut sauce; a delectable serving of boneless quail with sage stuffing and potato crisps with merlot butter; a moist pork tenderloin with bacon and port-soaked prunes which was at once fruity, tangy, and smoky. Crab and salmon hash-cakes with a silky mushroom sauce are a revelation for crab-cake fans, or try ratatouille-filled wonton ravioli with jumbo garlic prawns (prawns are handled nicely here). Plates are artfully arrayed, and side dishes—shredded carrots and ginger, for instance—are not forgotten. Bum dishes are few but memorable, as a recent run-in with a tough braised lamb shank attests, and servers could work on their polish. Always there is that backdrop, however—the whole glittering spread of Elliott Bay, as seen from this sophisticated room atop a Belltown office building—and desserts have consistently revealed the deft hand of a classical pro. ■ *1st and Cedar; (206) 441-4805; 2701 1st Ave, Seattle; $$; full bar; AE, MC, V; no checks; dinner Mon-Sat.* &

La Buca ★★ Rustic to its wooden beams in the manner of an Italian country house, this brick-walled basement restaurant is manned by the most visible front man in town, the voluble Luigi DeNunzio, who welcomes each guest as if he were the Italian lord of the manor. Most of the time, the inventive food is worthy of the welcome. Stunning starters include squid sautéed with garlic, tomatoes, raisins, and pine nuts, or a plate of French beans sautéed with smoky pancetta in a creamy Gorgonzola sauce. Entrées include pastas, risottos, meats, and chops; lamb is treated particularly respectfully. In one dish, tender disks of Ellensburg lamb are swathed in a silken sauce of port and figs, lightly marked with rosemary, and scattered with crumbs of Gorgonzola. Such meals are three-star excellent, but not every meal has been: chicken can arrive overcooked, pasta lukewarm. That and schizophrenic service compel us to withhold the third star and hold out for more consistency (especially on Luigi's day off)—by revisiting frequently. ■ *1st and Cherry; (206) 343-9517; 102 E Cherry, Seattle; $$; beer and wine; AE, MC, V; local checks only; lunch Mon-Fri, dinner every day.*

Mamounia ★★ We're happy to announce that this Moroccan restaurant is back in full force. It's a complete-immersion course in the cuisine, a long leisurely feast in a desert tent where you sit comfortably on the floor and eat with your hands (right hand preferred). The staff carefully guides you through the strange territory (with a sense of humor when warranted), offering bread from the big basket in the middle of the room, washing your hands for you before and after the meal, and pouring your tea from a standing position into your glass two feet below. Each dinner starts with harira (Moroccan lentil soup), followed by eggplant and tomato salad, and a lovely bastilla—a chicken, egg, and pistachio pastry in flaky dough, topped with cinnamon and sugar—an unusually perfect synthesis of flavors. Then come the entrées, a whole slew of them if you order the chef's special, which we recommend if you're in a group. You'll be tearing into fragrant meats and sauces—couscous with lamb, lemon chicken, lamb in honey sauce, hare with paprika. If there's any room left, you'll nibble on a honey pastry and wash it down with tea. Ramble slowly through your dinner and try not to fill up too fast, since there are no doggie bags here. Not for vegetarians or the terminally uptight. ■ *At E Olive and Denny; (206) 329-3886; 1556 E Olive Way, Seattle; $; beer and wine; MC, V; checks OK; dinner Tues-Sun.* &

Maple Leaf Grill ★★ This neighborhood haunt has become as much a destination restaurant as a local watering hole. It's not just northeast Seattleites mingling over burgers and beer or chicken and white wine, but folks from all over, who've heard tell of a marvelous chef (known simply as "Rip") and his skill in the kitchen. Everyone's comfortable in this Depression-era bar with lots of old wood, nine local brews on tap, a couple of TVs with the game on and the volume turned down, and Ry Cooder on the stereo. The menu lists the good burgers and the turkey sandwich (served with Yakima gouda), while a blackboard heralds the evening's specials, which have achieved a sort of local acclaim: a rabbit and pork pâté appetizer (a huge slice, more than enough for two), the spicy Rocker's Iko (an ample seafood stew). The menu seems to know what our collective appetite hankers for: fresh, timeless eats tweaked with the chic of chipotle chiles, cilantro vinaigrette, and mangoes. If occasionally a dish falls flat (a too-bitter soup of seasonal greens and ravioli, a pasta dish without great harmony), it seems to be affected more by honest curiosity about what foods work together than by carelessness. Best of all, this food is fairly priced. Reservations aren't a bad idea. ■ *89th and Roosevelt; (206) 523-8449; 8909 Roosevelt Way NE, Seattle; $$; beer and wine; MC, V; checks OK; lunch Mon-Fri, dinner Mon-Sat.* &

Panda's ★★ The sight of steaming pot-sticker dumplings, plates of rich orange beef, and sautéed eggplant in a spicy sauce has been known to tempt customers into ordering too much here. However, the skillful floorstaff will be happy to suggest the best dishes that night (and will try to cut you off if you're ordering too much). It's hard to go wrong with the extensive menu, and even harder to find a time when the line of customers isn't spilling out the door. All the cooking chores are handled by a single line, but somehow Panda's can handle a busy take-out and delivery service as well and has expanded to a Magnolia location. The same terrific specialties are at both locations: mu-shu pork with homemade pancakes; perfectly cooked, dry-sautéed green beans with almonds; a standout

Seattle

Restaurants

General Tso's chicken, which quietly explodes inside the mouth with tender meat and vibrant seasoning. There are almost 100 dishes to choose from. Delivery areas are limited, but it has always been faster than expected, and the food as hot as if it just came out of the kitchen. Both restaurants are nonsmoking. ▪ *NE 75th and 35th NE; (206) 526-5115; 7347 35th Ave NE, Seattle; $; beer and wine; AE, MC, V; local checks only; lunch Mon-Sat, dinner every day.* ▪ *Between 16th W and 17th W; (206) 283-9030; 1625 W Dravus, Seattle; $; beer and wine; AE, MC, V; local checks only; lunch Mon-Sat, dinner every day.* ♿

Phoenecia ★★ Seattle's Middle Eastern wizard, Husein Khazaal, has pulled the strengths of his two former restaurants (La Fontana and Phoenecia in the former Hansen Baking Company) into one location on the Alki beach strip, an area way overdue for an excellent restaurant. Those lamenting the loss of the old Phoenecia will be pleased with the warm glow inside (and outside) Khazaal's new home. Khazaal uncannily takes care of everyone who walks in the door. Appropriately for Alki, his new menu offers more seafood and vegetarian items than lamb. The antipasto plate might contain marinated and grilled eggplant, mozzarella with fresh leaves of basil, roasted red peppers, asparagus, and tender lemony-and-garlicky calamari; close your eyes and let the flavors identify themselves in your mouth. There are a lot of pasta combinations here—the tomato-based Moroccan eggplant on penne is reliable, but the specials, such as the oysters in a light cream sauce over fettuccine, can be outstanding. Unlike most other restaurants along Alki, Phoenicia draws a clientele that's not the happenstance beach crowd. These folks have come to Alki for one thing: Khazaal's addictive Italian and Middle Eastern creations. The addition of sunset over the Sound is merely a pleasing extra. ▪ *On Alki in West Seattle; (206) 935-6550; 2716 Alki Ave SW, Seattle; $$; beer and wine; MC, V; checks OK; lunch, dinner Tues-Sat.*

The Pink Door ★★ The idea is exemplary: a reasonably priced trattoria with cheap wine, good pasta, and a sort of built-in cachet (you enter through the pink door on Post Alley; there's no sign). At lunch, the large room grows noisy around a burbling fountain, and on summer days there's usually a wait for a table on the pretty rooftop terrace overlooking the Sound. Nothing is outstanding, but everything (from the pesto lasagne to tortellini Gorgonzola to the puttanesca) is perfectly satisfying. At night, when the pace slows down, the tables are lit by candlelight, and you can dine (prix-fixe) on four courses (no choices). Most people tend to order appetizers in the bar and watch the occasional entertainment. The cheerful place overflows with Italian kitsch. ▪ *Post Alley between Stewart and Virginia; (206) 443-3241; 1919 Post Alley, Seattle; $$; full bar; AE, MC, V; no checks; lunch and dinner Tues-Sat.*

Queen City Grill ★★ You sink into a glossy, high-backed booth and disappear from the world to schmooze with friends. Fashionable people perch at the bar with cigarettes and bottles of good wine. The ocher walls and art deco sconces give you the feeling that if something tragically wonderful were to happen to you tonight, it would be here. Here is a restaurant where the menu is pared down to a handful of dishes done really, really well and a couple of specials—a nice ethic in this era of multiethnic, pancontinental eateries. The disbelieving should sample the melting tuna carpaccio appetizer (tinged with peppercorns and wasabe). Or a genuine caesar salad, done as Cardini envisioned: hearts of romaine, simply dressed in olive oil, lemon, and Worcestershire. The entrées, too, are simply prepared, mostly from the grill, by cook Paul Michael, from swordfish to New York steak to Jamaican jerk chicken—spicy and charred on the outside, but fall-off-the-bone tender inside. Service is impeccable, if aloof. At lunch, reservations are recommended. This is one of the few downtown restaurants that are open until midnight (11pm on weekdays). ■ *Corner of Blanchard and 1st; (206) 443-0975; 2201 1st Ave, Seattle; $$$; full bar; AE, DIS, MC, V; checks OK; lunch Mon-Fri, dinner every day.* &

Rain City Grill ★★ Aside from the big bright bouquets of lilies, daisies, and sunflowers, this cloud-hued room raining umbrellas is very Seattle gray. Like the fresh flowers, the colorful food and sunny service make any day (or night) at the Rain City shine. Blue cheese, apples, and walnuts with romaine is a stunning beginning, as is sophisticated wilted savoy cabbage salad, hot with sausage, tinged with ginger and cooled with pear, and prettied with one or two plump sweet peas. The deliciously succulent fennel-encrusted salmon steak laced with leek cream sauce has become one of their signature pieces. Vegetarian entrées tend to be relatively simple concoctions; one stars a '90s version of macaroni and cheese decorated with deep red sun-dried tomatoes; however, not all dishes work so well. A special egg cavatappi (a pasta slightly thicker than fettuccine) came sauced in a too rich Sichuan-spiced puréed-eggplant-based sauce with grilled shrimp. The fricassee of pork resulted in somewhat dry (though nicely seasoned) pork. But when the waitress brings glasses of wine to help in your wine choice, then comes back later to introduce you to another she thought you might prefer...suddenly small lapses in the food seem even smaller. ■ *1 block south of Roanoke exit; (206) 325-5003; 2359 10th Ave E, Seattle; $$; full bar; MC, V; no checks; lunch Mon-Fri, dinner every day.*

Reiner's ★★ Reiner Greubel's small bistro is at the same time elegant and unstuffy, catering to a clientele put off by aggressively trendy restaurants; the fine food, too, has a continental feel. Soups (lobster bisque with crème fraîche and vegetable purée with chives) are complex and Greubel's home-smoked salmon appetizer served with a dill horseradish sauce is an excellent version of a Northwest classic. We recommend just about everything that comes out of the kitchen: the mushroom ravioli, the mosaic of smoked duck and chicken breast with a plum sauce and cinnamon apple, any of the beef or lamb offerings. Petrale sole—any way it's prepared—seems to be a house favorite. Touches are lovely (wine by the glass is served in miniature pitchers) and service is the right mix of professional and unobtrusive. Reiner's surely would have become a Seattle institution the day it opened—if only it weren't in such an odd location. ■ *8th and Spring, in the Lowell Apartments building, near Virginia Mason; (206) 624-2222; 1106 8th Ave, Seattle; $$; beer and wine; MC, V; checks OK; lunch Tues-Fri, dinner Tues-Sat.*

Romio's Pizza ★★ There's a scene in the movie *Mystic Pizza* in which the local restaurant critic, a real constipated sort, evaluates the product at Mystic Pizza while the staff watches, terrified, from the kitchen. The staff at Romio's surely wouldn't be so nervous. For one thing, these fine establishments (there are now five) are as busy as restaurants can get, particularly the larger Interbay and Eastlake branches (the last thing Romio's needs is press). Even more, Romio's delivers—literally and figuratively—a magnificent product. Pies here have thick, textural crusts—crisp outside, chewy in—and are coated with a blistered layer of mozzarella. In the Zorba, each part—onion, tomato, feta, Greek olives, gyro meat, and homemade tzatziki—contributes nobly to the whole. Romio's signature pizza, the GASP (which stands for garlic, artichoke hearts, sun-dried tomatoes, and pesto), achieves such integration of flavors and textures that it seems somehow inevitable, as if it had grown on a tree. Order it on a garlic crust (which they tend to run out of early), and you've got yourself a bona fide religious experience. The delivered pizzas don't deserve as much gasping, so if you have the choice, head to the original branch at Interbay, which is dim, cozy, and crowded; the bright new branch at Eastlake, 3242 Eastlake Avenue E, (206) 322-4453, which has notable service; or the branch in Greenwood, 8523 Greenwood Avenue N, (206) 782-9005. The other locations, in Pioneer Square, 616 First Avenue, (206) 621-8500, and downtown, 917 Howell, (206) 622-6878, are mostly just take-out. ■ *20th W and W Dravus; (206) 284-5420; 2001 W Dravus, Seattle (and branches); $; beer and wine; MC, V; local checks only; lunch, dinner every day.*

Salvatore ★★ Some Seattleites vote this neighborhood spot the most romantic restaurant around—what with the heady wines, the murals, and the Italianate heartiness, Salvatore gets the essentials right. Much of the warmth stems from Salvatore Anania himself, who brings his amore for the Southern Italian food of Basilicata to his North End landing. Penne puttanesca is a fine example of the region's fondness for red pepper; penne luciana is a lovely, simple toss of fresh ingredients—tomatoes, broccoli, and garlic. The antipasto rustico, rather than being a stack of Italian deli ingredients, is dealt with restraint: marinated, grilled eggplant, a couple of excellent quality tomato and mozzarella slices, and a pile of nutty wild greens. And all is fine until dessert, when you might be railroaded into ordering more than you really have room for, but life should be full of such problems. A great place to be a regular. ■ *1 block north of Ravenna Blvd on Roosevelt; (206)527-9301; 6100 Roosevelt Way NE, Seattle; $$; beer and wine; MC, V; checks OK; dinner Mon-Sat.* &

Toyoda Sushi ★★ Every neighborhood should be so lucky as to have a local sushi spot where an authentic production of Japanese dining comes without the shock of a high bill. And we mean production: the action flies behind the sushi counter, where chef/owner Natsuyoshi Toyoda seems to be working with more than one pair of hands while carrying on cheerful conversations with the regulars who jam the sushi bar and have their own engraved wooden sake cups lined up against the wall. With such speed comes a certain casualness: sushi rolls uncurling on the plate, missing chopsticks, a slightly frozen piece of hamachi (yellowtail). But then comes a spicy cucumber and noodle salad, a superb spinach and sesame salad, and an array of the freshest seafood: tender amoebi (sweet raw shrimp), lightly smoked salmon, and butter-sautéed geoduck seasoned and served on skewers. There are some unusual delights to be found here, including shiso, a hosomaki roll prepared with plum paste, beefsteak leaf, and mountain potato. Toyoda-san also makes some of the best gyoza in town. The intimate restaurant crowds quickly on weekend nights, when we've spotted City Council members and students waiting shoulder to shoulder for a seat. ■ *125th and Lake City Way; (206) 367-7972; 12543 Lake City Way NE, Seattle; $$; beer and wine; MC, V; local checks only; dinner Tues-Sat.* &

Tulio's (Hotel Vintage Park) ★★ This hotel restaurant in downtown Seattle feels more like a neighborhood restaurant in Tuscany. Tables with red-checkered cloths are packed in tightly, the sweet scent of roasted garlic hangs in the air, and service comes with big, sincere smiles. With Walter Pisano in charge, your meal is in good hands. Of the seven antipasti, two are especially outstanding: the bruschetta mista (a mix of breads, marinated mushrooms, goat cheese, tapenade, and tomatoes tossed with pine nuts and currants) and the homemade mozzarella with grilled eggplant and tomatoes in balsamic vinaigrette.

The menu's not large, but it's well balanced. The big, thin ravioli combine smoked salmon with a just tart lemon cream sauce; tender veal saltimbocca comes stuffed with prosciutto and mozzarella on a bed of spinach and roasted mushrooms. Breakfast offers welcome respite from typical hotel fare, what with vanilla French toast with baked apples, homemade sausages, spiced cider, and rosemary potatoes. ■ *5th and Spring; (206) 624-5500; 1100 5th Ave, Seattle; $$; full bar; AE, DC, DIS, MC, V; no checks; breakfast, lunch, dinner every day.*

Two Bells Tavern ★★ Starving artists tried not to tell anyone about the excellent, cheap burgers on sourdough at the funky Two Bells, but word got out, and now the tavern is packed all the time with an eclectic crowd, joining in common worship of the burger. It's big and juicy, smothered in onions and cheese, served on a roll with your choice of side orders, including rich, chunky potato salad. Another favorite with the Bells crowd is the hot beer-sausage sandwich. Satisfying doesn't say the half of it—this food is so full of flavor and freshness and goes so well with the beer (25 kinds) that you don't care about getting mustard all over your face. Food is served till 10pm every night, but the tavern stays open till 2am. Come prepared to roll with the punches—the place is staffed with career nonconformists. ■ *4th and Bell; (206) 441-3050; 2313 4th Ave, Seattle; $; beer and wine; no credit cards; no checks; lunch, dinner every day, breakfast Sat-Sun.* ⅋

Axum ★ This basement space off the Ave, scented with incense and exotic smells from the kitchen, is one of the most comfortable and inviting Ethiopian restaurants in town (and yes, there are now almost a half-dozen). These dishes are rich and exotically flavored, meant to leave a pleasant tingle, not a burn, in the mouth. Injera, a slightly sour flat bread, serves simultaneously as plate and eating utensil. With it you grab bits of beef and peppers from the zilzil tibs, chicken from the doro wat (Ethiopia's national dish, a chicken thigh simmered in a red sauce with peppery sweetness and served with a hard-boiled egg, traditionally given to the guest of honor), and stewed beef and aromatic berbere sauce from the zigni. Kitfo, a variation on steak tartare with an exotic kick of spices, may be overly rich for uninitiated palates, but some eaters find it shamefully delicious. With each entrée you choose two of five side dishes—spinach, red lentils, potatoes, collards, and onions —so with a party of three, you can sample them all. ■ *Corner of 42nd and Brooklyn; (206) 547-6848; 4142 Brooklyn Ave NE, Seattle; $; beer and wine; AE, DIS, MC, V; checks OK; lunch Mon-Sat, dinner every day.*

Cactus ★ Cactus, a spot of intense heat in the rainy Northwest, attracted crowds the day it opened, proffering its mélange of Spanish- and Southwestern-influenced cuisine. The first tapas seen in years in Seattle appeared on the tables in this South-western-decored *restoran*, and the menu changes seasonally at least once a month. Maybe you'll be there for a spicy round of chicken in chipotle-peanut sauce or mussels swimming in a sauce of Dijon mustard and roasted red peppers, or for grilled eggplant with pesto—all with lush, spice-infused sauces begging to be sopped up with coarse peasant bread. The tapas are tiny, but several strewn across your plate make a lovely light meal. The menu holds some of the Mexican standards and a couple of dishes that have become Cactus institutions, such as tequila chicken and cactus salad (grilled nopales leaf, jícama spears, roasted red pepper, and Mexican squash). Pay attention to the play of spices and ingredients: mild, fresh chunks of seafood smothered in the fiery bite of ancho chiles; the fruity zing of tequila infused in a piece of chicken. Some nights the kitchen seems to be out of *everything*. We continue to be baffled by this place: some nights it intrigues, others it disappoints, but we always return. ■ *In Madison Park near the lake; (206) 324-4140; 4220 E Madison, Seattle; $$; beer and wine; MC, V; checks OK; lunch Mon-Sat, dinner every day.*

Maximilien-in-the-Market ★ There is something so undeniably French about this place, something about the mismatched silverware and the broad Elliott Bay view, about the dark wood antiques and the light bonhomie of the waiters. All you seem to need here is a light, crusty loaf of bread and a bottle of wine to be truly happy. Luckily, you don't have to stick to bread and wine, when a simple lunch can be assembled out of steamed mussels with wine and cream, a salade Niçoise, or excellent fish 'n' chips. A four-course dinner is available, fronted by soup and salad, and then ultimately simple offerings: sweetbreads in mustard-caper sauce, halibut broiled with wine and herbs, scallop mousse in a creamy sauce nantua (down to a simple ham and cheese *omelette*). Sometimes there are flaws: the service *un peu* slow between courses, a slightly dry cut of fish, a salty soupe à l'oignon. But here, you simply sigh, pour another glass of wine, and nod, *c'est la vie.* ■ *Pike Place Market; (206) 682-7270; 81-A Pike Place Market, Seattle; $$; full bar; AE, DC, MC, V; no checks; breakfast, lunch, dinner Mon-Sat, brunch Sun.* &

McCormick's Fish House and Bar ★ This is certainly the most popular downtown fish house. Lunch is noisy and frenetic, the bar jams up with City Hall types after 5pm, and even dinners feel crowded, particularly during the tourist season. Somehow the waiters remain cheerful amid the bustle. The formula here is simple: the heavy-on-seafood menu, printed daily, offers several types of fish prepared in simple ways: grilled with a flavored butter, sautéed with another butter, baked elaborately. Preparation can be uneven—we've had both tough tuna and near-perfect halibut—but you can usually rely on decent cooking (especially when you order your fish broiled) and generous portions. Oysters are fine, salads pedestrian, the wine list carefully chosen and overpriced, the beautifully fresh sourdough bread always a treat. ■ *4th and Columbia; (206) 682-3900; 722 4th Ave, Seattle; $$; full bar; AE, DC, DIS, MC, V; local checks only; lunch Mon-Fri, dinner every day.*

Metropolitan Grill ★ This handsome haunt in the heart of the financial district does a booming business among stockbrokers and Asian tourists. The soul of the restaurant is its steaks, and you'd do well to stick to them, since they mostly live up to the hoopla. Pastas and appetizers are less well executed, but a list of large, appealing salads (and a terrific clam chowder) present good alternatives to beef for the lunch crowd. Waiters are of the no-nonsense school, which suits the table-hopping power brokers just fine. Financiers count on the Met's 30-person private room as a dependable dinner venue. ■ *2nd and Marion; (206) 624-3287; 820 2nd Ave, Seattle; $$; full bar; AE, DC, MC, V; no checks; lunch Mon-Fri, dinner Mon-Sun.* ＆

Omar Al-Khyam ★ Lebanese music wails softly in the background. Velvet paintings and New England calendar scenes hang on knotty pine paneling. Vivid plastic flowers adorn the tabletops. Last year's Christmas decorations stay up until August. One night we watched a party of 10 enter our dining room, the women swathed in veils. This is an authentically Middle Eastern restaurant (some call it the best of its kind in town), and thoroughly satisfying besides. Dinners are served with iceberg lettuce salad amply dressed with oil, lemon, and mint. Warm, soft pita and a choice of fries or a buttery pilaf with pine nuts (always our choice) also come with the meal. We've sampled much of the grilled meat: shish kabob, kafta kabob, and chicken wings, all perfectly cooked. It's easy to assemble a full dinner from the appetizer menu as well, particularly if you're there with a large party. Don't miss the baba ghanouj, infused with a heavy, smoky flavor (too smoky for some) and reeking of garlic. Have the zahrah, too—cauliflower florets fried until soft and pale gold, lightly sauced with tahini—and fatoush, a bread salad. ■ *77th and Aurora; (206) 782-5295; 7617 Aurora Ave N, Seattle; dinner Mon-Sat.* ■ *Next to the 7-11 on Sunset Blvd N; (206) 271-8300; 354 Sunset Blvd N, Renton; lunch Mon-Fri, dinner Mon-Sat. $; beer and wine; AE, DC, MC, V; no checks.*

Pirosmani ★ We are enchanted by the arrival of a truly *new* restaurant on the Seattle ethnic front. Pirosmani is a gentle education in the foods of the Georgian region of the former Soviet Union, foods with a slight Mediterranean lean, here redolent of coriander, garlic, and saffron, nuts, fruits, and meats.

The menu is small and the waitstaff helpful in guiding you through it. Appetizers with the strangest names yield the loveliest results: khachapuri and spinach pkhali resembles nothing so much as a disassembled spanakopita, a spinach pâté tweaked with walnuts, cilantro, and garlic scooped up with a gooey cheese bread; badrijani nigvzit (thin slices of eggplant wrapped around a rich, nutty walnut-and-herb purée) is served with gadazelili, a mild farmer's cheese and mint spread. Entrées so far are uneven: we've swooned over lamb chakapuli, a sustaining stew with plums and tender lamb, though a recent ajapsandali, a vegetarian stew, was on the gloppy, undistinguished side. Specials tend to be good; fish is well treated here. An altogether pleasant experience, from the mottled damson walls to the classical music at just the right pitch, to the olive oil lamps on the table. ■ *Queen Anne Ave N, between Boston and McGraw; (206) 285-3360; 2220 Queen Anne Ave N, Seattle; $$; beer and wine; MC, V; checks OK; dinner Tues-Sat.*

Ristorante Buongusto ★ The counterbalance hasn't been a destination for serious eaters for a long time, but you'll now find people who can orient themselves in the Queen Anne neighborhood in relation to Buongusto. It's a bright, active place, and it's almost always crowded (though the dining room has recently been expanded to make room for more devotees). Here are some of the most reliable (and the most fun) pastas in town—flirty creste di gallo in spicy red sauce with good Isernio sausage; rotolo di Mamma Flora, stuffed with bubbling veal, ricotta, and spinach; and robust linguine alla pescatora, chockfull of calamari and shellfish. For those feeling distinctly unrobust, there are grilled meats and seafoods. And many of these dishes have graced the Buongusto menu since it opened a couple of years ago. Service hasn't quite been the same since one unlucky night when appetizer and entrée were delivered, without apology, together. The Varchettas still own Buongusto, but don't seem to be around as much; we miss their happy, bustling presence. ■ *Queen Anne Ave and McGraw; (206) 284-9040; 2232 Queen Anne Ave N, Seattle; $$; full bar; AE, DC, DIS, MC, V; no checks; lunch Tues-Fri, dinner every day.*

Septieme ★ In the Paris of the *septième arrondissement*, a vigorous intellectual culture exists in tiny cafes, where the propriétaires let the literati linger, and conversation is fueled with coffee and rich pastries. Septieme is Kurt Timmermeister's tribute to the student life he remembers there. He features the same lush pastries, the same easy atmosphere, the same compact quarters and small brick courtyard. Septieme, equally winning by morning or by evening, pays attention to what's important: rich and delicious lattes served in china teacups (or bowls for the real addicts), on white linen-covered tables. Lush pastries, baked in-house, are arrayed at the counter—a pear tart dusted with nutmeg, a sticky pecan roll that tastes like a brioche with French caramel, a dense wedge of poppyseed cake—and are delivered on pretty gold-rimmed white china plates with heavy silver forks. Fans rhapsodize about them. Evenings under the stars, candles twinkle on tables where patrons happily savor calzones stuffed with soothing cheeses and roasted peppers, or oil-drizzled eggplant sandwiches, or fat wedges of vegetarian lasagne, with roseate glasses of Chianti. ■ *2nd between Battery and Bell; (206) 448-1506; 2331 2nd Ave, Seattle; $; beer and wine; no credit cards; checks OK; breakfast, lunch, dinner every day.* &

Siam on Broadway ★ Among Seattle's crowded collection of Thai restaurants, Chai Asavadejkajorn and John Sariwatanarong's tiny Siam on Broadway is one of the most aesthetically pleasing and smoothly run. The menu doesn't stray far from the Bangkok standards, but the food is distinctive. The open kitchen makes a fun diversion—it's probably the only place in town where you can enjoy Thai cooking from a front-row seat (and undoubtedly will if you don't make reservations at least 24 hours in advance for a table in back). A three-star chicken curry was no hotter than the two-star soup during a recent visit, so if you want tongue-tingling food, make yourself heard. Try the crisp yum wuun sen, a salad of bean threads with pork, squid, and onions, piquant with fresh lime and cilantro. Lately we've heard that Siam's high standards are slipping. We hope it doesn't fall prey to indifference. ■ *Broadway E and E Roy; (206) 324-0892; 616 Broadway E, Seattle; $; beer and wine; AE, MC, V; checks OK; lunch Mon-Fri, dinner every day.*

Viet My ★ In Saigon, Chau Tran was known as a good cook, both professionally and at home. When she fled Vietnam by boat in 1980 and eventually came to Seattle to learn English, she didn't stop cooking. She cooked at home and brought the food to school. Her meals were so popular that she opened this little restaurant on Prefontaine Place, and at lunchtime, this bright, busy spot is standing room only. Chau is a whirlwind of energy: she's either vigorously scraping the grill, doling out menus, or directing the kitchen, which turns out food that is always exact and delicious. Start with the rice-paper rolls, fatly filled with shrimp, pork, vermicelli, cilantro, and mint, and never failing to leave a fresh taste in the mouth. The pho (beef noodle soup and practically the national dish of Vietnam)—a fragrant broth, layered with herbs, scads of noodles, tender beef, and fresh sprouts for dunking—gets better the farther down you go in the bowl, as the herbs infuse and flavors assert themselves. Chau also offers several curries, a half-dozen chow meins, and eight or so soups. Even for such generous exotica as beef wrap, you won't pay more than $6, and usually much less. ▪ *Just off 4th near Washington; (206) 382-9923; 129 Prefontaine Pl S, Seattle; $; no alcohol; no credit cards; local checks only; lunch, dinner Mon-Sat.*

LODGINGS

Four Seasons Olympic Hotel ★★★ The Olympic has **⑳ YEARS** been a Seattle landmark since the 1920s. It has been refurbished in a style befitting its earlier grandeur; the 450 rooms are quite spacious, softly lit, and tastefully furnished in period reproductions. Welcome touches include valet parking, 24-hour full room service, a stocked bar, complimentary shoeshines, and a terrycloth robe for each guest. A team of well-informed concierges offers uncommonly good service; indeed, the staff usually exudes just the right blend of unobtrusiveness and thorough care. The hotel even goes out of its way for kids, right down to a teddy bear in the crib, a step stool in the bathroom, and milk and cookies for the ride home; however, a few recent gaffes in both service and maintenance leave us wondering if something's gone astray. The public rooms are grand verging on gaudy: armchairs, potted plants, marble galore, tapestries, wood paneling. You can lounge amid the swaying palms in the skylit Garden Court, taking high tea if you wish. The showcase dining room, the Georgian Room (see review in this section), is a handsome space; downstairs is the livelier Shuckers, an oyster bar with a full menu and excellent mixed drinks. There are several elegant meeting rooms and classy shopping in the retail spaces off the lobby. A health club rounds out the amenities with a pool, a Jacuzzi, and a licensed masseuse. Prices are steep, especially considering there are few views, but this is Seattle's one venerable world-class contender. ▪ *5th and University; (206) 621-1700; 411 University St, Seattle, WA 98101; $$$; AE, DC, DIS, MC, V; checks OK.* ♿

Alexis Hotel ★★★ The Alexis is a gem carved out of a lovely turn-of-the-century building in a stylish section of downtown near the waterfront. It's small (54 rooms), full of tasteful touches (televisions concealed in armoires, complimentary sherry upon arrival), and decorated with the suave modernity of Michael Graves' postmodern colors. You'll be pampered here, with Jacuzzis and real wood fireplaces in some of the suites, a steam room that can be reserved just for you, and nicely insulated walls between rooms to ensure privacy. Since there are no views to speak of in this centrally located hotel, we suggest booking a room that faces the inner courtyard—rooms facing First Avenue can be noisy, especially if you want to open your window (and we've received reports that some nonsmoking rooms can still be smoky, so if you want one, insist). Amenities include complimentary continental breakfasts, a morning newspaper of your choice, shoeshines, and a guest membership in the nearby Seattle Club ($12) or Northwest Nautilus ($5 per visit). There's only one meeting room here, as the Alexis favors well-heeled travelers who prefer quiet poshness. Flaws here seem to come by way of the service—young, unpolished employees—though front-desk personnel are helpful. The Painted Table serves innovative Northwest cuisine (see review in this section). Pets are accepted.

For a longer stay, book one of the 43 condos—some have limited water views, all have kitchens—across the street in the jointly managed Arlington Suites. The Alexis' turndown service, complimentary sherry, and maid and room services are available to condo patrons as well. ▪ *1st and Madison; (206) 624-4844; 1007 1st Ave, Seattle, WA 98104; $$$; AE, DC, DIS, MC, V; checks OK.* &

Inn at the Market ★★★ A stay in this hotel puts you within striking distance of the famous Pike Place Market. Looking out over fruit stands and fishmongers to the lovely bay beyond, this small hotel—65 rooms—features service that approximates that of a country inn. Despite the ideal location, you won't feel oppressed by conventioneers—conference facilities consist of one meeting room and one outdoor deck. The architecture features oversize rooms, bay windows that let occupants of even some side rooms enjoy big views, and a comfortable, pretty lobby. Lately, however, there have been reports of forgotten wake-up calls, missing newspapers, and no robes—something we've come to expect from a hotel of this caliber. Opening off the central courtyard are smart shops, a sumptuous spa, and the elegant Campagne restaurant (see review in this section). There is no complimentary breakfast (just mediocre coffee), but room service for that meal can be ordered from Bacco in the courtyard; dinner comes from Campagne. ▪ *1st and Pine; (206) 443-3600; 86 Pine St, Seattle, WA 98101; $$$; AE, DC, MC, V; checks OK.* &

Sorrento Hotel ★★★ When the Sorrento opened in 1909—in time for the Alaska Yukon-Pacific Exposition—it commanded a bluff overlooking young Seattle and Puget Sound. For years thereafter, it was the most elegant hotel in the city, with Renaissance architecture modeled after a castle in Sorrento, Honduras mahogany in the lobby, and a famous dining room on the top floor. The place faded badly, though, and the view was lost as the city grew up around the hotel. In 1981 it was fixed up and reopened. The view is gone forever, but the beauty is back. Downstairs there's the first-class Hunt Club restaurant (see review in this section), and the mahogany lobby is now a lounge perfect for afternoon tea. The 76 rooms are decorated in muted, tasteful coziness with a slight Asian accent. We recommend the 08 series of suites, in the corners. Suites on the top floor make elegant quarters for special meetings or parties—the showstopper being the 3,000-square-foot, $1,000 penthouse, with a grand piano, a patio, a Jacuzzi, a view of the bay, and luxurious multiple rooms. Some may find the location—uphill five blocks from the heart of downtown—inconvenient, but we find it quiet and removed. ■ *9th and Madison; (206) 622-6400; 900 Madison St, Seattle, WA 98104; $$$; AE, DC, DIS, MC, V; checks OK.* ♿

Westin Hotel ★★★ Westin international headquarters is in Seattle, so this flagship hotel has quite a few extras. The twin cylindrical towers may be called corncobs by the natives, but they afford spacious rooms with superb views, particularly above the 20th floor. Convention facilities, spread over several floors of meeting rooms, are quite complete. There is a large pool, along with an exercise room supervised by conditioning experts. On the top floors are some ritzy, glitzy suites. The location, near Westlake Center and the Monorail station, is excellent. For dinner, try superb Japanese food at Nikko (see review in this section) or continental dining at the Palm Court. For more casual dining, try the hotel's somewhat overpriced Market Cafe; for a drink visit Fitzgerald's long, dark cocktail bar. ■ *Between Stewart and Virginia on 5th; (206) 728-1000; 1900 5th Ave, Seattle, WA 98101; $$$; AE, DC, DIS, MC, V; checks OK.* ♿

The Broadway Guest House ★★ Built by Cecil Bacon in 1909, the three-story Edwardian-style Tudor mansion is now fit for a fine bed and breakfast—with some of the original wood and furnishings intact. Seven rooms in the main guest house (five with private bath) are appointed with antiques and brass fixtures. The top of the line is the Capitol Room, a huge suite on the second floor with a sun room, fireplace, French doors, and a view of the Space Needle. The basement Garden Room has 8-foot ceilings, a kitchenette, and stays quite cool in the summer. The unique Carriage House ($125), a separate, two-story building with hunter green decor, is appropriate for a small family or two couples. An expanded continental breakfast (cereal, fruit salad, homemade muffins and baked goods, juices, coffee, and tea) might be served on the spacious patio between main house and carriage house. New proprietor Daryl King is an enthusiastic, friendly host. ■ *Corner of Broadway E and E Prospect Ave on Capitol Hill; (206) 329-1864; 959 Broadway E, Seattle, WA 98102; $$; AE, MC, V; checks OK.*

Chambered Nautilus ★★ This blue 1915 Georgian colonial in a hillside woodsy setting in the University District offers six airy guest rooms beautifully furnished with antiques. Four have private baths, and four open onto porches with tree-webbed views of the Cascades. All rooms have robes, desks, flowers, and reading material. This location just across the street from shared student housing units and a few blocks from Fraternity Row can get noisy here during rush. Other times, though, it's surprisingly quiet. Innkeepers Bunny and Bill Hagemeyer serve a full breakfast and complimentary afternoon tea. A spacious public room, meeting facilities, a library of 2,000-plus volumes, and an enclosed porch/reading room with soothing chamber music round out this tasteful inn. Smoking is allowed on the porches and outside. Make prior arrangements for kids under 12. ■ *East on NE 50th St to 21st Ave, and circle left-right-right around the block; (206) 522-2536; 5005 22nd Ave NE, Seattle, WA 98105; $$; AE, DC, MC, V; checks OK.*

The Edgewater ★★ Alas, you can't fish from the famous west windows of this waterfront institution anymore. You can, however, still breathe salty air and hear the ferry horns toot. The place has been spiffed up quite a bit, giving the lobby and rooms a rustic tone, with bleached oak and overstuffed chairs, plaid bedspreads, and lots of duck motifs and antler art. It's like a lodge on a busy (and sometimes noisy) Northwest waterfront, but with a reputable restaurant (Ernie's Bar and Grill—and we've been hearing reports that the food is on the upswing), a decent bar with a piano, and an uninterrupted view of Elliott Bay, Puget Sound, and the Olympic Mountains. Waterside rooms have the best views, but can get hot on summer afternoons. The *Victoria Clipper* terminal is just two blocks south. ■ *Pier 67 at Wall St and Alaskan Way; (206) 728-7000; Pier 67, 2411 Alaskan Way, Seattle, WA 98121; $$$; AE, DC, DIS, MC, V; checks OK.* &

Gaslight Inn and Howell Street Suites ★★ Praised by repeat guests and bed-and-breakfast owners alike, the Gaslight is one of the loveliest, most reasonably priced, and friendliest bed and breakfasts in town. Trevor Logan and Steve Bennett have polished this turn-of-the-century mansion into a 10–guest-room jewel, six with private baths, two with fireplaces, each decorated in a distinct style—some contemporary, some antique, some art deco, some mission. Outside are two sun decks and a large heated swimming pool. The very new Howell Street Suites next door (five full and one studio) are outfitted with kitchens, contemporary furnishings and antiques, a coffeemaker and Starbucks coffee, wineglasses, fruit, and flowers. Targeted at businesspeople, the suites also offer phones, fax availability, off-street parking, maid service, and laundry facilities. At press time, the owners were finishing plans to install a hot tub and a garden area between the two houses. Weekly rates are available. No pets or kids, but smoking is okay. ■ *15th and Howell; (206) 325-3654; 1727 15th Ave E, Seattle, WA 98122; $$; AE, MC, V; checks OK.*

Holiday Inn Crowne Plaza ★★ This hotel bends over backward for the repeat and corporate visitor. The upper-floor rooms are corporate, comfortable, and very clean in striking maroons, mauves, and dark wood. Businesspeople receive individual attention: free newspapers, a lounge, and their own concierge desk (for a slightly higher price). Lower-floor guests stay in spacious but rather bland rooms. The lobby is elegant and comfortable, the staff attentive and accommodating. In addition to the pleasant Parkside Cafe, the pricier Parkside Restaurant features continental fare. Conference rooms and parking (for a fee) are available. The location is ideal—downtown, near the freeway, and two blocks from the Convention Center. ■ *6th Ave and Seneca St; (206) 464-1980; 1113 6th Ave, Seattle, WA 98101; $$$; AE, DC, DIS, MC, V; checks OK.* &

Mayflower Park Hotel ★★ Renovations have paid off at this handsome 1927 hotel right in the heart of the downtown shopping district. A coolly elegant lobby opens onto Oliver's (bar and lounge) on one side and Clipper's, one of the prettiest breakfast places in town, on the other. Rooms are small, bearing charming reminders of the hotel's past: lovely Oriental brass and antique appointments; large, deep tubs; thick walls that trap noise. Modern intrusions are for both better and worse: double-glazed windows in all rooms keep out traffic noise, but there are undistinguished furnishings in many of the rooms. The deluxe rooms are slightly bigger and have corner views; aim for one on a higher floor or you may find yourself facing a brick wall. ■ *4th and Olive; (206) 623-8700; 405 Olive Way, Seattle, WA 98101; $$$; AE, DC, DIS, MC, V; checks OK.* &

Roberta's ★★ Roberta is the gracious, somewhat loquacious lady of this Capitol Hill house near Volunteer Park and a few blocks from the funky Broadway district. Inside it's lovely: refinished floors throughout, a comfortable blue couch and an old upright piano, books everywhere, and a large oval dining table and country-style chairs. Of the five rooms, the blue-toned Hideaway Suite (the entire third floor), with views of the Cascades from the window seats, skylights, a sitting area with a futon couch and a small desk, and a full bath with a tub, is our favorite. Others prefer the Peach Room with its antique desk, bay window, love seat, and queen-size oak bed. Early risers will enjoy the Madrona Room, with its morning sun and bath. All five rooms have queen-size beds; four have private baths. In the morning, Roberta brings you a wake-up cup of coffee, then later puts out a smashing full breakfast (no meat). No children. No smoking except on the porch. ■ *16th E north of Prospect; (206) 329-3326; 1147 16th Ave E, Seattle, WA 98112; $$; AE, DC, MC, V; checks OK.*

Salisbury House ★★ A welcoming porch wraps around this big, bright Capitol Hill home, an exquisite hostelry neighboring Volunteer Park. Glossy maple floors and lofty beamed ceilings lend a sophisticated air to the guest library (with a chess table and a fireplace) and living room. Up the wide staircase and past the second-level sun porch are four guest rooms (one with a canopy bed, all with queen-size beds and down comforters) with full private baths. Our favorite is the Rose Room, with its bay window and walk-in closet; the Lavender Room, true to its color, comes in second. The full breakfast (without meat) is taken in the dining room or on the sunny terrace. Classy, dignified, nonsmoking, and devoid of children (under 12) and pets, the Salisbury House is a sure bet in one of Seattle's finest neighborhoods. ■ *E Aloha and 16th Ave E; (206) 328-8682; 750 16th Ave E, Seattle, WA 98112; $$; AE, DC, MC, V; checks OK.*

Seattle Sheraton Hotel and Towers ★★ Seattle's Sheraton is an 841-room tower rising as a sleek triangle, the Convention Center in its shadow. It, too, aims at the convention business, so the rooms are smallish and standard, and much emphasis is placed on the meeting rooms and the restaurants. Banner's offers mainstream continental fare, plus a 27-foot-long dessert spread; Gooey's is the night club; and the outstanding Fullers is adorned with fine Northwest paintings (see review in this section). Service is quite efficient. Convention facilities are complete, and the kitchen staff can handle the most complex assignments. Discriminating business travelers can head for the upper four "VIP" floors (31-34), where a hotel-within-a-hotel offers its own lobby, concierge, and considerably more amenities in the rooms (which are the same size as economy). The top floors feature a health club and a private lounge with a knockout city panorama. You pay for parking. ■ *6th and Pike; (206) 621-9000; 1400 6th Ave, Seattle, WA 98101; $$$; AE, DC, DIS, MC, V; checks OK.* &

Stouffer Madison Hotel ★★ This large hotel at the southeast edge of downtown successfully conveys a sense of warmth and intimacy inside. The lobby, dressed in signature greens and peach, is tasteful and uncluttered, and upstairs hallways are softly lit. The rooms sport elegant marble countertops, coffered ceilings, and wood cabinetry. Extras include feather pillows, oversize towels, and morning papers. The pricey "Club Floors" (25 and 26) offer exclusive checkin privileges, concierge services, hors d'oeuvres and continental breakfast at Club Lounge, a library, and the best views (although views from most rooms are quite good). Comfortable conference facilities, parking (for a fee), free in-town transportation, and coffee delivered to your room each morning round out the offerings. Prego, on the 28th floor, offers a surprisingly fine selection of seafood. ■ *6th and Madison; (206) 583-0300; 515 Madison St, Seattle, WA 98104; $$$; AE, DC, DIS, MC, V; checks OK.* &

Lake Union B&B ★ Shoes off. If you don't have any socks, they're provided. Then sink into the white cloud of carpet and couches of this modern three-story house (the B&B occupies the two top floors) not far from Gas Works Park—a refreshing break from the Victoriana that plagues most B&Bs. There are only two rooms upstairs, both stunning, though one—with its solarium, fireplace, and a view of Lake Union and the Seattle skyline from the Jacuzzi—is among Seattle's finest affordable bedrooms. In summer, though, when you'll want to open your windows (there's no air conditioning), street noise can be a bother. Modest visitors may not appreciate the downstairs location of the shared bathroom (with a sauna)—to get to it you have to waltz through the living and dining rooms. Smoking is prohibited and a two-night minimum stay is required, although exceptions to the latter have been made. In the evening, parking in this residential neighborhood can be a challenge. ■ *3 blocks north of Gas Works Park; (206) 547-9965; 2217 N 36th St, Seattle, WA 98103; $$; MC, V; checks OK.*

Marriott Residence Inn—Lake Union ★ Lake Union's first full-scale hotel is not exactly on the lake, but across busy Fairview Avenue. Still, the 234 rooms, most of which boast lake views (request the north-facing rooms on the highest level possible), are decorated in tasteful '90s colors, with touches of peach, mauve, and teal; the one-bedroom suites are spacious, but the studios feel cozier. All rooms have fully outfitted kitchenettes, and a continental breakfast is presented in the lobby—a light, plant-lined atrium and waterfall—or taken back to your room. There isn't a hotel restaurant, but guests can charge meals to their room at any number of lakeside eateries across the street. Amenities include five quiet meeting rooms, a lap pool, an exercise room, a sauna, and a spa. The nearby docks are a fun place to dream. ■ *Fairview and Boren, across from the marina; (206) 624-6000; 800 Fairview Ave N, Seattle, WA 98109; $$$; AE, DC, DIS, MC, V; checks OK.*

MV Challenger ★ If you've spent a night aboard a boat—and enjoyed it—you'll like this friendly little bunk and breakfast docked at the southeast end of Lake Union. When you come aboard, owners Jerry and Buff Brown may offer you a refreshment from the hardwood bar and a seat in the conversation pit—a sunken living space with two couches and a fireplace. On deck, you can loll in the sun. As for sleeping, you have two choices: the classic MV *Challenger* and the yacht *Arden/Mischief.* The former is the most charming, with three small main-floor berths that share a head, three top-floor cabins with private heads, and one room with a private bath on the main deck. More spacious accommodations, two rooms with double beds, are available aboard the *Arden/Mischief.* Breakfast is cooked in the *Challenger's* galley, using a diesel-powered stove and a microwave oven. In the evening, check out Opus Too, I Love Sushi (see review in this section), or one of the other restaurants a short stroll away. Despite close quarters, this is an authentic

Seattle experience. Park in the Opus Too restaurant parking lot. ■ *Yale St Landing; (206) 340-1201; 1001 Fairview Ave N, Seattle, WA 98109; $$; AE, DIS, MC, V; checks OK.*

WestCoast Camlin Hotel ★ Like many older hotels in Seattle, this 1926 grande dame has been remodeled and soundproofed with double-glazed windows. (The elevator and the ventilation system, however, both hark back to an earlier era.) Though its conference facilities are limited, the Camlin appeals to the business traveler, with large rooms that have small sitting/work areas. Rooms have been redecorated with sophistication, featuring spacious closets and spotless bathrooms; those whose numbers end in 10 have windows on three sides. Avoid the cabanas (they're small and dreary and for smokers) and room service, which is quite slow. There's rooftop dining and a bar in the newly restored Cloud Room. A good buy, the Camlin is closer to the shopping district and the Convention Center than it is to downtown offices. ■ *9th and Olive; (206) 682-0100; 1619 9th Ave, Seattle, WA 98101; $$; AE, DC, DIS, MC, V; checks OK.*

WestCoast Roosevelt Hotel ★ Gone is the grand skylit lobby that so distinguished the Roosevelt when it first opened its doors in 1930; the space is now inhabited by Von's Restaurant. The new lobby is low-ceilinged and cramped, but elsewhere the WestCoast installation has somewhat preserved the Roosevelt's art deco sensibilities. The hotel's 20 stories have been redivided for the contemporary traveler, but standards are still almost comically small. The Roosevelt Rooms (only $20 more than a standard) are a better choice, with adjoining sitting areas; the 13 Jacuzzi rooms each boast their namesake and a separate sitting area. Nine floors are nonsmoking. Considering its proximity to the Convention Center and the shopping district, the Roosevelt's prices—$85 to $170—are decent, but the service could be more polished. ■ *7th and Pine; (206) 621-1200; 1531 7th Ave, Seattle, WA 98101; $$$; AE, DC, DIS, MC, V; checks OK.* &

The Williams House ★ In its 89-year history, this south-slope Queen Anne residence has also been a gentlemen's boardinghouse and an emergency medical clinic for the 1962 Seattle World's Fair. Although it's been a bed and breakfast for quite some time, owners Doug and Sue Williams have lately been gearing their services toward family travelers. Kids are welcome. There are five guest rooms, four with views and two with private baths. The enclosed south sun porch is a nice gathering spot. Brass beds, original fixtures, fireplaces, ornate Italian tiles, and oak floors mirror the home's Edwardian past. A full breakfast is served in the first-floor dining room. ■ *Galer and 4th N; (206) 285-0810; 1505 4th Ave N, Seattle, WA 98109; $$; AE, DC, MC, V; checks OK.*

The College Inn Guest House Burgundy carpets, a couple of antiques, and pastel comforters create a cozy if somewhat spartan atmosphere in this hospitable inn designed along the lines of a European pension. Housed in the upper three floors of a renovated 1909 Tudor building that's on the National Register of Historic Places, it's in the heart of the lively U District. The College Inn Pub and Cafe are on street level (late-night noise travels quite handily into westside rooms). On the second and third floors, each of the 25 guest rooms has a double bed, a sink, and a desk; the nicest ones have window seats. Men's and women's bathrooms are at the end of each hall, and a guest living room is tucked away on the fourth floor where a generous continental breakfast—a good deal at these budget prices— is served. Smoke-free. ■ *40th and University Way; (206) 633-4441; 4000 University Way NE, Seattle, WA 98105; $; MC, V; checks OK.*

GREATER SEATTLE: EDMONDS

The area thought of as Edmonds is just a small village in a much larger area. Funky stores, wide sidewalks, and waterfront views encourage evening strolls through town. The ferry departs to Kingston; for information, call (206) 464-6400. Edmonds bills itself as the City of Celebrations. Most popular are the **Edmonds Art Festival** (in June) and **A Taste of Edmonds** (third weekend in August).

Brackett's Landing, just north of the ferry terminal, has a jetty and an offshore underwater marine-life park that draws lots of scuba divers. **Edmonds Historic Walk** was prepared by the Centennial Committee and offers a look at old Edmonds. Stop by the Chamber of Commerce, 120 N Fifth Avenue, (206) 776-6711, for a free map of the walk.

RESTAURANTS

Ciao Italia ★★ This Edmonds favorite combines a solid menu and lovely atmosphere—at once candlelit and casual—to fine effect. The menu is full of Italian meat and pasta standards done in better-than-standard fashion. Winners have included a tender pollo pesto, penne pasta with four cheeses and eggplant, and a noble (if slightly oversweet) chicken Marsala, covered in delectable mushrooms. Hints: Make sure someone at the table orders the simple, elegant pizza margherita, and order pastas off the special list, which here always seems to yield the best efforts of the chef. A recent special of tortellini in cream sauce with peas and prosciutto was velvety and ethereal. Dinners come with okay complimentary salads; meat dishes include outstanding grilled vegetables.

Ciao Italia's younger brother, Ciao Bella, 5133 25th Avenue NE, (206) 524-6989, is a terrific Ravenna *ristorante*, with a twin menu and similar ambience. ■ *5th and Walnut; (206) 771-7950; 512 5th Ave S, Edmonds; $; beer and wine; MC, V; local checks OK; dinner Mon-Sat.* &

Chanterelle Specialty Foods ★★ Jochen Bettag no longer operates the restaurant he put on the Edmonds map, but Chanterelle nobly maintains his fine record by remaining the best restaurant in town. A recent visit yielded much success off an appealing international list: a savory bowl of mussels in a delectable garlicky juice, a tender (though too thin of cheese) pork saltimbocca, a sautéed breast of chicken (perhaps too gooped up) in a dijon cream sauce with mushrooms and artichoke hearts, a robust four-cheese lasagne. Mysteriously underused for dinner, Chanterelle is best known for its more casual lunches, where it has received glowing word-of-mouth for everything from the falafel burger to the steak sandwich. We have no complaint about the space—sort of '70s fern-deli meets cozy bistro—but service could use polish. ■ *Up from ferry terminal, on Main; (206) 774-0650; 316 Main St, Edmonds; $; beer and wine; MC, V; checks OK; breakfast, lunch every day, dinner Tues-Sat.* &

Provinces Asian Restaurant & Bar ★★ Years ago, Asian fare was either Chinese, Japanese, Cambodian, or Vietnamese. The thought of a pan-Asian restaurant was too much for monoethnic eaters. Today, such culinary journeys actually work, especially in this serene, low-lit restaurant, filled with equally serene Edmondsites. Disappointments are few: Vietnamese salad rolls that are a little limp and a little lettuce-heavy, and service that is kind of slow (call it laid back). From there, everything gets better: seafood-stuffed wonton (hard to eat with chopsticks); spicy Mongolian ginger beef; fragrant basil scallops; deep-fried Sichuan eggplant with a sweet sauce; and garlicky brown rice served (by request) in place of the usual sticky white. There really is something for everyone on this menu. Desserts from Seattle's Pacific Desserts can be a big bite after such a feast, but no one seems to be complaining. ■ *In upper level of Old Mill Town Mall at 5th and Maple; (206) 744-0288; 201 5th Ave S, Edmonds; $$; full bar; AE, DC, DIS, MC, V; local checks only; lunch Mon-Sat, dinner every day.* &

LODGINGS

Edmonds Harbor Inn ★ Strategically located near the Edmonds ferry and train terminals (20 minutes north of Seattle), the inn is an attractive choice for a night in Edmonds. It features 61 large rooms (none with views), oak furnishings, continental breakfast, and access to a nearby athletic club. Get directions—the place is near the harborfront, but a little difficult to find in the gray sea of new office and shopping developments. ■ *Dayton and Edmonds Way; (206) 771-5021; 130 W Dayton St, Edmonds, WA 98020; $$; AE, DC, DIS, MC, V; checks OK.* &

▼
Edmonds

Restaurants

▲

GREATER SEATTLE: BOTHELL

The town stands at the north end of Lake Washington, on the way into more open country. **Sammamish River Park** is a pleasant spot, and from here you can take a 9.5-mile hike, bike ride, or roller-skating tour along the Sammamish River (often called the Sammamish Slough), stopping part of the way at the Ste. Michelle winery for a picnic; food and wine can be purchased at the winery (see Woodinville).

RESTAURANTS

Gerard's Relais de Lyon ★★★ French cuisine of stellar quality is happily right in our backyard, almost literally hidden under the pines along the Bothell Highway. Gerard Parrat very boldly opened his restaurant close to 20 years ago, back when deciding on a drive to Bothell for dinner took more than a second's thought and before escargot had become a household word. Through diligence, creative marketing, and sheer talent, Chef Parrat has endured, and very strongly so. No other French restaurant in the Seattle area has remained so French, so unaltered by current trends and regional influences, from the tiny amuse gueule offered to tease the palate before the first course, to the plate of miniature cookies and chocolates served with coffee. Each evening offers an ample list of nightly specials that only make choosing more difficult—will it be rabbit, or lobster, or roasted pheasant, or maybe beef tenderloin? Whatever you choose, it will be expertly executed and simply presented, full of flavor and devoid of frill. The voluptuous lobster bisque is a must. To appreciate the full extent of Parrat's talents, try the découverte (discovery menu) or dégustation (tasting menu), with six and seven courses respectively and at relatively reasonable prices. Gerard's Relais de Lyon is a charming, cozy restaurant for celebrating or simply indulging year-round, with warming fires during the colder months and an outdoor courtyard patio during the summer. Recently, the friendly and well-meaning service did not represent the polished style of French service that you would expect in such an establishment. ■ *Just inside Bothell city limits, north of Seattle; (206) 485-7600; 17121 Bothell Way NE, Bothell; $$$; full bar; DC, MC, V; checks OK; dinner Tues-Sun. &*

Woodinville

GREATER SEATTLE: WOODINVILLE

The suburbs have caught up with this formerly rural outback, paving the dirt roads and lining them with strip malls. Some of the country ambience remains, however, especially to the east where Woodinville fades into the dairy farms of Snoqualmie Valley. Woodinville's claim to fame is **Chateau Ste. Michelle**, the state's largest winery. The grapes come from Eastern

Washington, but experimental vineyards are on site, and tours of the operation, complete with tastings, run daily between 10am and 6pm (until 4:30pm on Mondays); 14111 NE 145th, (206) 488-1133. Just across the street from Ste. Michelle is **Columbia Winery**, the state's oldest premium-wine company. Columbia offers tours on weekends, and the tasting room is open daily from 10am to 5pm; 14030 NE 145th, (206) 488-2776.

Gardeners from around the region flock to **Molbak's**, the massive nursery at 13625 NE 175th, (206) 483-5000.

Woodinville also carries a leg of the **Sammamish River Trail**, a paved path that runs along the river from Bothell to Marymoor Park in Redmond.

RESTAURANTS

Armadillo Barbecue ★ This West Texas barbecue joint plopped down in west Woodinville serves tender, lean pork and extra-moist chicken, all smoky with a rich hot-sauce tang, and sides of molassesy beans and cakey corn bread. It all adds up to a fine Texas feast. The salads, most agree, are acceptable but undistinguished. Tasters stand in general agreement on one other point: the Armadillo should not be regarded as a take-out-only place. Brothers Bob and Bruce Gill have done up "222 Pork Avenue" according to the dictates of a freewheeling, slightly perverse sense of humor, making for surroundings at least as good as the eating. Specials of the day are scrawled on the front windows, there's always an old codger or two at the window table picking his teeth, and the menu includes some inspired descriptions. Need we say a relaxed attitude prevails at the Armadillo? Dinners, which include a salad and your choice of two side dishes, cost in the $8 to $9 range (except the Fat Man, a truckload of barbecued meat for $18.95); lunches ($3.50 to $5.95) are less expensive. An experience. ■ *Woodinville exit from 522E; (206) 481-1417; 13109 NE 175th St, Woodinville; $; beer and wine; AE, DC, MC, V; checks OK; lunch, dinner every day.* ♿

Sushi Kuma A clean, calm place in the middle of mall central. One side is lined with pretty blue-and-bamboo tatami rooms, and a small sushi bar is tucked in the back (though that's where the smoking section is). We recommend, without reservation, the sushi—knockout gems of sweet, tender fish: tuna, whitefish, trout, smoked salmon rolls. The mastermind with the sushi knife is Kuma-san, late of Takara in Seattle. Unfortunately, the rest of the menu is not quite so devastating, and slightly lax in the details (grilled cod, for example, that is overly greasy) and slow service. And we cannot understand why the otherwise lovely pot-stickers came with a blob of tuna salad (yes, with mayonnaise, onions, the whole works). ■ *Between NE 171st and NE 175th on 140th Ave NE; (206) 820-7676; 17321 140th Ave NE, Woodinville; $$; MC, V; no checks; lunch, dinner Mon-Sat.*

Italianissimo [*unrated*] With the closing of his lakeside Stresa, Luciano Bardinelli opened his new Italianissimo ("the most Italian"), which may just work better than his Stresa or Settebello. It's more relaxed than either of the two, set in semi-rural Woodinville, and attracting local families more than ultradiscerning foodies. There's a country-kitchen feel here, from the green-and-cream tiled floors to the casually scribbled menus. The service tends toward casual and the menu looks familiar to those who know Bardinelli—thin-crust pizzas, simple pastas (paglia e fieno, capellini with tomatoes and basil), and meats (a preponderance of veal). Early visits reveal an excellent veal scalloppine with olives and sage—somehow rich and light at the same time—and a calamari stew, spicy and satisfying. Appetizers, somewhat standard, are well attended to. The service, at this early stage in the game, gets some of the details exactly right (such as bringing a taste of the soup of the day to an uncertain customer) and gets some of the big picture exactly wrong (such as consistently forgetting to bring the check). Occasionally a lovely Italian tenor is heard from within the kitchen. ■ *At the corner of 140th and 175th; (206) 485-6888; 17650 140th NE, Woodinville; $$; beer and wine; AE, DIS, MC, V; checks OK; lunch, dinner every day.* ⅃

GREATER SEATTLE: MALTBY

RESTAURANTS

Maltby Cafe ★★ Four women have chased ghosts of cafeterias past from the old Maltby schoolhouse. It's now a country cafe worth finding—the first time might be tough, but you'll never forget the way. Unhurried breakfasts feature delicious, hearty omelets, good new potatoes, old-fashioned oatmeal, and thick slices of French toast. If you have to wait for a table (which is usually the case on weekends), order one of the legendary giant cinnamon rolls and savor it on the steps outside. Breakfast isn't the only meal done right, though—lunch is just as good. Sandwiches such as the Reuben (made with their own corned beef) and the grilled tuna, or a bowl of soup and a microbrew, bring customers back again and again. This is a great place to stop before heading up Stevens Pass. No smoking. ■ *From Hwy 405, go 4½ miles east (toward Monroe) on Hwy 522, turn left at the first light onto Paradise Lake Rd, take a left, a right, and a left onto 212th St SE; (206) 483-3123; 8809 212th St SE (Maltby Rd), Maltby; $; beer and wine; MC, V; local checks only; breakfast, lunch every day.* ⅃

Our evaluations are based on numerous reports from local experts and final judgements are made by the editors. Our inspectors never identify themselves (except over the phone) and never accept free meals or other favors. You can help too, by sending us a report.

It may be known for its corporate top gun **Microsoft**, but this city at the north end of Lake Sammamish is also the hub of a lot of local (and national) cycling activity. Every summer at the **Marymoor Velodrome**, the country's best bicyclists gather for the U.S. Track Cycling Championships in **Marymoor Park**. On the north shore of Lake Sammamish, the park is a huge expanse of ball fields and semi-wild grassland that makes for great bird-watching. On weekends, dog owners bring their pets to the vast and legally leashless dog run in the fields along the Sammamish River. Less ambitious peddlers enjoy the **Sammamish River Trail**, which runs north along the river.

Redmond's downtown is a traditional suburban amalgamation of strip malls and shopping centers, but Anglophiles should stop for afternoon tea at the **British Pantry**; 8125 161st Avenue NE, (206) 883-7511.

RESTAURANTS

Kikuya ★★ Stuck in the back of an undistinguished shopping center in Redmond is this small, family-run, informal Japanese restaurant where the food is wonderful. No kimonos or tatami rooms here—the draw is the excellent sushi bar. As for the rest, it's the kind of place where you order good, honest, simple things—spicy yakisoba (which you can see the chef cooking), gyoza, donburi, and a tempura you can always count on. The fresh, full-flavored meats and fish aren't overseasoned; they're allowed to command the entrée. Everything comes with pickled cucumbers, miso soup, a simple salad, and green tea. Kikuya doesn't take reservations. There's frequently a line at the door, and once seated you may find the service disarmingly rushed. ■ *Off Kirkland-Redmond Hwy on 161st NE; (206) 881-8771; 8105 161st Ave NE, Redmond; $$; beer and wine; MC, V; no checks; lunch and dinner Tues-Sat.* &

Big Time Pizza ★ Big Time stands out as purveyor of the best pies in byte-land, hands down. Homemade dough (made with unbleached flour and olive oil) is hand-tossed and then artfully arranged with fascinating decorations as specified. Our favorites remain the Pesto Plus (with fontina, sun-dried tomatoes, mushrooms, artichoke hearts, and pesto) and the Greek Pizza (feta, kalamata olives, Roma tomatoes, green peppers, and oregano). Best is Big Time's attention to unusually flavorful toppings: cappocolla ham, chorizo, blue cheese, Montrachet. The calzone oozes mozzarella, with that flavorful, chewy, handmade pizza crust for a casing. Rotating beers on tap are now available for that inimitable slice-and-brew combination. The staff resembles the local skateboarding team, but they get enough of the meaningful things right. ■ *Leary and W Lake Sammamish; (206) 885-6425; 7281 W Lake Sammamish*

▼ Redmond ▲

Pkwy NE, Redmond; $; beer and wine; DIS, MC, V; checks OK; lunch, dinner every day. &

GREATER SEATTLE: KIRKLAND

This city's comfortable downtown on Lake Washington's Moss Bay is a popular summer strolling ground. Art galleries, restaurants, bookstores, and boutiques line the two-story main street. Several restaurants look out over boats docked at the marina. Have breakfast at Cousin's, 140 Central Way, (206) 822-1076, or grab a muffin and coffee at Triple J's, 101 Central Way, (206) 822-7319, a storefront coffee shop, and walk a block to the recently renovated waterfront park, where ducks beg scraps and dodge children on the sandy beach.

On Yarrow Bay at the south end of town lies **Carillon Point**, a glitzy hotel and shopping complex lining a round, red-brick courtyard with view of the lake and the Olympic Mountains in the distance.

To the north, just outside of Kirkland, at **Saint Edward State Park**, spectacular rolling trails amble through old stands of Douglas fir and Western red cedar, eventually winding up on the lakefront.

RESTAURANTS

Cafe Juanita ★★★ It used to be that you couldn't get into Cafe Juanita without a reservation months in advance. That was back in '79 when Italian restaurants weren't a lira a dozen. Today Peter Dow's establishment still stands out as one of the standard-bearers of Italian cooking on the Eastside. Dow is often seen presenting a bottle of his own Cavatappi sauvignon blanc, cabernet sauvignon, or Maddalena, threading himself among the pasta eaters, and, now and then, preparing his favorite dishes behind the line. The menu is small, maybe eight items, and indeed, a lot of this eatery's notoriety has to do with its consistency. Dow is a cautious steward of his menu, rotating some of his favorite specials (such as the coteghino de milanese—homemade pork, pancetta, and pistachio sausage on lentils stewed with a savory stir of tomatoes, onions, and rosemary) without losing any tried-and-true successes (spiedini misti—two skewers of lamb and Italian sausage, roasted with onions and green peppers). Not every dish is a winner—some think the pollo ai pistachio arrives swimming in too much of a bland cream sauce, others think the gnocchi (which come with the sage-infused rabbit) are too dry, just a dusting of Parmesan. A private room with fireplace and sofa is particularly good for a party of up to 25 (more in the summer, when guests pour out onto the patio). ■ *116th exit off 405, west to 97th; (206) 823-1505; 9702 NE 120th Pl, Kirkland; $$; beer and wine; MC, V; checks OK; dinner every day.*

Izumi ★★ Tucked into taco-and-burger land in a Kirkland shopping center, Izumi is an oasis of bright blond wood. Part the dark blue half-curtain, step into the room, and suburbia is behind you; you're in the competent care of servers dressed in traditional sea green kimonos. Things move briskly at lunchtime, when Japanese families mingle with local businesspeople. (Lunch hours are 11:30 to 1:30, and they mean it. If you linger past 2:00, you're likely to realize that the background music has just stopped midphase. It's not brusque, just efficient.) Unagi (broiled freshwater eel) and mirugai (geoduck) sushi are outstanding; roe enthusiasts can sample the eggs of four different sea creatures, and more timid souls can pig out on the California maki. Tonkatsu, in a light, crisp breading, is juicy, tender, greaseless, and huge. Tempura can be underdone if the kitchen is rushed. Makunouchi comes in two sizes at dinner— the larger a real feast of sushi, sashimi, tempura, teriyaki, and cooked vegetables presented in a lacquer box. Wash everything down with a big Asahi beer. ■ *Totem Lake West Shopping Center; (206) 821-1959; 12539 116th NE, Kirkland; $$; beer, wine, and sake; AE, MC, V; checks OK; lunch Mon-Fri, dinner Mon-Sat.* &

▼

Kirkland

Restaurants

▲

Le Provençal ★★ We've said it before, and we'll say it again: you can get better French food in the Northwest, but in certain moods this is probably the most pleasant of French restaurants. On the whole, the food at Le Provençal is quite good and the atmosphere is very charming in a country-inn-meets-bistro sort of style. Waiters with thick accents and long white aprons set an authentically French mood, which continues through to the dessert tray being wheeled to the table for your selection. The menu emphasis is bistro, with a very reasonably priced prix-fixe four-course meal ($19.50). Begin with a full and flavorful onion soup, followed by a good crisp salad with a sprinkling of goat cheese. Among the five main-course selections is the Daube Avignonnaise (Avignon-style beef stew) which Chef Gayte has been preparing since the day his restaurant opened. Very simple, served with rice and vegetables, and quite good. Other options might include rabbit stew, steak au poivre, or duck breast with blackberries. You can also choose from more upscale items on the à la carte menu. Or try the prix-fixe "menu gastronomie" at $32.50 for five courses. The desserts, however tantalizing on the cart, were anticlimactic, though the Grand Marnier soufflé puts some of the area's more classy French establishments to shame. ■ *Downtown Kirkland; (206) 827-3300; 212 Central Way, Kirkland; $$; full bar; AE, DC, MC, V; local checks OK; dinner every day.* &

Ristorante Paradiso ★★ This place is a real sleeper. Unpretentious, tucked away behind Kirkland's main drag, it's an oasis of tender, loving care in the kitchen. Locals have made it theirs in touching ways: smokers tend to step outside to light up, and one patron has been known to don an apron and refill water glasses. Openers are a beautifully arranged plate of grilled vegetables—meltingly tender and complex eggplant, lighter zucchini, red and yellow peppers, and onions in a marinade with a hint of rice-wine vinegar—and a generous bowl of perfectly fresh and perfectly cooked cozze e vongole (mussels and clams), in white wine and lemon-Italian-parsley-garlic broth of which we scooped up every drop. Warm, floury, just-out-of-the-oven rounds of firm but soft yeast bread were a nice change from the currently trendy chew-toy texture of house bread elsewhere. Lasagne is homemade and rich; saltimbocca delicate; loin lamb chops expertly grilled. The weighty wine list assembled by wine steward Enrico Fabregas is a minitour of Italy. A 1986 Salice Salentino bloomed in the glass and complemented every dish. Service is knowledgeable and unhurried. A gem. ■ *Off Lake Washington St, across from Moss Bay; (206) 889-8601; 120 A Park Lane, Kirkland; $$; beer and wine; AE, MC, V; local checks OK; lunch Mon-Sat, dinner every day.* &

Shamiana ★★ Brother-and-sister team Eric Larson and Tracy Larson Devaan grew up as foreign service kids in East Pakistan (now Bangladesh), and after their return to the United States found themselves hankering for the food they remembered. Now Eric's in the kitchen, Tracy runs the front of the house, and their mother, Nancy (Memsahib) Larson, oversees the operation. Eastern cooking meets Western chefs here in the happiest of ways: stunning creations include a velvet butter chicken wallowing in cumin-scented butter, tomato, and cream sauce. A Pakistani barbecue turns out flame-broiled meats and some mouth-watering (and mouth-igniting) versions of traditional Indian curries. Vegetarians can select from crisp samosas stuffed with crunchy potatoes or aloo dum Kashmiri, potatoes simmered in spicy yogurt sauce. Instructively, the menu notes which dishes are made without dairy products and gives a heat guide to ordering curries. Dinner may top $20, but lunch is bargain city, with a buffet that changes daily. ■ *In the Houghton Village at 108th and 68th; (206) 827-4902; 10724 NE 68th St, Kirkland; $; beer and wine; AE, MC, V; checks OK; lunch Mon-Fri, dinner every day.*

Yarrow Bay Grill and Beach Cafe ★★ There are two restaurants here, sharing a stunner of a lake view as well as a kitchen from which emerges creative meals. In ways, it's reminiscent of the praiseworthy Shilshole formula (three of the four Ray's owners started Yarrow Bay, originally slated to be the Eastside's Ray's). Upstairs, in the formal dining room with teak booths and a fish theme (down to fish pulls on the window shades), the entrées are a bit more celebratory (and expensive). Vicki McCaffree in the kitchen plays fast and loose with unusual pairings of ingredients, and they usually work. Here is a place where you can feel good about ordering multifaceted dishes (such as a perfectly undercooked swordfish with fruit salsa) and feel confident that they'll be fine; our experience with the simpler dishes is that they tend to fall flat (attention to detail: a salad overdoused with dressing), but in general most things at this place seem to be on the upswing. Service is efficient and helpful, the bouillabaisse is spicy and loaded with crab, mussels, and clams, and there seems to be something on the menu for everyone's palate.

There's a lively scene downstairs in the Beach Cafe. You come as you are, sit on the west-facing deck over Lake Washington (or in one of the angled booths at sunset), and choose from equally sophisticated dishes at less sophisticated prices: ravioli stuffed with three cheeses, hazelnuts, and roasted garlic hidden in a mustard and salmon cream sauce; Whidbey Island mussels Dijonnaise; or fried calamari with an aioli dipping sauce. The wine list (same on both levels) is well conceived. ■ *In the Carillon Point Plaza, downtown Kirkland; (206) 889-0303 (Beach Cafe) or (206) 889-9052 (restaurant); 1270 Carillon Point, Kirkland; $$$; full bar; AE, DC, MC, V; local checks only; lunch Mon-Fri, dinner every day.* &

Third Floor Fish Cafe ★ This upstairs restaurant pulls out all the stops to lure patrons up to the view, to the flirty food, to the zany drinks (Electric Fish Bowl and Moss Bay Slimer). It's jazzy, in hues of vermilion, orange, aqua, and yellow—a place that can be either casual or an occasion spot. However, somewhere the execution has wavered, delivering meals that falter in the basics. A tough cut of meat, for example, in the peppercorn New York steak. A bland seafood fettuccine. Thick, mayonnaise-ish sauces on everything from the salads to the (otherwise good) crab cakes. This is not to say there aren't bright spots, such as utterly fresh oysters and the confetti relish that arrived next to the crab cakes, sweet and hot at the same time. You're better off sticking to dishes whose distinctive ingredients speak out for themselves—such as grilled sea scallops and mahi-mahi—or sitting in the bar grazing on appetizers; some swear they've never had a bad meal here. A banquet room with a view is available. ■ *In downtown Kirkland, above the marina; (206) 822-3553; 205 Lake St, Kirkland; $$$; full bar; AE, DC, MC, V; local checks only; lunch Mon-Fri, dinner Mon-Sat.* &

LODGINGS

Woodmark Hotel ★★★ On the eastern shore of Lake Washington, this hotel claims the only lodging actually on the lake. From the outside, it resembles a modern office building, but on the inside one encounters the soft touches of a fine hotel: 100 plush rooms (the best have lake views and sounds of geese honking and ducks quacking) with fully stocked minibars and refrigerators, VCRs (complimentary movies are available at the front desk), baths equipped with a second TV, terrycloth robes, and oversize towels, with service (from laundry to valet) to match. You'll get a complimentary newspaper with the full breakfast. Downstairs on the lake level there's a comfortable living room with a grand piano and a well-tended fire. The hotel has its own clubby restaurant, the Carillon Room, with a menu that harks back to a time of escargots and rack of lamb; seafood is the main event next door at the Yarrow Bay Grill and Beach Cafe (see review in this section). Check out the nearby specialty shops or rent a boat from the marina. Business travelers can take advantage of extra amenities such as a pager for off-site calls, a cellular phone, and complimentary use of a laptop computer and a printer. Parking access is a bit of a maze. ■ *Kirkland exit off SR 520, north on Lake Washington Blvd NE to Carillon Point; (206) 822-3700; 1200 Carillon Point, Kirkland, WA 98033; $$$; AE, DC, MC, V; checks OK.* &

Shumway Mansion ★★ When Richard and Salli Harris heard that developers wanted to demolish this historic 1909 building to make room for condos, they hauled the four-story house to a safe location near Kirkland's Juanita Bay. Now it's a gracious bed and breakfast with an equal emphasis on seminars and receptions. Seven guest rooms are furnished with antiques (each has a private bath), and antique-filled public rooms overlook the bay (just a short walk away) and the lower parking lots. An eighth room was being completed at press time. The ballroom downstairs is often used for weddings or special meetings, and in summer it opens onto a flowering patio. A full breakfast is served in the dining room on table linens. Guests can use the Columbia Athletic Club; downtown Seattle is 20 minutes away. Children over 12 are welcome. No pets or smoking. ■ *Near NE 116th on 99th Pl NE; (206) 823-2303; 11410 99th Pl NE, Kirkland, WA 98033; $$; AE, MC, V; checks OK.* &

▼

Bellevue

▲

GREATER SEATTLE: BELLEVUE

This former quiet suburban hamlet is developing into a sister-city of Seattle, boasting a true downtown skyline. Bellevue is the heart of the Eastside, the former suburbs of Seattle, east of Lake Washington, that now stand on their own. As many commuters now leave Seattle in the morning for work on the Eastside as make the traditional suburb-to-Seattle trek.

At the core of downtown Bellevue is **Bellevue Place**, a hotel, restaurant, and shopping complex. Daniel's Broiler on the 21st floor of the Seafirst Office Building offers stunning views of Seattle, Puget Sound, and the Olympics.

Across the street, **Bellevue Square** hosts Nordstrom and hundreds of other stores, but it's also one of the first malls in the country to house a museum—the **Bellevue Art Museum**, specializing in Northwest crafts, (206) 454-6021.

Much of what makes Bellevue such a livable city is the quiet neighborhoods that ring the downtown. The neighborhood surrounding **Bridle Trails State Park** on the Kirkland border looks like a condensed version of Virginia equestrian country, with backyards of horses and stables. The park features miles of riding and hiking trails through vast stands of Douglas fir. Day hikers can head east toward Issaquah to explore **Cougar Mountain**, the forested, westernmost hill of an ancient mountain range that stretches from Lake Washington to the younger Cascades.

RESTAURANTS

Tosoni's ★★ For ten years chef Walter Walcher has presided over a room of friendly diners diving into colossal portions of oldtime Middle European food dished out at reasonable prices. The strip mall storefront on a Bellevue thoroughfare gives little indication as to the delights inside. Tosoni's is a small (somewhat noisy) room filled with armoires of wine, lined with booths, and serviced by an open kitchen. The meals are a throwback to the copious servings of fifteen years ago—perhaps that's why the place is so refreshing. You will not find herb oils anointing tiny portions of pampered birds. Abundance is the key ingredient here, whether it's the crab-stuffed mushroom appetizer or the fork-tender veal chop in a savory reduction accompanied by parmesan-dusted cappelini, mashed potatoes, and a platter of lightly steamed vegetables. There is nothing slim or trim about this very popular place. ■ *Off 148th Ave NE; (206) 644-1668; 14320 NE 20th N, Bellevue; $$; beer and wine; MC, V; local checks only; dinner Tues-Sat.*

Azalea's Fountain Court ★ Azalea's stands out as something of an oasis in Bellevue, quietly elegant in chintz and cool colors. The menu is local and quite seasonal, to the point that summer dinners really *feel* summery. On recent visits, we enjoyed a sumptuous warm seafood salad, baked oysters with tomatoes and peppers, and grilled scallops over spinach, and the overall effect of the place, the quiet atmosphere, and the live jazz in the balcony above were such that small flaws (too much breadcrumb on the oysters, salad dressing that was overly sweet) hardly detracted from the meal at all. Service is excellent, as is the tequila-grapefruit ice. ■ *Off Main St on 103rd Ave NE; (206) 451-0426; 22 103rd NE, Bellevue; $$$; full bar; AE, DC, MC, V; checks OK; lunch Mon-Fri, dinner Tues-Sat.* ᕻ

Eques (Hyatt Regency at Bellevue Place) ★ Eques seems to have a bit of the Bellevue syndrome by attempting to please many by offending none. Indeed, the formal setting is warm and pleasing in pastel tones and natural wood; however, the

▼
Bellevue
▲

food is quite plain—flavors neither entice nor disappoint (a bland salmon chowder, a shrimp abruzzi served with spaghetti—not linguine as billed—and lacking much seasoning). You'll do best with dishes infused with strong individual ingredients such as Gorgonzola, mustard, and garlic. Prices in this glitzy Bellevue Place spot are quite reasonable and service properly subdued. Desserts are large and quite lovely. Children's portions are available at half price, although the atmosphere—with a roaring fire in the fireplace and a classical guitarist in the background—is only for the best behaved. ■ *Across from Bellevue Square; (206) 451-3012; 900 Bellevue Way NE, Bellevue; $$; full bar; AE, DC, MC, V; no checks; breakfast, lunch, Mon-Sat, dinner every day, brunch Sun.*

Noble Court ★ If the parking lot is jammed, don't worry. There's plenty of room inside. But Eastsiders (and some who actually journey across the lake) know that there is some fine Chinese food here. Oyster fans should venture the Sichuan-style appetizer, two huge Pacific oysters split and doused in hot (temperature), hot (spicy), sweet Sichuan sauce. Connoisseurs of the unusual can just cast their eyes down the menu for shark-fin soup, stewed abalone, and bird's nest with crabmeat soup. Anything in black-bean sauce is going to be dependable, from stir-fried clams (though not all of them were open on a recent visit) to something from the live tanks outside. Sizzling dishes are just that. Service is a little scattered, but our Chinese sources say that Noble Court serves the best dim sum on either side of the lake. ■ *Off the Bellevue-Redmond Rd; (206) 641-6011; 1644 140th NE, Bellevue; $$; full bar; AE, MC, V; no checks; lunch, dinner every day.*

Pogacha ★ Properly speaking, a pogacha is a chewy Croatian dinner roll baked in a wood-fired oven. Here, at the only Croatian pizza joint in Bellevue (or in all the Puget Sound area, for that matter), some liberties are taken: larger pogachas become sandwiches, and the dough is pulled out to make crusts for pizzas that owe as much to California as to Croatia. The Four Seasons Pogacha is subdivided to mesh classic flavors from four gourmet food groups: mushroom and pesto; five-cheese; tomato and basil; and artichoke hearts dressed with feta, red onion, and garlic oil. Request red sauce if you must have it. The daily special operates on the cook's whims and may feature a lovely smoked-salmon-caviar-with-sour-cream creation; for pogacha-phobes, there are smartly sauced pastas and a few meat and fish options. This eatery is practically hueless and slightly sterile. Luckily, you can jazz up the paper tablecloths (and your wait) with the crayons provided at each table. ■ *In Bellevue Plaza near 106th NE and NE 8th; (206) 455-5670; 119 106th Ave NE, Bellevue; $; beer and wine; AE, MC, V; no checks; lunch Mon-Fri, dinner Tues-Sat.*

▼

Bellevue

Restaurants

▲

Seoul Olympic Restaurant ★ Some of the best Korean food in the Seattle area is in a nondescript office complex in Bellevue. There are a lot of odd-sounding dishes (check out the "one cow" barbecue), and the waitstaff is good about steering you away from food that might ring strange with Western palates and stomachs (or might be raw or unbearably hot). You don't need to know the menu, however, to order the Korean barbecued beef (grilled beef that's been marinated in soy sauce, sugar, and wine), or crispy dumplings, or a fine dry Korean beer to wash it all down. Adventuresome eaters who do not heed the staff's advice might find themselves faced with (gulp!) a hearty soup of beef tripe and tubular animal innards. ■ *At the corner of NE 12th and 112th NE; (206) 455-9305; 1200 112th Ave NE, Bellevue; $$; full bar; MC, V; checks OK; lunch, dinner every day.* &

LODGINGS

The Bellevue Hilton ★★ With every amenity in the book, the Bellevue Hilton is the best bet on the Eastside's Hotel Row. Rooms are tastefully done in warm colors. Amenities include use of a nearby health-and-racquet club, free transportation around Bellevue (within a 5-mile radius), room service until 10pm weekdays and 10:30pm weekends, a Jacuzzi, a dry sauna, a pool, several free cable channels in every room, and three restaurants. Working stiffs will appreciate the hotel's business center and the desks in every room. Doubles run from $92 to $112; parlor suites, from $160 to $235, have sitting rooms, a wet bar and a refrigerator, and dining tables. ■ *Main and 112th NE; (206) 455-3330, toll-free (800) BEL-HILT; 100 112th Ave NE, Bellevue, WA 98004; $$$; AE, DC, DIS, MC, V; checks OK.* &

Bellevue Holiday Inn ★★ This understated two-story motel doesn't overload your senses or your budget; many regular visitors to Bellevue won't stay anywhere else. The units are arranged campus-style around a well-manicured lawn and heated pool. The suites are nothing special; the fancy dining room, Jonah's, is better than most. ■ *112th and Main; (206) 455-5240; 11211 Main St, Bellevue, WA 98004; $$; AE, DC, DIS, MC, V; checks OK.* &

Hyatt Regency at Bellevue Place ★★ Hyatt Regency is just one part of Kemper Freeman's splashy, sprawling retail-office-restaurant-hotel-health-club complex called Bellevue Place. The 382-room hotel with 24 stories (the highest in Bellevue) offers many of the extras: pricier "Regency Club" rooms on the top two floors, two big ballrooms, several satellite conference rooms, use of the neighboring Seattle Club (for a $10 fee), and a fine restaurant, Eques (see review in this section). The best rooms are on the south side above the seventh floor (if only the windows would open). Plenty of people come to Bellevue just to shop—and now they have a place to stay. ■ *NE 8th St and Bellevue Way; (206) 462-1234, toll-free (800) 233-1234; 900 Bellevue Way, Bellevue, WA 98104; $$$; AE, DC, DIS, MC, V; checks OK.* ♿

GREATER SEATTLE: MERCER ISLAND

RESTAURANTS

Caffe Italia ★ The bright, lemon yellow Caffe Italia is a less formal version of Subito (which used to live here), very casual and comfortable. The menu yields an interesting mix of authentic Italian dishes and a couple of health-conscious '90s-style adaptations. Hold true to the Italian side of the menu and you'll rarely be disappointed. The focaccia that comes to the table as you sit down is actually schiacciata—flat, chewy bread drizzled with olive oil and sprinkled with salt. Among the appetizers we found, to our delight, suppli al telefono, the classic Roman street food: fried balls of rice with a gooey mozzarella center, and a little tub of marinara for dipping. Chewy pizzas are piled with robust ingredients (although an overwhelmed palate may wish for a tamer version); pastas and meats are simple and lovely. Prices for food and wine are reasonable; service is young and uncommonly pleasant. ■ *Across from the Safeway on 76th Ave SE; (206) 232-9009; 2448 76th Ave SE, Mercer Island; $$; beer and wine; MC, V; checks OK; lunch Tues-Fri, dinner Tues-Sun.* ♿

GREATER SEATTLE: ISSAQUAH

Fast-food franchises now line Interstate 90, but the center of this old coal-mining town still resembles small-town America, complete with a butcher shop and a working dairy. On good days, Mount Rainier appears between the hills that form the town's southern and eastern borders.

Gilman Village on Gilman Boulevard is a shopping complex with a twist: the developers refurnished old farmhouses, a barn, and a feed store, then filled them with craft and clothing shops, restaurants, and a woodworking gallery. **Boehm's Chocolates** on the edge of town still dips its chocolates by hand and offers tours for groups (reservations are needed), (206) 392-6652.

The **Issaquah Farmers' Market** is open Saturdays throughout the summer, across from the **Issaquah State Salmon Hatchery**, on Sunset Way, which is open to visitors daily from 8am to 7:30pm (there aren't any tours, but there are instructional displays in the lobby).

Lake Sammamish State Park lies between town and Lake Sammamish, and offers swimming and boat access. **Tiger**

Mountain, the sprawling 13,000-acre state forest that looms to the east, is a favorite weekend destination for hikers and mountain bikers. Trails wind through alder and evergreen forests and past old coal-mine shafts.

RESTAURANTS

Mandarin Garden ★★ This Issaquah restaurant has the distinction of producing spiciness where promised—a rarity among Chinese restaurants in the area, and all the more admirable since chef and owner Andy Wang is a native of Shanghai. The minimal decor and the down-at-heels ambience mask Wang's understanding of Sichuan, Hunan, and Mandarin cooking and warm, efficient service. Praiseworthy dishes include melt-in-your-mouth kung pao chicken, mixed seafood Sichuan, and variations on bean curd. Two private rooms (one holding up to 50 guests) are available for banquets. Order Peking duck a day in advance. ■ *Exit 17 off I-90 to Sunset Way; (206) 392-9476; 40 E Sunset Way, Issaquah; $; beer and wine; MC, V; local checks only; lunch Mon-Sat, dinner every day.* ♿

▼

Issaquah

▲

Nicolino ★★ Day and night Nicolino's charming room virtually teems with diners who like the lively chatter, casual atmosphere, sunny courtyard, and low price tags (and who don't mind waiting a bit for a table). The pastas might transport you to another plane of existence, especially those in cream sauce (the pomodoro-based version is oddly, though not unpleasantly, sweet). Try the fettuccine della casa, with mushrooms, peas, and prosciutto; or penne sovietiche, with an original sauce of mascarpone cheese, butter, spiced vodka, and a kiss of tomato sauce. They aren't showy dishes, but they can be no less than stunning, sided with hearty slices of peasant bread to dredge in olive oil, a few swirls of Chianti. Unfortunately, if Dr. Jekyll is the genius of the noodle, Mr. Hyde seems to be the grill-and-sauté man. Prawns are overcooked when they should be bursting with fruitlike juices, veal is long past tender, chicken arrives shamefully tough. If Nicola Petruzzelli paid more attention to this side of the menu, he'd have a restaurant that had a shot at living up to its dazzling reputation. ■ *In Gilman Village; (206) 391-8077; 317 NW Gilman Blvd, Issaquah; $$; beer and wine; MC, V; checks OK; lunch, dinner every day.* ♿

LODGINGS

The Wildflower ★ Laureita Caldwell has decorated three guest rooms in her log-house bed and breakfast in floral themes, based on plants native to Issaquah. The Strawberry Room, the Fern Room, and the Rose Room all have raw pine walls, charming window seats (great for reading), handmade quilts, and private baths. Downstairs there's a cozy common room where guests can relax by the wood stove. All this and breakfast too for $55. The massive cabin sits impressively in the lonesome woods just north of Issaquah—a terrific base camp for travelers torn between the mountains and the metropolis. ■ *Exit 17 from I-90, head left 2 blocks, then right onto Issaquah-Fall City Rd for 1 mile, turn right at light, turn right into second driveway after next traffic light (look for a horse-crossing sign); (206) 392-1196; 25237 SE Issaquah-Fall City Rd, Issaquah, WA 98027; $; no credit cards; checks OK.*

GREATER SEATTLE: BAINBRIDGE ISLAND

Once a major logging port, Bainbridge Island is now a semirural haven for city professionals (who don't mind the half-hour commute via ferry from downtown Seattle), writers, artists, and people seeking simpler lives. It makes a pleasant tour by car or bike, during which you can see some small pastoral farms, enviable waterfront homes, and spectacular cityscapes (especially from **Fay Bainbridge State Park** on the northeast corner of the island). The wooded and waterfront trails in **Fort Ward State Park**, on the south end of the island, make for a nice afternoon stroll (good picnic spots, too).

Bloedel Reserve is 150 acres of lush, tranquil gardens, woods, meadows, and ponds. Plants from all over the world make the grounds interesting at any time of the year. Reservations are required and limited, taken for Wednesdays and Sundays only, (206) 842-7631.

A simpler trip is to ride over on the ferry, sans car, and walk a few strides up the road to the **Bainbridge Island Winery**, a small family winery which makes a number of good wines, including a superb strawberry. Then walk a few blocks to downtown, take in the shops, have coffee and pastry at **Pegasus Espresso House** at the foot of Madison Avenue S, and float back to Seattle. For Washington State Ferry information, call (206) 464-6400.

Bainbridge Island

Restaurants

RESTAURANTS

Four Swallows ★★ Islanders can't get enough of Geraldine Ferraro's cheery restaurant on the south end of Bainbridge Island. It's an inviting place with high booths, a comfortable couch, and upbeat jazz in the air. It's appreciated by locals both for its friendly neighborhood appeal and its consistently good food. The small, well thought-out menu changes weekly and somehow it's always exactly right. Familiar ingredients (roasted garlic, roasted red peppers, sun-dried tomatoes, and Gorgonzola) are part of the tiny kitchen's regular repertoire; however, they always seem to appear with a new inspiration. Count on one or two pasta dishes (perhaps fresh fettuccine with pancetta, roasted tomatoes, garlic, and mozzarella spiked with a touch of crushed red pepper and rosemary), and a soul-satisfying entrée of fish or chicken. Vegetarians eat well here too, what with a Gorgonzola, pear, and toasted walnut salad, a wild mushroom pizza, and an antipasti plate that stands up to any we've sampled in Seattle. Sometimes in the spring we go just for the warm rhubarb crisp. ▪ *Follow signs toward Fort Ward State Park; (206) 842-3397; 4569 Lynwood Center Rd, Bainbridge Island; $; beer and wine; MC, V; local checks only; dinner Tues-Sun.*

Pleasant Beach Grill ★★ Bainbridge Island's only white-linen restaurant remains quietly tucked away in a large Tudor house on the south end of the island. Islanders have always favored the pine-paneled bar, warmed by a fireplace and with two couches, as the place to sink into a drink and dessert (a luscious slice of rich shortcake crowned with crimson berries, or an excellent chocolate mousse). Under the direction of Hussein Ramadan, the grill has found a pleasant consistency which islanders truly appreciate. The menu is very continental in range, from a sauté of prawns, scallops, and white fish (in a sauce of curry, cool lemon grass, and coconut milk, adorned with mushrooms and a tricolored mosaic of peppers) to an excellent 10-ounce slab of New York pepper steak. Stick with the simpler grills and seafoods or opt for a mixed-grill plate if indecisive; enjoy the ample portions and skilled service. The dining room's pleasant, but in the summer, ask for the terrace. In winter, reserve a table in the appealing fireside bar. ▪ *Near Lynwood Center, follow signs toward Fort Ward State Park; (206) 842-4347; 4738 Lynwood Center NE, Bainbridge Island; $$; full bar; AE, MC, V; local checks only; dinner every day.* &

Streamliner Diner The Streamliner Diner (an easy walk from the ferry) has been an Island institution for almost a decade. This steamy restaurant built its reputation on satisfying breakfasts and inventive entrées—mom food with a creative twist. It's a local custom to savor a cup of Starbucks coffee for as long as you like, visiting friends and trading local gossip (though locals shy away from this place when weekend ferry riders line up out the door). With its kitchen-table decor and sweet saxophone swing coming through the sound system, this no-smoking restaurant oozes small-town personality. The omelet list is extensive, and the potatoes are chunky and oniony. More than one regular swears by the Potatoes Deluxe, a scramble of potatoes, mushrooms, spinach, green onions, tomatoes, and cheddar, with cumin-scented guacamole on top. Lunches (light on Saturdays) are homemade soups, salads, and sandwiches—maybe artichoke, tangy with a Dijon marinade and onions, or the BLT with garlic cream cheese and avocado. ▪ *Winslow Way and Bejune; (206) 842-8595; 397 Winslow Way, Bainbridge Island; $; no alcohol; no credit cards; checks OK; breakfast every day, lunch Mon-Sat.* &

The Bombay House ★★ This sprawling turn-of-the-century house with a widow's walk, set in a lavish flower garden with a rough-cedar gazebo overlooking scenic Rich Passage, is just a sweet stroll from Fort Ward State Park. With a hearty dose of island-hideaway atmosphere, the Bombay House has five bedrooms done up in country antiques. Three have private baths, and the vast second-floor Captain's Suite has a wood parlor stove and a claw-footed tub. The large living room has a fireplace. Innkeepers Roger, Bunny, and their charming daughter, Cameron, are friendly hosts. In the morning, you'll discover that, yes, Bunny wrote the book on breakfast. And what a feast it is. Smoking is restricted to outside. ■ *4 miles south of the ferry, just off W Blakely Ave; (206) 842-3926 or (800) 598-3926; 8490 Beck Rd NE, Bainbridge Island, WA 98110; $$; AE, MC, V; checks OK.*

Beach Cottage B&B ★ Right across Eagle Harbor from the ferry-stop town of Winslow is this charming, flower-bedecked four-cottage setup. Each cottage has a queen-size bed, a kitchen (stocked with breakfast fixings), logs for the fireplace, and a stereo. One is right on the beach, and all four boast decks and a view of Eagle Harbor and its marina (the two-bedroom on the hill even views Seattle and Mount Rainier on clear days). Smoking is allowed (pets and children under 16 are not), and there's a rowboat for use. ■ *4 miles from the ferry off Eagle Harbor Dr; (206) 842-6081; 5831 Ward NE, Bainbridge Island, WA 98110; $$$; no credit cards; checks OK.*

GREATER SEATTLE: SEA-TAC

LODGINGS

Seattle Airport Hilton Hotel ★★ This streamlined two-story building, camouflaged by trees and plantings, miraculously manages to create a resort atmosphere along an airport strip. Plush rooms (at posh prices) circle a large, landscaped courtyard with pool and indoor/outdoor Jacuzzi. The architecture is by the distinguished national firm of SOM. An exercise room and numerous meeting and party rooms are available. A versatile menu offers continental cuisine. ■ *188th St exit off I-5, north 1½ miles; (206) 244-4800, toll-free (800) HILTONS; 17620 Pacific Hwy S, Seattle, WA 98188; $$$; AE, DC, DIS, MC, V; checks OK.* &

Seattle Marriott at Sea-Tac ★ Another megamotel, though somewhat concealed by trees, it's a block from the airport strip. The Alaska motif is warm, though somewhat cluttered in the lobby. Rooms are standard, but suites are spacious. A pool and a courtyard area are part of an enormous covered atrium; there are also two Jacuzzis, a sauna, and a well-equipped exercise room. ■ *Just east of Pacific Hwy S at S 176th and 32nd Ave S; (206) 241-2000 or toll-free (800) 228-9290; 3201 S 176th St, Seattle, WA 98188; $$$; AE, DC, DIS, MC, V; checks OK.* ♿

WestCoast Sea-Tac Hotel ★ This WestCoast outpost was recently refurbished, and its 150 bright rooms each feature a writing desk (a slightly less upscale WestCoast across the street caters handily to the business traveler; 18415 Pacific Highway S, (206) 248-8200). Terrycloth robes, hair dryers, shoe-shine machines, and a stocked honor bar are available in the 32 limited-edition suites. Meeting facilities accommodate up to 200; an outdoor pool, Jacuzzi, and sauna accommodate everyone. It's the only airport hotel that offers free valet parking for seven days. ■ *Across from the airport entrance; (206) 246-5535 or (800) 426-0670; 18220 Pacific Hwy S, Seattle, WA 98188; $$$; AE, DC, DIS, MC, V; checks OK.* ♿

Wyndham Garden Hotel ★ You can't get much closer to the airport than this. Attractive styling inside, warm wood paneling in the lobby lounge, and an inviting library and fireplace make this a bit classier than your standard airport hotel. Accommodations include 180 guest rooms with writing desks, and 24 suites, with in-room coffeemakers, complimentary coffee, and hair dryers. Nonsmoking rooms, room service (early evening only), and meeting space are available. ■ *South of S 176th St; (206) 244-6666; 18118 Pacific Hwy S, Seattle, WA 98188; $$$; AE, DC, DIS, MC, V; checks OK.* ♿

GREATER SEATTLE: BURIEN

RESTAURANTS

Filiberto's ★★ Filiberto's is the most authentic and, on a good day, among the best of the local (and we mean local) Italian restaurants. The look is cheery and trattoria-perfect, with even the dishwashing section in back finished in imported tile. Service can be erratic, but the food seems to have gotten more consistent, with good attention to the basics. The long menu emphasizes Roman and other midregion preparations of pasta, veal, poultry, and rabbit, right down to the real stracciatella alla Romana egg-drop soup (not too salty, as it often is in Rome). Three special treats: the huge, very well-priced selection of Italian wines in a take-your-pick glass case, Filiberto's pizza oven—the realest in Seattle—and a bocce court out back (if you're lucky, you'll get asked to play). ■ *Off Hwy 518; (206) 248-1944; 14401 Des Moines Memorial Dr S, Burien; $$; full bar; AE, MC, V; checks OK; lunch Tues-Fri, dinner Tues-Sat.* ♿

Satsuma ★★ Plain as a box on the outside, this tranquil Burien hideaway has captured the interest of the local Japanese, who come to enjoy the cooking of Tak Suetsugu, formerly of the Mikado. The tempura is light as air, the sushi merely creditable. For a twist, try the Washington roll, with smoked salmon, tamagoyaki (similar to an omelet), cucumber, and strips of Washington apple. The black cod kasuzuke, marinated in sake lees and broiled, is a velvety ambrosia. Tatami rooms are available. ■ *Off 148th on Ambaum; (206) 242-1747; 14301 Ambaum Blvd SW, Burien; $; beer and wine; AE, MC, V; no checks; lunch Tues, Wed, Fri, dinner Tues-Sun.* &

GREATER SEATTLE: KENT

RESTAURANTS

Cave Man Kitchens ★ The late Dick Donley spent years experimenting with methods of smoking ribs, chicken, turkey, sausage, ham, and salmon over alder and (when available) applewood. What he finally achieved was outstanding—especially the moist smoked turkey. Donley's six children carry on after him, and nothing has changed. There is no inside seating, but in warm weather you can eat outside on picnic tables and go across the street to the neighborhood store for beer. Load up on the smoked goods and accompaniments such as beans, potato salad, coleslaw, and a terrific bread pudding with butterscotch-whiskey sauce. ■ *West Valley Hwy at the James intersection; (206) 854-1210; 807 West Valley Hwy, Kent; $; no alcohol; MC, V; checks OK; lunch, dinner every day.* &

▼

Des Moines

Restaurants

▲

GREATER SEATTLE: DES MOINES

RESTAURANTS

Le Bonaparte ★ This restaurant in a house has been known to draw diners from the entire region to the shoreline of Des Moines. But as things begin to slip, fewer are inspired to make an evening of it. Owner/chef Jacques Mason normally has up to four game birds (squab, duck, quail, pheasant) prepared in different sauces. Not all of them are successful—a recent lamb dish was overpowered by Pernod. There are, however, some surprising touches: the veal dishes are often exemplary, and the chocolate Marie Antoinette gâteau made without flour continues to wow even reluctant chocoholics. The service has been known to attempt to cover up incompetence with snobbery. Le Bonaparte is especially lovely in summer, when you can eat on the verandah in the shade of venerable old fruit trees. On Sundays, a five-course champagne brunch features everything from omelets and fruit to seafood and escargots. Chef Mason puts together imaginative customized menus for private groups of up to 150. ■ *S 216th St and Marine View Dr; (206) 878-4412; 21630 Marine View Dr, Des Moines; $$$; full bar; AE, DC, MC, V; no checks; lunch Mon-Fri, dinner every day, brunch Sun.* &

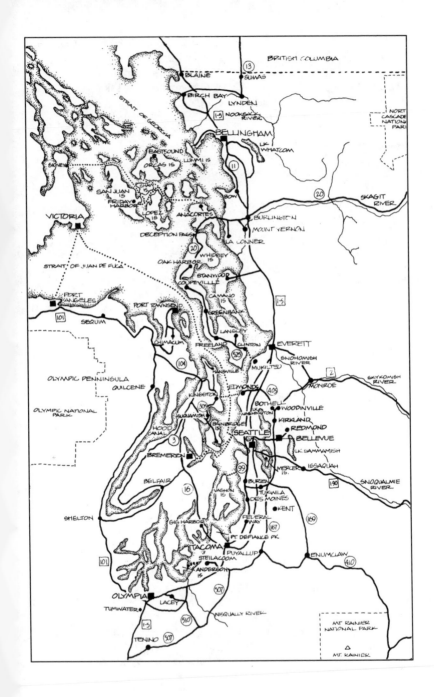

Puget Sound

North to south along the I-5 corridor, including side trips to the islands.

BLAINE

Blaine is plain. Not exactly the kind of spot you're likely to make a travel destination unless you have some other reason for visiting this little community snugged up against the border. The flower-bright gardens and the lawns at the border-crossing park around the **International Peace Arch** are quite lovely, so if you want to picnic en route to or from British Columbia, this a good, if sometimes crowded, place.

LODGINGS

Inn at Semiahmoo ★★ Semiahmoo Spit is a stunning site for a resort, with beachward views of the sea and the San Juans from many of the buildings. It sports lots of amenities: a 300-slip marina convenient to the inn; a house cruise vessel on which you can book excursions through the San Juans or scenic fishing trips; a thoroughly outfitted athletic club (an outdoor swimming pool—cold—racquetball, squash, tennis, aerobics, weight lifting, tanning, massage, sauna, and Jacuzzi); an endless stretch of beach. Three restaurants (Stars, the Northwest gourmet dining room, plus two more casual spots) provide the necessary range of culinary alternatives. The golf course, designed by Arnold Palmer, has long, unencumbered fairways surrounded by dense woods, excellent use of water (some very clever water shots here), and lovely, sculptural sand traps. However, lots of little things leave us feeling vaguely as though Semiahmoo is more glorified motel than luxury resort. The adjacent convention center, where revamped cannery buildings make top-notch meeting arenas, is really Semiah-moo's greatest strength: it's a nice place to do business. But vacationers might well be disappointed by the mindless clichés of decor. Systems noises have been far too audible through the walls. Views, splendid from the bayside rooms, are nonexistent in others. Recent changes in management make us wonder if the problems run even deeper. ▪ *Exit 270 off I-5, travel west, watch for signs at 9565 Semiahmoo Pkwy; (206) 371-2000; PO Box 790, Blaine, WA 98230-0790; $$$; AE, DC, MC, V; checks OK; breakfast, lunch, dinner every day.*

BIRCH BAY

It's just the place for 1950s teenage nostalgia. The crescent-shaped beach draws throngs of kids—cruising the strip, go-carting, hanging out in the arcade (open Memorial Day through Labor Day). Frankie and Annette are all that's missing. There's a state park for camping and lots of sandy beach to wiggle between your toes. Off season can be very off.

LODGINGS

Jacobs Landing Rentals ★★ This is the best of the condo developments, right in the "middle of town," across the main street from the beach. Units are set at angles among the beautifully maintained grounds—affording some of them better water views than others. Suites (one-, two-, and three-bedroom units) are modern and deluxe, with fireplaces, kitchens, and washers and dryers. There are outdoor tennis courts, an indoor heated pool, a Jacuzzi, and racquetball courts to keep everyone busy. ▪ *Exit 270 off I-5, head west for 5 miles, follow signs; (206) 371-7633; 7824 Birch Bay Dr, Birch Bay, WA 98230; $$; AE, MC, V; checks OK.*

LYNDEN

This picture-perfect, neat and tidy community sports immaculate yards and colorful gardens lining the shady avenue into downtown, which has adopted a Dutch theme (slightly overdone) in tribute to a community of early inhabitants. Be sure to visit the charming **Pioneer Museum** full of local memorabilia and antique buggies and motorcars; (206) 354-3675.

RESTAURANTS

Hollandia Riding on the tail of bigger Dutchified establishments is a slightly more tasteful and quiet bistro that offers a selection of authentic fare imported from The Netherlands. It's located just off the base of the windmill in the center of town. Chef Dini Mollink works competently on what is, to the American palate, rather heavy cuisine. A safe choice is, believe it or not, the Toeristenmenu: Groentesoep (Dutch meatball soup, firm, tasty meatballs in a luscious homemade broth with bits of vegetable), Schnitzel Hollandia (chicken breast in a just-crunchy light breading), and dessert (we adored the little almond tarts). A less filling selection would be the Koninginnesoep met crackers (the Queen's cream soup, a rich chicken soup served with fresh raisin bread and thin slices of Gouda cheese). A small spice cookie accompanies your after-dinner coffee—a nice touch. ■ *In the Dutch Village at Guide Meridian and Front St; (206) 354-4133; 655 Front St, Lynden; $; beer and wine; MC, V; local checks only; lunch Mon-Sat, dinner Tues-Sat.*

LODGINGS

Dutch Village Inn One might question an inn located in a windmill in a Dutch-theme village. This particular inn, however, provides six authentically designed, tastefully furnished, and luxuriously appointed rooms to please all but the most jaded of travelers. Not surprisingly, the rooms are named for the Dutch provinces; Friesland Kamer, the room named for the northernmost province, occupies the top of the windmill. Views are lovely, but interrupted rhythmically as the giant blades of the windmill pass by (turning, fully lit, until 10pm). There are special touches in all the rooms—two have extra beds fitted into curtained alcoves in true Dutch fashion, and several have two-person tubs. Breakfast is served from the full menu of the cafe, just off the lobby and along the village "canal." ■ *Front St and Guide Meridian; (206) 354-4440; 655 Front St, Lynden, WA 98264; $$; MC, V; checks OK.*

FERNDALE

Hovander Homestead Park. At this county-run working farm, kids can pet the animals or prowl the barn, and families can picnic along the Nooksack River. The centerpiece is the gabled farmhouse and its gardens, built in 1903 by a retired Swedish architect, Holand Hovander; 5299 Nielsen Road, south of Ferndale off Hovander Road, (206) 384-3444. Call ahead for hours.

Adjacent to Hovander Park, the **Tenant Lake Interpretive Center and Fragrance Garden** offers boardwalk access to an abundance of birdlife in a wetland setting. The garden was developed with the visually impaired and handicapped in mind, so many of the raised-bed plantings are identified with braille labels and the garden is very wheelchair accessible.

RESTAURANTS

Douglas House Settling down after a string of changes in ownership, Douglas House now belongs to Guy and Linda Colbert of Oyster Creek Inn. The emphasis is on seafood, from the unexpected—shrimp and pistachio seafood sausage with red pepper coulis—to steak and lobster. An intensely flavored mushroom strudel with rosemary and perfect raspberry-champagne sorbet both demonstrate a confident, careful kitchen. The service shows a bit less polish, but genuine warmth. The house was built in 1904 by a successful farmer, and the decor goes in for dried flowers and lace. Good beer and an adequate wine list with some nice dessert ports. The Colberts deserve more than zero stars, but we'd like them to settle in first. ■ *½ mile west of Ferndale city center; (206) 384-5262; 2254 Douglas Dr, Ferndale; $$; beer and wine; MC, V; checks OK; dinner every day.*

SUMAS

Although Sumas, a small border-crossing town east of Lynden, is not a destination community, it's a good jumping-off point for a trip to Canada. Tuesdays and Wednesdays have the shortest lines at the border.

RESTAURANTS

El Nopal Dos Jose and Wendy Gonzalez have a knack for the neighborhood hangout. In the spring of '93 they sold their thriving Mexican cafe in nearby Everson and relocated to a former burger joint in even smaller Sumas. Again, lines for a table stretched out into the parking lot. Immense margaritas, good, cheap carne asadas, chicken and mole, and other basics are part of the draw. The rest is a convivial mixture of local Anglo and Hispanic families. A strolling guitarist serenades tables on weekends. Nothing here is innovative or glamorous (except Jesus, who is surely the coolest waiter in north Whatcom County), but everything is prepared with care. The locals like to eat early, so come for lunch or after 7:30pm. ■ *Front St just east of the border route; (206) 988-0305; 120 Front St, Sumas; $; full bar; MC, V; checks OK; lunch and dinner every day.*

LODGINGS

Sumas Mountain Village ★ This place deserves a more rustic setting than Sumas' main drag, steps away from the Canadian border. This handsome log lodge is a small-scale replica of the classic Mount Baker Lodge, which was destroyed by fire in 1931. The nine rustic rooms recapture the aura of the old lodge, with peeled-log beds, wooden floors with braided rugs, and framed black-and-white reproduction photos of Mount Baker Lodge. Six rooms have Jacuzzis; two have river-stone fireplaces. Room 6, Twin Sisters, where the queen-size bed is supplemented with a dandy bunk bed and red tartan curtains, is perfect for families. Guests receive a $5-per-person credit toward breakfast in the lodge's attractive restaurant. In deference to the fiery finale of its predecessor, this is a nonsmoking establishment. ■ *Downtown Sumas; (206) 988-4483; 819 Cherry St, Sumas, WA 98295; $$; AE, MC, V; checks OK.*

The mishmash grid of Bellingham's streets is a reminder of its former days as four smaller towns. Only recently has the downtown architecture of this city, situated on three rivers flowing into one bay, been rediscovered: the town is full of fine old houses, award-winning architecture at Western Washington University, stately streets, and lovely parks. An economic boom is bringing change and expansion to Whatcom County, most notably at the handsome port facility that houses the southern terminus of the **Alaska Marine Highway System**. For information on weekly sailings for passengers and vehicles along the Inside Passage, call (800)642-0066 or (206)676-8445.

Bellingham

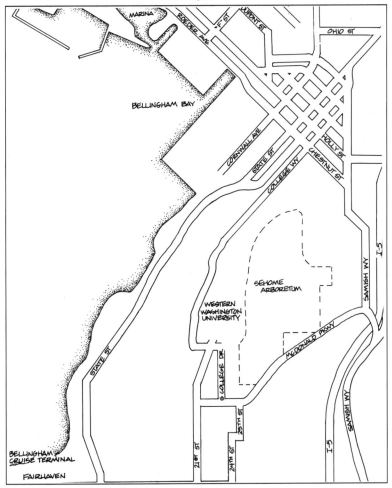

Art. The Whatcom Museum of History and Art, 121 Prospect Street, (206) 676-6981, a massive Romanesque building dating from 1892, was used as a city hall until 1940. It has been beautifully restored, and recent expansion into neighboring buildings has allowed for permanent exhibits on historic Bellingham as well as an adventurous art exhibition schedule. Check out the local wildlife and native American culture presentations in the education center down the block. One block from the museum is **R.R. Henderson**, one of the best used bookstores in the state; 112 Grand Avenue, (206) 734-6855.

Old Homes. Wonderful turn-of-the-century mansions abound in Bellingham: check out Utter Street, between Madison and Monroe; W Holly Street, from Broadway to C Street; Eldridge Avenue; and N Garden Street, from Myrtle to Champion. Also worth a visit, in the south end of town, are the homes on Knox Avenue from 12th to 17th and on Mill Street near 15th; the 1890 Roland G. Gamwell House at 16th and Douglas; and the Craftsman-style Roeder Home on Sunset Drive, open to the public.

Gardens of Art. The City of Bellingham now owns what was formerly called Big Rock Garden and privately run by the George Drake. A vast array of azaleas, rhododendrons, and Japanese maples share this wonderful woodland site with a unique outdoor gallery of garden art. Plans are in the works for free music in the garden on Sunday afternoons from May to August. 2900 Sylvan, near Lake Whatcom; (206) 671-1069.

▼

Bellingham

▲

The **Old Town** around W Holly and Commercial streets hosts antique and junk shops and some decent eateries. **Fairhaven**, the product of a short-lived railroad boom from 1889 to 1893, is good for exploring—there has been a resurgence of life in the red brick buildings. **The Marketplace**, the grand dame and central figure among the attractive old buildings, was restored in 1988 and houses a number of interesting shops and dining options. The district is rich with diversion: crafts galleries, coffeehouses, bookstores, a charming garden/nursery emporium, and a lively evening scene unique for Bellingham.

Western Washington University, on Sehome Hill south of downtown, is a fine expression of the spirit of Northwest architecture: warm materials, formal echoes of European styles, respect for context and the natural backdrop. The Ridgeway Dormitory complex by Bassetti and Morse demonstrates an extraordinary sensitivity to terrain; also notable are the Social Sciences Building, with its elaborate concrete structural patterns; Mathes and Nash halls, with a curvilinear echo of Aalto; and the Central Quadrangle, with its feelings of a Danish town square.

Lake Whatcom Railway—located not on Lake Whatcom, but on Highway 9 at Wickersham—makes scenic summer runs using an old Northern Pacific engine; (206) 595-2218.

Mount Baker Vineyards. This attractive, cedar-sided, sky-lit facility specializes in some of the lesser-known varietals, such as Müller-Thurgau and Madeleine Angevine, and various less exotic blushes and blends. The tasting room is located 11 miles east of Bellingham on Mount Baker Highway; (206) 592-2300.

The **Island Shuttle Express** provides passenger-only ferry service from Bellingham to the San Juan Islands, May through September. Call for reservations: (206) 671-1137.

RESTAURANTS

il fiasco ★★★ il fiasco (Italian for "the flask") has built a dedicated clientele who come often because the welcome is warm and sincere, the staff friendly and knowledgeable, the decor sophisticated and comfortable, and the food interesting and ambitious. Just as we put this book to bed, however, owner Teri Treat sold her restaurant to Andrew and Kay Moquin. They plan a few design changes (Kay runs an interior design business), but hopefully they'll maintain a similar menu to the one that has made il fiasco one of Bellingham's favorite restaurants. Diners here have come to expect a masterfully orchestrated menu featuring Northern Italian classics, often with a contemporary twist—for example, a traditional carpaccio (beef tenderloin sliced paper-thin) accompanied by fresh-grated Reggiana Parmesan and a caper/mustard sauce. All is accompanied by a choice of the day's soup (often rather eclectic combinations, consistently sensational) or mixed greens (always nicely done, making this a tough choice), vegetable, and an angel-hair soufflé. Cross your fingers as the new owners take over. ■ *Across from the Parkade at Commercial and Holly; (206) 676-9136; 1309 Commercial St, Bellingham; $$; full bar; MC, V; local checks only; lunch Mon-Fri, dinner every day.*

Bellingham

Restaurants

Cafe Toulouse ★★ In this quietly remodeled corner of the old Bon Marché, Vincent Nattress has created the essentials of a genuine French cafe, adding a carefully selected dinner menu to the breakfast and lunch offerings popular at Toulouse's former tiny space. The breast of free-range chicken is a standout, served with a perfect lemon-butter emulsion, and the pasta primavera is done with care. On the more substantial side are a seductive cassoulet and a steak in red sauce. The seasonal salad with wild greens is exceptional. The short wine list has some hard-to-find selections. The breakfast and lunch menus offer familiar favorites—Greek and Provençal frittatas, hefty sandwiches, soups, and pastas. If there's a weak spot, it's the soups. ■ *Downtown near Cornwall, next to the Federal Building; (206) 733-8996; 114 W Magnolia St, Bellingham; $$; beer and wine; MC, V; checks OK; breakfast, lunch every day, dinner Tues-Sat.*

Pacific Cafe ★★ The Pacific Cafe, tucked into the historic Mount Baker Theater building, has always been a leader on

Bellingham's gastronomic front. But recently there seems to have been something of a renaissance going on in Robert Fong's kitchen, and the results are even more exciting than usual. The menu—and the tasteful decor—reflects a bit of Fong's Asian influence (he comes to Washington via Hawaii, supplemented with years of travel in Europe, India, China, and Malaysia). The satay sauces are complex, light, and fragrant. Specials may include a buttery truffle-and-cognac pâté and perfectly fried Brie with fresh fruit. Entrées are prepared with care; the roast duck with ginger-shiitake mushroom sauce is rich and moist; lamb grilled with rosemary and garlic rock salt comes adorned with a sweet and tangy chutney. Fong is a serious wine collector, and the quality of the vintages presented reflects a fine-tuned palate. No smoking, please. ■ *Off Holly on Commercial; (206)647-0800; 100 N Commercial, Bellingham; $$; beer and wine; MC, V; local checks OK; lunch Mon-Fri, dinner Mon-Sat.*

Pepper Sisters ★★ Invigorated by a recent move into one of Bellingham's nice old brick commercial buildings downtown, Pepper Sisters has shown conclusively that it has outlasted Southwestern trendiness and now stands on its own with inventive, delicious food, very reasonably priced. Daily seafood specials are a good prospect. One standout is oysters in a light tomatillo–pumpkin-seed sauce, served on short-grain rice along with black beans and a toothsome posole. All that and a practically airborne sopaipilla with honey butter comes in at under $10. The kitchen shows the same verve with plainer fare: roasted potato and garlic enchilada with green chile sauce. Sangria blanco—white wine with raspberry juice—is refreshing, not cloying. Coffee flan is a standout dessert, and the coffee itself, the local Tony's brand, is brewed with a dusting of cinnamon on the filter. A raised area in back, with comfortable couches and a view of Bellingham Bay, makes your wait for a table more palatable. ■ *On State St south of Holly; (206)671-3414; 1055 N State St, Bellingham; $; beer and wine; MC, V; checks; dinner Tues-Sun.*

The Bagelry ★ In 1993, the Bagelry doubled its size and diminished the lines somewhat. Everything else is pretty much the same, with the addition of some desserts and the first-rate, intensely flavored juice from local McLean's farms (try the loganberry/Jonagold apple). Another nice addition is the bagel with a schmear of cream-cheese spread—a middle ground in cholesterol and price between the plain bagel and the standard overloaded cream cheese number. Expatriate East Coasters will delight in the dense, crusty New York-style bagels, six or seven kinds of which are offered hot from the ovens throughout the day. The pumpernickel is especially good, with onion running a close second. The tasty bialys make an addictive base for a sandwich—tender smoked Virginia ham, for example. No smoking. ■ *Railroad near Champion; (206) 676-5288; 1319 Railroad Ave, Bellingham; $; no alcohol; no credit cards; local checks only; breakfast, lunch every day.*

Bluewater Bistro ★ The Bluewater has filled a long-empty niche in downtown Bellingham, providing a cheerful atmosphere, energetic staff, an adventurous attitude in the kitchen, and even a live jazz brunch on Sundays. It's supposed to be fun—and for the most part it is. The delicious garlic burger is served on the Bistro's own brioche bun, with provolone and a tasty marinara dip. The Mexican quiche is a lesson in taco-as-quiche in a so-so crust. At brunch you might try the hearty Italian eggs (eggs on polenta with the house marinara) or the mild and creamy basil, chèvre, and tomato omelet. Wines here tend toward the less patrician (and less expensive), covering the territory from Australia to California to the Northwest, and the brews can take you from Kalama, Washington, to Eastern Europe. ■ *Holly and Cornwall; (206) 733-6762; 1215½ Cornwall Ave, Bellingham; $; beer and wine; MC, V; checks OK; breakfast, lunch Mon-Sat, dinner Tues-Sat, brunch Sun.*

Thai House ★ Peggy Sripoom has fashioned a most comfortable spot located (as many of the great Thai restaurants seem to be) in a strip mall. Bellingham's best Thai house caters to the most discerning lovers of Thai food. It's a nice environment in which to savor one's fish cakes or linger over the flavorful hot-and-sour soup chock-full of tender seafood and redolent of fresh lemon grass. Tried-and-true favorites include a whole flatfish, deep-fried and then smothered in a spicy red sauce, or any one of the curries. The Thai House offers a more restricted but reasonably priced menu for lunch, which includes steamed rice and a rather forgettable cup of soup. Thai House can also cater your next party. ■ *Across from Bellis Fair Mall; (206) 734-5111; 3630 Meridian Village, Bellingham; $; beer and wine; MC, V; checks OK; lunch, Mon-Fri, dinner every day.*

Colophon Cafe Located in the best bookstore in town, Colophon offers table service and an outdoor wine garden on its lower level, booths and sidewalk tables above. The African peanut soup (in vegetarian and nonvegetarian versions) is justly famed—chunky with fresh tomatoes, grainy with peanuts, and pungent with ginger. Real cream pies—rich, light, wonderful—are another specialty. Key lime, chocolate brandy, and peanut butter are among the favorites. The Colophon encourages patrons to tarry over their espresso with a book or with friends for a lively discussion. The gallery space around the walls is dedicated to local artists. ■ *11th near Harris (in Village Books) in Fairhaven; (206) 647-0092; 1210 11th St, Bellingham; $; no alcohol; MC, V; checks OK; breakfast, lunch, dinner every day.*

Taste of India Recently and tastefully remodeled, Taste of India has eliminated the last traces of the Greek restaurant that preceded it in this small strip mall (two doors south of Thai House). Tandoori meats and breads and other Punjabi creations are a specialty, but South Indian vegetarian cooking is well represented. The shrimp tandoori is just wonderful—sweet, tender-firm, with a perfect masala and a mint chutney. The vegetarian combination is another triumph of blending flavors. These are meals for lingering, which allows time to polish off a 22-ounce Taj Mahal beer. The lunch buffet, with two dozen selections for a fixed $5.50 price, is justly popular with the locals. ■ *Across from Bellis Fair Mall; (206) 647-1589; 3930 Meridian St #J, Bellingham; $; beer and wine; MC, V; local checks only; lunch Mon-Sat, dinner every day.*

LODGINGS

Schnauzer Crossing ★★★ This sophisticated and unique B&B overlooking Lake Whatcom attracts a surprising range of visitors, from newlyweds to businesspeople to discerning foreign travelers—and graciously accommodates them all. Donna and Monte McAllister open their lovely contemporary home, gardens, and grounds to their guests, many of whom return time and again. A charming new cottage will vie in popularity with the spacious and elegant suite, which also has a king-size bed, fireplace, Jacuzzi, TV/VCR, and a tranquil garden view. The McAllisters are sensitive to guests' needs for privacy and have a finely tuned sense of hospitality that's obvious in the details such as extra-thick towels and gorgeous flowers year-round. A superior gourmet breakfast might include jazzy French toast with fresh fruit and espresso. A private tennis court, hot tub in a Japanese garden setting, canoe, decks, and use of the living room are all available to guests. There really are schnauzers here. ■ *Exit 253 off I-5, go 3.2 miles on Lakeway Dr and turn left; (206) 733-0055 or (206) 734-2808; 4421 Lakeway Dr, Bellingham, WA 98226; $$$; MC, V; checks OK.*

Best Western Heritage Inn ★★ Three tasteful, Wedgwood-blue, shuttered and dormered structures nestling amid a small grove of trees and a stream seem incongruous adjacent to I-5 and a conglomeration of malls; however, this Best Western is one of the most elegantly furnished, professionally run hotels in the area. Exquisite cherry-wood four-poster beds (stair-step up included), high- and lowboys, wing-back chairs in rich fabrics, and stylish desks with a comfortable chair. Other thoughtful touches include in-room coffee and tea, hair dryers, guest laundry facility, an attractive outdoor pool (in season), and indoor hot tub. A free continental breakfast is served in front of the fire in the lobby or can be taken back to your room. Rates are extremely reasonable. Request a room that doesn't face the freeway.

■ *I-5 Exit 256; (800) 528-1234 or (206) 647-1912; 151 E McLeod Rd, Bellingham, WA 98226; $$; AE, DC, MC, V; checks OK.*

Anderson Creek Lodge ★ Once a private school, the main house is now an intimate bed and breakfast with six individually designed rooms, three of which have their own fireplaces (for the others, the massive stone hearth in the common area is quite inviting). The remainder of the facility has been developed as a conference center, though it is quite conceivable to nestle into the lodge without the slightest hint that 70 physicists are conferring just down the lane. Most guests will be lured out to the hot tub or to walk the parklike trail through the woods. An inviting pool and sauna are scheduled so as not to conflict with conference-attendee use. While exploring, be sure to seek out resident sculptor James Lapp's studio; his work is exhibited in the lodge. Strolling visitors are likely to catch part of a llama-training session (llamas can accompany your day hike by advance arrangement). ■ *East of Bellingham, off Mt Baker Hwy; (206) 966-2126; 5602 Mission Rd, Bellingham, WA 98226; $$; AE, MC, V; checks OK.*

DeCann House ★ Within this neighborhood of historic homes overlooking Squalicum Harbor Marina, Bellingham Bay, and the San Juan Islands, this unpretentious Victorian bed and breakfast welcomes visitors to a quiet and comfortable haven. Test your skills at the ornate pool table in the front parlor or the interesting collection of wooden mazes in the sitting room. Barbara and Van Hudson maintain an extensive current library of travel-related material and provide a log in which you can pass along your impressions to other travelers—a nice touch. A complete breakfast, beautifully served, assures a cheery start to the day. ■ *West on Holly, which turns into Eldridge; (206) 734-9172; 2610 Eldridge Ave, Bellingham, WA 98225; $$; no credit cards; checks OK.*

▼

Bellingham

Lodgings

▲

North Garden Inn ★ This Victorian house (on the National Register of Historic Places) boasts over two dozen rooms plus seven baths, the result of additions early in the century. Only 10 are rented as guest rooms (seven in winter); some have lovely views over Bellingham Bay and the islands. Five full baths are shared. All the rooms are attractive, clean, and with a bit more character than usual—due partly to the antique house, partly to the influence of the energetic and talented hosts. Barbara and Frank DeFreytas are both musical—two grand pianos in performance condition are available to guests, and musical or dramatic evenings take place here just as they probably did at the turn of the century. In the morning, Barbara serves a full breakfast and freshly ground coffee. ■ *Maple and N Garden; (206) 671-7828; 1014 N Garden St, Bellingham, WA 98225; $$; MC, V; checks OK.*

Sunrise Bay ★ Hosts Karen and Jim Moren have crafted a most attractive and welcoming retreat on the north shore of Lake Whatcom at Sunrise Cove. The Morens offer a cheerful pair of rooms in a detached cottage, where huge windows overlook their expansive lawn to the lake (at times at the expense of guests' privacy). Thoughtful touches reveal extensive travel experience and knowledge of what makes guests comfortable: TVs with VCRs, private phones, private baths (with skylights), and reading lights on both sides of the beds. A creative breakfast is served in the Morens' contemporary home. Families are welcome, and Katie, the youngest host, provides her special welcome. A heated swimming pool (seasonal), hot tub, beach, canoes, and dock are also available. ■ *On the north shore of Lake Whatcom; (206) 647-0376; 2141 N Shore Rd, Bellingham, WA 98226; $$; MC, V; checks OK.*

LUMMI ISLAND

Located just off Gooseberry Point northwest of Bellingham, Lummi is one of the most overlooked islands of the ferry-accessible San Juans. It echoes the days when the San Juan Islands were still a hidden treasure, visited only by folks who preferred bucolic surroundings and deserted beaches to a plethora of restaurants, resorts, and gift shops. Private ownership has locked up most of this pastoral isle, so you won't find state parks or resorts. The only restaurant has limited hours, the only store limited wares. Pastures, woodlands, and expansive views abound, and you're more likely to encounter a tractor than a BMW on the country roads, a heron than a sunbather on the sandy beaches.

Lummi is serviced not by the Washington State ferries but by the tiny **Whatcom County ferry**, which leaves Gooseberry Point on the hour from 6am to midnight (more frequently on busy Friday nights). It's easy to find (just follow the signs to Lummi Island from I-5, north of Bellingham), cheap ($4 roundtrip for a car and two passengers), and quick (a 6-minute crossing); call ahead for schedule, (206) 676-6730 or (206) 398-1310.

Just a few yards from the ferry landing is **The Islander**, the island's only mercantile, (206) 758-2190. Rental bikes are available next store ($6 half-day; $12 all day). The **Beach Store Cafe** is a fine way to start a Lummi Sunday; (206) 758-7406.

LODGINGS

Loganita ★★★ Beautifully situated on the north end of Lummi, with sweeping views across Georgia and Rosario straits, this elegant 100-year-old lodge invites contemplation and refined relaxation. The spacious downstairs area, divided into two rooms, is furnished with comfortable leather couches,

Oriental rugs, low, polished tables, and a fine collection of Northwest art. Huge stone fireplaces stand at either end, music fills the rooms, and windows on three sides open to unobstructed views of water, sky, and distant islands. Veteran innkeepers Ann and Glenn Gossage used to host only executive retreats, but now B&B guests have exclusive use of the expansive lodge, sprawling decks, manicured lawns, and long stretch of sandy beach. Upstairs, Laura Ashley bedding, antiques, comforters, and pillows fill three small guest rooms. A couple could happily hide away in the Sunset Suite for days. Its north-facing bedroom has a fireplace and couch; there's a separate sitting room and a private deck. Groups or families will enjoy the fully equipped, three-bedroom Carriage House out back. A tasteful breakfast of just the right proportions is served at a formal dining table in the main room. There's a hot tub on the back porch, pool and chess in the main rooms, and endless places to wander or curl up and read. ▪ *From ferry, north on Nugent for 3 miles; (206) 758-2651; 2825 W Shore Dr, Lummi Island, WA 98262; $$$; MC, V; checks OK.*

The Willows ★★★ Run as a resort since the late 1920s, the old Taft family house perches on a knoll 100 feet above the accessible beach, offering sweeping views of the San Juan and Gulf islands. There are four rooms in the main building (two view rooms upstairs share a bath, two downstairs in the back have their own baths), a small cottage for two (decor is a bit precious but the view and privacy are terrific), and a two-bedroom apartment that looks out over the rose garden to the ocean (with a little of the kitchen roof in between). For couples traveling together, the last is our favorite. It offers a convincingly toasty gas-log fireplace, a thoughtfully equipped kitchen, and a private bath for each bedroom (one with a Jacuzzi and the other with a shower for two). Hostess Victoria Taft Flynn quietly delivers a beautiful tray with coffee and a loaf of hot Irish soda bread first thing in the morning—to get you going and tide you over until you emerge for her superb breakfast.

The Willows is one of the few—and definitely the best— places on Lummi for an evening meal. During the summer season, a "peasant fare" supper is served on Thursday and Sunday nights, a four-course meal on Friday nights. But the real event takes place year-round on Saturday night, when innkeepers Gary and Victoria Flynn combine graciousness and culinary expertise with the inn's lovely location for a truly memorable dining experience. The six-course meal begins in the main room, where Gary Flynn greets 24 or so guests with sherry and appetizers. You can wander the deck, gardens, and patios, soaking in the expansive view to the strains of a harpist and a classical guitarist, until you're escorted into the carefully appointed dining room. After dinner, guests repair in civilized fashion to the sitting room for port. The feast has become quite popular among locals (who often come from Bellingham just for dinner) and requires reservations often months in advance. Friday night dinners (summers only) are casual, Saturdays are not. ■ *From ferry, north on Nugent for 3½ miles; (206) 758-2620; 2579 W Shore Dr, Lummi Island, WA 98262; $$$; beer and wine; MC, V; checks OK; dinner Thurs-Sun (Sat only in winter).*

West Shore Farm ★ Carl and Polly Hanson's hand-built octagonal house tucks into a slope overlooking the north tip of the island and the Strait of Georgia. Rough cedar paneling, brass fixtures, and odd-shaped angles lend a pleasant, nautical feel. Accommodations on the lower level are cozy and cabinlike, with sweeping views and ground-floor entrances. Readers will appreciate the plethora of interesting books and magazines, comfortable seating, and individual reading lights above the beds. The two guest rooms each have (not en suite, but handy) a thoughtfully appointed bath. A substantial breakfast is served at the big round table in the inviting quarters; lunch and dinner are available on request. Little to do but sleep late, walk the secluded beach, or laze on the deck. Don't bother to bring your car; the Hansons will pick you up at the ferry if you like. ■ *From ferry, north on Nugent for 3 miles; (206) 758-2600; 2781 W Shore Dr, Lummi Island, WA 98262; $; MC, V; checks OK.*

▼

Lummi Island

Lodgings

▲

CHUCKANUT DRIVE

This famous stretch of road between Bellingham and Bow used to be part of the Pacific Highway; now it is one of the prettiest drives in the state, curving along the Chuckanut Mountains and looking out over Samish Bay and its many islands. Unfortunately, if you're in the driver's seat, you'll have to keep your eyes on the road and wait for turnoffs for the view; the road is narrow and winding. Take the Chuckanut Drive exit off I-5 north, or follow 12th Street south in Bellingham.

Teddy Bear Cove is a nudist beach, and a pretty one at that, on a secluded shore along Chuckanut Drive just south of the Bellingham city limit. No signs; watch for the crowd of cars.

Interurban Trail, once the electric rail route from Bellingham to Mount Vernon, is now a 5-mile running, walking, riding, and mountain-biking trail connecting three parks at the north end of Chuckanut Drive: Fairhaven Park to Arroyo Park to Larrabee State Park.

Larrabee State Park, 7 miles south of Bellingham, was Washington's first state park. Beautiful sandstone sculpture along the beaches and cliffs provides a backdrop for exploration of the abundant sea life. Good picnic areas and camping.

Looking for a particular place? Check the index at the back of this book for specific restaurants, lodgings, attractions, and more.

As you wend your way through these bucolic communities of the Skagit Valley, it's hard to imagine I-5 is only minutes away. Removed from traffic and shopping malls you'll discover orchards, oyster beds, slow-moving tractors, and fields of mustard. In Bayview, visit the **Breazeala-Padilla Bay National Estuarine Research Reserve and Interpretive Center**. Learn about **Padilla Bay** (an estuary with fresh and salt waters) through displays, saltwater tanks, a nature trail, and a library. Open Wednesday through Sunday, 10am-5pm; 1043 Bayview-Edison Road, (206) 428-1558. Nearby **Bayview State Park** is open year-round with overnight camping and beachfront picnic sites, perfect for winter bird-watching; (206) 757-0227.

Permanent and part-time residents inhabit **Samish Island**, as do numerous oyster beds. **Blau Oyster Company** has been selling Samish Bay oysters, clams, and other seafood since 1935. Open Monday through Saturday from 8am-5pm (call 24 hours in advance and receive a 10 percent discount). Seven miles west of Edison via the Bayview-Edison Road and the Samish Island Road, follow the signs to the shucking sheds; 919 Blue Heron Road, Samish Island, (206) 766-6171.

RESTAURANTS

The Oyster Bar ★★ This Samish Bay restaurant has become somewhat of an institution on Chuckanut Drive. The toughest task for the Oyster Bar has been to match the quality of the food to the spectacular view, but chef David Buchannan seems to have things under control. The award-winning wine list can be a bit intimidating, but a veteran waiter steers you in the right direction. The seasonally changing menu selection is small but dimensional. The crab cakes, accompanied by a mango-ginger-chutney sauce, are a nice beginning. A creamy fresh pea soup might come tanged with apples. Entrées might include scallops with a garlic herb crust and lemon purée, and oysters touched with Pernod—these plump, extra-small jewels from Samish Bay are sautéed in a hazelnut and spinach breading. Ironically there's no oyster bar here, but there is an incredible selection of bivalves. A light cheese soufflé accompanies each meal. Skip dessert and have an after-dinner drink. No young children. ■ *Exit 250 off I-5; (206) 766-6185; 240 Chuckanut Dr, Bow; $$$; beer and wine; AE, MC, V; local checks OK; dinner every day.* ₺

Oyster Creek Inn ★ Walking into this creekside restaurant is a bit like entering an aquarium—windows full of water and fish—they're filled with views of lush, green trees and a busy creek below. Adjacent to the Samish Bay Shellfish Farm (open daily to visitors), the Inn has a long history of dedication to seafood. The menu is a bit overwhelming, making the end

Bayview,
Samish
Island,
Edison,
Bow

Restaurants

▲

result sometimes disappointing. Start with a glass of Oyster Creek Columbia Valley Méthode Champenoise, a light accompaniment to the humorous bowls of oyster crackers placed at every table. Unless you're famished, stay with the small side of the menu (large meals include a spinach timbale and stuffed potato). A pea-cucumber salad in a dill dressing starts the meal a bit slowly, but the mussels in garlic herb sauce served with cold vegetables in a creamy tarragon sauce is a potent entrée. Try the rhubarb crisp, made on location. ▪ *About ½-hour drive south of Bellingham on Chuckanut Dr; (206) 766-6179; 190 Chuckanut Dr, Bow; $$; beer and wine; MC, V; checks OK; lunch, dinner every day.* ৬

The Rhododendron Cafe ★ The Rhododenddron Cafe is the perfect starting or stopping point for a scenic trek on Chuckanut Drive. It does not have the view other Chuckanut eateries boast, but it serves up some darn good food. Once the site of the Red Crown Service Station in the early 1900s, the Rhody serves homemade soup (the chowder is excellent), a tasty veggie burger topped with provolone, or lightly breaded and sautéed Samish Bay oysters for lunch. Don't skip the desserts, whether it's homemade chocolate ice cream in a frosted dish or Rosie's brownie sundae. Dinner closely follows lunch. Write your postcards on the patio and put them in the mail at the post office across the street. ▪ *At the Bow-Edison junction; (206) 766-6667; 553 Chuckanut Dr, Bow; $$; beer and wine; MC, V; local checks only; lunch Fri-Sat (Wed-Sun spring to fall), dinner Wed-Sun, brunch Sun (closed late Nov-Dec).* ৬

LODGINGS

Benson Farmstead Bed & Breakfast As you walk through the back door you may wonder where John Boy is. But this is for real, not fiction. For the past decade, Jerry and Sharon Benson have been restoring their 1914 farmhouse to a true country bed and breakfast. Once part of a working dairy farm, the large 17-room house is packed with antiques and Scandinavian memorabilia. The four upstairs guest rooms are outfitted with iron beds and custom quilts. In the hallways are family photos and artwork by the young Benson brothers. The quietest rooms (a relative term in Bow), English Garden Room and Forget-Me-Not Room, both have private baths. In the evening, relax in the hot tub or in the parlor sharing Sharon's desserts and coffee. Jerry cooks a country breakfast. And don't be surprised to hear music in the air—the Bensons are talented pianists and violinists (including the four sons). Kids will like this place, especially the playroom, three cats, and two dogs. Baby-sitter available. ▪ *Exit 231 off I-5 north of Burlington; (206) 757-0578; 1009 Avon-Allen Rd, Bow, WA 98232; $$; MC, V; checks OK; (open weekends only Oct-March except by special arrangement).*

Anacortes, the gateway to the San Juans, is itself on an island—Fidalgo Island. Though most travelers rush through here on their way to the ferry, this town adorned with colorful, life-size cutouts of early pioneers is quietly becoming a place where it's worth it to slow down. If only for a good cup of coffee and baked goods, drop into **The New Bohemian**, 1008 Fifth Street, (206) 299-1051, open Tuesday through Saturday, a hip new-wave coffeehouse. For picnic or ferry food, try **Geppetto's**, 3320 Commercial Avenue, (206) 293-5033, for Italian take-out. Those with a little more time, head to **Gere-A-Deli**, 502 Commercial Avenue, (206) 293-7383, a friendly hangout with good, home-made food in an airy former Bank of Commerce building.

And stop by **Watermark Book Company**, 612 Commercial, (206) 293-4277, loaded with interesting reads. Seafaring folks should poke around **Marine Supply and Hardware** (since 1913), 202 Commercial Avenue, (206) 293-3014. Marine Supply is packed to the rafters with basic and hard-to-find specialty marine items. And for the history of Fidalgo Island, visit **The Anacortes Museum**, 1305 Eighth Street, (206) 293-1915.

RESTAURANTS

▼

Anacortes

Restaurants

▲

Janot's Bistro and Pub (Majestic Hotel) ★★ It's the most elegant dining room in Anacortes, surrounded by coral and teal sponged walls. Diners are welcomed by host Janot Rocchi to a room filled with white tablecloths, French music, and tall-paned windows overlooking a garden and patio. Fortunately, chef David Wightman's food matches the decor, and Janot's has succeeded in combining the harvest of the Pacific Northwest with classic French cuisine. Lunches might include a tasty Dungeness crab sandwich, fettuccine with wild mushrooms, and a slightly spicy curry chicken salad with raisins and coconut. At dinner, begin with the fresh local oysters on the half shell with a shallot-raspberry mignotte. Entrées range from Northwest bouillabaise to roast rack of baby lamb in a rosemary demi-glace, and a vegetarian dish. Janot's has recently added Wine Maker Dinners, a seven-course meal with selected wines for $49.95. There's also a Sunday champagne brunch, and live jazz Friday and Saturday nights in the pub. ■ *Between 4th and 5th on Commercial; (206) 299-9163; 419 Commercial Ave, Anacortes; $$; full bar; AE, MC, V; local checks only; lunch and dinner every day (closed Tues in winter).* &

La Petite ★★ La Petite has been a bright star on the Anacortes dining scene for a number of years, and it continues to shine. The Hulscher family, longtime owners of this restaurant at the Islands Inn motel, continues to deliver French-inspired food with a touch of Dutch. Seasonal items are personally selected for each evening's menu from local markets (don't expect shrimp in the winter). With only six entrées to choose from, quality is high. Appetizers range from fried squid to sautéed mushrooms stuffed with Dungeness crab. Try the lamb marinated in sambal and other Indonesian spices for a unique flavor, or the popular pork tenderloin served with a mustard sauce. If chateaubriand is on the menu, order it—it's delicious. Soup, salad, and oven-fresh baked bread come with each meal. La Petite has an interesting dessert list, with plenty for chocolate lovers. A fixed-price Dutch breakfast is intended primarily for (but not exclusive to) motel guests. ▪ *34th and Commercial; (206) 293-4644; 3401 Commercial Ave, Anacortes; $$; full bar; AE, DC, DIS, MC, V; local checks OK; breakfast every day, dinner Tues-Sun.*

LODGINGS

Channel House ★★ Just a mile and a half from the ferry dock, Dennis and Pat McIntyre's Channel House is a 1902 Victorian home designed by an Italian count. Although the exterior of the house could use a coat of paint, the four antique-filled rooms in the main house (all with private baths) are inviting and comfortable. Each has a grand view of Guemes Channel and the San Juan Islands. A cottage contains two suite-style units, complete with fireplaces and private whirlpool baths; the Victorian Rose room has its own deck and is especially nice. There is a large hot tub out back, and the McIntyres serve cozy breakfasts (before a roaring fire on chilly days). Freshly baked oatmeal cookies and Irish cream coffee await guests returning from dinner. ▪ *At Oakes and Dakota; (206) 293-9382 or (800) 238-4353; 2902 Oakes Ave, Anacortes, WA 98221; $$; DIS, MC, V; checks OK.*

The Majestic Hotel ★★ Truly majestic, this 1889 hotel has been through a number of incarnations (apartments, mercantile, offices), but this is surely the grandest. Located at the north end of town, the hotel is one of many historical buildings that have been renovated to their turn-of-the-century charm. Every one of the 23 rooms is unique, with individualized English antiques; some have oversize tubs with skylights above, some have decks, others have VCRs, and a few have everything. The best rooms are the showy corner suites. On the second floor (the only smoking level) there's a small library with a chess table. And up top, a cupola with a 360-degree view of Anacortes, Mount Baker, the Olympics, and the San Juans. There's no better perch in sight for a glass of wine at sunset. (See also Janot's Bistro and Pub in this section.) ▪ *Between 4th and 5th on Commercial; (206) 293-3355 or (800) 950-3323; 419 Commercial Ave, Anacortes, WA 98221; $$$; AE, DIS, MC, V; checks OK.*

There are 743 at low tide and 428 at high tide; 172 have names; 60 are populated; and only 4 have major ferry service. The San Juan Islands are varied, remote, and breathtakingly beautiful. They are also located in the rain shadow of the Olympics, and most receive half the rainfall of Seattle. The four main islands—Lopez, Shaw, Orcas, and San Juan—have lodgings, eateries, and some beautiful parks. Lopez, Orcas, and San Juan are discussed below; Shaw has little on it other than the world's only ferry landing run by nuns—and a campground with eight sites.

Getting there. The most obvious and cost-effective way of getting to the San Juans is via the **Washington State ferries** that run year-round from Anacortes, 1½ hours north of Seattle; for schedule and fare information, call (206) 464-6400. However, the sparsely populated islands are rather overrun in the summer months, and getting a ferry out of Anacortes can be a long, dull 3-hours-and-up wait. Bring a good book—or park the car and board with a bike. Money-saving tip: cars only pay westbound. If you plan to visit more than one island, arrange to go to the farthest first (San Juan) and work your way east.

San Juan Islands

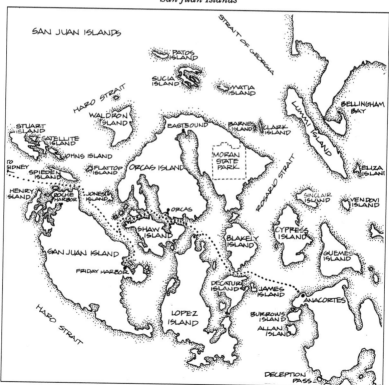

During the summer, there are other options for those who don't need to bring a car. The **Victoria Clipper** makes a once-a-day trip from downtown Seattle to Friday Harbor (with a quick stop in Port Townsend) from mid-May through mid-September. The summer-only ferry departs Pier 69 at 7:30am and arrives in Friday Harbor just before noon; for *Clipper* information, call (206) 448-5000 or (800) 888-2535. Another summertime option is via Bellingham; the **Island Shuttle Express** provides passenger-only ferry service to the San Juan Islands, May through September. Call for reservations: (206) 671-1137.

You can also fly to the islands. **Kenmore Air** schedules four flights a day during peak season. Round-trip flights start at about $99 per person; for more information, call (206) 486-8400 or (206) 486-1257.

SAN JUAN ISLANDS: LOPEZ

Lopez Island, flat and shaped like a jigsaw-puzzle piece, is a sleepy, rural place, famous for its friendly locals (they always wave) and its cozy coves and full pastures. It has the easiest bicycling in the islands: a 30-mile circuit suitable for the whole family to ride in a day.

There are numerous public parks. Two new day parks (**Otis Perkins** and **Upright Channel**) are great for exploring, with good beach access. You can camp at **Odlin County Park** (80 acres) or **Spencer Spit State Park** (130 acres), both on the north side. Odlin has many nooks and crannies, and grassy sites set among Douglas firs, shrubs, and clover. Spencer Spit has around 30 conventional campsites, and more primitive sites on the hillside. Both parks have water, toilets, and fire pits. **Agate County Park**, at the southwest tip of the island, has a pleasant rocky beach for the tired cyclist. A great place for a sunset. Seals and bald eagles can often be seen from the rocky promontory off **Shark Reef Park**.

Lopez Village is basic, but has a few spots worth knowing about, such as **Holly B's Bakery** in the Lopez Plaza, with celebrated fresh bread and pastries and coffee to wash them down (open June through September).

RESTAURANTS

Bay Cafe ★★ Entertaining a full house of both tourists and Lopezians most nights, this storefront restaurant seems only to be increasing in popularity. Specializing in ethnic dishes, owner Bob Wood changes the menu often to include innovative preparations which span many cuisines, from chicken satays with curried noodles (dressed with a Thai-style peanut and lime sauce) to an extraordinarily fresh king salmon with a subtle Creole mustard sauce and three creamy, crunchy potato cakes. Vegetarians can count on at least one option (the tapas are usually excellent). Prices are reasonable, especially considering the inclusion of both soup (perhaps a delicate chanterelle spinach) and a fresh tossed salad. The Bay Cafe is reason enough to come to this serene isle. ■ *Across from the post office in Lopez; (206) 468-3700; Lopez Town, Lopez Island; $$; beer and wine; MC, V; local checks only; dinner every day in summer (winter days vary).* &

LODGINGS

Inn at Swifts Bay ★★★ With their remarkable knack for knowing how to care for guests without ever appearing intrusive, Robert Herrmann and Christopher Brandmeir have turned this former summer home into the most appealing accommodation on Lopez Island. Choose from three large and comfortable bedrooms or two luxurious suites. The suites are very successful renovations of two separate attic spaces; one features an antique sleigh bed, and our favorite, the Red Cabbage suite, is a very private space with a separate sitting area and afternoon-sun deck. Both top-floor hideaways have private entrances. There's also a secluded outdoor hot tub that can be scheduled for private sittings (towels, robes, and slippers provided) and a first-class selection of recorded music and movies on tape for evening entertainment (but in temperate months you really ought to be outside). Expect to be pampered. Brandmeir is an excellent breakfast chef, and if you're lucky he'll fix you his crab cakes. Before you leave, you'll want to add to the mystery book of this wonderful place. ■ *Head 1 mile south of ferry to Port Stanley Rd, left 1 more mile; (206) 468-3636; Rt 2, Box 3402, Lopez Island, WA 98261; $$$; MC, V; checks OK.*

Blue Fjord Cabins ★ Lopez is the most secluded and tranquil of the three islands with tourist offerings, and the Blue Fjord Cabins are the most secluded and tranquil getaway on Lopez. The three log cabins are tucked away up an unmarked dirt road, each concealed from the others by thick woods. They're of modern chalet design, clean and airy, with full kitchens. Rates are a deal; $58 to $68 a night with a two-night minimum (three nights, in July and August). Doing nothing never had such a congenial setting. ■ *Elliott Rd at Jasper Cove; (206) 468-2749; Rt 1, Box 1450, Lopez Island, WA 98261; $$; no credit cards; checks OK.*

Edenwild Inn ★ Seattle architect Susan Aran designed her own inn a few years ago. It's definitely Lopez's biggest B&B and the most central, located a stone's throw from Lopez Village. There are eight rooms in this new Victorian-style, a very easy stroll from the best (and only) restaurants on the island. Each room has its own bath, a few have fireplaces. Ask for the one with the water or garden view; otherwise you may be stuck staring at the pharmacy. Breakfast is family-style (and for guests only) and lunch (open to the public) is a light treatment of soups, salads, and a few specials such as Thai peanut chicken. Our favorite room is Room 5 with a gracious bay window and a view of the channel, or the large, sunny Room 7. Room 1 has its own entrance, but is also too close to traffic through the front door. The only B&B on the island to accept children. ■ *In Lopez Village; (206) 468-3238; PO Box 271, Lopez, WA 98261; $$$; MC, V; checks OK; lunch, light dinner every day in summer (lunch only Mon-Fri in winter). &*

MacKaye Harbor Inn ★ Location, location, location. Bicyclists call it paradise after their sweaty trek from the ferry to this little harbor. The tall powder-blue house sits above a sandy, shell-strewn beach, perfect for sunset strolls or pushing off in one of their rented kayaks to explore the scenic waterways. Inside, the five rooms have been done up a bit sparsely, with a second-story deck for lounging and sunset ogling. There are too many signs directing you around the house—perhaps that's because the Bergstroms live in the house on a neighboring lot. But then, part of being on Lopez is being on your own. If you do come by bike, be warned; the closest restaurant is 6 miles back in town. Breakfast gets you started before a long morning of paddling out to play with the otters. ■ *12 miles south of the ferry landing on MacKaye Harbor Rd; (206) 468-2253; Rt 1, Box 1940, Lopez Island, WA 98261; $$; MC, V; checks OK.*

SAN JUAN ISLANDS: ORCAS

Named not for the whales (the large cetaceans tend to congregate on the west side of San Juan Island and are rarely spotted here), but for a Spanish explorer, Orcas has a reputation as the most beautiful of the four big San Juan islands. It's also the biggest (geographically) and the hilliest, boasting 2,400-foot **Mount Constitution** as the centerpiece of Moran State Park. Drive, hike, or, if you're feeling up to it, bike to the top, but get there somehow; from the old stone tower you can see Vancouver, Mt Rainier, and everything between. The 4,800-acre **Moran State Park** also has one lake for freshwater swimming, three more for fishing and boating, and nice campsites, but you must write at least two weeks ahead for reservations: Moran, Star Route Box 22, Eastsound, WA 98245.

The man responsible for the park was shipbuilding tycoon Robert Moran. His old mansion is now the centerpiece of **Rosario Resort**, just west of the park. Unfortunately, the resort doesn't live up to its extravagant billing and prices. But the mansion, decked out in memorabilia and mahogany trim and featuring an enormous pipe organ (still in use; check for concert dates), is certainly worth a stop; (206) 376-2222.

Although you probably won't see whales around Orcas, there's a plethora of other wildlife, including bald eagles and seals. One good way to get up close: **kayak trips**. Try Shearwater Adventures (206) 376-4699, or Doe Bay Village Resort, (206) 376-2291.

Adventure Limo & Taxi Service, (206) 376-4994, offers historic tours and trips up Mount Constitution, as well as car rentals for those who prefer to leave behind their vehicles (and the hassle of getting them on the ferry). Or you can rent bicycles by the hour, day, or week from **Dolphin Bay Bicycles**, (206) 376-4157, at the Orcas ferry landing and from **Wild Life Cycles**, (206) 376-4708, in Eastsound.

Every small, hip town has to lay claim to a small, hip bakery, and Eastsound has **Roses Bakery Cafe**, (206) 376-4220. Roses features simple breakfasts and lunches, but locals prefer the outdoor patio for blueberry and other innovative scones, fresh baguettes, muffins, and lattes served in enormous bowls.

RESTAURANTS

Christina's ★★ Christina's enjoys a reputation as the premier restaurant on the islands (and certainly the most expensive). At its best, the reputation is deserved. Chef/owner Christina Orchid changes the menu daily, and her innovative neo-Northwest cuisine has earned her accolades as far away as Europe. Trouble is, Christina's isn't always at its best. We've heard reports of sloppy dishes, kitchen tantrums, and small portions. And at times you may detect a certain snootiness (even with the recent attempt to tone down to meet the demands of the '90s). The prices are still high enough that you're entitled to expect near perfection and gracious hospitality—and not just occasionally. The decor in this converted 1938 gas station is purposefully casually elegant: no tablecloths on the copper-topped tables, but silver cutlery and cloth napkins. The enclosed deck and outdoor patio offer a fantastic view of Eastsound, but you can't reserve specific tables in advance. The more consistent desserts range from rhubarb spice cake with hazelnut ice cream to espresso shortbread sandwiches. ■ *North Beach Rd and Horseshoe Hwy; (206) 376-4904; Eastsound; $$$; full bar; AE, MC, V; checks OK; dinner every day June-Sept (Thurs-Mon off season)*.

Deer Harbor Lodge and Inn ★★ This expansive, rustic dining room with a large view deck is a cozy, soothing place despite its size, done up nicely in dark blue prints and natural wood. Pam and Craig Carpenter have rescued the inn from its long career as a purveyor of battered chicken and made it home to the island's best seafood, with generous portions and a strong emphasis on fresh, local ingredients. About a dozen entrées, including beef, chicken, and a staple vegetarian fettuccine, are outlined on the blackboard at the door and varied according to what's in season. Soups and salads arrive in large serving bowls, allowing each diner to partake according to capacity with a minimum of fuss. Fresh homemade bread comes with them. Both the wine list and the beer list are thoughtfully conceived, with novelties like German wheat beer. Dessert may be homemade ice cream.

For lodging, there's a two-story log cabin with eight rooms and two decks; breakfast arrives in a picnic basket outside your door. ■ *Follow signs to Deer Harbor; (206) 376-4110; Deer Harbor; $$; beer and wine; AE, MC, V; checks OK; dinner every day (weekends only in winter).* &

Bilbo's Festivo ★ Orcas Islanders speak of this cozy little place with reverence. Its decor and setting—mud walls, Mexican tiles, arched windows, big fireplace, handmade wooden benches, spinning fans, in a small house with a flowered courtyard—are charming, and the Navajo and Chimayo weavings on the walls are indeed from New Mexico. The fare is a fairly standard combination of Mexican and New Mexican influences, with improvisation on enchiladas, burritos, and chiles rellenos. Nightly specials grilled over mesquite might be carne asada (lime-marinated sirloin strips) served with Spanish rice, refried beans, and flour tortillas, or pollo en naranjas (chicken marinated in orange sauce) served with new potatoes, asparagus, and salad. Lunch includes ceviche salad (raw fish or seafood marinated for 24 hours in lime juice) and a wide array of soups, salads, and grilled whitefish. The staff is not always accommodating, but still, it's a great place to sit outside and dive into a margarita. ■ *Northbeach Rd and A St; (206) 376-4728; Eastsound; $; full bar; MC, V; local checks only; dinner every day (closed Mon in winter; seasonal lunch).*

Cafe Olga ★ You're likely to experience a wait at Cafe Olga, a popular lunch and late-afternoon stop for locals and visitors alike. Luckily, this cozy country kitchen is part of the Orcas Island Artworks, a sprawling cooperative crafts gallery cum New Age bookstore in a picturesque renovated strawberry-packing barn, so you can browse while you work up an appetite. The wholesome international home-style entrées range from a rich artichoke pie to cheese-spinach manicotti to Greek salad. For dessert, try a massive piece of the blackberry pie ("best in the world," according to islanders), or one of the wonderful chewy and dense chocolate chip cookies. Espresso or chilled applemint cooler washes it all down nicely. ■ *East of Moran State Park at Olga Junction; (206) 376-5098; Olga; $; beer and wine; MC, V; Washington State checks only; lunch every day.* &

La Famiglia ★ Here's a mainstream Italian lunch and dinner spot that seems to have achieved the consistency to match its pleasant, sunny decor, friendly service, and reasonable prices, as witnessed by the many discriminating locals who've become

▼

San Juan Islands: Orcas

Restaurants

▲

regulars. The emphasis is on fresh pasta, calzone, and other hearty family fare befitting the name; try the chunks of veal sautéed in butter, wine, and lemon, nestled nicely alongside pasta and vegetables. ■ *A St and North Beach Rd; (206) 376-2335; Deer Harbor; $; full bar; AE, MC, V; local checks only; lunch Mon-Sat, dinner every day (Mon-Sat in winter).* &

Ship Bay Oyster House As the new kid on the Orcas restaurant block, Ship Bay is developing a reputation as the spot for fresh local oysters. The comfortable old farmhouse offers a nice view of Ship Bay (ask for a window table); unfortunately, there's no deck dining. The entrées are not the most exciting on the island (and sort of remind us of something we'd get in a Seattle chop house), but they make up for their lack of innovation by sheer size. You'll do best if you head straight for the oysters on the half shell, oyster stew made to order, or a bowl of steamed mussels or clams. ■ *Just east of Eastsound on Horseshoe Hwy; (206) 376-5886; Eastsound; $$; full bar; AE, MC, V; checks OK; dinner every day (Tues-Sun off season).*

LODGINGS

Turtleback Farm Inn ★★★ The Turtleback is inland but still scenically located amid tall trees, rolling pastures, and private ponds. In 1984 it was just another dilapidated farmhouse, used to store hay. Bill and Susan Fletcher have redone it entirely and added a wing, but have kept the country flavor with natural wood, wide floor planks, private claw-footed tubs for six of the seven rooms, and excellent antiques. (Penny-pinching tip: one equally outfitted room is reasonably priced at $70 just because it's a bit small.) The Fletchers live in a separate house past the pond, so you won't suffer the B&B horror of feeling you're imposing on Aunt Irma and Uncle Ralph. A glass of sherry tops the evening. Their breakfasts, which may be taken in the well-appointed dining room or on the sunny deck, are the most praised on the island. Besides the usual bacon and eggs, they may include fresh yogurt, crêpes with lingonberry sauce, and an example of the ultimate B&B staple that reportedly won the San Juan granola contest. ■ *10 minutes from the ferry on Crow Valley Rd; (206) 376-4914; Rt 1, Box 650, Eastsound, WA 98245; $$$; MC, V; checks OK.* &

Beach Haven Resort ★★ The sign as you exit on the dirt road reads "Leaving Beach Haven. Entering the world." Cute, but appropriate, especially after the seven-day minimum summer stay. The cabins, shielded by tall trees, are of the genuine log variety, with wood stoves. Accommodations range through various grades of rustic to modern apartments and one "Spectacular Beachcomber" four-bedroom house. Everything faces on the long pebble beach, canoes and rowboats are ready if you feel energetic, and the air of tranquillity is palpable enough to chew. A great place to bring the kids but not pets. ■ *9 miles from the ferry at President Channel; (206) 376-2288; Rt 1, Box 12, Eastsound, WA 98245; $$; MC, V; checks OK.* &

Kangaroo House ★★ The location of this bed and breakfast, next to the Orcas airport, isn't scenic, but the 2-acre grounds are, and it's convenient to Eastsound and North Beach. The beautiful, enormous (6,700-square feet) 1907 Craftsman-style bungalow is done up in period style, with lovely antiques collected from the owners' world travels, a fieldstone fireplace in the living room, and a rear deck perfect for a late-afternoon cocktail. Three of the five rooms have their own wash basin but share a bath; a downstairs suite and large bedroom upstairs have private baths. The living room is full of informational books about the island; and there's a game room with cribbage and Trivial Pursuit if it's raining. Jan and Mike Russillo run their place with a professional blend of warmth and efficiency, and they serve an elegant full breakfast. ■ *North Beach Rd just north of Eastsound; (206) 376-2175; PO Box 334, Eastsound, WA 98245; $$; MC, V; checks OK.*

North Beach Inn ★ If you like funky, private settings with history and personality, North Beach Inn is the spot. Originally an apple orchard, then converted into a resort in the early '30s, North Beach Inn has remained relatively unchanged ever since (no small feat on this rapidly developing island). Eleven worn cabins are laid out on a prime stretch of the Gibson family beach. The spiffiest: Columbia; Frazier; and Shamrock, which has a loft that kids adore. Each cabin comes complete with a full kitchen, grill, Adirondack chairs on the beach (bonfires allowed), and a tremendous view. Also likely: duck-print flannel sheets, flimsy floral curtains, or artwork and furniture probably picked up at a local garage sale. In summer, guests can help themselves to the blackberries that proliferate here (and bring Fido if they'd like). Don't even think about visiting without a reservation. One-week minimum stay July through September; two-day minimum rest of the year. ■ *1½ miles west of the airport at North Beach; (206) 376-2660; PO Box 80, Eastsound, WA 98245; $$; no credit cards; checks OK (closed after Thanksgiving through mid-Feb).*

Orcas Hotel ★ This 1904 Victorian inn at the Orcas Island ferry terminal reopened in 1985. That same year, it was also exorcized of the ghost of former owner Octavia Van Moorhem. You can't blame her for wanting to stick around: the 12-room hostelry is a gem, with period pieces, white wicker in the lovely gardens, and a deck overlooking the water (though the gas tanks make for a less-than-perfect view). Ten rooms, three of which have half-baths, share showers down the hall, and two new, larger rooms have private balconies and whirlpool tubs. It feels like a small romantic hotel, but the accommodations include breakfast, served in a bright dining room downstairs. The pub with deck is a favorite local watering hole. The same management rents out Foxglove Cottage, a two-bedroom cabin on the water at Deer Harbor (very pricey privacy). ■ *Orcas ferry landing; (206) 376-4300; PO Box 155, Orcas, WA 98280; $$$; AE, MC, V; checks OK; breakfast, lunch, dinner every day.*

SAN JUAN ISLANDS: SAN JUAN

San Juan Island is the most populated in the archipelago; therefore it supports the biggest town, Friday Harbor, though typically nightlife is scarce even here. Attractions include the mid-19th-century sites of the **American** and **English Camps**, established when ownership of the island was under dispute. The conflict lead to the infamous Pig War of 1859-1860, so called because the sole casualty was a pig. The Americans and British shared joint occupation until 1872, when the dispute was settled in favor of the United States. The English camp, toward the island's north end, is wooded and secluded, while the American camp is open, windy prairie and beach, inhabited now only by thousands of rabbits. Either makes a fine picnic spot. So does **San Juan County Park**, where it's also possible to camp on the dozen often-crowded acres on Smallpox Bay (reservations suggested, (206) 378-2992). Another option is **Lakedale Campground** (reservations suggested), 4½ miles from Friday Harbor on Roche Harbor Road, (206) 378-2350, which sports 82 acres and three private lakes for swimming and fishing, and is popular with bicyclists. The best diving in the archipelago (some claim it's the best cold-water diving in the world) can be had here; **Emerald Seas Diving Center**, 180 First Street, Friday Harbor, (206) 378-2772, rents equipment and runs charter boats. It also rents sea kayaks, a wonderful way to see the island's wildlife up close. If you're lucky (best in late spring), you may even encounter whales which belong to the three native pods of orcas. Or you can join a guided kayak trip; **Shearwater Adventures** runs tours in conjunction with the Whale Museum, 62 First Street, Friday Harbor, (206) 378-4710. Several charter boats are also available for whale watching and fishing. Those distrustful of their sea legs can visit the nation's first official whale-watching park at **Lime Kiln Point State Park** on the island's west side. Bring binoculars and a lot of patience.

The **San Juan Historical Museum** is located in an old home in Friday Harbor filled with memorabilia from the island's early days. The 90-plus-year-old founder, a third-generation islander, is there two days a week. Admission is free; (206) 378-3949. Another bit of history is hidden away at the **Roche Harbor Resort** (see review in this section). Here you'll find a mausoleum, a bizarre monument that may tell more about timber tycoon John McMillin than all the rest of Roche Harbor. The ashes of family members are contained in a set of stone chairs that surround a concrete dining room table. They're ringed by a set of 30-foot-high columns, symbolic of McMillan's adherence to Masonic beliefs.

Oyster fans will be happy to visit **Westcott Bay Sea Farms** off West Valley Road just north of British Camp, (206) 378-2489, where you can help yourself to irregularly shaped oysters at bargain prices.

Jazz Festival. Throngs of people infest the streets of Friday Harbor for three days of Dixieland jazz, mid to late July; for information, call (206) 378-5509.

RESTAURANTS

Roberto's ★★ Word is, Roberto Carrieri has worked in about every restaurant on the island and finally decided to open one himself and do it right. He did. Now everyone's talking about Carrieri and Paul Aiello's tiny Italian restaurant in its little perch above the ferry parking lot. And if you want to get in, we suggest the first thing you do upon arriving at Friday Harbor is make reservations (even in the off season, since it's become a local fave). Come hungry. Portions are huge. Come early. The best dishes, such as the ravioli in an orange-zest cinnamon sauce or a sage, Parmesan cheese, and black pepper sauce, disappear early. But even when they do, the specials—such as a mound of creamy fettuccine with smoked salmon, goat cheese, sun-dried tomatoes—are outstanding. The spicy Pasta from Hell is only for those who already have fire coming out of their mouths. Who needs dessert? ■ *Corner of 1st and A sts; (206) 378-6333; 205 A St, Friday Harbor; $$$; beer and wine; MC, V; checks OK; dinner Tues-Sat.* &

Springtree Eating Establishment and Farm ★★ Since taking over this well-established cozy Friday Harbor restaurant, new chef/owner James Boyle has garnered praise from locals and tourists alike for his consistently excellent Northwest cuisine. Decor is simple—no tablecloths, plain wooden tables graced by a few fresh flowers, some photographs on the walls. But the menu, emphasizing seafood, organics, and local produce, is anything but simple. A recent dinner found us wowed by a spicy Dungeness crab cake, a heavenly fillet of salmon basted with basil and lemon, and an enormous plate of corkscrew pasta with smoked mussels, prawns, and crabmeat in a basil cream sauce. Try the superb eggless caesar salad; you'd never know it was made with tofu. The best food here is that which is the most adventurous (lunch sandwiches are clearly an afterthought). Vegetarians are well cared for since Boyle eschews meat. Portions are ample and beautifully presented. There's a great deal of attention paid to every detail here. Service is folksy and energetic; there's outdoor dining on the small patio, weather permitting. ▪ *Under the elm on Spring downtown; (206) 378-4848; 310 Spring, Friday Harbor; $$; beer and wine; MC, V; local checks only; lunch, dinner every day in summer (Wed-Sun off season).* &

Duck Soup Inn ★ Richard and Grechen Allison seem committed to continuing the ambitious reach of the kitchen with emphasis on fresh local seafoods and seasonal ingredients, adding game dishes and pastas to round out the selection. It's a charming restaurant that's tough to get to, but the playful entrées can be hit or miss. On any given day the menu might hint of Thai, Cajun, and German influences, as well as offer home-smoked salmon or oysters. The wine list has been expanded and internationalized by Richard, the maître d' and wine steward. ▪ *4½ miles north of Friday Harbor on Roche Harbor Rd; (206) 378-4878; 3090 Roche Harbor Rd, Friday Harbor; $$; beer and wine; MC, V; local checks only; dinner Wed-Sun (closed in winter).* &

Katrina's Out of her tiny kitchen in the back of a second-hand store, Kate Stone runs her one-woman culinary show. Except for her signature spinach-cheese pie and green salad with toasted hazelnuts and garlicky blue cheese dressing, you never know what you might find here. Stone's been known to arrive in the morning and ask her first customers if they have any preferences for the day's menu. Odds are, whatever she's serving will be a simple sensation: a Thai vegetable soup strongly flavored with lemon grass and galangal root; a baked potato with tarragon, fresh asparagus, and chicken. There are two stools inside and half a dozen tables in the ramshackle yard; the food's the real centerpiece here. ▪ *2 blocks up from the ferry terminal behind Funk & Junk; (206) 378-7290; 65 Nichols Street, Friday Harbor; $; no alcohol; no credit cards; checks OK; lunch, specialty dinners, and baked goods (closed Wed and Sun).*

LODGINGS

Duffy House ★★ New owners Mary and Arthur Miller haven't changed much about this 1920s farmhouse looking out upon Griffin Bay and the Olympics beyond, which is just fine with us. The house displays an architectural style (Tudor) that's rare in the islands, in a splendid, isolated site. Decorated with antiques and accented with classic mahogany trim, Duffy House offers five comfy guest rooms (all with shared bath). The sunken living room sports a large fireplace and a bounty of information about the islands. Even neophyte bird-watchers won't be able to miss the bald eagles here; they nest in the backyard. A secluded beach and nearby gardens, woods, and orchard offer plenty of room for contemplation. ▪ *Argyle Rd south from town to Pear Point Rd; (206) 378-5604; 760 Pear Point Rd, Friday Harbor, WA 98250; $$; MC, V; checks OK.*

Lonesome Cove Resort ★★ Back in 1945, Roy and Neva Durhack sailed their 35-foot yacht here from the Hawaiian Islands. They were getting ready to sail it around the world, but once they saw Lonesome Cove their wanderlust subsided. Now under newer management, the resort remains a pretty spot. The six immaculate little cabins (recently renovated with hand-laid red cedar walls) set among trees at the water's edge, the manicured lawns, and the domesticated deer that wander the 75-acre woods make the place a favorite for honeymooners—fully 30 percent of Lonesome Cove's guests are newlyweds. The sunsets are spectacular, and there's a fine view of nearby Speiden Island. Cabins start at $85 a day and have a five-night minimum in the summer months. No pets—too many baby ducks around. ■ *Roche Harbor Rd 9 miles north to Lonesome Cove Rd; (206) 378-4477; 5810 Lonesome Cove Rd, Friday Harbor, WA 98250; $$; MC, V; checks OK.* ⅖

Mariella Inn and Cottages ★★ In time—when all the cabins are remodeled, when they've refinished the two rowboats, when they build a shoreside barbecue pit, when they sponsor spontaneous classical concerts on the lawn—Mariella could become the finest establishment in the San Juans. Until then, enjoy watching it develop into all good things an inn should be. This 11-room inn, built in 1902, is set on a 9-acre point, an easy stroll from Friday Harbor. The rooms are simple and elegant. Our favorite is the Fleur du Soleil, a large room warmed with sunlight. Others prefer Arequipa, a corner waterside room with its own bath. (Robes are provided, but you might have to hunt for them.) There are seven small cabins (with kitchens, fireplaces, and four-night minimum in summer) set unobtrusively in the madronas on the waterfront, and three extra rooms in the farmhouse. Guests might spend the day exploring the island (sea kayaks, mountain bikes, daysailers for rent to guests), then return to relax before the parlor fireplace or soak privately in the cedar hot tub. A 65-foot classic motor yacht (1927) is available for charter. During the summer, the large lawn is often set for a game of volleyball or a round of croquet. There's a tennis court for racket enthusiasts.

At press time, the inn's restaurant—in the expert hands of Greg Atkinson—launched their dinner menu. Even without a liquor license, and without an experienced waitstaff as yet, the food was quite remarkable. Informality is the rule here, with inn guests perhaps sharing tables with others. The menu is a four-course prix-fixe affair. It reflects Chef Atkinson's recent sabbatical in France without indulging in it. Reservations necessary. ■ *Left on 1st St, follow until turns into Turnpoint Rd; (206) 378-6868; 630 Turnpoint Rd, Friday Harbor, WA 98250; $$$; MC, V; checks OK; dinner Wed-Sun (one seating; reservations necessary).* ⅖

Olympic Lights ★★ As you approach this isolated bed and breakfast, you may recall the movie *Days of Heaven*: the tall Victorian farmhouse sits lonely as a lighthouse in a sea of open meadow. The renovated interior is more modern, and quite elegant: four upstairs rooms, all with queen beds, done up in bright whites and soft pastels, and furnished with antiques. The downstairs room, however, is the only one with a private bath. You must remove your shoes to tread the off-white pile carpet. All the rooms are lavishly bathed in sunlight. The panorama of Olympic Mountains and Strait of Juan de Fuca from the south rooms adds to the effect. The proprietors, Christian and Lea Andrade, are San Francisco refugees who came to San Juan's empty south tip seeking a more calming, contemplative milieu. Breakfast includes fresh eggs from the resident hen; they also have four cats who roam downstairs. No smoking. ■ *Argyle Ave out of Friday Harbor to Cattle Point Rd; (206)378-3186; 4531-A Cattle Point Rd, Friday Harbor, WA 98250; $$; no credit cards; checks OK.*

Westwinds Bed & Breakfast ★★ Westwinds commands what may easily be the most magnificent view on all of the San Juan Islands. Unfortunately, too few people will enjoy the 10 acres of mountainside abundant with deer and quail. This private paradise remains a one-bedroom facility (but guests have the 1,200-square-foot house to themselves). Owners Chris Durbin and Gayle Rollins have built an extraordinary glass-and-wood home that uses the setting to optimal advantage: look from your cathedral-ceilinged bedroom, private bath, patio, living room, or virtually any seat in the house, and you're likely to feel in possession of a large part of the world (or at least the Strait of Juan de Fuca and the Olympic Mountains). Breakfast is almost as majestic. The owners breed miniature horses, which provide an unusual diversion. Particularly popular with honeymoon couples (privacy is never an issue), this bed and breakfast is to be enjoyed whatever the occasion, whatever the season. ■ *2 miles from Lime Kiln Whale Watch Park; (206) 378-5283; 4909-H Hannah Highlands, Friday Harbor, WA 98250; $$$; MC, V; checks OK.*

Blair House Bed and Breakfast Inn ★ Believe it or not, it's a country retreat—four blocks from the ferry (which is actually very convenient if you happen to arrive late). Owners Jane Benson and Jeff Zander have tastefully decorated their early 1900s home in pastels, floral prints, and antique furnishings, without overdoing the frou-frou, so just about anyone can feel comfortable here. Most of the six rooms have their own bath; the one-bedroom cottage is fully equipped. A bountiful morning meal featuring home-baked coffee cakes, fresh fruit, and other delights is included, and on sunny days breakfast may be taken to the attractive poolside patio. Since the salt water is too cold for leisurely swimming, the heated pool is a definite attraction. You share the parlor, equipped with a VCR (tape rentals nearby), as well as a huge, old-fashioned wraparound verandah. The owners are both attentive and businesslike, striking the perfect balance between warm hospitality and invisibility. ■ *4 blocks up Spring to Blair; (206) 378-5907; 345 Blair Ave, Friday Harbor, WA 98250; $$; AE, MC, V; checks OK.*

Friday's ★ The former Elite Hotel is finally starting to live up to its old name. Innkeepers Debbie and Steve Demarest have taken this longtime bunkhouse and given it a completely new life. Eleven rooms are decorated in rich colors of wine, water, and wings. The best room in the place is unquestionably the third-floor nest with its own deck (and water view), kitchen, double shower, and Jacuzzi tub. Heated floors in the bathrooms, bowls of candies, and bedtime mints are just some of the thoughtful touches; however, the inn is right in the middle of town and not always the most quiet retreat. Downstairs is a bistro with good pizzas and huge salads. The ambitious Demarests plan to open a second bed and breakfast not far from town. ■ *2 blocks up from the ferry; (206) 378-5848 or (800) 352-2632 (35-B AND B); PO Box 2023, Friday Harbor, WA 98250; $$; AE, MC, V; checks OK.*

Wharfside Bed & Breakfast ★ If nothing lulls you to sleep like the gentle lap of the waves, the Wharfside's the B&B for you. It's this region's first realization of the European tradition of floating inns. Two guest rooms have been installed on the 60-foot sailboat *Jacquelyn*, both very nicely finished with full amenities and that compact precision that only living on a boat can inspire. The fore cabin has a double bed and sleeping berths for kids or extras. When the weather's good, you can enjoy the huge breakfast on deck and watch the local fishermen gather their nets. And what other B&B can you hire for a sail around the islands? ■ *On the K dock in Friday Harbor; (206) 378-5661; PO Box 1212, Friday Harbor, WA 98250; $$; no credit cards; checks OK.*

Hillside House This 4,000-square-foot modern house on the outskirts of Friday Harbor distinguishes itself from other contemporary country-style B&Bs by, among other things, its full-flight aviary. Sleep in one of the four rooms adjacent to it and you might find yourself waking up and staring into the face of Bob, an enormous Reeves pheasant, or any of a dozen doves and exotic ducks. Three other guest rooms have views of the harbor in the distance. The plushest is the Eagle's Nest, a third-floor suite with TV, phone, wet bar, a small balcony, and a whirlpool tub. A full breakfast is served in the informal, sunny dining room on plastic patio chairs. Owners Dick and Cathy

Robinson keep a fax machine for those who just can't leave it all behind. ■ *On Carter Ave, west of the ferry landing; (206) 378-4730 or (800) 232-4730; 365 Carter Avenue, Friday Harbor, WA 98250; $$; AE, MC, V; checks OK.*

Moon & Sixpence Moon & Sixpence is a country B&B with a slightly artsy flourish (witness the nod to W. Somerset Maugham in the name). Charlie and Evelyn Tuller's sunny farmhouse in the middle of San Juan Island might need a new coat of paint, but inside it's done up tastefully in a gamut of folk arts. Of the four guest rooms, the Island suite is a favorite. The best spot is the Lookout—a converted water tower with exposed post-and-beam construction, a reading loft, bathroom, and pastoral views out of all four sides. The size of the breakfast seems to depend on the mood of the innkeeper. The farm pond is a dandy spot for picnics, barbecues, or just counting the clouds. ■ *3½ miles from the ferry dock on Beaverton Valley Rd; (206) 378-4138; 3021 Beaverton Valley Rd, Friday Harbor, WA 98250; $$; no credit cards; checks OK.*

Roche Harbor Resort When you walk out of the stately old ivy-clad Hotel de Haro at Roche Harbor and gaze out at the trellised, cobblestoned waterfront and yacht-dotted bay, you'll forget all about the creaky, uneven floorboards, the somewhat pieced-together wallpaper, the sparse furnishings. The resort evolved from the company town that John McMillin built a century ago for his lime mill, once the largest west of the Mississippi. It has seen some renovation since Teddy Roosevelt visited, but not tons. Still, the 107-year-old resort has a terrific view, and if it's all too quaint for you, try the cottages or the condos at the other side of the harbor. If you do stay in the hotel, at least be sure to reserve a room with a harbor view. Between gardens, swimming, tennis, and the mausoleum (really), there's plenty to do at Roche Harbor. Come by boat or plane if you'd like; just make sure you have a way to get into Friday Harbor for dinner. ■ *Roche Harbor; (206) 378-2155; PO Box 4001, Roche Harbor, WA 98250; $$$; MC, V; checks OK.*

LA CONNER

La Conner was founded in 1867 by John Conner, a trading-post operator, who named the town after his wife, L(ouisa) A. Conner. Much of what you see today was originally built before the railroads arrived in the late 1880s, when the fishing and farming communities of Puget Sound traded almost entirely by water. In an age of conformity and efficiency, the town became a literal backwater, and a haven for nonconformists (Wobblies, WWII COs, McCarthy-era escapees, beatniks, hippies, and bikers), with a smattering of artists and writers, including Mark Tobey, Morris Graves, Guy Anderson, and Tom Robbins.

This long-standing "live and let live" attitude of the town has allowed the neighboring native American Swinomish community to contribute to the exceptional cultural richness of La Conner. Even the merchants here have created a unique atmosphere, an American bazaar: **Chez la Zoom**, **Cottons**, **Nasty Jack's**, and the **Dinghy Baby**.

Tillinghast Seed Co., at the entrance to town, is the oldest operating retail and mail-order seed store in the Northwest (since 1885); in addition to seeds it has a wonderful nursery, a florist shop, and a general store, (206) 466-3329. **Go Outside** is a small but choice garden and garden-accessory store, (206) 466-4836.

Gaches Mansion, on Second Street overlooking the main drag, is a wonderful example of American Victorian architecture, with a widow's walk that looks out on the entire Skagit Valley. It is filled with period furnishings, and a small museum of Northwest art occupies the second floor. Open weekends, (206) 466-4288.

RESTAURANTS

Palmers Restaurant and Pub ★★ Another change of ownership could mean turmoil but Palmers (formerly Barkley's of La Conner) continues to be La Conner's favorite restaurant. Thomas and Danielle Palmers' place is perched on a knoll just behind town at the far end of the La Conner Country Inn. Locals like the hobbit-like pub with wall murals painted by La Conner artists; but for a more elegant atmosphere, climb the stairs. There are two rooms—one with lace curtains on the west-facing windows that pull in the golden evening sun, another cozy room with a wood stove to warm winter evenings. The deck is a pleasant spot too. Dinners are reliable; the massive lamb shank bergère is moist and savory with garlic, tomatoes, mushrooms, and herbs. A special prawns with papaya, kiwi, and cilantro shows the kitchen is successfully playful. The appetizers falter occasionally: too much salt overpowers the fresh mozzarella, tomato, and basil plate. Still, this is a place that likes to please—and usually does. ■ *2nd and Washington; (206) 466-4261; 205 Washington, La Conner; $$; full bar; MC, V; checks OK; lunch, dinner every day.*

Calico Cupboard ★ It's awfully cute—Laura Ashley meets Laura Ingalls Wilder—but the bakery is the reason to go, turning out excellent carrot muffins, pecan tarts, shortbread, raspberry bars, currant scones, apple Danish, and much more. Our advice for avoiding the weekend crowds is to buy your goodies from the take-out counter of the bakery and then find a sunny bench by the water. Hearty waffle and omelet breakfasts are offered, but let's face it, most folks come here for the pastries. Lunches run to sandwiches on homemade bread, salads, and terrific soups. There's another Calico in Anacortes. ■ *South*

end of the line on 1st; (206) 466-4451; 720 S 1st, La Conner;
$; beer and wine; no credit cards; checks OK; breakfast, lunch
every day.

LODGINGS

Downey House ★★ Just three miles out of La Conner, Downey House has perfect access to the tulip fields in spring. It's a lovely, neat, tidy place with five guest rooms (three with baths) and Victorian appointments. Jim and Kay Frey have lived in the house for 28 years and share their love of the Skagit Valley and its lore with guests. There's a hot tub out back. The full breakfast may include sourdough pancakes, omelets, or fruit-topped crêpes. Reserve now for tulip season. ■ *3½ miles southeast of La Conner; (206) 466-3207; 1880 Chilberg Rd, La Conner, WA 98257; $$; MC, V; checks OK.*

The Heron in La Conner ★★ The Heron is the prettiest hostelry in town, with 11 rooms done in jewelry-box fashion. We like those that show a little individuality, such as the Antiques Room with its lovely furnishings and an old claw-footed tub, or the View Suite with its gas fireplace and view of Mt Baker. All rooms have private baths and TVs. There's also a bridal suite with a two-person Jacuzzi. Downstairs is an elegant living room with wing chairs and lush carpeting, along with a formal dining room in which you can eat your continental breakfast. Out back you may barbecue in the stone fire pit or slump in the sun or the hot tub. ■ *On the edge of town at 117 Maple St; (206) 466-4626; PO Box 716, La Conner, WA 98257; $$; AE, MC, V; checks OK.*

Hotel Planter ★★ The most famous (and infamous) characters of La Conner's colorful past once inhabited this end of town. They drank at the raucous Nevada Tavern, ate at the steamy Planter Cafe, and slept one floor above in the Hotel Planter. The first two landmarks have long since been replaced by more genteel shops and galleries, but the 85-year-old Hotel Planter is up and running again. In 1988, owner Don Hoskins used his connoisseur's eye and artisan's care to create a style that is a tasteful blend of past (original woodwork staircase and entrance) and present (private baths and armoire-hidden TVs in every room). Six rooms face the waterfront; others, including a special bridal suite with Jacuzzi, overlook a Renaissance garden courtyard (with a hot tub for hotel guests only). The staff, well-versed in the Skagit Valley, are exemplary. ■ *End of the line on the south end of 1st St; (206) 466-4710; 715 S 1st St; PO Box 702, La Conner, WA 98257; $$; AE, MC, V; local checks only.*

La Conner Channel Lodge ★★ At the edge of the Swinomish Channel, the Channel Lodge is a fit urban version of its slightly dowdy country cousin a few blocks inland. It's an appealing place, from the attractive cedar-shingle building down to the gentle aroma of potpourri in the library just off the lobby. Your fireplace (gas) is lit upon arrival and some of the rooms have a Jacuzzi with a channel view. If you're not splurging for a splash, make sure to request a Channel view room away from (or at least not directly underneath) those with potentially noisy waterjets. The decks are nooks—just enough for a chair and fresh air while you watch the tugs work the waterway. Breakfast is a rather perfunctory continental array of granola, fruits, and tiny morning treats. ■ *Right on the water at 205 N 1st; (206) 466-1500; PO Box 573, La Conner, WA 98257; $$$; AE, DC, MC, V; checks OK.* &

Rainbow Inn ★★ On Chilberg Road on the way into La Conner sits an elegant turn-of-the-century farmhouse, the Rainbow Inn, amid acres of Skagit Valley flatlands. New owners Ron Johnson and Sharon Briggs are starting to spiff up the place, primarily with a new garden plan. From the eight guest rooms you get sweeping views of the region you came to see: lush pastures, Mount Baker, the Olympics. Inside is pretty too: most of the furnishings are American country-pine, consistent with the farmhouse, and some of the baths have claw-footed tubs (robes are provided for the hot tub). Even though one side of the Violet room faces the road, it's still our favorite, with a door to the second story porch, grand potbellied stove, and a huge armoire. Downstairs are plenty of lingering zones. Owner Sharon serves inventive breakfasts on an enchanting French-windowed front porch. ■ *½ mile east of town; (206) 466-4578; 1075 Chilberg Rd, La Conner; PO Box 1600, La Conner, WA 98257; $$; MC, V; checks OK.*

White Swan Guest House ★★ Poplars line the driveway, adirondack chair are placed throughout the garden grounds, wheat and tulip fields stretch beyond. Peter Goldfarb's bed and breakfast may be tough to find but getting lost on the back roads of Skagit Valley is not such a bad thing. The house is splashed with warm yellow, salmon, evergreen, and peach and seems to soak up the sunlight, even when it's raining. There are three guest rooms with an odd assortment of antiques (and handmade quilts on the beds); they share two baths down the hall. Pamper yourself with a soak in the large claw-footed tub, or curl up on the pink sofa in front of the wood stove. A charming guest house (one of the few in the valley) out back provides an especially private accommodation; great for family or romantics. Peter serves a breakfast of freshly baked scones or muffins, fruit from his garden, and coffee. Bring binoculars for bird-watching and bikes for easy touring around the flat farmlands of Fir Island. ■ *6 miles southeast of La Conner; (206) 445-6805; 1388 Moore Rd, Mt Vernon, WA 98273; $$; MC, V; checks OK.*

La Conner Country Inn ★ Despite its name, the La Conner Country Inn is not really a country inn—it's more of a classy motel with 28 spacious rooms with gas fireplaces. Breakfasts are complimentary and served in the library, where an enormous fieldstone fireplace and comfortable furniture beckon you to enjoy a good book. The rooms are starting to show their age but the place is comfortable and kid friendly. Those in search of spiffier (and pricier) accommodations should look to the 40-room La Conner Channel Lodge under the same ownership. Palmers restaurant, perched on a knoll at the far end of the hotel, is the town's best (see review). ▪ *2nd and Morris; (206) 466-3101; 107 2nd St, PO Box 573, La Conner, WA 98257; $$; AE, MC, V; checks OK.*

MOUNT VERNON

Mount Vernon is a rare working town: one in which there are more good restaurants and bookstores than taverns and churches. It is the Big City to residents of surrounding Skagit and Island counties, and a college town to a surprising number of local folk, even though Skagit Valley College is but a blip on the very outskirts of town.

The classy old town center of Mount Vernon heroically survived the terrible winter floods of 1990, the worst river flooding since the town was founded 101 years prior. The Mount Vernon Mall was not so lucky, virtually wiped out that same year by the opening of the Cascade Mall in neighboring Burlington.

To travelers on I-5, it is little more than a blur except during the spring when the lush farmlands are brilliantly swathed in daffodils (mid-March to mid-April), tulips (April through early May), and irises (mid-May to mid-June). The pastoral countryside is flat and ideal for bicyclists, except for the gridlock that occurs on the small farm lanes during the **Tulip Festival** (usually early April). Mount Vernon is really all about fresh food and beautiful flowers, products of surrounding Skagit Valley farms. For information on the many harvest festivals (June is Strawberry Month, September Apple Month, and October Redleaf Month), call the Chamber of Commerce, (206) 428-8547.

Little Mountain Park has a terrific picnic spot plus a knockout vista of the valley (look for migratory trumpeter swans in February). On the other end of the spectrum, **The Chuck Wagon Drive Inn** offers 50 different kinds of burgers, electric trains, and the largest collection of ceramic whiskey-bottle cowboys in the free world.

▼

**Mount
Vernon**

Restaurants

RESTAURANTS

Wildflowers ★★★ Without doubt, chef David Day and owner Michele Kjosen have created a restaurant worthy of considerable attention. And attention *is* the secret—attention to the smallest detail, in the kitchen, on the plate, in the surrounding ambience. It begins with Kjosen's attention to her guests, which verges on excessive but never crosses the line. Without her help we might have overlooked a marvelous entrée hidden on the menu under "salads": char-grilled prawns radiating atop a mound of brown rice and pecans, with lightly sautéed fresh orange slices in cilantro-cumin beurre blanc. Inspirations such as this come on a daily basis. Chef Day has succeeded in nurturing his wildflowers to full bloom year-round. ■ *3 minutes east of I-5 from College Way exit; (206) 424-9724; 2001 E College Way, Mt Vernon; $$$; full bar; AE, MC, V; checks OK; dinner Tues-Sat.*

The Longfellow Cafe ★★ Local people fill the Longfellow Cafe because they have come to expect good food. With high volume, high ceilings, and high expectations, chef/owner Peter Barnard also has a creative, playful twist or two to lavish on us. The "steamers" with lemon-dill butter off the daily-special blackboard were a mélange of butter clams, blue mussels, and pink singing scallops, all locally harvested and wonderfully prepared. The cafe features an excellent selection of wines by the glass, including vintage port, and a nice variety of beers. This brother-and-sister team, Peter and Annye Barnard, have worked hard to warm up the cavernous old brick granary, now a showcase of Skagit Valley produce and their solid culinary talents. The adjacent bookstore (Scott's) makes a happy ending. ■ *In the historic Granary Building; (206) 336-3684; 120-B N 1st St, Mt Vernon; $$$; beer and wine; MC, V; local checks only; lunch Mon-Sun, dinner Tues-Sat.*

Pacioni's Pizzeria ★ Wafts of fresh bread, fresh herbs, and fresh espresso tug at passersby. As the first weeks of opening turn into months, fewer pass by. They congregate at the red-and-white-checkered tables, enjoy a friendly glass of red wine, and savor the pungency of pizza. Young owners Dave and Paula Alberts have thrown their hearts into this restaurant as impressively as Dave throws the pizza dough into the air (remember the mad Italian baker in *Moonstruck?*). Paula (née Pacioni) is the keeper of family secrets, but we'll let you in on our favorite pie, the tricolor pizza (pesto, ricotta, and Roma tomatoes). All ingredients are fresh (even the biscotti are baked here), and *everything* is made to order. Pacioni's is showing signs of becoming one of the most gregarious spots in the Skagit Valley. ■ *In old downtown Mt Vernon; (206) 336-3314; 606 1st St, Mt Vernon; $; beer and wine; no credit cards; checks OK; lunch, dinner Mon-Sat.*

If you've found a place that you think is a best place, send in the report form at the back of this book. If you're unhappy with one of the places, let us know why. We depend on reader input.

STANWOOD

Stanwood is a sleepy little farm center with a Scandinavian heritage, a Midwestern air, and one good reason for a few minutes' sightseeing. Years ago, local daughter Martha Anderson started working at *rosemaling*, traditional Norwegian "flower painting," and teaching it to her fellow Stanwoodians. Now they've embellished many everyday businesses with charming rosemaled signs—not for tourist show as in Leavenworth, but out of an authentic impulse to express their heritage and make Main Street pretty.

Pilchuck School. Founded in 1971 by glass artist Dale Chihuly and Seattle art patrons John Hauberg and Anne Gould Hauberg, Pilchuck is an internationally renowned glass art school. Students live and study on this campus, situated in the midst of a country tree farm. An open house twice each summer gives folks a chance to see craftspeople at work; call first for times and directions. Summer: (206) 445-3111; winter: (206) 621-8422.

CAMANO ISLAND

LODGINGS

Willcox House ★ The clapboard house looks like a remodeled Victorian with its turrets and wraparound porch, but it was built just a few years ago. Out of 60 windows you get fine views of Skagit Bay, and in clear weather you can see Mount Baker from the meadowlike lawn. Four guest rooms are decorated with antiques and brass and iron beds. Only one has a private bath. The Captain's Room that adjoins the turret is a wonderfully sunny spot to read. The morning's meal might be an omelet of local wild mushrooms, muffins, fruit, juice, and coffee. ■ *1 mile west of Stanwood; (206) 629-4746; 1462 Larkspur Lane, Camano Island, WA 98292; $$; no credit cards; checks OK.*

Everett

EVERETT

Enormous regional population growth is forcing this sleeping bear to wake up and plant some roses. Progress is slow, but at least it is moving. Hanging flower baskets now decorate the main boulevard downtown, a large retail complex, Colby Square, is in the works, as are the plans for a city-financed performing arts theater. The city is experiencing new pride as it readies itself for the arrival of the Navy later this decade.

The **Everett Giants** are an exciting Class A minor league baseball affiliate of the San Francisco Giants. Games are played outdoors, tickets are cheap, and the ballpark food isn't bad. Call (206) 258-3673 for tickets and information.

The **Boeing 747/767 plant**, in South Everett on Highway 526, offers free 90-minute tours of the world's largest plant (measured in volume). No children under 10; (206) 342-4801.

Marina Village is a small but pleasant shopping center/restaurant complex on Port Gardner Bay. A ferry shuttle service runs from mid-July to September to Jetty Island, for beachcombing and bird-watching; schedules vary with the tide.

RESTAURANTS

Passport ★★ Passport is your ticket to good food in Everett. Owners/chefs Lil Miller and Nan Wilkinson began an ambitious dream to bring the world (at least, a culinary taste of the world) to this mill town. Believe it or not, they pull it off. If the menu's unfamiliar, just choose something, anything. It is all good: the Cantonese steamed clams, the spicy Brazilian coconut shrimp, the outstanding Greek steak salad, and the hot-and-sour Indonesian salad with plenty of fresh seafood. In addition to a good wine list and full bar, fresh coffee is served European-style in a bowl. Desserts are good but anticlimactic. Scribble your thoughts on the butcher-papered tables. ■ *Hewitt Ave between Oakes and Lombard; (206) 259-5037; 1909 Hewitt Ave, Everett; $$; full bar; MC, V; local checks only; lunch Mon-Fri, dinner Mon-Sat.*

▼

▲

The Sisters This place is as popular as it is funky. Soups such as mulligatawny, gazpacho, or just plain old beef barley can be outstanding. Salads are also consumer-friendly. Sandwiches range from average deli stuff to very healthful concoctions, including a vegetarian burger made with chopped cashews and sunflower seeds. Among the usual morning fare are some delights—the blueberry or pecan hotcakes; granola with yogurt and blueberry sauce; or scrambled eggs with bacon, onion, cottage cheese (or cheese of choice), sprouts, and salsa, wrapped in flour tortillas. Fresh-squeezed lemonade and strawberry lemonade are available year-round. A slice of blackberry pie weighs 10.5 ounces. ■ *8 blocks west of Broadway, in the Everett Public Market; (206) 252-0480; 2804 Grand St, Everett; $; no alcohol; MC, V; checks OK; breakfast, lunch Mon-Fri.*

LODGINGS

Marina Village Inn ★★ Waterfront accommodations are a surprising rarity on Puget Sound, making this 28-room inn on Port Gardner Bay all the more attractive. It offers all the sophistication of a big-city hotel without the parking problems and convention crowds, and is therefore becoming increasingly popular with corporate executives. Best to book rooms a month or more in advance.

Rooms in the old inn are very contemporary and stylish (we've actually picked up decorating tips), featuring oak chests of drawers, tasteful art and lamps, refrigerators, handcrafted ceramic sinks, color satellite TVs, extension phones in the bath-rooms, and trouser presses; some rooms have notably comfy couches and easy chairs. Four of the rooms have Jacuzzis; most have telescopes for gazing out over the water. Be sure to book a room on the harbor side; sea lions might be lollygagging in the sun on the nearby jetty. A new addition features 11 rooms, all with harbor views and Jacuzzis and some with decks. No room service. ■ *Exit 193 off I-5 onto Pacific Ave, turn right on W Marine View Dr to waterfront; (206) 259-4040; 1728 W Marine View Dr, Everett, WA 98201; $$; AE, DC, DIS, MC, V; no checks.*

SNOHOMISH

This small community, formerly an active lumber town, now bills itself as the "Antique Capital of the Northwest." It certainly has plenty of antique shops filling the downtown historic district; the **Star Center Mall** is the largest, with 165 antique dealers from all over the area; 829 Second Street, (206) 568-2131.

In addition to antiquing, get a lift in a **hot air balloon** at Harvey Field, (206) 568-3025, which also offers scenic flights, (206) 568-1541, and skydiving opportunities, (206) 568-5960.

RESTAURANTS

Sweet Life Cafe What began as a coffeehouse (reportedly the first of its kind in Snohomish County) has become the town's favorite restaurant. It's located on the second floor of the old brick Marks Building, where owners Dennis Lebow and Paula Inmon have maintained the classic coffeehouse appeal with secondhand mismatched tables, classical jazz on the sound system, and a separate room devoted to overstuffed couches and reading material. The counter servers at lunch are friendly and lightning-fast (weekends can get quite busy), ladling up generous bowls of ginger-carrot soup or making a roasted turkey and cranberry sandwich on hand-sliced five-grain bread. Dinners slow down a bit and the food takes a different approach: a lamb stew spiked with North African spices and dried figs and served over orzo, grilled fresh Alaskan white salmon with an orange sauce, or perhaps a vegetarian ravioli with grilled vegetables. The light and dark chocolate mousse confirms it is, indeed, a sweet life. ■ *1st and B on the 2nd floor of Marks Bldg; (206) 568-3554; 1024 1st St, Snohomish; $$; beer and wine; MC, V; checks OK; breakfast Sat-Sun, lunch Tues-Sat, dinner Wed-Sat.*

MUKILTEO

Unfortunately, Mukilteo is probably best known for the traffic congestion caused by the **Washington State ferry** to Clinton on Whidbey Island; (206) 355-7308. There are, however, a small state park and a historic lighthouse worth seeing. You can also stroll along the waterfront and fish off the docks.

RESTAURANTS

Charles at Smugglers Cove ★★★ The smugglers were none other than Al Capone and associates, who built this mansion in 1929 as a speakeasy and distillery complete with a secret tunnel to the docks below. (Mukilteo was Snohomish County's first port city.) Charles is the owner's father. Chef Claude Faure and partner Janet Kingma have turned this Northwest landmark building into an elegant French restaurant. There are two floors; for best atmosphere, reserve a table downstairs, where the country-French ambience is more appealing. The veal medallions with chanterelles and the sweetbreads were fork-tender, each in a delectable wine-based sauce and served with steamed vegetables. Portions were ample and rich; every vegetable bore its own sauce (too many sauces on the plate). Entrées come à la carte, but for an extra $6.50 you can get a dinner salad and dessert (worth the extra)—baked Alaska or chocolate mousse. Much of Charles' business is from nearby Boeing and, accordingly, weeknights tend to be busier than weekends. There's a small terrace with a view of the Sound, or ask for a table in the back with the same vantage. ■ *At intersection of Hwys 525 and 526; (206) 347-2700; 8340 53rd Ave W, Mukilteo; $$; full bar; AE, MC, V; local checks only; lunch Tues-Fri, dinner Mon-Sun.*

WHIDBEY ISLAND

Whidbey Island has let just about everyone know that in 1985 it officially became the longest island in the United States. But they haven't told too many people that Whidbey is only one of eight islands that make up Island County (the others are Camano, Ben Ure, Strawberry, Pass, Hope, Smith, and Deception). Named after Captain Joseph Whidbey, a sailing master for Captain George Vancouver, Whidbey Island was first surveyed and mapped by the two explorers in 1792. Nearly 200 years later, Whidbey's largest employer is the government (thanks to the Navy base in Oak Harbor). The island boasts pretty towns, historical parks, sandy beaches, and some lovely rolling farmland.

Whidbey's flat, relatively traffic-free roads make it good for biking, especially if you stay off the highway. Island Transit has free bus service Monday through Saturday from the Clinton ferry dock to Deception Pass, (206) 321-6688 or (206) 678-7771.

WHIDBEY ISLAND: CLINTON

You won't find a manicured course or even a clubhouse at **Island Greens**, 3890 E French Road, Clinton, (206) 321-6042, but the par-3, nine-hole course is challenging, the location is scenic, and fees are amazingly low ($5 per person). This is an "alternative" golf course built by Dave and Karen Anderson on former farmland and maintained with minimal pesticides and fertilizers.

Cultus Bay Nursery, 4000 E Bailey Road, Clinton, (206) 221-2329, has a wide array of perennials in a Victorian setting, and owner Mary Fisher is knowledgeable and helpful. **Jan Smith's Christmas House**, 6930 S Cultus Bay Road, Clinton, (206) 579-7838, located in a cabin, displays handcrafted items from more than 200 Whidbey Island artisans, year-round.

WHIDBEY ISLAND: LANGLEY

The nicest town on Whidbey still carries its small-town virtues well, even though it's getting a little too spit and polished for some. And with the recent addition of Langley Village on Second Street, it has grown into a two-street town. Local art abounds and can best be seen at **Childers-Proctor Gallery**, (206) 221-2978. Swap stories with Josh Hauser at **Moonraker Books**, (206) 221-6962, then grab a bag of popcorn from the antique popper in the **Wayward Son** gift shop, (206) 221-3911. Best bet for fashion statements are **Sister, Roberta, The Star Store**, and **Good Cheer Thrift Shop**, (206) 221-6454. For unique shopping, try **The Cottage**, (206) 221-4747, **Virginia's Antiques**, (206) 221-7797, and **Madhatter's Old Books**, (206) 221-2356. **JB's Ice Creamery & Espresso**, (206) 221-3888, is the place for both java and ice cream (and people-watching), **The Dog House**, (206) 221-9996, for a pitcher of ale after a movie at **The Clyde**, (206) 221-5525, and the pesto pizza at **Langley Village Bakery**, (206) 221-3525, is becoming a local favorite. **The South Whidbey Historical Museum** is located at 312 Second Street in Langley (open weekends from 1 to 4pm), and Whidbey Island Winery, 5237 S Langley Road, (206) 221-2040, has a tasting room.

Public fishing. The small-boat harbor has a 160-foot public fishing pier.

Whidbey Island: Langley

Restaurants

RESTAURANTS

Cafe Langley ★★ Cafe Langley was a most welcome addition to the Langley dining scene when it surfaced several years ago, and owners Shant and Arshavir Garibyan have maintained its appeal. The staff continues to be knowledgeable and friendly. Reserve a window seat (the place fills up fast on the weekends and summer) and prepare for a fine Middle Eastern dining experience. Don't overdo on the creamy hummus served with warm, chewy pita bread, even though it's both fresh and flavorful. The Greek salad is just the right taste before a feast of Mediterranean seafood stew or maybe the lamb shish kabob. Daily specials might include tuna, chicken breast with dried fruits (excellent), and Copper River salmon. Split a Russian cream with raspberry sauce for dessert. Reservations are often a necessity here. ■ *At the south end of town; (206) 221-3090; 113 1st St, Langley; $$; beer and wine; AE, MC, V; checks OK; lunch, dinner every day (Wed-Mon in winter).*

Star Bistro ★ Every town needs a restaurant like the Star Bistro. Chef Paul Divina has been on board for several years, and the restaurant's consistency rating has elevated significantly. Located above the Star Store, this not-too-trendy eatery sports a black-and-white tile floor and red-topped bar (which hops on the weekends and after local events). It's a fun place, portions are generous, and the martinis are good (the wine selection is fine, but best to order a bottle). Best bets are the caesar and spinach salads, pastas, Bistro burger (with onions, peppers, bacon, and cheese), and the daily specials. There's a kids' menu, and you can't beat dining out on the deck (but bring your sunglasses and windbreaker). ■ *Above the Star Store on First; (206) 221-2627; 201½ 1st St, Langley; $$; full bar; AE, MC, V; checks OK; lunch Mon-Sun, dinner Tues-Sun, breakfast Sun.*

▼

Whidbey Island: Langley

Restaurants

▲

Francisco's Northwest and Continental Cuisine There are many people who look to Francisco's as their fancy night out. No doubt about it, Francisco's has the best view in town. But ever since the doors opened to this old Victorian house, it's been rocky times for both diners and management. The semiformal decor is pleasant enough, but ask for a window table and your gaze will be turned outward. There have been too many chefs in the kitchen since Richard Francisco opened his restaurant three years ago, but under new chef Andy Elf, the menu is slowly beginning to find its mark. Here too many sauces and flavors are happening on the plate at once, regardless of whether it's pasta, steak, chicken, or seafood. Even the most elegant of sauces should allow the basic ingredients to contribute more than texture to the mouthful. Things have a way to go at Francisco's, but improvements seem imminent. ■ *Across from CMA church on Cascade Ave; 510 Cascade Ave, Langley; (206) 221-2728; $$$; full bar; AE, DIS, MC, V; local checks only; days open are inconsistent, call restaurant in advance.*

LODGINGS

Inn at Langley ★★★ Paul and Pam Schell's first private venture is one of Whidbey's finest. Architect Alan Grainger designed the building in a marriage of three themes: Frank Lloyd Wright's style, Northwest ruggedness, and Pacific Rim tranquillity. For the most part, it works—fabulously. Inside this roughhewn, cedar-shingled building (whose size is disguised by the clever design) are 24 rooms finely decorated with an eye for pleasing detail: quiet shades of tan and gray (a tad austere for some tastes), simple Asian furnishings, trimmings of three different woods, and a quarry-tiled bathroom (in a brown hue reminiscent of beach stones) with hooks made from alder twigs. Adjacent is a Jacuzzi from which you can watch the boat traffic on Saratoga Passage and the flicker of your fireplace through the translucent shoji-style sliding screen. All this opens onto a private shrubbery-lined balcony with cushioned bench seats overlooking Saratoga Passage. We prefer the upper-level rooms; others are approached by a dark concrete stairwell. The small conference room (equipped with up-to-the-minute business necessities) has the expansive view of the Passage that the dining room lacks. Friendly and gracious, Sandy Nogal arranges for all needs.

Chef Steve Nogal is making waves in his country kitchen with his four- and five-course prix-fixe weekend dinners. As you sip on your glass of sherry, expect the ultimate Northwest dining experience, with a simple yet creative touch (and a generous hand). Nogal gives his interesting spiel before the meal, indicating the origin of the foodstuffs, and whetting diners' appetites. A four-course meal might include chilled potato-leek soup; a salad of locally harvested greens; pork served with rice and asparagus; and fresh apricot cobbler delivered warm from the oven. After dinner, a glass of port completes the meal. ■ *At the edge of town at 400 1st; (206) 221-3033; PO Box 835, Langley, WA 98260; $$$; beer and wine; AE, MC, V; local checks only; continental breakfast Mon-Wed (guests only), dinner Fri-Sat (Nov-April), Fri-Sun (May-Oct); (by reservation only).*

Eagle's Nest Inn Bed & Breakfast ★★ Situated in a woodsy knoll overlooking the Saratoga Passage, Camano Island, and Mount Baker, this four-story, octagonal home makes the most of its view. The entire third and fourth stories are for guests, including a living room with a library of books, videotapes, and CDs. The adjacent balcony offers a Jacuzzi. A snack counter with coffee, tea, and drinks is open for guests, as is the "bottomless" cookie jar. Each of the four upstairs rooms offers a pretty, spotlessly clean setting with floral-printed quilts and a private bath. The best is the Eagle's Nest, an eight-sided penthouse suite rimmed with windows (and a balcony) giving a 360-degree view of the water and the surrounding forest. For less extravagance, stay one floor below in the balconied Saratoga Room. The Garden Room on ground level is the largest of the rooms (sleeps four). Nancy tries to accommodate your breakfast wishes, but if you leave the choice up to her you might dine on a feast of baked apples with whipped cream, followed by crisp-sweet French toast and scrambled eggs with turkey sausage. ■ *Call ahead for directions; (206) 221-5331; 3236 E Saratoga Rd, Langley, WA 98260; $$; DIS, MC, V; checks OK.*

▼

Whidbey Island: Langley

Lodgings

▲

Galittoire ★★ Galittoire is a sleek, contemporary B&B that's almost sensual in its attention to detail. Slanted ceilings, lots of windows, lovely oak trim throughout, and unexpected details, such as the variation on a four-poster bed in one of the rooms—silky, snow-white fabric hanging from the ceiling to all corners of the bed. The decor is spare and deliberate, and if a deer wanders through the rolling yard past the gazebo, he may just seem like part of the perfect plan. Amenities abound—hot tub, spa, hors d'oeuvres in the evening—and owner Mahésh Massand is an accommodating host. Two-night minimum on weekends. ■ *Off Highway 525 on Coles Rd; (206) 221-0548; 5444 S Coles Rd, Langley, WA 98260; $$$; AE, MC, V; no checks.*

Log Castle ★★ This is the house that Jack built—literally. And whenever there's time the former state senator, Jack Metcalf, builds on it some more, to his wife Norma's newest designs. As a result, the beachside castle has a slightly unfinished air about it—which shouldn't in the slightest detract from what can be a distinctly unusual experience. Every log tells a story (ask Norma about the log-end floor entrance, the branded-log table, the hollow-log sink), and the place can feel quite cozy on a winter evening. The loft suite comes with an antique ship's stove; two rooms on the other side of the house are built into a turret and feature remarkable views. Each room has its own bath. Breakfast usually includes Norma's homemade bread. The Metcalfs possess a genuine gift for the art of hospitality. ■ *1½ miles west of Langley on Saratoga; (206) 321-5483; 3273 E Saratoga Rd, Langley, WA 98260; $$; MC, V; checks OK.*

Lone Lake Cottage and Breakfast ★ You can't take your room out for a spin on Lone Lake anymore, but Delores Meeks' place is still one of the most unique B&Bs around. One of the four lodgings is *The Queen Whidbey*, a beamed-ceiling stern-wheeler that has been permanently moored on the lake since its maker, Delores' husband Ward Meeks, passed away. ("No one else knew how to run it.") However, guests staying on board the *Queen* now enjoy the same extras found in the two lakeside cottages: fireplace, VCR, CD player, and a private shoji-screened deck with Jacuzzi and barbecue grill. The one-bedroom Terrace Cottage is nicest; it looks into the domed top of an aviary housing some 300 rare birds from around the world. A suite built under the deck of the main house is cool and comfortable and sports a grand view. There are exotic ducks, pheasant, quail, peacocks, and swans in an outdoor pen. Each room has a full kitchen stocked with breakfast makings, plus seasonings for the barbecue should you get lucky and land a trout or two from the lake. Guests are welcome to use the canoes, rowboat, and bikes. ■ *5½ miles from the Clinton ferry, off Hwy 525 on S Bayview; (206) 321-5325; 5206 S Bayview Rd, Langley, WA 98260; $$$; no credit cards; checks OK.*

The unincorporated town of Freeland may not have sidewalks and matching buildings, but it's charming in its own free way, and home to Nichols Brothers Boat Builders. **Island Bakery**, Main Street, (206) 321-6282, is a good spot for picnic supplies, or try their salubrious soups with a garden fresh salad. Cruise through Whidbey Island's first drive-thru espresso stand, located in the Pay-Less grocery lot. Back on the highway at Tara Village, stop by **The Mutiny Bay Company**, (206) 331-2313, for your outdoor equipment and clothing. **Freeland Park** on Holmes Harbor has picnic tables, a play area, and sandy beach.

LODGINGS

Cliff House ★★ Seattle architect Arne Bystrom designed this dramatic house, which makes an extraordinary getaway. The home on a cliff above Admiralty Inlet is full of light from lofty windows, centering on a 30-foot-high atrium (open to the weather), and a sunken fireplace. For $265 a night ($365 for two couples) you have use of the entire house, with two large loft bedroom suites and a kitchen for cooking your meals. The house is strikingly decorated with an interesting arrangement of Oriental rugs, modern art, and Indian baskets, and is set amid 13 acres of woods with hammocks, bench chairs, and a platform deck with a hot tub built high on the cliff. The elfish one-bedroom Sea Cliff Cottage goes for $135 a night. Peggy Moore sets the country kitchen table (in both houses) with a continental breakfast. ■ *Bush Point Rd to Windmill Rd; (206) 321-1566; 5440 Windmill Rd, Freeland, WA 98249; $$$; no credit cards; checks OK.*

Whidbey
Island:
Greenbank

Restaurants

Here on the narrowest part of the island, stop by **Whidbey's Greenbank Berry Farm**, at one time the largest loganberry farm in the country. After a short self-guided tour, sample Whidbey's Loganberry Liqueur. Lots of pretty picnicking spots. And don't miss the two-day **Loganberry Festival** in July, featuring food and crafts booths and entertainment (and a pie-eating contest, of course). For more information, call (206) 678-7700.

RESTAURANTS

Whidbey Fish Market and Cafe ★★ Whidbey Fish has already become an island institution. Owners Thom and Jan Gunn are selling (and serving) some of the best fresh fish around. Recently they added their own line of retail products, including Clam Island Chowder, Dungeness Crab Cakes, and Smoked Salmon. For a truly unique dining experience, reserve a seat for the all-you-can-eat fish nights on Mondays and Saturdays. Clink glasses with old and new friends at the family-style table, and delight in the multicourse feast of salad, seafood chowder, steamed mussels, halibut or salmon, fresh vegetables, pasta with spot prawns or maybe scallops and smoked salmon, all topped off with a piece of Jan's famous loganberry pie. The Gunns and their staff do a swell job behind the burners, and their energy is contagious. Decor is early Route 66, so leave your heels at home. ■ *On Hwy 525; (206) 678-3474; 3078 Hwy 525, Greenbank; $; no alcohol; no credit cards; checks OK; lunch, dinner Fri-Mon (closed Jan-March).*

LODGINGS

Guest House Bed & Breakfast Cottages ★★ We love this place, partly for all its alternatives. You can stay in the $85 Wildflower Suite farmhouse (closest to the swimming pool and hot tub), a pricier log-cabin cottage, the one-bedroom carriage house, or the new Kentucky Pine Cottage. All have kitchens, baths, and VCRs. But our favorite—everybody's favorite—is the $225-a-night lodge cabin. Full of antiques, but built in 1979, the lodge combines the old (a wood stove next to the breakfast nook, a hammock and picnic tables outside by the pond) with the new (two-person Jacuzzi, remote-control TV, dishwasher) to a most appealing effect. Perched at the edge of a lovely pond and ringed by trees, the two-story home features a broad deck and views of the Cascades and the Sound from the loft bedroom. Breakfast makings are left in the fully equipped kitchens. ■ *1 mile south of Greenbank off Hwy 525 on E Christenson Rd; (206) 678-3115; 3366 S Hwy 525, Greenbank, WA 98253; $$$; AE, MC, V; checks OK.*

WHIDBEY ISLAND: COUPEVILLE

The second-oldest incorporated town in the state dates back to 1852, when farming commenced on this fertile isle. Coupeville was founded by sea captain Thomas Coupe, whose home still stands on Front Street. A fort was built in 1855 after some Indian scares, and part of it, the Alexander Blockhouse on Front Street, is open for touring. Amid the growing pressures of development, the town has set itself a strict agenda of historical preservation.

Coupeville's downtown consists of half a dozen gift and antique shops and several restaurants. **Toby's 1890 Tavern**, (206) 678-4222, is a good spot for burgers, beer, and a game of pool. Homemade breads, pies, soups, and salads make a memorable meal at **Knead & Feed**, (206) 678-5431, and real coffee has come to Coupeville at **Great Times Espresso**, (206) 678-5860. **Island County Historical Museum**, (206) 678-3310, tells the story of Whidbey Island's early history. Community events include the **Coupeville Arts & Crafts Festival** the second weekend in August, and the **Penn Cove Water Festival** every May; for information (206) 678-5434. **All Island Bicycles**, 302 N Main, (206) 678-3351, sells, rents, and repairs bikes and equipment. An extra bike lane follows Engle Road 3 miles south of Coupeville to **Fort Casey**, a decommissioned fort with splendid gun mounts, beaches, and commanding bluffs. The magnificent bluff and beach at the 17,000-acre **Ebey's Landing** and **Fort Ebey State Park** are good places to explore. The **Keystone ferry** (206) 678-6030, connecting Whidbey to Port Townsend, leaves from Admiralty Head, just south.

LODGINGS

Captain Whidbey Inn ★ The old inn, dating back to 1907 and built from madrona logs, nestles picturesquely in the woods overlooking Penn Cove: a lovable place with some serious quirks. The lodge has 12 upstairs rooms (two suites) and two shared bathrooms; there are four sparsely furnished cottages with fireplaces and baths, two with separate bedrooms, plus 13 lagoon rooms—the best choices—with private baths and verandahs. The problem is that the walls are so thin they seem to talk, and sniffle, and sneeze. Stay clear of those above the bar. The public rooms—a dining room with creaky wooden floors that seem to slope toward the sea, the deck (when the weather's warm), a cozy bar festooned with wine bottles and business cards, a well-stocked library, a folksy fireplace room—are quite attractive. In the past, the restaurant has suffered from a constant turnover of chefs; under the direction of current chef Ken Floyd, the food is still uneven. Stay with simple preparations off the very limited menu and you'll do well here (fresh Penn Cove mussels—you're looking at the mussel beds/pens—steamed in ginger, soy, and garlic, or the pasta primavera with just-steamed veggies in a zesty marinara sauce). Dessert (Washington apple cake, warmed and served with cream cheese topping) almost made up for the flaws of dinner. ■ *Off Madrona Way on W Captain Whidbey Inn Rd; (206) 678-4097; 2072 W Captain Whidbey Inn Rd, Coupeville, WA 98239; $$; full bar; AE, DC, MC, V; checks OK; breakfast, lunch, dinner every day (lunch Sat-Sun only during winter).*

Fort Casey Inn ★ Built in 1909 as officers' quarters for nearby Fort Casey, this neat row of nine houses now offers no-frills and tidy accommodations with a historical bent. Houses are divided into two duplexes, each with two bedrooms, a living room with small fireplace, private bath, and kitchen stocked with breakfast makings. Rooms are plain but comfortable, with original stamped-tin ceilings. Decor consists mostly of tied-rag rugs, old photographs of soldiers, and renditions of early U.S. presidents. Garrison Hall, which offers a small reception area with its own bedroom and bath, can be rented for weddings or private parties. Unlike most B&Bs on Whidbey, Fort Casey welcomes kids—and is truly a fun place to explore. Manager Gina Martin can tell you anything you need to know about the nearby Fort Casey State Park, the bird sanctuary at Crockett Lake, or nearby Ebey's Landing National Historic Reserve just north. ■ *2 miles west of Coupeville; (206) 678-8792; 1124 S Engle Rd, Coupeville, WA 98239; $$; AE, MC, V; checks OK.*

Inn at Penn Cove ★ Mitchell and Gladys Howard are carrying on the warm hospitality and friendly atmosphere established by the former owners, the Cinneys. The two pink buildings were built in 1887 and 1891; 100 years later, one of the buildings was moved to Main Street and opened as a gracious inn. The three guest rooms in the main house are prettily furnished, if slightly overdecorated (lots of frills and the occasional stuffed animal). The swankest room, Desiree's, has a king-size bed, Jacuzzi, its own miniparlor with a view of Penn Cove and the elusive Mount Baker. The three rooms in the more casual second house seem best for guests with children (there's a game room with puzzles). Breakfasts are a great send-off, with blueberry and lemon-poppyseed muffins, seasonal fruits, cereal, Scandinavian style breakfast cakes, waffles, or pancakes. ■ *Hwy 20 from Deception Pass or Hwy 525 from the ferry; (206) 678-8000 or (800) 688-COVE; 702 N Main St, Coupeville, WA 98239; $$; AE, DIS, MC, V; checks OK.*

The Old Morris Farm ★ This is no old farmhouse by any means. Owners Mario Chodorowski and Marilyn Randock have successfully transformed their 1909 farmhouse into an elegant countryside bed and breakfast. Once a former commune, the guest rooms are all individual in style and decor, but reflect the colonial feeling throughout the house. The Rose Room is done in a paisley motif, and has a private bath and a deck which leads out to the secluded spa. Enjoy a gourmet breakfast in the red, red dining room, and evening hors d'oeuvres (cheese balls or maybe pesto pinwheels) in the sunwashed living room. Notice the collection of Miguel Condé paintings (the Mexican artist is Marilyn's brother-in-law). Stroll the grounds and enjoy the flower, vegetable, and herb gardens. There's a gift shop, with locally made walking sticks and kaleidoscopes. ■ *Hwy 20, 3 miles from Coupeville overpass; (206) 678-6586; 105 W Morris Rd, Coupeville, WA 98239; $$; MC, V; checks OK.* &

WHIDBEY ISLAND: OAK HARBOR

Named for the thriving Garry oak trees, Oak Harbor is Whidbey's largest city and home to the **Whidbey Island Naval Air Station**, a large air base for tactical electronic warfare squadrons. For the most part, Oak Harbor is engulfed in new military and retired military folk, and has the largest concentration of fast-food restaurants on the island.

An interesting stop is **Lavender Heart**, which manufactures floral gifts on a 12-acre former holly farm. From the Hendersons' gift store, you can peek at the impressive 1,000-square-foot production facility; 3 miles south of Deception Pass at 4233 N DeGraff Road, (206) 675-3987. For the kids at heart, visit **Blue Fox Dri-Vin Theatre and Brattland Go-Karts**; 1403 Monroe Landing Road, Oak Harbor, (206) 675-5667.

Deception Pass. The beautiful, treacherous gorge has a lovely, if usually crowded, state park with 2,300 acres of prime camping land, forests, and beach. The pass can also be toured from the water by the Mosquito Fleet on a group charter basis; (206) 252-6800. **Strom's Shrimp/Fountain and Grill**, just north of the pass, sells fresh seafood and shrimp for your cookout. They also grill up a mean oyster burger to go, (206) 293-2531. **Lams Golf Links** is a par-3 golf course, located 1 mile south of Deception Pass Bridge, (206) 675-3412.

RESTAURANTS

Kasteel Franssen (Auld Holland Inn) ★ Half a mile north of Oak Harbor, this newish motel with the trademark windmill is just fine, if a shade close to the highway; however, the restaurant is quite delightful. Kasteel Franssen, owned and operated by Joe and Elisa Franssen, has quite a regal, European feel about it and a solid reputation among locals. There's a big gas fireplace, tapestry-upholstered dining chairs, and a lively piano bar. Chef Scott Fraser of Vancouver, B.C. has taken over the toque from longtime mentor Jean Paul Combettes, and the results are pleasing. Dinner offerings include seafood, chicken, beef, but Fraser is also preparing game—caribou and pheasant (a new taste for Oak Harbor diners). Particularly good is the Hollandaise Biefstuk, medallions of beef tenderloin sautéed and served with a brandy Dijonnaise cream sauce. The desserts are divine.

Whidbey Island: Oak Harbor

Restaurants

As for the inn, some upper-story rooms have antiques, and six impressive-looking rooms with Jacuzzis were scheduled to open at press time. There's a tennis court, hot tub, outdoor pool, and children's play area. Prices are good, and include a complimentary continental breakfast in the Auld Mill Room.
■ *8 miles south of Deception Pass on State Rd 20; (206) 675-2288; 5681 State Rd 20, Oak Harbor; $$; full bar; AE, DC, MC, V; checks OK; dinner every day (Mon-Sat in winter).*

Lucy's Mi Casita It doesn't look like much, lined up along a strip of fast-food joints and automotive-type stores. But it's good inside. Al and Lucy Enriquez keep locals coming back with their homemade food and lively atmosphere. The dining room is done in early Mexican motif: old calendars, beer ads, cutouts of flamenco dancers, and curtains made of beer-bottle caps. Upstairs is a lounge with a balcony (watch out for the 27-ounce Turbo Godzilla margarita). The menu is large and includes shredded beef tacos, chile poblano imported from Mexico, Lucy's authentic refried beans, tortillas shipped from California, and homemade hot sauce. Don't miss the entomatadas—a tortilla topped with tomato sauce, cheese, and onion—from Lucy's home town of Chihuahua. ▪ *On the main drag of Oak Harbor; (206) 675-4800; 1380 W Pioneer Way, Oak Harbor; $; full bar; AE, MC, V; local checks only; lunch, dinner every day.*

VASHON ISLAND

Faintly countercultural, this bucolic isle is a short ferry ride away from Seattle (take the Fauntleroy ferry) or Tacoma. It's a wonderful place to explore by bicycle, although the first long hill up from the ferry dock is a killer. Few beaches are open to the public.

Unlike Bainbridge, its northern neighbor, Vashon Island employs many of its own in island-based companies that market their goods both locally and nationally; many of these offer tours (it's a good idea to call ahead): **K-2 Skis, Inc.**, (206) 463-3631; **SBC** (popularly known as Seattle's Best Coffee), Island Highway, (206) 463-3932; **Maury Island Farms**, with berries and preserves, at 99th and 204th on Island Highway, (206) 463-9659. **Wax Orchards**, on 131st SW north of 232nd, is no longer open for tours, but you can stop by and pick up some fresh preserves, fruit syrups, and apple cider; (206) 463-9735. Island arts are on display at the **Blue Heron Art Center**, (206) 463-5131. **The Country Store and Farm** is an old-fashioned general store stocking most of the island-made products, along with natural-fiber apparel, housewares, sundries, dried herbs, and gardening supplies; (206) 463-3655. Although there are a myriad of small (one- and two-bedroom) bed and breakfasts on the island, there is only one with more than three rooms.

RESTAURANTS

Dog Day Cafe ★ The island's favorite hangout is, interestingly, on the island's busiest intersection. Inside this stylish (gothic '90s?) street-side cafe, you'd never know it. Steve Shanaman started this place in the same spirit as Seattle's beloved Septième. Same tête-à-tête tables, same great espresso (here made with SBC, of course), and similar lunch fixings (roasted eggplant sandwich with tapenade, mozzarella, and roasted red peppers; a chapati roll with black beans, brown rice and sprouts; a special casserole layered with vegetables). The soups are innovative and delicious (Thai peanut soup). Some just saunter by in the afternoon for a tall glass of lemonade and dessert of vanilla bread pudding or the ethereal mousse tart. ▪ *Corner of Vashon Hwy and Band Rd; (206) 463-6404; Vashon Island; $$; beer and wine; no credit cards; local checks only; breakfast, lunch, dinner Tues-Sat.* 占

Sound Food Restaurant It's a delightfully mellow place, an airy room with wood floors, fresh flowers, and pretty wisteria overhanging the windows. The restaurant, which started out as a hangout for the island's artsy population, experiences weekend rushes that result in interminably long waits for waiter, water, and menus. Brunch is the meal in demand: potato pancakes, crêpes, French toast, whole-wheat waffles, blintzes with fresh fruit toppings, omelets—perhaps with asparagus and ham, and topped with mornay sauce. Lunches offer healthful soups, salads, and sandwiches made from their own bread. Dinners have not been up to their usual snuff. An array of fresh-baked goods (which seem a bit tired these days) is offered for consumption on the spot or to take home.
■ *7 miles south of the ferry on Island Hwy; (206) 463-3565; 20312 99th Ave SW, Vashon Island; $$; beer and wine; AE, MC, V; checks OK; breakfast Mon-Fri, lunch, dinner every day, brunch Sat-Sun.* &

LODGINGS

Back Bay Inn ★ Stacey and Don Wolczkos purchased three dilapidated houses on the corner of Vashon Highway and Burton Drive with the dream of someday owning a country inn in the same location. Persistance paid off. The Wolczkoses opened their new inn (built in part from salvaged materials which you'll notice in the floor of the 1905 replica and in the small fireplace library). There are four guest rooms (each with bath en suite), but the best are the two large end rooms. Trouble is, Back Bay is located on Vashon's main road (though thermal-pane windows mute most noise) and there's not much to explore on the grounds. Fortunately, there's plenty to discover on the island and the Wolczkoses can point you in the right direction. Downstairs is their 40-seat restaurant—giving Vashon one more option for a formal meal—the first to offer Northwest cuisine on Vashon (and the first to dare such relatively high prices). Stacey Wolczkos and chef Todd Hughes both attended the South Seattle Community College culinary school. There's guest moorage at the yacht club just across the way. So, sail on over to Vashon for dinner, and if there's no room at the inn, stay on your yacht.
■ *In the community of Burton at 24007 Vashon Hwy SW; (206) 463-5355; PO Box 13006, Vashon Island, WA, 98013; $$$; DIS, MC, V; checks OK; dinner Wed-Mon (Wed-Sun in winter).*

▼
Puyallup
▲

PUYALLUP

At the head of the fertile Puyallup Valley, this frontier farm town serves as a major gateway to Mount Rainier. While much bulb, rhubarb, and berry farmland continues to be cultivated, a great part of it has been malled and auto-row ravaged around the edges. Avoid the fast-food strip to the south and head east up the valley to Sumner, White River, Orting, Wilkeson, and Carbonado.

The **Ezra Meeker Mansion** is the finest original pioneer mansion left in Washington. Its builder and first occupant, Ezra Meeker, introduced hops to the Puyallup Valley. The lavish 17-room Italianate house (built 1890), complete with fireplaces, carved cherry-wood staircases, and ornate brass doorknobs, now stands beautifully restored in the rear parking lot of a Main Street furniture store; 312 Spring Street, (206) 848-1770. Open Wednesday through Sunday, 1pm to 4pm, March through mid-December.

Puyallup is big on old-time seasonal celebrations, and it's home to two of the biggest in the Northwest: the **Daffodil Festival and Parade** in early April and the **Western Washington Fair**, better known as the Puyallup Fair, in September. It's one of the nation's biggest fairs; call (206) 845-1771 for dates and information. **Puyallup Downtown Farmers Market** is held every Saturday, starting at 9am, at Pioneer Park. It runs throughout the growing season, usually late May through September.

▼

RESTAURANTS

Balsano's Since Italian meals usually begin in the marketplace, it makes sense that there's an enjoyable Italian restaurant in the fertile Puyallup Valley. Tom Pantley has filled the menu with unusual regional dishes from his Sicilian roots. Photos of his mother's family line the walls (many of the staff *are* family). Homemade sausage of coarsely chopped pork and the subtle anise flavor of fennel are served, traditionally, with golden-fried cauliflower. Thin slices of tender veal are topped with mushrooms, onions, and dry, sweet Marsala wine from the western region of Sicily; spinach lightly braised with balsamic vinegar and hazelnuts is another treat. Do ask to have the accompanying spaghetti (with merely-average tomato sauce) served on a separate plate—it can overwhelm the selections with which it is automatically dished up. ■ *Between Pioneer and E Main; (206) 845-4222; 127 15th St SE, Puyallup; $$; beer and wine; MC, V; checks OK; lunch Tues-Fri, dinner Tues-Sun.* ♿

TACOMA

Sided by Commencement Bay and the Tacoma Narrows and backed by Mount Rainier, Tacoma is no longer just a blue-collar mill town, but a growing urban center with a thriving cultural core.

Pantages Center, 901 Broadway Plaza; (206) 591-5894. The restored 1,100-seat Pantages Theatre, originally designed in 1918 by nationally known movie-theater architect B. Marcus Priteca, is the focal point of the reviving downtown cultural life—dance, music, and stage presentations. And the nearby Rialto Theatre has been restored for smaller performance groups. Tacoma Actors Guild, Tacoma's popular professional theater—now in a new home at the Commerce Street level atop the park-covered transit center, (206) 272-2145—offers an ambitious and successful blend of American classics and Northwest premieres that draw an audience from throughout the Puget Sound region.

The Tacoma Art Museum, 12th and Pacific, (206) 272-4258, is housed in a former downtown bank. The small museum has paintings by Renoir, Degas, and Pissarro, as well as a collection of contemporary American prints. The Washington State Historical Museum, 315 N Stadium Way, (206) 593-2830, has some Native American artifacts—canoes, baskets, and masks from British Columbia and Puget Sound—and some early Tacoma memorabilia as well. The Historical Museum's projected move in 1995 will take it to a new residence near the Railroad Depot and Pacific Avenue.

Tacoma has fervently embraced the idea of preservation. The historic buildings in the downtown warehouse district are being converted from industrial use to residential and commercial functions, and some of the old warehouses are being used by a branch of the University of Washington now. The stately homes and cobblestone streets in the north end are often used as sets for Hollywood's moviemakers, and students still fill the turreted chateau of Stadium High School. Old City Hall, with its newly coppered roof, Renaissance clock, and bell tower; the Romanesque First Presbyterian Church; the rococo Pythian Lodge; and the one-of-a-kind coppered Union Depot—now the much praised Federal Courthouse—delight history and architecture buffs. The Ruston Way Waterfront, a 6-mile mix of parks and restaurants, is thronged with people in any weather.

OTHER THINGS TO DO

Point Defiance Park is situated at the west side of Tacoma, with 500 acres of untouched forest jutting out into Puget Sound. Aside from its many other attractions, this park is one of the most dramatically sited and creatively planned city parks in the country. The wooded 5-mile drive and hiking trails open up now and then for sweeping views of the water, Vashon Island, Gig Harbor, and the Olympic Mountains beyond. There are rose, rhododendron, Japanese, and Northwest native gardens, a railroad village with a working steam engine, a reconstruction of Fort Nisqually (originally built in 1833), a museum, a swimming beach, and the much acclaimed zoo/aquarium.

Watching the almost continuous play of seals, sea lions, and the white beluga whale from an underwater vantage point is a rare treat; (206)591-5335. **Wright Park** at Division and I streets is a serene in-city park with many trees, a duck-filled lake, and a beautifully maintained, fragrant conservatory, built of glass and steel in 1890. One of the area's largest estates, and the former home of the late Corydon and Eulalie Wagner, is now **Lakewold Gardens** (12221 Gravelly Lake Drive SW, (206)584-3360, located on a beautiful 10-acre site overlooking Gravelly Lake in Lakewood, just 10 minutes south of Tacoma. Recognized nationally as one of the outstanding gardens in America, Lakewold Gardens is opened Sunday, Monday, Thursday, Friday, and Saturday for guided and nonguided tours.

Tacoma

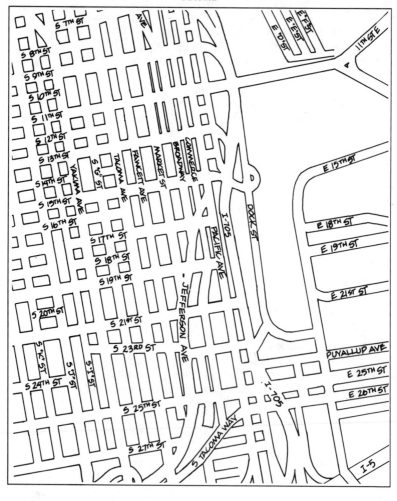

The **Tacoma Dome**, the world's largest wooden dome, is the site of many entertainment and trade shows as well as a sports center. The dazzling neon sculpture by Stephen Antonakos provides a dramatic background for events such as the **Tacoma Stars'** indoor soccer games, championship ice-skating competitions, and many other regional activities. Call (206) 272-6817 for ticket information. **Freight House Square** (the old Milwaukee Railroad freight house), just downhill from the Dome, houses a popular central dining commons, surrounded by take-out restaurants selling everything from Jamaican jerked chicken to Korean noodles and oversize cinnamon rolls.

Fans who like their baseball played outdoors in a first-class ballpark arrive in enthusiastic droves at **Cheney Stadium** to watch the **Tacoma Tigers**, the Triple-A farm team of the Oakland A's; (206) 752-7707.

Fishing/boating. With the waters of Puget Sound lapping at virtually half of Tacoma's city limits, it is to be expected that many Tacomans and visitors choose to spend their leisure time afloat or on the pier. There are two fishing piers along Ruston Way and public launches and boat rentals at Point Defiance.

RESTAURANTS

Pacific Rim ★★★ First-rate dining experiences have been in short supply in Tacoma, but Bill Nevins' downtown restaurant has changed all that. It's an elegant place, with marble facade outside and dark wood paneling inside, and provides a reflective atmosphere in which to dine. Chef Diana Prine's restless creativity is best shown off by her seafood cookery which she pairs with other unusual, compatible flavors in such combinations as grilled salmon perfectly mated with a slather of cilantro pesto, slightly lemony, slightly spicy, and served with a tangle of Chinese egg noodles, asparagus, and fiddlehead ferns. An added touch: Prine grows her own herbs on top of the renovated bank building that houses Pacific Rim. Many regular patrons choose to dine exclusively on an assortment of appetizers; a subtle ginger beef carpaccio and an order of magnificent crispy onion rings is a perfect light meal. Desserts run to the sinfully rich (baked chocolate pudding) and stylish and comforting (old-fashioned bread pudding).

Live music Wednesdays and weekends is played at the foot of the stairs in the open lounge and eating area, with the sound filtering up to the more intimate upper dining room. There have been some complaints about slow and indifferent service, but on most occasions patrons find their servers attentive and knowledgeable. ■ *Corner of 9th and A, 1 block north of Pacific; (206) 627-1009; 100 S 9th, Tacoma; $$$; full bar; AE, MC, V; checks OK; lunch Mon-Fri, dinner Mon-Sat.* &

Fujiya ★★ Absolute consistency continues to attract a loyal clientele to Masahiro Endo's stylish downtown Japanese restaurant. Using the freshest of seafood in its traditional sushi, Fujiya seldom disappoints, although the theatrical punch (and occasional surprises) of a *great* sushi bar is often missing. The food from the menu is of equally high quality. Begin your meal with gyoza (savory pork-stuffed dumplings) either fried or steamed (the latter allows the diner to better appreciate the flavor). The real test of a Japanese restaurant is the tempura, and Endo makes certain that his is light and airy, which assures that when fried it will be feathery crisp. For a fitting conclusion to the meal, have ginger or green tea ice cream, or a scoop of both. ■ *Between Broadway and Market on Court C, near the Sheraton Hotel; (206) 627-5319; 1125 Court C, Tacoma; $$; beer and wine; AE, MC, V; checks OK; lunch Mon-Fri, dinner Mon-Sat.*

Kabuki ★★ The lively, congenial sushi bar is the starring attraction of Joe Kosai's newish restaurant—the patrons are drawn by the fastidiously selected fresh seafood and the artistic presentation of the food. You'll see a substantial number of Japanese dining here, on crackly seaweed-wrapped rolls—a spicy roll of deep red tuna; smoky, grilled freshwater eel combined with cucumber and a firm layer of refreshingly sweet omelet; or the spider roll, a dramatic presentation of soft-shell crab. The more timid explorer of Japanese cooking will find comfort in broiled salmon delicately flavored with miso, or moist, tender salmon shioyaki (salt-broiled fish). Meat served as a main course is relatively new to the Japanese cuisine, but tonkatso (deep-fried breaded pork loin) is well done here. Not on the menu, nor on your bill, may be surprising tiny side dishes presented to you when you least expect it: tasty eggplant with fried bean curd or a refreshing fanlike spiral of flavored cucumber. An excellent selection of sake is available. After 9pm a sometimes raucous karaoke bar takes over the adjacent lounge. ■ *38th St W exit off I-5, turn right at Best Plaza; (206) 474-1650; 2919 S 38th St, Suite B, Tacoma; $$; full bar; AE, MC, V; local checks only; lunch Mon-Fri, dinner every day.* ⬇

Stanley and Seaforts Steak, Chop, and Fish House ★★ Every customer in this dramatically located restaurant is provided with a panoramic view of Tacoma and its busy harbor and waterways, with the Olympic Mountains as a backdrop on clear days. Here is a view restaurant that consistently provides excellent food and service to its patrons. The emphasis is on quality meats and seafood simply grilled over apple-wood with flavorings of herbs and fruits, although the pasta dishes, such as a Cajun fettuccine with a tongue-tingling Tabasco accent, are always good choices. Those passionate about their chocolate should try a rich, silky chocolate-mint cheesecake with the

▼

Tacoma

Restaurants

▲

muted contrast of crème de menthe. The spacious bar features a comprehensive and distinctive selection of Scotch whiskeys —a favorite spot to watch the sun go down. ■ *City Center exit off I-5 to 38th, right on Pacific Ave, right on 34th; (206) 473-7300; 115 E 34th St, Tacoma; $$; full bar; AE, DC, DIS, MC, V; local checks only; lunch Mon-Fri, dinner every day.* &

Bimbo's ★ Don't be dismayed by the seedy location or the name; this is a real family restaurant. Tacomans have been packing this lower Pacific Avenue Italian restaurant day in and day out for almost 75 years. Italians have always loved to feed people, and at Bimbo's, members of the original owner's family are still cooking their native recipes with little regard for today's trends. Rabbit was once the most common source of meat in their region of Tuscany, especially in the late summer after the wheat harvest, and at Bimbo's rabbit is served year-round in a hearty, full-bodied tomato sauce. The pork ribs are meaty and luscious, and aficionados of that Italian favorite, tripe, will find it judiciously treated here. Tuscans like their pasta sturdy, and a robust, garlicky tomato sauce with just a hint of hot red pepper and lemon turns the side-dish spaghetti into a meal in itself. ■ *15th and Pacific; (206) 383-5800; 1516 Pacific Ave, Tacoma; $; full bar; AE, DC, DIS, MC, V: no checks; lunch Mon-Sat, dinner every day.* &

C.I. Shenanigan's ★ For those looking for great views and lots of pizzazz, this is one of the best of the booming formula restaurants along Commencement Bay's scenic waterfront. In good weather, not even a sardine could wiggle in without a reservation, since the large deck and adjacent classy bar is packed with those wanting to enjoy a bowl of freshly cooked shrimp and a bottle of cold white wine. Seafood, as you might have guessed, dominates both the lunch and dinner menus. While there are plenty of fancier seafood dishes, a simple favorite is the Fisherman's Feast, a heaping serving of clams, salmon, and prawns. Those with really gargantuan appetites will finish with mud pie—a mile-high creation (well, almost) of ice cream, cookies, fudge, whipped cream, and nuts. Good it is; subtle it is not. ■ *City Center exit off I-5 and follow Schuster Pkwy onto Ruston Way; (206) 752-8811; 3017 Ruston Way, Tacoma; $$; full bar; AE, DC, MC, V; local checks only; lunch, dinner every day, brunch Sun.* &

Engine House #9 ★ For connoisseurs of taverns, this former firehouse, listed on the National Register of Historic Places and complete with hoses, ladders, rescue nets, and brass fire pole, is a definite smoke-free winner. It offers close to 50 brands of quality draft and bottled beer and ale, including Mamba from the Ivory Coast. Closer to home, Engine House #9 has recreated Tacoma's original beer, Tacoma Brew, once the premier

▼

Tacoma

Restaurants

▲

label of the Pacific Brewery (converted to a soap factory during Prohibition). An eatery it is too, specializing in such world-roving dishes as bangers and onions, soft tacos, and excellent pizzas. Habitués look forward to the soups and other dishes that are served up as daily specials—and some until midnight. ■ *6th and Pine; (206) 272-3435; 611 N Pine St, Tacoma; $; beer and wine; MC, V; checks OK; lunch, dinner every day.* &

Harbor Lights ★ Tacoma's pioneer Ruston Way waterfront restaurant still packs them in. Nothing trendy here. Decor is circa 1950, with glass floats, a stuffed marlin, and a giant lobster. The main concession to progress is a glassed-in sun deck. Up-to-the-minute it may not be, but that doesn't seem to bother the seafood fans who regularly crowd into the noisy dining room to consume buckets of steamed clams and plates of Columbia River smelt in season. Grilled fillet of sole is done to perfection; halibut and chips are the best around, as are the crisp hash-browns. The usual complaint is that portions are so gargantuan that only a trencherman can clean the plate. Oh bummer. Reservations are important. ■ *City Center exit and follow Schuster Pkwy to Ruston Way; (206) 752-8600; 2761 Ruston Way, Tacoma; $$; full bar; AE, DC, DIS, MC, V: checks OK; lunch Mon-Sat, dinner every day.* &

Katie Downs ★ Katie Downs' Philadelphia-style deep-dish pizza is a winner. You place your own order at the food counter for one of their classic combinations. Especially good is the "Fearless" which recklessly matches smoked bacon and provolone cheese with white onions, spicy peperoncini—and lots and lots of fresh garlic. Since the pizzas can take close to 30 minutes to make and bake, take advantage of the waterfront location and order some steamer clams to tide you over while you wait, and watch the tugs and barges, freighters and sailboats move across Commencement Bay. This place is noisy, boisterous, and fun, but remember it is a tavern, and no minors are allowed. ■ *City Center exit off I-5, follow Schuster Pkwy onto Ruston Way; (206) 756-0771; 3211 Ruston Way, Tacoma; $; beer and wine; MC, V; checks OK; lunch, dinner every day.* &

Lessie's Southern Kitchen ★ Let's face it—this is not a restaurant for everyone. Today's uptight calorie counters should pass by this little cafe (and you might anyway, seeing's how it's situated on an almost impossible-to-reach busy five-way corner). However, if you have a hankering for the authentic fare of the south, do stop. Abandon all restraint and order up some pork chops smothered with gravy, or liver with lots of lovely onions, all sided by a trio of vegetables, perhaps long-cooked collard greens served up in their own "pot likker," black-eyed peas, or sweet nuggets of yams. Lessie, who hails from southern Alabama, also dishes up some mighty fine fried chicken and barbecued ribs. Thin, light cornbatter cakes are served in lieu of rolls and most folks finish up their meal with the likes of bread pudding or a slice of homemade pie. Breakfasts are great here too: pan-fried butterfish with eggs, buttery grits, home-fries, and genuine Southern biscuits. ■ *6th and Division; (206) 627-4282; 1716 6th Ave, Tacoma; $; no alcohol; no credit cards; checks OK; breakfast, lunch, early dinner Mon-Sat.* &

The Lobster Shop ■ The Lobster Shop South ★ The Dash Point Lobster Shop could just as well be set next to the moorings of Maine lobster trawlers as it is to the docks of the small public beach on Puget Sound. This comfortable sea-weathered restaurant is a welcome change from the increasing number of pricey, slick eateries blossoming along the local waterfronts. As could be expected, lobster is the house specialty; here, unfortunately, it's Australian rock lobster, but oven-baked and rich with butter. Large juicy crab cakes, often paired with pan-fried oysters, are another favorite. There is a good selection of beer and wine, although the owners never bothered to put in a bar. It is totally nonsmoking.

The larger, swankier Lobster Shop South on the Ruston Way waterfront has a distinctly different atmosphere and menu. It provides good seafood dishes and a full bar, but has not half the personality of the original. No problem here about lighting up. ■ *Off Dash Point Rd; (206) 927-1513; 6912 Soundview Dr NE, Tacoma; $$; beer and wine; AE, DC, DIS, MC, V; checks OK; dinner every day.* & ■ *Schuster Pkwy to Ruston; (206) 759-2165; 4015 Ruston Way, Tacoma; $$; full bar; AE, DC, DIS, MC, V; checks OK; dinner every day.* &

Mandarin on Broadway ★ The ancient Chinese philosophy of yin (that which is feminine, shadowy, and yielding) and yang (that which is contrastingly masculine, bright, and hard) is evident in the handsome decor and in the kitchen. Sweet, crispy cashews and narrow slivers of spicy, crunchy cucumbers at the beginning of a meal can be contrasted with slippery bright green stir-fried spinach and some of the best pot-stickers around. For the main courses, balance a platter of crisp, mahogany-skin duck with sugar-sweet snow peas and white nuggets of scallops. Intersperse the explosive Hunan deep-fried pork with soothing stir-fried seafood and vegetables, served on top of a crispy bird's nest of deep-fried bean threads and a bed of shredded cabbage. Try intensely flavored sesame beef and rice noodles. For those in a hurry, noodles makes a wonderful one-bowl meal. ■ *On Broadway between 13th and 11th; (206) 627-3400; 1128 Broadway Plaza, Tacoma; $$; full bar; AE, MC, V; checks OK; lunch-dinner Mon-Sat.* &

Antique Sandwich Company A visit here is a little like returning to a storybook grandma's house. Plastic bears filled with honey adorn the shared tables; a roomy couch usually has several students curled up on it studying and eating; and everyone generally just has a good time. On the way to Point Defiance Park, it's also a favorite luncheon gathering place for the diaper set and their parents. Toys abound on a carpet-covered platform, which doubles as a stage when the folk or classical music concerts begin. Peanut-butter-and-jelly sandwiches with bananas and fresh-fruit milk shakes share the menu with big-people food such as hearty homemade soups, quiches, and a variety of other tasty sandwiches. The clam chowder is still, hands-down, the best in town. There is excellent coffee from your choice of beans. Tuesday is open-mike night, when locals perform. No smoking. ■ *Corner of 51st and N Pearl, 2 blocks south of Point Defiance Park; (206) 752-4069; 5102 N Pearl, Tacoma; $; no alcohol; no credit cards; checks OK; breakfast, lunch, dinner every day.* &

Park Bistro This tiny place near Wright Park has been transformed by Kim Paeper into a haven for light and healthy food. Chicken Kimberly is an all-out favorite, a colorful roll of chicken breast and spinach accented with lemon and garlic. Unique weekly specials draw on the regional cuisine of our country. Breakfasts are generally standard (as are the hamburgers), but such specials as a sauté of vegetables and cheese (with sausage if you like) do appear. No smoking. ■ *4th and Tacoma Ave S; (206) 272-5937; 322 Tacoma Ave S, Tacoma; $$; beer and wine; AE, DIS, MC, V; checks OK; breakfast, lunch every day.*

LODGINGS

Sheraton Tacoma Hotel ★★ This elegant hotel has filled a real need in Tacoma. Adjacent to the massive Tacoma Convention Center, it's quite suitable for conventions. Most rooms look out over Commencement Bay or have a view of Mount Rainier. The more expensive concierge rooms on the 24th and 25th floors include a continental breakfast and early-evening hors d'oeuvres. The mezzanine cafe, Wintergarden, is pleasant for casual meals; a new Italian restaurant is expected to replace the former Rose Room in late 1993. ■ *Take City Center exit off I-5 between 13th and 15th on Broadway; (206) 572-3200; 1320 Broadway Plaza, Tacoma, WA 98402; $$$; AE, DC, DIS, MC, V; checks OK; breakfast, lunch, dinner every day.* &

PARKLAND

RESTAURANTS

Marzano's ★ The reputation of Lisa Marzano's voluptuous cooking had people driving in from miles away, patiently standing in line, often in the rain, waiting for their turn at one of the eight tables in her tiny restaurant. Thankfully, her new place has double the interior size, with outside seating on two deck areas when the weather is balmy. The food, though, will stay the same—including the crusty bread at the beginning of each meal, ready to be topped with shredded Parmesan and spicy herbed olive oil. The holes in the stubby rigatoni are perfect for capturing the extraordinary boscaiola sauce made with mushrooms and ham; the lasagne is sumptuous and the elegant chicken piccata pungent with capers and lemons. Even the osso bucco —a dish usually not too well done in restaurants—is deeply flavored and succulent, with classic risotto with fresh asparagus on the side. Marzano's many-, many-layered chocolate poppyseed cake swimming in whipped cream is a hard thing to pass up. ■ *Adjacent to PLU; (206) 537-4191; 516 Garfield S, Parkland; $$; beer and wine; MC, V; checks OK; lunch Tues-Fri, dinner Tues-Sun.* ふ

GIG HARBOR

Gig Harbor, once almost undisturbed fishing village (and still homeport for an active commercial fleet), is now part suburbia, part weekend destination. Boating is still important here, with good anchorage and various moorage docks attracting gunwale-to-gunwale pleasure craft. When the clouds break, Mount Rainier holds court for all.

Interesting shops and galleries line Harborview Drive, the single street that almost encircles the harbor. **Mostly Books**, 3126 Harborview Drive, (206) 851-3219, the **Beachbasket**, 4102 Harborview Drive, (206) 858-3008, for gifts and clothes; **Bonneville's**, 3102 Harborview Drive, (206) 858-9890, for unusual clothes; and the **White Whale**, 7811 Pioneer Way, (206) 858-3286, for an excellent selection of cooking ware, all have longstanding reputations.

▼

Gig Harbor

▲

Gig Harbor was planned for boat traffic, not automobiles (with resulting traffic congestion and limited parking), yet it is still a real place for celebrations. An arts festival in mid-July and a jazz festival in mid-August are two main events. May through October (Fridays) the Gig Harbor Farmers Market features locally grown produce, plants, and Northwest gifts; Pioneer Way between Highway 16 and city center, (206) 851-4117.

Nearby, **Kopachuck State Park** is a popular destination, as are **Penrose Point** and **RFK state parks** on the Key Peninsula, all with numerous beaches for clam digging. (Purdy Spit and Maple Hollow Park are the most accessible spots.) At **Minter Creek State Hatchery** the public can watch the various developmental stages of over four million coho salmon (although call ahead as they're temporarily closed for repairs until spring of 1994).

Performance Circle, 6615 38th Avenue NW, (206) 851-7529, Gig Harbor's resident theater group, mounts seven enjoyable productions from July to March, with summer shows staged outside in the meadow at 9916 Peacock Hill Avenue NW. Theatergoers bring picnics and blankets, watching the shows beneath the stars. It's turning into a wonderful small-town custom.

RESTAURANTS

Tides Tavern ★ "Meet you at the Tides" has become such a universal invitation that this tavern perched over the harbor is often standing room only, especially on sunny days when the deck is open for eating. Originally a general store next to the ferry landing, it was rebuilt in 1973 as the Tides, complete with old Gig Harbor memorabilia. The Tides doesn't pretend to be anything other than what it is—a self-service tavern (no minors) with pool table, and live music on weekend nights. Indulge in good hefty sandwiches, huge charbroiled burgers, a gargantuan super shrimp salad, okay pizzas, and highly touted fish and chips. The distinct personality and unique location continue to draw in the locals and, increasingly, out-of-towners, who come by boat, car, and the occasional seaplane. ■ *Harborview and Soundview; (206) 858-3982; 2925 Harborview Dr, Gig Harbor; $; beer and wine; MC, V; checks OK; lunch, dinner every day.*

Marco's Ristorante Italiano [*unrated*] It's very new, but so far we like what we've tasted. The menu ranges from the traditional (spaghetti and meatballs, handmade tortellini in fresh pesto) to the more original (ravioli plumped with smoked salmon or fresh mushrooms; a dense, tender piece of tuna sautéed in red wine). Deep-fried olives are an unusual starter. Marco and his wife, Mimi, who tends the stove, have a 15-year history in the food business, and it shows; initial reports have been very positive. ■ *Turn up the hill on Pioneer Way at the only stoplight in Gig Harbor; (206) 858-2899; 7707 Pioneer Way, Gig Harbor; $$; beer and wine; AE, DIS, MC, V; checks OK; dinner Tues-Sun.* &

North by Northwest [*unrated*] This is one of the loveliest locations around for a restaurant but, since many years ago when it was run as a Scandinavian eatery, other managements have not made a go of it. Seasonal cuisine will be the guideword for the food due to come out of the kitchen of chef/owner Mike Borassi as he and his two partners Laura Schrock and Sean Derek open their new restaurant atop Peacock Hill. Expectations are high that North by Northwest will fill the need for a high-quality restaurant in Gig Harbor. ■ *Left on Peacock Hill Ave NW to top of hill; (206) 851-3134; 9916 Peacock Hill Ave NW, Gig Harbor; $$; full bar; MC, V; checks OK; lunch, dinner every day.* &

LODGINGS

The Pillars ★★ From the windows of this landmark house, you can see Colvos Passage, Vashon Island, and Mount Rainier. All three guest rooms are beautifully decorated with private baths and separate reading areas furnished with writing desks and telephones. An added bonus is the covered, heated swimming pool and Jacuzzi. Breakfasts feature home-baked breads and muffins. No smoking, no children (except by special arrangement), and no pets. ▪ *First Gig Harbor exit off Hwy 16; (206) 851-6644; 6606 Soundview Dr, Gig Harbor, WA 98335; $$$; MC, V; checks OK.*

No Cabbages B&B ★ If you are looking for an unstructured and relaxed environment in an old, well-loved beach house with a friendly hostess who happens to be an accomplished cook, No Cabbages may be perfect for you. After reluctantly getting out of your bed—which has an intimate view of the harbor—you might start the day with a large glass of freshly squeezed orange juice, a Brie and green apple omelet, and all the freshly ground coffee you can drink. There's boating, and it's a superb place for bird-watching—great blue herons nest nearby, and a clutter of gulls, terns, grebes, ducks, and cormorants are always around. The knotty-pine interior is filled with Northwest arts and crafts; the two guest rooms (with shared bath) have a separate entrance. ▪ *Follow the bay, on the east side of the harbor; (206) 858-7797; 7712 Goodman Dr NW, Gig Harbor, WA 98332; $; no credit cards; checks OK.*

STEILACOOM

Once an Indian village and later Washington Territory's second incorporated town (1854), Steilacoom today is a quiet village of old trees and houses, with no vestige of its heyday, when a trolley line ran from Bair's drugstore to Tacoma. October's **Apple Squeeze Festival** and midsummer's **Salmon Bake**, with canoe and kayak races, are popular drawing cards.

The **Steilacoom Tribal Museum** is located in a turn-of-the-century church overlooking the South Sound islands and the entire Olympic mountain range. Ferries run to Anderson Island, with restricted runs to McNeil Island (a state penitentiary); call the Pierce County Public Works Department for more information, (206) 591-7250.

RESTAURANTS

ER Rogers ★ View restaurants on Puget Sound are not novelties, but views like this one are still exceptional, particularly when seen from a restored Queen Anne-style home built about 100 years ago. The halibut baked in parchment paper is noteworthy, but the Steilacoom special prime rib, first roasted, then sliced and quickly seared, is still tops. You can't beat the huge Sunday buffet brunch, with its large selection of seafood: oysters on the half shell, cold poached salmon, flavorful smoked salmon, cracked crab, pickled herring, steamed clams, and fettuccine with shrimp. There is a beautiful upstairs bar with a widow's walk just wide enough for one row of tables. Fresh flowers appear in unexpected places, and chamber music plays softly in the background. ■ *Corner of Commercial and Wilkes, off Steilacoom Blvd; (206) 582-0280; 1702 Commercial St, Steilacoom; $$; full bar; MC, V; checks OK; dinner every day, brunch Sun.* ⟨

Bair Drug and Hardware Store Side orders of nostalgia are presented gratis when you step into Bair's. Except for the customers, little has changed since it was built—in 1895. Products your grandparents might have used—cigars, washtubs, perfume, and apple peelers—are still on display. Old post office boxes mask the bakery, which turns out pies and pastries such as flaky apple dumplings; the potbelly stove warms customers in the winter. Best of all, there is a 1906 soda fountain, where you can still get a sarsaparilla, a Green River, or a genuine ice cream soda. ■ *Lafayette and Wilkes; (206) 588-9668; 1617 Lafayette St, Steilacoom; $; beer and wine; MC, V; local checks only; breakfast, lunch every day.* ⟨

ANDERSON ISLAND

LODGINGS

Anderson House on Oro Bay ★★ Anderson Island is still one of the best-kept secrets on Puget Sound, although word is spreading. A short ferry ride from Steilacoom and a few miles' drive from the dock is a large red house surrounded by 200 acres of woods. Since Randy and B. Anderson stay next door at grandfather's home, guests have exclusive use of the whole house, with its four large bedrooms (some with private bath) and beautiful antique furnishings. Full farm breakfasts feature breads hot from the oven, fruit pizzas, and other treats. Since this is isolated country with no stores or restaurants, lunch and dinner—perhaps a five-course Greek meal—are also served. While both of the Andersons are superb cooks, it is Myrna Rieck who is the steady hand in the kitchen. A cedar fishing cabin (wood-stove heated) that sleeps eight is hidden away on outer Amsterdam Bay. A short bike ride from the Anderson House brings you to the west side of the island, where a mile-long secluded beach is backed by old-growth forest and has a dramatic view of the Olympics. Arrangements can be made to pick up guests at the ferry dock. Boaters and those with seaplanes have their own dock, but check the tides. ■ *Head south from ferry for 3½ miles to head of Oro Bay; (206) 884-4088; 12024 Eckenstam-Johnson Rd, Anderson Island, WA 98303; $$; no credit cards; checks OK.*

If you've found a place that you think is a best place, send in the report form at the back of this book. If you're unhappy with one of the places, let us know why. We depend on reader input.

The capitol's centerpiece is the classic dome of the Washington State Legislative Building. Lavishly fitted out with bronze and marble, this striking Romanesque structure houses the offices of the Governor and other state executives. The State Senate and House of Representatives meet here in annual sessions that can be viewed by visitors.

Just opposite the Legislative Building rises the pillared **Temple of Justice**, seat of the State Supreme Court. To the west is the red brick Governor's Mansion, open to visitors on Wednesday afternoons from 1pm to 2:45pm. Reservations must be made in advance, (206) 586-TOUR.

Handsomest of the newer state buildings is Paul Thiry's squarish **State Library**, directly behind the Legislative Building. Open to the public during business hours, it boasts artifacts from the state's early history. At 211 W 21st Avenue, the **State Capitol Museum**, (206) 753-2580, houses a permanent exhibit that includes an outstanding collection of Western Washington native American baskets.

Downtown, on Seventh Avenue between Washington and Franklin streets, is the restored **Old Capitol**, whose pointed towers and high-arched windows suggest a late medieval chateau. In another part of the downtown, just off the Plum Street exit from I-5, and adjacent to City Hall, is the newly installed **Yashiro Japanese Garden**, which honors one of Olympia's sister cities.

▼

Olympia

▲

There is also a triad of colleges here: **The Evergreen State College (TESC)**, west of Olympia, on Cooper Point; **St. Martin's**, a Benedictine monastery and college in adjacent Lacey; and **South Puget Sound Community College**, just across Highway 101. Though TESC is relatively new, its innovative educational policies have already won national praise. It offers a regular schedule of plays, films, and experimental theater, as well as special events such as its annual February Tribute to Asia. Its library and pool are both public; (206) 866-6000, ext. 6128.

In Olympia proper, the **Washington Center for the Performing Arts** (on Washington Street between Fifth Avenue and Legion Way) has brought new life to the downtown. In the same block is the **Marianne Partlow Gallery**, a leading outlet for contemporary painting and sculpture. Across Fifth Avenue, the **Capitol Theatre** provides a showcase for the offerings of the active Olympia Film Society as well as for locally produced plays and musicals. Toward the harbor, at the corner of North Capitol Way and West Thurston Street, is the lively **Olympia Farmers Market**, which displays produce, flowers, and crafts from all over the South Sound; open Thursday through Sunday during the growing season.

Wholly different in character is **West Fourth Avenue** between Columbia and Water streets, a hangout for students and ex-students, artists and would-be artists, gays, lesbians, and counterculture members. Increasingly, Percival Landing (a new waterfront park) is becoming a community focal point, the site of harbor festivals of all kinds. The historic heart of the whole area (Olympia, Lacey, and Tumwater) is **Tumwater Falls**, where the Deschutes River flows into Capitol Lake. Established here today is the chief local industry, the Tumwater Division of the **Pabst Brewing Company**, with free daily tours.

The area's finest nature preserve lies well outside the city limits. This is the relatively unspoiled **Nisqually Delta**—outlet of a river that rises on a Mount Rainier glacier and enters the Sound just north of Olympia. Take Exit 115 off I-5 and follow the signs to the **Nisqually National Wildlife Refuge**. From here, a 5-mile hiking trail follows an old dike around the delta, a wetland alive with bird life. Just south, a rookery of great blue herons occupies the treetops.

RESTAURANTS

Bristol House ★★ Adolf Schmidt (of the Olympia Brewery founding family) is owner and chef at this cheerful place, located in the rapidly developing professional office area south of the Thurston County courthouse. His Bacardi beef may be the best steak available in town, and he offers such unusual creations as curried prawns served with mushrooms, raisins, and grapes. An excellent dessert is chocolate mousse prepared with either Grand Marnier or crème de cacao. The wine list is conservative but sufficiently comprehensive. Go at dinner if you want to take full advantage of the chef's ingenuity; lunches are adequate, but relatively uninspired. Service is fast and professional. Overseeing all this, with an appropriately no-nonsense mien, is a gold-framed portrait of an avuncular Schmidt ancestor who looks as though he would tolerate no inefficiency. ■ *Off Evergreen Park Dr; (206) 352-9494; 2401 Bristol Ct SW, Olympia; $$; full bar; MC, V; checks OK; breakfast Sun-Fri, lunch Mon-Fri, dinner Tues-Sat.*

Gardner's Seafood and Pasta ★★ Loyal Gardner's fans aren't bothered by the change of ownership since Olympia's favorite seafood spot was purchased by Leon and Jane Longan, longtime employees. Here the rambunctious geoduck has been thoroughly tamed. A true Puget Sound specialty is an appetizer of a dozen Calm Cove Olympia oysters, each the size of a quarter, served on the half shell. Interesting soups include rock shrimp with dill; a variety of pastas are available with or without seafood. A Dungeness crab casserole is sautéed with bacon, green onions, mushrooms, chablis, and cream, and topped with mozzarella and cheddar cheeses. Connoisseurs of ice cream shouldn't pass up Gardner's homemade product. Because

▼

Olympia

▲

of the restaurant's small size and popularity, early reservations are advisable. ■ *North on Capitol Way to Thurston; (206) 786-8466; 111 W Thurston St, Olympia; $$; beer and wine; AE, MC, V; checks OK; dinner Tues-Sat.*

La Petite Maison ★★ This tiny, converted 1890s farmhouse—now overshadowed by a beetling new office building—is a quiet, elegant refuge for Olympians seeking imaginative, skillfully prepared Northwest cuisine. Among its specialty appetizers are steamed Kamiche clams and mussels, and delicate and flavorful Dungeness crab cakes served with a dill sauce. Entrées include perfectly sautéed medallions of pork with tangy Dijon mustard sauce and fresh poached petrale sole stuffed with salmon mousse. The tender sautéed venison comes with a rich juniper-berry sauce. In spring or summer, it's pleasant to sit on the restaurant's glassed-in porch—though the view of over-trafficked Division Street outside may make you long for the days when this place was truly a farm. ■ *1 block south of Division and Harrison; (206) 943-8812; 2005 Ascension Ave NW, Olympia; $$; beer and wine; DC, MC, V; checks OK; lunch Mon-Fri, dinner Mon-Sat.* &

Seven Gables ★★ Visually, this dinner house is the most striking restaurant in Olympia, occupying as it does the fine old Carpenter gothic residence built by the city's turn-of-the-century mayor, George B. Lane. The site takes full advantage of a splendid Mount Rainier view, and the surrounding gardens are tended with loving care by owner Sally Parke. The menu includes numerous steaks. Among seafood dishes are crab and prawns Indienne, or Dungeness crab and prawns sautéed with pea pods and chutney in a curry cream sauce. A daily special might be tilapia, a flavorful freshwater white fish, sautéed in sherry and topped with brandied pecans. ■ *¾ mile north of the 4th Ave bridge; (206) 352-2349; 1205 W Bay Dr, Olympia; $$; beer and wine; AE, DC, MC, V; checks OK; dinner Tues-Sat, brunch Sun.* &

Ben Moore's ★ One of the most talented chefs in the area holds sway behind Ben Moore's plain exterior, which looks as though it hasn't changed much since the time of the New Deal. Mike Murphy is in charge, and if you order any of his prawn, oyster, or steak dinners, you'll get a lot to eat, and none of it is likely to disappoint. Prices are out of a bygone era; the costliest complete dinner is a New York steak with prawns at $13.95. ■ *On 4th Ave, east of Columbia; (206) 357-7527; 112 4th Ave, Olympia; $; full bar; AE, DC, MC, V; checks OK; breakfast, lunch, dinner Mon-Sat.* &

Budd Bay Cafe ★ There's no doubt about it: the Budd Bay Cafe, with its long row of tables looking out across Budd Inlet, has suddenly become the preferred after-hours haunt of many of today's legislators, lobbyists, and state government movers and shakers. Restaurateur John Senner is on hand most of the time, seeing that everyone is satisfied. Don't look for elaborate dishes here; the menu (steaks, sandwiches, pasta, salads, seafood) is designed for boaters and people to whom good talk matters more than haute cuisine. It's also more expensive than many places in town. Sunday brunch features eggs Benedict and oysters on the half shell, either fresh or baked with pesto. This place has become such a scene that you wonder what people were doing before it opened. ▪ *Between A and B on Columbia; (206) 357-6963; 525 N Columbia St, Olympia; $$; full bar; AE, DC, MC, V; checks OK; lunch Mon-Sat, dinner every day, brunch Sun.* ੬

Chattery Down ★ This small dining room, which began as an annex to Ann Buck's gift shop next door, has proven so successful that it has almost taken over the whole place. For lunch, there are homemade breads, interesting soups such as lemon broccoli bisque, and salads. Many patrons prefer Fridays, when an oyster dish is always on the menu—angels on horseback, oyster stew, or chowder. Or Saturday mornings, when a full breakfast is served instead of the weekday continental fare. Dinner specials change daily, but might include paupiettes of sole stuffed with spinach and salmon mousse, or steak and prawns Monique, served in a dill cream sauce. Lighter dinners are offered at a lighter price; vegetarian dishes too. Some patrons (many single) come in only for the appetizers, such as oysters Rockefeller or baked Brie with pesto. High tea Wednesdays and Saturdays. ▪ *Across from the Capitol Theatre; (206) 352-9301; 209 5th Ave E, Olympia; $$; beer and wine; AE, MC, V; checks OK; breakfast, lunch Mon-Sat, dinner Tues-Sat.* ੬

▼
Olympia
———
Restaurants

▲

Falls Terrace ★ It would be hard to find an Olympian who hasn't had at least one meal at this longtime Tumwater institution; anyone wanting to eat during regular hours should get reservations. Part of the reason for its popularity is its splendid setting overlooking the Tumwater Falls of the Deschutes River. There's a wide variety of steak, lamb, and chicken dishes, along with a fried version of the delectable Olympia oysters (we prefer them raw). The menu also includes a bouillabaisse, containing prawns, lobster, salmon, crab, and clams. Ice cream desserts are featured; apple strudel crunch is essentially a generously portioned version of pie à la mode. The wine list is not for connoisseurs, but Irish coffee is available as an after-dinner drink. The adjacent bar is one of the most agreeable drinking spots in town. ▪ *Across the Deschutes River from the Olympia Brewery; (206) 943-7830; 106 Deschutes Way, Tumwater; $$; full bar; AE, DC, DIS, MC, V; checks OK; lunch, dinner every day.* ੬

The Spar ★ Above the restaurant's old-fashioned booths are blown-up Darius Kinsey photos of teams of old-time loggers beaming over unbelievably mammoth trees they've just brought to earth. Indeed, some 60-odd years ago, the Spar used to be known as a workingman's hangout. Today it's classless, with a volatile mixture of students, attorneys, businesspeople, artists, politicians, fishermen, tourists, and leisured retirees. The Spar's robust milk shakes, thick turkey sandwiches, and homemade bread pudding are all locally acclaimed, as is its water, which comes from its own artesian well. Willapa Bay oysters or fresh salmon from the Farmers Market are sometimes available; the prime rib dinner is popular on weekends. Conversations at the long, J-shaped counter range from state house scandals to the probable origin of the galaxies. ■ *1 block east of Capitol Way; (206) 357-6444; 114 E 4th Ave, Olympia; $; full bar; AE, MC, V; checks OK; breakfast, lunch, dinner every day.* &

Urban Onion ★ The site of many a power lunch for Olympia's rising breed of feminist politicians, the Urban Onion retains a faint flavor of the counterculture of the '60s. A signature dish is an especially satisfying lentil soup. The Mexican chicken grilled with mushrooms is also outstanding. Breakfasts include a hefty huevos rancheros. The Urban Onion has recently expanded into the lobby of the former Olympian Hotel, and meeting space is available. ■ *Legion and Washington; (206) 943-9242; 116 Legion Way, Olympia; $$; beer and wine; AE, MC, V; checks OK; breakfast, lunch, dinner every day.*

Wagner's European Bakery and Cafe ★ Almost as *echt deutsch* as an opera by that other well-known Wagner is the formidable collection of pastries regularly produced by Rudi Wagner's bakery, which effortlessly fabricates stuff like apricot squares, raspberry mousse tortes, pig's ears, cream horns, several species of doughnuts, and all kinds of fresh-baked breads. Toothsome Black Forest tortes whirl temptingly in a display case. An attached cafe, featuring light breakfast and lunch, has expanded to serve many more customers. German-born Wagner, chief baker as well as owner, gets new ideas on trips back to Europe. ■ *Capitol Way and Union; (206) 357-7268; 1013 S Capitol Way, Olympia; $$; no alcohol; no credit cards; checks OK; continental breakfast, lunch Mon-Sat.*

LODGINGS

Harbinger Inn ★ Occupying a restored 1910 mansion, this B&B offers Edwardian furnishings, a fine outlook over Budd Inlet and the distant Olympic mountains, and four choice guest rooms (two with views, two without). Nicest is the two-room suite on the view side, which has its own bath (all other rooms share); but rooms on the back side are farther from the street, with only the sound of a small artesian-fed waterfall to disturb the tranquillity. The inn is situated near excellent routes for bicycle riding, and complimentary bicycles are available. A light breakfast of fruit and home-baked pastry is served. Under new owners Terrell and Marisa Williams, the place remains pleasant and well maintained, with a garden in front to welcome you. ■ *1 mile north of State St; (206) 754-0389; 1136 E Bay Dr, Olympia, WA 98506; $$; AE, MC, V; checks OK.*

Westwater Inn ★ Few urban hotels around Puget Sound take such striking advantage of the Northwest's natural beauty as this one, dramatically perched on a high bluff above Capitol Lake, with much greenery in view, and the Capitol dome—illuminated by night—rising to the north. There are fairly large rooms, a heated outdoor pool (seasonal), a year-round Jacuzzi, and an entertainment lounge presenting live music Tuesday through Saturday nights. Some rooms can be noisy, so it's advisable to request one on the water side. Meals are served at an almost continuously operated coffee shop, and at Thurstons, a restaurant with as scenic an outlook as any in town. A Sunday brunch concentrates on an impressive variety of desserts. ■ *Exit 104 off I-5; (206) 943-4000 or (800) 551-8500; 2300 Evergreen Park Dr, Olympia, WA 98802; $$; full bar; AE, DC, DIS, MC, V; checks OK; lunch Mon-Fri, dinner Mon-Sat, brunch Sun.* &

TENINO

Wolf Haven, 3111 Offut Lake Road, (206) 264-4695, is an educational research facility that teaches wolf appreciation and studies the question of whether to reintroduce them into the wild. Come see the wolves or join them in a "howl-in."

RESTAURANTS

Alice's Restaurant ★ Located in a fine turn-of-the-century farmhouse on a lively little creek, Alice's serves hearty dinners, all including crudités, cream of peanut soup, a Waldorf salad, trout, an entrée, and choice of dessert. The price of each entrée determines the price of dinner (baked ham with pineapple glaze, fresh oysters, a selection of game dishes, perhaps quail, and even catfish). In conjunction with the restaurant, Ann and Vincent de Bellis operate the Johnson Creek Winery. (You will be invited for a pre-dinner tasting when you call for reservations.) Reservations are required. ■ *Call for directions; (206) 264-2887; 19248 Johnson Creek Rd SE, Tenino; $$; beer and wine; AE, DC, DIS, MC, V; checks OK; dinner Wed-Sun.* &

Wondering about our standards? We rate establishments on value, performance measured against the place's goals, uniqueness, enjoyability, loyalty of clientele, cleanliness, excellence and ambition of the cooking, and professionalism of the service. For an explanation of the star system, see "How to Use This Book."

RESTAURANTS

Arnold's Country Inn ★ Long known as one of Olympia's most accomplished chefs, Arnold Ball has established his latest restaurant just outside Yelm on the road leading from the state Capitol to Northwest Trek (see Eatonville section) and Mount Rainier. Steaks and meat dishes dominate here. But besides steak Diane, there are familiar Arnold's specialties such as chicken sautéed with raspberry brandy, roast duckling à l'orange, and traditional escargots. Arnold is careful with small details: his rolls baked on the premises are warm and delicious, as are his fine pies. His wine list is adequate, but many patrons are happy to drive all the way from Olympia just for the food.
■ *Across from the Thriftway Shopping Center; (206) 458-3977; 717 Yelm Ave E, Yelm; $$; full bar; AE, MC, V; checks OK; breakfast Sat-Sun, lunch, dinner Tues-Sun.* &

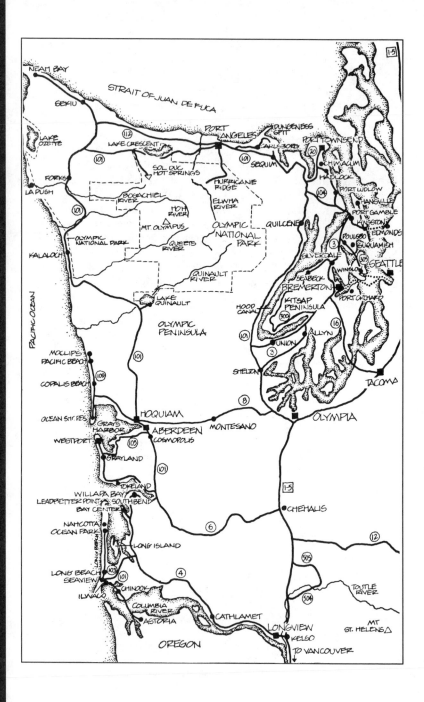

Olympic Peninsula

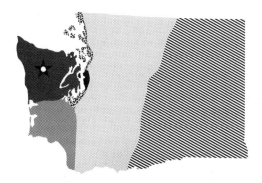

The Kitsap Peninsula north to Hansville, then north up the west shore of the Hood Canal to Port Townsend, west along the Juan de Fuca shore of the Olympic Peninsula and southward along the Pacific coast to Ocean Shores.

PORT ORCHARD

Fifteen minutes by car from Bremerton and a short drive from the Southworth ferry, Port Orchard is a waterfront town. Its main-street pavements are covered by overhanging roofs, bespeaking the reality of much rainy weather. There are numerous antique shops and the **Sidney Gallery** shows Northwest art on the first floor and has a collection of historic vignettes upstairs. Walk up the hill behind town for views of Sinclair Inlet, Bremerton's shipyards, and the Olympic Mountains. On Saturdays, from the end of April through October, the **Port Orchard Farmers Market** offers a tantalizing selection of fresh cut flowers (at good prices), as well as fresh vegetables and Hood Canal oysters.

A privately owned **foot ferry** service provides an economical means of travel between the main ferry terminals at Bremerton and downtown Port Orchard. It runs every half hour and costs less than a dollar.

RESTAURANTS

Hadi's Restaurant ★ Good Lebanese food—a marvelous mixture of Mediterranean influences—would be a welcome treat anywhere, and it's especially so in the west sound area. Assad Nakkour and his wife, Samiha, opened their small restaurant in a classic Port Orchard building. The appetizers are all tempting: hummus, baba ghanouj, tabouli, stuffed grape leaves, and cabbage rolls. Fresh, delicious ingredients—such as sesame, yogurt, eggplant, garbanzo beans, and plenty of garlic—go into these dishes. Beef, lamb, and chicken shish kabobs, cooked to order, make up the bulk of the entrées. Portions are plentiful, and Nakkour is a relaxed and helpful waiter who is happy to expound on Lebanese cuisine or Middle Eastern politics. ■ *On main street of Port Orchard, next to the movie theater; (206) 895-0347; 818 Bay St, Port Orchard; $$; beer and wine; no credit cards; checks OK; lunch, dinner every day.*

LODGINGS

Reflections Bed and Breakfast ★★ Well hidden from the road, Reflections is a spreading, shingled structure with enough gabled windows for Nathaniel Hawthorne. Massachusetts transplants Jim and Cathy Hall moved their collection of Early American antiques west and opened Port Orchard's best bed and breakfast. All four rooms face the northern view, which is an eyeful of Port Orchard Inlet (Bremerton is hidden slightly to the west). The house is light and airy, with a minimum of walls. The sheltered back garden is filled with the sound of wind chimes; the front terrace, lawn, and hot tub have a sweeping north view. Regional American dishes make up the breakfast menu: eggs and grits, eggs and crab cakes, or smoked salmon in an omelet. The only hitch is that all the guests must agree on the same thing. The Halls and their golden retriever, Maggie, are low-key, wonderful hosts. ■ *East of Port Orchard off Beach Dr; (206) 871-5582; 3878 Reflections Lane E, Port Orchard, WA 98366; $$; MC, V; checks OK.*

BREMERTON

Bremerton, as even many residents admit, can seem a pretty dismal place. It has a long history as the site of a U.S. Naval Shipyard and houses part of the Navy's mothball fleet—driving around the end of Sinclair Inlet, you can see the ghostlike gray ships lined up. The area is also home to a Trident nuclear submarine base, across the Kitsap Peninsula in Bangor, and the region is highly dependent on the military.

Bremerton sometimes seems built of tough sailors' taverns at the center and endless roadside sprawl at the edges. However, downtown near the ferry terminal, has undergone a facelift with a new promenade where Navy buffs can visit the **Bremerton Naval Museum** and the destroyer *USS Turner Joy*. The museum tells of shipbuilding history back to bowsprit-and-sail days; (206) 479-7447, closed Mondays. The *Turner Joy* is open for self-guided tours Thursday through Monday. Washington State ferries schedule runs between Seattle and Bremerton roughly every hour and a half; call (206) 478-4902.

RESTAURANTS

Boat Shed ★ A mile from the ferry landing is this nautical place, not far from the road but perched grandly out over the water. The food runs to seafood, sandwiches, and salads; at lunchtime you wait in a long line to look at the menu (during which you should commission one member of your party to grab a table on the deck), but the line moves fast and the hearty food is worth it. Try the Skipjack Sandwich, with three kinds of cheese, red onions, and chopped olives in hot pita bread. The nachos are perhaps the most generously bedecked in the region. We can't rave as much about their new Island Grill on Bainbridge, 321 High School Road, suites #1 and #2, (206) 842-9037. ▪ *East side of Manette Bridge, on the water; (206) 377-2600; 101 Shore Dr, Bremerton; $; full bar; MC, V; local checks only; lunch, dinner every day, brunch Sun.*

LODGINGS

Willcox House ★★ This copper-roofed art deco manse on 242-mile long Hood Canal was the original lavish home of Colonel Julian and Constance Willcox (and their eight servants); later it became a school for boys, then an adult retreat. Now it's a five guest-room B&B of some pretension, easily the Canal's most opulent retreat, in spite of the slightly worn quality of the enormous front rooms. (The parlor fireplace alone is as big as a small bathroom.) Downstairs is a bar and a game room, and a clubby library, which features a sweeping view of the Canal and the impressive garden and saltwater lap pool. Here tea is served for guests in the late afternoon. A delicious, hearty breakfast starts the day for guests; the day ends with an unprepossessing dinner (Saturday evenings only, by reservation). Best dinners are in summer, when you eat on the dusky terrace instead of in the rather characterless dining room. The five bedrooms are lavishly bedecked. Hope for a stormy night and reserve the lavish Mrs. Constance Willcox's Room with its stone fireplace and large tub. It's a half-hour drive from the Bremerton ferry, though some prefer to take a seaplane right to the dock. ▪ *9 miles south of Seabeck; (206) 830-4492; 2390 Tekiu Rd, Bremerton, WA 98312; $$$; MC, V; checks OK.*

RESTAURANTS

Yacht Club Broiler ★ In an office building on Dyes Inlet is Silverdale's swankiest restaurant, opened by Brett Hayfield (of Bremerton's Boat Shed), Andy Graham, and Alan Quick. The tables aren't packed every night, the prices are a bit more than locals would like, and there's no actual yacht club in sight (though it *is* on the water). For dinner, select from the specials sheet: perhaps roast duckling in a raspberry brandy sauce or baked halibut with a lightly breaded crunch, surrounded with a subtle vermouth-cream demiglace. The deck is a good spot for lunches and after-work appetizers. Each day Graham selects a dozen wines by the glass from the extensive list of over 90 bottlings. Desserts are refreshingly simple; the IBC Root Beer Float is a great way to go. ▪ *From 305 take Silverdale exit, first right into town, then left on Bayshore; (206) 698-1601; 9226 Bayshore Dr, Silverdale; $$; full bar; AE, DC, MC, V; checks OK; lunch, dinner every day, brunch Sun.*

LODGINGS

Silverdale on the Bay Resort Hotel ★★ Inside, tasteful design highlights serene views over Dyes Inlet. Most view rooms have private balconies, remote-control TV, and clock radio; mini-suites are the best. Extras establish it as the resort it aspires to be: an indoor lap pool with sliding glass doors that open onto a large brick sun deck (where you can sip cool drinks all afternoon if you'd like), a sauna, weight room, video game room, boat dock, and convention facilities. The Mariner Restaurant offers white-linened tables, professional service, and expertly prepared dinners that aren't too pricey. Young, conscientiously trained hands toss the caesar salads at tableside and light the flambés—showy food that sometimes misses the mark, but is often pleasing. ▪ *Silverdale Way and Bucklin Hill Rd; (206) 698-1000; 3073 Bucklin Hill Rd, Silverdale, WA 98383; $$; full bar; AE, DC, MC, V; checks OK; breakfast, lunch, dinner every day.* &

POULSBO

Poulsbo was once a community of fishermen and loggers, nearly all of whom were Scandinavian. Today its snug harbor is full of yachts, and the trees have given way to a town that fills the hillside. The Scandinavian heritage, however, is still going strong—Front Street sports its "VELKOMMEN TIL POULSBO" signs and the architecture is a dolled-up version of the fjord villages of Norway.

Visit the **Poulsbo Smokehouse**, 18881C Front Street, (206) 779-1099, if smoked salmon is your bag—these folks are serious about the quality of their product, using king salmon from Alaska which they smoke with bleached alder. They skip the nitrates and keep their brine low in salt. The **Poulsbo Country Deli**, across from the Anderson Park gazebo, (206) 779-2763, makes marvelous sandwiches, soups, quiche, and desserts (the park along the waterfront is a perfect spot for a picnic). If one of these doesn't suit, go back to Front Street and try to select something from the overwhelming choices at **Sluy's Bakery**, 18924 Front Street NE, (206) 779-2798; take home a loaf of Poulsbo Bread, the local specialty. Finally, **Boehm's Chocolates** has an outpost here, 18864 Front Street, (206) 697-3318. It's worth walking into its quiet, dark interior just for the smell that wraps around you at the door.

There's a growing population of antique dealers in Poulsbo, as well as numerous gift shops. Farther afield, the **Kemper Brewing Company**, 2 miles north of town at 22381 Foss Road NE, (206) 697-1446, follows the classic German brewing style and makes excellent lagers, on tap at the brewery's grill where a simple menu is served from 11am until early evening. Call ahead for tour time.

RESTAURANTS

Judith's Tearooms and Rose Cafe ★ The small storefront of this charming spot disguises a large interior space that runs back through several rooms. The farther back you go, the more claustrophobic you feel, but decorations with a mix of antique furniture and false windows help. The food more than makes up for a bad seat. Judith's team of efficient waitresses serve homemade food along with tea brewed in teapots. Sandwiches come on thick slices of delicious bread; soups, desserts, tea sandwiches, meat loaf, and quiche are prepared fresh every day. A special menu section offers Scandinavian delicacies —fruit and cheese board, pickled herring with rye crackers, and Swedish cream cake with dried apricots. Between 2pm and 4pm Judith's serves afternoon tea (an excellent alternative to lunch). ■ *At the east end of Front St; (206) 697-3449; 18820 Front St NE, Poulsbo; $; wine and champagne; MC, V; checks OK; lunch, tea every day.*

LODGINGS

Manor Farm Inn ★★★ A lavish retreat in the middle of nowhere, Manor Farm is a working farm with horses, sheep, dairy cows, chickens, and a trout pond—a beguiling mix of the raw and the cultivated that succeeds in spoiling even the city-bred. Jill Hughes, a Los Angeles native, is the proprietor who runs a superlative accommodation. There are eight bright, airy guest rooms (two have fireplaces; most have private baths), and a hot tub bubbles in what is maybe a too-central location. Best are the cottages. The farm cottage is across the road, with vaulted ceilings, French country-pine antiques, down comforters, and Robin's own watercolors. Or there's the beach house on Hood Canal with two-plus bedrooms, plenty of decks, and an inviting hot tub. Adjacent to the farmhouse is a conference center for small retreats.

Breakfast happens twice at Manor Farm: first a tray of hot scones and orange juice is left at your door; then (for non-guests as well) at 9am, there are fresh fruit, oatmeal folded with whipped cream, eggs from the farm chickens, and rashers of bacon. (Ample, but too simple for the $12 prix fixe.) Dinner is even more of an event: a (6:30pm) one-seating four-course affair that begins with sherry and hors d'oeuvres in the lovely drawing room. You proceed to the dining room for soup, salad, and appetizer. The entrée (which you choose upon making reservations) might be a lightly cooked salmon or a tender cut of lamb. The finish is dessert, port, coffee—a proper finale for what aspires to be a proper English meal. Wine and service not included in the $35 per person price tag. ▪ *½ hour from Winslow ferry dock off Hwy 3 on Big Valley Rd; (206) 779-4628; 26069 Big Valley Rd NE, Poulsbo, WA 98370; $$$; MC, V; local checks only; breakfast, dinner every day.*

SUQUAMISH

In Suquamish on the Port Madison Indian Reservation (follow the signs past Agate Pass), the **Suquamish Museum** in the Tribal Center is devoted to studying and displaying Puget Sound Salish Indian culture; (206) 598-3311. **Chief Sealth's grave** can be found nearby, on the grounds of St. Peter's Catholic Mission Church. Twin dugout canoes rest on a log frame over the stone, which reads, "The firm friend of the whites, and for him the city of Seattle was named."

KINGSTON

RESTAURANTS

Kingston Hotel Cafe [*unrated*] Not only is this inviting cafe exactly what Kingston needed, it's exactly where it needed to be: facing out across the Sound framed from this northern vantage by Mount Rainier and Mount Baker. Judith Weinstock (former owner of Bainbridge Island's famed Streamliner Diner) adopted this two-story western-front building and built a simple, wholesome menu. Still very new at press time, but early reports tell us that sunny mornings on the upstairs deck will be tough to beat. Bring the kids and let them play in the sandbox while you enjoy another latte. Custom jeweler David Weinstock has his shop upstairs. ▪ *A block north of the ferry terminal at Washington Blvd and 1st Ave; (206) 297-8100; Kingston; $; no alcohol; no credit cards; checks OK; breakfast, lunch every day.*

PORT GAMBLE

Built in the mid 19th century by the Pope & Talbot timber people, who traveled here by clipper ship from Maine, this is the essence of the company town. Everything is company-owned and maintained, and the dozen or so Victorian houses are beauties and in splendid repair. The town, which was modeled on a New England village, also boasts a lovely church, a vital and well-stocked company store, and a historical museum—down the steps and in back of the store—that is a gem. An ideal presentation of a community's society and industrial heritage, it was designed by Alec James, who designed the displays for the Royal Provincial Museum in Victoria. The lumber mill, incidentally, is still in operation and proves to be an interesting sight. Unfortunately, a grand hotel that sat on a splendid bluff overlooking the water was razed in the 1960s; the hotel's splendid lobby is re-created in the museum. For more information, call (206) 297-3341.

HANSVILLE

Just beyond the unassuming fishing town of Hansville are a couple of the prettiest, most accessible, and least explored beaches on the peninsula. To the east is **Point No Point**, marked by a lighthouse and great for kids and families, because there's a parking lot just steps away. Follow the road from Hansville to the west and you'll come across **Cape Foulweather**. The short trail through the woods is tough to find, so look for the Nature Conservancy sign on the south side of the road.

SHELTON

RESTAURANTS

Cafe Luna ★★ There is nothing about Shelton to prepare you for Cafe Luna—Alice must have felt the same sense of unreality when she fell into Wonderland. Cafe Luna is a muted art deco room with moons of magic. The real magic though, comes from the kitchen. The ravioli is made on the premises; the rest of the pasta is perfectly cooked and sauced enticingly. The menu changes with the availability of fresh ingredients (prawns come from Alaska, right off the boat at the Shelton dock) and the fancies of the chef. Wines are selected from West Coast vineyards and service is personal and professional. The quality of the cuisine and the service may have something to do with the fact that Cafe Luna is open only three nights a week—so the cook's creativity never dulls. No smoking. ■ *In the Mercantile Mall at 3rd and Railroad; (206) 427-8709; 221 W Railroad St, Shelton; $$; beer and wine; no credit cards; checks OK; dinner Thurs-Sat.*

UNION

RESTAURANTS

Victoria's ★★ Victoria's doesn't seem exceptional from the outside, but this only adds to the pleasant surprise once you're inside. The effect of high beamed ceilings, a fireplace, and green plants is cozy and enchanting. Large windows provide a view of a green parkland complete with a brook and sheltering firs. Seated at one of the 10 round tables in this understated dining room, one quickly forgets the adjoining trailer park that formed a first impression. The food and service are as good as the ambience. Pasta appears in several variations, and seafood is always fresh—the oysters are especially tender and tasty. Prime ribs are ample and delicious. There is a thoughtful wine list and knowledgeable help to take your order. Victoria's offers a refined choice of nonalcoholic beverages as well as beer, wine, and aperitifs. Desserts are imaginative and rich. ■ *¼ mile west of Alderbrook Inn on Hwy 106; (206) 898-4400; E 6791 Hwy 106, Union; $$; full bar; MC, V; checks OK; breakfast Sun, lunch, dinner every day (closed Mon-Tues, Jan-May).*

BRINNON

RESTAURANTS

Half-way House Restaurant ★ Brinnon is a town you can miss if you blink, but keep your eyes open for the Half-way House, especially around dinnertime. Tuesday evening is the night many locals comb their hair, wash their faces, and treat themselves to a gourmet five-course meal. Wednesday night is "pour night" when special seasonal cocktails come with your meal. Thursdays are for ethnic dinners, Fridays two-for-one steaks, Saturdays pizza, and Sunday it's fried chicken. Reservations required on Tuesday nights only. ■ *Set slightly back on the west side of Hwy 101 in Brinnon; (206) 796-4715; Brinnon; $ ($$ on Tues); full bar; MC, V; checks OK; breakfast, lunch, dinner every day.*

QUILCENE

RESTAURANTS

The Timber House ★ The Timber House, a charming place, resembles nothing so much as a large and rough-hewn hunting lodge. Although the menu is not without more pretentious items, the local seafood is the reason to go. Quilcene oysters come from right down the road, and there's much more from the waters around the Sound. Sautéed Dungeness crab is a winner, as are the scallops Timber House, sautéed with mushrooms and onions and bathed in a mornay sauce. Even the deep-fried selections that make up the Captain's Plate are nicely done and not over-battered. ■ *About ½ mile south of Quilcene on Hwy 101; (206) 765-3339; Hwy 101 S, Quilcene; $$; full bar; MC, V; checks OK; lunch, dinner Wed-Mon.*

Looking for a particular place? Check the index at the back of this book for specific restaurants, lodgings, attractions, and more.

PORT LUDLOW

LODGINGS

Port Ludlow Golf & Meeting Retreat ★★ While you're dining at the resort's Harbormaster Restaurant, imagine the same view being enjoyed by old Cyrus Walker— Pope & Talbot's legendary 1880s sawmill manager. His "biggest damn cabin on the Sound" (actually a splendid Victorian manse) once occupied this site with its eye-filling Olympic peaks, teardrop bay, and rolling, timber-covered hills. Now 180 units, year-round swimming pool, a marina, seven tennis courts, a 27-hole championship golf course, hiking and cycling trails, and a hidden waterfall fill the 1,500 developed acres. All of the individually decorated suites have fireplaces, kitchens, and private decks; many include views of the harbor. Views of the forests and countryside are equally pleasant. Port Ludlow also hosts a good number of conventions; at other resorts, these usually prove to be the kiss of death for a romantic weekend, but here a feeling of spaciousness acts as a serene buffer. The Harbormaster Restaurant has recently been renovated and now includes a deck that is delightful in the summer. They serve standard upscale food and have a pleasant bar. ▪ *6 miles north of Hood Canal Bridge on west side; (206) 437-2222; 9483 Oak Bay Rd, Port Ludlow, WA 98365; $$$; AE, DC, MC, V; checks OK; breakfast, lunch, dinner every day.*

Weatherford Inn ★ The Weatherford's site, on a hillside looking south down Hood Canal, seems to be a magnet for the changeable weather systems bouncing off the Olympic Mountains. The area, known as Shine, takes its name from the brilliance of its sunny days. The building is new, but its design was copied from the 19th-century Saratoga Inn on Whidbey Island. The common rooms are large and cozy, and a fireplace is especially welcome when the view to the south is stormy. The three view rooms have adequate bathrooms; the others (perhaps to make up for their lack of view) have large, luxurious bathrooms. Guests can dig and hunt for clams and oysters on the beach, though fishing rights are shared with a family of eagles. ▪ *From Poulsbo, turn left at the end of Hood Canal Bridge and drive about 1.4 miles; (206) 437-0332; 941 Shine Rd, Port Ludlow, WA 98365; $$; DIS, MC, V; checks OK.*

MARROWSTONE ISLAND

Marrowstone Island is off the northeast corner of the Olympic Peninsula (drive across the southern end of well-protected Indian Island). **Fort Flagler**, one of the old coastal fortifications at the north end of the island, is a beautiful spot for walks.

LODGINGS

The Ecologic Place A great spot for families who'd rather spend more time out than in. It's a basic gathering of rustic cabins in a natural setting that is simply breathtaking. Bordering on a tidal estuary that flows into Oak Bay and then Puget Sound, this property sees the Olympic Mountains and Mount Rainier whenever conditions permit. The cabins, each with their own character, have not been done by a decorator, but have everything you need to enjoy the beauty of the place—wood stoves, equipped kitchens, comfortable mattresses on the queen-size beds and fine-for-children bunks and twins. You can bring bikes, boats, books, bathing suits, binoculars, and children, and *should* bring groceries. ■ *Turn right at "Welcome to Marrowstone" sign—office is just ahead on right; (206) 385-3077; 10 Beach Dr, Nordland, WA 98358; $$; MC, V; checks OK.*

PORT HADLOCK

RESTAURANTS

Marrowstone Island

Lodgings

Ferino's Pizzeria ★ People from Port Townsend and Port Ludlow drive to Port Hadlock for this first-rate pizza—homemade crisp, tasty crust, loaded with fresh, plentiful toppings. The veggie pizza—loaded with cheese, olives, mushrooms, tomatoes, green peppers, onions, artichoke hearts, green onions, fresh garlic, and pineapple—is an exotic and delicious mix. The pepperoni's good too, and they've got the grease level under control. The restaurant is spotless and smokeless, the seating comfortable, and the pizza is available by the slice and to go. ■ *At the crossroads in Hadlock; (206) 385-0840; Kivley Center; PO Box 210, Port Hadlock; $$; beer and wine; MC, V; local checks only; lunch, dinner Wed-Mon.*

PORT TOWNSEND

Port Townsend's most noticeable boom came in the late 19th century, when speculators thought this busy port of entry would be the terminus of the Union Pacific. When the railroad stopped in Tacoma, the money evaporated in Port Townsend. The boom left behind an array of grand and modest Victorian homes and commercial structures, many of which have gradually been reclaimed and renovated during the boom swings of this century. The historic architecture and the wraparound water and mountain views lie at the heart of Port Townsend's charm.

Chetzemoka Park, in the northeast corner of town, has a charming gazebo, picnic tables, tall Douglas firs, and a grassy slope down to the beach; in autumn there are blackberries.

Fort Worden adds another dimension to Port Townsend. The 433-acre complex overlooking Admiralty Inlet mixes turn-of-the-century military structures, campgrounds, gardens, a theater, and a summertime concert shed. The Commanding Officer's house is furnished with antiques and is open to the public. A huge central parade ground is perfect for games or kite flying. This setting may look familiar to those who saw the movie *An Officer and a Gentleman*, which was filmed here. Down at the water, an enormous pier juts into the bay—it's the summer home to the **Marine Science Center**, with touch tanks and displays of sea creatures. There's a safe, protected swimming beach on one side of the pier, and access to miles of beaches. Up on the hillside you can spend hours exploring the deserted cement bunkers and massive gun mounts. The Cable House Canteen, across from the beach parking lot, provides excellent hamburgers and fish 'n' chips; (206) 385-9951.

Fort Worden is also home to **Centrum**, a sponsor of concerts, workshops, and festivals throughout the year. Many of these take place in the old balloon hangar which has been reborn as McCurdy Pavilion, the concert shed.

Events. A historic homes tour happens the first weekend in May and the third weekend in September. **The Rhododendron Festival** in May, with a parade and crowning of the queen, is the oldest festival in town. The **Centrum Summer Arts Festival**, one of the most successful cultural programs in the state—with dance; fiddle tunes; chamber music; the Seattle Youth Symphony; a writers conference; jazz, blues, and theater performances—runs at Fort Worden from June to September. The winter lineup includes classical performances and a jazz weekend; call (206) 385-3102 for information and schedules. The **Wooden Boat Festival**, at Point Hudson Marina, (206) 385-3628, the weekend after Labor Day, is a celebration of traditional crafts and a showcase for everything from prams to kayaks to yachts to tugboats. The **Women's Film Festival** in March uses the renovated Rose Theater, 235 Taylor Street, (206) 385-1089, to showcase a rich variety of films made by women.

Wandering. The Jefferson County Historical Society has a fascinating museum, 210 Madison Street, (206) 385-1003, complete with 1885-vintage jail cells and an extensive collection of Northwest Indian artifacts. Colorful shops line **Water Street: Franklin House Gallery**, 636 Water Street, (206) 385-0620, is a bazaar of local and imported arts and crafts; **Captain's Gallery**, 1012 Water Street, (206) 385-3770, has an amazing selection of pricy kaleidoscopes; **William James Bookseller**, 829 Water Street, (206) 835-7313, and **Melville and Co.**, 914 Water Street, (206) 835-7127, have well-organized inventories of used books; and **Imprint Bookstore**, 820 Water Street, (206) 385-3643, is well stocked with classics, best sellers, regional books and a great selection of contemporary verse. **Phoenix Rising**, 839 Water Street, (206) 385-4464, offers New

Port Townsend

Age culture, from self-help and astrology books to crystals and aromatic oils. The best ice cream cone can be had at **Elevated Ice Cream**, 627 Water Street, (206) 385-1156, the best pastry at **Bread & Roses Bakery**, 230 Quinsey Street, (206) 385-1044, and the best antique selection at **Port Townsend Antique Mall**, 802 Washington Street, (206) 385-2590, where about 40 antique merchants have convened under one roof. For a nip with the natives, head for **Back Alley Tavern**, Tyler and Water streets, (206) 385-2914, for live music and local color, or the historic **Town Tavern**, Water and Quinsey streets, where the pool tables, the huge bar, and the owner's great taste in music draw an interesting assortment of people. Finally, check out the retail revitalization of uptown Port Townsend at **Aldrich's**, Lawrence and Tyler streets (206) 395-0500, an authentic 1890s general store come to life with an upscale twist; **the 1004 Gallery**, 1004 Lawrence Street, (206) 385-7302, for excellent contemporary art; **Potpourri**, 625 Tyler Street, (206) 385-7162, for tasteful interior decor; **Jack and Jill**, 1044 Lawrence Street, (206) 385-3166, for darling children's clothing.

The *Victoria Clipper* runs a daily ferry from Seattle and Friday Harbor (May-September only); call (206) 448-5000 for reservations.

RESTAURANTS

Cafe Piccolo ★ In a welcome change from menus saturated with Port Townsend funk, Cafe Piccolo opts for the simple preparations and fresh ingredients of Italian food. Owner Farnham Hogue brought 20 years of cooking experience up from San Francisco, assessed the local dining scene, and opened his "little cafe" with the help of his wife, Nancy, and sister (and partner) Patricia Hodge. Hogue's menu borrows flavors and textures from all over the Italian boot, from a wonderfully marinated bistecca alla fiorentina to Sicilian fisherman's stew. There's a selection of pizzas (they're meant to be one-person, but they're *huge*) in different combinations. Pastas are nicely prepared, with a judicious choice of ingredients. Upstairs, a wine bar is planned for the near future. ■ *On Hwy 20 about a mile outside of town; (206) 385-1403; PO Box 1777, Port Townsend; $$; beer and wine; MC, V; checks OK; dinner every day May-Sept (Wed-Sun, Oct-Apr).*

Fountain Cafe ★ Locals like to bring their out-of-town guests here for a cozy storefront dining room with quirky local art on the walls. This really is cafe food—pastas and local shellfish, to be sure, but not a full dinner to be seen on the menu. Eggplant and oyster with pepper linguine pleasantly fuses flavors, while tangy Greek pasta, with olives, capers, and feta, is always in demand. Pasta dishes can be vast and gummy. The wine list is good, and you'd have to be loony not to try the loganberry fool for dessert (a "fool" is a wondrous blend of custard, fruit, and whipped cream). Service is courteous even with patrons queued in front. ■ *At the Port Townsend fountain steps; (206) 385-1364; 920 Washington St, Port Townsend; $$; beer and wine; AE, MC, V; checks OK; lunch, dinner every day.*

Khu Larb Thai ★ A pleasant mix of Thai and Port Townsend—a clean, spacious restaurant; muted, harmonious decor; and dependably good food. Thai cuisine here includes curries and a variety of spicy dishes with all the ingredients chopped fine. Soups are especially exotic, and vegetarian dishes made with tasty Thai noodles are good bets. Choose your spice carefully and be prepared for burnout if you go too high on the chart. Good black rice pudding for dessert. Xylophone music on some evenings can be annoying. ■ *Off Water St on Adams; (206) 385-5023; 225 Adams St, Port Townsend; $; beer and wine; MC, V; local checks only; lunch, dinner every day.*

The Public House ★ This large space with soaring ceilings has been brought into human scale by clever interior design. It feels comfortable, what with its antique lights, wooden floor, and dark green wainscoting; the bar is a marvel of the cabinetmaker's art. The best thing you can do here is select a beer from the impressive selection of drafts and order a hamburger. The menu ranges far beyond this standard fare, but the chef has a heavy hand with salt and seasonings, so the basics are the way to go. Play darts or chess, watch the world go by through the big front windows, or enjoy the live local music. The best nonsmoking bar in town. ■ *On the north side of Water St; (206) 385-9708; 1038 Water St, Port Townsend; $$; full bar; MC, V; checks OK; lunch, dinner every day.*

The Landfall This funky neighborhood standby, with its octagonal boathouse-style add-on and a wood stove for warming up Point Hudson winters, is frequented for its burgers and fish and chips. But the nicely seasoned cod and tender grilled salmon, with flavorful brown rice on the side, are also highly respectable. So are the prices. The menu features some Mexican selections. A typical Port Townsend touch: restrooms are out back. ■ *North end of Water St; (206) 385-5814; 412 Water St, Port Townsend; $$; beer and wine; no credit cards; checks OK; breakfast, lunch every day, dinner Wed-Sun.*

Salal Cafe Breakfasts are justly famous here, with a couple of morning newspapers circulating and locals trading stories back in the solarium. The omelets are legendary—we like the avocado with homemade salsa and the spinach and feta cheese—and cheese blintzes, oyster scrambles, and tofu dishes are satisfying. The light, cheerful cafe serves lunch, but is really more fitting for the morning meal. ■ *Quincy and Water; (206) 385-6532; 634 Water St, Port Townsend; $$; beer and wine; no credit cards; checks OK; breakfast, lunch Wed-Sun.*

▼

Port Townsend

Restaurants

▲

Silverwater Cafe Port Townsend's New Age slant is captured inside the four walls of the Silverwater. Light music floats through the air and meals are approached from a holistic, healthy angle. The Silverwater favors simple, fairly light preparations, which usually include rice, lots of veggies, and a couple of unusual ingredients (a tarragon pesto, for example, on a warm shellfish salad). The fish selections are most popular (Canterbury oysters, salmon, and an additional daily fresh shellfish), but there are chicken and beef entrées and a couple of wholesome standbys (stir-fry, pasta primavera) for vegetarians. Soups and stir-fries are lacking in flavor. Chocolate espresso cheesecake is a zinger. ■ *On Quincy St, near the old ferry dock; (206) 385-6448; 126 Quincy St, Port Townsend; $$; beer and wine; MC, V; local checks only; lunch, dinner every day.*

LODGINGS

The James House ★★★ Everything's up to snuff at the James House—one of the more pleasant places to stay in the state. This fine Victorian B&B rests in the competent hands of Carol McGough and Anne Tiernan, who are still improving it, continually freshening the rooms and the pretty garden. It's more an inn than a B&B with 12 rooms beautifully furnished in antiques; those in the front of the house have the best views out across the water. Not all rooms have private baths, but the shared facilities are spacious and well equipped. The main floor has two sumptuous adjoining parlors, each with a fireplace and plenty of reading material. A gardener's cottage with patio provides the most privacy. Guests can look forward to fresh fruit, granola, homemade baked goods, and quiche or eggs at breakfast, either at the big table in the formal dining room or in the kitchen with its antique cookstove. ■ *Corner of Washington and Harrison; (206) 385-1238; 1238 Washington St, Port Townsend, WA 98368; $$; MC, V; checks OK.*

Hastings House/Old Consulate Inn ★★ One of the most photographed Victorians in these parts, this former German consulate is one of the most comfortable and nonstuffy, with its wraparound porch and Sound views. Finishing touches are being made by owners Rob and Joanna Jackson, who keep the rooms immaculate and pretty. All of the rooms have private baths; most are closet-size (from their former incarnations as, well, closets), but guests in the Master Suite can soak and admire a gracious view at the same time. The third floor Tower Suite, with a sweeping bay view and dripping with lace, is a honeymooner's dream. Mammoth seven-course breakfasts—over which Joanna will be more than delighted to wittily recount the inn's history—are served. ■ *At intersection of Washington and Walker on the bluff; (206) 385-6753; 313 Walker St, Port Townsend, WA 98368; $$$; AE, MC, V; checks OK.*

20
YEARS

Heritage House ★★ An immaculate yard welcomes visitors to this hillcrest Victorian B&B. The sprightly variety of refinished antiques matches guest rooms with names like Lilac and Morning Glory. Four of the six rooms have private baths; the Peach Blossom has an oak-and-tin claw-footed bathtub that folds away when not in use. Relax in the evenings on the porch swing, in the mornings over breakfasts of decadent French toast with fresh fruit. Views over the north Sound and the business district come close to rivaling those of Heritage's venerable neighbor, the James House. Children over eight are permitted, but pets are not. ■ *Corner of Washington and Pierce; (206) 385-6800; 305 Pierce St, Port Townsend, WA 98368; $$; AE, DIS, MC, V; checks OK.* &

Quimper Inn ★★ When the Quimper was remodeled in 1904, it picked up some welcome architectural details as a result. A pillared porch (with a second-story porch above) was added out front, the windows were enlarged, and bay windows were added on both sides of the house. And through the years, the rooms have been painted in a variety of rich hues; the light from all the windows playing across these surfaces suffuses every corner of the large house with a mellow glow. A first-floor bedroom more resembles a library with a comfortable bed and a bath (with tub), and upstairs there is a lovely suite with period decor, more bookcases, and a private bath. Two rooms at each end of the hall share a delightful step-up bath, and the last room, with bay windows and a brass bed, has its own commodious bath with a six-footed tub, a pedestal sink, and wicker furniture. Sue and Ron Ramage treat their inn and their guests with thoughtful care. Breakfasts are as well executed as the rest of your stay. ■ *Corner of Franklin and Harrison; (206) 385-1060; 1306 Franklin St, Port Townsend, WA 98368; $$; MC, V; checks OK.*

Ravenscroft Inn ★★ This airy inn is a nonconformist among the surrounding Victorians. Built in 1987 (and borrowing its design from historic South Carolina), the structure is large and impressive with a long front porch, redwood-stained clapboards, and graceful end chimney. Owners Leah Hammer and John Ranney have taken great care with their B&B. A suite on the third floor sports dormer windows that overlook the town and harbor. Thick, warm carpeting throughout the house deadens sound and creates immediate coziness. The color scheme in every room is unique; each has wicker or antique reproduction furniture and custom upholstery (and one romantic room on the second floor has its own fireplace). Breakfast is the high point of a stay here, when, seated in the dining room with morning light streaming through the French windows, guests enjoy a gourmet meal and the musical accompaniment of John, a virtuoso pianist. Refrains from this breakfast will play in your

Port Townsend

Lodgings

head for the rest of the day. ■ *Corner of Quincy and Clay on the bluff; (206) 385-2784; 533 Quincy St, Port Townsend, WA 98368; $$; DIS, MC, V; checks OK.*

Ann Starrett Mansion ★ The most opulent Victorian in Port Townsend, this 1889 multigabled Queen Anne hybrid appears to have thrived under the ownership of Edel and Bob Sokol. The spiral stairway, octagonal tower, and "scandalous" ceiling fresco (the Four Seasons, complete with unclad winter maiden) are visually stunning. All rooms are antique-furnished and have high ceilings and lovely decorating touches. But all in all, it's not as impressive as it sounds, and not everyone feels comfortable here. The color scheme may throw the artistically inclined for a loop. The Drawing Room (with a tin claw-footed bathtub) opens to fabulous views of the Sound and Mount Baker, while the new, romantic Gable Suite, which occupies the whole third floor, has a skylight (also with a knockout view) and ample seating area. The less expensive brick Carriage Room feels more like a basement room, with old carriage doors and a sleigh bed. Sunday breakfast is a chocoholic's dream (or a dieter's nightmare). The house is open for public tours from noon until 3pm. ■ *Corner of Clay and Adams; (206) 385-3205; 744 Clay St, Port Townsend, WA 98368; $$; DIS, MC, V; checks OK.*

Bay Cottage ★ Susan Atkins has turned a cluster of old-fashioned waterside cottages into a delightful, private retreat. Discovery Bay is a magnificent stretch of water that reaches to the base of the Olympics; cottages on the south side look out on all this splendor and there are only a few houses visible to remind one of the building frenzy that has taken place all around. The cottages have good stoves and refrigerators, a tasteful mix of carefully selected antique furniture, comfy mattresses covered with feather beds, and direct access to a marvelous walking and swimming beach. Susan stocks the kitchens with the basic necessities (which include pancake mix and hot cereal), and when the mood strikes, she has been known to bake cookies. Each cottage has its own picnic basket, binoculars, and library. Perfect for families. ■ *½ mile west of Four Corners Grocery on S Discovery Rd; (206) 385-2035; 4346 S Discovery Rd, Port Townsend, WA 98368; $$; no credit cards; checks OK.*

Fort Worden ★ Fort Worden was one of three artillery posts built at the turn of the century to guard the entrances of Puget Sound. The troops have since marched away, and the massive gun mounts on the bluff have been stripped of their iron, but the beautifully situated fort has become a state park, a conference center, the site of the splendid Centrum arts festival, and an unusual place to stay. Twenty-four former officers' quarters, nobly proportioned structures dating back to 1904, front the old parade ground. These houses, including a few duplexes with period reproductions, have been made into decent lodgings. They are wonderfully spacious, each has a complete kitchen, and the rates are bargains. There are two more hidden lodgings in the park: the Castle, built in the 1890s, with a bedroom, kitchen, bath, and sitting room, and Bliss Vista, a small cottage at the edge of the bluff with a fireplace and plenty of romantic appeal. Reservations should be made well in advance (the office recommends a year to the date). At press time, a restaurant called Blackberries is scheduled to open. ■ *1 mile north of downtown; (206) 385-4730; 200 Battery Way, Fort Worden State Park Conference Center, Port Townsend, WA 98368; $$; no credit cards; checks OK.*

Lizzie's ★ Lizzie, the wife of a tugboat captain, put the deed of this model of Victorian excess in her own name; her name now graces a B&B as well as a line of lotions and sweet bubble-bath powders created by friendly owners Patti and Bill Wickline. Breakfast, served in a huge, cheerful farm kitchen, can turn into a friendly kaffeeklatsch; a soak in the tub in the black-and-white corner bathroom—especially if the sun is slanting in—is a Victorian treat. There are views from half of the eight bedrooms, and flowered decor. Two parlors, once frequented by former boardinghouse tenants, seem to have been plucked from the past; in one you'll even find a vintage stereoscope and a basket of photos to look at. ■ *Near the corner of Lincoln and Pierce in the historic district; (206) 385-4168; 731 Pierce St, Port Townsend, WA 98368; $$; DIS, MC, V; checks OK.*

SEQUIM

Sequim (pronounced *skwim*) was once one of Washington's best-kept secrets. The town sits smack in the middle of the "rain shadow" cast by the Olympic Mountains: cacti grow wild here, the sun shines, glaciated mountains border New England-style saltwater coves, and the fishing's just fine. Now Sequim's been discovered and is growing up fast. Farms have become subdivisions and golf courses sprout in what used to be grainfields. Retirees form the bulk of the new population, and their influence colors Sequim's transformation from a quiet cultural community into a semisuburban town.

Cedarbrook Herb Farm (open March through Christmas, 9am to 5pm daily) has a vast range of herb plants, scented geraniums, and fresh-cut herbs; 986 Sequim Avenue S, (206) 683-7733.

Olympic Game Farm breeds endangered species and raises a line of beasts for Hollywood—a nice drive-through; 5 miles north of Sequim in Dungeness, (206) 683-4295.

Dungeness Spit, 6 miles northwest, is a national wildlife refuge for birds and the longest sand spit in the country (a favorite spot for horseback riders during the off season and low tide). The driftwood displays are extraordinary, the winds are often good for kite flying, and a long walk down the 6-mile beach takes you to a remote lighthouse. Call (206) 683-5847 for camping information.

Two wineries are in the vicinity: **Lost Mountain Winery** offers tours and tastings when it's open, 3142 Lost Mountain Road, (206) 683-5229; **Neuharth Winery** is open daily for tastings in summer (winter hours vary, so call ahead); 148 Still Road, (206) 683-9652.

RESTAURANTS

The Buckhorn Grill ★★ Ignore the drab decor—the food, at any rate, will be lovely in presentation. Little slices of duck breast get carefully fanned out, paper-thin morsels of smoked salmon contrast with a sprinkle of capers and tomato. Happily, most of the food is as good as it looks. The main stumbling block is the fish, which for some reason doesn't take advantage of the local bounty. Why offer Atlantic salmon on the Olympic Peninsula? Why use frozen halibut when fresh is available? Everything else (meats, oysters, and duckling) is delicious. Vegetables and salads are handled with finesse. Service is professional; the wine list is comprehensive. A coat of paint and a consultation with the local fishermen would make this an even better restaurant. ■ *Hwy 101 east of Sequim; (206) 681-2765; 268522 Hwy 101, Sequim; $$; full bar; MC, V; local checks only; breakfast, lunch, dinner every day (closed Mon in winter).*

▼.

Sequim

▲

Casoni's ★ The popularity of Casoni's sparkling-clean Italian restaurant is undeniable. Perhaps it's the lingering memory of the fresh pasta served alongside veal Marsala, or the gray-haired warmth of Mama Casoni herself, that keeps diners returning for more. The tender calamari and the very fresh salads with homemade dressing are enough to bring us back, though we're still wary of the overpowering sauces that are sometimes too much for Mama's delicate noodles. The delectable desserts, such as the peanut butter chocolate-chip cheesecake, are another area in which Mama goes too far. ■ *1½ miles west of Sequim on Hwy 101 at Carlsborg Junction; (206) 683-2415; 104 Hooker Rd, Sequim; $$; full bar; AE, DC, MC, V; checks OK; dinner Wed-Sun (every day in summer).*

Hiway 101 Diner ★ It's not as aggressively kitschy as, say, the Beeliner Diner in Seattle, but for the laid-back folks in sunny Sequim, that's just fine. The retro-'50s theme extends to the back end of the '56 T-bird (which is actually a CD player) and a healthy dose of neon, but they don't push it much further than that: this is just a diner, and a pretty good one at that.

Breakfasts are standard omelets and combination fare, but it's in the burger-and-pizza area that this place really shines. Burgers are juicy, two-fisted events loaded with your choice of toppings (the Nifty Fifty, a fully dressed quarter-pounder, is quite popular), and chicken-breast sandwiches are uncommonly moist and tender. Pizzas come Chicago-style with all sorts of toppings. Service can be a gamble. ■ *Hwy 101; (206) 683-3388; 392 W Washington, Sequim; $; beer and wine; no credit cards; checks OK; breakfast, lunch, dinner every day.*

Oak Table Cafe ★ What's new here is an early Friday and Saturday dinner (until 8pm)—good, wholesome meals of Nebraska-fed beef, seafood specials, and mashed potatoes made from scratch. Breakfast is still a feast with huge omelets, fresh-fruit crêpes, and legendary puffy apple pancakes. Service is friendly and efficient—the coffee keeps coming—and the cream is the real thing. Lunches are lighter, with quiches, sandwiches, and seafood salads. It's noisy and boisterous and chatty. Espresso is served all day. ■ *1 block south of Hwy 101 at 3rd and Bell; (206) 683-2179; 292 W Bell St, Sequim; $$; no alcohol; no credit cards; checks OK; breakfast every day, lunch Mon-Fri, early dinner Fri-Sat.*

Jean's Mini Mart and Deli The mini mart is what you see from the road, but what you can't see are homemade soups, pastries, and fresh deli sandwiches. Jean started baking a little and making soup now and then for the odd customer, and word got around and now her home cooking is in demand full-time. Good muffins, cinnamon rolls, and honey buns are offered as early as 5am. Lunch is a choice of three of Jean's soups (curry cream of chicken, clam chowder, or tomato bacon), a thick tasty sandwich, and a piece of carrot cake or something called "lemon lush." This is what some fondly remember as roadside home cooking, though it was probably never as good as Jean's. ■ *At Hwy 101 and Carlsborg Rd across from Casoni's; (206) 683-6727; 20 Carlsborg Rd, Sequim; $; beer and wine; no credit cards; checks OK; breakfast, lunch Mon-Fri.*

 Three Crabs Dungeness crab is one of the major culinary delights of the Northwest, and this modest restaurant is the place where many pay tribute to the sweet, flavorful sea creature (unfortunately, almost everything else on the menu is fried). The location and reputation of Three Crabs have created a paradox—when it is really busy, as it is almost every night during the summer, it just isn't a pleasant dining experience. Kitchen smells creep in, reservations get mixed up, the food appears slapped together, and the waitresses haven't time for a smile. Instead, go in the afternoon. Order the whole, crack-it-yourself Dungeness crab (they get it all year round) and try to find room for some fresh-from-the-kitchen pie. ■ *Turn north from Hwy 101 onto Sequim Ave and head*

*5 miles toward the beach; (206) 683-4264; 101 Three Crabs Rd,
Sequim; $$; full bar; MC, V; checks OK; lunch, dinner every day.*

LODGINGS

Groveland Cottage ★ Simone Nichol's place is only a spit
away from Dungeness, and the rooms have that comfortable
salty-air feel of an old beach house, plus fair weather that's al-
most a guarantee. This 90-year-old building has four cheerful
rooms upstairs (with cheerful names to match) and—it comes
with the territory—a gift and food store below. Avoid the dark
one-room cottage out back with its awkward approach through
the cluttered yard. The place fills up in the summer with guests
addicted to Nichol's amenities, such as receiving the newspa-
per and coffee in your room before her four-course breakfast.
■ *Follow signs from Sequim toward Three Crabs; (206) 683-
3565; 1673 Sequim Dungeness Way, Dungeness, WA 98382;
$$; DIS, MC, V; checks OK.*

Juan de Fuca Cottages ★ You can't go wrong at any of these
five charming and comfortable cabins overlooking either Dungeness Spit or the Olympics (and a two-bedroom suite has both
views and a lovely fireplace). In fact, each is equipped with a
Jacuzzi, kitchen utensils, a clock radio, and reading material,
as well as cable TV, VCR and over 250 free films from which to
choose. Outside is the spit, begging for beach walks and clam
hunts. Two-night minimum stay on weekends. ■ *7 miles north
of Sequim; (206) 683-4433; 561 Marine Dr, Sequim, WA
98382; $$; MC, V; checks OK.*

Sequim

Restaurants

▲

PORT ANGELES

Port Angeles is the jumping-off point to both **Victoria**, via the
privately owned Black Ball Ferry, (206) 457-4491, and the north
(and most popular) end of **Olympic National Park**. The park
fills the interior of the peninsula. The often inclement weather
ensures a low human population and large numbers of elk,
deer, bear, and (on the highest crags) mountain goats. Follow
the signs to the visitors center, (206) 452-0330, and stop in for
an orientation. Then drive 17 miles along winding precipices to
an expansive view that few mountains with twice the altitude
can offer (the Olympics make only the 6,000- to 8,000-foot
range). **Hurricane Ridge**, with restrooms and snack facilities,
sits among spectacular vistas. The best time to see wildflowers
is after mid-July; in winter there is good cross-country skiing
and a Poma-only downhill area (weekends only). Check cur-
rent road conditions by calling a 24-hour recorded message,
(206) 452-9235, before you set out. If you prefer the low road
to the high, you'll find the **Elwha natural hot springs** in the
backcountry west of Port Angeles a more relaxing form of
recreation; call information at (206) 452-0330.

At the downtown **Arthur D. Feiro Marine Laboratory** on the City Pier, (206) 452-9277 x264, 80 species from nearby waters—including octopuses, wolf eels, sculpins, and sea slugs—have been collected, and a touch tank keeps children occupied. **Port Book and News**, 106 Laurel, (206) 452-6367, sells a healthy selection of magazines, the daily *New York Times* and *Wall Street Journal*, as well as new and used books. **Bonny's Bakery**, 502 East First, (206) 457-3585, is housed in a lovely old church and is a good place to stock up for ferry-ride food.

RESTAURANTS

C'est Si Bon ★★ It is "so good," this restaurant. The French still have the most sophisticated cuisine in the world, and believe it or not, Port Angeles has a fine example of it. It's an understated, elegant place with deep burgundy walls and large windows overlooking a rose garden (in winter, the dining room feels more intimate). There are three realities of fine French cuisine: it is expensive, it cannot be hurried, and it is delicious—all three apply here. Expect to have a leisurely meal, and be warned that sometimes (on weekends and in the summer), you may feel a cousin of your escargot is working in the kitchen. But be patient. The fresh halibut or salmon will spoil you forever. Rack of lamb comes pink in the center and accented with just the right amount of subtle brown sauce. Even just a simple salad of bibb lettuce turns into an amazing treat. Leave your busy schedule and your Americanized palate at home, and you'll enjoy a classically French evening. ■ *4 miles east of Port Angeles on Hwy 101; (206) 452-8888; 2300 Hwy 101 E, Port Angeles; $$$; full bar; AE, MC, V; local checks only; dinner Tues-Sun.*

China First ★ China First won't seem like much more than a typical Chinese joint on the main road out of Port Angeles, but Khoan Vong, a Vietnamese chef trained in Hong Kong, whips up some exceptional fish selections with remarkable flair. Pick a table by the little carp-filled pool and you'll rave about tender stir-fried oysters with black beans and spicy sautéed squid; the lemon duck and marinated barbecued pork ribs are outstanding as well. The standard combinations are exactly that, but at least not swimming in grease and a nice amount of food for the price. Service is quite slow; the restaurant is large, and there is only one chef behind the grill. ■ *Between Eunice and Francis; (206) 457-1647; 633 E 1st St, Port Angeles; $; full bar; MC, V; local checks only; lunch and dinner every day.*

The Coffee House Restaurant and Gallery ★ It's bigger than it was; however, this is still the place that Port Angeles' countercultural minority calls home. The bulletin board lists all the alternative events that the newspaper skips, and the menu lists adventurous, mostly healthful fare as well as eclectic espresso

▼

Port Angeles

Restaurants

▲

drinks. There's frequently evening entertainment, from dinner theater to music, and there's always art on the walls. We like their original sandwiches (try the Middle Eastern), the sweet-potato biscuits, and other inventions. Hang out with a cup of caffeine and a sweet, sumptuous truffle or two. No smoking—this *is* an art gallery. ■ *1st and Lincoln; (206) 452-1459; 118 E 1st St, Port Angeles; $$; beer and wine; no credit cards; local checks only; breakfast, lunch, and dinner every day.*

Downriggers ★ This is the place to look out on this seascape and dream and eat—seafood, of course. Downriggers is awfully proud of their fish and guarantee its freshness, and the menu subsequently crosses into the realm of overwhelming, a sign of caution at many restaurants. But most things are well done here, local oysters and crab among them. A miraculous range of nonalcoholic drinks graces the menu. Waitstaff is young, efficient, and pleasant. ■ *Upstairs at the Landing Mall, adjacent to the Victoria ferry landing; (206) 452-2700; 115 E Railroad, Port Angeles; $$; AE, DIS, MC, V; checks OK; lunch, dinner every day.* &

First Street Haven ★ It's just a skinny slot of a restaurant, easily missed among the storefronts if you're not paying attention, but it's the best place in Port Angeles for informal breakfasts and lunches. Fresh and unusual salads with homemade dressings, hearty sandwiches, pastas, and quiche constitute the menu, with pleasing arrangements of fresh fruit on the side. We've heard great things about the chili and fajitas. Expertly made espresso and their own coffee blend are fine jump-starters, especially with a fresh blueberry muffin or sour-cream coffee cake. The prices are reasonable, the service is friendly and attentive, and the air is smoke-free. ■ *1st and Laurel, next to the Toggery; (206) 457-0352; 107 E 1st St, Port Angeles; $; no alcohol; no credit cards; checks OK; breakfast, lunch Mon-Sat, brunch Sun.*

LODGINGS

Domaine Madeleine On Finn Hall Road ★★★ Romantic is almost an understatment. This elegant bed and breakfast overlooking the Strait of Juan de Fuca has witnessed (or perhaps inspired) proposals, wedding parties, honeymoons, and anniversary celebrations. What with the garden fashioned after Monet's Petites Allees in Giverny, the deer grazing in the field at the entrance, the sea air, and the silence, John and Madeleine Chambers have cultivated a natural-feeling, lovely spot. And that's just outside. There are two rooms at ground level and a suite upstairs with a balcony and Jacuzzi. A large central room with a dining table boasts a hand-carved Flemish-style mantlepiece and a massive basalt fireplace. Full windows facing the water disperse soft light throughout. Breakfast, in the hands of Madeleine, is a thorough indulgence. On antique porcelain, fresh fruit, hot baguettes, and perhaps the best omelet to be had outside of France are served with coffee with a hint of hazelnut flavor, and then dessert in the form of crème caramel decorated with a flower blossom. ■ *North of Hwy 101 between Sequim and Port Angeles (ask for detailed directions); (206) 457-4174; 146 Wildflower Lane, Port Angeles, WA 98362; $$$; MC, V; checks OK.*

Lake Crescent Lodge ★★ Some places never change, and in the case of Lake Crescent Lodge, it's a good thing. The lodgings are comfortable and well worn, but well kept up. The main building has a grand verandah (marvelous for reading or for afternoon tea) overlooking the placid, enormous, mountain-girt lake, and the cabins have nice porches. The service is just fine: eager college kids having a nice summer. Fishing (for a fighting *crescenti* trout, found only in this lake), hiking, evening nature programs, and boating are the main activities. The food is merely adequate, but the bar is above average. We recommend staying in the motel rooms or in one of the cabins that have fireplaces; the rooms in the main lodge are rustic—a euphemism that means, among other things, the bathroom is down the hall—and noisy. ■ *20 miles west of Port Angeles on Hwy 101; (206) 928-3211; HC 62, Box 11, Port Angeles, WA 98362; $$; AE, DC, MC, V; checks OK (closed mid-Nov–April).*

Tudor Inn ★★ One of the best-looking buildings in town, a completely restored Tudor-style bed and breakfast, is located 12 blocks from the ferry terminal in an unassuming neighborhood. Owners Jane and Jerry Glass are friendly hosts and well versed in Port Angeles political and cultural life; even their popular cat, Toby, is a character. Their house boasts a well-stocked library, fireplace, crisp linens, and antique touches here and there. The rooms are quite small (the Glasses are in the process of adding a private bath to each one), but the best one has wonderful views of both the Strait of Juan de Fuca and the Olympics. Breakfast is usually English traditional, although Jane will surprise her guests occasionally with treats such as sourdough pancakes. Other pluses include transportation to and from the ferry dock and the airport (with advance notice), afternoon tea, winter ski packages, and hosts who really know the town. ■ *11th and Oak, (206) 452-3138; 1108 S Oak St, Port Angeles, WA 98362; $$; MC, V; checks OK.*

Pond Motel ★ Six rooms overlook an acre-big pond where bufflehead ducks and mallards float by and two pet rainbow trout occasionally stir the serene water. Frank and Jo Kelly, the friendly owners of this unassuming arrangement, are gradually relandscaping the area; pretty little meadows and quiet moments show up unexpectedly here and there. The rooms are

Port Angeles

clean and spare—and very reasonably priced. There are two single rooms (dark, but sort of cozy) next to the office, and two bigger rooms equipped with vintage '40s kitchenettes. There's occasional noise from Highway 101, which runs right by, but the *place* is so quiet, it hardly seems to matter. ■ *½ mile west of city limits; (206) 452-8422; 196 Hwy 101 W, Port Angeles, WA 98362; $; MC, V; checks OK.*

SOL DUC HOT SPRINGS

Centuries ago, Native Americans believed that two dragons living in deep caves created the hot springs at the edge of the Sol Duc River. At the turn of the century, travelers seeking to soak in the sulfuric water made the long trek to **Sol Duc Hot Springs** via Stanley Steamer and ferry; (206) 327-3583. Today, there is nothing in this location to conjure up antiquity. The 32 brown cabins spread out on the river bank without benefit of shade or even a flowerpot to brighten them. If the dragons are still there, they must be staggering under the weight of the cement, tile, and piping that controls the hot water and keeps it circulating in three round tile pools. Where the natives probably cooled off in the river, there is now a large swimming pool ($5 admission). The hike to Sol Duc Falls is through one of the loveliest stands of old-growth forest anywhere. Camping facilities and RV hookups are also available. Open mid-May to the end of September.

SEKIU

LODGINGS

Van Riper's Resort The only waterfront hotel in Sekiu, Van Riper's is family-owned and -operated, low-key, and comfortable. The protected moorage of Clallam Bay draws picturesque fishing boats, so views from six of the 11 rooms are great. The best room is the Penthouse Suite: it sleeps six, has a complete kitchen and three walls of windows, and goes for just $65. Other rooms are smaller and cheaper, some with thin walls. ■ *Corner of Front and Rice on the main street; (206) 963-2334; PO Box 246, Sekiu, WA 98381; $; DC, MC, V; checks OK.*

NEAH BAY

The little town of Neah Bay, located on the Makah Indian Reservation, was the site of an 18th-century Spanish settlement. It offers some fine fishing (charters are available and fishing permits may be obtained from the tribal council), but it is most famous for its museum and research center, housing some fine artifacts from the magnificent archaeological dig nearby at **Lake Ozette**. The Makah Indian fishing village there was obliterated suddenly by a mudslide over 500 years ago. The clay soil sealed the contents of the houses, retarding the decay of a wealth of wooden and woven items. Discovered in 1970, the village has yielded some 55,000 artifacts.

The Makah Cultural and Research Center displays photomurals from pictures taken by Edward S. Curtis in the early 1900s; dioramas; a life-size replica of the longhouse that was the center of village life; and whaling, sealing, and fishing canoes. A cedar carving of a whale fin inlaid with 700 sea otter teeth is one of the most prized possessions; (206) 645-2711.

Cape Flattery, the northwesternmost point of mainland America, is supposedly the most perfect "land's end" in the United States, with the longest unbroken expanse of water before it. It can be reached by a short trail that leads to a viewpoint of Tatoosh Island. Call the Parks Department for coastal access information, (206) 452-4501.

FORKS

RESTAURANTS

South North Garden ★ A surprisingly good Chinese restaurant in the middle of logging country. The restaurant expanded into the space next door in 1989 and continues to be popular, especially considering its remoteness. The food inlcudes standard Cantonese and Sichuan dishes, which the chef will spice up if you ask. Wonton soup is made with flavorful chicken stock; Mongolian beef is a generous serving of tender, spicy beef strips. Hot pepper diced chicken (kung pao) is an excellent example of that popular dish. ■ *North end of town, 100 yards off Main St (Hwy 101) behind totem pole; (206) 374-9779; Sol Duc Way, Forks; $; beer and wine; MC, V; local checks only; lunch, dinner Tues-Sun.*

LODGINGS

Miller Tree Inn ★ A large, attractive house, Miller Tree Inn was one of the original homesteads in Forks. Conveniently located a few blocks east of Highway 101, it's popular with hikers and fisherfolk. The six rooms are attractive, if a bit small, with comfortable furnishings. Three have private baths. There's a new hot tub on the back deck. Breakfast is served in the big farmhouse kitchen. The atmosphere is relaxed and friendly— kids and well-behaved pets are welcome. At $55 a couple (summer rate), the price is at least as good as the motel down the road. ■ *6th St and E Division; (206) 374-6806; PO Box 953, Forks, WA 98331; $; MC, V; checks OK.*

Misty Valley Inn ★ If guests can walk away from Rachel Bennett's breakfast table, she hasn't done her job. Hospitality is the key to this lovely contemporary home with three guest rooms, decorated in English, Irish, and French styles (all share a bath). In summer she opens up the Dutch Room—the master suite with private bath. There's a baby grand piano in the living room, Nintendo in the family room, and a deck (where breakfast is sometimes served) overlooking the Sol Duc Valley. Rachel's breakfast might include waffles, or apple soufflé, or she is happy to honor special requests. The inn is on Highway 101 but separated from the road by a large screen of trees and shrubs. ■ *Milepost 195 on Hwy 101; (206) 374-9389; RR 1, Box 5407, Forks, WA 98331; $; MC, V; checks OK.*

LA PUSH

The town is a Quillayute Indian village noted for its rugged seascape, fine kite flying, salmon charter boats, and Indian fishing by canoe. Offshore stacks of rocks give the coastline its haunting appeal. One of the finest beach walks in the world is the 16-mile stretch south from Third Beach to the Hoh River Road; trailheads to the beaches are along the highway coming into La Push. Be sure to stop in at the ranger station in nearby Mora to get a backcountry use permit and tide tables; (206) 374-5460. Due to extreme tide changes, it's easy to get stranded on the beaches if you're not careful.

▼
Forks

Lodgings

▲

LODGINGS

La Push Ocean Park Resort If you request one of the remodeled cabins, you can count on a clean one. Most of the front row of cabins have queen-size mattresses and new ovens and refrigerators (good thing, since there's no restaurant in La Push). Front-row cabins also have their own well-stocked fireplaces (numbers 36 and 37 have huge stone fireplaces). The water (laden with harmless sulfur) tastes even worse than we remembered. If you plan to drink or cook, bring your own water or purchase bottled water in the convenience store across the street. The motel units on the top floor have nice views but thin walls; all have balconies overlooking the beach. The campers' cabins, about as rustic as you can find on the coast, are small A-frame structures with wood stoves and toilets (and showers in a couple); you lug your wood from the woodshed and shower in the communal washroom. The beach, the main reason for going to La Push, is beautiful and just beyond the driftwood logs. ■ *La Push Rd; (206) 374-5267; PO Box 67, La Push, WA 98350; $$; DIS, MC, V; checks OK.*

[20 YEARS]

KALALOCH

The attraction here is the beach, wide and wild, with bleached white logs crazily pitched on the slate gray sand. The road from the Hoh River to Kalaloch hugs the coast and offers magnificent vistas if the weather isn't too foggy. A good way to learn about the area is to take one of the guided walks and talks conducted out of the ranger station; summer only, (206) 962-2283. You can see whales offshore during fall and spring.

Rain forests. These shaggy regions lie along the Bogachiel, Hoh, Queets, and Quinault rivers, all within easy drives from Kalaloch. The Hoh, 25 miles north, has a nice visitors center, (206) 374-6925, and many moss-hung trails leading into the mountains. There are self-guided nature hikes, lots of wildlife to spy, and some of the most amazing greenery you're likely to see anywhere. Some of the world's largest Douglas fir, Sitka spruce, and red cedar are in the area, reachable by trails of varying difficulty. You can find out details in the Hoh ranger station. Rainfall in these parts reaches 140 inches annually.

LODGINGS

Kalaloch Lodge ★ Note that Kalaloch Lodge is quite impossible to get into on short notice during the summer; long stays may require reservations half a year in advance. The attractions are obvious: a wonderful beach, cabins dotted around the bluff, a wide variety of accommodations (the lodge, cabins, duplex units, and a modern motel). This formerly family-owned resort is now run by ARA (the same organization that took over Lake Quinault a while ago). The rooms in the lodge, which allows no cooking, are quite good—bright, clean, and quiet—and rooms 1, 6, 7, and 8 have ocean views. Sea Crest House is the modern motel, set amid wind-bent trees; rooms 407 to 409 have glass doors that open onto decks with ocean views, while suites 401, 405, 406, and 410 have fireplaces and more space. The old cabins can be rather tacky and hard to keep warm; the 21 new log cabins are a bit expensive, but they have nice facilities (except for the annoying practice of not providing eating utensils in the kitchenettes). Six duplexes on the bluff all feature ocean views. Prices for two range from $68 to $135. Two-day minimum stays on weekends; pets allowed in cabins only. The mediocre food in the dining room rarely matches the splendid ocean view. ■ *Hwy 101; (206) 962-2271; HC 80, Box 1100, Forks, WA 98331; $$; AE, MC, V; checks OK.*

▼

Lake Quinault

▲

LAKE QUINAULT

The lake, dammed by a glacial moraine, is carved into a lovely valley in the Olympic Range. The coast-hugging highway comes inland to the lake at this point, affording the traveler the easiest penetration to the mountains. You are near a mossy rain forest, the fishing for trout and salmon is memorable, and the ranger station can provide tips on hiking or nature study.

Big Acre is a grove of enormous old-growth trees, an easy hike from the lodge. **Enchanted Valley** is a 10-mile hike into the fabulous old forests, with a 1930s log chalet at the end of the trail.

LODGINGS

Lake Quinault Lodge ★ A massive cedar-shingled structure, the lodge was built in 1926 in a gentle arc around the sweeping lawns that descend to the lake. The public rooms are done up like Grandma's sun porch in wicker and antiques, but the gift shop seems inappropriately large. There's a big fireplace in the lobby, the dining room overlooks the lawns, and the rustic bar is lively at night. You can stay in the main building, where there are nice (small) rooms, but only half of them with a view of the lake; all have private baths (but the towels look a little ratty). The adjoining wing has balconies and queen-size beds in each unit; the decor is tacky, including plasticky fireplaces. Summer reservations take about two months' advance notice. Amenities consist of a sauna, an indoor heated pool, a Jacuzzi, a game room, canoes and rowboats for touring the lake, and well-maintained trails for hiking or running. The dining room puts up a classy front, but the food is uninspired. Stick with simpler items—waffles for breakfast, seafood for dinner—and brown-bag it when you can. There are often too many conventioneers around (mainly in the winter months), drawn by the spalike features of the resort, but somehow the old place manages to exude some of the quiet elegance of its past. Prices for two range from $80 for a basic room to $210 for a suite. ■ *S Shore Rd; (206) 288-2571 or (800) 562-6672; PO Box 7, Quinault, WA 98575; $$$; AE, MC, V; no checks.*

MOCLIPS

LODGINGS

Ocean Crest Resort ★★ Nestled in a magnificent stand of spruce on a bluff high above one of the nicest stretches of beach on the Olympic Peninsula, the Ocean Crest has always offered rooms with memorable views (and some with kitchens). There's a handsome wing featuring modern units done up in smart cedar paneling, with fireplaces and European-style showers. The ocean views from these rooms are even better. A handsome recreation center is just across the road, with a swimming pool, sauna, Jacuzzi, weight rooms, tanning beds, and massages. They'll sell you a vinyl swimsuit if you forgot to bring yours. An annex a quarter mile down the road offers two apartments with complete kitchens, porches, and two bedrooms each ($84). Maids are hard-pressed to trek the extra distance and may need to be requested.

Access to the beach is along a winding walkway through a lovely wooded ravine. There are few views on the Northwest coast outside of Cannon Beach that can rival the panorama from the dining room at the Ocean Crest. For many, the best news here is that the Ocean Crest's food is now consistently excellent, with prompt and friendly service. Breakfasts, especially, are outstanding. One floor above, there's a cozy bar, furnished with Northwest Coast Indian artifacts and offering the same view. ■ *18 miles north of Ocean Shores; (206) 276-4465; Hwy 109, Moclips, WA 98562; $$; AE, DIS, MC, V; checks OK.*

PACIFIC BEACH

LODGINGS

Sandpiper ★★ Here's the place to vacation with four other couples, or to bring the kids, the grandparents, and the family dog: miles of beach and a fleet of kites and volleyball players. The resort consists of two four-story complexes containing large, fully equipped suites—usually a sitting room with a dining area and a fireplace, a compact kitchen, a small porch, and a bedroom and bath. There are splendid views of the beach (and a childrens' play area) from every deck. Penthouse units have an extra bedroom and cathedral ceilings. We prefer the rooms in the older complex (the northern one), since they are a tad larger. There are also five cottages, and one-room studios are available too. This resort knows enough not to try to compete with the draws of the Pacific: there's no pool, no TV, no restaurant, no in-room telephones, no video machines—but the gift shop does sell board games, kites, and sand buckets. Prices remain very good. Minimum stays are imposed on weekends and summers, and reservations usually take months to get. Housekeeping drops by every day to see if you need anything (but you'll need to pay extra for logs for the fireplace); otherwise you're on your own...just like home. ■ *Hwy 109, 1½ miles south of Pacific Beach; (206) 276-4580; PO Box A, Pacific Beach, WA 98571; $$; MC, V; checks OK.*

COPALIS BEACH

LODGINGS

Iron Springs Resort ★ Friendly owners maintain this complex of cabins along a well-forested bluff, overlooking a beautiful stretch of beach. Some cabins are quite old and spacious—and amiably dowdy: light bulbs can be dim, and the sun can beat its way through the roof in the summer. Decor is mid-century chartreuse and orange, but each cottage has its own fireplace. Other cabins are newer, with vast view patios (number 8) and beautiful corner windows (number 14).

Number 6 is the only one with no view; newer (and quite spiffy) are those numbered 22 to 27. The beach is especially fine here, with a river meeting its destiny with the surf just south of the resort. The heated pool is covered for year-round use, and Olive Little's famous clam chowder, cinnamon rolls, and cheese rolls are still available. As a family place, where nobody's kids and pets seem to bother other people, Iron Springs is at its best. ▪ *Hwy 109, 3 miles north of Copalis Beach; (206) 276-4230; PO Box 207, Copalis Beach, WA 98535; $$; AE, MC, V; checks OK.*

OCEAN SHORES

As the big, silly gate to the city might indicate, Ocean Shores would like to become Atlantic City West. In May, June, and October, families flock here for kite-flying competitions and related events.

A good way to avoid downtown altogether is to reserve one of the private beach houses that owners occasionally put up for rent. Reservations need to be made weeks in advance; (206) 289-2430 or toll-free (800) 562-8612 in Washington only. For charter-fishing arrangements, call (206) 289-3391.

LODGINGS

The Grey Gull ★ This condominium-resort looks like a ski lodge (a rather odd style here on the beach), with jagged angles, handsome cladding, and a front door to strain the mightiest triceps. There are 36 condominium units, facing the ocean at a broad stretch of the beach (although not all have views; prices are calibrated accordingly), each outfitted with a balcony, fireplace, kitchen, and attractive furnishings. The resort has a pool, a sauna, and a spa. You are right on the beach, the main plus, and the lodge has been built with an eye for good Northwest architecture. Prices for the suites get fairly steep, but there are smaller rooms and you can save money by doing your own cooking in the full kitchens. ▪ *In town on Ocean Shores Blvd; (206) 289-3381; PO Box 1417, Ocean Shores, WA 98569; $$$; AE, DC, MC, V; local checks only.*

Southwest Washington

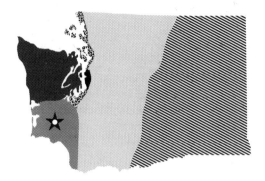

A clockwise route: southward on the southern half of I-5, west along the Columbia River, north along the Long Beach Peninsula and the south coast, and eastward at Grays Harbor.

CENTRALIA

RESTAURANTS

Winter Kitchen ★ Julie Norman owns this little green house decorated year-round in tasteful Christmas attire. The lunch menu is short and sweet—cheap too, with sandwiches, salads, and an oyster stew, all (except a seafood salad) less than $5. Red floats, green floats, apple cider, and hot chocolate make this a fun spot to stop on a wearying highway drive. Friday-night candlelight dinners (until 8pm) come complete with a candle on your plate. This place is as cozy as all get-out. ■ *2 blocks east of exit 81 off I-5; (206) 736-2916; 827 Marsh St, Centralia; $; no alcohol; no credit cards; checks OK; lunch Mon-Fri, dinner Fri.*

CHEHALIS

RESTAURANTS

Mary McCrank's ★ This is plain, unexciting food, but a good, homemade value. The 1935 dinner house occupies a large home, with fireplaces in some of the dining rooms; windows overlooking the garden, lawns, and stream; and armchairs scattered around the comfy rooms. Dinner starts with breads, jams, and a tray of homemade relishes. Offerings

343

include fried chicken, chicken with dumplings, pork chops, steaks, and other country fixings. Grilled chicken livers and onions are a local favorite (soups and salads, however, are perfunctory). A glorious pie comes for dessert: we never turn down the sour-cream raisin. Your girth may have widened, but your wallet will only be out $15 (tops) per person. ■ *4 miles east of I-5 on the Jackson Hwy, 4 miles south of Chehalis; (206) 748-3662; 2923 Jackson Hwy, Chehalis; $; beer and wine; MC, V; checks OK; lunch Tues-Sun, dinner Tues-Sun.* ⟨⟩

LONGVIEW

Longview has the unusual distinction of having been a totally planned community, ever since R.A. Long appeared in 1918 and hired Kansas City planners to make a town for his sawmill workers. **Lake Sacajawea Park**, a lovely stretch of green alongside a necklace of ponds, is the best evidence of this design.

RESTAURANTS

Henri's ★ The Longview big shots all come here for lunch, when the large place can be fun and reliable; at dinner, when the pretension level rises and the number of customers dips, things can be rather lonely and the food not really worth the money. Still, the steaks are perfectly good, you can have some nice seafood bisques, and the rack of lamb with béarnaise is quite tasty. There is a fancy wine room, into which guests are escorted by owner Henry Paul, who learned how to do this kind of thing years ago at Seattle's Golden Lion. Service and decor are only passable. ■ *45th and Ocean Beach; (206) 425-7970; 4545 Ocean Beach Hwy, Longview; $$; full bar; AE, DIS, MC, V; local checks only; lunch Mon-Fri, dinner Mon-Sat.* ⟨⟩

20 YEARS

LODGINGS

Monticello Hotel It fronts on Civic Center Park with an impressive facade of brick and terra-cotta, obviously the heart of town. But the 1923 edifice has suffered a loss of confidence over the years; now the hotel rooms are rented out as senior housing and offices, and the public rooms are showing their age. However, four executive suites have recently opened in the old hotel, and you can stay in a motel-like wing to one side, where the rooms are perfectly standard but the cost is low. The dining room, old-fashioned and a little dowdy, serves some inventive seafood dishes and a very spicy blackened beef dish that overshadows the restaurant's small-town presence. ■ *Larch and 17th; (206) 425-9900; 1405 17th Ave, Longview, WA 98632; $ to $$; AE, DIS, MC, V; no checks; breakfast, lunch, dinner every day.*

RIDGEFIELD

RESTAURANTS

Victoria Bakery & Restaurant Huge homemade meals come out of Victoria Cornea's kitchen. Cornea, a red-haired Romanian who cooks, bakes, and waits tables here, knows what her regulars like. She prepares one and only one meal per day, and that's what you'll eat: perhaps meatball soup with chicken breast, hollandaise, and potatoes for lunch on Tuesday, beef with mashed potatoes and mushroom gravy for dinner that evening. Call ahead to see what the day has in store. All reflects Victoria's talent and generosity, as do the thick slabs of freshly baked bread. Mismatched tableware, Top 40s music, and Victoria's bustle add to the delightful incongruity of a small-town gem. The Ridgefield National Wildlife Reserve is around the corner.
■ *Exit 14 off I-5, look for the hardware store; (206) 887-8001; 807 Pioneer St, Ridgefield; $; beer and wine; no credit cards; checks OK; breakfast, lunch, dinner Tues-Sat.* &

VANCOUVER

Vancouver, long known as a bedroom community of Portland, is coming into its own with the advent of new industry, including a number of up-and-coming restaurants. Unfortunately, we can't say the same about their lodgings. If you must stay close to Vancouver, cross the river to one of Portland's two Red Lions (either the Columbia River or Jantzen Beach). Among the modest tourist attractions is the Northwest's oldest apple tree (in Old Apple Tree Park, east of I-5 on Columbia Way). Locals claim that it was planted in 1829 by a member of the Hudson's Bay Company.

Vancouver

Fort Vancouver was the major settlement of the Hudson's Bay Company from the 1820s to the 1860s, when it passed to the Americans. The stockade wall and some of the buildings have been reconstructed, and the visitors center has a decent museum; 1501 E Evergreen Boulevard, (206) 696-7655. On your way to Officers Row, you'll pass the active military post, **Vancouver Barracks**. The Heritage Trust of Clark County gives walking tours of the restored officers' quarters nearby; (206) 737-6066. The Grant House on Officers Row now houses the **Folk Art Center**, a tribute to regional art. It's open Tuesday through Sunday. Call (206) 694-5252. **Clark County Historical Museum** reconstructs pioneer stores and businesses; 1511 Main Street at 16th, (206) 695-4681. **Covington House** is the oldest log house (1846) in the state; 4201 Main Street, (206) 695-4106.

Ridgefield National Wildlife Refuge, 3 miles west of I-5 exit 14, has nature trails leading to the bird refuge on the lowlands of the Columbia River; (206) 887-3883.

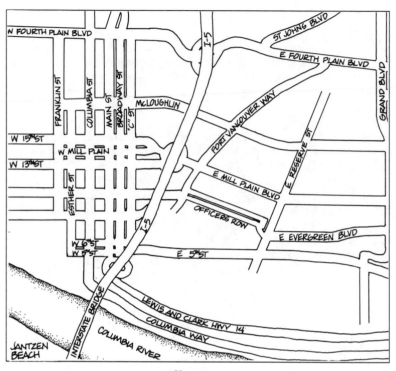

Vancouver

RESTAURANTS

Grant House Cafe ★★ The 1849 Grant House, named for Ulysses Grant, has reopened, this time as a folk art museum and cafe. Its location, with verandah and herb garden, is quite charming, and the food is rapidly catching up. For lunch, soups, salads, quiches, seafood, and sandwiches are the bill of fare, with Northwest bistro fare for dinner—pasta, salmon, Willapa Bay oysters, and gourmet burgers, with seasonal fruit tarts or a chocolate fudge sundae for dessert. We'd come back any time for the tomato-basil-blue cheese soup and the free regional folk art exhibit. ■ *Midtown Vancouver on Officers Row off Evergreen Blvd; (206) 699-1213; 1101 Officers Row, Vancouver; $ to $$; beer and wine; AE, MC, V; checks OK; lunch, dinner Tues-Sat (Thurs-Sat in winter), brunch Sun.*

Pinot Ganache ★★ Downtown Vancouver, forever struggling to buff up its image, shows off a glimmer of sophistication at Pinot Ganache. The interior is slick (and not just by Vancouver standards), with well-spaced tables and a cart of fresh flowers. The rest of dinner has caught up with the impressive desserts: brandied espresso chocolate mousse, chocolate decadence with white chocolate mousse, and a hazelnut toffee torte. Multiethnic describes the food here, with such international items as Asian-style game hen, Arabic falafel pita, and enchiladas con pollo, though the juicy sirloin burger with sautéed onions and mushrooms continues to draw regulars. Lunch consists of smaller portions of the creative standards and originals served during the evening. It's a popular enough place to demand minimum charges at peak hours. The place brightens in summer, when pink geraniums bloom in the sidewalk cafe. ■ *Corner of Washington and Evergreen; (206) 695-7786; 1004 Washington St, Vancouver; $$; beer and wine; AE, MC, V; checks OK; lunch, dinner Tues-Sat.*

Bernabe's Family Cafe ★ Pedro and Mary Bernabe run this tiny restaurant on an undistinguished strip of highway, where the Mexican flavors are as big as a sombrero. Traditional rellenos, quesadillas, and fajitas are served with homemade tortillas (available by the dozen for take-out). Let Pedro's posole stew (hominy with lettuce and radishes) and carne asada with grilled green onions and guacamole take you into perhaps unfamiliar Mexican territory. Sauces are prepared to order, to your spiciness specifications. For breakfast, choose from traditional American fare or south-of-the-border specialties (scrambled eggs and hot salsa, or a breakfast burrito with chorizo, eggs, and potatoes). ■ *Off Hwy 99 north of Vancouver; (206) 574-5993; 9803 NE Hwy 99, Vancouver; $; no alcohol; MC, V; checks OK; breakfast, lunch every day, dinner Mon-Sat.*

DeCicco's Italian Ristorante ★ Some come here for the homemade almond biscotti and good coffee, others like the outdoor seating that lends this little Italian cafe in Vancouver a more European air. Lunch is refreshingly unpretentious—polenta with Gorgonzola cheese; seafood pasta or spinach lasagne; a focaccia sandwich; an array of fresh, imaginative salads (from roasted eggplant to an Asian noodle variation). Best of all, nothing exceeds $6. Arrive early because there's not always enough food to last until they close at 5pm. ■ *Between Grant and Franklin sts across from the Courthouse in Vancouver; (206) 693-3252; 611 W 11th St, Vancouver; $, beer and wine; MC, V; checks OK; breakfast, lunch Mon-Fri.*

Hidden House ★ The Hiddens, a leading family in these parts since 1870, made their money with a brick factory. Their handsome (brick, of course) home was opened by Susan Courtney as a restaurant in 1976, and she has succeeded in turning it into a reliable, if old-fashioned, place for an intimate dinner. You are offered a combination of slightly dated small-city standards (pasta primavera, scampi, tenderloin, pork loin medallions with plum sauce). The lunch menu changes every 10 days, providing loyal customers with new combinations of beef, chicken, fish, or salad dishes. A "beggar's banquet" of soup, salad, and homemade poppy seed or banana bread is a midday favorite. If you call ahead, Courtney and her staff will prepare specials such as an unusual Indonesian chicken dish. There's a fairly in-clusive Northwest wine list. A satellite cafe, the Paradise Cafe, is open for breakfast and lunch next door; 304 Main St, (306) 696-1612. Service could be faster in both places. ■ *Corner of 13th and Main in downtown Vancouver; (206) 696-2847; 100 W 13th St, Vancouver; $$ to $$$; beer and wine; AE, MC, V; checks OK; lunch Mon-Fri, dinner Tues-Sun.*

Thai Little Home ★ It's not as fancy as similar joints across the river in Portland, but Serm Pong and his family prepare fresh, homecooked Thai food that locals think is just fine. Yum Nuer (sliced beef salad with cucumber, seasoned with chile and lime juice) rivals the popular Pra Koong (shrimp with chile paste, lemon grass, and lime juice); we've enjoyed both mee krob (Thai crispy noodles) and chicken satay at the beginning of meals. Service is friendly, informed, and fast. ■ *Just north of downtown Vancouver and Clark College; (206) 693-4061; 3214 E Fourth Plain Blvd, Vancouver; $; beer only; AE, MC, V; checks OK; lunch, dinner Mon-Sat.*

Tyrone's Patisserie ★ Gary Galland, who roasts his own cof-fee beans, has had a good thing going for several years in his downtown patisserie, although few other than loyal locals know about it. He cooks up curries, pastas, fresh soups, croissant sandwiches, and generous salads. His place is open for espres-so drinks (made with his own beans), gargantuan bran and car-rot muffins, or scrambled eggs with diced ham for breakfast. Come midday, this countertop restaurant on Vancouver's res-taurant boulevard has a choice of good, fresh bargains: try the angel-hair seafood pasta, any of the soups, or the hearty rata-touille served with a buttery croissant. Around town, Galland's reputation rests as solidly on his fudge cake as on his stew-ardship of jazz—his place often doubles as an afternoon get-away for Northwest musicians. ■ *Downtown Vancouver between Broadway and Main St; (206) 699-1212; 106 E Evergreen Blvd, Vancouver; $; no alcohol; MC, V; checks OK; breakfast, lunch Mon-Fri.* &

CATHLAMET

Cathlamet, seat of Wahkiakum County, is an old-style river town, tied almost as closely to the Columbia as Mark Twain's Hannibal was to the Mississippi. Fishing is everyone's recre-ation—in season, for trout, salmon, and steelhead; all year round for the Columbia's mammoth, caviar-bearing sturgeon. Nearby **Puget Island**, reachable by bridge, is flat dairyland, ideal for cycling; a tiny ferry can take you from there directly across to Oregon.

Send us your feedback on the report form at the back of this book.

Country Keeper in the Bradley House ★ It's not exactly in the country (Main Street, Cathlamet is more exact), but it's certainly a keeper. This former town library is an immaculate 1907 mansion—original decorative hardwood floors, Oriental rugs, light fixtures, period pieces and all. As a tribute to the mansion's former incarnation, the comfortable bedrooms are filled with books. A porch with a distant view of the Columbia invites long afternoon visits in summer. ■ *Just off SR 4, on Main St, north end of town; (206) 795-3030; 61 Main St, Cathlamet, WA 98612; $$; MC, V; checks OK.*

CHINOOK

Nestled on the shores of Baker Bay, part of the broad Columbia River estuary, Chinook was formerly a profitable salmon fish-trapping center. The too-efficient fish traps were outlawed earlier this century. Most of the thousands of wooden pilings visible in the bay at low tide are all that remains of these harvesting contraptions.

Nearby, on Scarborough Hill, is **Fort Columbia State Park**. The former commander's house is now a military museum (nearby is the youth hostel); foreboding concrete bunkers once held huge cannons. Open daily, mid-May to September, but hours vary; (206) 777-8221.

Long Beach Peninsula

RESTAURANTS

The Sanctuary ★ You dine in a deified setting, an old Methodist church, complete with pump organ, stained-glass windows, statues of angelic cherubs watching over you—even pews to sit in, for God's sake. Amid the finery, owner/chef Joanne Leech serves an eclectic array of food, from steak and seafood to svenska kottbullar (Swedish meatballs) and fiskekaker (Scandinavian fish cakes)—both of which can be sampled as appetizers. Preparations can be imaginative, as in a risotto, red pepper, and bean mixture accompanying a recent meal (vegetarians should inquire carefully into their meals). For dessert, homemade sherbet—blackberry one time, lemon another—is, er, heavenly. Light lunches are served in the herb house. ■ *Hwy 101 and Hazel; (206) 777-8380; Chinook; $$; full bar; AE, DC, DIS, MC, V; checks OK; dinner Wed-Sun (Wed-Sat in winter).*

LONG BEACH PENINSULA

The slender finger of land dividing Willapa Bay from the Pacific is famous for its 37-mile-long flat stretch of public beach (reputedly the longest such stretch worldwide); its gentle marine climate; its exhibition kite flying; its cranberry bogs, clamming, and rhododendrons; and for its food, which is unequaled by any like-size area on the Northwest Coast.

Willapa Bay's **Long Island**, reachable only by boat, harbors a 274-acre old-growth cedar grove. Some trees are over 200 feet tall, with trunks 11 feet in diameter. Campsites are available. The island is part of the **Willapa National Wildlife Refuge**, with headquarters on Highway 101, 10 miles north of Seaview; (206) 484-3482.

LONG BEACH PENINSULA: ILWACO

Named after a Chinook Indian chief, Ilwaco is best known as the sport-fishing hub of the lower Columbia River. Two popular sport-fishing operators, both located at the port docks, are **Sea Breeze Charters**, (206) 642-2300, and **Coho Charters**, (206) 642-3333.

The **Ilwaco Heritage Museum** is one of the better small-town museums you're bound to find. It offers not only a look at Southwest Washington history (including native American artifacts and a scale-model glimpse of the Peninsula in the 1920s) but also contains an excellent research library, art gallery, and a whole separate building of train memorabilia; 115 SE Lake Street, in the Convention Center, (206) 642-3446.

Fort Canby State Park covers 2,000 acres stretching from North Head south to Cape Disappointment at the Columbia's mouth. Good surf fishing and wave watching can be had from the North Jetty, two miles of massive boulders separating the ocean and river, with an observation platform for good views. The park also includes hiking and biking trails and 250 campsites; open all year, (206) 642-3078.

Also in the park is the **Lewis and Clark Interpretive Center**, which depicts the explorers' journey from St. Louis to the Pacific, explains the history of Cape Disappointment and North Head lighthouses, and enjoys the best view of the Columbia River bar—a great storm-watching spot. The lighthouses are not open to the public, but may be approached on foot; (206) 642-3029.

LODGINGS

Inn at Ilwaco ★ Located atop a quiet dead-end street overlooking the town of Ilwaco, this bed and breakfast is housed in the old Ilwaco Presbyterian Church. The church has been transformed into a performing arts center (but still a good place for a wedding) that hosts a myriad of community theater productions. The former Sunday school has been converted into nine guest rooms (seven with private bath) with plush bedding, lacy curtains, original wood floors, some even with window seats; privacy seekers will find the walls unfortunately thin. A couple of rooms can accommodate two twin beds, a good choice for families. In the spacious public room, guests take their ample breakfast (quiche, frittata, fruit, baked goods) and read the morning papers. Innkeeper Laurie Blancher provides first-rate hospitality. ■ *Off 4th at 120 Williams St NE; (206)642-8686; PO Box 922, Ilwaco, WA 98624; $$; MC, V; checks OK.*

LONG BEACH PENINSULA: SEAVIEW

RESTAURANTS

The Shoalwater (The Shelburne Inn) ★★★ The Shoalwater remains the finest eating establishment on the Northwest coast and teeters on the verge of winning that fourth star. It's an elegant, understated atmosphere, where the service is easygoing (though sometimes *too* leisurely). Kitchen maestro Cheri Walker continually produces imaginative, artful offerings, always using the Northwest's finest seasonal foods. The fresh seafood is often your best choice, especially if it is locally harvested. Begin with a robust bowl of the innkeeper's mussel and clam chowder, or the sautéed Dungeness crab cakes served with a smooth and understated roasted red pepper mayonnaise. Anything connected with local Willapa Bay oysters is worth a taste, and memorable entrées include a lusty winter cioppino chock full of briny ingredients, or grilled garlic rabbit sausage served on fragrant tomato-onion-cumin fettuccine. A fresh halibut steak might be afforded a reverential cranberry, blueberry, and mustard sauce—pretty to look at as well as to taste. As to dessert, lemon cheesecake is heavenly, bread pudding is perfection, and anything with cranberries is out of this world. The wine list is superlative. Reservations imperative. ■ *In the Shelburne Inn, Pacific Hwy 103 and N 45th; (206) 642-4142; Seaview; $$$; full bar; AE, DC, MC, V; checks OK; dinner every day.* ᕆ

42nd Street Cafe ★ The 42nd Street Cafe is not a cafe at all, but rather a house transformed into an Americana-style restaurant that's warm, unpretentious, and smells good. In fact, the eating experience here is akin to a crowded family reunion. Tables are so closely packed you feel as though you could reach around and tap the woman behind you—is it Aunt Martha?—and inquire about her latest baking exploits. Everyone appreciates a good deal and that's what you get here. Dinners include soup, salad, homemade bread (with corn relish and cranberry conserves), *and* dessert. The food is American Gothic (country-fried steak, pot roast, and fried chicken with overcooked veggies) joined by Peninsula favorites (oysters, often heavily breaded, and halibut). There's an expansive (and inexpensive) array of wine, mostly Washington vintages. Desserts are straightforward and sweet. ■ *42nd St and Pacific Hwy; (206) 642-2323; Seaview; $; beer and wine; MC, V; checks OK; lunch Wed-Sat, dinner Wed-Mon.* ᕆ

The Heron and Beaver Pub ★ There's a feeling of serendipity here. You might slip in for a beer as you wait for your table at the Shoalwater, across the foyer. Then you discover that most of the pub's patrons aren't going anyplace else. They're here because the handsome, pint-size Heron and Beaver is a destination in its own right. If only it weren't so small. Just think of it as cozy as you sip something with a head on it, select from the excellent wine list, or savor a single-malt Scotch. Light meals are available—pasta, pâté, sandwiches, soup, a delectable cheese fondue, or a stout chicken cordon bleu burger—all prepared with the same meticulousness as the food next door. You might even decide to stay. ■ *Pacific Hwy 103 and N 45th; (206) 642-4142; in the Shelburne Inn, Seaview; $$; full bar; AE, DC, MC, V; checks OK; lunch, dinner every day.*

LODGINGS

The Shelburne Inn ★★ You can't see the ocean from here, but you most definitely can feel its allure throughout the historic Shelburne, a creaky but dignified almost century-old structure. Trouble is, there's a busy highway out front, with a well-lit supermarket across the way. Consequently, request a westside room to assure peace and quiet. They're bright and cheerful, with antiqued interiors, private baths, and cozy homespun quilts covering queen-size beds. Don't expect the modern amenities (sauna, Jacuzzi) that have become de rigeur at so many chic hideaways. The third floor offers the best buys ($85), lots of tongue-and-groove woodwork, and gently slanted floors (the entire building was pulled across the street by a team of horses in 1911). Breakfasts are superb: innkeepers David Campiche and Laurie Anderson whip up satisfying eye-openers of razor-clam cakes or scrambled eggs with smoked salmon, chives (from the herb garden out front), and Gruyère cheese—not to mention the pastries. The separately owned Shoalwater (see review in this section) is the dinner restaurant. ■ *Pacific Hwy 103 and N 45th; (206) 642-2442; PO Box 250, Seaview, WA 98644; $$$; AE, MC, V; checks OK.* ♿

Sou'wester Lodge ★ This place is definitely not for everyone, but those who appreciate good conversation, a sense of humor, and rambling lodgings on the beach will find Leonard and Miriam Atkins' humble, old-fashioned resort just what the doctor ordered. The main structure was built in 1892 as a summer home for U.S. Senator Henry Winslow Corbett; you can also stay in fully equipped cabins or a collection of classic trailers. The hosts are as much a draw as the lodgings. Originally from South Africa, they came to Long Beach by way of Israel and Chicago. The view from the lodge's balcony—across windswept, grassy dunes to the sea—is enough to keep them here permanently. Interesting books and periodicals clutter the living room, which also occasionally hosts lectures, chamber music concerts, and informal (but stimulating) conversations. Leonard has deemed this joint the official outpost of the "B & (MYOD)B club"—Bed and (Make Your Own Damn) Breakfast. ■ *1½ blocks southwest of Seaview's traffic light on Beach Access Rd (38th Pl); (206) 642-2542; PO Box 102, Seaview, WA 98644; $; DIS, MC, V; checks OK.*

LONG BEACH PENINSULA: LONG BEACH

Long Beach, the town, boasts a half-mile-long elevated boardwalk (with night lighting) stretching between S 10th and Bolstad streets, accessible by wheelchairs, baby strollers, and, of course, by foot.

Kite lovers can visit the **Long Beach World Kite Museum and Hall of Fame**, Third and N Pacific Highway, (206) 642-4020, or purchase kites at Ocean Kites, 511 S Pacific, (206) 642-2229. August's **International Kite Festival** brings thousands of soaring creations to the skies. The entire peninsula swells with visitors for this event, so plan ahead; (206) 642-2400.

RESTAURANTS

The Lightship Restaurant and Columbia Bar ★ The Lightship is a rare find: a view restaurant with good food. It's housed on the top floor of a boxy Nendel's Inn, and looks like just another poor-quality, high-priced, ocean-front eatery, the type of establishment that seems to proliferate wherever land and sea meet. Disregard all that, for the ocean view, fair prices, and the food make it all worthwhile. Begin with something as unusual as grilled scallops wrapped in bacon with citrus-jalapeño sauce. Pan-fried Willapa Bay oysters are served either lightly floured or heavily dusted with herbed cornmeal. Linguine is fresh, the sauces herby and flavorful. There's breakfast (try the hangtown fry), and lunch selections are extensive; everything done here must pass muster with owners Ann and Tony Kischner (of Shoalwater Restaurant fame). ■ *Between 10th St and the beach; (206) 642-3252; at Nendel's Inn on S 10th, Long Beach; $$; full bar; AE, DC, MC, V; checks OK; breakfast, lunch, dinner every day, brunch Sun (breakfast Sat-Sun in winter).* &

My Mom's Pie Kitchen The name says it all. This is a small establishment that serves a host of homemade pies. Banana cream, pecan, sour-cream raisin, rhubarb, raspberry, and a myriad other concoctions are offered, depending on the time of year and, in some cases, the time of day. Arrive too late (especially in summer), and baker Jeanne McLaughlin might be sold out of your favorite (but it's easy enough to find a satisfying replacement). Before a sweet slice, satisfy yourself with a steamy bowl of chowder or a silky Dungeness crab quiche. Locals wish they could keep this place to themselves, but it has become increasingly popular with summer folks. ■ *Pacific Hwy and 12th St; (206) 642-2342; Long Beach; $; no alcohol; MC, V; checks OK; lunch Tues-Sun.*

LONG BEACH PENINSULA: OCEAN PARK

Ocean Park, founded as a religious settlement, is now a tranquil retirement community with a quiet beach. The **Wiegardt Watercolors Gallery**, 2607 Bay Avenue, (206) 665-5976, displays Eric Wiegardt seascapes in a restored Victorian house.

At the end of the Ocean Park beach approach is **Kopa Wecoma** (no phone), a great place to stop for a good burger or fish 'n' chips in between volleyball games or foot-tingling forays into the cold Pacific. On summer evenings, there's often a line (and lots of wind), so bring a coat.

LODGINGS

Klipsan Beach Cottages ★ This cozy operation, a row of nine small, separate, well-maintained older cottages, stands facing the ocean in a parklike setting of pine trees and clipped lawns. Since these are individually owned condominiums, interior decoration schemes can vary widely, but all of the units feature fireplaces (or wood stoves), full kitchens, and ocean-facing decks just a couple of hundred feet from the beach. Children are fine, but no pets. ■ *Hwy 103, 2 miles south of Ocean Park; (206) 665-4888; 22617 Pacific Hwy, Ocean Park, WA 98640; $$; MC, V; checks OK.* ᕑ

LONG BEACH PENINSULA: NAHCOTTA

Nahcotta has become almost synonymous with oysters. At the **Nahcotta Oyster Farm**, 270th and Sandridge Road, on the old rail line, you can pick up some pesticide-free oysters (or gather your own for half-price); **Jolly Roger Seafoods**, across from The Ark, (206) 665-4111, is also a good bet.

RESTAURANTS

The Ark ★★ The debate continues: Is it or isn't it as good as its reputation? Accolades from up and down the West Coast have built it up to legendary status; unfortunately, such renown is hard to uphold, and in the process, the restaurant has gained some snob appeal but lost some epicurean excitement. On some nights, we wonder where the inventiveness and flair that we have so admired have gone. Recent specials have been bathed in identical sauces billed as a hollandaise and a béarnaise, Boston chowder can be bland, and grilled swordfish has been something less than fresh. Then again, on some nights the restaurant with the picture-perfect setting is still darn good. Calamari Dijonnaise and traditional French onion soup are heavenly meal starters; halibut and salmon (try it pan-fried with chanterelles, lime, and cilantro) are solid entrées. The legendary Ark oyster feed, an unlimited amount (the record is 100) of Willapa Bay bivalves lightly breaded and pan-fried, continues to be the best in, at least, our universe. ■ *On the old Nahcotta dock, next to the oyster fleet; (206) 665-4133; 273rd and Sandridge Rd, Nahcotta; $$$; full bar; DC, DIS, MC, V; checks OK; lunch Thurs-Sat, dinner Tues-Sun, brunch Sun (hours vary off-season).*

LODGINGS

Moby Dick Hotel Although it looks fairly institutional at first glance, this friendly place is one of those that grows on you. Fritzi and Edward Cohen of the Tabard Inn in Washington, DC, first spied the Moby Dick from a window table at the Ark and knew it just needed the care of good innkeepers. So today, the hotel, originally built in 1929 by a railroad conductor with his gold-prospecting money, is under their careful ownership. It's quite beachy (without really having a beach), with a couple of spacious public rooms, 10 small and modest bedrooms (most with shared bath), and a rambling bay front (loaded with oysters). In the afternoon, join the innkeepers for a few Pacific oysters on the half-shell. Full breakfasts (included) make use of the hotel's own garden produce. Like virtually every other place in Nahcotta, you can buy oysters here too. Pets welcome. ■ *South of Bay Ave on Sandridge Rd; (206) 665-4543; PO Box 82, Sandridge Rd, Nahcotta, WA 98637; $$; MC, V; checks OK.*

LONG BEACH PENINSULA: OYSTERVILLE

Oysterville dates to 1854 and was the county seat until (legend has it) a group from South Bend stole the county records in 1893. South Bend remains the county seat to this day, but Oysterville has its own charm. It's listed on the National Register of Historic Places and features a distinctive row of shoreside homes, surrounded by stately cedars and spruce trees. (Follow Sandridge Road north to the Oysterville sign.) Also known for bivalves, **Oysterville Sea Farms**, at the old cannery in Oysterville, sells 'em by the dozen (open weekends, year-round).

   Leadbetter Point State Park, on the northern tip of the peninsula, is a stopover site for over 100 species of birds, and a nature-lover's paradise with miles of sandy trails as well as un-trampled ocean beaches. Hiking trails abound (3 miles north of Oysterville on Stackpole Road).

SOUTH BEND

The sleepy Pacific County seat perches picturesquely on the low bluffs that ring the inside curve of the north arm of Willapa

Bay. The outsize **County Courthouse** two blocks south of US 101 atop "Quality Hill" rules over the town like a medieval castle. On Highway 101 just north of town, **H & H Cafe** is the place to stop for transcendent pie, in rhubarb, blackberry, or four other flavors and fresh-baked daily by the owner (or her granddaughter).

RESTAURANTS

Boondocks ★ South Bend, the historic county seat of Pacific County, bills itself as "The Oyster Capital of the World." That's a classic bit of boosterism, but the oysters *are* world-class, and this pretty little town is coming out of its shell. Boondocks is right on the waterfront, with an outdoor deck and a fine view, not to mention pan-fried fresh Willapa Bay oysters and razor clams. The delicious hangtown fry is a crowd-pleaser at breakfast, and the dinner menu now features combination plates and blackened prime rib. ■ *Hwy 101; (206) 875-5155; 1015 W Robert Bush Dr, South Bend; $$; full bar; MC, V; checks OK; breakfast, lunch, dinner every day.* ♿

TOKELAND

▼

South Bend

▲

Set on the long peninsula reaching into northern Willapa Bay, this crabbing community named after 19th-century Chief Toke is the loneliest part of the southwest coast, where the omnipresent tackiness of contemporary resort life is least apparent. Pick up a container of crabmeat and some cocktail sauce from **Nelson Crab** (open daily 9am-5pm) to enjoy on a driftwood log at the beach across the street, or bring a crab trap and try your luck off the pier at **Toke Point** (warning: seals steal bait).

LODGINGS

Tokeland Hotel This chaste, century-old structure teetered for several years on the edge of genteel collapse until its rescue by two couples who aim to restore fully "the oldest resort hotel in Washington." The remodeling's probably never complete, but all 18 rooms are open. Rooms, some with views of Willapa Bay, are somewhat spartan, and bathrooms are shared. The creaky-floored restaurant is often filled with folks from the surrounding community, who take advantage of reasonable prices, large helpings, and a peaceful setting. Breakfast (included in the price of a room) offers ample choices for everyone, including kids with a yen for pigs in a blanket. ■ *Kindred Ave and Hotel Rd; (206) 267-7006; 100 Hotel Rd, Tokeland, WA 98590; $$; beer and wine; MC, V; local checks only; breakfast every day, lunch Mon-Sat, dinner every day.*

*All the places in this book are recommended; even "no stars"
are worth knowing about.*

GRAYLAND

RESTAURANTS

The Dunes ★ Follow the bumpy gravel road a quarter of a mile down to the dunes. You will discover a funky kind of place that's as comfortable as an old windbreaker: a beachcomber's hideaway, eclectically decorated with shells, ship models, stained glass, and blooming begonias. The main dining room is always warm and wonderful, with a fireplace in the middle and linen-draped oak tables. Unfortunately, the non-smoking section is in the less appealing upstairs. Families are everywhere, especially on Sunday mornings, dressed in their Sunday best or outdoor gear. The restaurant offers a front-row seat on the ocean just beyond the dunes, and you won't find fresher seafood—clams, salmon, crab, and oysters. ■ *Right off Hwy 105 at the sign of the giant razor clam; (206) 267-1441; 783 Dunes Rd, Grayland; $$; beer and wine; AE, MC, V; checks OK; breakfast, lunch, dinner every day (winter hours vary).*

GRAYS HARBOR

Nature's abundance in the area around the estuary continues to help support the economies of its communities, including timber milling and shipping operations in Aberdeen and Hoquiam; charter fishing, whale watching, crabbing, and clam digging in Westport; and cranberry bogging in Grayland. The wild beauty of the expansive bay and the obvious attractions of the coastal beaches draw retirees, tourists, surfers, and migrating shorebirds.

▼

Westport

▲

A half million Arctic-bound shorebirds migrate from as far south as Argentina and congregate on the tidal mudflats at the wildlife refuge of **Bowerman Basin** each spring from about mid-April through the first week of May. At high tide, the birds rise in unison in thick flocks that shiver through the air, twisting and turning, before settling back onto their feeding grounds. There are trails through the marsh (located just beyond the Hoquiam airport). Be sure to wear boots. For more information call the Grays Harbor National Wildlife Refuge, (206) 753-9467.

WESTPORT

For a small coastal town that regularly endures the flood tide of tourists out to catch the Big One, the city of Westport remains surprisingly friendly and scenic. Most fisherfolk rise early and join the almost comically hasty 6am exodus from the breakwater to cross the dreaded bar and head for the open sea. The short **salmon fishing** season has changed charter-boat marketing, so many now feature whale-watching cruises as well. **Gray whales** migrate off the coast March through May on their way toward Arctic feeding waters, where they fatten up for the trip back down to their breeding lagoons in Baja come fall (when waters are too rough to go out and greet them). Breakfast cafes are open by 5am, some much earlier (especially those down by the docks).

You can drop by and pick up a bushel of Brady's Oysters (a shack at water's edge) or take home some great chorizo, kielbasa, or beef jerky, all made on the premises of **Bay City Sausage Company**.

Charter rates vary little from company to company. Some of the **best charters** include Cachalot, (206) 268-0323; Deep Sea, toll-free (800) 562-0151 or (206) 268-9300; Westport, toll-free (800) 562-0157 or (206) 268-9120; Islander, toll-free (800) 562-0147 or (206) 268-9166; Ocean, toll-free (800) 562-0105 or (206) 268-9144; Northwest Educational Tours, (206) 268-9150; Travis, (206) 268-9140. (Toll-free numbers are in operation only during the season.)

Things quiet down until the 3:30pm return of the fleets. You can explore the town during this lull, or head for the expansive beaches—open for driving, jogging, clamming, or picnicking—along the coast from Grayland to Westport. **Surfers** can be found year-round hoping to catch their own Big One at the jetty in Westhaven State Park.

RESTAURANTS

Constantin's Constantin "Dino" Kontogonis, who came to Westport in 1987 "to get away from Seattle," is a Greek with a gift for cooking. Beware only of calories—and garlic. From behind the plastic grapes emerges some chewy, fresh pita bread. Use it to scoop up dollops of skordalia, a delicious garlic-potato-almond dip. A mixed grill combines marinated lamb chop, prawns, and chicken for a Greek spin on the surf-and-turf concept (the lamb was undercooked for our tastes). You're only a stone's throw from the Westport docks, so there's fresh seafood (unfortunately often breaded and fried). A joint venture with the wine shop next door provides Constantin's with an inexhaustible wine list and over three dozen varieties of beer. ■ *½ block from the dock; (206) 268-0550; 320 E Dock St, Westport; $$; beer and wine; AE, MC, V; local checks only; lunch, dinner Wed-Mon (call for winter hours).* ♿

LODGINGS

The Chateau Westport ★ This is considered the fanciest motel lodging in Westport—though it bears no resemblance to any chateau we know. Prices for the 108 units range up from $63; indoor pool and hot tub are available. Studio units have fireplaces and can be rented alone (with a queen-size hide-abed) or in conjunction with adjoining bedrooms to form a suite. It's not the quietest place, and the continental breakfast is nothing to get excited about, but the ocean views are

magnificent; those from the third and fourth floors are best.
■ *W Hancock and S Surf sts, (206) 268-9101; PO Box 349, Westport, WA 98595; $$; AE, DC, DIS, MC, V; no checks.*

Glenacres Inn Turn-of-the-century entrepreneuse Minnie Armstrong ran a horse 'n' buggy service from the docks of Westport to her bed and breakfast, long before B&Bs became the latest thing in charming accommodations. The trees are taller now (so you don't have a sense of the ocean) and you probably won't be arriving by carriage, but the place is back in service—a gabled gem with lots of lodging alternatives and a hot tub, no less. In addition to the five plush bedrooms (all with private baths), there are three simpler "deck" rooms and four cottages on the property. Cleanliness and comfort, however, do not make up for a recent obvious lack of hospitality. And we'll withhold any stars until guests *at least* get a bottomless cup of coffee and a spare towel. ■ *1 block north of the stoplight at 222 N Montesano; (206) 268-9391; PO Box 1246, Westport, WA 98595; $$; MC, V; checks OK.*

COSMOPOLIS

LODGINGS

Cooney Mansion ★★ For many years this 1908 manse housed timber tycoon Neil Cooney, his servants, and his out-of-town guests. There's a very masculine feel to the place (Cooney was a bachelor): spruce wainscoting in the living room, large windows with dark wooden frames, heavy furniture throughout. There are the five main bedrooms, each with private bath. A clubby feel prevails: from the deck on the second floor you can sit and watch golfers on the public course next door, and you see tennis courts as you head up the driveway (they are part of Mill Creek Park, but are available for guests' use). Upstairs in former servants' quarters, new owners Jim and Judi Lohr are opening up three extra bedrooms with more of a comfortable cottage feel. ■ *Follow C St to 5th; (206) 533-0602; 1705 5th St, Cosmopolis, WA 98537; $$; DIS, MC, V; checks OK.*

ABERDEEN/HOQUIAM

With the timber industry in slow decline, these old Siamese-twin lumber towns are in transition, as they have been since the sawmilling and shipping glory days of the early 1900s. At the **Grays Harbor Historical Seaport,** east side of Aberdeen, (206) 532-8611, you can tour a replica of Captain Gray's *Lady Washington*, a 105-foot floating museum offering afternoon and evening cruises in summer around Grays Harbor. **Hoquiam's Castle** gives tours of the mansion, built for a lumberman in 1897; 515 Chenault Avenue, Hoquiam, (206) 533-2005.

Polson Park is a fine house by Arthur Loveless, with a rose garden; 1611 Riverside Avenue, Hoquiam, (206) 533-5862.

RESTAURANTS

Parma ★★ Fortunately for Aberdeen, French-Italian chef Pierre Gabelli loves rain and doesn't like cities. Few urban trattorias can match his excellent pastas and gnocchi—all of it made fresh daily. The place is as spotless as it was when it was Misty's. Gabelli named his restaurant after his birthplace—the northern Italian city where Parmesan cheese was also born. The spaghetti arrabbiata with fresh tomatoes, olives, peppers, and hot spices made a huge hit with Governor Booth Gardner. The fresh-baked bread is wonderfully chewy, and there's a mondo selection of beers and ales, including several Northwest microbrews on tap. The espresso machine is always on. An Italian logger would pronounce it "great ciao." ■ *On Heron, 1 block west of Broadway; (206) 532-3166; 116 W Heron St, Aberdeen; $$; beer and wine; AE, MC, V; checks OK; lunch Tues-Fri and Sun, dinner Tues-Sun.* &

Billy's Bar and Grill ★ The best little whorehouse in town used to be right across the street from this historic pub, and the walls at Billy's sport some original artwork that recalls Aberdeen's bawdy past. The place is named after the infamous Billy Gohl, who terrorized the Aberdeen waterfront in 1907. Billy shanghaied sailors and robbed loggers, consigning their bodies to the murky Wishkah River through a trapdoor in a saloon only a block away from the present-day Billy's—where you get a square-deal meal and an honest drink without much damage to your pocketbook. The thick burgers and ranch fries are popular with everyone. ■ *Corner of Heron and G; (206) 533-7144; 322 E Heron St, Aberdeen; $; full bar; AE, DC, MC, V; local checks; lunch, dinner every day.* &

Bridges ★ Sonny Bridges started out with a corner cafe and kept expanding his horizons, both in space and in taste. An extensive remodel produced an airy, pastel restaurant with casual class. The diverse menu features fresh seafood, including razor clams and salmon, plus prime rib and pasta. Bridges is bolder now, offering some tasty Cajun-style specials, albeit with few surprises. The bar is first-class, with Northwest wines, beers, and espresso drinks. The staff, as always, is extraordinarily professional. ■ *1st and G; (206) 532-6563; 112 N G St, Aberdeen; $$; full bar; AE, DC, DIS, MC, V; local checks only; lunch, dinner every day.* &

The Levee Street ★ With a riverside park, a centennial dock, and some handsome office buildings, Hoquiam is rediscovering its picturesque waterfront. Roy Ann Taylor spent 12 years as a cook at a logging camp, serving up "acres of flapjacks and mounds of meat and potatoes." But apart from good food and

▼

**Aberdeen/
Hoquiam**

▲

generous portions, her restaurant has nothing in common with a cookhouse. There are plum-colored carpets, soft music, and a great view of swooping seagulls and tugboats. The menu offers everything from "Raging Bull"—a logger-size portion of prime rib coated with a port and peppercorn sauce —to salmon fresh from the docks, veal Marsala, and bouillabaisse. Chewy homemade bread sticks accompany the soups and salads. ■ *7th and Levee; (206) 532-1959; 709 Levee St, Hoquiam; $$; full bar; DIS, MC, V; checks OK; dinner Tues-Sat.*

LODGINGS

Lytle House Bed & Breakfast ★ In 1900, when Robert Lytle built what was to become Hoquiam's big architectural landmark, Hoquiam's Castle, his brother Joseph erected a smaller version next door. This has become Lytle House with the almost requisite Victorian embellishments throughout. The front parlor feels too formal for anyone to hunker down in a big chair for reading, but there are more than enough parlors for all and the eight guest rooms are spacious enough. On the second floor the Windsor Room has a small library, an antique wood stove, and a balcony overlooking the town. Guests share the bathrooms, with huge claw-footed tubs that remind you how long it once took to draw a bath. Breakfasts are ample. Owners Robert and Dayna Bencala—he an antique-furniture refinisher and she an Air Force helicopter mechanic—are B&B hosts of the best kind: genuinely hospitable yet unobtrusive. Hoquiam's Castle is somewhat of a tourist attraction, which can sometimes be disruptive to guests. ■ *Head west on Emerson, turn right on Grant, go 3 blocks; (206) 533-2320; 509 Chenault, Hoquiam, WA 98550; $$; MC, V; checks OK.*

MONTESANO

RESTAURANTS

Savory Faire ★ This is a charming place a block away from the handsome and historic Grays Harbor County Courthouse. The restaurant grew out of Candi Bachtell's popular cooking classes at Montesano's ambitious Community School. Breakfasts are wonderful: omelets, country-fried potatoes, and homemade breads. At lunchtime, she can elevate a French dip sandwich to a veritable event. An outdoor patio is available for fair-weather seating. Fresh-baked breads, rolls, and cakes, pasta, and specialty coffees are available for take-out. If a glass of fresh lemonade fails to do the trick, take a dip in Lake Sylvia at the north end of town. ■ *Take Montesano exit off Hwy 12; (206) 249-3701; 135 S Main St, Montesano; $; beer and wine; AE, MC, V; checks OK; breakfast, lunch Mon-Sat (dinner the second Sat of each month by reservation only).*

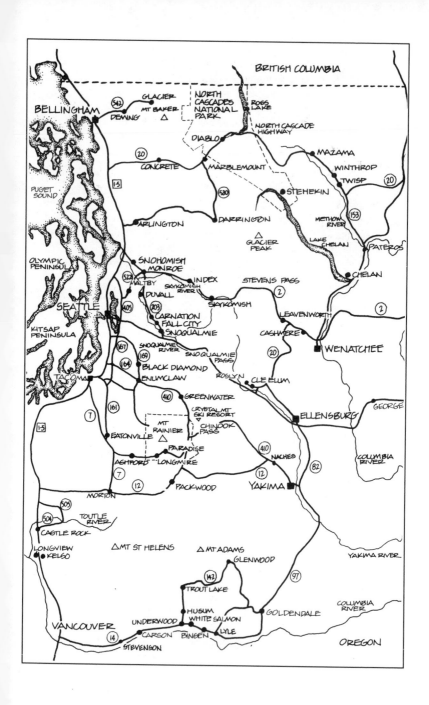

Washington Cascades

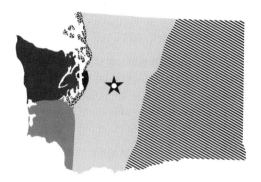

*Easterly crossings, starting in the north from Deming
to Mount Baker, then Concrete to the Methow Valley along
the North Cascades Highway. Farther south in the Cascade
Loop: eastward along Highway 2 to Cashmere, south to Cle
Elum, westward again on I-90. The two Mount Rainier
approaches—Maple Valley to Chinook Pass or Eatonville to
Ashford—followed by a southward route through the heart of
the Cascades, past Mount St. Helens, and a short easterly jog
along the Columbia River (including Mount Adams).*

DEMING

RESTAURANTS

Deming Tavern ★ In operation since 1922, this is one of the
few real steak houses left hereabouts. It's not a fancy place, but
everyone (a mix of loggers, suburbanites, and Bellingham city
slickers) comes for the steak. You can get a tender, well-aged
6-ounce tenderloin for $8.50, a 16-ouncer for $14.50. The ultimate challenge here: you can have a 72-ounce steak, with a
baked potato and spaghetti, for *free*—provided you can eat the
whole thing in half an hour. If you can't, it's $36.95. Reserve
in advance. So far, everyone has paid up. Twelve beers on tap.
■ *Off Mount Baker Hwy at Deming Rd and 1st St; (206)
592-5282; 5016 Deming Rd, Deming; $$; beer and wine; no
credit cards; checks OK; lunch, dinner every day.*

Carol's Coffee Cup Carol's is a local institution: a pleasant little hamburger joint/bakery/cafe, long a favorite with loggers, skiers, and hikers. The hamburgers are fine, but the big cinnamon rolls and homemade pies are best. Be prepared for a long wait on summer weekends and during the peak of the Koma Kulshan (Mount Baker) ski season. ■ *1½ miles east of Deming at Mt Baker Hwy; (206) 592-5641; 5414 Mt Baker Hwy, Deming; $; no alcohol; MC, V; checks OK; breakfast, lunch, dinner every day.* ⌖

GLACIER

RESTAURANTS

Innisfree ★★ Discriminating folks are lured from Seattle and Vancouver to Fred and Lynn Berman's special treatment and food at Innisfree. The Bermans are organic farmers, and they opened the restaurant as a reliable outlet for their produce (you'll find fresh berries, light steamed vegetables tossed in creative combinations). Over the years they've honed their cooking skills to the point of excellence at this cabin-in-the-woods experience. The menu is simple but intriguing. This cuisine is pure, ever-changing Northwest eclectic: Nooksack Valley fowl, beef and veal, or halibut (with strawberry butter, perhaps). The finisher, tart local blueberries with the Bermans' homemade kefir (from a culture they brought back from Norway), was exceptionally flavorful. You can sit up front, but it's better to wait for a seat in the light and airy dining room. For a getaway evening in Washington's own north woods, you can't do better. ■ *31 miles east of Bellingham on Mt Baker Hwy; (206) 599-2373; 9393 Mt Baker Hwy, Glacier; $$; beer and wine; MC, V; checks OK; dinner Thurs-Mon (summer), Fri-Sun (winter).*

Milano's Market and Deli Popular with locals and carbo-loading hikers and skiers alike, this tiny, clean restaurant is really three: a deli (with meats and sandwiches), a casual Italian restaurant (with hearty pastas and a good, well-priced wine selection), and a nice place for dessert and coffee. The pasta is made fresh daily and stars in dishes ranging from two different lasagnes to a filling chicken Gorgonzola to a slew of wonderful raviolis (including a woodsy porcini mushroom ravioli in a delicate, herby marinara). The deck outside boasts a Mt. Baker view. ■ *Mt Baker Hwy in Glacier; (206) 599-2863; 9990 Mt Baker Hwy, Glacier; $$; beer and wine; MC, V; checks OK; lunch, dinner every day, breakfast Sat-Sun (closed Tues in winter).*

LODGINGS

The Logs ★ Five log cabins nestled among dense stands of alder and fir at the confluence of the Nooksack River and Canyon Creek comprise this rustic retreat. The only remaining signs of the floods that caused a lot of damage a few years ago are the extensive piles of rock which widened the riverbed considerably. Cabins are comfortable, not luxurious: they sleep up to 10 people in bunk-bedded rooms and on pull-out couches. The centerpoint of each cabin is the large fireplace (built from river cobbles and slabs of Nooksack stone), stocked with lots of firewood. Each cabin also has a fully equipped kitchen, as well as a charcoal grill. There's a pool and a volleyball court as well. A great place to bring the kids and the family dog. ■ *30 miles east of Bellingham on Mt Baker Hwy; (206) 599-2711; 9002 Mount Baker Hwy, Deming, WA 98244; $$; no credit cards; checks OK.*

MOUNT BAKER

Mount Baker Ski Area, 56 miles east of Bellingham, has gained quite a reputation with snowboarders. It's now open from mid-November through May (the longest season in the state). The mountain never lacks for snow, and runs are predominantly intermediate, with bowls, meadows, and trails. Call (206) 734-6771.

Hiking in the area is extensive and beautiful, especially in the late summer when the foliage is turning, the wild blueberries are ripe, and the days are hot and dry. The end of the road (which in winter doubles as the Mount Baker Ski Resort) is a jump-off point for some easy day hikes and spectacular views of both Mount Baker and the most photographed mountain in the world, the geographically eccentric **Mount Shuksan**. For trail and weather conditions call the Glacier Public Service Center, (206) 599-2714.

Concrete

Lodgings

CONCRETE

LODGINGS

Cascade Mountain Inn ★★ Here's one of the few bed and breakfasts that began life as an inn, not as a residence. Ingrid and Gerhard Meyer celebrated their retirement by building this spacious log inn on 10 acres in the Upper Skagit Valley, near where hundreds of bald eagles gather in the winter. There are six immaculate guest rooms, each named after a different country where the Meyers have lived; in the German room, piles of down gently pillow you to sleep. Breakfast is served in a cozy dining room or on the patio with its calming views of the North Cascades. The convivial Meyers will pack you a picnic for your jaunt into the surrounding countryside if you'd like—they're close to both Baker Lake and the North Cascades National Park. A lovely place. ■ *5 miles west of Concrete, off Hwy 20; (206) 826-4333; 3840 Pioneer Lane, Concrete-Birdsview, WA 98237; $$; MC, V; checks OK; closed Oct 1–May 14.*

MARBLEMOUNT

Eagle watching. Hundreds of bald eagles perch along the Skagit River from December through March. The best area to view these scavengers is along Route 20 between Rockport and Marblemount (bring your binoculars). You'll be able to spy a number from the road; however, the best way to view them is from the river; call **Downstream River Runners**, (206) 483-0335; **Northern Wilderness River Riders**, (206) 448-RAFT; or **Orion Expeditions**, (206) 322-9130.

RESTAURANTS

Mountain Song Restaurant This serve-yourself restaurant makes for a nourishing stop along the North Cascades Highway. Homemade breads and organically grown vegetables become big sandwiches; soups, salads, and quiches round out the menu along with pasta, chicken, and fish on the specials list (but never anything deep-fried). A lunchtime buffet of soup, salad bar, and homemade breads is a filling bargain. For dessert, try a slice of fresh berry pie. Northwest microbreweries and vitners are well represented. The feeling is rustic and faintly countercultural, with a wood stove and hanging plants inside, a pleasant, tree-ringed garden outside. No smoking. ■ *In middle of town on Hwy 20; (206) 873-2461; 5860 Hwy 20, Marblemount; $; beer and wine; AE, DIS, MC, V; checks OK; breakfast, lunch, dinner every day May-Sept (closed Nov-March; open part-time April and October).*

▼
Marblemount
▲

DIABLO

Since the only road access to Ross Lake is south from Hope, BC, the best way to get to the southern end of the lake—save by a 3½-mile hike—is on the Seattle City Light tugboat from Diablo. Here Seattle City Light built an outpost for crews constructing and servicing the dams on the river. The tugboat leaves twice daily (8:30am and 3pm), runs from mid-June through the end of October, and the ride costs $2.50; (206) 386-4393.

Worth visiting are the dams themselves, built by a visionary engineer named James Delmage Ross. **Skagit Tours** offers 4-hour journeys through the Skagit Project, including an informative slide presentation, a ride up an antique incline railway to Diablo Dam, then a boat ride along the gorge of the Skagit to Ross Dam, a construction of daring engineering in its day. Afterward there is a lavish chicken dinner back in Diablo; Seattle City Light, 1015 Third Ave, Seattle, WA 98104, (206) 684-3030; summer only; reserve well in advance.

Our evaluations are based on numerous reports from local experts and final judgements are made by the editors. Our inspectors never identify themselves (except over the phone) and never accept free meals or other favors. You can help too, by sending us a report.

MAZAMA

LODGINGS

Mazama Country Inn ★★ With a view of the North Cascades from nearly every window, this spacious 6,000-square-foot lodge makes a splendid year-round destination (especially for horse-back riders and cross-country skiers), with 10 good-size rooms of wooden construction with cedar beams (a wing offers four additional rooms). Some of the guest rooms now have air conditioning, which is a plus, especially on hot summer nights. Each room has a private bath, thick comforters on the beds, and futonlike pads that can be rolled out for extra guests. The four rooms behind the sauna have individual decks, two with views of Goat Peak and two looking out into the woods. Prices are reasonable, and many winter packages include three meals. Although the kitchen works at serving big, family-style meals in the winter, summers are à la carte with about 10 entrées to choose from (salmon to prime rib to spaghetti). Pasta remains the best choice for dinner. Meals for non-guests require reservations (even though seating is made only every 15 minutes); even guests must reserve for dinner in the summer.

The original inn, a converted ranchhouse, lacks the charm of the new one. The six rooms there (which share two baths) are used only during busy periods (or rented to groups). Families might want to try one of the two cabins that sleep up to six, especially since children under 13 are discouraged in the quiet lodge during the winter. ■ *14 miles west of Winthrop; (509) 996-2681 or (800) 843-7951; PO Box 275, Mazama, WA 98833; $$; beer and wine; MC, V; checks OK; breakfast, lunch, dinner every day.*

Winthrop

WINTHROP

Stroll through this Western-motif town and stop in at the **Shafer Museum**, housed in pioneer Guy Waring's 1897 log cabin on the hill behind the main street. Exhibits tell of the area's early history and include old cars, a stagecoach, and horse-drawn vehicles. It is said that Waring's Harvard classmate Owen Wister came to visit in the 1880s and found some of the material for *The Virginian* here.

The Early Winters' plan for a destination downhill resort took the proverbial plunge last year, but pilgrims to the valley know there is plenty to do here for the outdoor enthusiast even without the help of a lift. The valley offers fine whitewater rafting, spectacular hiking in the North Cascades, horseback riding, fishing, and cross-country or helicopter skiing (call Central Reservations for more information; see below). An excellent blues festival in the summer brings in such talents as John Mayall and the Bluesbreakers and Mick Taylor (see Calendar).

Methow Valley Central Reservations is a booking service for the whole valley—Mazama to Pateros—as well as a good source of information on things to see and do and on current ski conditions. Write PO Box 505, Winthrop, WA 98862, or call (800) 422-3048 or (509) 996-2148.

Hut-to-Hut Skiing offers miles of cross-country ski trails connecting with three spartan huts in the Rendezvous Hills. Each hut bunks up to eight people and comes equipped with a wood stove and a propane cookstove. Open for day skiers—a warm, dry lunch stop. For Rendezvous Huts information, call the Central Reservations office listed above.

RESTAURANTS

Riverside Rib ★ This unassuming restaurant smack in the middle of town is a local favorite, day after day after day. Huge platters of quesadillas come stacked with either sausage, barbecued chicken, or soy burgers, then heaped with Riverside's own beans, cheese, salsa, chiles, and sour cream. All summer long what you get will probably be off the grill out front. In the winter, owners Patty Yeats and Jim Gerlach let the chefs cut loose and cook some of their whimsy on the stove. Dive into the mud pie for dessert or slither down the espresso moose mud slide (named after the gooey mess left on the North Cascades Highway last spring). Locals lament when the Riverside closes for the months of November and March. ■ *At the corner of Riverside Rd (Main St) and Hwy 20; (509) 996-2001; 207 Riverside Dr, Winthrop; $$; beer and wine; no credit cards; checks OK; lunch, dinner every day May-Sept (dinner Thurs-Sun in winter).*

Duck Brand Cantina, Bakery, and Hotel Built to replicate a frontier-style hotel, Duck Brand is a Winthrop standby for good, filling meals at good prices. The menu ranges from bulging burritos to fettuccine to sprout-laden sandwiches on whole-grain breads. The smooth homemade salsa has plenty of zip. The American-style breakfasts feature wonderful cheesy Spanish potatoes and billowing omelets. The in-house bakery produces wonderful baked goods from biscotti to giant cinnamon rolls to 3-inch-thick berry pie. When you're not in the mood for painfully slow service, just take the sweets to go. Upstairs, the Duck Brand Hotel has six homey, sparsely furnished rooms, but the price is right (around $49 for two). ■ *On the main street; (509) 996-2192; 248 Riverside Ave, Winthrop; $; beer and wine; AE, MC, V; local checks only; breakfast, lunch, dinner every day.*

LODGINGS

Sun Mountain Lodge ★★★ When the European-based Haub family took over this resort, they made a few changes—$20 million worth. The location has always been dramatic, set on a hill high above the pristine Methow Valley and backed by the North Cascades. Now the massive timber-and-stone resort is equally impressive. Ask for one of the rooms in the 28 Gardner unit. They are dressed in natural colors, from the hand-painted bedspreads to the bent-willow headboards. Each new room has a gas fireplace (only those in the suites burn wood) and a view of the spectacular Methow Valley. Rooms in the main lodge are more standard. In addition there are eight rustic cabins available just down the hill at Patterson Lake. In winter, over 50 miles of well-groomed cross-country trails make this a haven for Nordic skiers (with 150 miles available throughout the valley). Expert instructors are available for skiers of any level. Close by are a heated pool (summers only), a hot tub, and tennis courts. In summer there are also guided nature hikes through the wilderness, brisk breakfast trail rides, and outfitter pack trips as well. The restaurant now offers a great table to every guest, whether it's a warm spot by the massive stone fireplace or a window table with a sweeping view of the valley. The food takes second place to the setting. The best dishes are those that don't challenge the kitchen. And although the wine list is well chosen, we wish the staff were more informed on the bottlings. ■ *9 miles southwest of Winthrop on Patterson Lake Rd; (509) 996-2211; PO Box 1000, Winthrop, WA 98862; $$$; full bar; AE, MC, V; checks OK; breakfast, lunch, dinner every day.*

WolfRidge Resort ★ Finally, with a total of 12 condo-style units in three big new log buildings and a conference pavilion, it appears as if construction at this resort, at the edge of a Methow meadow, is beginning to settle down. The resort itself sits both literally and metaphorically somewhere between the home-style Mazama Country Inn and the more showy Sun Mountain Lodge. The lodgings are tastefully, if simply, furnished and provide families and small groups with a full kitchen in each unit. The design allows the flexibility of being able to rent an entire unit (complete with kitchen) or a suite or just a single room. Whatever suits your needs. The 50-acre setting includes a pool, hot tub, playground, and barbecue area. Horseback riders are referred to the local outfitters. ■ *5 miles northwest of Winthrop on Wolf Creek Rd; (509) 996-2828; Wolf Creek Rd, Rt 2, Box 655, Winthrop, WA 98862; $$; DIS, MC, V; checks OK.* &

TWISP

RESTAURANTS

The Queen of Tarts and Confluence Gallery ★ This cafe with adjoining gallery makes for a new twist in Twisp, a town dominated by hardware and feed stores. The breakfast-and-lunch cafe features delicious homemade soups, such as curried lentil served with a crusty chunk of bread, and fresh salads and sandwiches, as well as the specialty, quiche tarts (try tomato mushroom or crab). The gallery showcases works of local and regional artists. ■ *On the main street; (509) 997-1335; 104 Glover St, Twisp; $; no alcohol; no credit cards; checks OK; breakfast, lunch Mon-Fri, Sat from May-Oct.*

METHOW

RESTAURANTS

Cafe Bienville ★ Jim and Louise Swickard might be newcomers to the area but they're not newcomers to the restaurant scene. You might recognize some of the dishes (blackened catfish, gumbo, or bouillabaisse) from their New Orleans Kitchens in Wenatchee or South Lake Tahoe. You can find select Creole, Cajun, or classic French eats from the menu, which has more entrées than the restaurant has tables. There's lots of flavor here, and it's not all in the food. Jim Swickard loves to pour you a glass of wine, and he's got a great list to choose from. ■ *Can't miss it; (509) 923-2228; Methow; no credit cards; checks OK; dinner Wed-Sat.*

PATEROS

LODGINGS

Amy's Manor ★★ Orchardists Barb and Rodney Nickell opened their enchanting three-bedroom home as a B&B a few years ago to keep it in the family. Built in 1928, the manor is dramatically situated at the foot of the Cascades overlooking the Methow River, and the rooms are country-quaint, with patchwork quilts tossed over rocking chairs and comfortable beds. The 170-acre estate includes a small farm where chickens and rabbits wander freely. A continental-plus breakfast is served (something easy but filling). ■ *5 miles north of Pateros on Hwy 153; (509) 923-2334; PO Box 411, Pateros, WA 98846; $$; MC, V; checks OK.*

LEAVENWORTH

A railroad-yard-and-sawmill town that lost its industry, Leavenworth, with its stunning alpine setting in the Cascade Mountains, decided years ago to recast itself as a Bavarian-style town with tourism as its primary industry. The architecture in the city center features some excellent craftsmanship in the Bavarian mode. We recommend browsers head to the **Gingerbread Factory** for authentic decorated gingerbread cookies and a delightful village of gingerbread houses, 828 Commercial Street; **Images and Sounds** for distinctly non-Bavarian posters, prints, and notecards, Ninth and Commercial; the **Black Swan** and

Ugly Duckling for boutique fashions and children's wear, 827 Front Street; Village Books for an excellent collection of books about the Northwest, books by Northwest authors, and cookbooks, 215 Ninth Street; The Wood Shop for colorful wooden children's puzzles and Christmas tree ornaments, 719 Front Street; Die Musik Box for a dazzling (and sometimes rather noisy) array of music boxes, 837 Front Street; and the Alpen Haus's miniature shop for a fascinating collection of dollhouse furniture and miniatures, downstairs at 807 Front Street.

Oberland Bakery and Cafe relies largely on whole-grain breads, but also does a great raspberry Danish. The restaurant is spare, but they also serve hearty soups and sandwiches on their substantial breads; 703 Front Street, (509) 548-7216. Other attractions include Homefires Bakery, where visitors can see the German-style, wood-fired oven (the nine-grain bread is the thing to get, but don't pass up the dark German rye bread) and during fair weather can sit at the picnic table on the lawn and have cinnamon rolls and coffee; 13013 Bayne Road (off Icicle Road). There's also the new Leavenworth Brewery at 636 Front Street, which has six or seven beers made on the premises on tap (the types of beers rotate with the season), and offers daily tours of the small brewery itself.

Outdoor activities include river rafting on the Wenatchee; fishing and hiking at Icicle Creek; touring the national fish hatchery on Icicle Creek to watch the chinook salmon run (June and July) and spawn (August and September), 12790 Fish Hatchery Road (off Icicle Road), (509) 548-7641; golfing at the scenic 18-hole Leavenworth Golf Club, (509) 548-7267; downhill skiing at Stevens Pass, (206) 973-2441, or Mission Ridge, (509) 663-6543; fabulous cross-country skiing around the area, at the golf course, on Icicle Road just past the Fish Hatchery, or at the Leavenworth Nordic Center, (509) 548-7864; horseback riding at Eagle Creek Ranch, (509) 548-7798; sleigh rides behind Belgian draft horses at Red-Tail Canyon Farm, (509) 548-4512; walking along the river on a new city center trail system which leads via wheelchair-accessible ramps to Blackbird Island; mountain biking with rentals available at Icicle Bicycle at the Leavenworth Nordic Center, (509) 548-7864; and rock climbing in the new Peshastin Pinnacles State Park just 10 miles east of Leavenworth (no camping, just climbing).

Scottish Lakes Snomad Camps, 8 miles into the backcountry west of Leavenworth, is a cluster of primitive plywood cabins at the edge of the Alpine Lakes Wilderness Area. It's most popular with backcountry skiers, but open (and less expensive) for hikers come summer. You can ski up the 8 miles or be carted up in a snowmobile and ski home the 3,800-foot descent; PO Box 312, Leavenworth, WA 98826, (509) 548-7330, by reservation only.

Edel Haus Inn ★ Edel Haus got its start as a bed and break-fast; however, today it's a quiet, pleasant restaurant with an international menu. The pot-stickers could use a slight crisping and the cream of broccoli soup a few fresh herbs; but the caesar salad remains true to the original recipe. The menu changes about once a month, and its biggest fault is that it tries to do too much. But what it does is at least more than satisfactory. A special of swordfish served with a saffron-shallot sauce and grilled red and yellow peppers is moist and delicious; the chicken piccata, though tasty, could benefit from a lighter sauce. Desserts are bound to be legendary: mocha espresso sour-cream cheesecake with a chocolate amaretto sauce. Upstairs, there are several pretty rooms, and next door there's a cottage suite with a Jacuzzi and gas fireplace. The Edel Haus Inn doesn't serve breakfast to its overnight guests, but does offer them a 50 percent discount on the other meals. ■ *On 9th between Commercial and the river; (509) 548-4412; 320 9th St, Leavenworth; $$; beer and wine; MC, V; local checks only; dinner every day (Wed-Sun from Jan-April), lunch weekends only.*

▼

Terrace Bistro ★ Locals continue to recommend the Terrace as one of the best restaurants in Leavenworth. At least one good reason: this second-floor eatery leaves the German food alone (okay, there is *one* wiener schnitzel on the menu). At the bistro, favorites are chicken Jerusalem (chicken breasts grilled with bread crumbs, parsley, basil, Parmesan cheese, and served with artichoke sauce) and tortellini with shrimp. The medallions of pork tenderloin sautéed in a brandied cream sauce were rich and tender. As the name implies, there's a terrace for fair-weather dining. The meal is unhurried and it's easy to linger over coffee and dessert. Service is attentive and hospitable, though the atmosphere and presentation are a bit heavy-handed; reservations recommended. ■ *On the corner of 8th and the alley between Commercial and Front; (509) 548-4193; 200 8th St, Leavenworth; $$; full bar; AE, DIS, MC, V; checks OK; lunch, dinner every day.*

Walter's Other Place ★ Locals frequented the Terrace Bistro so often that Walter Wilmouth opened a second restaurant just so they wouldn't have to go to the same restaurant two nights in a row. Turns out we're not the only ones who actually prefer the downscaled atmosphere of this place to the more affected Terrace. On ground level (just down from the Terrace Bistro), this place is smaller and simpler in decor and menu. The prices are lower (where they should be), and the food, primarily unfussy Italian and Greek, is just as good. ■ *Commercial St; (509) 548-6125; 820 Commercial St, Leavenworth; $$; beer and wine; DIS, MC, V; checks OK; dinner every day.*

Reiner's Gasthaus For the quintessential Bavarian culinary experience in Leavenworth, Reiner's is the place. The menu offers Austrian and Hungarian specialties as well. The smoked Bavarian-style farmer's sausage with sauerkraut and German rye bread is a safe selection for the uninitiated. More adventuresome eaters can try the homemade dumplings (boiled liver, egg, and bread) served with melted cheese for lunch; or the schnitzel topped with paprika sauce or the Hungarian goulash for dinner. Seating is European-style (which means tables are sometimes shared); service is prompt and knowledgeable. Because it's located on the second floor at the back of the buildings on Front Street, the views of the town from the restaurant are slim (although a tiny balcony seats a few patrons in good weather). There's a wide selection of imported wines and beers. Have dessert somewhere else. ■ *Across from the gazebo; (509) 548-5111; 829 Front St, Leavenworth; $; beer and wine; MC, V; local checks only; lunch, dinner every day.*

LODGINGS

All Seasons River Inn ★★ Each of the five guest rooms in this outstanding inn takes advantage of the Wenatchee River view with a private deck or patio and an indoor seating area in front of sliding glass doors. Rooms are furnished with unusual antiques. Each room has a spacious, gleaming private bath, and several offer Jacuzzis. Owners Kathy and Jeff Falconer encourage socializing with other guests by offering dessert each night in front of the living room fireplace. A hearty, filling breakfast is served family-style at 8:30 each morning. Mountain bikes are available, and the owners have a wealth of knowledge about the area and its restaurants. ■ *1 mile off Hwy 2 on Icicle Rd; (509) 548-1425; 8751 Icicle Rd, Leavenworth, WA 98826; $$$; MC, V; checks OK.*

Run of the River ★★ Built on the bank of the Icicle River, this log-construction bed and breakfast boasts such solitude and comfort that you may want to spend the entire day on the deck, reading or watching the wildlife in the refuge across the river with the provided binoculars. Hosts Monty and Karen Turner run Leavenworth's finest B&B, and every year it just keeps getting better. There are six rooms, each with hand-hewn log bed, private bath, TV (cable), deck, and terrycloth robes. The rooms facing the river have commanding views of the mountains. The Aspens, warmed by a wood stove, has perhaps the best river view, but the Jacuzzi in the Pinnacles suite is a nice attribute. Hearty breakfasts emphasize the seasonal discoveries from a local organic farmer and the Turners' own herb farm. There's a Jacuzzi on the deck near the river, and mountain bikes are available for off-road explorations (a complimentary cruise up Icicle Canyon is offered to guests). This is an excellent getaway for adults, and the in-room massage gives a new meaning to R and R at the R of the R. No smoking whatsoever. ■ *1 mile east of Hwy 2 at 9308 E Leavenworth Rd; (509) 548-7171 or (800) 288-6491; PO Box 285, Leavenworth, WA 98826; $$; AE, MC, V; checks OK.*

Haus Lorelei Inn ★ Here's a rarity: a bed and breakfast that not only welcomes kids but is run by several of them (and their mom). The two-acre site, surrounded by towering pines and flanking the Icicle River, is only two blocks from Leavenworth's main street and provides many activities for the younger guests. Elisabeth Saunders and her children offer eight bedrooms furnished in comfortable European tradition, all with private baths. Each of the rooms affords gorgeous views of the Cascades; at night you can hear the river rushing over the boulders. During the summer months, guests eat on the screened sun porch and may use the private tennis court. There's a hot tub overlooking the river, and a short walk away there's a sandy swimming beach. ■ *2 blocks off Commercial on Division; (509) 548-5726; 347 Division St, Leavenworth, WA 98826; $$; no credit cards; checks OK.*

Haus Rohrbach Pension ★ It's a true European pension, with alpine architecture, gracious hosts, and breakfast included with the room. Most rooms now have private baths. The lodge is tucked into the base of Tumwater Mountain, so it has a nearly Bavarian view over the valley farmland back toward town and the snow-clad mountains. Most of the rooms open onto a flower-decked balcony facing this direction, and the delicious, ample breakfast is served on a large deck with the same majestic vista. The rooms are decorated rather austerely; those on the uppermost floor facing the valley have the most light and appeal, unless you want to spring for one of the very appealing, newly renovated suites, which offer king-size beds, whirlpool tubs, gas fireplaces, and private decks. Bring the kids—there's a swimming pool, and a sled hill out back (although the new suites are reserved for adults and children over 12). Sometimes a naturalist will drop by to give an evening talk. ■ *About ½ mile off Ski Hill Dr; (509) 548-7024; 12882 Ranger Rd, Leavenworth, WA 98826; $$; AE, DIS, MC, V; checks OK.*

Mountain Home Lodge ★ There's a lot to do here. Miles of tracked cross-country ski trails leave from the back door; you can snowshoe and sled, and there's a 1,700-foot toboggan run. Complimentary cross-country ski loans are available at the lodge. There's a Jacuzzi on the deck looking out to a broad meadow and the mountains across the valley. Summer activities include hiking, horseshoe pitching, badminton, swimming, and tennis. And that's a good thing, because there aren't many places to gather when the weather's not cooperating. The nine rooms themselves are very plain (almost motelish), and noise still travels from bedroom to bedroom. No children.

Straightforward meals are included in the price during the winter. Winter weekend reservations should be made a few months ahead of time. A heated snow-cat will pick you up from the parking lot at Duncan Orchard Fruit Stand, just east of Leavenworth. In the summer, Mountain Home is accessible over 3 miles of dirt road, appropriately labeled primitive. ■ *Mountain Home Rd off E Leavenworth Rd and Hwy 2; (509) 548-7077; PO Box 687, Leavenworth, WA 98826; $$$; AE, MC, V; checks OK.*

Mrs. Anderson's Lodging House ★

Though it has been through other incarnations (it originally opened in 1903 as a boardinghouse for sawmill workers), this 10-room inn right in the center of Leavenworth has charm to spare and very friendly operators. It's basic—rooms are minimally, crisply furnished, boardinghouse-style—but sparkling clean, with pristine white-washed walls and lace curtains. It's a bargain: the two that share baths cost $44 and $49; the rest, with private baths, average $63 a night. (All prices include breakfast of muffins, cereal, juice, tea, and coffee.) We fancy the room upstairs with the deck facing town, or the room with the splendid view of the North Cascades. ■ *Just off the center of town at 917 Commercial St; (509) 548-6173 or (800) 253-8990; PO Box 158, Leavenworth, WA 98826; $$; DC, MC, V; checks OK.*

Leavenworth

Lodgings

River Chalet ★

An ideal vacation spot for groups of couples, this contemporary guest house on the east side of Leavenworth gives the visitor a real feel for the Northwest. It's right on the Wenatchee River, and large windows look out toward the mountains. Three bedrooms sleep 10 comfortably (but slumber parties of 22 sleeping-baggers have occurred); wood stoves keep you warm. Outside there's a hot tub. In winter there's ample skiing all around, and a large kitchen makes gourmet collaborations a pleasure. Cost is $200 for four. Catering can be arranged on request. ■ *4 miles west of Leavenworth off Hwy 2; (509) 663-7676 or (800) 323-2920; 1131 Monroe St, Wenatchee, WA 98801; $$$; no credit cards; checks OK.*

Enzian Motor Inn

This is the best hotel/motel place in town. Built by former contractor Bob Johnson and his son, Robert, it is now owned by the father/son team and their wives. Equal parts owners and contractors, they were meticulous about detail throughout. Stair rails and ceiling beams are hand-carved by a true Bavarian woodworker. The suites offer in-room spas and fireplaces; even the standard rooms are tasteful and a cut above most "motor inns." Breakfast (included with the price of a room) is served in the large fourth-floor breakfast solarium. During the summer the older Johnson plays the alpenhorn on the balcony outside the dining room. ■ *On the north side of*

Hwy 2 in the center of town; (509) 548-5269 or (800) 223-8511; 590 Hwy 2, Leavenworth, WA 98826; $$; AE, DC, DIS, MC, V; checks OK. &

CASHMERE

If you're not in a Bavarian mood, this little orchard town gives cross-mountain travelers an alternative to stopping in Leavenworth. The main street has put up Western storefronts; the town's bordered by river and railroad.

Chelan County Historical Society and Pioneer Village has an extensive collection of Indian artifacts and archaeological material; the adjoining pioneer village puts 19 old buildings, carefully restored and equipped, into a nostalgic grouping. 600 Cottage Avenue, (509) 782-3230.

Aplets and Cotlets. These confections, made with local fruit and walnuts from an old Armenian recipe, have been produced for decades; you can tour the plant at Liberty Orchards and (of course) consume a few samples. 117 Mission Street, (509) 782-2191.

RESTAURANTS

The Pewter Pot Here you can get Early American food such as apple country chicken topped with owner Kristi Biornstad's own apple cider sauce, Plymouth turkey dinner, and New England boiled dinner. Desserts are tasty. The restaurant, short on atmosphere, has been prettied with lace curtain dividers which help soften the lone room. Biornstad works hard to serve dishes that reflect the area, using local ingredients. Try one of the daily specials. But if you want dinner, arrive early; the place closes promptly at 8pm even on Saturdays. ■ *Downtown Cashmere in the business district; (509) 782-2036; 124 Cottage Ave, Cashmere; $$; beer and wine; MC, V; checks OK; lunch, dinner Tues-Sat.* &

LODGINGS

Cashmere Country Inn ★★ In the middle of Aplet-and-Cotlet country, consummate innkeepers Patti and Dale Swanson have created a first-class inn. The Swansons are energetic but never intrusive, full of enthusiasm about the area, and genuinely concerned for the well-being of their guests; the farmhouse and its gardens are fitted out with a keen eye for aesthetics. The four guest rooms are a bit smaller than what you might expect for a place of such ambitions, but we'll trade in extra dimension for such attention to details any day (turndown service, a lit fire in the fireplace, complimentary Saturday night dessert). A fifth room with French doors opening to the swimming pool and hot tub area should be available by publication time. Breakfasts here don't taste like an innkeeper's duty so much as an accomplished cook's delight. Patti will also do a lovely candlelit five-course dinner with advance notice (by the pool if you'd like). Take advantage of this place any time of the year: in winter for the ski packages, in summer for poolside lounging, in fall for the apples (and the fresh cider). ■ *Off Hwy 2, follow Division to Pioneer; (509) 782-4212; 5801 Pioneer Ave, Cashmere, WA 98815; $$; AE, MC, V; checks OK.*

THORP

LODGINGS

Circle H Holiday Ranch ★★ Sweeping views of the Kittitas Valley and the Cascade foothills and a small herd of horses are the big draws to the Circle H, located an easy hour and a half from Seattle. The sprawling, modern ranch house was bought out of bankruptcy from an agriculture baron who hit hard times; Betsy Ogden converted ranch-hand bunkhouses into two-room suites, decorated with the overflow from Betsy's collection of Westernalia. Each suite sleeps four and contains a kitchenette and bath; books, puzzles, and playing cards fill the shelves, but no phones or TVs (there's a big-screen TV in the day room). Meals, included in the price of your stay, are served family-style in the summer (breakfast only in winter). Some of the suites can connect to accommodate bigger families.

The corral supports a small menagerie, from a family of Angora rabbits to burros. Oliver, the ranch collie, playfully herds guests around the landscaped grounds. The Ogdens welcome young hands to help with ranch chores, while others opt for a trail ride on one of the horses. The 100,000-acre L.T. Murray Wildlife Area backs up to the ranch and is prime for hiking, biking, and riding (bring your own horse, if you like). The nearby Yakima River provides quality fly-fishing and lazy-day river rafting. ■ *Exit 101 off I-90; (509) 964-2000; Rt. 1, Box 175, Thorp, WA 98946; $$$; MC, V; checks OK.*

CLE ELUM

This former coal-mining town is now undergoing a modest rediscovery. **Cle Elum Bakery** is a longtime local institution. From one of the last brick-hearth ovens in the Northwest come delicious torchetti, cinnamon rolls, and great old-fashioned cake doughnuts. Closed Sundays. First and Peoh, (509) 674-2233.

Cle Elum Historical Telephone Museum. Open Memorial Day to Labor Day only, this museum incorporates the area's original phone system, which was operating well into the 1960s; 1st and Wright, (509) 674-5702.

RESTAURANTS

Mama Vallone's Steak House & Inn ★ Talk to the regulars and they'll tell you about the warm welcomes, great steaks, and good homemade pasta at Mama Vallone's. It's definitely the best Cle Elum has to offer, but it doesn't always quite live up to its reputation. One of the big deals is bagna cauda, a "hot bath" of garlic, anchovy, olive oil, and butter into which you dip strips of steak, chicken breast, or your favorite seafood. Or simply order steak, the tastiest version of which tosses Sicilian-spiced steak slices over homemade fettuccine. Wines are okay; service (you're cared for by several members of the staff) is exceptional. Upstairs there are two bedrooms with private baths, decorated in antique reproductions, that rent for $55 a night. ■ *On the main drag at the west end of town; (509) 674-5174; 302 W 1st St, Cle Elum; $$; full bar; AE, DC, MC, V; checks OK; dinner Tues-Sun.*

LODGINGS

Hidden Valley Guest Ranch ★ A short hour from Seattle is the state's oldest dude ranch. Owners Bruce and Matt Coe have brought a little pride of ownership back to this pastoral 700 acres. The 13 cabins are still quite rustic and thin of wall (the ones with the fireplaces are the best in the winter), but miles of wildflower-lined trails, horseback riding, nearby trout fishing, a pool, a hot tub, and splendid cross-country skiing terrain make up for the basic accommodations. All meals, included in the package price, are taken in the cookhouse, a dining room serving country-style buffets (open to the public by reservation). Here you'll also find treats such as cookies and lemonade throughout the day. On Sunday mornings they load up the chuck wagon with blueberry pancakes, muffins, and wrangler-style coffee for a hearty breakfast out in the fields. We're talkin' country, so don't forget the bug repellent. ■ *Off SR 970 at milepost 8, Hidden Valley Rd; (509) 857-2322; HC 61, Box 2060, Cle Elum, WA 98922; $$; MC, V; checks OK.*

The Moore House ★ This bed and breakfast was originally built in 1913 to house transient employees of the Chicago, Milwaukee, St. Paul & Pacific Railroad. Now on the National Register of Historic Places, the bunkhouse with 10 guest rooms is light and airy, and pleasantly furnished with reproduction antiques. Four of the rooms have their own baths. Throughout the house the railroad motif is evident: rooms are named for men who actually stayed in the house decades ago, and railroad memorabilia—vintage photographs, model trains, schedules, and other artifacts—are displayed in the hallways and the public rooms. Two cabooses in the side yard are fully equipped with baths, fridges, queen beds, and private sun decks. Unfortunately, the current owners aren't the railroad buffs the former owners aimed to be. Should you feel the spirit, there's an outdoor hot tub that the proprietors will rev up for your use. ■ *Adjacent to Iron Horse State Park Trail at 526 Marie St; (509)*

674-5939 or (800) 22-TWAIN; PO Box 629, South Cle Elum,
WA 98943; $$; AE, MC, V; checks OK.

ROSLYN

Until the TV series "Northern Exposure" introduced Roslyn to
the nation (and called it Cicely), it was just a sleepy reminder
of its rough-and-tough days as a thriving coal-mining town. To-
day, people come from all over the world in search of the ficti-
tious Cicely, Alaska. Modest turn-of-the-century homes have
become weekend places for city folk, and the former mortuary
is now a video store and movie theater, but the main intersec-
tion still offers a cross-section of the town's character: the his-
toric Northwestern Improvement Company building (which
once housed the company store) occupies one corner, while
the old brick bank across the way still operates behind the orig-
inal brass bars and oak counters.

"Northern Exposure" fans will recognize the old stone
tavern, inexplicably called **The Brick**, which has a water-fed
brass spittoon running the length of the bar; (509) 649-2643.
Down the road, behind the town's junkyard, you'll find **Carek's
Market**, one of the state's better purveyors of fine meats and
sausages. Notable are the Polish sausage, the pepperoni, and
the jerky; 4 South A Street, (509) 649-2930.

Roslyn

RESTAURANTS

Restaurants

Roslyn Cafe ★ The Roslyn Cafe remains the kind of funky

eatery that every picturesque, slightly chic town like Roslyn
should have. It's an old building with high ceilings, a short bar
that is now a counter, neon in the window, hard chairs, a juke-
box with original 78s—full of a sense of different types be-
longing. Dinners try to be a bit more fancy—grilled halibut
with dill sauce, Chinese pepper steak. But it's best earlier in the
day, when you can get really good burgers, a fine corn chow-
der, or a super Philadelphia steak sandwich at lunch. Breakfast
is also worth the side trip (but it begins a little later than what
we call normal breakfast hours): bacon and eggs, blueberry
short stacks, homemade fried potatoes, gooey cinnamon rolls,
and huevos rancheros. The help is gratifyingly spacey, and the
patrons—all the politically correct types—fill up before head-
ing back to Seattle on a Sunday afternoon. ■ *2nd and Penn-
sylvania; (509) 649-2763; 28 Pennsylvania Ave, Roslyn; $;
beer and wine; MC, V; local checks only; breakfast Sat-Sun,
lunch, dinner Tues-Sun (winter hours vary).*

Village Pizza ★ You've found the local hangout, run by a real
couple of characters, Nan and Darrel Harris, a mother/daugh-
ter team from San Francisco. Their urban literary passions
(they'll have copies of the *New York Review of Books* and *Ar-
chitectural Digest* arrayed on the tables) are well in evidence.

This is good pizza too, some bordering on *molto delizioso* (the pungent fresh garlic pizza is out of this world). Interesting toppings include sauerkraut and cashews (not at once), all of which are inexplicably popular. Everyone is here—gangs of wild children with their bicycles piled outside, longhairs, local ranchers, yuppies—peacefully coexisting, which is perhaps the biggest tribute to the Harrises and their pizza. ■ *Main and Pennsylvania; (509) 649-2992; 6 Pennsylvania Ave, Roslyn; $; beer and wine; no credit cards; checks OK; dinner every day.*

SNOQUALMIE

This lovely country, where the dairyland folds into the mountains, was once best known for its falls. Today it's familiar to most as the setting for "Twin Peaks." The series is over, but the town's diner still serves Twin Peaks pie, and Peakers can still purchase a T-shirt almost anywhere (even at the bank). The 268-foot **Snoqualmie Falls** just up the road is, as it has always been, a thundering spectacle. There is an observation deck; better is to take a picnic down the 1-mile trail to the base of the falls.

Puget Sound Railway is a volunteer-operated steam locomotive that runs Saturdays and Sundays from April through October, up to Snoqualmie Falls gorge. There's also a railroad museum. Call Snoqualmie Depot for schedule; (206) 746-4025.

The **Snoqualmie Winery** is now under the ownership of Stimson Lane. It is a splendid stop on the way through the Cascades, with tours, tastings, and a marvelous view; 1000 Winery Road, (206) 888-4000.

Snoqualmie Pass. The four ski areas—Alpental, Snoqualmie, Ski Acres, and Hyak, (206) 434-6161—are all under the same ownership, and offer the closest downhill and cross-country skiing for Seattle buffs (with a free shuttle that runs between the areas on weekends). Alpental is the most challenging, Snoqualmie (with one of the largest ski schools in the country) has excellent instruction for beginners through racers, Ski Acres has some challenging bump runs, and the smallest of the four, Hyak, is a favored spot for downhill telemark skiers, with lit, groomed cross-country tracks and many kilometers of trails. In summer, the relatively low-lying transmountain route is a good starting point for many hikes.

LODGINGS

The Salish Lodge ★★ The falls may be the initial draw. But since you really can't see much of them from the rooms, it's a good thing the owners have rebuilt the lodge with rooms that are as much a selling point as the falls themselves. Each room is designed in a tempered country motif: light, clean-lined wooden furnishings, pillowed window seats (or balconies in some), flagstone fireplaces (and a woodbox full of split wood

▼

Roslyn

Restaurants

▲

and kindling), and a cedar armoire. The details are covered here: TV cleverly concealed, bathrobes and even a telephone in the bathroom. Jacuzzis are separated from the bedrooms with a swinging window to invite the full effect of the fire. Only 8 (out of 91) with a falls view; most have views of the upper river (and the power plant). The rooftop open-ceiling hot tub is another nice feature. There are two banquet rooms downstairs and every detail is well attended to.

The five-course brunch—filling but disappointing—lives on. We prefer dinner these days, which might begin with a successful terrine of smoked duck with brandied melon, ringed with mustard sauce. Follow this with an exquisite pumpkin crab bisque, thick with morsels of succulent crabmeat, and finally a simple but well prepared choucroute of Puget Sound (salmon, scallops, and shrimp on sauerkraut) or sea scallops on creamy polenta with tomato sauce. The wine list is almost legendary (some say overwhelming), but the sommelier is friendly and helpful. The chocolate truffles with the check is a nice touch. Think ahead and reserve a window booth. ■ *Exit 27 off I-90, follow signs to Snoqualmie Falls, (206) 888-2556; 37807 SE Fall City-Snoqualmie Rd, Snoqualmie, WA 98065; $$$; full bar; AE, DC, DIS, MC, V; checks OK; breakfast, lunch Mon-Fri, dinner every day, brunch every day.*

FALL CITY

RESTAURANTS

The Herbfarm ★★★★ What began as a front-yard wheelbarrow filled with a few extra chives for sale has become, among other things, a trustworthy haven of *gourmandise* in the Cascade foothills. Whether more attention is lavished upon the herbs grown for sale, or the gourmet lunch and dinner preparations they give rise to, is hard to say. (The legendary difficulty in securing reservations has been slightly alleviated since the proprietors began leaving ¼ of their 24-seat dining room unreserved until 1pm Friday of the week before the weekend in question. Best to call no later than 1:01pm.) It is easier to claim that no other restaurant works with such devotion and delight to transform a meal into a memorable occasion.

What the Herbfarm presents is not simply a meal, but an opportunity for tasting, learning, and talking about what you have eaten. Prix-fixe luncheons or dinners generally begin with a short tour of the 17 herbal theme gardens, and the education continues throughout, as owner Ron Zimmerman and chef Jerry Traunfeld narrate from the open kitchen, and servers circulate with plants for guests to sniff and sample. Unfortunately, co-owner Carrie Van Dyck brings a stuffed bear named Herb into the act, providing the only oversweetened moments of the whole feast. And a feast it is. Traunfeld and his minions make every attempt to gather ingredients as close to home as possible. At autumn harvest dinner, which begins with guests selecting snippets of herbs to perfume glasses of sparkling wine, we've tasted a sorbet made from Douglas fir needles, and a fondue of Oregon white truffles served with salsify and Jerusalem artichoke chips. The entrée was a redolent fillet of wild king salmon, smoked over herb stems, draped with a braised leek, and served alongside a purée of celery root and apple. At the other end of the calendar in spring, we've encountered memorable soups—particularly a duo: morel mushrooms with caraway and wild stinging nettle with lovage, served in the same bowl and topped with swirls of crème fraîche and tiny cheese puffs. Desserts are elaborate and sumptuous—a warm bosc pear poached in riesling with persimmon-caramel and chocolate hazelnut sauces, for instance—and each course comes with a matched wine. Plan on two hours for luncheon, four for dinner, and plan on paying dearly for this extraordinary celebration of Northwest bounty: $42 (lunch) and $100 (dinner) per guest. ■ *3½ miles off I-90 from exit 22, (206) 784-2222; 32804 Issaquah-Fall City Rd, Fall City; $$$; wine only; MC, V; checks OK; lunch Fri-Sun (late April-Dec only).*

CARNATION

Twenty-five miles northeast of Seattle is the home of the **Carnation Research Farm**, where self-guided tours let you glimpse several stages in the pasteurizing process. Kids love it; (206) 788-1511. Closed Sunday and during the winter.

At **MacDonald Memorial Park**, meandering trails and an old-fashioned suspension bridge across the Tolt River provide a great family picnic setting; Fall City Road and NE 40th Street.

Remlinger Farms. The sky's the limit for your favorite fruits and vegetables at this U-pick farm. The Strawberry Festival in mid-June starts off the season. Throughout the summer you can choose from the best in raspberries, apples, corn, and grapes. The kids, young and old alike, love tromping through the fields in search of the perfect jack-o'-lantern-to-be in October. Call (206) 333-4135 or (206) 451-8740 for more information.

RESTAURANTS

The Original Brown Bag Restaurant and Bakery ★ The Brown Bag still fills Carnation's air with the sweet fragrance of fresh cinnamon rolls and breads. The historic 1913 building (spruced up with a coat of paint and wallpaper) holds only 10 tables (plus six outdoors for the overflow) and gets pretty packed on weekends. Alex and Allison Awaski serve up wholesome and hearty soups and sandwiches to the teeming (and pleased) mobs. ■ *On the main drag; (206) 333-6100; 4366 Tolt Ave (Hwy 203),*

Carnation; $; no alcohol; no credit cards; checks OK; break-fast, lunch every day.

BLACK DIAMOND

Black Diamond Bakery, now much more than just a bakery, boasts the last wood-fired brick oven in the area. The bread that comes out of it is excellent: 26 different kinds, including raisin, cinnamon, sour rye, potato, seven-grain, honey-wheat, and garlic French. To get there, take the Maple Valley exit from I-405; at Black Diamond, turn right at the big white Old Town sign; at the next stop sign, veer left; the bakery is on the right; 32805 Railroad Avenue, (206) 886-2741, closed Monday.

ENUMCLAW

RESTAURANTS

Baumgartner's ★ Stop here to collect picnic supplies for a trip to Mount Rainier, or sit at a pink-draped table in the atrium for an early supper after a day at the mountain. It's a full delicatessen with a range of European sausages and cheeses, coffee beans, teas, and spices, and even hand-dipped ice creams and Boehm's chocolates. The friendly staff make up delectable sandwich combinations on fresh bread and croissants (huge). Try Marsha's special with your pick of cheese and meat, avocado, green peppers, lettuce, tomato, sprouts, mustard, and a pickle; or a poor boy with ham, pastrami, salami, Swiss, provolone, and the works. The freshly baked desserts have made a name for themselves: raspberry tarts filled with a heavenly white chocolate-almond mousse, German chocolate cake, and a slew of cheesecakes—the chef's specialty. ■ *On Hwy 410½ block west of the Pickle Factory; (206) 825-1067; 1008 E Roosevelt, Enumclaw; $; beer and wine; MC, V; checks OK; lunch every day.* &

GREENWATER

RESTAURANTS

Naches Tavern ★ Now *this* is the way to do a country tavern. The fireplace is as long as a wall and roars all winter long to warm the Crystal Mountain après-ski crowd. The food is bountiful, homemade, and modestly priced—deep-fried mushrooms, chili, burgers, pizza, four-scoop milk shakes. There's a countrified jukebox, pool tables, a lending library (take a book, leave a book) of yellowing paperbacks, and furniture so comfortable that the stuffing is coming out. It's not pretty—Big Don, the "chef," wouldn't want it pretty—but he's a gracious host and a no-nonsense barkeep. The group assembled is a peaceable mix of skiers, hunters, loggers, and locals—depends on the season.

Bring your own good company, play a little cribbage, stroke the roving house pets, nod off in front of the hearth. ∎ *North side of Hwy 410; (206) 663-2267; Greenwater; $; beer and wine; no credit cards; no checks; lunch, dinner every day.*

CRYSTAL MOUNTAIN

The ski resort is the best in the state, with runs for beginners and experts, plus fine cross-country touring. Less well known and less used are the summer facilities. You can ride the chair lift and catch a grand view of Mount Rainier and other peaks; rent condominiums with full kitchens, balconies, or other facilities from Crystal Mountain Reservations, (206) 663-2558, and play tennis. Other than that, there's just a grocery store, a sports shop, and Rafters, the bar-and-buffet restaurant atop Crystal's lodge. In summer, the Summit House offers weekend dinners. Off Highway 410 just west of Chinook Pass.

ELBE

▼

Greenwater

Restaurants

▲

The advent of the Morton Dinner Train (and an enterprising restaurateur) has turned this onetime sawmill town into more of a museum (some say graveyard) for antique cabooses. The **Morton Dinner Train**—$55 per person, (206) 569-2588—is a 4-hour, 40-mile round-trip train ride from Elbe to Morton. The dinner (shrimp cocktail, prime rib, and the works) is surprisingly good, and the conductor is well versed in the area's lore. You don't get dinner on the hour-long **Mount Rainier Scenic Railroad**—summers only; (206) 569-2588—but the scenery (to Mineral and back) is equally attractive.

EATONVILLE

Northwest Trek is a "zoo" where animals roam free while people tour the 600-acre grounds in small, open-air trams. The 5-mile tour passes by a large collection of native wildlife, with all kinds of Northwest beasts from caribou to mink. The buffalo herd steals the show. The whole tour is impressive for kids ($3.50) and adults ($5.75) alike; you can also combine your visit with breakfast at the in-park food service concession, the Fir Bough. Open daily February through October, weekends only the rest of the year. Group rates available. Seventeen miles south of Puyallup on Route 161, (206) 832-6116.

LODGINGS

Old Mill House Bed and Breakfast ★ A 1920s mill baron's mansion in an unassuming neighborhood is now a delightful B&B, re-created in the flair of the period—there's even a Prohibition-era bar (and dance floor) accessible through a secret panel in a bookcase. The enormous mauve, gray, and ice green Isadora Duncan Suite resonates with the free spirit of this dancer—private his-and-hers dressing rooms, a prettily tiled bath with a tub and a shower (boasting seven shower heads), and a king-size bed. The three other rooms share a bath and have equal character (Will Rogers, Bessie Smith, and F. Scott Fitzgerald). The latter comes with an ongoing novel penned by guests (reportedly *full* of cliff-hangers). ■ *Off Hwy 161 (called Michelle Ave in town) at 116 Oak St; (206) 832-6506; PO Box 543, Eatonville, WA 98328; $$; MC, V; checks OK.*

ASHFORD

Wellspring is a privately operated, judiciously situated hot tub/sauna/massage center, where the tub is nestled into a sylvan glade surrounded by evergreens. Perfect after a day on the Hill. On Kernahan Road 2¼ miles east of Ashford. Call ahead to schedule a massage: (206) 569-2514.

LODGINGS

Alexander's Country Inn ★★ This quaint country inn has gained such a following that it now rivals the mountain itself as the best reason to visit Ashford. First opened in 1912 by lumberman Alexander Mesler as a hotel, it's owned by Gerald Harnish and Bernadette Ronan, who have lovingly restored the rambling inn to much of its early grandeur.

Best is the Tower Room: a lofted suite in the turret of the manor. A large wheelchair-accessible suite has been added on the second floor—very private, with its own deck. Most of the bathrooms are shared, but they're large, modern, and immaculate. Indeed, this blending of old and new is the real genius here; it feels turn-of-the-century, but the comforts such as carpeted rooms and a new outdoor Jacuzzi, with a view of Heron Pond, are pure 1990s. Full breakfast is included.

The dining room, open to guests and non-guests alike, is your best bet in these parts for a fine meal. We've heard that the artichoke soup is exquisite in texture and taste; and we'll vouch for the perfectly pan-fried fresh trout—caught out back in the holding pond—and the satisfying beef stroganoff. During the summer, get a table on the brick patio, ideal for summer dining. ■ *4 miles east of Ashford on Hwy 706, (206) 569-2300, (800) 654-7615; 37515 Rt 706 E, Ashford, WA 98304; $$; beer and wine; MC, V; checks OK; breakfast (summer only), lunch, dinner every day (weekends only in winter).*

Mountain Meadows Inn and B&B ★ Logger-turned-innkeeper Chad Darrah saved this 1910 mill superintendent's home from fading away in the ghost town of National, Washington. It is now situated near a trout pond on 14 acres of landscaped grounds in Ashford. There are three large guest rooms (each has its own bath) filled with antiques, books, and extensive train memorabilia—everything from model Lionels to full-size lanterns. Nothing kitschy here; trains are conductor Darrah's passion. There's a VCR with rare train footage in the living room, if you're so inclined, and a player piano if you're not. If you need more space, ask about the guest house with two studio apartments. Full breakfasts of homemade sausage and muffins from the wood stove are fuel enough for a locomotive. ■ *¼ mile west of Ashford at 28912 Rt 706 E; (206) 569-2788; PO Box 291, Ashford, WA 98304; $$; MC, V; checks OK.*

Nisqually Lodge ★ Reasonably priced and clean, this lodge just a few miles before the west entrance to Mount Rainier offers welcome respite from the train-memorabilia theme that's pervading the area. This two-story lodge (owned by the same folks who run the Cowlitz River Lodge in Packwood and the Seasons Motel in nearby Morton) is well visited—returnees like the stone fireplace in the pinewood lounge and the hot tub outside (though we hear reports about the thin walls). Coffee and doughnuts are served for breakfast. If it's a view that you want, book a room at the Cowlitz, 13069 US Highway 12, Packwood, (206) 494-4444. ■ *Hwy 7 to Rt 706, 5 miles from park entrance; (206) 569-8804; 31609 Rt 706, Ashford, WA 98304; $$; AE, DC, MC, V; no checks.*

MOUNT RAINIER

The majestic mountain is the abiding symbol of natural grandeur in the Northwest and one of the most awesome mountains in the world. Its cone rises 14,410 feet above sea level, thousands of feet higher than the other peaks in the Cascade Range. The best way to appreciate the mountain is to explore its flanks: 300 miles of backcountry and self-guiding nature trails lead to ancient forests, dozens of massive glaciers, waterfalls, and alpine meadows, lush with wildflowers during its short summer. Chinook and Cayuse passes are closed in winter; you can take the loop trip or the road to Sunrise only between late May and October. The road from Longmire to Paradise remains open during daylight hours in winter. It is advisable to carry tire chains and a shovel during winter, and it is always wise to check current road and weather conditions by calling a 24-hour information service: (206) 569-2211. Backcountry permits for overnight stays must be obtained (any of the ranger stations).

Longmire. A few miles inside the southwestern border of the park, the little village of Longmire has the simple **National Park Inn**, (206) 569-2275, a small wildlife museum with plant and animal displays, a hiking information center, and a cross-country skiing rental outlet. It also has the only place that sells gas in the park.

Paradise. At 5,400 feet, Paradise is the most popular destination point on the mountain. On the way to this paved parking lot and visitors center, you'll catch wonderful views of Narada Falls and Nisqually Glacier. The visitors center, housed in a flying saucer-like building, has a standard cafeteria and gift shop, extensive nature exhibits and films, and a superb view of the mountain from its observation deck. Depending on the season, you could picnic (our advice is to bring your own) among the wildflowers, explore some of the trails (the rangers offer guided walks), let the kids slide on inner tubes in the snow-play area, try a little cross-country skiing, or even take a guided snowshoe tromp. The ice caves, 3 miles northeast of Paradise, still exist, but entering the deteriorating caves has become extremely dangerous.

Sunrise. Open only during the summer months, the visitors center at Sunrise (6,400 feet) is the closest you can drive to the peak. The old lodge here has no overnight accommodations, but it does offer a snack bar and exhibits about the mountain. Dozens of trails lead from here, such as the short one leading to a magnificent viewpoint of Emmons Glacier Canyon.

Climbing the mountain. There are two ways to do it: with **Rainier Mountaineering**, the concessionaire guide service, or in your own party. Unless you are qualified to do it on your own—and this is a big, difficult, and dangerous mountain on which many people have been killed—you must climb with the guide service. Call Paradise (206) 569-2227 in the summer, Tacoma (206) 627-6242 in the winter. If you plan to climb with your own party, you must register at one of the ranger stations in Mount Rainier National Park, (206) 569-2211. Generally, the best time to climb the mountain is from late June through early September.

LODGINGS

Paradise Inn ★ The hotel at Paradise, just above the visitors center, is a massive, old-fashioned 1917 lodge, full of exposed beams, log furniture, and native American rugs. Unlike the modest inn at Longmire, the Paradise Inn has 125 rooms, a comfortable full-service dining room, a small, smoky bar, and a lobby with two big stone fireplaces. The greatest advantage to staying here, however, is the proximity to the summit; the rooms are nothing grand, the bathrooms can be antiquated, and the expensive meals in the restaurant tend toward routine beef and frozen seafood dishes. Open late May to October only.
■ *Hwy 706 to Paradise in Mt Rainier National Park; reservations (206) 569-2275; PO Box 108, Ashford, WA 98304; $$; full bar; MC, V; checks OK; breakfast, lunch, dinner every day.*

PACKWOOD

LODGINGS

Packwood Hotel Just 10 miles west of White Pass Ski Area, Packwood makes for a good base camp for wintertime skiers and summer hikers into the Goat Rocks Wilderness. There are a couple of motels in town with more modern appliances but this spartan lodge (open since 1912) is a favorite. The woody aroma from the wood stove in the lobby permeates the place just enough to make you feel like you're really in the middle of the mountains (but you're actually in downtown Packwood). A small narrow staircase climbs up to the simple shared-bath rooms upstairs. ■ *104 Main St; (206) 494-5431; PO Box 130, Packwood, WA 98361; $; no credit cards; no checks.*

MOUNT ST. HELENS

The temperamental **Mount St. Helens** simmers about two hours south of Seattle off I-5. On a clear day it is well worth the trip to see the 8,365-foot remains as well as the mountain's re-growth since the incredible eruption of May 18, 1980 (it's 1,300 feet shorter than before the blast). The US Forest Service's wood-and-glass **Mount St. Helens National Volcanic Monument Visitor Center**—3029 Spirit Lake Highway, Castle Rock; (206) 274-6644 or (206) 274-4038 for weather conditions —sits in a stand of timber in the Gifford Pinchot National Forest 5 miles off I-5, near Silver Lake. On clear days the view of the mountain is stunning, either with the naked eye or through one of the center's telescopes. The center commemorates the blast with excellent exhibits, a walk-through volcano, hundreds of historical and modern photos, geological and anthropological surveys, and a film documenting the destruction and rebirth. A network of trails, some for wheelchairs, are good for short, scenic strolls. The new **Coldwater Ridge Visitors Center**, 38 miles closer to the mountain down State Highway 504, is a state-of-the-art facility with mind-boggling multimedia exhibits; (206) 274-2100.

Or for the better view from the north, the side on which the blast carved out a crater 2 miles across and half a mile deep, from I-5 turn east on Route 12 into Randall, then take Route 25 to connect with 26, which will lead you to **Windy Ridge**; park at the end of the road (closed winters). Many of the trails have been created or reconstructed to allow further exploration. The big thrills are to see the volcano from the air, which can be arranged with any of the numerous charter companies in the nearby towns of Kelso and Longview, or to climb it. Most climbers take one of two trails (Butte Camp or Monitor Ridge) up the south face—more of a rugged hike than real alpine climbing, but an ice ax is still recommended. The all-day climb (8 miles round-trip) is ideal for novice alpinists: the only big dangers are some loose-rock cliffs and the unstable edge around the crater. Permits are required mid-May through October, and only 100 are given out each day (for free). *Everyone* must register with the Forest Service headquarters in Amboy; (206) 247-5473 or (206) 247-5800. Call well in advance for details.

MOUNT ADAMS

Mount Adams and its surrounding area are a natural splendor largely overlooked by visitors from Portland and Seattle, who seldom venture in from the Columbia Gorge. Besides climbing to the summit of the 12,276-foot mountain—greater in mass than any of the five major volcanic peaks in the Northwest— hikers and skiers can explore miles of wilderness trails in the Mount Adams Wilderness Area and the Gifford Pinchot National Forest.

Volcanic activity long ago left the area honeycombed with caves and lava tubes, including the **Ice Caves** near Trout Lake with stalactites and stalagmites formed by dripping ice. To the southwest of Trout Lake is **Big Lava Bed**, a 12,500-acre lava field filled with cracks, crevasses, rock piles, and unusual lava formations. Contact the Mount Adams Ranger Station in Trout Lake, (509) 395-2501, to register for ascents and for information on area activities.

In the warm months, Klickitat County is a land of abundance: morel mushrooms in the Simcoe Mountains (April through June), wildflowers in the Bird Creek Meadows (part of the only area of the Yakima Indian Reservation open to the public) in late July, and wild huckleberries—reputedly the best in the state—in and around the Indian Heaven Wilderness (mid-August to mid-September).

TROUT LAKE

LODGINGS

Mio Amore Pensione ★ Tom and Jill Westbrook's restored 1904 farmhouse sits alongside Trout Lake Creek, with a view of Mount Adams from the Jacuzzi. The inside is decorated with memorabilia collected from spots around the world. Our only quibble is that everything here is a little *too* precious (even more so with the gift shop of local and imported crafts nearby). Bedrooms are small, but the Venus Room is the most spacious, with a private bath and a two-seat sitting room with a view of Adams. The converted stone icehouse in the corner of the yard is quiet and rustic, and it sleeps four. Breakfast includes a bountiful array of Jill's award-winning baked goods, with a hot dish such as French toast soaked in Grand Marnier. Tom, a trained chef, will prepare a dinner (the entrée is chosen by the first person to make a reservation) for $25 extra (including appetizer, dessert, coffee, and wine). You don't need to be a pensione guest to sample these savories, but you do need a reservation. ■ *Just off Hwy 141, take a sharp right onto Little Mountain Rd; (509) 395-2264; PO Box 208, Trout Lake, WA 98650; $$; MC, V; checks OK.*

GLENWOOD

LODGINGS

Flying L Ranch ★ We love the Flying L; this 160-acre ranch is like a big kids' camp in some of the most spectacular country around. Except for here, you're on your own. Bicycle the backroads, hike the trails, observe the birds in the Convoy Wildlife Refuge, or ski Mount Adams. The Lloyd family has lived here all their lives. Darvel and Darryl Lloyd, who both know the area well, can point you in the right direction for anything. Or just stick around. The pace here is relaxed. You'll feel quite comfortable putting on some classical music and curling up with an old issue of *National Geographic* by the fireplace in the main lodge's spacious living room or watching evening fall over Mount Adams from the hot tub in the gazebo. The bedrooms, named after Old West notables or cowhands, are nothing fancy— but we love 'em that way. Those in the main lodge have shared baths (the Charles Russell and the George Fletcher have fireplaces); those in the adjacent guest house are less charming, but face the Mountain. Two cabins back in the woods offer the most privacy. As you dig into your huckleberry pancakes in the cookhouse at breakfast, think about all the ways to spend the day. For lunch and dinner you'll have to bring your own food to prepare in one of the two well-equipped community kitchens. ■ *Off Trout Lake-Glenwood Rd on Flying L Lane; (509) 364-3488; 25 Flying L Lane, Glenwood, WA 98619; $$; AE, MC, V; checks OK.*

STEVENSON

LODGINGS

Skamania Lodge ★★ The Gorge's grand new lodge was constructed by a $5 million grant to spur on the economic development of Washington's side of the gorge—the side forgotten by development, left behind by timber companies, and favored by the hottest boardheads. The lodge was not meant to be a luxury resort: you won't encounter valet parking, nightly turndown service, or private decks, and you'll find only one complimentary Presto log per night in your fireplace. It's best to think of the lodge as a park resort or a conference center, and go and enjoy without expectations of grandeur. Then you will have a grand time indeed. Its massive stone and wood lobby absorbs the warm glows of morning and evening, and a little library nook on the second floor offers guests more quiet respite with the same view. Still, with 195 rooms, this place is meant for people, lots of people. Even on days absent of conventions there are too many echoes in the restaurant and too many voices through the walls (and some of the most expensive view suites are located directly above the bar with live music on weekends.) Guests have use of a lap pool, saunas, and an appealing outdoor hot tub. The golf course is scheduled to be completed in 1993. There's not a lot of choice on the menu for appetizers or desserts, so concentrate on the entrées (the wood-oven roasted chinook salmon on top of a creamy bed of roasted potatoes and leeks is the best of an otherwise unexciting menu). ■ *Just the west side of Stevenson on 1131 Skamania Lodge Way; (800) 221-7117; PO Box 189, Stevenson, WA 98648; $$$; AE, DC, DIS, MC, V; checks OK; breakfast, lunch, dinner every day.* ♿

HOME VALLEY

RESTAURANTS

Sojourner Inn ★ At the Sojourner, breakfast in bed is just the beginning. Word is getting out that Bob Davis, a Cordon Bleu chef, cooks what might be some of the best dinners on the Washington side of the Gorge. At first you won't believe it, driving up to this modest-looking home on the hill. And at 7:30pm sharp, it could be an awkward moment of just the two of you or a festive group of 20 others. Either way, the evening continues smoothly with a salad tossed with subtle Oregon blue cheese, perfectly ripened pears, and a light minty dressing; a heaping plate of spinach fettuccine with prawns, asparagus, and tomatoes topped with fresh-shaven Parmesan; and a sweet finish of apple pie loaded with thinly sliced apples and baked with a cheddar cheese crust. At $30 for two (including everything except tip), you'll never care that everyone else in the room is getting the same thing. Call before 10am for same-day dinner reservations. Of the six rooms, we recommend the three upstairs (the downstairs ones are serviceable but too dark). The Gorge view room seems altitudes above the rest. ■ *Follow signs from Hwy 14 in Home Valley; (509) 427-7070; Berge Rd, Home Valley; MC, V; local checks only; $$; dinner by reservation only, Thurs-Sun.* ♿

CARSON

The eccentric 1897 **Carson Hot Springs**—PO Box 370, Carson, WA 98610; (509) 427-8292—reminiscent of days when the sickly "took the waters" to improve their health, is today a bit worn; but we still recommend the hot mineral bath ($5), after which you're swathed in towels and blankets for a short rest. Massages are available, but reserve these well in advance. Don't expect as healthy a treatment from the restaurant.

HUSUM

LODGINGS

Orchard Hill Inn ★★ You're asked to leave your shoes by the doormat (and they might even get a shine) at this B&B on 13 acres overlooking pear and apple orchards and the White Salmon River valley. The three bedrooms, decorated with family antiques, offer refreshing respite. Two bathrooms—one with a whirlpool bath—are shared. The bunkhouse out back has its own bath and sleeps six. A full breakfast includes homemade breads, huckleberry bran muffins, baked apples, eggs, and local produce. Children are welcome and have a place of their own in a two-story tree house in front; hosts James and Pamela Tindall will even supply parents with a list of local babysitters. There's pitch-and-chip golf at the inn, and a nine-hole course at nearby Husum Hills. ■ *2 miles up Oak Ridge Rd out of Husum, milepost 2; (509) 493-3024; 199 Oak Ridge Rd, White Salmon, WA 98672; $$; MC, V; checks OK.*

▼
Carson

▲

BINGEN

RESTAURANTS

Fidel's ★ This Mexican restaurant seems transplanted straight from California; in fact, Fidel and Martha Montanez and their family recipes recently arrived from San Diego. Lively Mexican music sets the mood. Enormous margaritas go with the warm chips and disappointing salsa. The menu offers a chili verde, a chili colorado, and machaca (a shredded beef omelet). Portions are generous (often big enough for two). The chile relleno is encased in a thick layer of egg whites so that it resembles a big pillow on your plate, and is bathed in a delicious, spicy sauce. ■ *1 mile east of Singing Bridge (toll bridge) on Hwy 14; (509) 493-1017; 120 E Stuben St, Bingen; $; full bar; MC, V; checks OK; lunch, dinner every day (call ahead in winter).* ċ

LYLE

RESTAURANTS

Lyle Hotel [*unrated*] The Lyle Hotel is a very modest place in a very humble town, but its most recent incarnation by owners Cal Wood and Valya Coole is beginning to convince people to give Lyle a second chance. Upstairs are nine clean and serviceable guest rooms; biggest hopes, however, are for the restaurant. Chef Steve Phillips has modelled the menu after something you might find in a Seattle bistro—a big feat, considering this is probably the first time any Lyle establishment has ever offered halibut with three-citrus cilantro or ahi tuna with a light mustard sauce. But here Phillips uses not only produce from the fertile Hood River Valley but also locally hunted game from just up the Klickitat River. The restaurant is wheelchair-accessible; the rooms are not. ■ *10 minutes east of the Hood River toll bridge; (509) 365-5953; 100 7th, Lyle; $$; full bar; MC, V; checks OK; dinner Wed-Mon.* &

GOLDENDALE

Maryhill Museum perches rather obtrusively upon the barren Columbia River benchlands. Constructed in 1917 by the eccentric Sam Hill, son-in-law of railroad tycoon James J. Hill, Maryhill began as the Palladian dream home for Hill and his wife, Mary, but became instead what it is today: a fine art museum. With one of the largest collections of Rodin sculptures in the world, a whole floor of classic French and American paintings and glasswork, unique exhibitions such as chess sets, and splendid Northwest tribal art, the museum makes for quite an interesting visit. Peacocks roam the lovely landscaped grounds; Highway 14, 13 miles south of Goldendale, (509) 773-3733. Up the road is another of Sam Hill's bizarre creations: a replica of **Stonehenge**, built to honor World War I veterans.

Goldendale Public Observatory, on a hill overlooking town (20 minutes north of Goldendale on US 97), was a popular spot when Halley's comet dropped in. High-powered telescopes give incredible celestial views through unpolluted skies. Open daily and some evenings; call ahead, (509) 773-3141.

LODGINGS

Three Creeks Lodge Changes in ownership have taken their toll on the Three Creeks Lodge. It is a collection of vaulted-ceiling cedar chalets, some with wood-burning fireplaces and private spas, scattered throughout the beautiful backwoods wilderness. You fish in summer and go on sleigh rides in winter. The place capitalizes on the romance of seclusion, yet the simple fourplex creek houses with thin walls between units make televisions a bother. The dining room in the main lodge makes splendid use of its situation at the confluence of three creeks, with glass and cedar walls that seem to bring the trees inside. But the beauty of the place ends here, so stay in a chalet with a kitchen. ■ *18 miles north of the Columbia River on Hwy 97; (509) 773-4026; 2120 Hwy 97, Goldendale, WA 98620; $$; full bar; AE, MC, V; checks OK; breakfast, lunch Mon-Sat, dinner every day, brunch Sun (call for winter hours).*

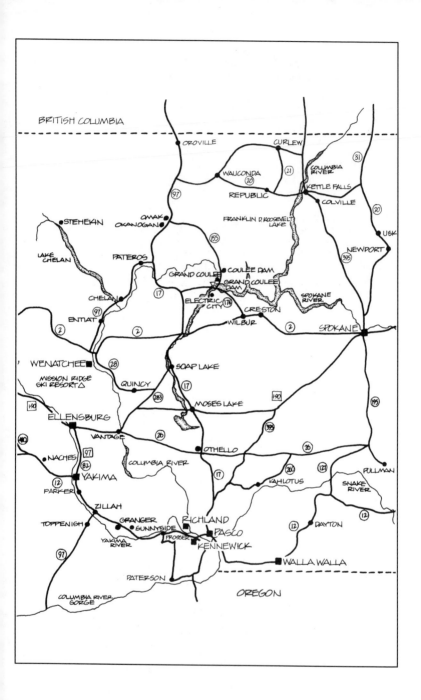

Eastern Washington

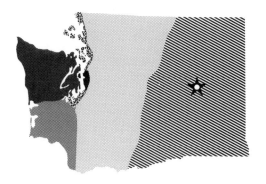

*An eastward route along I-90, Ellensburg to Spokane,
then a northwesterly arc through the northeast corner of the
state to the Okanogan and Colville national forests. The
Wenatchee loop begins in Okanogan and continues clockwise
through Grand Coulee, Soap Lake, and north again to
Wenatchee and Chelan (and Stehekin, accessible from
Chelan). Finally, an eastward drive along the
bottom of the state—Yakima to Pullman.*

ELLENSBURG

If you get away from the tourist ghetto by the freeway, as you
should, this college-and-cowboy town projects a pleasant ease.
Its famous Labor Day rodeo draws many for its slice-of-life view
of rural America.

Architecture. Ellensburg has more than its share of interesting buildings. The downtown area was rebuilt after a
devastating fire in 1889. Among the handsome structures still
standing are the Davidson Building, on the corner of Pearl and
Fourth, and the Masonic Temple, with its intriguing asym-
metrical facade. Off on the fringes of town, at Third and Wenas,
is a prime example of the Great American Train Station, built
late in the last century for the Northern Pacific. Art deco is represented by the Liberty Theater, at Fifth and Pine, and by the
Valley Cafe, whose interior is prime.

Central Washington University. For modern architecture, turn to the campus of Central Washington University,

which displays Fred Bassetti's library and dormitory compound and Kirk/Wallace/McKinley's fine-arts complex. The campus makes for a wonderful stroll, especially through the serene Japanese Garden, designed by Masa Mizuno. The curious should call ahead and arrange a Saturday or Sunday workshop with the Chimpanzee and Human Communication Institute (at 14th and D at the north end of campus). Here you can observe a human and chimps communicating through American sign language. Call in advance for workshop times and prices; (800) 752-4380.

Art. Sarah Spurgeon Gallery, on 14th Street in the fine-arts complex at Central, presents regional and national exhibits in all media, Monday through Friday (closed in September), (509) 963-2665. The Clymer Museum and Gallery, at 416 N Pearl Street, honors Ellensburg's own chronicler of the Western frontier, John Clymer, whose work appeared in several editions of *Saturday Evening Post*, (509) 962-6416. Community Art Gallery, 408½ N Pearl, (509) 925-2670, has nice quarters in an old building, displays good contemporary art, and sells local crafts; open noon to 5pm Tuesday to Saturday.

Theater. Central Washington's only professional repertory theater presents over 35 performances by the energetic Laughing Horse Company during July and August (Wednesday through Saturday at 8pm); for reservations, call (509) 963-3400. Plays are staged in the architecturally stunning Tower Theater on the Central campus.

Ellensburg oddities. Close to the Central Washington campus along Ninth Street are tree-lined blocks of attractive turn-of-the-century homes. For something a bit out of the ordinary, check out the Ellensberg Bull statue by Richard Beyer, located in the historic downtown business district, the cowboy sculpture by Dan Klennard that guards the corner of Fifth and Pearl, or stop by 101 N Pearl for a gander at Dick & Jane's Spot, a blend of unusual yard art, including reflector gyros, statues, and other unique offerings. Or perhaps treat the kids to an ice cream straight from the dairy at Winegar Family Dairy, 419 W 15th, (509) 925-1821 (Monday to Saturday 11am-6:30pm). Or down an espresso while sitting in the saddle at the Cowboy Espresso Bar in Jaguar's, 423 N Pearl, (509) 962-2125.

The hills surrounding Ellensburg are speckled with blue agates found nowhere else in the world except the Kittitas Valley. If you don't stumble upon any, you can purchase some at any of the local gem shops, particularly the Ellensburg Agate Shop, 201 S Main; (509) 925-4998.

Olmstead Place, 4 miles east of town on Squaw Creek Trail Road (off I-90), is a cottonwood log cabin from an 1875 cattle ranch now coming back to life; tours Thursday to Monday, 8am to 5pm; (509) 925-1943. Nearby Ellensburg is the Thorp Mill, an 1883 gristmill still in mint condition after 110 years. Open for tours by appointment; (509) 964-9500 or write PO Box 7, Thorp, WA 98946.

The big event in Ellensburg is the **Ellensburg Rodeo**, held Thursday through Monday of every Labor Day weekend at the fairgrounds (see calendar); (509) 962-7831.

Yakima River. There are fine canoe and raft trips to be made through the deep gorges, and the river is one of the finest trout streams in the country. Fly fishermen know the river for its wild trout. Highway 821, south of town, follows the gorge. Information about floats and river trips: (509) 925-3137.

RESTAURANTS

The Valley Cafe ★★ This 1930s-built bistro, with mahogany booths and back bar, would be an oasis anywhere—but is especially so in cow country. People traveling on business to Ellensburg arrange to arrive around lunchtime just to eat at this airy art deco spot. Salads are the choice at lunch, or one of the deli sandwiches. For breakfast you'll find French toast or a breakfast sauté of vegetables, chiles, eggs, and cheese. Eclectic concoctions, fresh seafood, and Ellensburg lamb compose most of the dinner menu: tortellini and chicken sauté, pan-blackened salmon, and prawns with a peanut sauce over rice. There's a well thought-out list of Washington wines, and there are some bracing espresso drinks. Service, though tending to favor regulars, has on recent visits been quite efficient. If you're just passing through (and require faster service), there's a take-out branch next door. ■ *Near the corner of 3rd and Main; (509) 925-3050; 105 W 3rd, Ellensburg; $$; beer and wine; AE, DC, DIS, MC, V; checks OK; breakfast Sat-Sun, lunch, dinner every day.*

Ellensburg

Restaurants

Giovanni's on Pearl ★ Welsh-born owner John Herbert started in the food and hotel business at age 12 in his parents' hotel on the Isle of Jersey. He landed here a few years ago and took over the fledgling Carriage House, and Ellensburg is all the better for it. The prime rib is gone (replaced by the oft-requested Ellensburg lamb), but there's a good sampling of fish and lotsa pasta. A chef's special might feature chicken breast baked in puff pastry with basil leaves and dried mushrooms. Candlelight, flowers on the tables, and green chintz tablecloths with a slight English country air add to a fresh and relaxing atmosphere. The college-bound servers are knowledgeable and prompt. The outstanding desserts (blackberry cobbler and an unmatched Dutch apple pie) are made by a former employee in her nearby farmhouse. ■ *1 block east of Main in the historic district; (509) 962-2260; 402 N Pearl, Ellensburg; $$; full bar; AE, DIS, MC, V; checks OK; lunch, dinner Tues-Sat.* &

The facts in this book were correct at press time, but places close, chefs depart, hours change. It's best to call ahead.

VANTAGE

Situated on a splendid stretch of the Columbia, Vantage has nothing much in the way of food, but the view from the parking lot of the A&W surpasses that of other root-beer stands.

Ginkgo Petrified Forest State Park has an interpretive center—open daily in summer, 10am to 6pm (by appointment only otherwise), (509) 856-2700—that takes you back to the age of dinosaurs; then you can go prospecting for your own finds. It's a lovely spot for a picnic, by the way.

GEORGE

The naturally terraced amphitheater looking west over the Columbia Gorge at **Champs de Brionne** offers a spectacular summer-evening setting for musical performances and attracts thousands of people with a diverse slice of big-name performers from Lollapalooza to the Moody Blues, Def Leppard to Barry Manilow, Bonnie Raitt to George Thorogood. For information on upcoming concerts, call (509) 785-6685. You can bring a picnic, but no booze (some wine is for sale on the premises, which used to be a winery and now just sells grapes to regional vintners). Arrive early; the one country road leading to George is not fit for crowds of this kind. For tickets, call Ticketmaster in Seattle, (206) 628-0888. George is a three-hour drive from Seattle; although you may find camping nearby, the closest lodgings are found in Ellensburg, Vantage, or Ephrata.

▼
Vantage
▲

SPOKANE

The friendly city by Spokane Falls is far more attractive to visit than is generally recognized. It is full of old buildings of note, marvelous parks, and splendid vistas, and the compact downtown is most pleasant for strolling. The Gold Rush of the 1880s brought it wealth and the railroads brought it people.

Architecture. The three blocks on W Riverside Avenue between Jefferson and Lincoln contain a wealth of handsome structures in the City Beautiful mode—doubtless the loveliest three blocks around. The **Spokane Club** on W Riverside is a fine example of the work done by Kirtland Cutter, who rebuilt most of the city after the fire of 1889; the **Spokesman-Review Building**, also on W Riverside, is everybody's idea of what a newspaper building should look like, especially one that is the seat of power for the dominant Cowles family. The **Spokane County Courthouse**, north of the Spokane River on W Broadway is a Loire Valley clone built in 1895 by Willis A. Ritchie. **City Hall**, on Spokane Falls Boulevard, occupies an old Montgomery Ward building, now elaborately restored in an award-winning blend of the profoundly practical and the aesthetic.

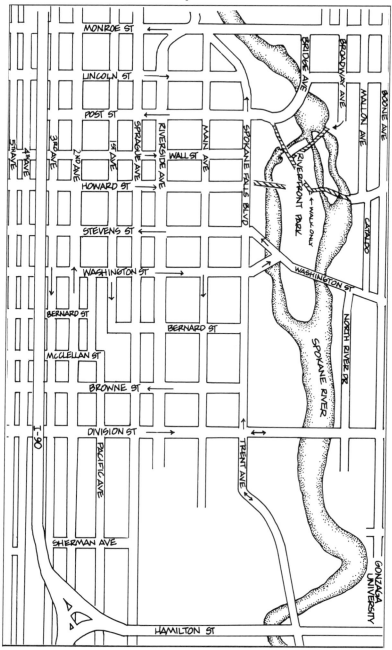

Old homes. Tour Overbluff Drive to see the small palaces of the upper crust, and Cliff Drive or Sumner Avenue on the South Hill to view some splendid older homes. Browne's Addition, west of downtown, is full of late-Victorian homes.

Parks. Riverfront Park is the pleasant green heart of the old city. Developed from old railroad yards by Expo '74, the park is now an airy place full of meandering paved paths, with entertainments ranging from ice skating to an IMAX theater. The 1909 carousel is a local landmark, hand-carved by master builder Charles Looff. The music is too loud for children under about four (and most adults), but older kids love riding the menagerie. **Manito Park**, at Grand Boulevard and 18th, has a splendidly splashable duck pond and theme gardens. **Finch Arboretum** (west of downtown Spokane), a pleasant picnic site, hosts a modest but attractive collection of trees and shrubs among ravines and a stream. For a panoramic vista of Spokane, visit **Cliff Park** at 13th and Grove.

Nature. Two natural areas just a couple of miles outside Spokane's city limits offer excellent places to hike and see birds and wildlife: the **Little Spokane Natural Area**, (509) 456-4730, and the **Spokane Fish Hatchery**, (509) 625-5169. The fishery is at 2927 W Waikiki Road; for the Natural Area, look for the Indian Rock Paintings parking lot on Rutter Parkway. The **Dishman Hills Natural Area**, a 460-acre preserve in the Spokane Valley, has a network of trails with mixed wildlife habitats. Take I-90 east to Sprague Avenue exit, go east 1½ miles to Sargent Road; turn right ½ mile to parking area. Just 45 miles south of Spokane you'll find the 15,000-acre **Turnbull National Wildlife Refuge**, especially interesting during fall and spring migration; excellent. Take I-90 west, exit at Cheney. Take I-90 west, exit at Cheney, go through the town and turn left on Smith Road.

Culture. New Brazilian-born conductor Fabio Machetti has been working with the **Spokane Symphony** since June 1993, and programs, including a pops series, are lively and innovative. An annual free Labor Day concert in Comstock Park draws thousands of picnicking spectators; (509) 326-3136. The **Spokane Civic Theatre**, 1020 N Howard, offers a mixed bag of amateur performances each season; the **Interplayers Ensemble Theatre**, 174 S Howard, is a professional company with a full season. **Riverfront Park** often hosts concerts of jazz, bluegrass, and popular music during the summer; call (509) 456-6675 for information.

Museums. Cheney Cowles Museum displays pioneer and mining relics, and one of the fine old mansions from Spokane's mining era, **Clark Mansion**, is open for viewing; 2316 W First Avenue, (509) 456-3931.

Sports. Golf is very good here. **Indian Canyon**, (509) 747-5353, and **Hangman Valley**, (509) 448-1212, two of the most

▼

Spokane

▲

beautiful public courses in the nation, have recently attracted a number of professional tournaments. There are no less than nine others. Spokane's parks and hilly roads and the new **Centennial Trail** (flanking the river from downtown to the Idaho border) offer great bicycle riding. Runners will find themselves in good company, especially during Spokane's annual Bloomsday Run (see calendar). The good ski areas nearby are 49 Degrees North, 58 miles north of Spokane near Chewelay, (509) 935-6649, a good place for beginners; Mount Spokane, 31 miles north on Highway 206, (509) 238-6281, with fair facilities and some challenging runs; Schweitzer Mountain Resort in Sandpoint, Idaho, (208) 263-9555, with excellent facilities for family skiing; and the country's newest destination ski resort, Silver Mountain at Kellogg, Idaho, (208) 783-1113. Mount Spokane also has 17 kilometers of groomed cross-country ski trails along with two warming huts; a SnoPark pass is required. Summers, Mount Spokane State Park, (509) 456-4169, is prime huckleberry terrain.

Brewery tour. Hale's Ales, which now has breweries in Spokane and Kirkland, is a microbrewery that welcomes visitors—when the day's brewing work is done. Call ahead for a reservation for a tour and a taste of their pale ale, bitter, porter, Moss Bay ale, and seasonal specialties: E 5634 Commerce Street, Spokane, (509) 534-7553.

RESTAURANTS

Milford's Fish House and Oyster Bar ★★ Spokane's oldest fish house offers simple decor—exposed brick, red-and-white checkered tablecloths, a few green plants—and good food at reasonable prices. Check the fresh list, updated daily, for best bets, and don't hesitate to ask the waiter for recommendations. Fresh salmon, baked or poached, is available in season, and the halibut is always a winner. On the weekend, service can be slow, especially in the trendy Oyster Bar. Reservations are a must unless you don't mind a wait. ■ *Corner of Broadway and Monroe; (509) 326-7251; 719 N Monroe St, Spokane; $$; full bar; MC, V; checks OK; dinner every day.* ⅋

Auntie's Bookstore and Cafe ★ This cheerful cafe-in-a-bookstore makes a great place to settle with a cup of coffee and a good read. The atmosphere is so inviting, in fact, that many lingerers fall prey to the vigilant parking meter patrol. Soups, salads, pasta, and dessert are all made daily from scratch—the thick and hearty lentil soup is the obvious favorite. On a chilly day, try the melted cheese and mushroom sandwich, spiced with a mild salsa. Breakfasts consist of muffins, cinnamon rolls, or bagels, and espresso. ■ *Between Washington and Bernard; (509) 838-0206; 313 W Riverside Ave, Spokane; $; no alcohol; MC, V; local checks only; breakfast, dinner Mon-Sat, lunch every day.*

Clinkerdagger's ★ Clinkerdagger's has broadened its menu from the basic chicken and steak selection to include more Northwest-oriented dishes, but in the end, it's the basic but well-handled (and attractively presented) food that wins us over. When fresh seafood is available, there might be four or five specials. Reservations recommended, especially for the coveted window seats. In the spring, when the Spokane River is rushing, the views from the window tables are exciting. ■ *East of Monroe in Flour Mill; (509) 328-5965; 621 W Mallon Ave, Spokane; $$; full bar; AE, DC, MC, V; local checks only; lunch Mon-Sat, dinner every day.*

The Downtown Onion ★ The magnificent old bar is a relic of the days when the building that houses this eatery was a fine hotel, the St. Regis. Some of the furnishings—the pressed-tin ceiling, the wood dividers—are also from the original hotel. The Onion set the standard in Spokane for gourmet hamburgers, and they're still local classics. The beer selection would be outstanding anywhere; fruit daiquiris are a specialty. (The huckleberry daiquiris—and the other huckleberry offerings such as huckleberry layer cake and huckleberry milk shakes—are available year-round). A young, informal crowd dominates on most nights, especially on Monday nights during NFL season. Being part of the chaos is part of the fun of this place, so don't take a booth in the sun room. Service is attentive. The

▼

Spokane

Restaurants

▲

same menu is served at the North Onion at 7522 N Division, (509) 428-6100. ■ *On Riverside at Bernard; (509) 747-3852; 302 W Riverside Ave, Spokane; $; full bar; AE, MC, V; checks OK; lunch, dinner every day.* &

Knight's Diner ★ Eggs the way you want them and crispy hashbrowns have been served up in this renovated circa-1900 railroad car for four decades, with only a brief interruption a few years ago when the diner was moved to its new site at the south end of Hillyard. Those seeking an old-fashioned breakfast flock to this former Pullman passenger car where they sit on stools and eat at a mahogany counter that runs the length of the car. If you go with a group, be prepared to take whatever seats open up. Those on grill-front stools get to watch the cook keep the dozens of orders all cooking at once. Hungry diners can order the 24 dollar-size pancakes or can opt for the even dozen. Our favorite, however, is the standard fried eggs, bacon, hashbrowns, and wheat toast. There's a lunch menu, but few bother. ■ *At the intersection of N Market and Green St; (509) 484-0015; 2909 N Market, Spokane; $; no alcohol; no credit cards; checks OK; breakfast, lunch Tues-Sun.*

If you've found a place that you think is a best place, send in the report form at the back of this book. If you're unhappy with one of the places, let us know why. We depend on reader input.

Marrakesh ★ The Moroccan restaurant, originally of Seattle and now in Portland, has come to Spokane. It is located in the Audubon district in a former used-appliance store. Diners sit on benches along the walls or on tippy hammocks. The meal begins with a traditional finger-washing ceremony and ends with the sprinkling of fragrant rosewater over your hands, practical since your fingers are your utensils. A set price of $14.50 buys a five-course meal in which you choose only the entrée. It begins with a flavorful lentil soup and continues with a Moroccan eggplant salad scooped up with a pita bread. The bastela royale, a chicken pie in phyllo dusted with powdered sugar, was the highlight of the meal on our visit. Entrées include a variety of lamb and chicken dishes. If it's crowded and there are only two, you may be seated with another couple, or a larger group. ▪ *West of Monroe on Northwest Blvd; (509) 328-9733; 2208 Northwest Blvd, Spokane; $$; beer and wine; MC, V; checks OK; dinner Tues-Sun.*

Niko's Greek & Middle Eastern Restaurant ★ Niko's is deservedly popular locally for traditional Greek food, much of which is homemade in this modest taverna-style restaurant. Lamb is especially well treated here, and the garlicky, smooth hummus can be ordered as an entrée at lunch with a plate of vegetables or pita. Several Indian entrées have been added to the dinner menu, most notably the keema mater, chunky beef with yogurt and Indian spices served with pita. The Greek salads have plenty of salty, strong feta and Greek olives; the baklava is loaded with honey and nuts between layers of phyllo (one version is a chocolava). Thursday is belly-dancing night. Niko II, downtown at W 725 Riverside Avenue, (509) 624-7444, and is a popular lunch spot. ▪ *2 blocks off Sprague; (509) 928-9590; 321 S Dishman-Mica Rd, Spokane; $; beer and wine; AE, MC, V; local checks only; lunch Mon-Fri, dinner Mon-Sat.*

Patsy Clark's ★ Patrick F. Clark, "Patsy" to his friends, arrived in America in 1870 at the age of 20, and by the time he was 40 he was a millionaire many times over, thanks to the success of Montana's Anaconda Mine. Naturally anxious to display his success, he instructed architect Kirtland Cutter to build him the finest mansion he could conceive—never mind the cost. Marble was shipped in from Italy, wood carvings and clocks from England, a mural from France, and a spectacular stained-glass window (with more than 4,000 pieces) from Tiffany's of New York. Locally, the restaurant isn't famous for its entrées (the kitchen cuts corners with the quality of its ingredients); rather, we like Patsy's for formal special occasions. An elegant spot it is, and you should find some excuse to stop by, even if it's only for a drink (the wine list is one of the best in the area). Sunday brunch—a memorable experienced based on the sheer quantity of the offerings—requires reservations.

■ *15 blocks west of downtown at 2nd and Hemlock; (509) 838-8300; 2208 W 2nd Ave, Spokane; $$$; full bar; AE, DC, DIS, MC, V; local checks only; lunch Mon-Fri, dinner every day, brunch Sun.* &

Thai Cafe ★ You won't just stumble into this ethnic oasis in the Eastern Washington desert. Its location off the beaten track keeps this Thai restaurant exclusive to those in the know. A waft of curry greets patrons at the door; and you'll find such seasonings, along with coconut milk and peanuts, in most of the entrées. The cooks will spice the dishes to the desired hotness. We've yet to be disappointed with any of the 12 chicken selections (and we've tried them all). If you can't decide, try the pra ram long song—chicken with peanut sauce, served on a bed of fresh spinach. And don't miss the desserts—black rice pudding over ice cream or warm bananas in coconut milk. ■ *Sprague at Washington; (509) 838-4783; 410 W Sprague Ave, Spokane; $; Thai beer only; no credit cards; local checks only; lunch Mon-Fri, dinner Mon-Sat.* &

Amore This small Italian eatery adjacent to a Baskin-Robbins is easy to miss while driving by on busy Grand Boulevard. To eat here is to engage in a veritable garlic-fest. Indeed, whole cloves of garlic arrive on everything, save the green salad, which is not devoid of garlic either. Despite the casualness of the place, the waitstaff works hard to make dining here an occasion by pacing the arrival of the food to the moment you are ready for the next course. A good opener to the meal is the crostini caponata, toasted bread rounds baked with eggplant and parmigiano-reggino. Entrées are all the usual Italian choices, all competently prepared (if a tad heavy on the olive oil). The à la carte menu adds up quickly. We leave it up to you to figure out the wall embedded with bowling balls. ■ *At Grand Blvd and 13th; (509) 838-8640; 1128 S Grand Blvd, Spokane; $$; beer and wine; MC, V; checks OK; lunch Mon-Fri, dinner every night.*

Coyote Cafe The walls of this Mexican place are covered with offbeat art, and the service is prompt and relentlessly cheerful. If you want to be in and out in 20 minutes, that's no problem. Food includes reasonably priced, standard south-of-the-border fare—tacos and burritos, refried beans and fajitas—all of which are enhanced by the large, icy margaritas. Try the grilled chicken tacos. ■ *Corner of 3rd and Wall; (509) 747-8800; 702 W 3rd Ave, Spokane; $; beer and wine; MC, V; checks OK; lunch, dinner every day.* &

Europa Pizzeria Restaurant Exposed brick walls and bare wood give this place a certain Old World charm, and the relaxed atmosphere attracts good-tempered students from adjacent downtown college branch campuses. The food, baked pasta entrées and large calzones, can be overwhelming as a midday meal. The service is cheerful, advice reliable, and the pace relaxed (sometimes too much so for those on a lunch hour) enough for you to feel entirely comfortable settling in with a beer and a book. ■ *North side of the railroad trestle downtown, next to the Magic Lantern Theater; (509) 455-4051; 125 S Wall St, Spokane; $; beer and wine; MC, V; checks OK; lunch, dinner Mon-Sat.*

LODGINGS

Waverly Place ★★ Across the street from what was a racetrack, Waverly Place retains the elegance of the Victorian era. The track is now Corbin Park, a lovely oval with a couple of tennis courts, a tree canopy, and plenty of places to walk. Guests at this bed and breakfast can sit on the broad porch overlooking the park and sip lemonade or swim in the new pool. There are three guest rooms: the Skinner Suite, decorated with all oak furnishings—including a sleigh bed—and a private bath; Anna's Room, with a window seat overlooking the park; and the Mill Street Room with its big brass bed. Fresh fruit, Swedish pancakes with huckleberry sauce, sausage, and coffee are a sample of the breakfast fare. ■ *Division St exit off I-90 and head north to Waverly Pl; (509) 328-1856; 709 W Waverly Pl, Spokane, WA 99205; $$; AE, DIS, MC, V; checks OK.*

Cavanaugh's Inn at the Park ★ This hotel on the bank of the river across from Riverfront Park now has 408 rooms (with a new tower opening soon), many with southern views of downtown Spokane (and a few of the hydropower weir). The spacious lobby is the center of the main building, and all seven stories of rooms open out to it; it can be noisy, so specify a quiet corner room or perhaps one in the wing at the east end of the hotel, away from the lobby and busy Washington Street, or in the new tower at the west end of the complex. The attractive Windows on the Seasons restaurant overlooks the river, but the food is perfunctory. The lounge has comedy on Wednesday nights. ■ *Division St exit from I-90, north to N River Dr; (509) 326-8000 or (800) 843-4667; 303 W N River Dr, Spokane, WA 99201; $$; AE, DC, DIS, MC, V; checks OK.* &

West Coast Ridpath Hotel ★ The 340 rooms are pleasant and spacious, and those in the tower overlook the city. The downtown location is as convenient as they come. This place is popular with conventioneers and tourists, and some of the public areas can be crowded, but the mood here is always convivial. The rooftop restaurant, Ankeny's, boasts a grand view of Spokane. At night, when all is glittering and reflected repeatedly by the smoked glass and mirrors of the interior decor, the effect can be dazzling, glitzy, or just plain bewildering. The food is somewhat predictable, Sunday brunch is a buffet; the Silver

Grill, a coffee shop, provides more low-key fare. ▪ *In the heart of downtown; (800) 426-0670; 515 W Sprague Ave, Spokane, WA 99204; $$; AE, DC, DIS, MC, V; checks OK.*

COLVILLE

The Colville River Valley has tiny farming communities, but outdoor recreation—fishing and cross-country skiing, primarily—is beginning to draw many to the pristine area. Highway 20 from Colville to Tonasket was dedicated last year as a National Scenic Byway. It climbs over **Sherman Pass**, amazingly, the highest pass in Washington.

KETTLE FALLS

LODGINGS

My Parent's Estate ★ This 118-year-old house has also been a mission school, an abbess's home in a Dominican convent, a home for troubled boys, and a private residence; it's now a quiet haven in the woods. The 49-acre estate on the Colville River boasts a gym, a barn, a chicken coop, a caretaker's house and a cemetery; more modern additions include a Jacuzzi and private baths. Hosts Al and Bev Parent are proud of their home; Bev's arts and crafts collection is displayed around the house, and Al is always eager to take guests on a historical tour of the grounds. The three guest rooms encourage quiet country relaxation, with comforters on the queen-size beds, refinished vanities, and antique washbasins. The lofty living room is dominated by a floor-to-ceiling stone fireplace. There's cross-country skiing in the winter; in more temperate months guests can float the Colville River, hike, or play in the water at nearby Franklin D. Roosevelt Lake. ▪ *7 miles past downtown Colville on Hwy 395; (509) 738-6220; PO Box 724, Kettle Falls, WA 99141; $$; MC, V; checks OK.*

CURLEW

RESTAURANTS

The Riverside Restaurant and Lounge ★ Curlew's downtown cafe has gained quite a reputation among backcountry hikers and mountain climbers. The setting is pleasant and comfortable: wooden tables and chairs and a wooden bar. The dining room has a large wood stove. There's a view of the river, the produce is fresh, and the food is fairly simple but always good. You can get the all-American thick sirloins, accompanied by steamed vegetables, but there's a recent bent toward Mexican, and where else can you get a shredded beef enchilada sided by gently steamed asparagus? There's usually great cheesecake for dessert. An oasis in Washington's northeastern corner. ▪ *On*

the main drag, on the river; (509) 779-4813; 813 River St,
Curlew; $$; full bar; MC, V; checks OK; dinner Wed-Sun.

WAUCONDA

RESTAURANTS

The Wauconda Cafe, General Store and Post Office If you
want atmosphere, here it is in this small general store cum gas
station cum post office cum restaurant. A lunch counter with a
few booths is squeezed between the general store and the din-
ing room. It's a popular hangout for the local folk, both rancher
types and counterculturalists. The view is out across the rolling
meadows so typical of the Okanogan Highlands, with a few
weatherbeaten barns enhancing the horizon and wildflowers in
the spring. The food is homemade and simple: tasty burgers,
milk shakes, sandwiches, and homemade soups for lunch;
sautéed prawns, prime rib, and big salads for dinner. ▪ *The only
place in town; (509) 486-4010; 2432 Hwy 20, Wauconda; $;
beer and wine; MC, V; local checks only; breakfast, lunch, din-
ner Mon-Sat.*

OROVILLE

LODGINGS

Sun Cove Resort ★ Sherill and Bruce Evans now run this
cozy lakefront hideaway that's both comfortable and away from
it all. Reasonably priced cabins are squeaky clean and fully
stocked with kitchen utensils (even soap for the dishes), bed-
ding, and linens. Ten of these rustic cabins comfortably sleep
four each. There are also two- and three-bedroom cottages for
families of six or eight in which a one-week minimum stay is
required. You'll undoubtedly want to stay longer, though.
There's excellent rainbow trout fishing in 2-mile-long Wanna-
cut Lake, swimming in a heated pool, kayaking, canoeing, a
game and toy center for youngsters, even a small library and
a tanning center. Horseback riding is available at extra cost. If
there's a drawback, it's the dusty, narrow drive in to the re-
sort—but that's a small price to pay for such seclusion. Chil-
dren are more than welcome. ▪ *11 miles southwest of Oroville
on Wannacut Lake; (509) 476-2223; Rt 2, Box 1294, Oroville,
WA 98844; $$; MC, V; checks OK.* &

OMAK

The famous—and controversial—Suicide Race is the climax of
the Omak Stampede the second weekend each August. At the
end of each of the four rodeos that take place over the three-
day weekend, a torrent of horses and riders pours down a steep
embankment, across the Okanogan River, and into the arena.

No one's ever been killed during the races since the event started in 1933, but plenty of horses have broken their legs.

RESTAURANTS

Breadline Cafe ★ Here in the heart of steak and Stampede country, the Breadline offers a choice of fare. In the front of an old bottling-works building, owner Paula Chambers has expanded her eatery to include a low-tech bistro/nightclub offering full dinners and live music—from small folk bands to big-name blues artists like Charlie Musselwhite. The country-style menu includes steak and scampi, Cajun chicken, and pasta dishes. We like the big, informal, cheerfully cluttered cafe in the back. Here, the food takes a more New Age twist: home-style breakfasts and creative lunches. You watch the whole-grain bread come out of the oven as your hearty sandwich or salad is prepared. The Washington's Best Salad combines lettuce, smoked salmon, tomato, and cucumber in a unique cranberry dressing (especially tasty). Hot apple fritters with cream maple sauce finish you off. ■ *Ash and 1st; (509) 826-5836; 102 S Ash St, Omak; $; beer and wine; AE, MC, V; checks OK; breakfast, lunch Mon-Sat, dinner Tues-Sat.*

▼

Omak

▲

OKANOGAN

LODGINGS

U and I Motel The name suits this family-run place's folksiness. It's not much to look at from its front on the old back road between Okanogan and Omak, but a closer look uncovers a more than usually pleasant little nook for hiding away from it all. The two-room cabinettes are less than spacious, but they're clean and cozily done up in rustic paneling. They are a deal, starting at $32, as are one-roomers with a double bed for $25. Best of all, the whole backyard of the motel is a grassy lawn and flower garden fronting on the tranquil Okanogan. Grab a deck chair, cast a fishing line, and watch the river flow. Pets okay. ■ *Off Hwy 97 on old 97 at 838 2nd Ave N; (509) 422-2920; PO Box 549, Okanogan, WA 98840; $; MC, V; local checks only.*

COULEE DAM

LODGINGS

Coulee House Motel With a great view of the dam, this motel has decent amenities—pool, sauna, and refrigerators in some of the large, clean rooms, to name a few. At night you can sit on the tiny lanai outside your room (smoking or non) and watch the new animated laser light show (summers only) over the dam as the water cascades past. ■ *Birch and Roosevelt; (509) 633-1101; 110 Roosevelt Way, Coulee Dam, WA 99116; $$; AE, DC, DIS, MC, V; no checks.*

Four Winds Once a dormitory for engineers on the dam, the
Four Winds is now Coulee Dam's most personable inn *and*
within walking distance of the dam itself. There are 11 spotlessly clean rooms with many combinations of baths: some
share with one other, and others down the hall. At one end of the
building is a foyer for reading, conversation, or board games.
Nothing fancy here, but all competently overseen by Richard
and Fe Taylor, who at 8:30am serve a virtual smorgasbord.
■ *Lincoln St is across from the Grand Coulee Dam visitors
center; (509) 633-3146 or (800) 786-3146; 301 Lincoln St,
Coulee Dam, WA 99116; MC, V; checks OK.*

GRAND COULEE

Grand, yes—this is a wonderful area from which to appreciate
the outsize dimensions of the landscape and the geological
forces that made it. The Columbia, as it slices through central
Washington, has an eerie power: the water rushes by in silky
strength through enormous chasms. The river, the second
largest in the nation, traverses a valley of staggering scale; in
prehistoric times glacier-fed water created a river with the
largest flow of water ever known.

Grand Coulee Dam is one of the largest structures on
the earth—tall as a 46-story building, with a spillway twice the
height of Niagara and a length as great as a dozen city blocks.
The dam, completed in 1941, was originally intended more to
irrigate the desert than to produce electricity; so much power
was generated, however, that the dam became a magnet for the
nation's aluminum industry. The north-face extension (completed in 1975) was designed by Marcel Breuer, a great practitioner of the International Style, and the heroic scale of the
concrete is quite magnificent, especially when illuminated by
the inspirational light show. There are daily self-guided tours
of the dam; hours vary according to season: (509) 633-9265.

Eccentric inventor Emil Gehrke amassed an oddly com-
pelling **windmill collection** at North Dam Park on Highway
155 between Electric City and Grand Coulee. Four hardhats
tilted sideways catch the wind, cups and saucers twirl around
a central teapot—it's whimsical and fascinating.

Houseboating. Until two years ago, Lake Roosevelt was
untapped by the RV-on-pontoons fleet. Now there are 40 houseboats available to explore the 150-mile-long lake, and most book
up early for the summer. The sun's almost guaranteed, and all
you need to bring is food, bed linens, towels, and your bathing
suit; boats are moored at Kelly Ferry Marina, 14 miles north of
Wilbur, 1-800-648-LAKE.

*Inspectors for the Best Places series accept no free meals or
accommodations; the book has no sponsors or advertisers.*

▮
409

CRESTON

RESTAURANTS

Deb's Cafe The glory days of Deb Cobenhaver, a world-champion rodeo rider back in the mid-1950s, are kept in a kind of time capsule here. Outside there is a wooden porch, like a stage-set saloon; inside, the place is strewn with trophies, photos, and saddles. Cowboy-hatted men and women shoot pool in the bar or line up at the lunch counter. The main cafe opens at 5am for its hearty breakfasts with homemade cinnamon rolls; at lunch there are a few decent sandwiches, served with home-cut fries; dinner is steaks—natch. ■ *Hwy 2; (509) 636-3345; 600 Watson, Creston; $; full bar; MC, V; local checks only; breakfast, lunch, dinner every day.* ᕕ

SOAP LAKE

Early settlers named the lake for its unusually high alkali content, which gives the water a soapy feel.

Dry Falls, off Route 17 north of town, is the place where the torrential Columbia once crashed over falls 3 miles wide and 400 feet high; an interpretive center (Wednesday through Sunday, 10 to 6, summer) explains the local geology, which has been compared to surface features of Mars. From this lookout, you can also see **Sun Lakes**, which are actually puddles left behind by the ancient Columbia. It's RV territory, but the waters are prime spots for swimming and fishing; (509) 632-5583.

LODGINGS

Notaras Lodge On the shores of Soap Lake, you can stay in the Norma Zimmer Room (the bubble lady on the "Lawrence Welk Show"), complete with a jukebox, or the Bonnie Guitar Honeymoon Suite (named for a local country-western celeb whose own guitar is memorialized in an epoxied table along with other souvenirs of the singer's career). Such memorabilia are owner Marina Romary's passion; the Western Nostalgia Room boasts a pool table as well as a whirlpool. The healing waters of Soap Lake are available to guests on tap in the bathrooms (eight of which have Jacuzzis). Romary also owns the nearby Don's Restaurant, 14 Canna Street, (509) 246-1217, a popular steak-and-seafood-and-Greek eatery, where man-size meals are served in a dark, slightly seamy interior. ■ *236 E Main St; (509) 246-0462; PO Box 987, Soap Lake, WA 98851; $$; MC, V; checks OK.* ᕕ

WENATCHEE

You're in the heart of apple country, with an Apple Blossom Festival the first part of May. **Ohme Gardens**, 3 miles north on Route 97, is a 600-foot-high promontory transformed into an Edenic retreat, with a fastidiously created natural alpine eco-system patterned after high mountain country. Splendid views of the valley and the Columbia River; (509) 662-5785.

Mission Ridge, 13 miles southwest on Squilchuck Road, offers some of the best powder snow in the region, served by four chair lifts (cross-country skiing too); (509) 663-7631. On the third Sunday in April, the Ridge-to-River Pentathlon is an impressive sporting event.

Rocky Reach Dam, 6 miles north on Route 97, offers a beautiful picnic and playground area (locals marry on the well-kept grounds), plus a fish-viewing room. Inside the dam are two large galleries devoted to the history of the region.

RESTAURANTS

The Windmill ★★ A constantly changing number on a blackboard keeps track of the steaks sold at this celebrated steak house. On our last visit it was 219,478. That's not the number of steaks sold since the Windmill opened 69 years ago—that's since January, 1982, when Pat and Linda Jackson took over as owners, and we haven't heard of even one that wasn't terrific. Waitresses here don't come and go—they stay and stay, sporting pins that proudly declare the number of years they've served. The meals, too, are time-tested and classic. They start you off with bread sticks and a relish tray, a lettuce salad, and a bottle of wine. There are seafood and pork chops, but don't be a fool—order the well-aged, perfectly cooked steak! Ritual dictates that you finish with a piece of one of the magnificent pies, baked fresh daily. ■ *1½ blocks west of Miller, on the main thoroughfare; (509) 663-3478; 1501 N Wenatchee Ave, Wenatchee; $$; beer and wine; AE, MC, V; checks OK; dinner Mon-Sat.*

Steven's at Mission Square ★ Steven's is a handsome place where Wenatchee's premier chef, Steve Gordon, serves Northwest cuisine with a few international excursions. The split-level dining room with potted plants is elegant in a trendy sort of way; full-length mirrors reflect the well-dressed clientele. Pasta and seafood dishes are served here with pride and a flourish, from fettuccine with asparagus and prosciutto to apricot-honey-mustard chicken with sweet basil on a bed of spinach, pecans, and Bermuda onions. We've had best luck with the specials (East Coast scallops sautéed with red and green bell peppers, artichoke hearts, and scallions, in a tomato sauce). Bread is freshly baked and warm, and desserts are first-rate, especially rich triangles of chocolate peanut-butter ice cream pie or chocolate hazelnut cheesecake. ■ *1 block off Wenatchee at 2nd and Mission; (509) 663-6573; 218 N Mission St, Wenatchee; $$; full bar; AE, MC, V; checks OK; lunch Mon-Fri, dinner every day.* &

Tequila's ★ Go ahead, salvage your high school Spanish; the friendly staff may even give you a few extra lessons. Tequila's takes Mexican food one step beyond the norm. Onions, pepper, and cilantro spice the fresh salsa. The baskets of warm tortilla chips are refilled often. Margaritas are generous and the re-fried beans have never seen the inside of a can. Best is any dish with the excellent carnitas or the tangy verde sauce. Or try the sizzling fajitas. It's all priced as if you were south of the border and you'll leave muy feliz. ■ *On Wenatchee Ave south of 9th; (509) 662-7239; 800 N Wenatchee Ave, Wenatchee; $; full bar; MC, V; checks OK; lunch, dinner every day.*

Visconti's Italian Restaurant ★ All the standards are on the menu, from spaghetti to caesars to thick slabs of lasagne. Fresh garlic and herbs permeate each generously sized dish. Try the mostaccioli (a tube-shaped noodle) with Italian sausage and mushroom sauce. Many wines are available by the glass, and Candy Mecham will offer sips to those unsure of the choice. Reports on dessert are good, especially the chocolate espresso cheesecake. ■ *At the west end of town on Wenatchee; (509) 662-5013; 1737 N Wenatchee, Wenatchee; $; beer and wine; AE, DC, DIS, MC, V; checks OK; lunch Mon-Fri, dinner every day.*

Golden East A remodeled bank is now a vault of red vinyl booths, paper lanterns, and Chinese food. George Chang and his wife, Marisa, prepare both Cantonese and more potent Sichuan favorites (even so, you might need to tell them you like it hot). Chang trained and worked in Seattle before going east to seek his fortune. He has a light hand with oil and favors cook-to-order preparation. The combination plates are fine, but you'll do better to order mu-shu pork with tender rice pancakes or chicken with cashews, soul-warming with hot peppers. Ask for a window table with a view of the Wenatchee River and Mission Ridge beyond. ■ *Across the Columbia River and up Grant Rd; (509) 884-1510; 230 Grant Rd, East Wenatchee; $; beer and wine; MC, V; local checks only; lunch, dinner Tues-Sun.* ⅙

LODGINGS

West Coast Wenatchee Center Hotel ★ This is the nicest ho-tel on the strip, with its view of the city and the Columbia River. It's elegant, but not overdone for this city. The nine-story hotel has three floors designated nonsmoking, with a total of 146 large, moderately priced rooms. A restaurant on the top floor is open for breakfast, lunch, and dinner, and the city's convention center is next door, connected by a skybridge. The outdoor pool is great under the hot Wenatchee sun. Also available are an indoor pool, a Jacuzzi, and a weight room. ■ *Center of town on Wenatchee; (509) 662-1234; 201 N Wenatchee Ave, We-natchee, WA 98801; $$; AE, DC, DIS, MC, V; checks OK.* ⅙

The Chieftain The motels all line up along Wenatchee Avenue, but this one stands out for its dependable quality year after year (since 1928). Outside it looks like it needs a new paint job, but it's popular with the locals, who come for "executive lunches," brunches after church on Sunday, or the famous prime rib in the evening. Guests will note that rooms are larger than those of the Chieftain's cousins down the pike. Ask for rooms in the newer wing, the "executive rooms," and you'll be surprised what spacious quarters you've got for about $55. There's a swimming pool, a hot tub, and a helicopter pad (which doubles as a basketball court). You can bring your pet with advance notice. Ugly views. ■ *On Wenatchee off 9th; (509) 663-8141, toll-free (800) 572-4456; 1005 N Wenatchee Ave, Wenatchee, WA 98801; $$; full bar; AE, DC, DIS, MC, V; checks OK; breakfast, lunch, dinner every day.* ♿

CHELAN

This resort area is blessed with the springtime perfume of apple blossoms, a 55-mile lake thrusting like a fjord into tall mountains, 300 days a year of sunshine, and good skiing, hunting, fishing, hiking, and sailing. It's been trying to live up to its touristic potential since C.C. Campbell built his hotel here in 1901, but with mixed success so far. Now that time-share condos are springing up near the golf course and B&Bs are blooming near the cross-country trails, the amenities are improving. No one need improve the scenery.

▼

Chelan

▲

The top attraction is the cruise up Lake Chelan on an old-fashioned tour boat, *The Lady of the Lake*, or the newer *Lady Express*. The lake is never more than 2 miles wide (it's also one of the deepest in the world), so you have a sense of slicing right into the Cascades. At Stehekin, the head of the lake, you can check out craft shops, take a bus tour, eat a barbecue lunch, and get back on board for the return voyage. The tour boat departs Chelan at 8:30am daily in summer, three or four days a week off season, and returns in the late afternoon; rates are $21 per person round-trip; kids 6-11 years are half price. No reservations needed. The faster *Lady Express* shortens the daily trip to just over 2 hours, with a 1-hour stop in Stehekin before heading back; round trip tickets are $38, and reservations are suggested. More info: The Lake Chelan Boat Company, (509) 682-2224. Or you can fly up to Stehekin, tour the valley, and be back the same day: Chelan Airways, (509) 682-5555.

Chelan Butte Lookout, 9 miles west of Chelan, provides a view of the lake, the Columbia, and the orchard-blanketed countryside.

Sports. Echo Valley, northeast of Chelan, offers rope tows and a Poma lift on gentle slopes; Lake Chelan Golf Course, (509) 682-5421 for tee times, is an attractive, sporting course near town; fishing for steelhead, rainbow, cutthroats, and chinooks is very good, with remote, smaller lakes desirable.

One thousand feet above Lake Chelan sits **Bear Mountain Ranch**, a 5,000-acre estate with 50 kilometers of tracked and skating trails for cross-country skiers. There's a warming hut with picnic tables and ski videos, and what are wheatfields in the summer provide gentle slopes for beginning telemarkers. Bigger plans are in the works, but for now you just go here to ski. Open for two weeks at Christmas, and weekends December through mid-March; (509) 682-5444.

Nostalgia. St. Andrew's Church, downtown Chelan, is a log edifice, reputedly designed by Stanford White in 1898, and still in service; from the Chelan Museum (Woodin Avenue, 1 to 4pm in summer) you can learn about other restored houses nearby, such as the old Lucas Homestead.

RESTAURANTS

Goochi's Restaurant ★ After years of abuse as a tavern in the historic Lakeview Hotel building, this pretty space with its huge antique cherrywood back bar is now a smart stop for lunch or dinner. Classic rock 'n' roll plays on CDs and neon sculpture decorates the cedar-planked walls. Burgers and pasta selections are popular with children; for the adults, however, the restaurant strives for a slight twist on the usual, offering black-eyed peas in lieu of potatoes or rice pilaf. A moist chicken breast may come with a tart lemon-thyme cream sauce. Soups (such as cream of green pepper) are often light and flavorful. Chelan's Riverfront Park, just around the corner, is good for a postprandial stroll. ■ *Across Woodin from Campbell's Lodge; (509) 682-2436; 104 E Woodin, Chelan; $; full bar; AE, DIS, MC, V; local checks only; lunch, dinner every day, brunch Sat-Sun.* ♿

LODGINGS

Campbell's Lodge ★★ Chelan's venerable resort, whose history goes back to 1901 and includes the absorption of its once rival to the north, Cannon's, continues to be the most popular place for visitors, with its prime lakeside properties and 148 rooms, many with kitchenettes. Among the facilities, you'll find three heated pools and an outdoor Jacuzzi, a sandy beach, and moorage should you arrive by boat. The convention center services up to 250 people. The most dependable restaurant at the lake is here: Campbell House Restaurant. Off a crowd-pleasing dinner menu one can order grilled chicken, beef stroganoff, breaded trout, a selection of seafoody pastas, and more; beware unbalanced sauces. Sourdough rolls, desserts, and informed service are first-rate. Reservations here, as at the lodge, can be scarce in high season. ■ *104 E Woodin, Chelan; (509) 682-2561;*

PO Box 278, Chelan, WA 98816; $$$; full bar; AE, DC, DIS, MC, V; checks OK; breakfast, lunch, dinner every day. &

Darnell's Resort Motel ★ Situated right on the shore of the lake, this is a resort especially suited to families. Suites are large and attractive and all have views ($75 to $145 for a suite for four). Lots of amenities are included with the price of the room: putting green, heated swimming pool, sauna, hot tub, exercise room, shuffleboard, volleyball, badminton, tennis, barbecues, bicycles, rowboats, and canoes. Down the road from Campbell's and the center of town, Darnell's is removed from the seasonal hurly-burly. ■ *Off Manson Hwy at 901 Spader Bay Rd; (509) 682-2015; PO Box 506, Chelan, WA 98816; $$$; AE, MC, V; checks OK.*

Kelly's Resort ★ Kelly-owned for about 45 years, this resort is a favorite for families because it is right on the shore and not right in town. The original 10 fully equipped cabins are set back in the woods; they're dark and rustic (request the one above the volleyball courts—it has the most sun), but they're great for those on a budget ($82 for three) and families seeking a playground. But we prefer one of the four new condo units on the lake (from the lower units you can walk right off the deck into the lake). There's a nice deck near the grocery store (a good spot to have a beer) and a knotty-pine common area with a pingpong table and a fireplace. A very friendly spot. ■ *14 miles uplake on the south shore; (509) 687-3220; Rt 1, Box 119, Chelan, WA 98816; $$$; MC, V; checks OK.*

▼
Stehekin
▲

STEHEKIN

A passage to Stehekin, a little community at the head of Lake Chelan, is like traveling to another world, where there is no telephone service. This jumping-off point for exploring the rugged and remote North Cascades National Park can be reached only by a four-hour *Lady of the Lake* boat trip or the faster *Lady Express* (daily from mid-April to mid-October, less frequently in winter), (509) 682-2224; by Chelan Airways floatplane, (509) 682-5555; by hiking (write Chelan Ranger District, PO Box 189, Chelan, WA 98816); or by private boat. The boat and the plane will take you to Stehekin from the town of Chelan. For a shorter ride, catch the *Lady* uplake at Field's Point.

Exploring the area is the prime reason for coming here. There are several day hikes, including a lovely one along the lakeshore and another along a stream through the Buckner Orchard, and many more splendid backcountry trails for the serious backpacker. In winter there are some fine touring opportunities for cross-country skiers or snowshoe enthusiasts, although the town pretty much shuts down then. The ranger station at Chelan (open year-round), (509) 682-2576, is a fine source of information for these activities. A National Park Service shuttle bus provides transportation from Stehekin to trailheads, campgrounds, fishing holes, and scenic areas mid-May to mid-October; for information, call either (206) 856-5700 or (509) 682-2549. There are also bicycle and boat rentals at the North Cascades Lodge.

Stehekin Valley Ranch. The Courtney family picks you up at Stehekin in an old bus and takes you to the farthest end of the valley for seclusion and hearty family-style meals at their ranch. Open in the summer months, their rustic tent-cabins offer a place to bunk and just the basics (a kerosene lamp, showers in the main building), plus hearty, simple food at a decent price ($49 per night per person). **Cascade Corrals**, also run by the family, arranges horseback rides and mountain pack trips; (509) 682-4677 or write Stehekin Valley Ranch, Box 36, Stehekin, WA 98852.

The **Stehekin Pastry Company** fills the void the Honey Bear Bakery left when the bakery migrated to Seattle; this spot is a local favorite for sweet desserts and rich conversation.

LODGINGS

Silver Bay Inn ★★ The Silver Bay Inn, located where the Stehekin River flows into Lake Chelan, is a wonderful retreat for those who want to explore the Stehekin Valley. Friendly Kathy and Randall Dinwiddie welcome their guests to this passive solar home with hikes and stories only the locals know. Guests get a continental breakfast, and for snacks later in the afternoon the Stehekin Pastry Company is just a short stroll down the road. The setting is spectacular: 700 feet of waterfront with a broad green lawn rolling down to the lake. The main house has a master suite (with a two-night minimum to ensure you'll take time to enjoy yourself) decorated in antiques, with a separate sitting room, two view decks, a soaking tub, and a faraway view. Three separate lakeside cabins are remarkably convenient (dishwasher, microwave, all linens) and sleep four and six. Bicycles, canoes, croquet, and (for the less active) hammocks are available. A hot tub has a 360-degree view of the lake and surrounding mountains. Silver Bay could be a perfect place for families; however, two of the three cabins are adult-only. ■ *Take the* Lady of the Lake *to Stehekin; (509) 682-2212; PO Box 43, Stehekin, WA 98852; $$; no credit cards; checks OK.*

NACHES

LODGINGS

Whistlin' Jack Lodge ★★ There are a number of fishing lodges nestled in the pines on the Naches River, but this one, on the east side of Mount Rainier's Chinook Pass, is our favorite. Ideal for all manner of outdoor activity, from hiking and fishing to alpine and cross-country skiing, this mountain hideaway (originally built in 1957) has all the comforts of home and then some. There are six cabins, two bungalows, and eight motel units here, but best are the cabins—specifically, the Naches (with a riverfront lawn and hot tub on the deck) or the Grandview (so close to the rushing river you could almost fish from your deck). If you book a bungalow or room without a kitchenette, the pan-fried trout in the restaurant is not such a bad deal (especially if you plan ahead and ask for a package deal). Access via Chinook Pass near Mount Rainier (where the lodge's namesake marmots call home) is closed almost seven months a year, but lodge patrons (many families) are used to driving the winding road from Yakima any time of year. ■ *40 miles west of Yakima on Hwy 410; (509) 658-2433 or (800) 827-2299; 20800 Hwy 410, Naches, WA 98937; $$; DIS, MC, V; checks OK.*

YAKIMA WINE COUNTRY

If your last visit to the Napa Valley recalled rush-hour traffic on the freeway to Disneyland, you may be ready for the less traveled, more organic pleasures of the Yakima wine country. Get off the freeway at virtually any point between Union and the Tri-Cities and you'll find a scene of unspoiled pastoral splendor. (See also Tri-Cities Wine Country.) Vineyards and orchards follow the meandering Yakima River. Cattle graze the pastures. And the small towns scattered here and there provide constant surprises and unexpected small pleasures. The burgeoning wine industry (there are close to two dozen wineries in the valley, and more on the way) has encouraged small businesses to go after the tourist trade. Warm welcomes in the shops and tasting rooms are genuine; they really are glad to see you.

Yakima Wine Country

Since vineyards were first planted about two decades ago, the valley's unique weather patterns—warm days, cool nights, with seemingly more daylight than down in Napa—have encouraged winemakers to develop new approaches to winemaking. A Northwest style has emerged: bright fruit flavors underscored by crisp acids. The white wines are mostly dry (even the rieslings tend that way) and firmer than their counterparts in California, while the reds are rich and textured, with the structure of fine Bordeaux. Prices are low, and wineries often sell special bottlings unavailable elsewhere.

The Yakima Valley Wine Growers Association (PO Box 39, Grandview, WA 98930) publishes a useful brochure that lists member wineries along with tasting-room hours, easy-to-follow maps, and a bit of history. Big or small, all offer a taste of what's new and a chance to chat about the vintage in the most relaxed circumstances. Here's a quick rundown, as you head east from Yakima. **Thurston Wolfe**, 27 N Front, Yakima, (509) 452-0335, dessert wine specialists, with a Sauterne-style "Sweet Rebecca" and a landmark Zinfandel port. **Staton Hills**, 71 Gangl Road, Wapato, (509) 877-2112, in an attractive building, with a view of Union Gap, picnic grounds. **Bonair Winery**, 500 S Bonair Road, Zillah, (509) 829-6027, a small, friendly, family-run winery, with a flair for chardonnay. **Hyatt Vineyards Winery**, 2020 Gilbert Road, Zillah, (509) 829-6333, fine dry white wines and a lovely view. **Zillah Oakes Winery**, Zillah, (509) 829-6990, off-dry white wines, gift shop, and a tasting room with a Victorian motif, faces right on the highway. **Covey Run**, 1500 Vintage Road, Zillah, (509) 829-6235, one of the larger wineries, expansive tasting room, picnic grounds, view, and a full line of well-made wines, particularly rieslings. **Portteus Vineyards**, 5201 Highland Drive, Zillah, (509) 829-6970, new, family-owned, with estate-bottled reds—cabernet, merlot, and lemberger. **Horizon's Edge Winery**, 4530 E Zillah Drive, Zillah, (509) 829-6401, another spectacular view and good lineup of wines. **Washington Hills Cellars**, 111 E Lincoln Avenue, Sunnyside, (509) 839-9463, large selection of pleasant wines in a no-frills facility. **Eaton Hill Winery**, 530 Gurley Road, Granger, (509) 854-2508, new winery and B&B in a restored homestead and cannery, all white wines so far. **Stewart Vineyards**, 1711 Cherry Hill Road, Granger, (509) 854-1882, one of the oldest vineyards in the state, rieslings and cabernets are worth noting. **Tefft Cellars**, Outlook, (509) 837-7651, Washington's newest winery produces a small number of handcrafted wines. **Tucker Cellars**, Sunnyside, (509) 837-8701, a family enterprise offering an extensive selection of Yakima valley fruit and produce as well as wines. Excellent tours at **Chateau Ste. Michelle**, W Fifth and Avenue B, Grandview, (509) 882-3928, where the state's biggest winery set up shop in the late '60s, and the highly regarded reds are still made, in a facility dating back to the repeal of Prohibition. **Yakima River Winery**, Prosser, (509) 786-2805, riverside location, full-blown reds and superb dessert wines. **Pontin del Roza**, Prosser, (509) 786-4449, family-owned and operated. **Hinzerling Winery**, 1520 Sheridan, Prosser, (509) 786-2163, one of the state's pioneering wineries, now under new ownership; look for tannic reds and fine late-harvest "Die Sonne" gewürztraminer. **Chinook Wines**, Prosser, (509) 786-2725, a charming, intimate setting in which small quantities of some of Washington's best wines are produced. Don't miss the merlot. The **Hogue Cellars**, Wine Country Road, Prosser, (509) 786-4557, spectacularly successful family enterprise making superb whites and cellar-worthy reds; look for "Reserve" wines. **Oakwood Cellars**, Benton City, (509) 588-5332, one of the newest additions to the growing number of wineries in the vicinity of Red Mountain. **Kiona Vineyards Winery**, Benton City, (509) 588-6716, a small estate winery, the first to plant on Red Mountain, making remarkable cabernet, lemberger, and dry and sweet rieslings. **Seth Ryan Winery**, Benton City,

▼

Yakima Wine Country

▲

(509) 588-6780, a winery with its first bottlings already getting recognized for its riesling and chardonnay. **Blackwood Canyon**, Benton City, (509) 588-6249, just up the road from Kiona, a no-frills facility making controversial but distinctive wines; the late-harvest wines are excellent. **Columbia Crest Winery**, Paterson, (509) 875-2061, off the beaten track a half hour south of Prosser, this impressive facility showcases sophisticated winemaking on a grand scale.

YAKIMA

Irrigation (first tried by the Indians and missionaries here in the 1850s) has made this desert bloom with grapes, apples,

Yakima

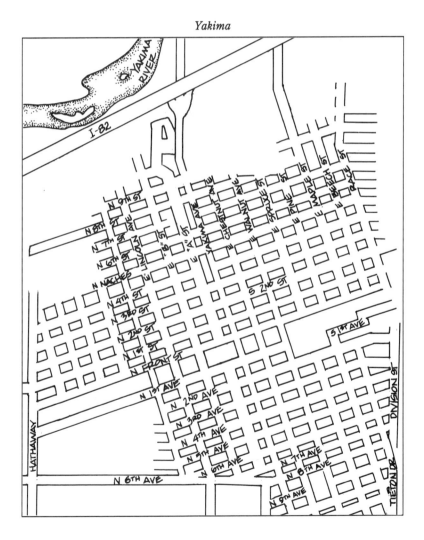

mint, asparagus, and hops. The town also blooms with small conventions.

Front Street Historical District includes a 22-car train that houses shops and restaurants, and the renovated Pacific Fruit Exchange Building, which holds a local farmers market.

The Greenway Bike Path winds along the Yakima River for 4.6 miles. Start out in Sherman Park on Nob Hill and go to the Selah Gap. Along the way, look for bald eagles and blue herons, or pick out a fishing hole; (509) 453-8280.

The Wine Cellar is a fine place to sample local vintages and orient yourself for a more extended foray into the wine country. Lenore Lambert, the owner, is a good source for local lore. Food products sold; 5 N Front Street, (509) 248-3590.

Interurban Trolley. A restored 1906 trolley provides summer-evening and weekend rides around Yakima. Call (509) 575-1700 for schedules.

Horse racing. Yakima Meadows has live races November through March. It's a dandy place to see small-town, old-West racing. 1301 S 10th, (509) 248-3920.

Yakima Valley Museum has handsome pioneer pieces, plus a collection from Yakima's most famous native son, Justice William O. Douglas. 2105 Tieton Drive, (509) 248-0747.

RESTAURANTS

Gasperetti's Restaurant ★★★ Almost a quarter-century after its beginning, John Gasperetti's Northern Italian restaurant continues to be one of the most innovative establishments in the region. You feel comfortable here in this intimate, leisurely, and friendly place—even if it's your first visit. Originally a family-style restaurant, the place still offers spaghetti with meat sauce (and great thin-sliced onion rings), but the daily specials display the real skill of chef Brad Patterson. Those in the know head to the room on the right; first-time patrons may find themselves shunted to the more austere left-hand room. Either way, you'll find pastas made fresh daily with seasonal sauces—light tomato cream, fresh pesto, rabbit with Chianti. You might want to split an appetizer of roasted garlic and Rollingstone chèvre, or asparagus vinaigrette. The light touch extends to both the pastas and the meat dishes. And save room for dessert—fresh berries in season; praline cheesecake; something chocolatey. The wine list (one of the best in the Valley) offers excellent bottlings of Washington wines, including many hard-to-find reds. Service is informed, attentive, anticipating, and unobtrusive. The location, on a busy street, is a little less desirable. ■ *6 blocks south of the N Front St exit off I-82; (509) 248-0628; 1013 N 1st St, Yakima; $$; full bar; AE, DIS, MC, V; checks OK; lunch Tues-Fri, dinner Tues-Sat.* &

Birchfield Manor ★★ All in all, Birchfield Manor offers elegant French country dining. As you arrive for your appointed seating, owners Wil and Sandy Masset greet you at the door and show you to your table in the large living room of this antique-filled historic home. Meals here are preceded by their reputation, which is taken *very* seriously. Young children are not welcome, lest they disturb others' enjoyment of the evening. Wil's European training as a chef produces an ambitious, imaginative meal. That said, Birchfield Manor is one of a kind in Central Washington, and therefore worth visiting when you're in the mood for a formal evening. Of the four entrées, we selected the double breast of chicken florentine and a very authentic bouillabaisse. Washington wines are featured, and the courses—dutifully explained by a friendly waitperson—are both individualistic and complementary to each other. There are five B&B rooms upstairs ($60 to $90 with baths). In contrast to the dark color scheme of the restaurant, bright colors and continental appointments fill each bedroom. An outdoor pool and hot tub are for guest use only. ■ *Exit 34 off I-82 onto Hwy 24, head east 2 miles, then south on Birchfield; (509) 452-1960; 2018 Birchfield Rd, Yakima; $$$; beer and wine; AE, MC, V; checks OK; dinner Thurs-Sat.*

The Blue Ox ★★ White linens, fresh flowers—and just homey enough to be a very comfortable restaurant. Several favorable reports have crossed our desks rating the steaks as some of the best in the area. With no less than 12 steak choices (from an aged top sirloin to a chateaubriand for two—carved at tableside), you won't go wrong. Care is put into all aspects of your dinner here right down to the carrots touched with ginger on the side of your plate. It's located in a large blue house near the center of town; the wine list stands up to the high expectations of the region. ■ *1 block north of Yakima Ave; (509) 248-5930; 15 N 6th St, Yakima; $$$; beer and wine; AE, DIS, MC, V; local checks only; dinner Mon-Sat.* &

Cafe European and Coffee Company ★★ What started out as Jerry Pardo's Viennese and French pastry shop has grown into one of Yakima's favorite eateries, all day long. Breakfast comes in the form of eggs and homemade scones or waffles. Lunch offers a number of sandwiches, but you'll do best to choose from the list of other selections such as a cold curry chicken and pasta salad or a true-to-the-anchovies caesar salad. Of course, this is also the kind of place you don't—no, you can't—leave without sampling a truffle or a vanilla génoise for dessert. Hands down, the best espresso in Yakima. ■ *Between 31st and 32nd on Summitview; (509) 248-5844; 3105 Summitview Ave, Yakima; $$; beer and wine; AE, MC, V; checks OK; breakfast, lunch Mon-Sat, dinner Wed-Sat, brunch Sun.*

The Brewery Pub ★ Bert Grant, one of the creators of the Northwest's boom in microbreweries, has brought back full-flavored, fresh, locally made ales, stouts, and hard cider. The pub is now located in the old train station. Small experimental batches are brewed here while the bulk of the beer is made at the original location across the street (open for tours by reservation only). It's a popular place (especially on weekends) that serves up a British pub menu to accompany the ales. (Only Grant's brews are served.) Homemade soups and Mexican food occasionally appear at lunch. A good place to meet friendly residents. ▪ *Head west on Yakima, turn right on Front; (509) 575-2922; 32 N Front St, Yakima; $; beer; MC, V; checks OK; lunch, dinner every day.*

Deli de Pasta ★ The North Front Street area is a comfortable blend of the old, the funky, and the hip. A half block south of Grant's, this intimate Italian cafe is quite popular with the locals. Owners Bob and Diane Traner have a flair for decor, making simple touches (red wooden chairs, red tablecloths, white linen napkins) seem somehow extraordinary. Fresh pastas and sauces, made on the premises, can be mixed and matched to suit your mood. The kitchen has been more consistent with their pastas lately; locals favor the salmon ravioli. The service is friendly, the coffee's fine, and the congenial atmosphere encourages many happy returnees. ▪ *½ block off Yakima on N Front St; (509) 453-0571; 7 N Front St, Yakima; $; beer and wine; AE, MC, V; checks OK; lunch, dinner Mon-Sat.*

Santiago's ★ The high ceiling, huge murals, and Southwestern art are festive—if the effect is somewhat overdesigned. Still, the price of the Mexican offerings is right, and the taste is quite good. The chalupas and the tacos Santiago (with beef, guacamole, and two kinds of cheese) are especially popular. Steak picado (their version of fajitas) was on the menu long before the sizzling sirloin strips became chic at every other Mexican restaurant. Owners Jar and Debra Arcand are especially proud of their all-Washington list of wines; however, only a few are available by the glass. Locals know Jar can do so much more than just Mexican food, so if he's got something else on the special list, give it a try. ▪ *Close to the intersection of 1st and Yakima; (509) 453-1644; 111 E Yakima Ave, Yakima; $; full bar; MC, V; checks OK; lunch Mon-Sat, dinner every day.*

LODGINGS

The Tudor Guest House ★★ This stately Tudor mansion was built in 1929 by a prominent Yakima philanthropist, whose standards of quality are evident throughout the house. Oriental carpets cover hardwood floors, leaded-glass windows look out onto the gardens and well-maintained grounds, and graceful archways lead into many of the rooms. Each room is tastefully decorated with beautifully restored antiques. The five guest rooms ($55 to $75 for a double), all on the second floor, share three bathrooms. The mansion is peaceful and sedate, and so tends to attract mature customers. The home has three working fireplaces, one in a guest room, the other two back-to-back affairs in the large living room/morning room, where breakfast is served. Summer use of the formal garden and lawn is encouraged. ■ *32nd and Tieton; (509) 452-8112; 3111 Tieton Dr, Yakima, WA 98902; $$; AE, MC, V; checks OK.*

Rio Mirada Motor Inn ★ Just off the I-82 freeway and right next to the shimmering Yakima River, this Best Western motel doesn't look like much from the road. A peek inside reveals 96 attractive rooms, each with a small balcony and a view of the river. (Second-story rooms are the best.) Most rooms have tiny refrigerators and a few have kitchenettes. For exercise there's an outdoor heated pool, an indoor exercise room with a Jacuzzi, and a recently expanded 7-mile path along the riverbank. All the rooms have recently been updated, and the convenience and views are worth the stay. The staff could use some orientation about the sights and events in the Yakima area. ■ *Exit 33 off I-82; (509) 457-4444; 1603 Terrace Heights Dr, Yakima, WA 98901; $$; AE, DC, DIS, MC, V; local checks only.* &

TOPPENISH

Western artist Fred Oldfield was raised here and returns occasionally at the request of the Toppenish Mural Society, (509) 865-6516, to lead a mural-painting posse. As a result, the whole town is an art gallery, with 10 large walls covered with murals and more planned. Clusters of Western shops, antique stores, and galleries make strolling and shopping pleasant, and there are rodeos scheduled throughout the summer months.

Yakima Nation Cultural Center, located on ancestral grounds, houses an Indian museum and reference library, plus a gift shop, a native American restaurant, a commercial movie/performing arts theater, and the 76-foot-tall Winter Lodge, for conventions and banquets. Open every day (closed January and February). On Fort Road off Highway 97, Toppenish, (509) 865-2800. **Fort Simcoe** was built in 1856, and its gothic revival officers' quarters still stand in desolate grandeur; 28 miles west of Toppenish on Route 220.

ZILLAH

RESTAURANTS

El Ranchito ★★ Here in hops- and fruit-growing country, where many Mexican-Americans live, is a jolly tortilla factory-cum-cafeteria that makes a perfect midday stop. You eat in the large dining area or in the cool, flower-shaded patio during the summer. After lunch you can browse in the gift shop, a mercado with pottery, rugs, and hard-to-find Mexican

20 YEARS

peppers, spices, canned goods, very fresh tortilla chips, and even south-of-the-border medicines. The authentic food is ordered à la carte. The smooth burritos, tasty nachos, and especially the barbacoa, a mild, slow-barbecued mound of mushy beef served in a tortilla shell or a burrito, are generous and recommended. There is a Mexican bakery on the premises, but no cerveza. ▪ *Exit 54 off I-82, follow the signs; (509) 829-5880; 1319 E 1st Ave, Zillah; $; no alcohol; no credit cards; checks OK; breakfast, lunch, dinner every day.*

SUNNYSIDE

RESTAURANTS

Taqueria La Fogata A small, simple roadside Mexican taqueria doing a lot of things right. The clientele is clearly local, the help clearly Mexican, and the menu expansive enough to include specialties such as pozole (Michoacán stew of pork back and feet and hominy) and menudo (Michoacán tripe and cow's-feet stew in a spicy sauce), along with all the usual tacos and burritos. Prices are prehistoric, the service friendly, the smells sublime. ▪ *In Sunnyside; (509) 839-9019; 1204 Yakima Valley Hwy, Sunnyside; $; no alcohol; MC, V; checks OK; breakfast, lunch, dinner every day.*

LODGINGS

Sunnyside Inn Bed and Breakfast ★ The eight bedrooms in this 1919 home are huge (so big they sometimes feel empty), four have outside entrances, and all come with phones, cable TV, air conditioning, and private baths with pedestal sinks and double Jacuzzi tubs. The bathrooms alone are bigger than most bedrooms. On the main floor, ask for the Jean room (king-size bed, outside entrance) or the Karen room (gas fireplace). Upstairs, the cheerful Viola room is decorated in peach, and the Lola room features a pleasant sun porch. For those who like the friendliness of B&Bs but need their fair share of privacy, this place is a godsend. Breakfast is a bountiful affair of blueberry pancakes, warmed syrups, fruit, and classical music.

On weekend evenings, the Sunnyside Inn offers a prix-fixe gourmet dinner ($18 for guests and non-guests) prepared by former Waldorf-Astoria chef James Graves. Call for reservations. ▪ *Exit 63 or 69 off I-82; (509) 839-5557; 800 E Edison Ave, Sunnyside, WA 98944; $; no alcohol; AE, MC, V; checks OK; dinner Fri-Sat, lunch every day (reservations required).* &

GRANDVIEW

RESTAURANTS

Dykstra House Restaurant Who can resist a restaurant that features bread made from hand-ground whole wheat grown in the Horse Heaven Hills? Rich desserts and a few choice Washington State wines complement this mansion's simple menu which changes daily. If you go with an open mind, you won't be disappointed. Proprietor Linda Williams takes the time to make visitors feel at home in the gray stone 1914 home of Grandview's former mayor and in the town at large. Local groups often reserve the upstairs for meetings or parties. Reservations are required for Saturday dinner, at which time there is a choice of two entrées only. A screened front porch is used for summer meals. ■ *Exit 73 off I-82; 1½ miles on Wine Country Rd; (509) 882-2082; 114 Birch Ave, Grandview; $$; beer and wine; AE, DIS, MC, V; checks OK; lunch Tues-Fri, dinner Fri-Sat.*

PROSSER

Cherries have always grown well in the Yakima Valley, except when the weather doesn't cooperate. Too much rain cracks cherries, too little leaves them small. **Chukar Cherries** turns imperfect cherries into a year-round delicacy—dried cherries. In the showroom of their production center you'll also see chocolate-covered cherries, cherry poultry sauce, and even cherry waffle mix; 306 Wine Country Road, Prosser, (509) 786-2055.

LODGINGS

Wine Country Inn Bed & Breakfast A welcome addition to the limited overnight options in Prosser, this riverside home has four rooms up and one down, with attached restaurant and gift shop. The river winds lazily by the front door and the restaurant, from which owners/innkeepers Chris Flodin and Audrey Zuniga turn out terrific country breakfasts and ample, hearty dinners. The thin-walled rooms are clean and comfortable. A deck and gazebo open onto the river, with outside restaurant seating on warm summer nights. No smoking, pets, or young children, please. ■ *Exit 80 off I-82, near bridge in Prosser; (509) 786-2855; 1106 Wine Country Rd, Prosser, WA 99350; $; beer and wine; AE, MC, V; checks OK; dinner Wed-Sun.* ら

TRI-CITIES WINE COUNTRY

The Tri-Cities wine country is the hub of the huge Columbia Valley viticultural appellation, which includes both the Yakima Valley and Walla Walla Valley appellations within its borders. Here its three principal rivers (Columbia, Snake, and Yakima) converge. A few miles to the west, at Red Mountain, the Yakima Valley wineries begin; and a few miles to the east is the small cluster of Walla Walla Valley wineries. The Tri-Cities Visitor and Convention Bureau, (509) 735-8486, can provide up-to-date wine-touring maps and tasting-room schedules, and visitors can explore some of the state's oldest wineries and vineyards (reportedly, 90 percent of the state's vineyards are located within a 50-mile radius of Red Mountain). In the immediate area are **Bookwalter Winery**, 2708 Commercial Avenue, Pasco, (509) 547-8571, a small facility located just off the cloverleaf joining Highway 395 and I-82; **Gordon Brothers Cellars**, 531 Levey Road, Pasco, (509) 547-6224, one of the state's best vineyards, with a special flair for merlot and a nice view of the Snake River; **Preston Wine Cellars**, 502 E Vineyard Drive, Pasco, (509) 545-1990, a large, family-owned enterprise with an expansive tasting room and park; and **Quarry Lake Vintners**, 2520 Commercial Avenue, Pasco, (509) 547-7307, another big operation, whose success is built on the excellent Balcom & Moe Farms vineyard. Southwest of Tri-Cities is Stimson Lane's $25 million showcase **Columbia Crest Winery**, Highway 221, Paterson, (509) 875-2061.

TRI-CITIES: RICHLAND

Richland was once a secret city, hidden away while the atomic bomb workers did their thing in the 1940s; now "the Atomic City" is the second largest of the Tri-Cities. Interestingly, Hanford now employs more people to dismantle the site than it ever did in its heyday. However, as nuclear reactors close and the controversy over hazardous waste continues, civic leaders are working hard on industrial diversification. **Hanford Science Center** in downtown Richland tells a bit of the saga of atomic energy; the energy displays are quite instructive; 825 Jadwin Avenue, (509) 376-6374.

▼
**Tri-Cities
Wine Country**
▲

Howard Amon Park, along the bank of the Columbia, makes a very nice spot for picnics, tennis, golf, jogging, or just ambling. **Allied Arts**, 89 Lee Boulevard, (509) 943-9815, located at the edge of the park, displays the work of mostly local artists in one of Richland's historic buildings.

RESTAURANTS

The Emerald of Siam ★★ One of the most authentic Thai restaurants in Eastern Washington is improbably located in a converted drugstore in a Richland shopping center. The space, not only a restaurant, includes a cultural center for visiting school groups, a display of Thai handicrafts for sale, and an Asian grocery. Thai-born Ravadi Quinn and her family have created the feel of a small Southeast Asian restaurant, and they are serving delicious native recipes. The curries, satays, and noodles all get high marks. Thai salad, a favorite in Asia, is a good bet. Weekday buffet lunches are popular. Quinn's many projects include occasional cooking classes and her own cookbook, *The Joy of Thai Cooking*. ■ *William and Jadwin; (509) 946-9328; 1314 Jadwin Ave, Richland; $; beer and wine; MC, V; local checks only; lunch Mon-Fri, dinner Mon-Sat.*

Giacci's ★ In Richland's oldest building (1906), wonderful aromas waft from the busy kitchen and Puccini arias float through the air. Good salads and Italian sandwiches are the lunch offerings at this attractive deli/restaurant in Richland. A similar menu makes for a rather ordinary dinner, even with the addition of a few specials such as eggplant Parmigiana or spinach ravioli in a marinara sauce. Still, you'll finish on a fine note if you add a glass of Chianti and one of their excellent desserts. Outdoor tables in summer. ▪ *Corner of George Washington and Lee; (509) 946-4855; 94 Lee Blvd, Richland; $; beer and wine; V, MC; local checks only; lunch, dinner Mon-Sat.* &

Gaslight Restaurant and Bar The Gaslight was here long before Shakey's and Pizza Hut, and for a long time it was the only place to get pizza in Richland. It looks like just another tavern on the outside, and the image is not dispelled by the giant TV screen inside, but the Gaslight has evolved into a place where everybody goes to get a good pizza and super potato skins. There's the usual excess of period brass lamp fixtures and Gay '90s mirrors, but there are also cozy booths and an outdoor deck that overlooks the Columbia River. ▪ *At the first main intersection on George Washington; (509) 946-1900; 99 Lee Blvd, Richland; $; full bar; AE, DIS, MC, V; local checks only; lunch, dinner every day.* &

LODGINGS

Red Lion Hanford House ★ Location, location, location. For conventions you might do better at the Best Western Tower Inn down the street, but the Hanford House has secured Richland's finest piece of real estate right on the Columbia (aka Lake Wallula), stretched with more miles of park than most guests can manage in an afternoon jog. Due to the unusual shape of the hotel there aren't many riverfront rooms (best bets are 175 to 187 and 275 to 287). If the riverfront rooms are booked, get one of the large rooms facing the attractive grassy courtyard and the dandy pool area (a must on the broiling Tri-Cities summer days). This is *the* place to stay in the Tri-Cities. The lounge is pleasant; the popular dining room serves standard Red Lion fare. ▪ *Richland exit off I-82 to George Washington; (509) 946-7611; 802 George Washington Way, Richland, WA 99352; $$; AE, DC, DIS, MC, V; checks OK.*

TRI-CITIES: PASCO

This was the first of the Tri-Cities, a railroad town started in 1884. Today it's home to more and more Mexicans who tend the surrounding farms. Not surprisingly, a number of authentic Mexican eateries, such as **Santos Cafe** (510 Lewis), are beginning to attract the attention of more clientele than just their extended families. **Columbia Basin Community College,** near the airport, puts on shows and lectures; the Performing Arts Building is a splendid, virtually windowless building in the brutalist mode.

LODGINGS

Red Lion Inn ★ The large, sprawling motel (281 rooms) in half-timbered style has several notable attractions. There is a nice outdoor pool, surrounded by the rooms, and a new exercise facility, and the 18-hole municipal golf course is right alongside, making the motel appear to be set in a park even though it's right on the freeway. It's exceptionally convenient to the Tri-Cities airport and Columbia Basin Community College. Local residents like the dining room for "dressy" occasions. The room is big and dark (perhaps so the blue flaming desserts and coffees can be seen clear across it) and the menu is very eclectic—usually a bad sign. Here we're proven wrong; this is one of the few restaurants in Eastern Washington that really knows how to cook seafood, *and* duck, *and* beef. The service is unpolished but eager to please. Given the location, the wine list could be a bit more adventurous. ■ *20th St exit off Hwy 395; (509) 547-0701; 2525 N 20th St, Pasco, WA 99301; $$; AE, DC, DIS, MC, V; checks OK; breakfast, lunch, dinner every day.*

TRI-CITIES: KENNEWICK

RESTAURANTS

Chez Chaz ★ A fun collection of salt shakers sits on the counter and every table has its own sodium centerpiece, but that's as whimsical as this restaurant in an office building on Clearwater Avenue gets. The dinner menu is quite limited, probably because most people choose to do Chez Chaz for a well-executed lunch. There is a long list of sandwiches, a favorite being a hot version of the Smoky Tom (turkey, cream cheese, provolone, and barbecue sauce on sourdough). But chef Chaz can do so much more—as evidenced by the specials: a spicy, peanutty Thai beef sauté on gently cooked vegetables; linguine with a light tomato and basil cream sauce; Moroccan vinaigrette with couscous. The Caesar is a local fave. Few diners leave without taking a sweet treat with them. ■ *Between Edison and Union on Clearwater; (509) 735-2138; 5001 Clearwater Ave, Kennewick; $$; no credit cards; checks OK; lunch, dinner Mon-Sat.*

The Blue Moon Owners Linda, Dale, and Dean Shepard opened this restaurant with first-class food as an adjunct to their catering business. Unfortunately, it's tough to pay such prices for such good food and receive nothing in the sense of surroundings in return. If you don't need atmo to enjoy your dinner you'll appreciate this seven-course prix-fixe meal (one seating at 7:30pm Friday, 7:00pm Saturday; private parties of 10 or more can book Tuesday through Thursday). The lobster bisque is full-flavored, rich, and spicy. After a good caesar salad, a tasty cabernet sorbet cleanses the palate. Entrée selections include perhaps a rack of lamb Provençal, tournedos Blue Moon, sautéed pork Dijon, and breast of chicken Grand Marnier. The wine list is composed entirely of local bottlings. Reservations are essential. ■ *½ block from Washington; (509) 582-6598; 21 W Canal Dr, Kennewick; $$$; wine only; MC, V; checks OK; dinner Fri-Sat.* ⟨

Casa Chapala The Tri-Cities' most endearing eatery is run by a couple so young that when they opened, they couldn't legally get a liquor license. They're old enough now, but that's not the point. Here is a very festive place where the help speak little English but do their best to assist. Come on a Tuesday, Thursday, or Friday between 5pm and 8:30pm and request a seat near the tortilla factory. Tortillas are that fresh, and you can be sure anything inside of them will be too. The honey-drizzled sweet-fried tortillas make a fine finish. ■ *Columbia and Washington; (509)586-4224; 107 E Columbia Dr, Kennewick; $; full bar; AE, MC, V; checks OK; lunch, dinner every day.*

LODGINGS

Quality Inn on Clover Island It's truly on an island, and thus offers wonderful river views from many of its 150 rooms. Otherwise, even under its new ownership (Quality Inn), there's not much to distinguish it from its Red Lion and Holiday Inn cousins except its comparatively inexpensive rates. Avoid dining here. ■ *Columbia Dr and Washington; (509) 586-0541; 435 Clover Island, Kennewick, WA 99336; $; AE, DC, DIS, MC, V; checks OK.* ⟨

WALLA WALLA

The Walla Walla valley is an important historical area: the Lewis and Clark Expedition passed through in 1805, fur trappers began traveling up the Columbia River from Fort Astoria in 1811 and set up a fort in 1818, and in 1836 missionary Marcus Whitman built a medical mission west of the present town, and he and his wife, Narcissa, and a dozen fellow settlers were slain by a band of Cayuse Indians in the famous massacre of 1847. Walla Walla was founded in 1856 by Colonel Edward Steptoe, first named Steptoeville, later named Walla Walla, an Indian phrase for "small, rapid streams." Main Street was built on the Nez Percé Indian Trail. Walla Walla has grown into a pleasant vale of 26,000 with fecund wheatlands all around and a pretty private college anchoring the city. The community boasts the oldest continuous symphony west of the Mississippi River, which performs a season of winter concerts. A free art gallery walk is staged the second Wednesday of every month, September through June.

Downtown. Walla Walla underwent a prettification in 1992. Many of the 25 brick buildings built near the turn of the century were restored to their original elegance and style. Two particular shops worth mentioning: China 'n Things, 11 E Main, (504) 529-8460, for beautiful china, glass and linens, kitchen utensils, and other gifts; and **Soper's Leather Goods**, 27 W Main, (504) 525-8823, for Western hobbyists or those interested in checking out the latest in English saddles and tack.

Old houses. Kirkman House Museum, listed on the National Register of Historic Places, is a fine period-home museum; 214 N Colville Street, (509) 529-4373. Mature trees and Colonial architecture lend a New England feeling to Catherine Street, S Palouse Street, and W Birch Street. Pioneer Park, on E Alder Street, is a good example of the urban park style of 80 years ago and was designed by the Olmsted brothers, the landscape architects whose father created New York City's Central Park and Seattle's Lake Washington Boulevard. The park has an excellent open-air aviary with a fine collection of pheasants, pigeons, and native waterfowl.

Whitman Mission. Seven miles west, off Highway 12, you can learn the story of the mission and the massacre; there aren't any historic buildings, but the simple outline of the mission in the ground is strangely affecting. A hike up an adjacent hill to an overlook offers the best impression of what the area looked like to the Whitmans and fellow settlers. The mission became an important station on the Oregon Trail, and Narcissa Whitman's arrival was notable in that she and Eliza Spalding, also with the Whitman party, were the first white women to cross the continent overland. Call (509) 529-2761 for tour hours.

Fort Walla Walla Museum. In Fort Walla Walla Park on the west edge of town, there's a collection of 14 historic buildings and pioneer artifacts. Call (509) 525-7703 for hours; camping and picknicking available in the park adjacent to the museum complex. Open summers only.

Whitman College. The lovely tree-filled campus is worth a stroll, and Memorial Building, an 1899 Romanesque revival structure, is worth admiring for its architecture; (509) 527-5176. The college stages many plays in the Harper Joy Theater, which also houses a professional summer theater company; Penrose Library has a strong collection of Northwest materials; and there are summer workshops.

Onions. Walla Walla Sweets are spendid, truly sweet onions, great for sandwiches; here you can get the "number ones," with thin skins. For information on the July onion festival or the May hot air balloon stampede, call the Chamber of Commerce.

Wines. Walla Walla is home to some of the state's most brilliant wineries. Most notable is **Woodward Canyon**, Lowden, (509) 525-4129, which produced a cabernet in 1987 that was judged one of the top 10 in the world by *Wine Spectator.* Others are **L'Ecole No. 41**, Lowden, (509) 525-0940; **Leonetti Cellars**, Walla Walla, (509) 525-1428; **Waterbrook Winery**, Lowden, (509) 529-1918; **Seven Hills Winery**, (509) 529-3331, with production facilities over the state line in Milton-Freewater, Oregon, (503) 938-7710; and **Biscuit Ridge**, (509) 529-4986, with a Waitsburg address but located just north of Dixie.

Juniper Dunes Wilderness. This 7,140-acre wilderness includes some of the biggest sand dunes—up to 130 feet high and a quarter-mile wide—and the largest natural groves of western juniper—some 150 years old—in the state. No camping or fires are allowed in the wilderness and there is no drinking water available. The most scenic portion of the wilderness is a 2-mile hike northeast from the parking area. Getting to the parking area, which is 15 miles northeast of Pasco, involves driving some unmarked back roads; for directions to the parking area, contact the BLM, (509) 353-2570.

RESTAURANTS

Merchants Ltd. ★★ It's a cluttered New York-style deli, with tempting culinary merchandise piled ceiling-high on broad shelves; a deli counter loaded with breads, cheeses, sausages, salads, caviar, and such; and a glass-fronted bakery from which enticing smells waft into the rooms. The homemade soups are deservedly popular, but you won't be disappointed in the chicken salad or tabouli. There are tables inside, or you might sit out front under the awning at a sidewalk table with a latte and watch Walla Walla waltz by. Upstairs is a more sedate dining room where the food is quite good. Lunch is served buffet-style (as is the Wednesday spaghetti dinner). Excellent wine list. ■ *2nd St exit off Hwy 12, turn left on Main; (509) 525-0900; 21 E Main St, Walla Walla; $$; beer and wine; MC, V; checks OK; breakfast, lunch Mon-Sat, dinner Wed.* &

Jacobi's For dining with a historic ambience, head for the former Northern Pacific Railroad Depot, home to Jacobi's, a cafe partially located in a former railroad dining car. The college crowd hangs out here, where they converse over espresso and beer from regional microbreweries. For more ambience, reserve a table in the railroad dining car. The 20-page menu includes local offerings such as Washington apples with Jacobi's caramelized dip (an appetizer), stuffed potatoes, sandwiches (try the eggplant sandwich for something different), steak, seafood, and ribs, as well as assorted Italian offerings and a selection of interesting salads. The eatery offers an impressive array of wines produced in area wineries, and microbrews from Redhook in Seattle and Widmer in Portland. ■ *2nd St exit off Hwy 12 to the old Northern Pacific Depot; (509) 525-2677; 416 N 2nd St, Walla Walla; $; beer and wine; AE, MC, V; checks OK; lunch, dinner every day.* &

Green Gables Inn A former hospital across the street is now a women's dormitory for the college. Margaret Buchan and husband Jim, the sports editor at the local newspaper, converted this historic manse (a block from Whitman College) to a bed and breakfast and reception facility. True to the architectural style, a broad covered porch sweeps across the front of the mansion and around one side, an ideal setting for relaxing on a warm afternoon, lemonade and book in hand. Inside, the large foyer is flanked by two sitting areas, both with fireplaces and one with a TV where guests can watch ball games with Jim. A love seat tucked into a corner of the second floor creates a cozy library for guests. Of the five guest rooms, the Idlewild is the only one with a fireplace, private deck, and a Jacuzzi. Dryad's Bubble, a room spacious enough to accommodate a reading area with overstuffed chair and ottoman, also opens through French doors to a small balcony. Those traveling with children should choose Birchpath and its accompanying room. ■ *Clinton exit off Hwy 12 to Bonsella; (509) 525-5501; 922 Bonsella St, Walla Walla, WA 99362; $$; AE, DIS, MC, V; checks OK.*

Stone Creek Inn In 1883 this mansion (the home of the last governor of Washington Territory) was a home in the country; now it's a a four-acre oasis surrounded by a modest residential neighborhood. Stone Creek still runs through the estate and century-old trees tower over the grounds. Greg and Gwena Petersen bought the Queen Anne-style mansion in 1991, but so far the place only has two guest rooms: a bright first-floor room with large windows overlooking a broad sideyard (the opulent bath has marble counter, gold-plated faucets, and crystal light fixtures); and a second-floor room with a fireplace and a private screened porch. A busy arterial runs by the property; however, a thick hedge of trees and foliage is an effective sound barrier. The Petersens have added their own quirky dimension to the place: an extensive collection of mounted insects and butterflies in the formal parlor and an assortment of classic cars in the back garage. Greg often takes interested guests for a spin; or if they prefer, he'll give them a bicycle tour of the area (there are five loaners on hand). ■ *Call ahead for directions; (509) 529-8120; 720 Bryant, Walla Walla, WA 99362; $$; no credit cards; checks OK.*

DAYTON

An impressive 88 Victorian buildings on the National Register of Historic Places make tiny Dayton a worthy stop, but don't expect to find all of the buildings restored. The town profited from a Gold Rush in 1861 in Idaho, as Dayton was on the main stage route between Walla Walla and Lewiston. Merchants and farmers built lavish houses during the boom years. The Italianate Columbia County Courthouse, the oldest courthouse (1886) in the state, is still in use for county government. One block off Main Street and adjacent to the railroad tracks that run through all of the farming communities of the Palouse, the historic 1881 Dayton Depot was in use until 1971. Restored, it's now a small railroad museum. There are a lot of firsts here: Dayton boasts the oldest family-run hardware store in the state, Dingle's; the state's oldest volunteer fire department and oldest rodeo; and the state's first high-school graduating class. Golfers are welcome at the nine-hole, par-72 Ironwood golf course, N Pine Street, (509) 382-4851, at the west edge of town.

Skiing. In season, skiers can head for Oregon's Blue Mountains and Ski Bluewood, (503) 382-4725, 21 miles southeast of Dayton (52 miles from Walla Walla), for cross-country and downhill skiing. The area, with the highest base elevation in the state, gets more than 300 inches of snow a year on its 26 runs. Forty miles southeast of Walla Walla, just outside Oregon's North Fork Umatilla Wilderness, Spout Springs ski area, (503) 566-2164, has two chair lifts and two T-bars along with a cross-country skiing trail system. Some runs are lit for night skiing.

RESTAURANTS

Patit Creek Restaurant ★★★★ Bruce and Heather Hiebert have achieved the seemingly impossible: they've turned a small rural cafe into an excellent regional restaurant. Serving good food to the locals (both conservative farmers and more liberal college types) has been an experience—at times frustrating and educational—but the effort has paid off. There is now a steady and very appreciative clientele who don't mind driving long distances to eat superbly roasted meat at Patit Creek, named after the creek which meanders through town and located in what was a service station in the 1920s and later a soda fountain. Call ahead, however, as this is considered one of the best restaurants in the region and sometimes it's difficult to get in. The menu features regional dishes, and changes in fall and spring. Appetizers are notable, particularly the smoked-salmon cheesecake (non-sweet) and the chèvre-stuffed dates wrapped in bacon and broiled. Bruce uses only the freshest vegetables and herbs. In the spring, fresh morel mushrooms are offered in a different entrée each night. A little later in the season, he'll wander into the hills in search of extraordinarily sweet wild onions to use in some of his sauces. Try the steak in green peppercorn sauce. The wine list is short but carefully chosen, including some fine Walla Walla-area wines. Heather's pies and desserts provide a proper conclusion to such delightful fare. Reservations are crucial on weekends. Urbanites may sneer at fine food being served in a room with such folksy decor—a small gripe that disappears shortly after the first bite. ■ *On Hwy 12 at north end of town; (509) 382-2625; 725 E Main, Dayton; $$; beer and wine; MC, V; local checks only; dinner Tues-Sat.* &

LODGING

The Purple House B&B Although it's only a block off Dayton's main street, the Purple House B&B is quiet (traffic is never oppressive in Dayton). A native of Southern Germany, owner Christine Williscroft brought her passion for China to the B&B and filled the formal living room with Chinese antiques and Oriental rugs. Breakfasts reflect Williscroft's heritage and include European pastries such as strudel or huckleberry pancakes. She can pack a picnic luncheon for explorers and on request will cook a European dinner, served family style. A typical dinner (guests only) would be Hungarian goulash or trout in season when Williscroft goes fishing in the Touchet River. French doors in the first-floor guest room open to a patio and backyard swimming pool. This decidedly feminine room has a sunken tub in the bedroom as well as private bath. The two upstairs guest rooms get quite hot in the summer. Small pets with advance warning. ■ *1 block off Hwy 12 in downtown Dayton; (509) 382-3159; 415 East Clay, Dayton, WA 99328; $$$; MC, V; checks OK.*

PULLMAN

Pullman's population swells in the fall with Washington State University students, while the permanent residents are a mix of wheat farmers and university faculty. The largest of the Palouse towns, Pullman retains some of its cowpoke image, but covets an international reputation as a university town. The central business district consists mostly of one main street crowded with shops and some restaurants. There is abundant free parking just off the main street. Browsers might visit the Nica Gallery for an excellent representation of Eastern Washington artists, 246 E Main Street, (509) 334-1213; Bruised Books for used books that sometimes include hard-to-find first editions, 105 N Grand, (509) 334-7898; and The Combine for deli sandwiches, salads, desserts, espresso, and teas and herbs, 215 E Main, (509) 332-1774.

Washington State University. The campus is expanding constantly. The Fine Arts Center is a showcase with a spacious gallery that attracts exhibits of notable artists. Martin Stadium, home of the WSU Cougar football team, can now hold Pac-10 Conference-size crowds; the baseball team plays on the new Bailey Field near the 12,000-seat Beasley Performing Arts Coliseum, which houses both the basketball team and frequent rock concerts; (800) 325-SEAT for tickets and an events calendar. Visitors might want to drop by Ferdinand's, located in the new Agricultural Science Building and open weekdays only, which offers ice cream, milk shakes, and Cougar Gold cheese, all made from milk and cream from WSU's own dairy herd, (509) 335-4014. Tours at the university, (509) 335-4527, can keep visitors busy for a couple of days. For an impressive insect collection, visit the Museum of Anthropology and Maurice T. James Entomological Collection in Johnson Hall. Other campus destinations include the Marion Ownbey Herbarium in Herald Hall for a quick course on herbs; the Beef, Dairy, and Swine centers; and the Jewett Astronomical Observatory, (509) 335-8518 for tours. Pick up a campus map and a visitor's parking pass from the visitors center adjacent to the fire station (follow the signs on Stadium Way).

Kamiak Butte, 13 miles north on Route 24, offers a good place for a picnic and nice overlooks of the rolling wheat country.

Steptoe Butte. About 30 miles north of Pullman on Highway 195, this geologic leftover towers above the Palouse and affords an impressive panoramic view of the Palouse or great stargazing. There's a picnic area at the top, but plan for wind, which is constant.

Steptoe Battlefield. History buffs will find Steptoe Battlefield near Rosalia interesting, but as at the Little Bighorn, the U.S. Cavalry lost this one to the Indians.

Palouse Falls. Just north of the confluence with the Snake River, the Palouse River gushes over a basalt cliff higher than Niagara Falls and drops 198 feet into a steep-walled basin. Hiking trails lead to an overlook above the falls and to streamside below the falls. The falls are best during spring runoff starting in late March. Camping allowed. Just downstream from the falls is the Marmes Rock Shelter, where remains of possibly the earliest known inhabitants of North America were discovered by archaeologists. At the confluence of the Snake and Palouse rivers, there is a public boat launch at Lyons Ferry State Park. The Marmes site is accessible via a 2½-mile unmaintained trail from Lyons Ferry State Park and by canoe. Much of the actual shelter area is flooded by the backwaters of Lower Monumental Dam, but the area is still popular with canoeists.

RESTAURANTS

The Seasons ★★ No doubt Pullman's finest dining experience. This elegant eatery occupies a renovated old house atop a flower-covered cliff. A winding wooden staircase leads diners to the front door. The interesting menu changes often, and dinner is presented in a proper and elegant fashion; chicken and seafood are good choices. Salad dressings are made on the premises and salads are served with scrumptious homemade breads such as whole-wheat with cornmeal, poppy seeds, and sesame seeds. Offerings from the dessert tray are worth saving room for. ■ *On the hill about ½ block off Grand; (509) 334-1410; 215 SE Paradise St, Pullman; $$; beer and wine; AE, DC, MC, V; checks OK; dinner Tues-Sun.* ⅋

Swilly's ★★ This eatery is located in what in the 1920s was a photography studio. It flanks the Palouse River and sports a small outdoor cafe in good weather. Across the street is one of the 20 artesian wells, drilled between 1890 and 1909, that were the deciding factor in locating a state college in Pullman. Inside, the warmth of the hardwood floors, the exposed brick walls, and the rich smell of espresso invite lingering. The eatery boasts fresh local ingredients, right down to cream from a nearby dairy and bread from a local bakery. The menu (which changes seasonally) offers pastas with tempting ingredients such as marinated artichoke hearts, a lemon-caper combination, or an Asian fish sauce. (There's a whole separate menu for calzone cravers.) For a different lunch treat, try the tarragon chicken sandwich with apples and Indian curry mayonnaise served on a sourdough roll. Plan to spend enough time to enjoy a second cuppa joe. ■ *1 block east of Grand; (509) 334-3395; 200 NE Kamiaken St, Pullman; $$; beer and wine; AE, MC, V; checks OK; lunch, dinner Mon-Sat.* ⅋

Hilltop Steakhouse This motel and restaurant has probably the best steaks in Pullman, family-style chicken dinners Sunday afternoons, Sunday brunch, and a wonderful view of the university and surrounding hills. The food is consistently good, albeit standard, fare. ■ *At city limits off Hwy 195; (509) 334-2555; Davis Way, Pullman; $$; full bar; AE, DC, DIS, MC, V; checks OK; lunch Mon-Fri, dinner every day, brunch Sun.*

(20 YEARS)

LODGINGS

Paradise Creek Quality Inn Just far enough off Route 270 to afford guests quiet nights away from traffic noise, this motel is also within walking distance of the WSU campus. It's situated over the meandering creek for which it's named. ■ *¼ mile east of the WSU campus near the junction of Hwy 270 and Bishop; (509) 332-0500 or toll-free (800) 669-3212; 1050 SE Bishop Ave, Pullman, WA 99163; $$; AE, DC, MC, V; checks OK.*

BRITISH COLUMBIA

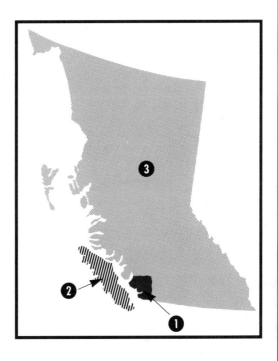

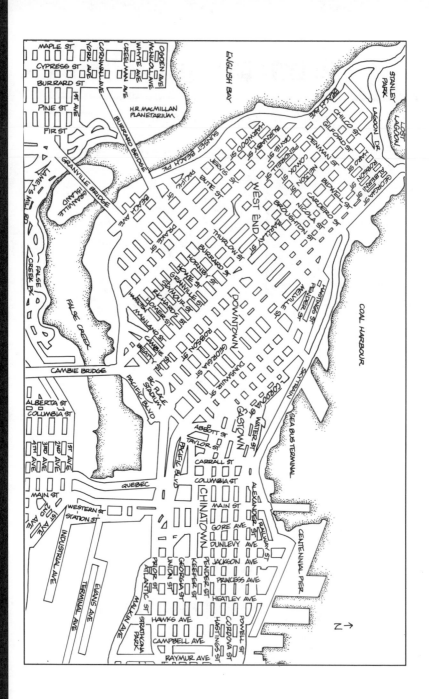

Vancouver and Environs

Vancouver and Environs

Vancouver restaurants and lodgings (including Richmond) followed by those recommended on the North Shore.

VANCOUVER

Vancouver has long touted itself as Canada's gateway to the Pacific Rim. But only when Hong Kong billionaire Li Ka-shing scooped up the old EXPO site, two hundred acres of prime development land, did the realization sink in that the city was also becoming the Pacific Rim's gateway to Canada. The new arrivals, especially those from Hong Kong, have taken advantage of immigration regulations designed to lure investors and have bought up billions of dollars worth of real estate since 1985.

Yet Vancouver has always accepted the waves of immigrants that have broken on its shores. Indeed, the city seems living proof that a benign environment will produce an easygoing disposition. Despite a stiffening of the work ethic of late, this is still a place of leisure and relaxed enjoyment.

Glance away from the opulence of the shops as you saunter along Robson and you will see why; at the end of a side street lap the peaceful waters of Burrard Inlet. Beyond, the mountains on the north shore glitter with snow for half the year. Vancouver, residents are fond of saying, is one of the few cities in the world where you can go skiing and sailing on the same day. How remarkable, then, that it should also be one of the few where, sitting outside a Neapolitan cafe, you can eavesdrop on an impassioned argument in Hungarian and see graffiti in Khmer.

Vancouver's chameleon identity is that of home to the children of the dispossessed, whether they be Scottish Highlanders or Hmong tribespeople. From the sculptors and the screenwriters, the dancers, jugglers, retired war correspondents and exiled aristocrats, to the drifters and dreamers who have settled here in such disproportionate numbers, this is as close to the Promised Land as it's possible to get.

THE ARTS

Visual Arts. Francis Rattenbury's elegant old courthouse is now the Vancouver Art Gallery, which holds more than 20 major exhibitions a year and whose permanent collection includes works by Goya, Carr, Gainsborough, and Picasso (750 Hornby, (604) 682-4668). Many of the city's commercial galleries are located on the dozen blocks just south of the Granville Bridge, and Granville Island, site of the Emily Carr College of Art and Design, has a number of potteries and craft studios. The avant-garde is most often found on the east side of the city, at spaces such as Pop Media Culture (154 W Hastings, (604) 681-7440) and the Pitt Gallery (317 W Hastings, (604) 681-6740). The Museum of Anthropology at the University of British Columbia (UBC, 6393 Northwest Marine Drive, (604) 228-5087) has an extensive collection of Indian cultures of coastal British Columbia (including an impressive display of totem poles), as well as artifacts from Africa to the Orient.

▼

Vancouver

▲

Music. Thanks to vigorous fund-raising by the musicians and their supporters and injections of government cash, the Vancouver Symphony Orchestra is back on its feet after a couple of bumpy years. The main season starts in October at the Orpheum, an old vaudeville theater (884 Granville). The Vancouver Opera puts on five productions a year at the Queen Elizabeth Theater (630 Hamilton): the program is a balance of popular and traditional. For information about any musical event, call Ticketmaster, (604) 280-4444.

Theater. The Vancouver Playhouse is entering the world of contemporary and classical theater; in the Vancouver Playhouse off Hamilton and Dunsmuir, (604) 872-6622. The Arts Club is a commercial theater with two locations and, usually, less production panache than the Playhouse; Granville Island, (604) 687-1644. Contemporary theater in Vancouver is largely centered in the VECC—Vancouver East Cultural Center, 1895 Venables Street, (604) 254-9578.

OTHER THINGS TO DO

Parks and Gardens. The city is blessed with a climate—very similar to Britain's—well-suited for flowers and greenery. Take a walk through the quiet forest in the heart of Stanley Park. The western edge is rimmed by three swimming beaches; you'll find tennis courts, a rose garden, an aquarium, and kiddie attractions on the southern fringes. Also great for kids is Science World British Columbia, across town at the old EXPO site. Here, hands-on exhibits, films, and working models will keep families busy for hours; 1455 Quebec Street, (604) 687-7832. At Queen Elizabeth Park, dramatic winding paths, sunken gardens, and waterfalls skirt the Bloedel Conservatory, (604) 872-5513 (stop in for lunch at Seasons in the Park). The University of British Columbia campus boasts three superb gardens—the Botanical Garden, Nitobe Memorial Gardens, and Totem Park—along with a top-drawer Sunday-tea setting at Cecil Green Park House, 6251 Cecil Green Park Road, (604) 228-6289. The new Chinese Classical Garden within Dr. Sun Yat-Sen Park (E Pender and Carrall streets), is a spectacular model of the Oriental garden complex with pavilions and water-walkways. Near Queen Elizabeth Park, the VanDusen Botanical Garden stretches over 55 acres. Each part of the garden offers flora from different regions of the world, as well as those native to the Pacific coast. Open every day, year round; 5251 Oak Street, (604) 266-7194.

Shopping. Vancouver has always been bursting with storefronts. Robson Street has a pleasant, European feel, with few high rises, colorful awnings, and a proliferation of delicatessens, boutiques, and restaurants. Downtown is full of outstanding shops. In poor weather, head underground for the Pacific Centre and Vancouver Center malls, with shops like Holt Renfrew, Eatons, The Bay, Birks, and Marks & Spencer. At Granville Island Public Market on the south shore of False Creek, you can get everything from just-caught salmon to packages of fresh herbs to fine unpasteurized lager (at the Granville Brewery) to a wonderful array of fresh produce in late summer. Or visit the lesser-known public market at Lonsdale Quay in North Vancouver with two levels of shops and produce right at the North Shore sea-bus terminal. It's a 15-minute sea-bus ride from the terminal near Canada Place across Burrard Inlet. Gastown is a restored 1890s precinct, once touristy, now anchored by some really good shops of more use to locals. Book Alley, the 300 and 400 blocks of West Pender, has bookstores specializing in everything from cookbooks to radical politics to science fiction.

Nightlife. On a warm summer night, the music spilling out from Vancouver's clubs and bars will range from down-and-dirty R&B at the suitably raunchy Yale Hotel (1300 Granville, (604) 681-9253) and the sprung-floored Commodore Ballroom (870 Granville, (604) 681-7838), through local alternative bands at the Town Pump (66 Water, (604) 683-6695) and disco thump at Richard's on Richards, the yuppie meat market (1036 Richards, (604) 687-6794), to swing at Hollywood North (856 Seymour, (604) 682-7722). The Railway Club (579 Dunsmuir, (604) 681-1625) has a remarkably varied membership and presents consistently

Vancouver

Other Things to Do

good music, whether pop or rock. Top names perform at BC Place Stadium (777 Pacific Blvd South, (604) 669-2300). To find out who's playing where, pick up a copy of the *Georgia Straight* or Thursday's *Vancouver Sun*. Jazz fiends can call the Jazz Hotline, (604) 682-0706.

Sports. The Vancouver Canucks, who made the playoffs in 1993, are the obvious draw when they play (Pacific Coliseum, (604) 280-4400). The Vancouver 86ers, the local soccer team, has a devoted following, especially since their 1988 Canadian championship (1126 Douglas, in Burnaby; (604) 299-0086). The BC Lions haven't had a very good track record in the past, but the 1991 season stirred up some hopeful fans (BC Place, (604) 669-2709). Visiting baseball enthusiasts should try to catch a Vancouver Canadians game at the Nat Bailey Stadium, a venue of which many locals have fond memories (Queen Elizabeth Park, (604) 872-5232). But most Vancouverites would rather play than watch. Golf, sailing, hefting weights, exploring the local creeks and inlets by any kind of boat you can name—the city has first-rate facilities for these activities and many more. For information, contact Sport, BC (1367 West Broadway, (604) 737-3000).

Ethnic Vancouver. The oldest and biggest of Vancouver's ethnic communities is Chinatown. The 200 block of East Pender is the main market area; to get started, try Yuen Fong for teas or the Dollar Market for barbecued pork or duck. More recently, a growing number of Asians are moving into Richmond, as evidenced by the increasing number of outstanding Chinese restaurants and the New Aberdeen Centre, where you can get ginseng in bulk, durian from Thailand, and eat home-style Chinese food while you bowl. Italian commercial and cultural life thrives in the distinctive neighborhood around Commercial Drive, east of downtown. A second, less discovered Italian district is on Little Italy's northern border—the 2300 to 2500 blocks of East Hastings. Vancouver's 60,000 East Indian immigrants have established their own shopping area called the Punjabi Market in south Vancouver at 49th and Main streets, where you can bargain for spices, chutney, and sweets. Vancouver's longest-established group of ethnic inhabitants, the Greeks, live and shop west of the intersection of MacDonald and West Broadway.

RESTAURANTS

Bishop's ★★★★ The fashionable dining crowd may flirt with newer places, but in the end they remain faithful to Bishop's. When the 1993 Summit came to Vancouver, the White House summoned John Bishop to create his wonderful grilled Pacific salmon fillet for presidents Clinton and Yeltsin (Bishop now has a standing invitation to the White House). Hollywood knows about Bishop's as well—Goldie Hawn, Richard Gere, and others have been spotted here. Bishop warmly greets his guests (celebrity and otherwise) and, assisted by the most professionally polished young staff in the city, proceeds to demonstrate he understands the true art of hospitality. Attention to detail is important in this minimalist Kitsilano restaurant. Appetizers might include grilled baby calamari, fresh local clams or mussels, or a delicate wild mushroom soup with sage. Entrées are uncomplicated. Lamb is always tender and excellent, as is daily fish (recently, halibut roasted with strawberry mint salsa). We favor tandoori chicken marinated in yogurt and cumin, then oven-roasted and served with mango chutney, Marsala-soaked raisins, roasted tomatoes, and basmati rice—but you really can't go wrong here. Everything bears the Bishop trademark of light, subtly complex flavors and bright, graphic color. Desserts, too, are not to be missed. The Death by Chocolate is easily the most talked-about dessert in Vancouver, and if you want President Clinton's choice, order the blueberry tart with homemade maple syrup ice cream. Nothing comes closer to dining perfection than Bishop's. ■ *Corner of Yew and 4th; (604) 738-2025; 2183 W 4th Ave, Vancouver; $$$; full bar; AE, DC, MC, V; no checks; lunch Mon-Fri, dinner every day.*

Chartwell (The Four Seasons) ★★★★ This welcoming, classic restaurant is a mecca for lovers of food and wine. Chartwell, named after the famous abode of Sir Winston Churchill, evokes an upper-class English men's-club atmosphere. Executive chef Wolfgang von Wieser has expanded the menu's horizons to include Pacific Northwest food graced with Chinese, Japanese, Thai, and Indian touches. Savor lightly smoked yellow snapper with garlic ravioli and chile orange oil, grilled organic beef fillet, or chardonnay steamed lobster—all lovely. From the city's most imaginative vegetarian menu come zucchini carpaccio with lemon vegetable crudités; potato tart and Mediterranean vegetables with arugula oil; and spinach sautéed in garlic and seasoned with just the right amount of sugar. Dessert is brilliant; plans just to taste may be foiled when the apple tartin and cherry soufflé arrive. Master host Angelo Cecconi and his staff give Chartwell its distinctive stamp of personal service—warm, discreet, and attentive. A pretheater dinner menu with valet parking is an outstanding value. ■ *W Georgia between Howe and Granville; (604) 689-9333; 791 W Georgia St, Vancouver; $$$; full bar; AE, DC, MC, V; no checks; lunch Mon-Fri, dinner every day.* &

Le Crocodile ★★★★ France without a passport, that's Le Crocodile. Chef and owner Michel Jacob named his bistro after his favorite restaurant in Strasbourg (his hometown) and his Franco-Germanic culinary heritage is all over the menu. There's a wonderfully savory onion tart he accompanies with chilled Alsatian wine in green stemmed glasses. Salmon tartare and sautéed scallops in an herb sauce are both showstoppers; luscious Dover sole, duck (lacquer-crisp outside, moist inside) accompanied by a light orange sauce, calves' livers with spinach butter—it's a trauma to choose. The best desserts are the traditional ones, such as a tangy lemon tart, a soothing crème brulée, and of course a tarte Tatin. And what with the well thought-out wine list and the European atmosphere, a dinner at Le Crocodile is an affair to remember. The new location on a one-way street can be difficult to find. ■ *Burrard St (enter off Smithe St); (604) 669-4298; 100-909 Burrard Street, Vancouver; $$$; full bar; AE, DC, MC, V; no checks; lunch Mon-Fri, dinner Mon-Sat.* ⎷

Tojo's ★★★★ *Cin-cin* Tojo Hidekazu *is* Tojo's. This beaming Japanese chef has a loyal clientele who regularly fill his spacious upstairs restaurant, though most people want to sit at his 10-seat sushi bar—not big enough for his devoted patrons, but the most Tojo likes to tend at one time. He's endlessly innovative, surgically precise, and committed to fresh ingredients. Show an interest in the food, and if the restaurant isn't frantically busy, he'll offer you a bit of this and that from the kitchen: Tojo tuna or perhaps special beef (very thin beef wrapped around asparagus and shrimp). Getting to be a regular is not difficult, and it's highly recommended. Sushi and sushi bar aside, the restaurant is still excellent. The dining room has a view of the stunning North Shore mountains and plenty of table seating; Japanese menu standards like tempura and teriyaki are always reliable and daily specials usually superb. We've enjoyed pine mushroom soup in the fall, shrimp dumplings with hot mustard sauce from October to May, cherry blossoms with scallops and deep fried sole with tiger prawns in the spring, and stuffed salmon and homemade egg tofu in the summer. Plum wine and fresh orange pieces or a green tea and some mango ice cream complete the meal. ■ *Broadway and Willow; (604) 872-8050; 202-777 West Broadway, Vancouver; $$$; full bar; AE, DC, MC, V; no checks; dinner Mon-Sat.* ⎷

CinCin ★★★ *Cin-cin* is a hearty Italian toast, a wish of health and good cheer, all of which is implied in this sunny Mediterranean place. The scent from wood-burning ovens, the warm surroundings—what more could one need? If you can, sit in the northeast corner by the window, where it's cozy and you can survey the entire room. CinCin's breadsticks and baked breads (vegetable-herb-seed and Tuscan) are irresistible, delivered with a spill of balsamic vinegar in a pool of olive oil. Launch your meal with a wonderful roasted red pepper, goat cheese, and sweet onion relish, or a carpaccio of lightly smoked beef. Name your noodle—it's made fresh daily and nicely sauced. Lasagne is layered with house-made sausage, fresh spinach, and mozzarella; linguine ribbons are laced with pesto or a mingling of sea creatures; and rotini is dotted with juicy roast chicken morsels and porcini mushrooms. The well-crafted wine list is international in scope, uncompromising in quality, and markups on high-end wines are reasonable. Desserts are all homemade in the best sense of the word, including the inevitable tiramisu. A great place to sip wine with the gang in the lounge (food's served until 1am). ■ *Between Bute and Thurlow; (604) 688-7338; 1154 Robson St, Vancouver; $$$; full bar; AE, MC, V; no checks; lunch Mon-Fri, dinner every day.*

Dynasty Restaurant (Vancouver Renaissance Hotel) ★★★

The masterful Lam Kam Shing has left our favorite Cantonese restaurant and at press time the consensus on the effects of this change is still not in. While recent visits have been reassuring, we'll withhold the fourth star until we can again attest that the Renaissance Hotel's restaurant is indeed unsurpassed by any other. The serene white-walled room is beautiful with etched glass and myriad visual details. The focus on freshness is also unchanged. Whole steamed rockfish with ginger and scallions scores top marks as does the drunken prawns steamed tableside (the broth is carefully ladled into silver-lined bone china bowls and served as a second course). A recent dim sum lunch was unhurried and prepared to order—excellent shark's fin soup, dumplings, and shrimp and mango rolls. The wine list remains the best in any Chinese restaurant in Vancouver. It seems that the efficient hotel-based management structure is not about to let this hard-earned success story slip into obscurity while waiting for chef Lam's replacement. ■ *On W Hastings between Thurlow and Burrard; (604) 691-2788; 1133 W Hastings St, Vancouver; $$$; full bar; AE, DC, MC, V; no checks; lunch, dinner Tues-Sun.* ⴺ

Hoshi Sushi ★★★

One of the few redeeming features of the unlovely Golden Gate Centre on the fringe of Chinatown is Tsutomu Hoshi's very Japanese restaurant. Tucked upstairs in its relatively obscure location, Hoshi Sushi is powered by Hoshi-san's reputation from his vast experience in Tokyo restaurants and at Vancouver's Aki (one of the city's first Japanese restaurants). Making head or tail of the extensive list of specials can be amusing—especially with the young Japanese staff eager to practice their English. Be insistently demonstrative about your adventuresome spirit; efforts are generously rewarded with seasonal delicacies such as steamed monkfish livers with wasabe and ponzu or crisp soft-shelled crab tempura accompanied by daikon, green onion, and soy dipping sauce. The chef's superior technique and total dedication to quality and freshness are evident throughout; utter simplicity is the key. ■ *Main St at Keefer; (604) 689-0877; 645 Main St, Vancouver; $$; full bar; AE, DC, JCB, MC, V; checks OK; lunch, dinner Mon-Sat.*

Il Giardino di Umberto ★★★ Stars, stargazers, the
movers and shakers come to Umberto Menghi's Il Giardino to mingle amid the Tuscan-villa decor: high ceilings, tiled floors, winking candlelight, and vine-draped terrace
for dining alfresco (no better place in summer). The emphasis
is on pasta and game with an Italian nuova elegance: farm-raised
pheasant with roasted-pepper stuffing and port wine sauce, tender veal with a mélange of lightly grilled wild mushrooms. An
accompanying slice of pan-roasted polenta adds a comforting
homey touch. Be warned: the prices on the specials are in their
own category. For dessert, go for the tiramisu—the best version of this pick-me-up in town. ■ *Pacific and Hornby; (604)
669-2422; 1382 Hornby St, Vancouver; $$$; full bar; AE, DC,
E, MC, V; no checks; lunch Mon-Fri, dinner Mon-Sat.*

Imperial Chinese Seafood Restaurant ★★★ The Imperial
may lay claim to being the most opulent Chinese dining room
around. There's a feeling of being in a grand ballroom of eras
past: a central staircase leads to the balustrade-lined mezza-
nine, diplomatic dignitaries and rock stars dine in luxurious pri-
vate rooms, and windows two stories high command views of
Burrard Inlet and the north-shore mountains. The food can be
equally polished, as in superb pan-fried prawns in soy, addic-
tive beef sautéed in chile with honey walnuts, crunchy-sweet
gai lan (Chinese broccoli) with garlic and bonito. Dim sum are
consistently good. If it weren't for a bit of unevenness in the ser-
vice, this could be a perfect restaurant. Reservations recom-
mended on weekdays. ■ *Burrard St and W Hastings; (604)
688-8191; 355 Burrard St, Vancouver; $$; full bar; AE, MC,
V; no checks; lunch, dinner every day.*

Kirin Mandarin Restaurant ■ Kirin Seafood Restaurant ★★★
Kirin's postmodern decor—high ceilings, slate green walls,
black lacquer trim—is oriented around the two-story-high mys-
tical dragonlike creature that is the restaurant's namesake. The
menu reads like a trilingual (Chinese, English, and Japanese)
opus spanning the culinary regions of China: Cantonese, Sichuan, Shanghai, and Beijing (live lobsters and crabs can be ordered in 11 different preparations). Remarkably, most of the
vastly different regional cuisines are authentic and well executed, but the Northern Chinese specialties are the best.
Peking duck is as good as it gets this side of China, and braised
dishes such as sea cucumber with prawn-roe sauce are "royal"
treats. Atypical of Chinese restaurants, desserts can be excellent—try the red bean pie, a thin crêpe folded around a sweet
bean filling and fried to a fluffy crisp. The Western-style service
is attentive though sometimes a tad aggressive. Unless you are
in the mood to splurge, stay away from the Cognac cart.
    The second, equally fine, outpost is in City Square with a
passable view of the city. It focuses more on seafood with great

dim sum (including a definitive hargou or shrimp dumpling). ■ *Alberni St at Bute; (604) 682-8833; 1166 Alberni St, Vancouver; $$$; full bar; AE, DC, E, JCB, V; checks OK; lunch, dinner every day.* ■ *12th Ave at Cambie; (604) 879-8038; 201-555 W 12th Ave, Vancouver; $$$; full bar; AE, DC, E, V; checks OK; lunch, dinner every day.* ᕗ

La Brochette ★★★ The focus of this Gastown hideaway is a huge, antique Normandy *tourne-broche*, the granddaddy of modern rotisseries, and its practitioner, Dagobert Niemann, is a master of the art. A true *rotiseur*, Niemann uses hardwood chips to attain his unique flavor, and works for three uninterrupted hours in front of his glowing fire. He stokes, turns, carves, sauces, tests, cuts, and grills, coordinating the arrangement and delivery of every order. His leg of lamb is minced with fresh herbs and served with a pungent aioli, the strong garlicky flavors of the creamy sauce combined with jus (replenished on cue to keep things hot) in an intense dose of flavor. Watch for roast half of duckling, which emerges from the rack with crisp skin and tender, moist flesh. Also from the grill come great vegetables—grilled baby asparagus in season, lightly buttered and salted, are an extra treat. Lead up to the main event, perhaps, with Brie en feuillette or with mussels in a light, creamy broth flavored with Pineau des Charentes. The wine list is one of the city's more comprehensive and well presented. After dinner, head downstairs to the fireplace with cozy wraparound seating. Reservations are a good idea. ■ *At Columbia and Alexander; (604) 684-0631; 52 Alexander St, Vancouver; $$$; full bar; AE, V; no checks; dinner Tues-Sat (may be closed in summer, July and Aug).*

▼

Landmark Hot Pot House ★★★ Hotpotting—traditionally for the warming of body and soul on long wintry nights—seems to have transcended its seasonal limits to emerge as a Chinese culinary trend. In the Landmark, the center of each table is cut out for the built-in natural-gas stove and its settings, which include a personal strainer and chopsticks. The menus are simply lists of available ingredients and prices; the rest is up to you. We ordered the Duo Soup Base of satay and chicken broth and happily experimented with platters of fish, chicken, beef, dumplings, vegetables, and noodles. This is heartwarming, healthy food at its simplest, embellished only by the chef's exquisite knifework and perfect presentation.

For more conventional dining, try Landmark's sister restaurant, Landmark Seafood Restaurant, 3338 Cambie Street, (604) 873-3338. In the glass-lined open kitchen you can watch your excellent food being prepared. ■ *Cambie St near Queen Elizabeth Park; (604) 872-2868; 4023 Cambie St, Vancouver; $$; full bar; MC, V; no checks; dinner every day.* ᕗ

Le Gavroche ★★★ Arguably the most romantic restaurant in the city, Le Gavroche is perfect for a lingering lunch or special occasion dinner. In the charming dining room, complete with blazing fire and glimpses of snowcapped mountains, your meal isn't so much served as orchestrated, with subtle but attentive service. The food tends to creative versions of the classics, though the recent return of chef Scott Kidd possibly signals a shift toward a more contemporary approach. À la carte selections include an excellent house hot-smoked salmon, homemade pâté, and delicious salmon baked with goat cheese. Look for the lobster bisque, fork-tender biftek entrecote in green peppercorn sauce, and tender house-smoked pheasant breast. Thorough, indulgent, and still very French, with one of the city's better wine cellars, Le Gavroche is a delight. ■ *Alberni at Cardero; (604) 685-3924; 1616 Alberni St, Vancouver; $$$; full bar; AE, DC, MC, V; no checks; lunch Mon-Fri, dinner Mon-Sat.*

Montri's Thai Restaurant ★★★ Top marks to Montri Rattanaraj for presenting an authentic cuisine not watered down for Vancouver tastes. Thai cuisine is a careful balancing act, based on six interconnecting concepts: bitter, salty, sweet, hot, herbaceous, and fragrant. The heat content is rated on a scale of one to five chile symbols, five being the level for masochists and Thai nationals. What to order? Everything is good. Tom yum goong is just that, yum, a lemony prawn broth that is Thailand's national soup. The tod mun fish cakes blended with prawns and chile curry are excellent, as is the salmon simmered in red curry and coconut sauce. Rattanaraj's Thai gai-yang, chicken marinated in coconut milk and broiled, is a close cousin to the chicken sold on the beach at Puhket. Have it with som-tam, a green papaya salad served with sticky rice and wedges of raw cabbage; the cabbage and the rice are coolants, and you *will* need them (Thailand's Singha beer also helps). ■ *W 4th and Trafalgar; (604) 738-9888; 2611 W 4th, Vancouver; $$; full bar; AE, MC, V; no checks; dinner every day.* ♿

Phnom Penh Restaurant ★★★ Once Vancouver's best-kept secret, this restaurant is now winning a steady stream of accolades, from local magazine polls to the *New York Times*. The decor is still basic, but the menu has expanded from its original rice and noodle dishes to include the cuisines of China, Vietnam, and Cambodia. Hot-and-sour soup with sablefish is richly flavored, redolent of lime and purple basil. An excellent appetizer of marinated beef sliced carpaccio-thin is seared rare and dressed with nuoc mam (a spicy, fishy sauce—the Vietnamese staple). Sautéed baby shrimp in prawn roe and tender slivers of salted pork cover hot, velvety steamed rice paste—a real masterpiece. Butterfly prawns with lemon-pepper dip are crisp and vibrant, chicken salad with cabbage is a refreshing twist on a pedestrian vegetable, and the oyster omelet is a dream. Service is knowledgeable and friendly. ■ *Close to Chinatown at Main and Georgia; (604) 682-5777; 244 E Georgia, Vancouver.* ■ *W Broadway and Oak; (604) 734-8898; 955 W Broadway, Vancouver; $; full bar; DC, MC, V; no checks; lunch, dinner Wed-Mon.*

Raintree ★★★ The Raintree of old never quite lived up to its self-promotion, but there's an exciting renaissance afoot—a new chef in the kitchen, a cooking school, and a winemaker series. The concrete-walled space is prettied with huge flower arrangements, decorated with a simple sophistication, and, provided you are seated facing the right way, offers a spectacular view of the North Shore skyline. Chef Karen Barnaby maneuvers the Northwest harvest of game and seafood and grape with skill, working flavor magic with pork and Alaskan black cod and delivering an on-target grilled spring salmon with bold beet-and-apple purée. It's a struggle to choose between the salmon bounty (kippered, smoked wild sockeye and Indian candy-salmon jerky) and the seafood bowl. Dessert provokes a similar conflict, so we order the sampler and taste everything, including Raintree's signature apple pie which contains 7 pounds of Okanagan fruit. The wine list echoes the Northwest Coast theme. At press time, Raintree is opening a similar restaurant in Victoria. ■ *Between Bidwell and Cardero; (604) 688-5570; 1630 Alberni St, Vancouver; $$$; full bar; AE, DC, E, MC, V; no checks; dinner every day.* ♿

Sun Sui Wah Seafood Restaurant ★★★ These two restaurants are actually an extension of a Hong Kong chain, with food that has a proven track record and dining rooms that are full most nights of the week. The reason: specialties and preparations that are tried and true (and much ordered): crisp, tender roasted squab; deftly steamed scallops on silky bean curd topped with creamy-crunchy tobikko (flying-fish roe) sauce; and Kirin Fish—steamed rock cod slices interwoven with paper-thin slices of ham and fleshy mushrooms and presented on a fresh lotus leaf. The Richmond location is renowned for its platter of deep-fried "milk"—fragrant, sweet coconut in a fluffy crust. With only a few minor lapses in service, their success is richly deserved. ■ *Alderbridge Plaza; (604) 273-8208; 4940 No. 3 Rd, Richmond; $$; full bar; MC, V; no checks; lunch, dinner every day.* ♿ ■ *At Main and 32nd; (604) 872-8822; 4818 Main St, Vancouver; $$; full bar; MC, V; no checks; dinner every day.*

Villa del Lupo ★★★ Owners Julio Gonzales and Vince Piccolo boast a culinary pedigree born of several fine Italian restaurants in Vancouver, and it shows. The "House of the Wolf" is a simple, elegant space with white walls and forest green trim that balances heritage with contemporary. Prices here tend to be high, but portions are generous (some enough for two). Almost everything is wonderful: crab cakes bursting with crabmeat and served with a surprisingly subtle aioli; pumpkin gnocchi dressed in a lovely combination of roughly chopped hazelnuts and basil oil; and veal medallions served with a garnish of Italian mushrooms, filament-thin shoestring potatoes, and julienned vegetables in an Armagnac sauce. The osso bucco is for serious appetites only: two shanks bearing fork-tender meat in a richly seasoned sauce, sided with orzo (rice-shaped pasta). Italy isn't the only region on the wine list (though it is well represented), and grappa and eaux de vie are available as well. Service is always correct, if a little slow. ▪ *On Hamilton between Robson and Smithe; (604) 688-7436; 869 Hamilton St, Vancouver; $$$; full bar; AE, DC, E, MC, V; no checks; dinner every day.*

The William Tell (The Georgian Court Hotel) ★★★

[20 YEARS] The elegance and charm of this Old World restaurant are a reflection of Erwin Doebeli, its dedicated owner. Doebeli, the consummate restaurateur, seems to be here, there, and everywhere, enthusiastically greeting arrivals at the door or flamboyantly whipping up a cafe diablo. Outstanding appetizers include Swiss-style air-dried beef and British Columbia salmon tartare with fennel and wild mushrooms on toasted homemade brioche. We recommend the Fraser Valley duck flavored with an apple-cucumber wine sauce, the scalloppine of veal in a sherry sauce, or the chateaubriand. The desserts, all homemade, just get better: an unequaled meringue glace au chocolat, perfect hot fruit soufflés (try the passion fruit), and opulently rich crêpes suzette or cherries jubilee prepared at your table. The sommelier reigns over one of the best wine cellars in the city (aficionados should ask to see the "reserved wine menu"). ▪ *Across from BC Place Stadium; (604) 688-3504; 765 Beatty St, Vancouver; $$$; full bar; AE, DC, MC, V; no checks; breakfast every day, lunch Mon-Fri, dinner Mon-Sat.* ⅊

Bandi's ★★ At Bandi's, chef/owner Bandi Rinkhy produces the robust country food of Hungary, with maître d' and co-owner Kader Karaa's sense of humor providing the dash of paprika. Start with an excellent sour-cherry soup and the dangerously addictive langos, a deep-fried peasant bread served with raw garlic (order one for your friends, one for yourself, and one to take home). Duck aficionados who haven't experienced Bandi's signature dish—crisp duck served with red cabbage braised in Tokay wine—should by all means do so. Goulash is presented in a little kettle set over a portable flame, and the paraszt sonka (smoked farmer's ham with fresh horseradish and green onions) is served in large, hearty portions. Uborkasalata (cucumber with sour cream dressing) may be the only concession to a timid palate. Desserts are mostly rich, sweet crêpes. A bottle of Badacsonyi off the good wine list is a decent value and is among Hungary's best white wines. You will exit in a fog of garlic.

■ *Between Beach and Pacific on Howe; (604) 685-3391; 1427 Howe St, Vancouver; $$; full bar; AE, MC, V; no checks; lunch Mon-Fri, dinner every day.*

Bianco Nero ★★ Bianco Nero's bold black-and-white decor with splashes of color never fails to impress, though, unfortunately, the service doesn't always live up to the surroundings. Attitude is always the unknown ingredient—sometimes warm and accommodating, at other times unfriendly and condescending. Luckily, the well-prepared food remains the most consistent factor. The kitchen has a healthy regard for garlic, onions, and olive oil (but a macho disregard for presentation). You may feel overwhelmed by all the choices; a sheet of daily specials is so crammed that they hardly seem special. Every Italian dish imaginable makes an appearance here, as do some surprises, such as sole in aquavit with Danish caviar, radicchio alla griglia (oven-broiled with garlic cloves and splashed with olive oil, lemon juice, and salt), tortellini alla nonna (in a delicate mustard cream sauce), and osso bucco. A recent penne with four kinds of mushroom was outstanding. This is the place for lovers of Italian wine, with one of the most comprehensive, sophisticated selections in Canada, including a full range of vintage Barolo. ■ *W Georgia and Richards; (604) 682-6376; 475 W Georgia St, Vancouver; $$$; full bar; AE, MC, V; no checks; lunch Mon-Fri, dinner Mon-Sat.*

▼

▲

The Bread Garden ★★ The Bread Garden is Vancouver's original bakery cafe, and still the most successful. Opened in 1981 as a croissant bakery, it quickly turned into an all-night coffee bar. Now there are five Bread Gardens and all but the Park Royal branch are open 24 hours. As the Bread Gardens proliferate, the deli cases grow bigger and bigger. The First Avenue Bread Garden is still the scene for early weekday coffee and (much later) weekend brunch, but now, for under $25 for two, you can also eat a quick and entirely satisfying dinner: wholesome, homey food such as shepherd's pie, lasagne (vegetarian and meat), fruit salad, potato salad, or black bean and corn salad. Desserts are homey too, including cheesecakes, fruit crumbles, Rice Krispie squares, double chocolate brownies, and bread pudding made from croissants. ■ *W 1st Ave between Burrard and Cypress, and branches; (604) 738-6684; 1880 W 1st Ave, Vancouver; $; no alcohol; E, MC, V; no checks; breakfast, lunch, dinner every day.* &

Caffe de Medici ★★ As you enter Caffe de Medici you are immediately made to feel like a favored guest. The high moulded ceilings, serene portraits of members of the 15th-century Medici clan, chairs and drapery in Renaissance green against crisp white table linen, and walls the color of zabaglione create a slightly palatial feeling; diplomatic waiters seem pleased to be looking after your needs. Businesslike by day, romantic by night—the mood changes, but the quality of the Northern Italian food does not. Skip the soups and order the beautiful antipasto: a bright collage of marinated eggplant, artichoke hearts, peppers, olives, squid, and Italian cold meats. The bresaola della Valtellina (air-dried beef, thinly sliced and marinated in olive oil, lemon, and pepper) is lovely. Pasta dishes are flat-out *magnifico*—a slightly chewy plateful of tortellini alla panna comes so rich with cheese, you'll never order any of the others. Although it's mostly a Florentine restaurant (with a knockout version of beefsteak marinated in red wine and olive oil), we've also sampled a fine Roman-style rack of lamb. ■ *Between Burrard and Thurlow on Robson; (604) 669-9322; 1025 Robson St, Vancouver; $$$; full bar; AE, JCB, DC, DIS, MC, V; no checks; lunch Mon-Fri, dinner every day.* ⅃

The Cannery ★★ A Vancouver original, serving "salmon by the sea" for more than 20 years, though the building has been cleverly refurbished to look and feel even older than that. Salmon selections run the gamut, from house-smoked items to the restaurant's hallmark, salmon Wellington. Seared salmon fillet, infused with flavors imparted from a cedar plank, has a subtle quality; by contrast, a mesquite-grilled smoked fillet has a lovely, truly strong barbecued flavor. An award-winning wine list offers one of the city's best selections, but service can be inconsistent. ■ *Powell and Victoria; (604) 254-9606; 2205 Commissioner St, Vancouver; $$$; full bar; AE, DC, DIS, MC, V; no checks; lunch Mon-Fri, dinner every day.*

Chez Thierry ★★ Restaurateur Thierry Damilano shops at the market in the morning, goes off windsurfing, and later in the day comes back to roll out the red carpet for regulars. He presides over his cozy restaurant with sunny good nature and flirtatious (very French) charm. Chef François Launay leaves experimentation to the nouveaux chefs and instead prepares simple, traditionally based meals without a lot of ornamentation. The house pâté is good but not outstanding; try a watercress and smoked salmon salad instead, or the impossibly melting chicken mousse, served warm in port sauce. A find: fresh tuna grilled with artichoke, garlic, and fresh tomato. Chocolate desserts are rich and just bitter enough; the tarte Tatin is superb, served upside down and flamed with Calvados. The wine list is carefully chosen; some may even be stored under your seat. For an unusual show, order a bottle of champagne and ask Damilano to open it for you—his favorite party trick is slashing off corks with a military saber, decked out in his flashing Napoleonic uniform. ■ *Robson between Bidwell and Cardero; (604) 688-0919; 1674 Robson St, Vancouver; $$; full bar; AE, DC, E, MC, V; no checks; dinner every day.*

Chili Club ★★ Despite the name, with a few exceptions, Chili Club's fare is not particularly hot. The staff, however, are well

informed and helpful, and if you want it spicy, they'll gladly oblige. We've enjoyed pork satay and Tom Yum Kung soup (prawns and mushrooms married in good broth with hot spice and deep-scented lemon grass), and when giant smoked New Zealand mussels, stuffed with a mild, thick curry paste are available, order them; the same goes for solidly spiced chicken curry, made with coconut milk and bite-size Thai eggplant. There's plenty to choose from. Popular wines and beers are available at realistic prices. For the best view of False Creek, try the holding bar upstairs with ceiling-to-floor windows on all sides. Even when the food is fiery, the decor is rather cold.
■ *Under the Burrard Bridge, near the water; (604) 681-6000; 1000 Beach Ave, Vancouver; $$; full bar; AE, MC, V; checks OK; lunch, dinner every day.* &

Chiyoda ★★ In a town full of sushi restaurants with robata grills on the side, Chiyoda is a robata restaurant with a sushi bar. Built on a generous scale, the robata bar was designed in Japan. Robata selections are arranged in wicker baskets on a layer of ice that separates the customer's side of the bar from the cook's side. Order from the simple menu: it lists a score of dishes, including snapper, squid, oysters, scallops, eggplant, and shiitake. The cook prepares your choices and hands the finished dishes across the bar on the end of a long wooden paddle. Seafood is excellent, but don't miss a foray into the cross-cultural world of robata-cooked garlic, potatoes, and corn. A popular spot for downtown businesspeople, the Chiyoda also attracts Japanese visitors exhausted from shopping in the huge gift shop downstairs. ■ *Alberni and Burrard; (604) 688-5050; 1050 Alberni St, Vancouver; $$; full bar; AE, MC, V; no checks; lunch Mon-Fri, dinner every day.* &

Cipriano's Ristorante & Pizzeria ★★ This compact and friendly pasta-pizza house is approaching institution status for its basic and most plentiful (for some, too plentiful) portions. Strains of Tony Bennett and Frank Sinatra fill the air as straightforward Italian home cooking arrives at your table, preceded with great garlic bread, dripping with butter and deluged with Parmesan. The caesar salad, an exercise in excess, is garlic-laden, crammed with croutons, and comes in a giant bowl which is, according to the menu, "Made to Share, Amore Style." Deep-dish pizza, pasta puttanesca, and chicken cacciatore are all worth your attention, though some sauces can be remarkably similar. Short routines from owner and onetime standup comic Frank Cipriano punctuate the meal. For atmosphere and value, few places compare, and lots of folks think so—reservations are a must.
■ *Main St and 24th; (604) 879-0020; 3995 Main St, Vancouver; $$; full bar; V; no checks; dinner Tues-Sun.*

Delilah's ★★ The unlamented three-martini lunch may be gone, but let's hear it for the one-martini cocktail hour with hors d'oeuvres at Delilah's. Start with valet parking (the quickest in town) and if you're early enough, grab a red plush banquette. People line up to get into Delilah's (if you'd rather not, arrive shortly after 6pm), and it really doesn't matter what you eat here, the place is a giggle. Food comes in small portions, but is good and reasonably priced. Your menu is your bill; simply check off your selections and hand it to your waiter. The peanutty yam soup is a good choice, and so is Jimmy's grilled beef tenderloin with mushrooms in a red-wine demiglace. The house specialties are the 30-plus varieties of martinis which you shake (or stir) yourself. Tucked away under the old Buchan Hotel, Delilah's is an intimate room with beautiful young things of every possible sex gathered at the bar under the frescoed ceilings. Reservations are accepted only for groups of six or more. ■ *Corner of Haro and Gilford; (604) 687-3424; 1906 Haro St, Vancouver; $$; full bar; MC, V; no checks; dinner every day.* ♿

Five Sails (Pan Pacific Hotel) ★★ From this restaurant's perch the view of the city is magic, gentled in the daylight, jeweled by nighttime. Facing the harbor from your table, you could vicariously be aboard a luxury liner sailing smoothly to Alaska. Loyal fans know what to expect in the serene and civilized world of chef Ernst Dorfler's domain—attentive service, spare luxury, and the joy of lots of space between tables. Dorfler's pièce de résistance, an appetizer of succulent warmed salmon gravlax delicately sandwiched between two crêpes, is evidence of his talents with seafood, as is a perfectly charbroiled fillet of salmon swimming in an orange and rosemary sauce, or a wonderful caramelized swordfish served with a Thai green curry hash. Desserts are not exceptionally creative, but you'll be pleased with the poached pear in puff pastry. ■ *On the waterfront at the north end of both Burrard and Howe; (604) 662-8111; 999 Canada Place, Vancouver; $$$; full bar; AE, DC, E, MC, V; no checks; dinner every day.* ♿

Floata ChiuChow Restaurant ★★ The Lam family has been in the restaurant business for generations, giving Vancouver its first ChiuChow restaurant and, most recently, the Floata. Connie Lam, number-one daughter and most amiable hostess, makes excellent recommendations from the menu. Traditional favorites such as double-boiled duck soup with dried lemons and ChiuChow poached duck in five spices and soy are once again true to form. Cold steamed Dungeness crab with vinegar dip offers a different take on our favorite regional crustacean; sautéed satay beef served over sweet and crunchy gai lan (Chinese broccoli) can be most memorable. Another restaurant, open for dim sum and with a seafood focus, is located in Richmond. ■ *Main St and E 27th; (604) 879-8118; 4316 Main St, Vancouver;*

$$; full bar; AE, V; no checks; lunch (dim sum), dinner every day. ▪ *In the Parker Place Shopping Center; (604) 270-8889; 1425-4380 N Columbus, Richmond; $$; full bar; V; no checks; lunch, dinner every day.* &

Kamei Sushi ★★ Kamei Sushi just keeps growing. Now at six locations, Kamei may no longer be the best Japanese restaurant in town, but its simple, Westernized dishes certainly make it one of the most popular. The Thurlow Street location, though a bit dated, is still our favorite and is particularly lively at night when the theaters empty out. Try for a seat at the sushi bar so you can watch the antics of the sushi chefs. Combination platters contain all the standards (tuna, salmon, octopus, abalone, salmon roe), or try the red snapper usuzukui, thinly sliced and fanned on the plate accompanied by a citrus sauce. Robata dishes are the special focus at the Broadway Plaza locale and can be very good. The luxury-class Kamei Royale on W Georgia seats over 300 with open and private tatami rooms. ▪ *Thurlow and Robson, and branches; (604) 684-4823; 811 Thurlow St, Vancouver; $$; full bar; AE, DC, E, MC, V; no checks; lunch Sun-Fri, dinner every day.*

Koji Japanese Restaurant ★★ In our opinion, it's the most beautiful garden in a downtown Vancouver restaurant—an island of pine trees and river rocks on a patio above Hornby Street. The best seats are the nonsmoking ones by the windows looking out on the garden, or at the sushi and robata bars. The rest is a crowded, smoky room often full of Japanese tourists. Sushi is not the best in town, but selections from the robata grill are dependable; grilled shiitake, topped with bonito flakes and tiny filaments of dry seaweed, are sublime. The Japanese boxed lunch might contain chicken kara-age, superb smoked black cod, prawn and vegetable tempura, two or three small salads, rice with black sesame seeds, pickled vegetables, miso soup, and fresh fruit—all for around $10. Finish with green tea ice cream. ▪ *Hornby and Georgia; (604) 685-7355; 630 Hornby St, Vancouver; $$; full bar; AE, DC, MC, V; no checks; breakfast, dinner every day, lunch Mon-Fri.* &

Le Coq d'Or ★★ Bruno Born's French bistro has a touch of urban chic, in a sunny room with tall windows and rich mustard-colored walls. Meals are simple and well executed, perhaps a half chicken roasted with fresh herbs, caramelized garlic, and lemon, or an extra-thick pork chop served with Le Coq's famous crisp pommes frites. There are specific dishes we'd return for: steak tartare, for example, and an eggplant and roasted red pepper appetizer baked with goat cheese. When it comes to the wine list, what you save on the reasonably priced food, you'll spend on the wine. Born's weekend brunch is one of the best in the city. Jazz piano happens on Friday and Saturday nights. ▪ *W Broadway and Trutch; (604) 733-0035;*

3205 W Broadway, Vancouver; $$; full bar; MC, V; no checks; breakfast, lunch Tues-Fri, dinner Tues-Sat, brunch Sat-Sun. &

Mescalero ★★

The very good Mescalero has become a most popular hangout (especially on Thursday nights) for Southwestern food and atmosphere. The rustic decor works well (though you may end up with some very authentic splinters). For best value, order from the tapas list; you can piece together a meal from spicy ceviche with marinated scallops, tuna, and jalapeños; roasted mussels in shellfish broth; and grilled eggplant salad with fresh spinach leaves and tangy blue cheese dressing, generously garnished with pine nuts—among others. A dark chocolate " pizza" with pistachios and walnuts in ginger and nutmeg chocolate sauce at the end of the meal will send you rolling out. Trendy and casual (though service may be a touch *too* casual). The wine list is made up of Chilean popular wines with more than half of them available by the glass. ■ *Bidwell and Davie; (604) 669-2399; 1215 Bidwell St, Vancouver; $$$; full bar; AE, E, MC, V; no checks; lunch Mon-Fri, dinner every day, brunch Sat-Sun.* &

▼

Vancouver

Restaurants

▲

Mocha Cafe ★★

Lunch here is the way Vancouverites have liked it all along: muffins, soups, salads, and sandwiches. But at dinner, the Mocha goes a little wild. It's the home of—among other things—Vancouver's best oyster stew, served with cheddar cheese bread. Other things include a great designer pizza, lamb chops with blueberry sauce, and creamy agnolotti with chicken, rosemary, and mushrooms. Salads make a statement—like Belgian endive, with impeccably fresh walnuts and blue cheese. The wine list is a careful collection of moderately priced British Columbia, Washington, and California wines; 10 or so are available by the glass. ■ *W Broadway at Granville; (604) 734-5274; 1521 W Broadway, Vancouver; $$; beer and wine; MC, V; no checks; breakfast, lunch, dinner Mon-Fri.*

Ouzeri ★★

Traditionally, the Greek ouzeri is a place to go to sit, drink, and eat appetizers before going to dinner. In Vancouver, the Ouzeri is where you can go any time of the day and compose a meal of appetizers. The food here involves all the expected Greek specialties and then some. Chicken livers are wonderful—crisp on the outside and tender on the inside. Prawns dressed with ouzo and mushrooms are simply amazing. Friendly, casual, happy (with surely the most reasonably priced menu this side of Athens), Ouzeri proves that being Greek doesn't mean you can't be trendy until 2am. ■ *Corner of Trutch and Broadway; (604) 739-9378; 3189 W Broadway, Vancouver; $$; full bar; AE, MC, V; no checks; lunch, dinner every day.* &

Passionate Pizza ★★

The humble pizza has come a long way, and you don't have to order the Wolfgang Puck (mozzarella, smoked bacon, sweet red peppers, red onions, feta and Asiago cheeses, and eggplant) to see why. The crust is traditional (white, crisp in the thin places, chewy in the thick ones, drizzled with good olive oil, and adorned with bits of baked-on cheese), though toppings tend not to be. Vegetarians, for example, can do well here with the Granville Island Gourmet (mozzarella and Gorgonzola, caramelized onions, pine nuts, and roast garlic). The Caesar-with-a-Twist has strips of sun-dried tomatoes and giant capers hiding among the romaine and croutons. Carrot cake, peanut butter, and chocolate chip cookies fill that last bit of room. ▪ *W 7th Ave at Hemlock; (604) 733-4411; 1387 W 7th Ave, Vancouver; $; no alcohol; MC, V; local checks only; dinner every day.* &

The Pink Pearl ★★ Tanks of fresh fish are your first clue that the Cantonese menu is especially strong on seafood. If you order the crab sautéed with five spices, you'll be further convinced. It's a spectacular dish—sometimes translated as crab with peppery salt—crisp, chile-hot and salty on the outside, moist on the inside. A good dim sum is served every day (be sure to arrive early on weekends to avoid the lineups), and cart jockeys always seem to have time to smile as you select from among sticky rice wrapped in lotus leaf, stuffed dumplings, and fried white turnip cakes. Table-clearing is an event in itself: the tablecloth is actually a stack of thick white plastic sheets; when you finish eating, a waiter will grab the corners of the top sheet and with a quick flip scoop everything up, dishes and all, and haul the lot away. A great place for kids. ▪ *Hastings St at Glen; (604) 253-4316; 1132 E Hastings St, Vancouver; $$; full bar; AE, MC, V; no checks; lunch, dinner every day.* &

Raincity Grill ★★ This newcomer has proved to be the dark horse in Vancouver's culinary sweepstakes, garnering plenty of attention and awards early on. The view of English Bay from the patio is stunning; inside, a clean, contemporary look—with white linen, maroon and gray contrasts, natural wood, and plenty of greenery—is most inviting. Owner Harry Kambolis and chef Gregory Walsh have created an imaginative, regional menu based on fresh available produce from Granville Island. Smoky seafood chowder (with plenty of fish and flavor) is worth a taste, as are littleneck clams. A healthy, al dente portion of lemon-pepper linguine comes with pistachio-nut pesto and grilled vegetables; juicy halibut swims in a gentle lime and chile cream and is sided with black Thai rice. Daytime offerings include one of the city's best burgers (with fresh basil mayo and excellent fries). Desserts are paired with wines (optional), such as a blockbuster Belgian chocolate and cocoa lasagne served with a glass of Quady's Elysium. ▪ *Near the corner of Davie and Denman; (604) 685-7337; 1193 Denman St, Vancouver; $$; full bar; AE, DC, E, MC, V; no checks; lunch, dinner every day, brunch Sat-Sun.* &

Raku Kushiyaki ★★ This almost too stark restaurant sports an innovative fusion menu that sometimes outreaches itself. It globetrots with offerings of skewered tidbits and tiny preparations from the Far East, Middle East, India, Thailand, France, and the Caribbean. There are some delicious surprises here, and some pitfalls as well. Those looking for the unusual will find perfectly prepared asparagus spears with orange and pistachio butter that we have not seen elsewhere, and an excellent barbecued squid yaki. But skip the cloying grilled tofu with peanut sauce and the untrimmed fiddleheads with mustard sauce. Raku stocks four brands of sake; if you're unfamiliar with them, try a taster-glass cold (the flavors are more distinct when sake is unheated). You can nibble, nosh, and share at Raku, but watch out—it adds up. ■ *10th and Trimble; (604) 222-8188; 4422 W 10th Ave, Vancouver; $; full bar; DC, MC, V; checks OK; dinner Tues-Sat.*

The Red Onion ★★ Forget drive-ins and head to Kerrisdale for the best double dogs, cheeseburgers, and fries in town. You simply have to order the sour cream and dill french fries dip. The menu is designed to please everyone (we like the Hot Chicken salad; others pick the veggie soup). The wieners are the Onion's own and so are the buns. At breakfast, the muffins (blueberry, chocolate chip, or banana) and aromatic cinnamon buns are baked on the premises (as are fantastic desserts) and served all morning. There's also take-out. The best of its kind in the city. ■ *At 41st and Maple; (604) 263-0833; 2028 W 41st Ave, Vancouver; $; beer and wine; E, MC, V; no checks; breakfast, lunch, dinner every day.* &

Rubina Tandoori ★★ Son Shaffeen Jamal is the congenial host; mother Krishna cooks the authentic East Indian fare. Rubina's menu is built around tandoori dishes, South Indian seafood, and Punjabi and Mogul dishes. Not surprisingly, tandoori breads are outstanding, and you can watch them being made in the new tandoori oven at the entrance of the restaurant. Fish masala is worth trying, as is a dry curry with potatoes—or any of the dishes that include Rubina's homemade paneer cheese. If you're a beginner at Indian food, try a duet (for two or more)—for example, Moglai Magic, a great, not-too-hot introduction to the cuisine. Don't pass up dessert, since the Gulab Jamun, deep-fried milk dough smothered in syrup and scented with rose water, is a soothing finale. Rubina has separate smoking and nonsmoking rooms. ■ *Kingsway and Victoria Dr; (604) 874-3621; 1962 Kingsway, Vancouver; $$; full bar; AE, MC, V; no checks; lunch Mon-Fri, dinner Mon-Sat.*

Saltimbocca ★★ Maverick chef Ken Bogas' perch has plenty of atmosphere and is something of a see-and-be-seen scene. A lively buzz, contemporary and casual surroundings, and distinctive

Mediterranean flair make tables here eagerly sought. The Italian-inspired menu (with some Asian influences) is prepared almost entirely on the compact open grill by three or four dexterous chefs, who add considerably to the theater. There's no question that Bogas can work marvels, as evidenced by the much-celebrated tuna fillet with lime wasabe, which is indeed superb and beautifully balanced. However, for meals preceded by such fuss and for a place with such a following, the fare can be surprisingly inconsistent and presentation haphazard. Starters such as fresh scallops with black beans are worthwhile, and a solitary crab cake (with plenty of crabmeat) is tasty and deeply spiced with coriander. The wine selection is well thought-out, though with few bargains. A reservation, while advised, doesn't necessarily guarantee dining on schedule, and service at times can be just short of nonchalant. ■ *At 1st and Yew; (604) 738-0101; 2201 W 1st Ave, Vancouver; $$$; full bar; AE, MC, V; no checks; dinner every day.* ♿

Santa Fe Cafe ★★ Anyone who has chowed down at the Santa Fe Cafe knows it is about as close to New Mexico as Vancouver can get. And the Santa Fe team seems to have what Vancouverites want these days: food that is earthy and vibrant and a setting that is casual. No one goes to Santa Fe for privacy; at this 46-seat, storefront-size restaurant, the people sitting at the next table are sitting at your table, and are practically sharing your conversation. But nobody seems to mind—the place sizzles on Friday nights. Tiger prawns on a bed of spinach, an appetizer, is a winner, giving the perfect zap of spices. Sante Fe's chili con queso, with perfectly prepared seafood and a healthy lacing of ancho and Anaheim chiles, may be a new classic. A new location has opened in the Barclay Hotel. ■ *Between Fir and Pine on W 4th; (604) 738-8777; 1688 W 4th Ave, Vancouver; $$; beer and wine; AE, DC, MC, V; no checks; lunch Mon-Fri, dinner every day.* ■ *Next to the Barclay Hotel; (604) 687-3003; 1348 Robson St, Vancouver; $$; full bar; AE, DC, MC, V; no checks; lunch, dinner every day.* ♿

Seasons in the Park ★★ A facelift and considerable attention in the kitchen have contributed to Seasons' rapidly rising reputation. While the park setting and stunning perspective of downtown and the North Shore mountains still guarantee a line of tour buses outside, today's visitors to Seasons (including recent visiting presidents Clinton and Yeltsin) come as much for the food as the view. Diners are treated to a menu of just-picked produce, succulent seafood, and local wines, with such highlights as fresh crab- and spinach-stuffed ravioli, veal medallions with sage butter sauce, and constantly changing salmon entrées. For dessert, a lemon espresso mousse cake with a dark-and-white chocolate sauce is a knockout. ■ *33rd Ave at Cambie in Queen Elizabeth Park; (604) 874-8008; Queen Elizabeth Park,*

Vancouver; $$; full bar; AE, MC, V; no checks; lunch Mon-Fri, dinner every day, brunch Sat-Sun.

Shijo Japanese Restaurant ★★ Shijo is a pleasant, uncluttered sushi bar serving excellent sushi, sashimi, and robata. Oysters, grilled on the half shell and painted with a light miso sauce, are a good bet, as are butterflied tiger prawns or shiitake foilyaki—mushrooms sprinkled with lemony ponzu sauce and cooked in foil. Meals end in a refreshing manner, with orange sherbet served in a hollowed-out orange. ■ *On 4th Ave between Cypress and Maple, on the 2nd floor; (604) 732-4676; 1926 W 4th Ave, Vancouver; $$$; full bar; AE, MC, V; no checks; lunch Mon-Fri, dinner every day.* &

Sophie's Cosmic Cafe ★★ Where "Leave It to Beaver" meets Pee Wee Herman—this funky diner-cum–garage-sale is a fun place to be. Don't worry about the wait—there's plenty to look at, including Sophie's collection of colorful lunch boxes and hats once stashed in her attic. People rave about the huge spicy burgers and chocolate shakes, but the best thing here is the stick-to-the-ribs-style breakfast. Try the great mash of Mexican eggs (with sausage, peppers, onions, and spiced with hot pepper sauce poured from a wine bottle) that's served right through lunch. Dinners run along a similar line with the addition of chicken enchiladas, ribs, cosmic pastas, and lamb chops. ■ *W 4th Ave and Arbutus; (604) 732-6810; 2095 W 4th Ave, Vancouver; $; beer and wine; MC, V; no checks; breakfast, lunch, dinner every day, brunch Sat-Sun.* &

Tai Chi Hin ★★ Tai Chi Hin was one of the first Chinese restaurants in Vancouver to set high standards, and many other places followed suit. The decor is postmodern (glass-block and pastel), the waiters are tuxedoed and give the same polished service as Swiss hotel school graduates, and the overall look is so glamorous, it makes the food appear to be more expensive than it actually is. We recommend the fried smoked duck (served in crisp chunks with coriander and dumplings); the crab and white asparagus soup; and the garlic eel in a smooth brown sauce. The rock cod comes to your table live in a plastic case for your premeal inspection (though you're welcome to skip the preview). For something special, the Peking duck does not need to be ordered in advance, but the Beggar's Chicken does. This dramatically different dish comes as a whole stuffed chicken wrapped in lotus leaves and baked inside a two-inch coating of dough. Ask them to remove the rock-hard crust at the table—it's fun to watch. ■ *On Burrard St at Smithe; (604) 682-1888; 888 Burrard St, Vancouver; $$; full bar; AE, E, JCB, V; no checks; lunch, dinner every day.* &

The Teahouse at Ferguson Point ★★ This stunning location is a magnet for tourists, with its park setting and spectacular view overlooking English Bay, but a faithful following of locals attest to the consistency of fare. Appetizers run the gamut from shrimp-and-crab avocado cocktail to carpaccio with wild mushroom salad, from Pernod-spiked fresh seafood soup to excellent crab-stuffed mushroom caps. Salmon is always a good bet, served sometimes with a rich topping of crab and shrimp in a dill hollandaise. Rack of lamb in fresh herb crust is also a perennial favorite and certainly one of the city's best—even without the view. Recent interior changes suggest the Teahouse may be updating its slightly staid style. ■ *Enter the park from Georgia St, follow road to Ferguson Point; (604) 669-3281; Stanley Park, Vancouver; $$; full bar; AE, MC, V; no checks; lunch Mon-Fri, dinner every day, brunch Sat-Sun.* &

Top Gun Chinese Seafood Restaurant ★★ A visit to Top Gun is somehow a bit larger than life (by the end of 1993 the area in which it's located, known as "little Asia," will be going full force, with a huge Japanese mall, an education center, and Buddhist temple). The menu is generic Cantonese, but specials can be quite interesting, as in sautéed spiced frog's legs with fagara, chicken marinated in bean paste and then nicely fried, or sea scallops and fresh pears in a potato nest. For dessert, amble across the mall to the Rhino Cafe (next to the bowling alley) and try some of the unusual Eurasian cakes and pastries. ■ *Hazelbridge Way, between No 3 Rd and Cambie; (604) 273-2883; 2110-4151 Hazelbridge Way, Richmond; $$; full bar; V; no checks; lunch, dinner every day.* &

Vassilis Taverna ★★ You'll feel transported to the Mediterranean, down to the paper placemats adorned with maps of the Greek Islands. Vassilis, one of Vancouver's original Greek restaurants, is located in what is loosely referred to as Little Greece. The menu is more traditional than original, but quality here is consistent. Worthy starters include lightly battered calamari (among the city's best) and rich, salty, and scalding-hot saganaki (Greek kefalotiri cheese fried in oil and sprinkled with lemon juice). Spiced roast lamb is superb and the house specialty—perfectly juicy kotopoulo: chicken pounded flat, simply seasoned with lemon juice, garlic, and oregano, and then barbecued—is special indeed. The Greek salad makes a sufficient meal in itself, or side it with a succulent pile of quick-fried baby smelts. For dessert, there's honey-sweet baklava or truly luscious navarino. Service is friendly, if at times sporadic. In summer the restaurant's front opens onto the sidewalk. ■ *Between McDonald and McKenzie; (604) 733-3231; 2884 W Broadway, Vancouver; $$; full bar; AE, DC, MC, V; no checks; lunch Tues-Fri, dinner Tues-Sun.* &

Vong's Kitchen ★★ With new upscale Chinese restaurants cropping up all over the city, one could get positively nostalgic about Vong's. It seems to have been around forever: the same tiny place on unfashionable Fraser Street, same steamy windows and almost stark decor inside. If you are serious about food and not into making impressions, then Vong's is the choice. The place is owned and run by the Vong family, who prepare each dish with loving attention. Order the chile-sauced prawns and atomic rice (rich broth is poured on top of the crisp-cooked rice and vegetables, producing a loud, sizzling racket). Although the execution of some dishes can be inconsistent, you are getting as close to a home-cooked meal as you are going to get in a restaurant. The service also gives you a sense of having just come home. If you don't plan on arriving before 6pm, reservations are essential—even then, be prepared to wait. It's worth it. ▪ *Corner of Fraser and E 44th; (604) 327-4627; 5989 Fraser St, Vancouver; `$; no alcohol; no credit cards; no checks; dinner Wed-Sun.*

Bo-Jik Vegetarian Restaurant ★ As part of a well-established Buddhist vegetarian tradition—there are hundreds of these restaurants in Hong Kong—Bo-Jik brings all of the force of Chinese culinary tradition to bear on the problem of eating well without eating meat. Generally, you want to avoid the gluten dishes (which substitute textured soy protein for meat)—though the barbecued satay delight and the basic gluten with chile black-bean sauce aren't bad—and steer toward the vegetable dishes. The Bo-Jik veggie pancake, for example. It's a tangle of stir-fried vegetables, a generous stack of paper-thin Mandarin pancakes, and a hoisin sauce—altogether like mu-shu pork without the pork. Pair it with shiitake on vegetables, big fresh mushrooms on a bed of brilliant green sautéed gai lan, and you have, with a few bowls of rice and some tea, a splendid dinner for under $25. Portions are extremely large, and only two of Bo-Jik's 100-odd dishes cost more than $10. Service is friendly, if somewhat disorganized. Unfortunately, it's on one of the uglier stretches of West Broadway. ▪ *W Broadway between Laurel and Willow; (604) 872-5556; 820 West Broadway, Vancouver; $; no alcohol; MC, V; no checks; lunch, dinner every day.*

English Bay Cafe ★ A candidate for the quintessential Vancouver restaurant. Downstairs, a casual bistro with a summertime deck is one of the city's favorite spots. The upstairs room has a comfortable, woodsy, West Coast feel, with plenty of greenery and a view of English Bay. The kitchen is conservative, if at times uninspired, but there are standouts in the diverse menu, including rack of lamb, filet mignon Oscar, and a combination of veal scalloppine and prawns. Brunches are still well attended, although the quality of the legendary fare that once made this one of the city's hottest brunch spots has waned. An award-winning wine list features a good selection of West Coast vintages. ▪ *Bottom of Davie St; (604) 669-2225;*

1795 Beach Ave, Vancouver; $$; full bar; AE, DC, E, DIS, JCB, MC, V; no checks; lunch Mon-Sat, dinner every day, brunch Sat-Sun.

Isadora's ★ Parents with young kids frequent Isadora's on Granville Island. Its children's menu (clown-faced pizzas and grilled cheese with potato chips), in-house play area, and tables next to the outdoor water park in summer make this a family favorite. Isadora's wholesome menu also features more grown-up items such as smoked wild salmon sandwiches, organic salads, great nut burgers, and plenty of choices for vegetarians and vegans. Open at 7:30am weekdays for early morning business meetings over their own blend of organic coffee, Isadora's is busiest at Sunday brunch. Service is generally slow. ■ *On Granville Island; (604) 681-8816; 1540 Old Bridge St, Vancouver; $; full bar; MC, V; no checks; breakfast, lunch, dinner every day, brunch Sat-Sun.* &

Moutai Mandarin Restaurant ★ The menu at this tiny restaurant was modeled after the one at the well-patronized Szechuan Chongqing; West Enders don't have to leave their territory to get good versions of Szechuan Chongqing favorites such as green beans with pork and plenty of chile pepper. We particularly like the specials: spicy black-bean sauce clams and the blistering stir fry with tiger prawns known as dai ching. Moutai's acid green tabletops and arborite trim in a pebble-pattern gray are miles removed from red-dragon tacky or Hong Kong slick, which seem to be the city's dominant Chinese restaurant styles. A tropical fish tank divides the room into two tiny sections (smoking and non). ■ *Davie and Denman; (604) 681-2288; 1710 Davie St, Vancouver; $; full bar; AE, MC, V; no checks; dinner every day.* &

Nazarre BBQ Chicken ★ There are rubber chickens on the turntables decorating the new storefront location, but only tender barbecued chicken finds its way onto your plate. Owner Gerry Moutal, French-born and Mexican-raised, bastes the birds in a mixture of rum and spices in the rotisserie—the chickens drip their juices onto potatoes roasting and crackling below, and are delivered with mild, hot, or extra hot garlic sauce. There are a few other goodies (vegetarian empanadas, tacos), but it's the chicken you've come here for. Eat in, at one of four tables, or take out. ■ *Commercial St and E 3rd Ave; (604) 251-1844; 1859 Commercial St, Vancouver; $; no alcohol; no credit cards; no checks; lunch, dinner every day.*

Olympia Fish Market and Oyster Co. ★ The Olympia is first and foremost a fish shop, but it purveys some of the best fish 'n' chips in the Lower Mainland. Eight years ago, Robson Street fish merchant Carlo Sorace decided that what the street really needed was a good place to get fish 'n' chips. Whatever is on

Vancouver

Restaurants

▲

special in the store is the day's special at the 12-seat counter; it might be halibut cheeks, scallops, catfish, or calamari, along with the tried-and-true halibut and cod versions. Soft drinks include Chinotto (Italian herbal and fruit-flavored sparkling water) and root beer. Eat in or take out. ■ *Robson and Thurlow; (604) 685-0716; 1094 Robson St, Vancouver; $; no alcohol; V; checks OK; lunch, dinner every day.*

Pho Hoang ★ As common in Vietnam as the hamburger is here, pho is a quick lunch, dinner, or snack, and a great bargain besides. A large bowl of heartwarming broth with rice noodles and your choice of flank, rump, brisket, tripe, or a dozen other beef cuts and combinations will cost you less than $5, complete with a side dish of bean sprouts, a sprig of fresh basil, sliced green chiles, and a wedge of lime with which to customize your soup. A cup of strong Vietnamese coffee, filter-brewed at the table, is the only other thing you need—an iced version, on a hot day. A second, equally busy, location is on E Georgia Street in Chinatown. ■ *20th and Main; (604) 874-0810; 3610 Main St, Vancouver; $; no alcohol; no credit cards; checks OK; lunch, dinner every day.*

Quilicum West Coast Native Indian Restaurant ★ A meal here is certainly an unusual culinary foray. You'll sample dishes you've never dreamed of—oolichan grease, for example, prepared from the oil of a native fish and spread on baked bannock bread (or as a unique side dish). Another taste thrill is caribou, barbecued or stewed, and herring roe served on a bed of healthy kelp. Not all the dishes are as spectacular as the impressive Quilicum Special—succulent parts of salmon (head, tail, and belly) barbecued and presented in a carved ceremonial bowl—but other, tamer variations on the salmon (wind-dried and steamed-smoked) are also good. The potlatch platter for two ($43.95) is heaped with barbecued salmon, smoked cod, oysters, prawns, and caribou, and will easily serve three. There are some flubs, such as overcooked fried oolichans, less-than-fresh hazelnuts, and a poor showing on the wine list. The totem poles, Indian masks, and artifacts among which you dine are for sale. ■ *Between Bidwell and Denman on Davie; (604) 681-7044; 1724 Davie St, Vancouver; $$; full bar; AE, MC, V; no checks; lunch Wed-Fri, dinner every day.*

Shinla Korean Restaurant ★ Shinla is a Korean restaurant for Koreans. The second-story location on E Broadway has minimal signage, giving it the feeling of a private club. Private rooms surround a center area with booth seating—all functionally decorated—with bulgogi grills on every table. The special combination for two (a hearty undertaking) is a bargain at $22.95: rib-eye steak slices, short ribs, chicken, prawns, and pork come neatly arranged on a large platter ready to be seared to taste, complemented by interesting side dishes of kimchi, pickled garlic, grilled dry minnows, sesamed spinach, and other vegetables. Sushi, tempura, and noodle dishes are also available with sometimes inconsistent execution. But when they're good, they're very good. ■ *At Kingsway and E Broadway; (604) 875-6649; 206-333 E Broadway, Vancouver; $$; full bar; MC, V; checks OK; lunch, dinner every day.*

Szechuan Chongqing ★ For a long time, Chongqing was the only Chinese restaurant offering authentic Sichuan specialties. The robust flavors, piquant sauces, and the searing heat of fresh and dry chiles quickly became familiar signposts of Chinese food in Vancouver, and when it closed many were left wondering where they would find that addictively haunting plate of fried green beans. Luckily, there's a new Chongqing. Live seafood tanks line one wall and a couple of VIP salons bring up the rear. Waiters in sleek vests briskly whisk away silk arrangements from the tables as you're being seated. The old haunt has gone upscale, and, not surprisingly, the reception has been ambivalent. While some pine for the lost cozy, friendly feeling, others complain that the service is confused. All this is trivial indeed, because the food remains eminently true to form. The fried prawns with chile sauce are quite simply magnificent: sweet and masterfully seasoned. The rich smooth-crunchy Tan Tan noodles, the lingering orange-peel beef, the melt-in-your-mouth sliced pork with garlic sauce, and, of course, those worth-their-weight-in-gold beans; they're all there to attest that the Chongqing dynasty is going to be long-lived. ■ *At Commercial and 12th; (604) 254-7434 or 879-8454; 2808 Commercial Dr, Vancouver; $$; full bar; AE, E, MC, V; no checks; lunch, dinner every day.* 👌

Tio Pepe ★ Tio Pepe—a shoebox of a restaurant, one long, narrow room crammed full of tables, with the kitchen at the back—has reasonable prices and food unlike any other Mexican food in town. Start with margaritas and a double order of chicken flautas—some of the best around. Charbroiled lamb is marinated in wine and spices with a haunting, bittersweet taste of Seville oranges. Pascaya con huevo, date-palm shoots fried in an egg batter and served with tomato sauce, is an unusual appetizer, with a pleasantly astringent taste. The food is flavorful without being too spicy: a mildness typical of Yucatan cooking. However, if fire is your style, on your table you'll find a bottle of habanero hot sauce, distilled from the hottest peppers known to anyone. ■ *Between the pier and William; (604) 254-8999; 1134 Commercial Dr, Vancouver; $; beer and wine; MC, V; no checks; dinner Mon-Sat.* 👌

Tomato Fresh Food Cafe ★ Tomato is two experiences, both noisy. One is a row of tables and chairs down the center of the restaurant, placed so close your elbows touch your neighbor's. The other (our choice) is a set of roomy booths around the edge, with plenty of space to lounge. For years, this was an undistinguished diner; now it has an overlay of young, retro energy, most lucidly expressed in the big, chunky, wildly colored bowls used for serving specialties such as "teapuccino"—cappuccino made with tea. Modern young waitstaff serve a variation of Mom food: vegetarian chili with really good corn bread, a whacking slab of turkey in the turkey sandwich, a tomato and pesto sandwich, real milk shakes, brownie sundaes, and a wide selection of fresh juices. ▪ *Cambie St and W 17th; (604) 874-6020; 3305 Cambie St, Vancouver; $; beer and wine; MC, V; no checks; breakfast, lunch, dinner Tues-Sat, brunch Sat-Sun.*

Ezogiku Noodle Cafe If it wasn't for the word "noodle" in its name, one would expect to find a trendy espresso-and-pastry bar here; instead, ramen dishes are the order of the day. There are only 10 seats at the counter and four at the window. The menu offers ramen in regular (pork) broth, miso, or soy, a fried rice dish, a fried noodle dish, a curried dish, gyozas, and that's all. Ezogiku's size and focus are the secret to the large bowls of perfectly cooked chewy noodles in rich, steaming broth. Do what the old master in the movie *Tampopo* instructed: study, sniff, and savor. Lineups are common, but it's always worth the wait. A new, much larger location now accommodates 70 noodle fanatics with equally focused food; 1329 Robson St, (604) 685-8606. Other branches are in Honolulu and Tokyo. ▪ *On Robson at Bidwell; (604) 687-7565; 1684 Robson St, Vancouver; $; no alcohol; no credit cards; no checks; lunch, dinner every day.*

LODGINGS

The Four Seasons ★★★★ After leaving your car in the porte cochère, you take an escalator up to a lively and elegant lobby, filled with marble, plants, and people. The rooms, with $14 million worth of new furnishings, come in three color schemes: terra-cotta, beauvais (a regal rose), and black-and-white; the last is the most stunning. Furnishings are tasteful without being ostentatious, and the many small amenities that are offered as a matter of course—outstanding 24-hour room service, terrycloth robes, hair dryers, VCRs (with rentals from reception desk), complimentary newspapers, fresh flowers—make this place a refined and welcome refuge. Evening tea service and slippers on arrival are given to Japanese tourists; however, if you would like the same, just ask. Aside from the split-level suites (there are two of them), our favorite rooms are those on a corner above the 20th floor. There are 24 floors of rooms, eight of which are smoking floors. There's a big deck off the spa with an indoor/outdoor pool, a Jacuzzi, and a sauna. The atriumlike Garden Lounge, off to one side, provides a bosky retreat for cocktails and conversation and serves an excellent buffet brunch on Sundays. An informal restaurant, Seasons Cafe, opens into the rotunda of the Pacific Centre mall. The formal dining room, Chartwell (see review in this section), is a first-class restaurant. ■ *Howe and W Georgia; (604) 689-9333, toll-free from US (800) 223-8772; 791 W Georgia St, Vancouver, BC V6C 2T4; $$$; AE, DC, MC, V; no checks.* &

Le Meridien ★★★★ Le Meridien is the most elegant hotel in Vancouver. The large pinkish stone building holds the refined, patrician decor that you would expect in an aristocratic European hostelry. Built just prior to Expo '86, the place is fairly big—397 rooms and 47 suites—and well suited to its address, close to the Vancouver Art Gallery and the fashionable browsing district of Robson Street. The lobby—decorated in soft shades of coffee and peach, with Asian-inspired rosewood furniture and dramatic flower arrangements in glazed pottery urns—sets the tone for the whole place. The ample-size rooms are soothing spaces with city views out of floor-to-ceiling windows (ask to face north for the best views). Prices in season are high—$185 to $240 for a standard-size double, over $1,000 for the presidential two-bedroom suite—but regardless of the size, accommodations *all* include twice-daily maid service, shoeshine, a downtown limousine at your disposal, an umbrella, and membership in Le Spa (a fitness and beauty and tanning salon complete with indoor and outdoor pool and sun deck). Of the restaurants, the dark, polished, publike Gerard Lounge is the current after-work gathering place for locals; Cafe Fleuri offers a good breakfast, pleasant Sunday brunches, and weekend chocolate buffets; and Le Club (formerly Gerard) is now a continental restaurant. The business center is complete with stock market TVs, computer workstations, and a bar. ■ *Corner of Smithe and Burrard; (604) 682-5511, toll-free from US (800) 543-4300; 845 Burrard St, Vancouver, BC V6Z 2K6; $$$; AE, DC, MC, V; no checks.* &

Delta Place ★★★ Original owners Mandarin International spared no expense with design and fixtures (the standard rooms, with large baths and extra amenities, are labeled deluxe). All the extras—wool carpeting, solid oak cabinetry, marble shower stalls, cast-iron bathtubs, balconies off most rooms, a health club (sauna equipped with a color TV, towels on ice, and racquetball *and* squash courts)—tipped the scales, and Mandarin had to sell. Now that it's owned by a local investment group (and managed by Delta), business has picked up a bit. Summer rates hover at around $225. Located in the center of Vancouver's financial district, Delta Place has ample facilities for the business traveler (boardrooms, secretarial services, and fax, among others). ■ *Dunsmuir and Howe; (604) 687-1122, toll-free from US (800) 877-1133, toll-free from Canada (800) 268-1133; 645 Howe St, Vancouver, BC V6C 2Y9; $$$; AE, DC, MC, V; no checks.* &

The Georgian Court Hotel ★★★ This exclusive, brick-clad
hotel, just across the street from BC Place, combines the business amenities traditionally associated with a "name" hotel with
the luxury and personality of a small one. Exceptional meeting
facilities, three phones in each room, a health club (with whirlpool, sauna, and exercise room), and its prime location are practical advantages. The amiable lobby is small and appealing, in
tasteful green with peach and gray accents. Doubles (starting
at about $125 a night) and one- and two-bedroom suites (from
$145 to $350) are smartly furnished with mahogany, antiques,
and Audubon prints—more reminiscent of a fine home than of
a hotel. For these prices, however, we'd expect a little more
precision: sounds of the heating system found their way into
our room on a recent visit, and the bathroom was curiously un-
derstocked with towels. Perhaps the biggest plus is the city's
best continental restaurant, the William Tell, just down the
stairs (see review in this section). Rigney's is a casual, less
pricey alternative. ■ *Cambie and Beatty; (604) 682-5555, toll-
free from US (800) 663-1155; 773 Beatty St, Vancouver, BC
V6B 2M4; $$$; AE, DC, MC, V; checks OK.* ♿

Pacific Palisades ★★★ The tri-tower complex (owned by
Shangri-La International) takes up an entire city block of the ul-
trafashionable Robson Street. It was formerly an apartment
complex (long-term rates are still available), and the rooms are
some of the most spacious in the city. Call them suites, as ev-
ery one has a kitchenette (no stoves, just microwaves) and is
supplied with thoughtful extras such as umbrellas, hair dryers,
and robes. Reserve a room above the fourth floor and you'll be
guaranteed a choice of view. There's a courtyard with a health
center (pool, sauna, weight room, whirlpool, masseuse, and
table tennis), where pick-up badminton or barbecues might be
held in the summer. Or rent a mountain bike and work out in
Stanley Park. Businesspeople will appreciate the business cen-
ter, with a number of small meeting rooms, a fax machine, and
computers; you can even rent a cellular phone.

Live jazz is often heard in the comfortable Monterey Lounge
(with pleasant sidewalk tables)—a good place to meet for a
drink before dinner at the Monterey Grill. ■ *Between Bute and
Jervis on Robson; (604) 688-0461; 1277 Robson St, Vancou-
ver, BC V6E 1C4; $$$; AE, DC, MC, V; no checks.* ♿

Pan Pacific Hotel ★★★ As part of Canada Place in the heart
of Vancouver's harborfront, the Japan-based Tokyu Corpora-
tion's 507-room hotel stands in all its white-sail magnificence
overlooking the docking cruise ships and the whole expanse
of the inner harbor. The five signature sails (made to resemble a flotilla of sailboats racing up Burrard Inlet) have attracted
a lot of attention, but that's not always a good thing: the entrance
is a bit awkward (past the Trade and Convention Centre, then

up two escalators to the reservation desk), and the big atrium space leans more toward a tourist attraction than a first-class hotel. Rooms are smallish but some of the prettiest in town, with bird's-eye maple armoires and marble bathrooms (shower early, there's not always enough hot water for everyone). All have views—on the west side toward Stanley Park and the Lion's Gate Bridge, and on the east overlooking the city; ask for a corner room (any room ending with "10") and you'll even have a view from the bathtub. Suites are spacious and lovely. Service is first-rate, and health facilities are endless: an outdoor lap pool (heated to 86 degrees) and hot tub, saunas, a running track, high-tech exercise equipment, indoor hot and cold pools, squash and racquetball courts, and, in keeping with the hotel's Asian connection, shiatsu massage.

The main floor features the Cascades Lounge with its marvelous water outlooks, the five enormous sculptured sails poised on the outside deck, and a waterfall. Other restaurants (all overpriced due to the hotel's popularity with conventioneers) are Cafe Pacifica, a casual place serving continental cuisine and dim sum lunches; Suntory, with Japanese food; and Five Sails, a French restaurant (see review in this section). ■ *At the north foot of Burrard St, across from Stanley Park; (604) 662-8111, toll-free from Canada (800) 663-1515, toll-free from US (800) 937-1515; 300-999 Canada Pl, Vancouver, BC V6C 3B5; $$$; AE, DC, MC, V; no checks.* &

Vancouver Renaissance Hotel ★★★ Hong Kong-based New World Development brought this former Holiday Inn up to the level of the better hotels in the city. A wavelike design (the hotel is just above Coal Harbour) is carried throughout the hotel—from the confetti-patterned rug in the lobby to the contoured hallways (leading to the meeting rooms) to the rotating dining room (Vistas) on the top floor. The rooms are standard hotel size; however, they include unusual features such as heated bathroom floors and hair dryers, even in the most inexpensive. Ask for a room with a view of the North Shore, and if you want extra-special treatment, request a room on the exclusive 18th floor. A ballroom is one of the few in the city, with a spectacular entryway with a view of the harbor. A pool, sauna, workout room, and sun deck are on the fourth floor. Dynasty Restaurant is one of the finest Chinese restaurants in the city (see review in this section). ■ *Above Burrard Inlet between Bute and Thurlow; (604) 689-9211; 1133 W Hastings St, Vancouver, BC V6E 3T3; $$$; full bar; AE, DC, DIS, MC, V; no checks; lunch, dinner Tues-Sun.* &

Waterfront Centre Hotel ★★★ Although this classy hotel is situated across the street from the Pan Pacific, its pie-shaped design allows equal views of Burrard Inlet and the North Shore mountains. There are 489 guest rooms and a good 75 percent of them have water views. Of the tastefully decorated standard rooms, the corner ones are the best, with two walls of windows. The Royal Suite comprises two floors with views from every room (including the closet and the bathrooms with Jacuzzi). Ten rooms on the business-class level open onto the terrace level, a nice feature if privacy isn't a factor. Around the corner on the terrace level is an outdoor heated pool and spa with a whirlpool and steam room. For personalized service (private checkin, concierge, lounge, shoeshine, and complimentary hors d'oeuvres, newspapers, and continental breakfast), request the Entrée Gold floor. The hotel is well suited to host meetings of any size (there's over 20,000 square feet of meeting space from small boardrooms with kitchen facilities to expansive ball-rooms), but it does not feel like a convention hotel. The Herons Restaurant and Lounge is on the main floor. ■ *Across the street from Canada Place; (604) 691-1991, toll-free from Canada (800) 268-9411, toll-free from US (800) 828-7447; 900 Canada Place Way, Vancouver, BC V6C 3K2; $$$; full bar; AE, DC, DIS, MC, V; checks OK; breakfast, lunch, dinner every day.* &

Coast Plaza Hotel ★★ This tall hotel, located in a pleasant residential neighborhood, has seen a few owners and a few names. It is currently being operated by the Coast Hotel chain. The pastel lobby and the rooms have recently been upgraded. Because this was originally an apartment building, rooms are larger than average and have individual balconies with wonderful views. All have minibars and some have kitchens. Upstairs floors constitute Limited Edition, a private businesspersons' territory where guest rooms have more personal service. All guests enjoy membership privileges in the newly renovated Olympic Athletic Club next door—*the* place to play squash in Vancouver. Breakfast and lunch are served in the Brasserie, dinner of West Coast fare at Windows on the Bay. The location—a few steps from English Bay and not far from the zoo and aquarium—makes this a good choice for families with kids. ■ *At Stanley Park; (604) 688-7711, toll-free (800) 663-1144; 1733 Comox St, Vancouver, BC V6G 1P6; $$$; AE, DC, MC, V; checks OK.* &

Delta Vancouver Airport Hotel and Marina ★★ This big (416 units) hotel is near the airport, but you can get a room over-looking the Fraser River and a small marina if you'd rather not gaze at jets. Prices range from $130 to $150; rooms are comfortable and spacious. The 10-story hotel has plenty of facilities: a nearby jogging trail, a sauna, and summer barbecues for lunch around the pool. In its main dining room, the Pier, you'll find French cuisine. ■ *On Cessna Dr before airport; (604) 278-1241, toll-free from Canada (800) 268-1133, toll-free from US (800) 877-1133; 3500 Cessna Dr, Richmond, BC V7B 1C7; $$$; AE, DC, DIS, MC, V; checks OK.* &

English Bay Inn ★★ When Bob Chapin exchanged teaching English for innkeeping on English Bay, he rounded up a whole new class of devotees. His Tudor house is tiny in comparison to the other places of this caliber; however, Chapin's impeccable taste measures up on every level. Most of the five rooms echo Chapin's passion for 18th- and 19th-century history with Louis Phillipe sleigh beds, antique armoires, and paisley-patterned down comforters. The two-level suite with a fireplace in the top-floor bedroom is, no doubt, the best. But a stay in any of the other four rooms (all with small bathrooms) is no less exquisite. Two rooms open out to the small cloisterlike garden out back. Complimentary robes, phones in each room, and tea upon arrival are nice thoughts. A formal breakfast is served upstairs in the dining room, often warmed with a fire. You're only steps away from English Bay and Stanley Park (bring your tennis racket and bike). ■ *1 block from English Bay on Comox at Chilco; (604) 683-8002; 1968 Comox St, Vancouver, BC V6G 1R4; $$$; AE, V; checks OK.*

Granville Island Hotel and Marina ★★ The Granville Island Hotel is a bold combination of an old stucco building (now pink) and a dramatic new complex of glass and corrugated iron, the latter reminiscent of Granville Island's industrial past. A glass atrium, extending toward the water like the bow of a ship, splits the building down the middle and lets in a stream of natural light all the way to the first floor. A whimsical, brightly colored sculpture, the *Cyrus P. Windless Kite Flying Machine*, fills the atrium space in the lobby. The small 54-room hotel has a lot to recommend it: the custom-furnished rooms are decorated in muted tones with light wood accents, and some have shutters that open onto small balconies. Avoid rooms that face the atrium: the nightclub can make for a sleepless night. Prices range from $150 for a double to $250 for a one-bedroom suite. Boats can hook up to the dock and connect with the hotel's television and telephone system, power and water lines, and even use its room service. There are two new restaurants here: the casual Pelican Pub and Grill and the more formal Pelican Bay. ■ *Far east corner of Granville Island; (604) 683-7373, toll-free (800) 663-1840; 1253 Johnston St, Vancouver, BC V6H 3R9; $$$; AE, MC, V; no checks.* &

⑳ Hyatt Regency ★★ Located in the city's core, the Hyatt is popular for conventions and business meetings, with more than 25,000 square feet dedicated to this purpose. But this is also a good spot for the vacationer: one block to Robson Street shopping, a 15-minute walk to Stanley Park. Harborside rooms with a terrific view onto busy Burrard Inlet and the surrounding mountains run $195 to $220. Suites cost $425 to $725. Each room comes with its own electronic safe. A fitness club and pool round out the amenities. Cafes and lounges abound, but most noteworthy is the casual Fish & Company, under chef Othmar Steinhart. ▪ *Burrard and Georgia; (604) 687-6543, toll-free (800) 233-1234; 655 Burrard St, Vancouver, BC V6C 2R7; $$$; AE, DC, MC, V; checks OK.* ♿

Park Hill Hotel ★★ This urban hotel, owned by Mainami Canada, is lovely and coolly sophisticated. The marble lobby is all pastels—peach and dusty rose—and the garden court lounge is particularly fine. Rooms are large and nicely furnished; each has a balcony and, from the 18th floor, there is an incomparable view of English Bay and the islands beyond. Extras include sauna, outdoor swimming pool, exercise room, and secretarial services. Prices are competitive. You're a 15-minute walk from the hub of the city, but the lively street life right outside your door in Vancouver's West End is a show in itself. ▪ *Davie and Thurlow; (604) 685-1311, toll-free (800) 663-1525; 1160 Davie St, Vancouver, BC V6E 1N1; $$$; AE, DC, MC, V; no checks.*

The Sylvia ★★ This charming and rather shabby brick landmark, completely covered with ivy, offers one of the best locations in the city: right on English Bay in the heart of the West End. Families with children especially enjoy its proximity to the beaches and playgrounds of Stanley Park, but the major attraction is its incredibly low prices (especially for Vancouver). Doubles run $55 to $80, triples (an extra bedroom for the kids) are $72 to $85, and suites are $70 to $120. Children under 18 traveling with a parent stay free. Avoid the cheaper rooms, which tend toward the tacky—opt for a room with a view of the bay or for one of the 16 newer rooms, which are pleasant and slightly less dowdy, although somewhat characterless. Ask to see the room first; the difference in price doesn't necessarily mean much difference in rooms here. The English Bay-view bar can get rowdy in the evenings with neighborhood apartment dwellers. The new dining room, Sylvia's, offers great sunset-watching but mediocre food. ▪ *Beach and Gilford; (604) 681-9321; 1154 Gilford St, Vancouver, BC V6G 2P6; $$; AE, DC, MC, V; checks OK.*

The Wedgewood Hotel ★★ Veteran hotelier Eleni Skalbania virtually custom-ordered this hostelry, which emerged like a butterfly out of the dilapidated Mayfair in the center of town. The place exudes Skalbania's presence, with her effort and care stamped on almost every facet of the operation. Businesspeople may prefer the corporate atmosphere of the bigger properties, but the Wedgewood is the place Vancouverites recommend to their friends. Doormen usher you into a lobby decorated handsomely with antiques and Oriental fixtures. There are 93 bedrooms; the suites are decorated in shades of dusty rose and cool green, and many of them include fireplaces. Doubles start at $180. All the rooms have patios, remote-control TVs, stocked

20 YEARS

▼

Vancouver

Lodgings

▲

minibars, and morning newspaper delivery. Recent reports indicate that careless service can be a problem here—curious for such a small place run by such an exacting taskmaster. Guests enjoy membership privileges at the Chancery Squash Club next door. In the Bacchus Ristorante, the 150-seat oyster bar and bistro serves rusticiana (country-style) cuisine created from local, organically grown foods. ■ *On Hornby between Smithe and Robson; (604) 689-7777, toll-free (800) 663-0666; 845 Hornby St, Vancouver, BC V6Z 1V1; $$$; AE, DC, MC, V; no checks.* ⅄

Westin Bayshore ★★ The setting is grand: gaze out over a small harbor, with Stanley Park beyond and the mountains beyond that. The city is behind you, but as you look north from your room you're at the edge of Stanley Park's wilderness. A great round pool fills up the courtyard, so in the summer you can sunbathe in this secluded setting. Or you can rent a boat (or a bike) for a little tour, or go jogging in Stanley Park. There is also an indoor pool for the cooler months. Problem is, the rooms are small and the staff doesn't go to any extra effort to justify the high price of a room. If you've a boat, moorage at the nearby marina is cheap and allows for full use of the hotel facilities and room service. The Garden Restaurant, a pleasant, open area facing the pool, serves modest breakfasts, lunches, and suppers. The big-deal restaurant is Trader Vic's. ■ *Georgia and Cardero, just south of Stanley Park; (604) 682-3377, toll-free (800) 228-3000; 1601 W Georgia St, Vancouver, BC V6G 2V4; $$$; AE, DC, MC, V; checks OK.* ⅄

▼
Vancouver
Lodgings
▲

West End Guest House ★★ Here's an alternative to the big, expensive hotels: a quasi-Victorian home nestled amid the newer and larger architecture of the last few decades. The place is bright pink, so you can't miss it. Vancouverite Evan Penner took over the place a few years ago, and poured money into spiffing it up. There are seven bedrooms, all with private baths, ranging in price from $90 to $170 for a double. Most have writing tables and queen beds. Each wears a different theme: Oriental, Laura Ashley, or old master (in stately blues). Best is the suite, with its own fireplace and fine touches (Louis Nichol linens, horsehair and wingback chair). The living room is comfortable, even if its collection of furnishings is somewhat odd. Breakfast is a special event. Turndown service, afternoon iced tea on the sun deck, and an evening sherry are part of the routine—so civilized. ■ *1 block south of Robson, between Jervis and Broughton, (604) 681-2889; 1362 Haro St, Vancouver, BC V6E 1G2; $$; AE, DIS, MC, V; checks OK.*

Hotel Georgia ★ It may not have the flash of some of the newer hotels in town, but this old, familiar face in the center of downtown has pleasant rooms adorned with new oak furniture and done in a calming jewel-toned palette. In all, it's an unpretentious place. The Cavalier Grill features a casual breakfast and lunch menu as well as fine dining in the evening; two other popular spots are the Night Court Lounge and the raucous George V pub, with sing-alongs Thursday to Saturday evenings and authentic pub lunches. ■ *Howe and Georgia; (604) 682-5566, toll-free (800) 663-1111; 801 W Georgia St, Vancouver, BC V6C 1P7; $$$; AE, DC, MC, V; no checks.* ⟨

Hotel Vancouver ★ Built in the French château style favored by the Canadian railways, this grand hotel comes complete with a steep green copper roof, BC stone exterior, menacing gargoyles and griffins, and rich ornamentation. Even so, the dowager has been made into a convention hotel, owned and managed by Canadian Pacific. Its location is about as central as you can get, near the big stores, the Law Courts complex, and the Vancouver Art Museum. The 508 rooms are moderately sized, sophisticated, and quiet; and service is good. A brand-new health club adds a modern touch to the old place. Dining is not the high point of staying here, but the Roof Top Restaurant and Lounge has a grand view; it's one of the very few places in town that still offers the dinner dance. ■ *Georgia and Burrard; (604) 684-3131, toll-free (800) 441-1414; 900 W Georgia St, Vancouver, BC V6C 2W6; $$$; AE, DC, DIS, MC, V; checks OK.* ⟨

GREATER VANCOUVER: THE NORTH SHORE

RESTAURANTS

Beach Side Cafe ★★ Owner Janet McGuire and chef Carol Chow have turned this little Ambleside haunt into one of the area's more serious kitchens, with a creative and varied approach to regional cuisine. The goat cheese salad alone—a sizable slice presented with endive and a pungent sun-dried vinaigrette—is worth a visit. In season, look for steamed mussels and swimming scallops in a zesty garlic and wine sauce. Choices are plentiful, with emphasis on daily specials as well as a cutting-edge list of better West Coast wines. Sweet-toothers swear by crème brulée and homey lemon meringue pie. Well-informed staff are happy to make recommendations. The surroundings are woodsy, the mood is relaxed, and in summer one of the city's best decks opens up, with views of Stanley Park and Kitsilano across the water. ■ *On Marine Dr between 14th and 15th; (604) 925-1945; 1362 Marine Dr, West Vancouver; $$; full bar; MC, V; no checks; lunch Mon-Fri, dinner Mon-Sun, brunch Sat-Sun.* ⟨

Cafe Norte ★★ The tortilla chips and addictive salsa that arrive while you peruse the extensive menu are a good sign of things to come. A full range of serious nontraditional nachos includes warm black bean guacamole, chili con queso topped with chorizo, sweet pineapple with jalapeño, and more. And things *look* good too: smooth, rich cream of crab soup comes with a garnish of finely chopped red peppers and parsley, and fajitas arrive with tender pieces of still-sizzling chicken nudged up against onions and green peppers. San Pedro pizza and smoked turkey quesadillas are also worthwhile. Margaritas (by the pitcher if desired) are appropriately slushy. Vancouver does not have a plethora of Mexican restaurants, and this is the best of the bunch. ■ *On the north side of Edgemont; (604) 255-1188; 3108 Edgemont Blvd, North Vancouver; $$; full bar; MC, V; no checks; lunch Mon-Sat, dinner every day.* &

Cafe Roma ■ Corsi Trattoria ★★
Mario Corsi (also of the Park Royal Hotel and Corsi Trattoria) operates this room with a view in a friendly, casual way, and the very Italian food is very good. Focaccia appears at your elbow while you contemplate the menu, and some of the pasta dishes—such as the ultraspicy spaghetti Trasteverini (with a sauce of minced chicken, black beans, garlic, and peperoncini)—are rarely seen outside the old country. There are several pizza choices, as well as many nicely prepared fish and meat dishes. Lighter appetites will be satisfied with halibut cooked on a slate with fresh herbs and olive oil; the undecided can pick over combination dishes. The deck is superb in summer, with an impressive view of downtown. ■ *Semisch St at Esplanade; (604) 984-0274; 60 Semisch St, North Vancouver; $$; full bar; AE, DC, E, MC, V; no checks; lunch Mon-Fri, dinner every day.* & ■ *Across from the Lonsdale Market; (604) 987-9910; 1 Lonsdale Ave, North Vancouver; $$; full bar; AE, DC, E, MC, V; no checks; lunch Mon-Fri, dinner every day.* &

La Cucina Italiana ★★
La Cucina is an Italian restaurant stuck rather incongruously in the middle of North Vancouver's strip of car dealerships and video shops. It's an attractive, rustic place, where Italian opera plays at just the right volume. When it's available, try bresaola—air-dried beef imported from Switzerland—as an appetizer. Pastas range from the traditional (spaghetti with tomato-and-meat sauce) to the original (fettuccine with squid and sweet red peppers). Fish specials are usually good; or try pollo alla diavola, a grilled chicken breast with black-pepper-crusted skin. The house lasagne is outstanding. Don't leave without sampling the homemade ice cream. ■ *Marine Dr and McGowan; (604) 986-1334; 1509 Marine Dr, North Vancouver; $$; full bar; AE, MC, V; no checks; dinner Mon-Sat.* &

La Toque Blanche ★★
This cozy, '70s-retro woodsy retreat tucked away behind the Cypress Park Mohawk gas station is still a well-kept culinary secret. Owner Peter Wieser has a passion for detail, manifest in appetizers such as duck liver terrine with cassis coulis, phyllo-wrapped escargots served with mild

pepper salsa, and wickedly rich lobster bisque. His entrées are no slouch either, as proved by breast of duckling glazed with Calvados, and morsels of lamb, cooked perfectly pink in a mustard sauce. A moderately priced wine list complements the menu. Prices are almost a bargain, by today's standards—especially considering the quality, detail and presentation. ■ *Next to the Cypress Park Market; (604) 926-1006; 4368 Marine Dr, West Vancouver; $$; full bar; AE, MC, V; no checks; dinner Tues-Sun.* ᕳ

Salute ★★ Great martinis are created in the elaborate (though dimly lit) bar, and the food in this cozy, relaxed spot is good too. Carpaccio here is one of the best around—lean and moist, attractively garnished with capers and fresh parsley and drizzled with a piquant grainy mustard. Salads can be too oily, but some are more successful, as is the carciofi: colorful mixed greens with a tasty combination of shrimp, chopped marinated artichoke hearts, and sun-dried tomatoes. A good list of pastas is punctuated with some rustic dishes such as ciocicara, a gutsy, earthy combination of fusilli with potatoes and spicy sausage; Spaghetti Salute is a well-spiced mix of pink and green peppercorns, garlic, chicken, black beans, a few chiles, and al dente pasta. Owner/chef Gamal Hanna spent several years at one of Vancouver's respected trattorias honing his skills, and it shows. A predominantly Italian wine list definitely caters to a more well-heeled clientele, but there are some less expensive options. Save a corner for chocolate salami, a plate of sliced dark chocolate and coconut flake pâte with starfruit and fresh blackberries. ■ *On Marine between 17th and 18th; (604) 922-6282; 1747 Marine D, West Vancouver; $$; full bar; AE, MC, V; no checks; lunch Mon-Fri, dinner Mon-Sat.*

The Salmon House on the Hill ★ The view from the Salmon House stretches from Lions Gate to Vancouver Island. West Coast Indian artifacts lend an appropiate cultural nod to the menu. A recent renovation was accompanied by changes in the menu that suggest the kitchen here is working toward a more regional identity. The hallmark BC salmon cooked over green alder wood (which delivers the distinctive, delicate, and smoky flavor) certainly warrants the drive halfway to Horseshoe Bay to sample it. A variation on the theme finds spring salmon marinated in dark sugar, Canadian whiskey, dill, and salt before being grilled. Crab cakes come with crab that you can actually taste, set off with apple and cherry salsa. The indecisive can try the Salmon House sampler, with generous tastes of smoked and alder-wood barbecued salmon, an intriguing roulade and gravlax, all served with homemade relish and chutneys. ■ *21st St exit off Hwy 1 W; (604) 926-3212; 2229 Folkestone Way, West Vancouver; $$$; full bar; AE, E, MC, V; no checks; lunch, dinner every day, brunch Sun.*

The Tomahawk ★ The Tomahawk just might be the original inspiration for all those hokey, totem-pole-theme restaurants on highways across North America. In Vancouver, it's an institution, deservedly famous for its hungry-man-size meals. The eye-opening Yukon Breakfast, for instance, gives you five rashers of bacon, two eggs, hashbrowns, and toast for $7.50 and is served throughout the day. At lunch there are several hamburger platters (named after Indian chiefs), sandwiches, fried chicken, fish 'n' chips, and even oysters. The pies (lemon meringue, Dutch apple, banana cream) are baked on the premises, and the staff will even wrap one up to go. For children there is a special breakfast menu for braves and princesses. ■ *Philip Ave at Marine Dr; (604) 988-2612; 1550 Philip Ave, North Vancouver; $; no alcohol; AE, MC, V; no checks; breakfast, lunch, dinner every day.* ⑁

LODGINGS

The Park Royal Hotel ★★★ Every city should have a hotel like this one (only 10 minutes from downtown): 30 spacious units surrounded by a couple of acres of lovely gardens and a walking path along the Capilano River. There's more: a rollicking English pub in the basement, a fine dining room, and a garden lounge (the Terrace) with gazebo for drinks and lunch. It's tough to get a reservation here. If you do make it, ask for one of the top floor ivy-clad riverside rooms, overlooking the gardens and the river (even though reservations in these rooms cannot be guaranteed); rooms facing the parking lot are somewhat noisy. Prices range from $105 to $225 for a double and include a morning newspaper and tea and coffee with your wake-up call. A note of caution to light sleepers: the pub tends to be quite noisy into the night. The Tudor Room serves continental fare, and host Mario Corsi will take good care of you. ■ *6th and Clyde; (604) 926-5511; 540 Clyde Ave, West Vancouver, BC V7T 2J7; $$$; AE, DC, MC, V; local checks only.*

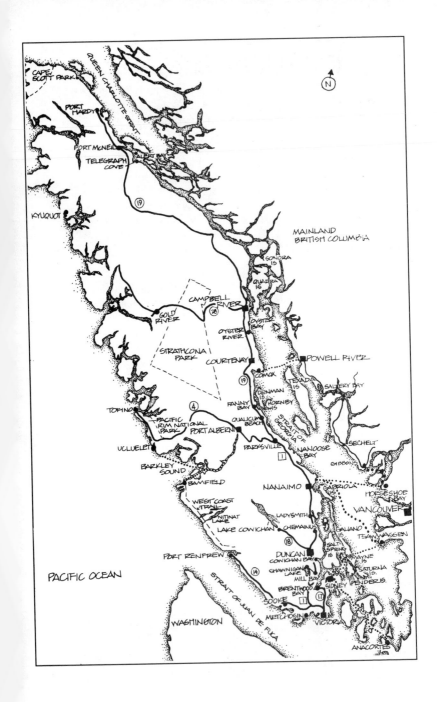

Victoria and Vancouver Island

From Victoria and environs—westward to Sooke, northward to Sidney—up-island along the east coast to Parksville. From there a short jog inland to Port Alberni (and access to west coast towns); then back to Qualicum Beach and north along the coast to Port Hardy. Finally, the Gulf Islands, north to south.

VICTORIA

Romantic as Victoria may be, with its delightful natural harbor and the Olympic Mountains of Washington State on the horizon, the provincial capital of British Columbia is less a museum piece nowadays than it is a tourist mecca. Visitors pour in to gawk at huge sculptured gardens and London-style double-deck buses, shop for Irish linens and Harris tweeds, sip afternoon tea, and soak up what they believe is the last light of British imperialism to set on the Western hemisphere. Raves in the travel press have brought a new crop of younger residents to upset Victoria's reputation as a peaceful but dull sanctuary for retiring civil servants from eastern Canada. The quality and variety of restaurants is improving as a result, and no longer are Victoria's streets silent after 10pm.

Getting There—ferries. The passenger-only **Victoria Clipper**, a jet-propelled catamaran, makes its 2½-hour voyages up and back four times daily, all year round ($85 round trip).

The good seats on the upper deck by windows are quickly taken, so board early; (604) 382-8100, (206) 448-5000, or (800) 888-2535 (good outside of Seattle and outside of British Columbia). Other ferry services **from Washington** to the Victoria area leave from Anacortes (destination Sidney, 27 kilometers north of Victoria), one of the most scenic routes in the Pacific Northwest; (206) 464-6400 or (604) 381-1551, $31.25 round trip in summer or $26.05 in winter; and from Port Angeles (via the privately run Black Ball Ferry), a 1½-hour voyage (year-round) on which cars are allowed, but for which no reservations are taken (call a day in advance to find out how long the wait will be); (206) 457-4491 or (604) 386-2202, $25 one way car and driver. Ferries **from British Columbia** depart from Tsawwassen (destination Swartz Bay, 32 kilometers north of Victoria) every hour from 7am to 10pm in summer, following a scenic route through the Gulf Islands; $48 round trip car and driver; call BC Ferries at (604) 386-3431.

Air Transportation—seaplane. The fastest link from Seattle (Lake Union) to Victoria (Inner Harbour) is provided several times daily for about $135 round trip on Kenmore Air, toll-free (800) 826-1890. You also can fly from Vancouver via Air BC, (604) 688-5515, or Helijet Airway, (604) 273-1414.

Attractions. First stop should be Tourism Victoria, a well-staffed office dispensing useful information on the sights; 812 Wharf Street, (604) 382-2127. The **Royal British Columbia Museum** is one of the finest of its kind in the country, offering dramatic dioramas of natural BC landscapes and full-scale reconstructions of Victorian storefronts. Of particular interest is the Northwest Coast Indian exhibit, rich with spiritual and cultural artifacts. Open every day, Belleville and Government, (604) 387-3701. The **Art Gallery of Greater Victoria** houses one of the world's finest collections of Oriental art (including the only Shinto shrine in North America), with special historical and contemporary exhibits on display throughout the year. Open every day, 1040 Moss Street, (604) 384-4101. **McPherson Playhouse**, a former Pantages vaudeville house done up with baroque trappings, offers evening entertainment throughout the summer. The box office, (604) 386-6121, also has information about plays and concerts at the Royal Theatre and other sites. The free *Monday Magazine* offers the city's best weekly calendar of events. Spreading out over 184 acres, **Beacon Hill Park** provides splendid views of the water, but the real interest here is in the landscaping (much of it left wild) and the hand-holding couples who stroll the walkways and give retirement a good name. A lovely spot to get away from the shopping mania downtown. **Crystal Garden** is a turn-of-the-century swimming-pool building converted into a glass conservatory with a tropical theme (lush greenery, live flamingos and macaws). It's a fine place to spend a rainy day; admission is $3. Open every day, 713 Douglas Street, (604) 381-1213. Just across the street is the **Victoria Conference Centre**, linked to the Empress by a beautifully restored conservatory and accommodating 1,500 delegates. **Butchart Gardens**, 21 kilometers north, shows what can be done with dug-out limestone quarries (with help from a small army of Chinese workers). The 50 acres of gardens are beautifully manicured, lovely displays in many international styles; they're lighted after dark. Take the time to look beyond the profusion of blooms to the landscape structure and its relationship to the setting of rocky bays and tree-covered mountains. In the summer it's best to go late in the afternoon, after the busloads of tourists have left. Concerts, fireworks on summer evenings, a good afternoon tea, and light meals provide

Victoria

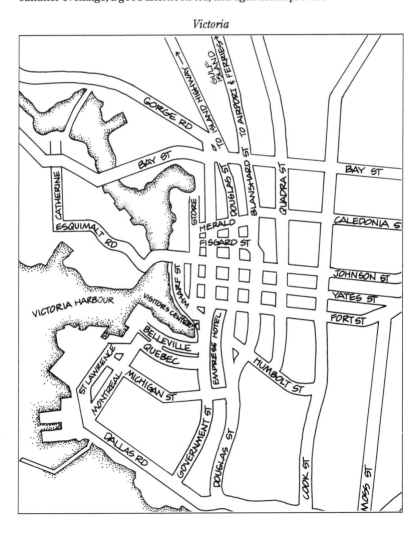

diversions. Open every day, (604) 652-5256. **Craigdarroch Castle** puts you back into an era of unfettered wealth and ostentation. Vancouver Island coal tycoon Robert Dunsmuir built this 19th-century mansion to induce a Scottish wife to live in faraway Victoria. Open every day, 1050 Joan Crescent, (604) 592-5323. **Victoria heritage homes.** You can visit five of the better restored old-Victoria homes, (604) 387-4697: Helmcken House, behind Thunderbird Park, east of BC Royal Museum; Point Ellice House, at Bay Street and Pleasant Street; Craigflower Manor, 110 Island Highway; Craigflower Schoolhouse (Admirals and Gorge Road W); and Carr House, at Government and Simcoe. Admission to all five is $3.25. The **Esquimalt and Nanaimo (E&N) Railway** leaves early in the morning from a mock-Victorian station near the Johnson Street bridge and heads up-island to towns with fine resorts. The trip is slow but scenic; no food service. For an autoless vacation, take the ferry to Victoria and the train from there. Call Via Rail, (604) 383-4324 or toll-free (800) 561-8630.

Specialty Shopping. For British woolens, suits, and toiletries, the downtown area north from the Empress on Government Street is the place to shop. **George Straith Ltd.** is the best of the clothing stores, and you can be measured for a suit here that will be tailored in England; **Piccadilly Shopper British Woolens** specializes in good-quality women's clothes; **W & J Wilson Clothiers** sells English wool suits and women's clothes; **Sasquatch Trading Company, Ltd** offers some of the best of the Cowichan sweaters; **EA Morris Tobacconist, Ltd.** carries a very proper, Victorian mix of fine pipes and tobaccos; **Munro's** books, a monumental 19th-century bank-building-turned-bookstore, has a thoughtful selection of books; **Murchie's Teas and Coffee** offers the city's best selection of specially blended teas and coffees; and don't forget **Roger's Chocolates** and the **English Sweet Shop** for chocolates, almond brittle, blackcurrant pastilles, marzipan bars, Pontefract cakes, and more, and **Bernard Callebaut Chocolaterie** for picture-perfect chocolates in the Belgian style. Farther north, on Yates and lower Johnson streets, are the trendier shops and designer boutiques. Market Square is a restored 19th-century courtyard surrounded by a jumble of shops, restaurants, and offices on three floors. A few blocks farther on at Fisgard Street, the entrance to Victoria's small and seemingly shrinking **Chinatown** is marked by the splendid, lion-bedecked Gate of Harmonious Interest. Visit the tiny shops and studios on Fan Tan Alley and check out Morley Co. Ltd, a Chinese grocery. **Antique hunters** should head east of downtown, up Fort Street to Antique Row—block after block of shops, the best of which are the Connoisseurs Shop and David Robinson, Ltd., with excellent 18th-century English pieces. Visit **Bastion Square** for sidewalk restaurants, galleries, the Maritime Museum, the alleged location of Victoria's old gallows, and a great gardener's shop called Dig This; Trounce Alley for upscale clothing; and Windsor Court for boutiques and gifts.

RESTAURANTS

Da Tandoor Restaurant ★★★ Da Tandoor (no connection with Vancouver's similiarly named establishment) is Victoria's most popular Northern Indian restaurant. A blend of exotic spices wafts around the room, raising expectations that are not only met but surpassed. The aromatic tandoori-style meats and breads baked in the huge red clay oven are easy to like; if you're a stranger to the style, try the murgh shorba to accustom your palate, a mild but flavorful chicken soup seasoned with garlic, ginger, cinnamon, cardamom, and other Indian spices, or try the $17 combination plate, which gives you a feast of poppadums and chutney, butter chicken, chicken tandoori, lamb curry, curried lentils, basmati rice, and much more. A glass of sweet (but not too) lassi is an ideal finish. ■ *Fort and Vancouver; (604) 384-6333; 1010 Fort St, Victoria; $; full bar; MC, V; no checks; dinner every day.*

Victoria

Restaurants

Camille's ★★ Never has a basement been so romantic. Chef David Mincey creates with fresh local produce, seafood, rabbit, and lamb, and occasionally borrows his grandmother's superb recipe for rich, smoky jambalaya (loaded with chicken, prawns, sausage, vegetables, and spicy tomato sauce). Three-cheese soup is a creamy delight. Most appetizers are meatless, and tofu lovers will appreciate it in a pepper steak incarnation with blueberry cream sauce which, unbelievably, seems to work. Over 200 wines are available, kept in a huge, walk-in vault and helpfully described; wine-tasting dinners (monthly Sundays) are highly popular—reserve early. ■ *Fort and Langley in Bastion Square; (604) 381-3433; 45 Bastion Square, Victoria; $$; full bar; MC, V; no checks; dinner Tues-Sun.* &

Cecconi's Pizzeria and Trattoria ★★ Suppertime at Cecconi's is a noisy affair, with lots of families and live music on some nights. The wood-oven pizzas can sometimes be a little too L.A. (such as Cajun shrimp, mushroom, leek, and cheddar), but the basic pizza pomodoro is perfectly rich and satisfying. Bruschetta al pomodoro is a generous serving of chewy bread rubbed with garlic and topped with chopped tomatoes. Enjoy the fresh, hard-working chunk of Reggiano Parmesan which staff will grate over almost everything except drinks and dessert. We've enjoyed excellent homemade pasta here, including Fettuccine Paradiso (prawns, scallops, clams, crab, and leeks in a luscious cream sauce), and rotini alla barese (hot Italian sausage, peppers, onions, and tomatoes). Cheesecake is big in Victoria and you will find a good sample or two here. Watch for

the novel ice buckets made from old olive oil cans. ■ *Shelbourne
and N Dairy Rd, across from Hillside Mall; (604) 592-0454;
3201 Shelbourne, Victoria; $$; full bar; MC, V; no checks;
lunch, dinner every day.* ♿

Chez Daniel ★★ Chez Daniel is one of Victoria's finest French
restaurants, tucked in Oak Bay a long way off the tourist track.
Daniel Rigollet has been pleasing people here for a long time—
people who come back again and again. The decor is pleasant,
and the wine list shows great care in selection—this place re-
cently won the coveted *Wine Spectator* Best Award of Excel-
lence. The expensive menu, though conservative French in ap-
proach, is wide-ranging in flavor: Dover sole, lamb, salmon in
vermouth and cream sauce, fresh young rabbit, or duck in a
fine chestnut sauce. The food can be very rich, but accompa-
nying al dente vegetables are a fine antidote. A few nouvelle
touches find their way into some presentations: tender pieces
of lamb cooked just enough, sauced in reduced cream, and fin-
ished with shreds of fresh ginger, and chicken breast wrapped
around fresh thyme, quickly roasted and served with pan
juices. Service can be understandably slow (Daniel works alone
in the kitchen). Plan to make an evening of it. ■ *Estevan and
Beach, past Sea Land, 10 minutes from downtown; (604) 592-
7424; 2524 Estevan Ave, Victoria; $$$; full bar; AE, MC, V;
checks OK; dinner Tues-Sat.* ♿

Herald Street Caffe ★★ The combination of Mark Finnigan
in the kitchen and Helen Bell presiding over desserts and bread
has created one of the most popular eateries in town. Unfortunately, recent reports on slacking service and greasy pasta leave
us wondering if they're at times overrun. Best to stick with the
tried and true favorites here: Fish Steamer (fresh, local whitefish, served in an Oriental bamboo steamer with black bean
sauce), bouillabaisse (as an appetizer), the rack of lamb, or the
beef tenderloin are very good. Shaker Lemon Pie, based on a
heritage recipe, wins raves, though the fruit crumbles are also
worth digging into. The reasonably priced wine list has won
prestigious awards. For evenings or weekends, reserve or be
prepared to wait. Great for post-theater (open until midnight).
■ *Government and Herald, 1 block past Chinatown; (604)
381-1441; 546 Herald St, Victoria; $$; full bar; AE, MC, V;
no checks; lunch Wed-Sun, dinner every day, brunch Sun.* ♿

La Petite Colombe ★★ The menu in this cozy, upscale restau-
rant is simple and French. Prawns in orange sauce make a very
pleasing appetizer, full of flavor but not too sharp. Indonesian
leg of lamb is a rewarding departure from the usual Franco
fare, and if you're really hungry, the huge rack of lamb ($20.95)
should satisfy. For dessert, La Petite Colombe maintains a de-
served reputation for sorbets and accompanying fruit sauces.
■ *On Broughton just off Government, 2 blocks north of Empress*

Hotel; (604) 383-3234; 604 Broughton, Victoria; $$; full bar; MC, V; no checks; dinner Mon-Sat. &

San Remo Restaurant ★★ The theme here is Mediterranean, with an Italian and Greek emphasis (the more interesting dishes seem to come from the Greek side). The pita bread is superb and perfect for dipping tzatziki or hummus. Saganaki—pan-fried goat cheese flamed at your table with brandy and lemon—will excite the youngsters at your table. Conservative diners can depend on charbroiled chicken salad; those suffering indecision might try the dinner platter for two, which at $37.50 is a good way to sample moussaka, lamb chops, chicken souvlaki, calamari, spinach pie, tzatziki, Greek salad, rice, and fresh veggies. ■ *Quadra and Hillside; (604) 384-5255; 2709 Quadra St, Victoria; $; full bar; AE, MC, V; no checks; lunch Mon-Sat, dinner every day.*

Siam ★★ The Thai food found here (and at the affiliated Bangkok Seafood Palace on Wharf Street) is very authentic and very good. The 54-item menu can be seasoned anywhere from mild to painful; the flavors of lemon grass, basil, peanuts, chiles, lemons, and limes work their magic in each imaginative presentation. Especially good are Siam Curry (red curry with coconut milk, bamboo shoots, sweet basil, and your choice of meats) and Siam Delight (sautéed bamboo shoots, black mushrooms, straw mushrooms, peanuts, baby corn, chiles, and your choice of meats). Stir-fried Chicken Cashew Delight, with onions, carrots, and peppers, has been earning raves recently. Siam's interior is not the most bright and cheerful, but it's up-scale and immaculate. ■ *Government and Johnson; (604) 383-9911; 1314 Government St, Victoria; $$; full bar; AE, MC, V; no checks; lunch Mon-Sat, dinner every day.* &

Spinnakers Brew Pub ★★ Spinnakers is simply the best pub in town (and seems to be constantly getting better). It certainly has the best selection of natural beers, most of which are made on the premises. All the necessary elements for a bar full of regulars are here: a cheerful, noisy atmosphere, friendly staff, dart board, live music every day (discreet enough that it doesn't offend), and, of course, hearty, casual food. Minors are welcome downstairs in the restaurant with the same good view and a touch more dining sophistication than is offered with the pub fare upstairs. Fish 'n' chips (of cod, salmon, or halibut), burgers, potpies, and the odd Mexican-style treat are worth sampling. But it's the beer that brings people back from all over—solid, dark stouts, aromatic bitters and brown ales, connoisseur lagers, and a range of seasonal brews, each kept and lovingly served at the right temperature. ■ *Travel west over the Johnson St Bridge to Catherine, or water taxi from the inner harbor; (604) 386-2739; 308 Catherine St, Victoria; $; full bar; MC, V; no checks; breakfast, lunch, dinner every day.* &

▼

Victoria

Restaurants

▲

Szechuan ★★ If you tell him you like spicy food, Joseph Wong will give your tastebuds something to tingle about. Try the Pon Pon Chicken as an appetizer—a tender chicken breast with thick sesame sauce. For the main course we recommend the very crisp whole rock cod, served with either hot bean, sweet-and-sour, or fermented rice sauce; spicy chicken with a hot garlic-soy sauce; Mandarin pork (sweet-and-sour style); tongue-tantalizing ginger beef; and shrimp. The service here is lightning-fast (and a good thing, since Szechuan is located right across from the Memorial Arena). It's best to order in relays; otherwise the dishes won't come in any particular sequence. Reports of occasionally greasy food have yet to be proven by us. ■ *Across from the Memorial Arena parking lot; (604) 384-5651; 853 Caledonia Ave, Victoria; $$; full bar; AE, MC, V; no checks; lunch, dinner Tues-Sun.*

Barb's Place ★ If the weather behaves, eating at Barb's is an alfresco treat: the fishing fleet bobs nearby as you sit on the dock at one of two open-air picnic tables, eating your fish 'n' chips out of newspaper. The fish is fine and fresh—tender halibut (cod during midsummer) encased in crisp batter accompanied by homefried chips with skins left on. Help yourself to vinegar and catsup from large vats on the counter. Take the water taxi back to the inner harbor or across to the local pub (there's no beer served at Barb's) to wash down this beautifully basic meal. ■ *At Fisherman's Wharf; (604) 384-6515; 310 St Lawrence St, Victoria; $; no alcohol; no credit cards; no checks; breakfast, lunch, dinner every day.* ঙ

Victoria

Restaurants

Blethering Place ★ "Blethering" is Scottish for voluble, senseless talking. What could be bordering on too quaint and precious works well here, and kids love it. This is one of the better British teas to be found in Victoria (Oak Bay can be more British than the real thing), and also one of the better values. Enjoy a decent pot of tea, Devonshire cream, fruity jam, and scones, as polite conversation mingles with the gentle, civilized clatter of authentic British crockery. Afternoon tea is $7.95, and can be enjoyed from 11am until 7pm (long, lazy afternoons are de rigueur around here), and then the dinner menu is offered. Farmhouse English food is excellent, though not for the calorie-conscious, most of it fitting into the "comfort food" category (sandwiches, quiche, and meat pies). Ask about teddy bears while you're here. ■ *Oak Bay and Monterey; (604) 598-1413; 2250 Oak Bay, Victoria; $; beer and wine; AE, DC, MC, V; local checks only; breakfast, lunch, dinner, tea every day.* ঙ

Chez Pierre ★ This is reputedly the oldest French restaurant in town. Atmospherically it's a bit dark, but the à la carte menu presents standard French classics such as tournedos, veal in cream and mushroom sauce, duck à l'orange, and rack of lamb, and also boasts fresh local seafood. A table d'hôte menu brings scallops in white wine sauce, butter lettuce salad, boeuf bourguignon, and crème caramel. It's much more bistro fare at lunch. ▪ *Yates and Wharf; (604) 388-7711; 512 Yates St, Victoria; $$; full bar; AE, MC, V; no checks; dinner every day.* ⑤

Demitasse ★ Coffeehouses have enjoyed a resurgence in Victoria, land of tea, so a decent cup of espresso is never far away. Demitasse has a broad selection of coffee by the cup (or by the bag) and a long-standing reputation to back it up. A favorite haunt of the committed, but not too trendy, java-and-croissant set. Lunch features homemade soup (try the borscht), thick sandwiches, and excellent desserts, but the real Demitasse fan comes for breakfast—for hot almond croissants, for croissants filled with steam-scrambled eggs and cheese (or add avocado, artichoke hearts, and smoked sausage). There's one small table outside and good service, simple decor, and a window-bar with a great people-watching view inside. ▪ *Corner of Blanshard and Johnson; (604) 386-4442; 1320 Blanshard St, Victoria; $; beer and wine; no credit cards; checks OK; breakfast, lunch, dinner every day.* ⑤

Futaba ★ This Japanese restaurant has a casual, Western air about it—no tatami rooms or kimono-clad waitresses, but nevertheless a good place to try some Japanese dishes that you won't find anywhere else in Victoria. The sushi bar is not outstanding, but appetizers are interesting and varied, the menu is distinctly health-conscious, and Futaba has become something of a mecca for a few of Victoria's more discriminating vegetarians and macrobiotic eaters (brown rice is the norm, though white is offered). The vegetarian dumplings in various flavors are good, and be sure to ask for matsutake, delicious pine mushrooms, when they're in season. Tofu appears in several tasty guises, though beef and chicken are also well represented. ▪ *Quadra and Pandora; (604) 381-6141; 1420 Quadra St, Victoria; $$; full bar; MC, V; no checks; lunch Mon-Sat, dinner every day.* ⑤

Victoria

Restaurants

John's Place ★ Breakfast or brunch at John's Place has become a Victoria institution: some love it (especially the younger crowd) and some don't. Small, usually busy with windsurfers, and consequently noisy, John's has the casual, party atmosphere of a student union bar. The Belgian waffles here are good, as are omelets. Portions are ideal for young, ravenous appetites, and desserts are generous too. Not for those who dislike smoke. ▪ *Douglas and Pandora; (604) 389-0711; 723 Pandora Ave, Victoria; $; full bar; MC, V; no checks; breakfast, lunch, dinner every day, brunch Sun.* ⑤

The Met Bistro ★ A long and narrow restaurant that's broad on service. The long walls and high ceiling sport a baroque touch (clouds and cherubs), and martini fans can indulge in over a dozen original variations on their favorite theme—need we say it's a trendy, post-theater kind of spot? The French chef rings the changes on the European menu every two weeks, but there's a regular mix of seafood and meat appetizers, decent salads, a few interesting pastas, and limited vegetarian fare. We've liked roasted tomato and gin soup, as well as a generous dish of steamed clams and mussels in white wine with garlic, tomato, shallots, and fresh herbs. Desserts are modest. Lunch and dinner menus vary slightly in content and price, but the biggest change is the cosmopolitan atmosphere that arrives around sunset. ■ *Herald and Government; (604) 381-1512; 1715 Government St, Victoria; $$; full bar; AE, MC, V; no checks; lunch Mon-Fri, dinner every day.* ᕋ

Pounder's ★ It's all a bit gimmicky, but it's fun. You arm yourself with a stainless steel bowl, select meats and vegetables from a long table and have them weighed, stir-fried Mongolian style, and served to you, and charged to your bill by the pound (lunch is almost half the price of dinner). Farm-raised meats and fish are truly international—tombo, mako shark, swordfish, Australian bluenose, caribou, wild boar, ostrich, musk ox, buffalo, even rattlesnake and alligator—and definitely create quite a stir here (but honestly, rattlesnake is tough and bony, and most settle with the more standard prawns, sea bass, or chicken). The secret is to make several trips with your bowl and work through the light, then dark fish, and then tackle the meats. Desserts are limited, but Pounder's Cheesecake is something special—a huge Oreo-type cookie topped with light cheesecake and covered with a mixture of dark and light chocolate. Every 10th customer at lunch wins a lottery ticket. ■ *Near the bottom of Yates St at Wharf; (604) 360-1875; 535 Yates St, Victoria; $$; full bar; MC, V; checks OK; lunch, dinner every day.* ᕋ

Soho Village Bistro ★ Recently installed chef/owner Jack Morrisey has kept the old favorites (such as falafel and souvlaki) and has livened things up on the vegetable front (baby turnips, candy-cane beets). The fish and pommes frites are very good, curiously delivered in a Chinese bamboo steamer. Morrisey's inventiveness is manifest in lamb scalloppine covered in Javanese tropical curry, sautéed with Asian gremolata and glazed with smoked pepper marmalade. Both dinner menu and atmosphere become more sophisticated as evening approaches. Parking is a problem, but if you turn off Chambers onto Gladstone, you can usually park west of Fernwood near the school. ■ *Gladstone and Fernwood, across from the Belfry Theatre; (604) 384-3344; 1311 Gladstone, Victoria; $; full bar; MC, V; no checks; lunch Tues-Sun, dinner every day.* ᕋ

Yoshi Sushi ★ Sushi originated in Southeast Asia as a means of preserving fish. Fermenting fish and salted rice destroys harmful bacteria, and vinegar gives the fish flavor. Care and sensitivity are vital when dealing with such delicate flavors—and Yoshi knows just how to do it. At the sushi bar, the robata bar, or in one of the 12 tatami rooms, you'll get consistent service and excellent traditional Japanese food. If sushi isn't for you, sample shabu shabu (sliced beef and vegetables in delicate broth). All of the entrées (including tempura, teriyaki, sukiyaki) are preceded by miso soup, sunomono, and an appetizer of yakitori or sushi. ■ *In Gateway Village Mall just outside of town on Hwy 17; (604) 383-6900; 601 Vernon Ave, Victoria; $$; full bar; AE, MC, V; no checks; lunch Mon-Sat, dinner every day.*

Pagliacci's Owner Howie Siegel is a mile-a-minute talker who turned the old Red Swing tearoom into a boisterous, Jewish-flavored Italian restaurant and Victoria institution. Siegel is a movie buff who names dishes after such mediagenic types as Veronica Lake and comes up with entrées such as Last Chicken in Paris and My Little Chickadee (a box-office hit of boneless breast of chicken with a creamy white sauce). Hollywood mugshots, Manhattan murals, and occasional live music contribute to an atmosphere that is somewhat chaotic (not a place for an intimate dinner); service can be slow. Modest food is reasonably priced, such as the interesting Pagliacci Salad ($7.25), a mix of romaine, tomato, egg, garbanzo beans, feta, carrot, green onion, and olives, served with foccacia bread. This is also the appropriate place to discuss wild Saturday nights over Sunday brunch, if you're prepared to line up. ■ *Between Fort and Broughton on Broad near Eaton Centre; (604) 386-1662; 1011 Broad St, Victoria; $$; full bar; MC, V; checks OK; lunch Mon-Sat, dinner every day, brunch Sun.* ⅄

Re-bar Lime green walls, a purple bar, and mismatched vinyl tablecloths can be something of a shock to the system, but what you eat here is very good for you (as is the smoke-free environment). The house salad (one of seven offered) is a positively juicy combination of red and green leaf lettuce, sprouts, cucumber, tomato, chick peas, shredded carrot, and shredded beet, with an especially good basil vinaigrette. Beer and wine are available, though healthy patrons sip a variety of vegetable juices and cocktails, some of them fortified with wheatgrass (growing in a rack of trays), bee pollen, amino acids, electrolytes, protein powder, or other dietary shots-in-the-arm. The chocolate espresso cheesecake is light and sweet—though not necessarily healthy. Closes at 6pm. ■ *Langley and Bastion Square; (604) 361-9223; 50 Bastion Sq, Victoria; $; beer and wine; V, MC; local checks only; breakfast, lunch, dinner Mon-Sat, brunch Sun.*

Six Mile Pub The Six Mile is a large, rangy pub/restaurant that boasts the longest-established liquor license in British

Columbia and a fiercely loyal clientele. A patio overlooks a small inlet and busy Parson's Bridge—inside it's darker and smokier. You stand in line to order substantial pub fare from a take-out window: garlicky caesar salad; mammoth savory roast beef sandwiches au jus served on slabs of fresh French bread; and daily lunch specials such as chicken fajitas or veal cordon bleu. Portions are quite generous. Vegetarians are limited to pizza, or possibly the ploughman's lunch if you hold the deli meat. Ten draft beers are available, though only three (Hermanns, Okanagan Pale, and Shaftebury Cream) are natural. ■ *Colwood exit off Island Hwy; (604) 478-3121; 494 Island Hwy, Victoria; $; full bar; MC, V; no checks; lunch, dinner every day.* ᗱ

LODGINGS

Abigail's ★★★ The feminine counterpart of the Edwardian Beaconsfield, just two blocks away, the Tudor Abigail's is all gables and gardens and crystal chandeliers, with three floors of odd-shaped rooms, each with a shiny-tiled bathroom. Not a lavish detail is missed: guest rooms are decorated in restrained tones (rose, peach, periwinkle, mint); crystal goblets sit in each room; the halls smell faintly of good coffee and beautiful women. Practicalities, too, are all well in place—there are electrical outlets wherever you might need them, a light shines in the shower, the walls are well soundproofed (light sleepers, however, may want to request a room as far from noisy Quadra Street as possible). In short, Abigail's combines the beauty of the Old World with the comforts of the New. Third-floor guest rooms are grandest: the Foxglove Room has a canopy bed, and a few of the bathrooms are equipped with Jacuzzis. Breakfast is served from 8am to 9:30am in the sunny downstairs dining room. The sitting room is inviting in the sort of way that makes one want to linger, with a glass of port and a hand of whist, after a day of traipsing about Victoria. ■ *Vancouver and McClure; (604) 388-5363; 906 McClure St, Victoria, BC V8V 3E7; $$$; MC, V; checks OK.*

The Beaconsfield ★★★ Of all the imitation England spots, this is the best. The Beaconsfield opened its Edwardian gates in 1984 and since then has quietly and capably assumed its place at the forefront of Victoria's accommodations. Tree-lined Humboldt Street is closer to the hub of downtown than its quiet demeanor would suggest, so the Beaconsfield's location here, just a block and a half from Beacon Park, is prime. It's meant to convey a sense of romance and hideaway and does, with 12 antique-filled bedrooms, all with private baths and down comforters. The Attic Room occupies the entire top floor, features its own Jacuzzi and wet bar, and is exceedingly private. Lillie's Room is a little more feminine, with inlaid mahogany pieces and an unusual wood-enclosed period bathtub. The antiques are offset by rediscovered "modernities" such as steam-heated towel racks. Public areas are elegantly crafted, with so much dark, gleaming mahogany that one can feel a bit cloistered on a sunny day, but this is easily remedied in the sun room/conservatory. The place is so popular for breakfast that you sign up for your morning meal when you check in. ■ *Vancouver and Humboldt; (604) 384-4044; 998 Humboldt St, Victoria, BC V8V 2Z8; $$$; MC, V; checks OK.* &

Holland House Inn ★★★ The house is a modern beauty (just the antidote to the endless Olde England theme so prevalent in Victoria), decked with rose trellises and a picket fence outside, skylights and stark white walls inside. Fine art and sculpture, many of the pieces by owner Lance Olsen, fill the 10 sparkling guest rooms. The result is startlingly chic and about as avant-garde as you're likely to find in Quaintville. The Lilac Room has an intriguing art deco-inspired headboard. Rooms 20 and 30 have fireplaces, the former with a unique lace-draped bed. All of the rooms have immaculate private baths (the fixtures in room 11 are equipped for wheelchair access); all but one of the rooms have their own balconies or patios. This is consistent with the inn's other orientation, a healthy one: Olsen's wife, Robin Birsner, is an occupational therapist. No smoking in the rooms, natch. Owners and the managers are always at the ready with hospitality, but the service is never fawning. A full breakfast can be had anywhere from the gallery to your balcony. Most of the art is for sale. ■ *2 blocks behind the Parliament buildings, at Government and Michigan; (604) 384-6644; 595 Michigan St, Victoria, BC V8V 1S7; $$$; AE, DC, MC, V; checks OK.* &

Laurel Point Inn ★★★ A massive brick-and-glass ziggurat addition now overlooks the harbor; inside there's a subtle Oriental touch. The angular construction of the lodge means that all of the rooms have good views of the harbor or the ship channel, but the upper floor of the newest wing has the best. Rooms on each floor can be connected to form two-room suites, a particularly nice touch if you are traveling with children. Junior suites, $200, make up most of the new pyramid-shaped addition. These spacious rooms have the niftiest bathrooms—floors and walls entirely of marble, and extremely comfortable bathtubs. A separate shower graces each of the new rooms. The channel-side rooms offer the best view of the comings and goings of boats and seaplanes and the Japanese garden at channel's edge, completed in 1991. The dining room, Cafe Laurel, is a wicker-and-fern place with better-than-adequate food. Sunday brunch is the best in town. Underground parking is adjacent to the hotel. Reservations are tough to make, and the front desk and bell staff are poorly trained or nonexistent. When these areas are given the same degree of attention that the rest of the hotel has received, Laurel Point Inn will be as close to perfect as you will find in the city. ■ *On the west side of Inner Harbour; (604) 386-8721; 680 Montreal St, Victoria, BC V8V 1Z8; $$$; AE, MC, V; no checks.* &

The Bedford ★★ The liveried doorman is gone, but the carefully maintained flower boxes, thick and pillowy bed quilts, private Jacuzzis, and a dozen rooms with fireplaces are still here. In a renovation that proved frogs can still become princes, Victoria's reigning dukes of hospitality transformed what used to be downtown's shoddiest hotel, the Alhambra, into a small showcase of European-style elegance. Today the Bedford is owned by Brittingham Properties. Most of the 40 rooms don't boast much of a view, and they're pricey ($135 to $185 in season), but the hotel's central location—smack in the middle of the shopping district—is hard to beat. There's no room service, and afternoon tea is an extra $11.95, but a full breakfast is included in the price. ■ *½ block north of Fort St; (604) 384-6835 or toll-free (800) 665-6500; 1140 Government St, Victoria, BC V8W 1Y2; $$$; AE, MC, V; no checks.* &

The Haterleigh ★★ The Haterleigh House was built in 1901 by Thomas Hooper, an architect who designed many of Victoria's Victorian homes. Owners Les and Mary Lane Anderson went to great lengths to preserve (and in many cases restore) the original character of the home. Fine curved, stained-glass windows grace the parlor; plaster moldings were recast from molds made from sections of existing molding. All six rooms each have a private bath. Four have large Jacuzzi whirlpool tubs. Stay on a Friday night and you'll get one night free. Vegetarian breakfasts are generous. ■ *Take Belleville west to Pendray until it dead-ends; (604) 384-9995; 243 Kingston St, Victoria, BC V8V 1V5; $$$; MC, V; checks OK.*

Joan Brown's B&B ★★ Joan Brown may monopolize the conversation at the breakfast table, but most really enjoy listening to the tales of her life. This lovely house draped with wisteria is in the renowned Rockland neighborhood, but Joan's personality, the spacious rooms (a few are the size of a small ballroom), and her quirky ways of running an inn make this stately bed and breakfast a very comfortable stay. The elegant Georgian-style house, like a few of the rooms, is huge. You walk literally *through* a trimmed bay laurel hedge to get to the front door. In the rooms, there's a definite Laura Ashley appeal. There are many rooms to choose from, but our favorite is the one with a second-empire flavor furnished with a king-size bed, fireplace, bath, and bay window. Nothing could be better for a rainy afternoon than her well-stocked library. ■ *Pemberton and Fort; (604) 592-5929; 729 Pemberton Rd, Victoria, BC V8S 3R3; $$; no credit cards; checks OK.*

Oak Bay Beach Hotel ★★ Presiding over the Haro Strait, this Tudor-style hotel is the loveliest—and most British— part of Anglophile Victoria, a nice place to stay if you want to be removed from downtown. Even so, it's a very busy spot— especially its bars. Yet it still evokes another world: handsome antiques dot the comfortable public rooms, and the private rooms, lavishly furnished, are full of nooks and gables. The best rooms are those with private balconies and a view of the sea, but the price runs up to about $175. Full breakfast for two is included. For a special treat, take lunch on the hotel's yacht.

The dining room is prettily done, overlooking the gardens, but isn't up to the rest of the place. Opt for the Snug—quite possibly the coziest bar in the whole city—where you can sit before the fire. For more status assurance, walk across the street and play a round at Victoria Golf Club, a Scottish-style links with windswept holes dramatically bordered by the sea. And don't forget the hotel's afternoon tea—a proper affair where you will feel more than a wee bit conspicuous dressed in jeans.
■ *Near the corner of Oak Bay Ave and Beach Dr; (604) 598-4556; 1175 Beach Dr, Victoria, BC V8S 2N2; $$$; AE, DC, MC, V; checks OK.*

The Prior House ★★ No imitation here: this grand, tranquil B&B occupies an English mansion built during the Edwardian period for the King's representative in British Columbia. It is in a quiet neighborhood about 1½ miles from downtown. Five of the six rooms have fireplaces and views of water, and all rooms have private baths. The Lieutenant Governor's suite ($210) has a luxurious Jacuzzi bath, gold fixtures, crystal chandeliers, and a view of the strait and the Olympic range. The three-room Windsor Suite occupies the entire top floor (quite a hike for some), and though it's the only room without a fireplace, the green marble Jacuzzi is a stunner. Innkeeper Candis Cooperrider fixes simple breakfasts every morning and tea at 4pm. No-smoking premises. Well-behaved children welcome (there's even a trampoline outside). ■ *St Charles and Rockland; (604) 592-8847; 620 St Charles, Victoria, BC V8S 3N7; $$$; MC, V; checks OK.*

Victoria Regent Hotel ★★ For those with a taste for very luxurious condo living, the modern Victoria Regent is a posh apartment hotel with grandstand views of the harbor from the north. Don't let the unadorned exterior put you off. Inside, huge, nicely decorated one- and two-bedroom suites range from $185 to $295 per night for two people (but double up with another couple and the price is more within reach, especially if you do your own cooking). Each apartment has a living room, dining room, deck, and kitchen, and most have two bedrooms and two bathrooms. All are furnished with quiet taste, and most have views of city and harbor. Full room service from the Water's Edge Cafe and Lounge is available. ■ *Corner of Yates and Wharf; (604) 386-2211; 1234 Wharf St, Victoria, BC V8W 3H9; $$$; AE, DC, DIS, MC, V; checks OK.*

The Captain's Palace ★ What was once a charming one-guest-room B&B with a mediocre restaurant is now a charming 16-guest-room B&B (in three Victorian houses) with a mediocre restaurant. The B&B outgrew the original handsome 1897 mansion near the harbor and spread into the adjacent property, where the quarters are newer and decorated in florals and muted pastels. Some have balconies; all have private baths—some with cute claw-footed tubs. Early morning coffee is brought to your door before the orange-blossom-special breakfast. High season prices range from $125 to $225, the latter offering views of the water and Beacon Hill Park. ■ *2 blocks west of the Empress; (604) 388-9191; 309 Belleville St, Victoria, BC V8V 1X2; $$$; AE, DC, MC, V; no checks.*

The Coast Victoria (Harbourside Hotel) ★ The Coast Victoria features Victoria's only indoor/outdoor pool. Rooms view the Olympic Mountains, the Strait of Juan de Fuca, and the Inner Harbour. Other features are underground parking, whirlpool, sauna, exercise and steam rooms, and a 42-slip marina. The 132 air-conditioned rooms range in price from $138 to $178. Suites come in different sizes and run $195 to $475. ■ *Between Laurel Point and Fisherman's Wharf; (604) 360-1211; 146 Kingston St, Victoria, BC V8V 1V4; $$$; AE, DC, MC, V; checks OK.* ＆

Craigmyle Guest House ★ Built as a guest house early in the century, the Craigmyle stands next to Craigdarroch Castle (a grand, well-preserved mansion). Best rooms are those with views of the neighborhood castle. A large breakfast with homemade preserves and good coffee is served in the dining room, and the main lounge features traditional wainscoting, lofty ceilings, an enormous fireplace, and (on our visit) annoying easy-listening music. Rooms are quite reasonable ($55 for a single, $85 for a double), but you're 1½ kilometers from city center. We appreciated the quiet neighborhood. The Craigmyle is one of the few guest houses in Victoria that allows children. ■ *1½ kilometers up Fort St from city center, look for the castle; (604) 595-5411; 1037 Craigdarroch Rd, Victoria, BC V8S 2A5; $$; MC, V; no checks.*

The Empress ★ The hotel that once stood as the quiet, ivy-clad dowager of the Inner Harbour has gone through a $45 million facelift. A separate guest entrance pavilion has been added, the Palm Court and the Crystal Ballroom have been polished up, and 50 new rooms have been added, bringing the total to 480. The grounds have been landscaped, and a restored conservatory at the rear of the hotel connects it to the new Victoria Conference Centre. Unfortunately, the attitude of the place was not much improved: many of the rooms received little or no attention, and you pay a lot for the view. You might have to endure a cold shower, go without decaf coffee, and wake up at 5am due to a short in the fire alarm. The valet parking staff is unreliable. Nevertheless, the Empress is the most notable landmark in town and is worth a stroll (you might even want to take the excellent historic tour). High tea is served daily by reservation; it may be overpriced, but it's still the best value at the Empress. ■ *Between Humboldt and Belleville; (604) 384-8111 or toll-free (800) 828-7447 from US, toll-free (800) 268-9411 from Canada; 721 Government St, Victoria, BC V8W 1W5; $$$; AE, DC, MC, V; checks OK.* ⅃

Heritage House ★ This 1910 beauty is 5 kilometers from the center of town. The five rooms (soon to be six) have been redecorated to the original Craftsman style of the house. They're still enchanting, and the bright Garden Room, with its three walls of windows, is still a favorite. The four bathrooms are shared. Downstairs the fireplace parlor is a cozy place to linger; in warm weather, a wraparound porch provides ample seating for garden appreciators (the garden is splendid). Gourmet breakfasts consist of several courses and—if you're lucky—Sandra's much-praised salmon quiche. Two-day minimum stay; no kids, pets, or smoking. ■ *Hwy 1 north, right on McKenzie, left to 1100 Burnside Rd W; (604) 479-0892; 3808 Heritage Lane, Victoria, BC V8Z 7A7; $$; MC, V; no checks.*

Huntingdon Manor Inn ★ A comfortable antique-furnished parlor with a blazing log fireplace and an indoor whirlpool and sauna make for a pleasant stay at the Huntington. Unfortunately, it's behind the very touristy stuff near the harbor and views can be rather odd. Rooms are nicely furnished, some with four-poster beds, and the spacious two-story gallery suites have bedroom lofts. This is a full-service hotel including room service, but some rooms have full kitchen facilities. Kids under 12 stay free in their parents' suite. ■ *Downtown across from the harbor; (604) 381-3456; 330 Quebec St, Victoria, BC V8V 1W3; $$$; AE, DC, DIS, MC, V; no checks.* ⅃

SOOKE

This relatively undiscovered area, half an hour west of Victoria, offers spectacular beach scenery and seclusion. The road at Port Renfrew peters out into the famous **West Coast Trail**, one of the greatest (and most demanding) hikes in the Northwest (see Pacific Rim National Park in Ucluelet). **Botanical Beach**, just south of Port Renfrew, has exceptionally low tides in the early summer that expose miles of sea life and sculpted sandstone. The entire coast has excellent parks, with trails to the beach or into the forest, and good waves for surfers.

Royal Roads Military College, on the road to Sooke, is a Dunsmuir family castle turned military college; the beautiful grounds are open to the public each day 10am-4pm; call (604) 363-4660.

East Sooke Park, a wilderness park, offers hiking trails in the forest, spectacular views, and good swimming beaches.

Sooke Region Museum mounts some interesting displays of logging and pioneer equipment, Indian artifacts, and a fully restored historic cottage showing turn-of-the-century lifestyles. The museum also sponsors BC's largest juried fine arts show, held every August in the Sooke Arena. Museum open daily; call (604) 642-6351 for more information.

Between Sooke and Port Renfrew are dozens of trails leading down to ocean beaches (Mirror Creek is a favorite), all of which offer fine beachcombing possibilities. Ask at the Sooke Region Museum for details.

Lester B. Pearson College of the Pacific, on Pedder Bay, has been open since 1974 with a two-year program to foster international understanding; the setting and the architecture are both worth seeing; call (604) 478-5591.

▼

Sooke

▲

RESTAURANTS

Sooke Harbour House ★★★★ At the end of the road in a modest Sooke neighborhood, this white clapboard farmhouse gives little indication that it is one of British Columbia's finest inns. Over the past 15 years, owners Sinclair and Frederica Philip, along with their team of four chefs, have gained international attention for their rare dedication to the freshest natural ingredients blended with a good deal of energy and flashes of searing innovation. The focus is seafood—same-day fresh free-swimming scallops, octopus, sea urchins, whelks, red rock crabs—but innovation extends to locally farmed meats and some 200 varieties of herbs, grown in decorative profusion around the grounds. These herbs, along with a tangle of wild greens and perhaps a fistful of roasted seeds, comprise the famous Sooke house salad—de rigueur in this dining room. A recent dinner featured a fascinatingly complex spinach and fennel-bulb cream soup, garnished with smoked steelhead and shrimp, and a couple of winning entrées: rich sablefish baked over fennel and served in a ginger, rhubarb, and mint glaze; and organic leg of lamb, tenderly roasted over herb fronds and served in a mustard sauce, deepened with morels. It's not perfect—on busy nights, innovation might outshine execution (to the point of overcooking scallops, a capital sin in this seaside kitchen), the reception at the door can be frosty, and servers can be mightily overtaxed. It's also not cheap. Plan to drop at least $160 for two.

The original 1931 inn, which includes the airy country dining room, features three spectacularly angular suites upstairs (the Blue Heron Room has the best view, a Jacuzzi, and a fireplace) and sits adjacent to a sparkling new house with 10 rooms. Each room is lovingly, singularly decorated: the Victor Newman longhouse room creates a theme rich in the spirit of the Northwest, with a vaulted ceiling, native American accoutrements, and an enormous bathtub positioned before a breathtaking view; the Herb Garden Room, in shades of mint and parsley, opens out through French doors onto a private patio with a broad vista over the green lawn and the pewter harbor toward the Olympic Mountains. Views, decks (or patios), and artful extras such as bouquets of fresh flowers in every room, a decanter of fine port, and terrycloth bathrobes are a given. A platter of lavish breakfast (delivered to your room) and a light lunch are included in the cost of a night's stay. ■ *At the very end of Whiffen Spit Rd; (604) 642-3421; RR 4 1528 Whiffen Spit Rd, Sooke, BC V0S 1N0; $$$; full bar; AE, MC, V; checks OK; dinner every day.* &

Good Life Bookstore and Cafe ★ The good life is, indeed, good food served among books. This is a funky establishment with a mishmash of furnishings in an old house where the former living room is now the dining room and a couple of the bedrooms a bookstore. Locals will tell you the food is not zanything fancy but it's quite good and well priced. Breakfast is just coffee and muffins (eggs only if Phippen is not too busy). Lunches usually entail two soups served with homemade soda bread and a number of vegetarian entrées (lots of seafood too). Seafood and chicken star at dinner. ■ *In downtown Sooke; (604) 642-6821; 2113 Otter Point Rd, Sooke; $$; beer and wine; MC, V; checks OK; lunch Tues-Sun, dinner Fri-Sat.* &

Margison House ★ An elegant cottage just off the highway in downtown Sooke serves up the best afternoon tea in these parts, along with light lunches of seafood chowder, raisin scones, sausage rolls, and the like. The view is fine, the grounds are pretty, and amiable owner Sylvia Hallgren has a charming B&B cottage next door with a bathroom and full kitchen. Hallgren stocks the fridge with freshly laid eggs and breakfast goodies from her garden. ■ *In the center of Sooke Village, look for signs; (604) 642-3620; 6605 Sooke Rd, Sooke; $; beer and wine; V; local checks only; lunch, tea Thurs-Sun (May-Sept).* &

LODGINGS

Malahat Farm ★★ Diana Clare's 45-acre "gentleman's farm" is a perfect escape for any city slicker longing for a little taste of the country. From the charming upstairs rooms, you can keep an eye on the well-grazed fields of Herefords (with a solitary Angus bull), sheep, chickens, and a couple of peacocks.

The two grand downstairs rooms have fireplaces but lack the farm view of the upstairs ones. Clare lives in the cottage next door, but in the morning she comes over to prepare a farm-hand's breakfast, an abundant spread of which virtually everything—muffins, blackberry jam, granola, grilled potatoes, honey, and eggs—comes from the farm. The tranquil setting provides sweet rejuvenation (especially with the addition of a hot tub in the gazebo), but if you're inclined to exploring, Clare is a wealth of local knowledge and will point out the best walks, loan you a good mountain bike, and maybe even pack you a thermos of coffee and muffins to go. ■ *15 minutes west of Sooke off West Coast Rd at Anderson Rd; (604) 642-6868; RR2, Sooke, BC V0S 1N0; $$; no credit cards; checks OK.*

Ocean Wilderness ★ This log cabin is a good choice if you want to leave pretensions behind. The rooms are big (and so are the bathrooms) and filled with an odd assortment of furnishings. Best are the upstairs suites, each with its own balcony. Captain Marion Paine added a full wing onto her house and opened her seven-room B&B a few years ago. It's been swarming with honeymooners ever since, who come primarily for the location, set back in a cove with a nice trail to the beach, but leave with a tree planted in their romantic memories. There's a separate Jacuzzi in its own Japanese-style enclosed building (reserved soakings). ■ *10 minutes west of Sooke; (604) 646-2116; 109 West Coast Rd, Sooke, BC V0S 1N0; $$$; MC, V; checks OK.* ♿

Point No Point Resort ★ The Soderberg family owns a mile of beach and 40 acres of wild, undeveloped, quintessentially Northwest coastline facing the Strait of Juan de Fuca and west to the Pacific. They rent 20 cabins ($64 to $130 for two) among the trees on or near the cliffside, catering to those who eschew TV and telephones and seek remote beauty and tranquillity (only cabins 3 and 4 allow pets; the five new, pricey cabins have hot tubs). Four hang right over the water. The only distractions here are the crashing of the rolling swells and the crackle of the fireplace. Firewood is supplied, but stop on the way to Point No Point and buy your own food. The cabins are rustic (and some are quite dark), but they're clean—besides, you're really here for the coast. Trail access to the shoreline promotes a relaxed appreciation of the area, including tidepools with all manner of marine life to discover. Afternoon tea (with mediocre pastries) and light soup-and-sandwich lunches are served in a dining room that is both worn and convivial. ■ *Hwy 14, 24 kilometers west of Sooke; (604) 646-2020; West Coast Rd, RR2, Sooke, BC V0S 1N0; $$$; no credit cards; checks OK.* ♿

If you've found a place that you think is a best place, send in the report form at the back of this book. If you're unhappy with one of the places, let us know why. We depend on reader input.

BRENTWOOD BAY

LODGINGS

Brentwood Bay Bed & Breakfast ★ Inside this restored Victorian you'll find seven guest rooms (soon to be nine) with antique furniture, glossy wood floors, lace curtains, colorful braided rugs, and hand-crafted coverlets. There's also a cottage (summers only), and a suite designed especially for the handicapped with a kitchenette and a full bath. Most rooms have en suite bathrooms. Ask for a room away from the fairly busy highway. Owner Evelyn Hardy serves spicy sausage and pear cobbler for breakfast in a glassed-in sun porch. No smoking. Future plans include a few more guest rooms, a honeymoon suite, *and* a chapel. ■ *Corner of Stelly and W Saanich; (604) 652-2012; 7247 W Saanich Road, Brentwood Bay, BC V0S 1A0; $$; no credit cards; checks OK.*

SIDNEY

RESTAURANTS

Deep Cove Chalet ★★★ Scrupulously manicured lawn rolls down to the cove. Even in winter the fragrance of an extravagant English flower arrangement greets you at the door. The service is professional without being stuffy, although sometimes it can be forgetful (especially on busy Saturday nights). Pierre Koffel is one of the most gifted chefs on Vancouver Island—and one of the most entertaining. He's not above taking on whatever task needs attention in the Chalet: on any given night he might be spied clearing a table, ceremoniously decanting a bottle of wine, or greeting a guest with the warmest of welcomes. As eccentric as he is, regulars know he's a stickler for freshness and quality. The wine list touts lots of high-priced California bottlings. The traditional menu has a light contemporary touch. You may choose from a prix-fixe menu, or you can put together your own meal—either way your check will add up quickly. Finish your meal with classic crêpes suzette, prepared with a flourish at your table—an appropriate finale. ■ *40 kilometers north of Victoria on the Trans-Canada Hwy; (604) 656-3541; 11190 Chalet Rd, Sidney; $$$; full bar; AE, MC, V; checks OK; lunch, dinner Tues-Sun.*

Cafe Mozart ★★ James and Marietta Hamilton have a fascination with Mozart; they even married on the day of his death (well, a couple of hundred years later). So it's not surprising that they (with their Austrian ties and their Swiss training) named their small European cafe after him. It's stark with lots of shiny black furniture and a few framed posters of Germany on the wall, but reports on the food continue to be good. Two outstanding dishes include the veal schnitzel (from humanely raised animals) topped with smoked ham in a cheese cream sauce, and the prawns with garlic and saffron in a pastry shell. Desserts might be an aromatic rose petal sorbet or a delightful crème caramel. Guess who's playing on the stereo? ■ *Downtown Sidney, between 2nd and 3rd; (604) 655-1554; 2470 Beacon Ave, Sidney ; $$; beer and wine; MC, V; local checks only; lunch Fri-Sat, dinner every day.*

The Latch ★★ The Latch—rough logs outside, refined wood paneling inside—was built for the provincial lieutenant governor in 1926 and converted to a tranquil restaurant half a century later. Fancy dining rooms feature views of the peerless gardens and the harbor yachts. This is one of the Saanich Peninsula's most accessible dress-up restaurants. In summer, the Latch bustles with an international clientele who expect good food and usually get it. Locals prefer winter, when the food might not be up to par but the price is down: a prix-fixe four-course dinner is $14.95. The entrées are dependable and sometimes superb (coquilles St. Jacques chock-full of tender scallops and shrimp; a succulent full rack of lamb). The wine list offers selections ranging from Summerland, British Columbia, to Wyndham, Australia, with a half dozen or so offered by the glass. ■ *3.2 kilometers out of Sidney on Harbour Rd; (604) 656-6622; 2328 Harbour Rd, Sidney; $$; full bar; AE, MC, V; checks OK; lunch Tues-Fri and Sun, dinner Tues-Sun.*

Blue Peter Pub and Restaurant Blue Peter is the international flag yachtsmen use to signal their ship is about to sail. There are plenty of boats here, but the sailors are often found moored to the deck of this pub. The food is as comfortable and as considerate as the place itself: salmon and spinach wrapped in phyllo dough, tangy caesar salad, garlic-ginger prawns. Other expected pub items include tasty burgers, clubhouse sandwiches, and fish 'n' chips. A lovely interpretation of a beachfront home, with petunias and nasturtiums, this place is especially inviting when the sun sets sail over the marina. ■ *3 kilometers north of Sidney on Harbour Rd; (604) 656-4551; 2270 Harbour Rd, Sidney; $; full bar; MC, V; no checks; lunch, dinner Tues-Fri (Mon in summer only).*

Pelicano's Cafe and Bakery A quick cafeteria-style bakery, espresso, and salad nook that is overwhelmingly popular because it fills a niche: inexpensive lunch with a view of the water. The food runs from muffins that aren't too heavy or sweet to meat pies, sausage rolls, and a harvest of good salads. The menu also includes a new selection of fresh pasta dishes. In the summertime the crowds overflow onto the deck. ■ *At Port of Sydney Marina; (604) 655-4116; 1B-9851 Seaport Pl, Sidney; $; no alcohol; MC, V; no checks; breakfast, lunch, dinner every day.*

MALAHAT

LODGINGS

The Aerie ★★ Maria and Leo Schuster's "Castle in the Mountains" roosts on a hill they built (yes, a hill) to look out over the Saanich Inlet's Finleyson Arm. On a nice day Mount Baker looms to the east and the Olympics spread out across the south; at night, the lights from Port Angeles glimmer in the distance. The building is impressive, with nooks and crannies, odd angles, and arched doorways (with as much pretentious service as you'd expect). Some rooms have private decks, built-in Jacuzzis, or fireplaces (rooms with all three weigh in at a hefty $290). Prepare yourself for a formal getaway (those not celebrating a special occasion may feel a bit out of place). That said, you still can hear (but not see) the cars from the Trans-Canada Highway from your deck. Amenities here include a sauna, hot tubs, multilevel lounging decks with unsurpassed views, and a helipad for those who like to arrive in style (and service pretentious enough to match). A tennis court is in the works. An excellent complimentary breakfast is especially bountiful on Sunday—eggs Benedict with smoked salmon and creamed mushrooms are just the beginning of the feast (which attracts a dressy crowd).

Mill Bay

Lodgings

Cooked by Leo (originally of Innsbruck, Austria), meals are many-coursed, highly sauced, and accompanied by perfectly prepared vegetables. Starters such as shrimp bisque, asparagus vichyssoise, and seasonal greens are excellent. The poached salmon is capably cooked; black tiger shrimp—accompanied by angel-hair pasta and basil—are firm and tender. The filet mignon and lamb entrées were cooked precisely to order and deliciously sauced. Desserts—such as port-marinated local strawberries with chocolate, or chilled cheese soufflé with raspberry sauce—are not to be missed. Presentation is unfailingly pleasing; the piano player is a nice thought, though sometimes intrusive. Ask for a window table in advance. ■ *Trans-Canada Hwy, look for signs; (604) 743-4055 or (604) 743-7115; PO Box 108, Malahat, BC V0R 2L0; $$$; full bar; AE, MC, V; no checks; breakfast, dinner every day.*

MILL BAY

LODGINGS

Pine Lodge Farm Bed & Breakfast ★ The word "farm" may be misleading. This is a classy country inn. When former antique dealers Cliff and Barbara Clarke retired, they built their dream house—a sprawling knotty-pine affair—on 30 acres overlooking Satellite Channel and the Gulf Islands. It's an impressive place. The living room is appointed with rich Oriental rugs, plush velveteen turn-of-the-century furniture, and intricately carved wooden chests dating back as far as the 1700s. The fieldstone fireplace acts as a centerpiece, unless there's someone around who knows how to play the organ or piano (there's one of each). Each of the seven smallish rooms (all with private baths; rooms 1 and 7 have full views) opens onto a balcony that wraps around the massive two-story living room. Privacy seekers can opt for a cabin down the drive which includes two bedrooms and a hot tub. Breakfast eggs are courtesy of the hens kept on the property and, in season, there are berries from the garden. Trails meander through the farm. ■ *Merideth and Mutter rds; (604) 743-4083; 3191 Mutter Rd, Mill Bay, BC V0R 2P0; $$; MC, V; checks OK.*

SHAWNIGAN LAKE

RESTAURANTS

Jaeger House Inn ★ An informal pub-style eatery in a massive building, with a big stone fireplace and a new outdoor garden. The 65-item menu is just as substantial, with German standbys such as a mushroom-laden veal cutlet with brown gravy side by side with teriyaki chicken and seafood casserole. It's still good, though, and situated on the skirt of pretty Shawnigan Lake. ■ *Follow Shawnigan/Mill Bay Rd off Trans-Canada Hwy 6.4 km to Renfrew; (604) 743-3515; 2460 Renfrew Rd, Shawnigan Lake; $$; full bar; MC, V; no checks; breakfast Sun, lunch, dinner every day.*

COWICHAN BAY

RESTAURANTS

The Bluenose Have breakfast or lunch at the coffee shop—either indoors at its horseshoe-shaped counter or out on the deck, where one waitress handles the whole place with savvy. For dinner, the restaurant is the local favorite in Cowichan Bay, with a menu of steaks and seafood (go for the seafood—ask your waitress to tell you what's fresh) and a great water view. Check out the Wooden Boat Society's museum next door. ■ *40 kilometers north of Victoria; (604) 748-2841; 1765 Cowichan Bay Rd, Cowichan Bay; $$; full bar; AE, MC, V; no checks; breakfast, lunch (coffee shop), dinner (restaurant) every day.*

LODGINGS

Old Farm Bed & Breakfast ★ Don't be discouraged by the Astroturf-covered stairs. Inside this charming turn-of-the-century house (formerly Caterham Court), you'll find three comfortable rooms furnished in overdone Laura Ashley style (the canopied beds are a little girl's dream). Ask for one of the two rooms facing the bay. The grounds are manicured for croquet, or you can take a rowboat out into the bay. ■ *1st Cowichan Bay turn-off on Trans-Canada Hwy 1 N; (604) 748-6410; 2075 Cowichan Bay Rd, Cowichan Bay, BC V0R 1N0; $$; V; checks OK.*

DUNCAN

The **Native Heritage Centre** is a must-see for admirers of native arts and crafts. Permanent exhibits include Cowichan sweaters, which are hand-knit in one piece with unique patterns, usually from homespun wools. In the summer, the Centre features an open-air carving shed, where a native carver whittles away at a traditional 12- to 20-foot totem pole; each pole interprets a traditional design in the carver's own artistic language. There are, at present, 66 such totem poles in Duncan, both downtown and along a half-kilometer section of the Trans-Canada Highway. The Native Heritage Centre is at 200 Cowichan Way, (604) 746-8119; call for schedule.

RESTAURANTS

The Quamichan Inn ★★ Set in the midst of several acres of lawn and garden, this comfortable turn-of-the-century home has been nicely transformed into a bed-and-breakfast-cum-dinner-house for boaters moored at the nearby marinas. Dinner might include roast Salt Spring Island lamb, Indian curry, or roast prime rib with Yorkshire pudding. There are Fanny Bay oysters, locally produced clams, and wines from France and California. A seasonal dessert might be a Pavlova made from raspberries, whipped cream, and meringue; there's always homemade ice cream. You can drink after-dinner coffee in the garden among wisteria, fuchsias, and dahlias. Each of the guest rooms has its own bath. Morning begins with an English hunt breakfast (sausages, mushrooms, bacon and eggs). However, if you're not staying here, the proprietors of Quamichan Inn will pick you up at Maple Bay or Genoa Bay and return you when dinner's over. ■ *Just east of Duncan; (604) 746-7028; 1478 Maple Bay Rd, Duncan; $$; full bar; MC, V; checks OK; dinner every day (closed Mon-Tues during winter).*

The Inglenook ★ The traveler may well have grown a little weary of Vancouver Island's fascination with restaurants in Tudor houses, but under the ownership of Jeannette and Eberhard Hahn, this one's a notch or two above the standard: roast rack of lamb, oysters coquille, New York steak with Pernod, crab, shrimp, and scallops. The dessert list showcases the apple strudel. There's a cozy library that calls for an after-dinner brandy. ■ *8 kilometers north of Duncan; (604) 746-4031; 7621 Trans-Canada Hwy, Duncan; $$; full bar; MC, V; local checks only; dinner Wed-Sun.*

Duncan

Restaurants

Arbutus Cafe This small vinyl and Formica corner cafe packs in the locals. They come for inexpensive real home cooking with a twist; surprisingly spicy vegetarian curry and steaming espressos are as voraciously devoured as the burgers and rich cream pies. Service is young and upbeat; the radio blares from the kitchen. Everyone knows each other and their musical tastes. ■ *Kenneth and Jubilee; (604) 746-5443; 195 Kenneth St, Duncan; $; beer and wine; MC, V; no checks; lunch Mon-Sat, dinner Mon-Fri.*

LODGINGS

Fairburn Farm Inn ★★ Once it was an Irish millionaire's country estate; now it's a 130-acre organic farm and country inn, literally at the end of the road. The farmhouse, built in the 1880s, occupies a sloping dale, and the working-farm orientation is the charm of the place, especially for families. Six large guest rooms feature comfortable furniture and private baths with Jacuzzi tubs. There's also a cottage available in summer that will house six comfortably. Guests are welcome to use two downstairs parlors (family reunions often book Fairburn) and to roam the grounds, where a sheepdog minds the lambs and a creek flows idly by. The bed comes with a hearty breakfast that always begins with porridge. For a more replete vacation, you arrange ahead for lunch and dinner to be served here. In this modern-day Eden you can witness a stunning example of how it is still possible to live off the land: almost everything you eat is organically home-grown. ■ *11.2 kilometers south of Duncan at 3310 Jackson Rd; (604) 746-4637; RR 7, Duncan, BC V9L 4W4; $$$; no credit cards; checks OK (closed Nov-March).*

Grove Hall Estate ★★ It's all very secluded: it's not always open and there isn't a sign out front. Captain Frank and Judy Oliver want it that way; tough for the curious, but an undisturbed retreat for guests. Seventeen wooded acres surround this 1912 Tudor-style manse near Lake Quamichan. From the outside it looks as if there would be far more than three rooms—until you see the size of the rooms. Each room has an Oriental theme (Indonesian, Malaysian, Thai) and magnificent rugs (you're provided with Chinese slippers), but no private baths. The master bedroom, decorated with pieces from Djakarta and Bali, expands into a sitting area and then onto a balcony. There are two full and one half baths in the mansion. Play tennis on the private court or games in the billiards room, or stroll along the quiet lakefront. Just remember: call ahead. ■ *Turn east at Trunk Rd, continue to Lake Rd, go north 1.6 kilometers; (604) 746-6152; 6159 Lakes Rd, Duncan, BC V9L 4J6; $$$; no credit cards; checks OK.*

▼

Duncan

Restaurants

RESTAURANTS

Crow and Gate Neighbourhood Pub ★ This magnificent English country pub makes a nice destination for a lazy afternoon. It is set back from the road, with a rose-arbor entrance, a backyard patio, a duck pond, and a noisy peacock. The homesick fellow who built it remembered the English original well, recreating it scrupulously from beamed ceiling to Oriental rugs, with a blazing hearth and a dart board. The pub food is topnotch, especially the pasties encased in flaky crusts, the steak-and-kidney pie, and the buttery Yorkshire pudding. The staff is chatty, the draughts are foamy, and at night everyone's having a ruddy good time. ■ *About 12.8 kilometers south of Nanaimo; (604) 722-3731; 2313 Yellow Point Rd, Ladysmith; $; full bar; MC, V; no checks; lunch, dinner every day.*

LODGINGS

Yellow Point Lodge ★★★ On a rocky promontory overhung with tall trees is Yellow Point Lodge, perhaps the most serene of all the classic British Columbia resorts. It's creaky and delightful, not exclusive in any sense of the word. The hours still pass with six meals a day—of standard but wholesome quality—as if you were on a cruise ship. In truth, it's a little more like summer camp for grown-ups (though it's popular year-round): you eat family-style at shared tables in the lodge, with no kids under 16 to detract from the mood. Many of the good-sized rooms have private baths. Rooms 4 and 5 have balconies. You'll want a cabin, however; the best are the small White Beach cabins with wood stoves and delightful beds with tree-trunk bases. There are two kinds of cabins: those on the beach (the Cliff Cabin is most remote, and the nicest) and the field cabins (Eve's is the most private). And there are the very popular beach barracks, ramshackle quarters with thin walls, built right on the shoreline rocks, with a "tree shower."

Ladysmith

Lodgings

Best of all is the site: two tennis courts, a huge seawater pool, 130 acres of meadow and forest for strolling, a hot tub, a sauna, windsurfing gear, a classic 32-foot boat for picnic cruising, and big slabs of rock jutting into the sea for sunbathing. Mountain bikes and canoes are also available. ■ *Yellow Point Rd, 14.4 kilometers east of Ladysmith; (604) 245-7422; RR3, Ladysmith, BC V0R 2E0; $$$; MC, V; checks OK.*

Inn of the Sea Inn of the Sea's nicest feature is the scenery, especially the long stretch of beach along Stewart Channel. Deluxe suites have fireplaces, kitchens, and balconies; large parties can request rooms that connect vertically via a spiral staircase. Many of the rooms are smaller than standard, and there have been recent grumblings about less-than-clean rooms. In the dining room, chefs arrive and depart almost as often as guests, so play it safe: cook in your own suite. Play tennis, or swim in the large heated pool at the water's edge. A pier out front allows for boat moorage, with water and power hookup. ■ *3600 Yellow Point Rd, 14.4 kilometers east of Ladysmith; (604) 245-2211; RR3, Ladysmith, BC V0R 2E0; $$; AE, MC, V; no checks.*

NANAIMO

This former coal-mining town is evolving into something very different. It now has a clean, accessible waterfront, cultural festivals in the summer, a university campus with a marvelous view, and vastly improved dining. Of the new attractions, Nanaimo claims itself as the home of North America's first (and only) bridge built specifically for **bungee jumpers**. You can watch or jump ($95) from this 140-foot bridge above the Nanaimo River; contact Bungy Zone, (604) 753-5867. Or for $3, ferry over to the **Dinghy Dock Pub**, a very nautical floating bar off Protection Island. Other attractions are: **the Bastion**, one of the few Hudson's Bay Company forts still standing, built in 1853 as protection against marauding Haida Indians. There's a cannon-firing every day at noon in the summer. **The Nanaimo Centennial Museum**, 100 Cameron Road, (604) 753-1821, has a to-scale replica of a coal-mine entrance, among other displays.

▼

Ladysmith

Lodgings

▲

Wandering. The waterfront promenade extends from the downtown harbor, past the modern seaplane terminal, and through Swy-a-lana Lagoon Park (Canada's only man-made tidal lagoon), over the new pedestrian bridge, by the Nanaimo Yacht Club, as far as the BC Ferry Terminal. The **Bastion Street Bookstore**, 76 Bastion Street, (604) 753-3011, houses an impressive collection of children's books, natural history texts, guidebooks, and Canadian authors. On nearby Commercial Street, the Scotch Bakery concocts the namesake **Nanaimo bar**. Several companies offer wildlife and harbor tours; **Bastion City Wildlife Cruises**, (604) 754-8474, provides informative commentary, and fresh fruit and baked goodies too.

Parks. Pipers Lagoon, northeast of downtown, includes a spit that extends into the Strait of Georgia backed by sheer bluffs great for bird-watching. **Newcastle Island**, (604) 753-5811, is an autoless wilderness island reached by ferries that leave hourly from behind the civic arena; it has a long shoreline trail, a trail for the handicapped, and some fine old-growth timber.

Golf. Nanaimo and the area to the north have seen the proliferation of new or recently upgraded golf courses. Most noteworthy is the **Nanaimo Golf Club**, 5 kilometers north of the city, a demanding 18-hole course with beautiful views; (604) 758-6332. Others include Pryde Vista Golf Club in Nanaimo, (604) 753-6188; FairWinds at Nanoose, (604) 468-7766; and

Morning Star, (604) 248-2244, and EagleCrest, (604) 752-9744, near Qualicum.

Gabriola Island. A 20-minute ferry ride from Nanaimo will take you to this rural spot.

RESTAURANTS

Old Mahle House ★★ It's intimate: three elegant, airy rooms done in a country motif seat 55 people. The affable and intelligent owners, Delbert Horrocks and Maureen Loucks, emphasize fresh, locally produced ingredients. A dozen daily specials fill a whiteboard: thick, savory carrot-and-ginger soup; homemade pasta tossed with salmon and cream, capers and scallions providing a tart counterpoint; or a succulent beef tenderloin in a green peppercorn sauce. The regular menu competes with fresh-caught prawns in zesty tarragon sauce or boneless lamb loin from Australia. End the meal with one of a battery of homemade desserts—the silken chocolate banana cheesecake alone was worth the drive. Visit during the summer, or attend one of

Nanaimo

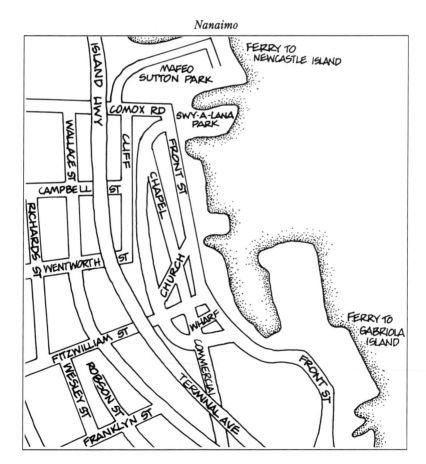

the monthly four-course dinners with six excellent wines included in the meal (about $45) and you could possibly encounter a three-star evening. ■ *Corner of Cedar at Hemer Rd;
(604) 722-3621; Nanaimo; $$; full bar; MC, V; local checks
OK; dinner Wed-Sun.* &

Gina's Cafe ★ Gina's is a comfortable place with all the down-home ambience of a Tex-Mex roadside cafe. A healthy, imaginative menu reflects the Korfields' vegetarian leanings. We enjoyed the daily special, a ricotta and spinach enchilada lavishly smothered in salsa, and barely managed dessert—a fruit burrito topped with ice cream. ■ *1 block up from the waterfront;
(604) 753-5411; 47 Skinner St, Nanaimo; $; full bar; MC, V;
local checks only; lunch Mon-Sat, dinner every day.*

Maffeo's ★ A favorite of Nanaimo-ites, this was once the home of former mayor Pete Maffeo and now houses Nanaimo's most *real* Italian restaurant. A deli occupies the main floor: made-on-the-premises pasta and Italian cheeses and meats. (Where else on the island are you going to find authentic prosciutto or cappocolla?) You dine upstairs in one of the two rooms prettied with antiques: pastas are done well here, and the cioppino with a dash of saffron is a local favorite. ■ *Prideau
and Wentworth; (604) 753-0377; 538 Wentworth, Nanaimo;
$$; full bar; AE, MC, V; no checks; lunch Mon-Fri, dinner
every day (closed Sun Nov-April).*

The Grotto The Grotto, a Nanaimo perennial for over 30 years, has completely outgrown its wharfish name. Its ample menu has many proven favorites—fresh salmon and Zum Zum (a seafood platter)—and cafe entrées such as gourmet burgers, veal, and pasta dishes. ■ *On the waterfront near the BC ferries; (604) 753-3303; 1511 Stewart Ave, Nanaimo; $; full bar;
AE, MC, V; no checks; dinner every day.*

LODGINGS

Coast Bastion Inn ★★ All 179 rooms of this swanky hotel have views of the restored Hudson's Bay fort; all are tastefully styled in postmodern hues. There is a new, formal meeting room and a trio of formula eateries—the family-style Cutters Cafe, the Offshore Lounge, and Sgt. O'Flaherty, a New York-style deli. A sauna, a hot tub, and a cool tub make the Bastion a self-sustaining entity. It's right in the middle of things downtown. ■ *Bastion St and Island Hwy; (604) 753-6601 or (800) 663-
1144; 11 Bastion St, Nanaimo, BC V9R 2Z9; $$$; AE, DC,
MC, V; no checks.*

The Dorchester Hotel ★★ It was built in the late 1880s on the site of an opera house and the residence of a coal baron, but there's little hint of the past at this newly refurbished Nanaimo landmark. That's partly because the original third floor, with its archways and detailing, was removed sometime during the '50s (after a fire) and replaced with utilitarian block architecture. The rooms are tastefully decorated; many have lovely views of the harbor and the Bastion. One really nice touch: there's a library on the second floor, complete with an extensive collection of old *National Geographics*. The lobby is light and airy, with a fireplace and complimentary newspapers; the restaurant, Café Casablanca, offers good food at surprisingly reasonable rates for a hotel (and a view too). It is popular with locals, who venture in for the smoked-on-the-premises scallops with saffron and lime or the rack of lamb with whole hazelnuts and blackberry demiglace. Service is extremely on the ball; the wine list is touted even in Vancouver. ■ *Church and Front St; (604) 754-6835; 70 Church St, Nanaimo, BC V9R 5H4; $$; AE, DC, MC, V; no checks; breakfast, lunch, dinner every day.*

PARKSVILLE

The town offers good sandy beaches; lovely picnic sites on Cameron Lake, Englishman River Falls, and Little Qualicum Falls; and fine fishing. **MacMillan Nature Park**, 32 kilometers west of Parksville on Route 4 heading for Port Alberni, has preserved Cathedral Grove, a haunting old-growth forest of Douglas firs and cedars ranging up to 200 feet high and 1,000 years old. The annual **Brant Festival** is held in April (see Calendar).

LODGINGS

▼

Port Alberni

▲

Tigh-Na-Mara Hotel Owners Jackie and Joe Hirsch's complex of rustic log cottages is no longer so rustic, and it's always busy. They've acquired more acreage and have added condominiums on the beach, all of which have views of the Strait of Georgia; some have their own Jacuzzis. The 40-or-so log cabins are spread among the 22 acres of natural arbutus and fir. The 12 suites in the lodge are surprisingly cozy, and although none has a view, each has a fireplace, fridge, and full bath, and a few have their own kitchens. Reports on the log-cabin restaurant have been favorable. With the indoor pool and Jacuzzi, outdoor tennis courts, volleyball, and 700 feet of beachfront, you'll have no problem working up an appetite. ■ *2 kilometers south of Parksville on Island Hwy; (604) 248-2072; 1095 E Island Hwy, Parksville, BC V0R 2S0; $$; AE, DC, MC, V; local checks only.*

PORT ALBERNI

The **Lady Rose** departs from the Harbour Quay at the end of Argyle Street in Port Alberni and voyages to Bamfield on Tuesdays, Thursdays, and Saturdays, with special Sunday trips during July and August. Round-trip fare is $32. Early June to late September, she sails for Ucluelet on Mondays, Wednesdays, and Fridays. Round-trip fare is $36. Besides being a better way to reach these remote towns than over rough roads, the 4-hour cruise down Alberni Inlet and through the Broken Islands Group is breathtaking. Breakfast and lunch are served; (604) 723-8313 or (800) 663-7192. Or take along a loaf of cheese bread from the Flour Shop, (604) 723-1105.

BAMFIELD

Bamfield is a tiny fishing village heavily populated by marine biologists. The *Lady Rose* from Port Alberni comes on Tuesdays, Thursdays, and Saturdays (and Sundays in summer); see above. Main Street is salt water with a charming board walk on the west side. It is a safe and welcomes port for those cruising the powerful waters off the adventurous West Coast of Vancouver Island. The **Bamfield Marine Center**, a science facility operated by a consortium of western Canadian universities, maintains a very fine small aquarium. Currently the BMC is doing research on commercial kelp growth, agar production, and whale behavior. You are advised to take the boat rather than the bumpy dirt road, which has some frightening logging traffic. For hikers, it's the end (or the start) of a five- to six-day beach trek along the **West Coast Trail** from Port Renfrew (see Pacific Rim National Park under Ucluelet). It is one of the premier places for finding a wilderness beach all to yourself, all week long. Photographers, bring your cameras. In Bamfield you can rent boats for fishing or exploring the islands.

▼

Port Alberni

▲

  Whale watching. During March and April, pods of migrating gray whales can be seen off the coast: book whale-watching trips through either Ocean Pacific Whale Charters Ltd., Box 590, Tofino, BC V0R 2Z0, (604) 725-3919, or SeaSmoke Sailing Charter & Tours, Box 483, Alert Bay, BC V0N 1A0, (604) 974-5225.

LODGINGS

Aquilar House Resort ★★ Far and away the most spectacular setting and guest ambience in Bamfield is this hidden-away resort now run by Jim and Lindsey McKelvey, who have taken the place two steps beyond the expectations of the former owners. While the whole village of Bamfield focuses on the harbor, Aquilar House, just around the bend, faces almost due west out into Barkley Sound toward the Broken Island group. Sunsets here are mindbenders. Not only do the resort's rooms and cabins share the spectacular view, but the cuisine shares the enthusiasm. Two Norwegian chefs prepare a properly paced feast which begins with drinks and appetizers (two huge platters appear with a symmetry of shrimp, smoked salmon, fresh local oysters, and baked herbed clams) in the living room, where guests share stories of the day. Lindsey directs attention to the dining room, where romaine lettuce is topped with generous slices of braised chicken breasts and a sweet-and-sour dressing. The entrée following might be a mini-smorgasbord of seasoned roast whitefish, a steak medallion cooked perfectly to order, and several braised shrimp, all surrounded by a fan of potatoes and carrots.

Fishing here is superb and Jim is a vigorous guide. The resort provides all the equipment you need for some of the continent's best salmon sportfishing; however, you can also plan to do absolutely nothing. A nearby bluff, allegedly the site of an Indian fort, now provides a dramatic coastal perch for guests. The resort is open year round; prices are dramatically reduced September through May. ▪ *Guests are met at the point of arrival; (604) 479-8964 or toll-free (800) 665-2533; Bamfield West, Bamfield, BC V0R 1B0; $$; MC, V; checks OK.*

UCLUELET

Pacific Rim National Park, the first National Marine Park in Canada, comprises three separate areas—Long Beach, the Broken Islands Group, and the West Coast Trail—each conceived as a platform from which visitors can experience the power of the Pacific Ocean. Long Beach, an 11-kilometer expanse of sand and rock outcrops backed by forest and mountains, can be reached by car from Port Alberni over a winding mountain highway. The Broken Islands Group—more than 100 in all, at the entrance to Barkley Sound—are accessible only by boat. This area is famous for sea lions, seals, and whales, and is very popular with fishermen, skindivers, and kayakers. The West Coast Trail is a rugged 72-kilometer stretch that was once a lifesaving trail for shipwrecked sailors. It can be traveled only on foot, and it's a strenuous but spectacular five- to six-day hike for hardy and experienced backpackers. For more information on the park, go to the information center at the park entrance on Highway 4 or call (604) 726-4212. Pacific Rim National Park, Box 280, Ucluelet, BC V0R 3A0.

The Wickaninnish Interpretive Center has interesting oceanic exhibits and an expansive view: (604) 726-7333, 10 kilometers north of Ucluelet off Highway 4. The same building houses the Wickaninnish Inn (see review in this section).

RESTAURANTS

Whale's Tale ★ Perhaps because it doesn't have a view, locals regard this as the best dinner house in town. Built on pilings that sway on windy evenings, the Whale's Tale is intimate and quiet. Fresh, simply cooked seafood is on the menu; we found the halibut, sautéed in butter, to be refreshingly clear-tasting. ▪ *Behind the Thornton Motel, 4 blocks from downtown; (604) 726-4621; 1861 Peninsula Rd, Ucluelet; $$; full bar; AE, MC, V; local checks only; dinner every day (Feb-Oct).*

The Wickaninnish Inn ★ In a dramatic setting on an otherwise untouched 3-kilometer-long beach, it's a striking building with glass on three sides, a beam-and-stone interior, and a rock fireplace serving as excellent backdrop for white linen tablecloths and pastel-cushioned chairs. Unfortunately, by the time you're seated you've seen the best of the Wick. Service has been known to be slow and forgettable, but at least once your food arrives it will be well prepared, from the Wickaninnish salad with a raspberry vinaigrette to a saffron-laced bouillabaisse, fresh halibut with pesto, or tender veal draped in a savory blackcurrant and mushroom sauce. The popular chowder is heavily clammed. The wine list includes a few selections difficult to find in British Columbia. ■ *10 kilometers north of Ucluelet in Pacific Rim National Park; (604) 726-7706; Ucluelet; $$; full bar; AE, MC, V; checks OK; lunch, dinner every day (closed mid-Oct–mid-March).*

LODGINGS

Canadian Princess Fishing Resort ★ A retired 235-foot survey ship in the Ucluelet Boat Basin has been converted to 30 cabins for lodging and a below-decks dining room for meals. The accommodations are comfortable but not at all luxurious: the small cabins have from one to six berths and share washrooms. If you want something a little more spacious, ask for the captain's cabin with adjoining bathroom. The nautical gear has been left in place—the ship's mast goes right through the dining room—but the conversion is rather spiffy. The newer 46 shoreside units, a little roomier and more modern, are for dryland sailors. The galley serves reasonable food, with steaks and seafood predominating, and opens at 4:30am for breakfast during the fishing season. A small ship's bar and a roomier stern lounge are pleasant places; there's a fine supply of cold beer. The *Canadian Princess*, with 10 charter boats, serves as a base for fishermen who flock to the Barkley Sound area. ■ *In the boat basin; (604) 726-7771; PO Box 939, Ucluelet, BC V0R 3A0; $; full bar; AE, MC, V; no checks; breakfast, lunch, dinner every day (closed Oct-Feb).*

Ucluelet

Restaurants

TOFINO

Literally at the end of the road on the west coast of Vancouver Island, Tofino, once a timber and fishing town, is quietly becoming a favored destination for Northwest and European travelers alike. Local environmentalists and artists have banded together to suspend destruction of one of the last virgin timberlands on the west coast of Vancouver Island and to halt the rapid development for which the area is prime. It boasts miles of sandy beaches, islands of old-growth cedar, migrating whales (March through April, September through October), natural hot springs, colonies of sea lions, and a rather temperate climate.

Neophyte paddlers should contact the **Tofino Sea-Kayaking Company** for guided day trips with an experienced boater and naturalist; or explore the wilds of the west coast with one of the eight charter **water taxi companies** (which are as available as their four-wheeled counterparts in New York City); or contact the seaplane company, **Tofino Air Lines**, to venture out to the sea lion caves or other remote places on the west coast of Vancouver Island.

Galleries. There are two excellent galleries in town, Roy Henry Vickers' hand-hewn longhouse called **Eagle Aerie Gallery** and the newer **House of Himwista**, both native-run.

RESTAURANTS

Alley Way Cafe ★★ Christina Delano-Stephens thinks the way of life in Tofino is the closest thing to her Latin-American roots she'll ever see in Canada. Christina has livened up a little sun-filled house with some pink and turquoise paint, put two picnic tables outside and cactus-shaped balloons in the window, and opened one of the most heart-filled spots north of Victoria. Today, Vancouver Island's only organic restaurant outside Victoria is thriving with a menu that just won't stop growing, as there's nothing she or the locals want to drop. The litany above the counter is getting stuffed with extraordinary vegetarian burritos; clam burgers; organic rice salad with onions, parsley, and carrot; excellent enchiladas; and, if you're lucky, pickled geoduck. Or try the cornmeal squares with seaweed and cheese. The huevos verdes for breakfast are quite popular. And all, *all*, right down to the mayonnaise on the clam burgers, is made by Delano-Stephens herself. ■ *Behind bank; (604) 725-3105; Box 439, Tofino; $; no alcohol; no credit cards; local checks only; breakfast, lunch, dinner every day (may close for a short time in winter).*

Tofino

Restaurants

Orca Lodge Restaurant ★★ There's no view, the dining room is only moderately attractive, and service is rather slow and confused, but the food is wonderful and prices reasonable. Grilled slices of focaccia are served with a plate of olive oil and vinegar for dipping. Try one of the delicious pasta dishes such as linguine pescatore, served with lots of fresh fish, scallops, and clams. A special of grilled halibut and salmon, served with a basil purée and crisp shoestring potatoes, was exquisite. The selection of wines by the glass is very limited. The adjoining pub offers a fireplace and an English-style pool table (smaller balls and even smaller pockets) and draws a mellow local crowd. ■ *Just south of Tofino on Rte 4; (604) 725-2323; 1258 Pacific Rim Hwy, Tofino; $$; full bar; MC, V; no checks; dinner every day (closed Jan-Feb).*

Blue Heron Dining Room at the Weigh West Motel ★ This is the motel that locals recommend. Not necessarily for the rooms; most venture here for the restaurant and bar. The Blue Heron restaurant in the Weigh West Motel is not perfect, and the supportive locals know it—and forgive it. The view is an immediate hit: a working marina backed by Meares Island, where old-growth forests grow and bald eagles nest. At least once during your meal the restaurant's long-winged namesake will probably swoop by your window. You can get the same view from the bar. Dinner's a bit less striking: a caesar salad generously doctored with crab and avocado, a tender charbroiled steak au poivre, and an overcooked halibut fillet (billed as halibut steak). The motel is neither on the beach nor right in town, but its 63 rooms are clean and well equipped. Reserve a room with a kitchen: they're the ones with the views, and the refrigerator will definitely come in handy for lunch. ▪ *Just south of town on Rt 4; (604) 725-4266; 634 Campbell St, Tofino; $$; full bar; AE, DC, MC, V; local checks only; breakfast, lunch, dinner every day.*

Common Loaf Bake Shop ★ A town meeting place—with save-the-whale buttons at the cash register and save-the-trees pleas on the bulletin board—has moved to a new location, but the rest of the place (the wonderful cheese buns and healthful peasant bread) has stayed the same. Come summer, the bread dough becomes pizza dough and it's the busiest nook in town. A fabulous seafood combo pizza is topped with smoked sockeye salmon, shrimp, and mushrooms; a European version has beer sausage and cheese. Waitstaff is young and easily distracted. ▪ *Just behind the bank; (604) 725-3915; 180 1st St, Tofino; $; no alcohol; no credit cards; no checks; breakfast, lunch, dinner every day (in winter, baked goods only).*

LODGINGS

Chesterman's Beach Bed and Breakfast ★★ With its location on Chesterman's Beach, you can't go wrong: kilometers of beach stretch out at low tide to nearby islands, with ever-changing tidepools. Joan Dublanko designed her home around driftwood and travelers. Each space is different and very much your own: a romantic nook with a comfortable bed, small bath, and a beach-view sun deck (Dublanko brings hot muffins and fruit in the morning; you make coffee); a separate one-bedroom cabin with a kitchen, living room, and bath (no view, sleeps up to four); or the main floor of the house with its own entrance, two bedrooms, kitchen, bath, and sauna. Showers should be quick: the hot water sometimes runs low. In the evening, you can have beach bonfires long into the night. ▪ *1345 Chesterman's Beach Rd; call ahead for directions; (604) 725-3726; PO Box 72, Tofino, BC V0R 2Z0; $$$; V; checks OK.*

Middle Beach Lodge ★★ Until the Middle Beach Lodge opened, lodging options in Tofino meant either a motel or a bed and breakfast. This 26-room lodge, with its forest green and natural wood color scheme, blends nicely into its wooded setting on rocks above a private beach. It's exactly the kind of place Tofino needed. The common room has floor-to-ceiling windows, beautiful wood floors, and a huge stone fireplace. There are multilevel decks from which to enjoy the ocean views. The rooms are small, but perfectly appointed with a European feel: crisp cotton sheets, fluffy down duvets, and colorful throws on the beds; thick cotton towels on the tiled sink. The best rooms are the west-facing balcony rooms. Friends traveling together will probably want to take two adjoining rooms, since the size and layout of the rooms make them rather small for non-couples. Families can save a few dollars by putting the kids in the bunk room. ▪ *South of Tofino off Rt 4, look for signs; (604) 725-2900; PO Box 413, Tofino, BC V0R 2Z0; $$; MC, V; no checks (closed Jan-Feb).*

Paddler's Inn Bed and Breakfast ★★ Ahh, simplicity. White 100 percent cotton sheets, down comforters, clean-lined Scandinavian-style furnishings. The five rooms in Tofino's original hotel are as basic and lovely as Tofino itself: no phones, no TVs, no distractions but the ocean breeze and friendly conversation. Owner Dorothy Baert (whom you'll often find in her Tofino Sea-Kayaking Company downstairs) comes in to cook you a fitting breakfast in the kitchen—and lets you take over for dinner. Checkin is at the kayak shop. ▪ *Just above the Front St dock at 322 Main St; (604) 725-4222; PO Box 620, Tofino, BC V0R 2Z0; $; MC, V; no checks.*

Vargas Island Inn ★ Where else can you find an inn on an island all to itself? You're a couple of hours by kayak or a half-hour by skiff from Tofino, so you should expect a few sacrifices: there aren't any refrigerators or chefs (though owner Marilyn Buckle is an expert on cookies and crab). But that's a small price to pay to be so far from civilization and so close to the warmth of a living-room fireplace, sipping tea in the wood-furnace–heated kitchen or sleeping in absolute silence. Upstairs, there are five modest rooms. What more? There's a wood-burning sauna, a hobbitlike A-frame (great for groups of six or so), not to mention all the crab or cod you (and the Buckles) happen to catch. ▪ *3 miles by water taxi from Tofino; (604) 725-3309; Box 267, Tofino, BC V0R 2Z0; $; MC, V; checks OK.*

Qualicum

Restaurants

QUALICUM

RESTAURANTS

Old Dutch Inn It's a funny place, a motel and dining room done in a Dutch motif with a spectacular view of the expansive

Qualicum Bay. The 36 rooms that make up the hotel portion of the inn are comfortable enough; some feature views, but be aware that there's a major thoroughfare between the motel and the beach. The real draw is the Dutch cuisine. We liked the uitsmyter—an open-faced sandwich topped with Dutch smoked ham and Gouda cheese—and the lekkervekje—Dutch-style fresh fish 'n' chips. Be sure to save room for dessert: the traditional Dutch apple cake with fresh whipped cream is delicious. ■ *On the Island Hwy; (604) 752-6914; 110 Island Hwy, Qualicum Beach; $$; full bar; MC, V; no checks; breakfast, lunch, dinner every day.*

FANNY BAY

RESTAURANTS

The Fanny Bay Inn Ever wonder what a real roadhouse looks like? It's called the "FBI," an unassuming haunt with ma-and-pa vibes, a fine fireplace, the obligatory collection of tankards, a dart board, and hearty pub fare. Low-key and lovely. Stop in for a pint and darts at this classic slice of Canadiana. ■ *In the center of town—you can't miss it; (604) 335-2323; 7480 Island Hwy, Fanny Bay; $; full bar; V; no checks; lunch, dinner every day.*

COURTENAY/COMOX

The Comox Valley has skiing in winter, water sports in summer, the best restaurants around, and scenic access to Powell River on the Sunshine Coast via the *Queen of Sidney*, which leaves four times daily from Comox, (604) 339-3310. Cross-country and downhill skiers flock to a pair of surprisingly decent hills: **Mt. Washington**, where four chair lifts operate over 140 days of the year and there are 29 kilometers of cross-country tracks, (604) 338-1387; and **Forbidden Plateau**—named for an Indian tale—a half hour from downtown Courtenay, (604) 334-4744.

RESTAURANTS

La Crémaillère ★★ One of the few area restaurants capable of answering the challenge of the Old House, La Crémaillère, a two-story Tudor with a charming Puntledge River view, relies on the culinary skills of Michel Hubert, a menu that transforms the region's delicacies into fine French cuisine, and an ambience that offers more intimacy than the bigger restaurant down the road. Start your meal with huîtres Rockefeller (using local oysters) or an extraordinarily delicate pheasant pâté. Enjoy your dinner in a plush private dining room for two if you like. The emphasis on regional products stops at the wine cellar—La Crémaillère features quite an excellent selection of French wines. ▪ *17th St Bridge Rd off Island Hwy; (604) 338-8131; 975 Comox Rd, Courtenay; $$; full bar; AE, DC, MC, V; no checks; lunch Wed-Fri, dinner Wed-Sun.*

The Old House Restaurant ★★ A carefully restored pioneer home is set amid lovely trees and colorful flower gardens. Cedar shakes cover the outside; inside, the exposed heavy beams, large stone fireplace, copperware, and old porcelain combine to create an air of simple, rough-hewn charm. The Old House was one of the first restaurants in the area to divide into distinct formal and casual areas (others are following suit, competently). It features—upstairs—linen, fresh flowers, a pricier, more innovative menu, and—downstairs—a more informal restaurant with a latticed deck and simpler fare: sandwiches, salads, pastas (which are also served upstairs at lunch). Both levels are extremely popular, placing heavy burdens on a generally competent serving crew; lunch can be disastrously slow. The upstairs menu changes every six months, reflecting the freshest of local seafood, fruit, vegetables, meat, and herbs. Recently we've encountered signs of skimping on quality, but we've still enjoyed fine lunches of beef pie made with dark beer and lots of vegetables or house pâté with fruit chutney. Dinner's invention may yield veal timbales stuffed with sweetbreads or roasted pecan chicken with peaches and apricot tarragon sauce. You'll also do well with time-tested French classics: a savory quenelle of escargots, milk-fed veal medallions with basil and wild mushrooms, a full-bodied pepper steak. The wine list is well chosen.

▼

Courtenay/ Comox

Lodgings

▲

Owner Michael McLaughlin's latest addition is Stan's, 1760 Riverside Lane, (604) 338-0050, in the hand-crafted wood cottage next door, with a few tables and glass cases filled with torta rustica, chicken and shrimp pasties, a smorgasbord of salads, and desserts (including their own homemade chocolates). ▪ *Turn right on 17th from Island Hwy north, take the first right before the bridge; (604) 338-5406; 1760 Riverside Lane, Courtenay; $$; full bar; AE, DC, MC, V; checks OK; lunch, dinner every day, brunch Sun.*

LODGINGS

Greystone Manor ★ Conveniently close to the booming ski scene at Mount Washington and Forbidden Plateau, midway between boaters' havens of Nanaimo and Campbell River, this elegant four-room B&B is a welcome alternative to a night in a featureless Island Highway hotel. Authentic Victoriana and other splendid period furnishings and a lawn that gently slopes to an unobstructed view of the water are just some of Greystone's winning attributes. Owners Mike and Mo Shipton serve a hearty breakfast—fruit, homemade muffins, fruit pancakes,

▮

Did we lead you astray? Send us your gripe on the report form at the back of this book.

517

or quiche—from 7:30 to 9am. ■ *5 kilometers south of Courtenay on Island Hwy, watch for signs; (604) 338-1422; 4014 Haas Rd, Site 684/C2, Courtenay, BC V9N 8H9; $; no credit cards; checks OK.*

Kingfisher Beach Resort Set off the highway among a grove of trees, 5 minutes south of Courtenay, this motel with its clean lines, cedar-shake roof, and white stucco walls is pleasing to the eye after the dozens of run-of-the-mill places that line the route. The lobby invites with a large fireplace, skylight, and hanging plants; and the rooms are spacious, with striking, simple furnishings, refrigerators, and decks overlooking the heated pool and the Strait of Georgia. Diversions include a tennis court, sauna, and whirlpool. ■ *4330 S Island Hwy, 8 kilometers south of Courtenay; (604) 338-1323; RR6, Site 672, Courtenay, BC V9N 8H9; $$; AE, DC, MC, V; no checks.*

OYSTER BAY

RESTAURANTS

**Courtenay/
Comox**

Lodgings

Gourmet-by-the-Sea ★ They've surprised us with a strong comeback since the place was razed by a fire in 1986. The new incarnation is larger than the old—and all tables look out to the same magnificent view. A bistro section is a nice addition, with four or five lighter specials; the main dining room offers 14 or so entrées. Chef Michel Rabu has made a name for himself with townspeople and travelers alike, who return for the fresh leeks wrapped in prosciutto and cheese sauce, a simple watercress salad sprinkled with a lovely raspberry vinaigrette, and a mousseline of scallops in a sauce of puréed lobster reduced in whipping cream and accented with Cognac. His seafood specialties are utterly fresh—don't miss his bouillabaisse. ■ *14.4 kilometers south of Campbell River on Discovery Bay; (604) 923-5234; 4378 S Island Hwy, Oyster Bay; $$; full bar; AE, DC, MC, V; no checks; dinner Wed-Sun (Oct-May).*

CAMPBELL RIVER

A town of over 16,000 people, Campbell River is big as Island cities go. It's completely ringed with shopping malls, yet the city center still looks and feels as it undoubtedly did in the '50s. Here you'll find some of the best fishing outfitters on the island, and during the Salmon Festival in July, the town is abuzz with famous and ordinary fisherfolk. For information on the region's wealth of short trails and dive sites, call the Chamber of Commerce, (604) 286-0764.

    Strathcona Provincial Park, to the west, is a park of superlatives. It has Canada's highest waterfall and Vancouver Island's highest mountain and offers a wide variety of landscapes to explore, including alpine meadows and lakes and large forests of virgin cedar and Douglas fir. Easily accessible by road (take Highway 28 from Campbell River), the park has campgrounds and boat-launching facilities at Buttle Lake, and a surprisingly deluxe lakeside accommodation, **Strathcona Park Lodge** (see review in this section). The park also has fine trout lakes and an extensive trail system for backpacking.

RESTAURANTS

Koto ★★ It makes sense: a very fresh sushi bar smack in the middle of fishing country. Still, it's tough to find essential Japanese ingredients where most people opt for loggers' cuisine. In his pleasant Campbell River restaurant, Takeo Maeda (Tony) is single-handedly turning that around. Locals are becoming familiar with (and fond of) his sushi specialties and other Japanese fare from teriyaki to sukiyaki. It's a nice meal, especially if you pull into town late. There's only one sushi chef—so when it's busy (especially in summer) the service can be slow. ■ *Behind the Bank of BC building; (604) 286-1422; 80 10th Ave, Campbell River; $$; full bar; AE, MC, V; no checks; lunch Tues-Fri, dinner Tues-Sat.*

Royal Coachman Inn ★★ We like everything about this place, from the hearth bearing soccer trophies to the savory aroma of the soup du jour (if it's French onion, order it) to the practiced pouring arm of the bartender. A steady stream of regulars crowds the Coachman from lunch into the wee hours, and the chef meets demands with a small, hard-working kitchen staff. A blackboard menu changes daily. Meals include surprisingly ambitious dishes that you don't expect to see in a pub: crêpes; schnitzel cordon bleu; sole topped with asparagus, shrimp, and hollandaise. Tuesday and Saturday nights are prime-rib nights—come early. ■ *2nd and Dogwood; (604) 286-0231; 84 Dogwood St, Campbell River; $; full bar; AE, MC, V; no checks; lunch, dinner every day.*

LODGINGS

Painter's Lodge ★ You'd never know this was a 60-year-old fishing lodge. Due to a fire in 1985, the place is brand-spanking-new. Old photos of big-name types and their award-winning fish line the plush lobby, lounge, and dark Tyee pub, where unkempt fishermen seem almost out of place—but aren't. Pandemonium breaks out at 4am as the seaplanes and 50 Boston whalers zoom in to pick up the anglers and shatter any non-fisherman's sleep. Packages run from $259 to $419 a night, which includes eight hours of fishing. Painter's is a growing resort, now with four buildings (in addition to the main lodge) totaling 80 rooms, and more in the works. Best are rooms in the main lodge (no longer for anglers only), with two steps down into the bedroom and a porch overlooking Discovery Passage and Quadra Island. In the evening, appetizers in the lounge are our choice: try the moist smoked salmon marinated in a honey-mustard-seed-and-lime vinaigrette. Dinners are inconsistent and service incompetent. ■ *1625 McDonald Rd and Island Hwy, 4 kilometers north of Campbell River; (604) 286-1102; Box 460, Campbell River, BC V9W 5C1; $$; AE, MC, V; no checks; open April-Oct.*

Strathcona Park Lodge ★ A week-in-the-woods experience: canoeing, day hikes, lake play. Stay in one of the attractive cabins with kitchens or one of the modest motel units—we think they're a bit overpriced for what you get, but you couldn't ask for a better location. There are lots of outdoor activities (including rock-climbing and rope courses), perfect for families seeking fresh-air fun. Family-style buffet meals at strictly regulated hours feature healthful food—plenty of vegetables and limited amounts of red meat. Don't be late. ■ *At the edge of Strathcona Park, 44.8 kilometers west of Campbell River; (604) 286-8206; PO Box 2160, Campbell River, BC V9W 5C9; $$; full bar; MC, V; checks OK (closed Jan-Feb).*

GOLD RIVER

**Campbell
River**

Lodgings

The *Uchuck III* will take you for a magnificent 10-hour chug from Gold River along Vancouver Island's broken western coastline to the remote settlement of Kyuquot. You spend the night at a bed and breakfast and return the next day ($145 all-inclusive); PO Box 57, Gold River, BC V0P 1G0; (604) 283-2325. Book these tours well in advance.

PORT MCNEILL

The major asset of this remote spot is proximity to all things wild and wonderful—great boating, diving, whale watching, salmon fishing, and tidepooling.

The U'mista Cultural Centre in Alert Bay, an inspiring Kwakiutl museum, is a short ferry ride from Port McNeill. This one examines cultural origins and potlatch traditions. Seasonal hours, closed Sundays, (604) 974-5403.

Whale watching is superior (July through October only) from Telegraph Cove, 16 kilometers south of Port McNeill. Stubbs Island Charters, (604) 928-3185, takes groups out for morning and afternoon cruises to view the cetaceans on their migration down Johnstone Strait, and can accommodate groups of five or more in a cluster of modest harborfront cabins; two suites are suitable for couples.

RESTAURANTS

The Cookhouse ★ The minimalism of Port McNeill makes the amenities of the Cookhouse shine all the brighter. Located in

Pioneer Mall, Walter and Sue Schinner's elegant restaurant and carry-out deli/bakery feature tasty continental fare prepared on the spot in a central kitchen midway between deli counter and dining room. The Schinners' subtle Eastern European influence is most evident in dishes such as chicken Budapest or chicken à la brochette in a light lemon-hazelnut sauce. More traditional fare served on brown stoneware includes chateaubriand, filet mignon, crab béarnaise, and veal Oscar. Eat hearty—it could very well be your last high-quality feast before plunging into the North Country. ■ *In Pioneer Mall on Hwy 19; (604) 956-4933; Port McNeill; $$; full bar; MC, V; local checks only; lunch, dinner Tues-Sat.*

PORT HARDY

You'll feel as though you're on the edge of the world in Port Hardy—venture any farther north and you'll have to go by boat. It's a town full of loggers, fishermen, miners, and travelers stopping long enough to catch the 15-hour ferry to Prince Rupert, (604) 949-6722. The boat leaves every other day in summer and once a week in the winter.

The famous Edward S. Curtis film *In the Land of the War Canoes* was filmed in nearby **Fort Rupert**, still one of the best places to purchase authentic native American art.

Cape Scott Park. A drive of 1½ hours on a dirt road west of Port Hardy and then a short hike on a rickety boardwalk through old-growth forest bring you to spectacular San Josef Bay. For exact directions or information on other hikes at the northernmost tip of the island, contact the Chamber of Commerce, (604) 949-7622.

THE GULF ISLANDS

The Gulf Islands, a 240-kilometer string of small islands in the Strait of Georgia, are British Columbia's more remote version of Washington's San Juans to the south. Similar in geography and philosophy, the Gulf Islands also enjoy the same rain-shadow weather and offer wonderful boating and cycling opportunities. The best-known and most populous islands, the Southern Group, stretch from Campbell River to Victoria: Gabriola, Valdes, Galiano, Mayne, Salt Spring, North and South Pender, and Saturna. North of Nanaimo are Lasqueti, Texada, Denman, Hornby, Quadra, Cortes, Sonora. Ferries from Tsawwassen and Horseshoe Bay on the mainland and various spots on Vancouver Island service the islands. For more information, call BC ferries, (604) 669-1211. BC ferries does not take checks or credit cards (and few islands have bank machines), so be sure to bring extra cash.

THE GULF ISLANDS: SONORA

LODGINGS

Sonora Resort ★★ Sonora is posh and it's big. Even so, the $1,795 you shell out for two nights and three days includes *everything*. Everything: airfare, guided fishing, meals, drinks, rain gear, fishing rods, seven hot tubs, and five steam rooms. Some suspect, however, that this impeccable multimillion-dollar spot has gotten too big too fast. They cater to a number of executive vacations, and though the staff won't let you lift a finger, sometimes you wish the kitchen could handle groups better. There are five buildings with some very luxurious suites (some have their own Jacuzzis). Other amenities include a world-class billiards table, a small convention center, and five fully stocked self-service bars open 24 hours. Special needs are catered to here. The kitchen is competent and serves a well-selected variety of fresh fish. Occasionally a special chef is brought in for a fête around the Teppan cooker. ■ *48 kilometers north of Campbell River (accessible by boat or plane only); (604) 287-2869; 625-B 11th Ave, Campbell River, BC V9W 4G9; $$$; full bar; DC, MC, V; checks OK.*

THE GULF ISLANDS: QUADRA

Quadra is the northernmost of the Gulf Islands, a 10-minute ferry ride away from the salmon-fishing mecca of Campbell River. A lot of artists and craftspeople live here, so it makes a fine place to sleuth around for pottery and other wares. You can pick up a detailed map of the island at the **Kwakiutl Museum**, an outstanding collection of native art; three kilometers south of the ferry dock on Green Road, (604) 285-3733. Their masks, blankets, and carvings rival Indian displays in the finest international museums.

LODGINGS

April Point Lodge ★★★ Between April and October this famous resort draws serious fishermen and celebrities from all over the world for the extraordinary salmon fishing: bluebacks in April and May, tyee July through September, coho throughout the summer. The staff, nurtured by generations of experience, expertly pair guides with guests. About 8 kilometers in either direction are exceptionally lovely beach walks: the lighthouse to the south, Rebecca Spit Provincial Park to the east. The cabins facing west are spacious, beautifully furnished, and graced with large fireplaces; they're also expensive. Facing north are thin-walled cabins overlooking the marina; you might be kept awake most of the night by late-drinking or early-rising fishermen in adjoining rooms. There's a seawater pool, but if you're not here to fish—really fish (the cost of which is *not* included in your already hefty fee)—you will probably feel like a tolerated outsider; there are no other amenities. Reserve at least three or four months in advance. The main lodge is sunny and cheerful; the food is always very good. ■ *10 minutes north of the ferry dock on April Point Rd; (604) 285-2222; PO Box 1, Campbell River, BC V9W 4Z9; $$$; AE, DC, MC, V; checks OK (open April-Oct).*

Tsa-Kwa-Luten Lodge ★★ The Cape Mudge Band of the Kwakiutl opened this contemporary lodge, built in the spirit of a longhouse, a few years ago. The 33 rooms (which include three fully equipped beach cabins) all overlook Discovery Passage; some have fireplaces. As at April Point, fishing is the primary attraction here, although nonfishers can also explore the beach, with its ancient petroglyphs, as well as the nearby Cape Mudge lighthouse. Mountain bikes are available for rent, and the staff can arrange transportation if you want to explore. Local seafood is the catch in the dining room. In summer, the Lodge offers a weekly buffet of regional foods, with a tribal dance following. ■ *10 minutes south of the ferry off Lighthouse Rd (look for signs); (604) 285-2042 or (800) 665-7745; PO Box 460, Quathiaski Cove, BC V0P 1N0; $$$; AE, DC, E, MC, V; checks OK; breakfast, lunch, dinner every day.* ♿

THE GULF ISLANDS: DENMAN AND HORNBY

Tranquil and bucolic, the sister islands of Denman and Hornby sit just off the coast of Vancouver Island. Denman, the larger (10 minutes by ferry from Buckley Bay, south of Courtenay), is known for its pastoral farmlands and its population of talented artisans. Its relatively flat landscape and untraveled roads make it a natural for cyclists. Hornby (10 minutes by ferry from Denman) boasts Helliwell Park, with dramatic seaside cliffs and forest trails, as well as a lovely long beach at Tribune Bay.

LODGINGS

Sea Breeze Lodge ★ Sea Breeze Lodge may have a reputation among islanders for being posh and exclusive, but off-islanders will find it quite unpretentious. Catch the ferry from Denman before 6pm (10pm Fridays) and find 13 warm and comfortable cottages on the beach. If you come at any time other than the height of summer, reserve a cabin with a kitchen. Gail and Brian Bishop have enlarged their dining room to accommodate nonguests (by reservation) for Gail's home cooking (from June to the end of September), which is fresh and inventive, and for the convivial atmosphere around the rustic oak tables. Alternatives to the beach here include tennis on a grass court or a soak in the new hot tub (enclosed in winter, open in summer). ■ *Tralee Point; (604) 335-2321; Hornby Island, BC V0R 1Z0; $$; full bar; no credit cards; checks OK.*

THE GULF ISLANDS: GALIANO

A secluded, narrow strip of lushly forested hills, 22 miles long, Galiano preserves the most countercultural feel of the southern Gulf Islands and a sparse number of services, most clustered at the southern end. With fewer than 1,000 permanent residents, there is one gas station, no bank, a couple of small grocery/health food stores, and a popular pub with a mean burger, the Hummingbird Inn, junction of Sturdies Bay and Georgeson Bay roads, (604) 539-5472. A ferry from Tsawwassen arrives in Sturdies Bay twice a day.

Watch eagles, ferries, and sweeping tides from **Bluffs Park** overlooking Active Pass, or bike the unpaved eastern coast untroubled by traffic. Canoe or kayak under high cliffs and rest in secluded coves; Gulf Islands Kayaking, (604) 539-2442, can accommodate paddlers of all abilities. Breathtaking sunsets can be seen (weather permitting) at **Montague Harbour**, where camping and supplies are available; for moorings: (604) 539-5733. More secluded camping is available at the ruggedly beautiful **Dionysio Point Provincial Park** at the north tip of the island, where two sandstone-sculpted coves are joined by a rocky point.

▼

RESTAURANTS

La Berengerie ★ The quaint 40-seat restaurant boasts devoted fans. Owner/chef/hotelier Huguette Benger, who learned the trade running a small hotel in Paris, offers a $22 four-course menu that might offer something like mushroom soup, romaine salad with vinaigrette, a gingered beef with saffron rice and crisp vegetables, and cheesecake. Items change daily and may run out altogether by the end of the evening (in which case Benger will whip up something you may never have heard of). Service and atmosphere are casual. Benger is often your server as well as chef. Many of the vegetables come from the restaurant's own garden. Reservations are a must. Upstairs are five modest guest rooms, two with private (but not spotless) bath, and all with paper-thin walls. But the hot tub on the deck up at Benger's house and the good breakfast make up for the flaws. ■ *On the corner of Clanton and Montague Harbour rds; (604) 539-5392; Montague Harbour Rd, Galiano Island; $$; full bar; V; checks OK; dinner Wed-Mon in summer, Fri-Sun off season (closed Dec-Feb).*

LODGINGS

Bodega Resort ★★ The seven spacious chalets are furnished with care: you might find lace country curtains, custom cherrywood cabinets, or a cast-iron wood stove in the living room. Each unit has three bedrooms, two baths, a fully equipped kitchen, and two view decks. The ranch-style unit has three bedrooms, kitchen, living room, bath, and a large sun deck surrounded by a rose garden—perfect for family getaways. A lodge with a conference room also has a few rooms available. For fun there's horseback riding, a trout pond, hiking trails amid the 25 acres of meadows and trees, and Dionysio Point, just 3 (unpaved) miles away. Prices are remarkable for such generous accommodations. ■ *Follow Porlier Pass Dr 22.4 kilometers north of Sturdies Bay to Cook Rd; (604) 539-2677; PO Box 115, Galiano Island, BC V0N 1P0; $$; MC, V; checks OK.*

Mount Galiano Eagle's Nest ★★

Just about the time you think you must have turned onto a logging road by mistake, you finally come upon Francine Renaud and Bernard Mignault's unusual home, nestled in its roost at the foot of Mount Galiano with an eagle's-eye view of Trincomali Channel. Built from a combination of slash wood from the property and castaways from various doomed architectural structures (a wood floor from a Victoria home, a slate floor made from old blackboards, a slew of windows incorrectly sized for someone else), the house sits on 75 acres of land and a whole kilometer of waterfront—all abutting the Galiano Mountain Wilderness Park. Renaud and Mignault's love of the island is seen in their commitment to the Galiano community; their love of the land translates into a garden that is a work of art (and a prolific producer). And the breakfasts: melon and grapefruit served with nasturtium blossoms, followed by waffles accompanied by all manner of toppings. Our favorite of the three rooms by far is the romantic, peach-colored upstairs chamber that looks out over the water. An absolute treat unless you have something against shared bathrooms or friendly cats. ■ *Ask for directions: you'll need them; (604) 539-2567; 2-720 Active Pass Dr, Galiano Island, BC V0N 1P0; $$; no credit cards; checks OK.*

Woodstone Country Inn ★★

If this fancy manse straddling wood and field seems a little out of its element on casual Galiano, it will appeal to those whose tastes run to adult (children are discouraged), urban-style comforts or who need a peaceful venue for a business retreat. The 12 rooms, each named for a meadow flower, are sweet and bright (if somewhat sterilely decorated); all have private baths and most have fireplaces. The best rooms possess a dreamy view of green pastures; but even those on the other side feature tall windows allowing dramatic vistas of the backyard forest. The inn maintains a walking trail (and gumboots to borrow) leading guests through the woods to a viewing platform overlooking a tranquil marsh. The morning meal is usually something rich and delicious—creamy herbed eggs on a buttered croissant—and in the afternoon, guests regroup for tea.

The dining room here has given Galiano its first taste of elegant cuisine. The windows open onto an expanse of green,

The Gulf Islands: Galiano

Lodgings

▲

visited by deer and bald eagles and dotted with horses. The lighting is low and the servers soft-spoken. For $21.50, you might encounter a deliciously hot spinach salad with curry vinaigrette, freshly baked soda bread laced with thyme, a small plate of pasta in a red-pepper sauce, and an exquisite lightly braised salmon in béarnaise sauce accompanied by crisp vegetables and a rich almond butter. Dessert is extra. ■ *Bear left off Sturdies Bay Rd to Georgeson Bay Rd, follow signs; (604) 539-2022; RR1, Georgeson Bay Rd, Galiano Island, BC V0N 1P0; $$$; full bar; AE, MC, V; no checks; dinner every day.* &

Sutil Lodge ★ Ann and Tom Hennessy have done a period renovation of their rambling 1928 clapboard, situated on 20 secluded acres of beachfront on Montague Harbour, and the rooms retain a charming old-fashioned flavor, with the original fir paneling and authentic 1930s furnishings. Rusticity remains: the seven guest rooms are tiny, the walls are thin, the neighboring cabins have their facilities in a nearby bathhouse. But something about this place reflects better than any other the laid-back spirit of Galiano. Front rooms have stunning water views up the shaft of placid Montague Harbor; the others face (in season) lush cherry blossoms and an expansive lawn which was, in early days, a grass tennis court. The communal sitting room and dining area both have fireplaces. Morning makes a serene time for an otter-watching canoe paddle; come back to Ann's freshly baked croissants and smoked salmon scrambled eggs. Or take advantage of another of the Hennessys' seagoing vessels: a 46-foot catamaran, on which they take guests on tours of the islands followed by picnic suppers on the beach. Fabulous off-season rates. ■ *Follow signs for Montague Harbour, after long steep hill, turn left on Southwind, last drive on left; (604) 539-2930; 637 Southwind Rd, Galiano Island, BC V0N 1P0; $$; MC, V; checks OK.*

▼

**The
Gulf Islands:
Galiano**

Lodgings

▲

Galiano Lodge *[unrated]* The big news on the island is this handsome remodel of the Galiano Lodge, a stone's throw from the ferry dock. Though not quite completed on our early visit (there was substantial detail work left to be done on the new building), the spot has great potential. The original beachside building houses seven modest rooms with sitting areas and private baths and sensational views of Active Pass and Mount Baker; however, it's the ten deluxe rooms in the new building, particularly those on the second floor, that are the real stars: sweeping views, wood-burning fireplaces, down comforters, private balconies (in need of patio furniture), soaker tubs or Jacuzzis in elegant mustard-walled bathrooms, and pretty French country accoutrements. A lovely continental breakfast delivered to your room in a picnic basket is included in the considerable cost of a night's stay. The reasonably priced, bistro-style dinner menu is designed to cater to guests and islanders alike;

though it changes daily, it's sure to feature seafood (perhaps the terrific trout amandine with a buttery potato cake and perfect roasted red peppers, or the linguine con vongoli in a red sauce). Proprietors Frank Leung and Leslie McKay have many plans for the place: a more publike bar, a warmer dining room, tennis courts, a swimming pool, an exercise room, and—following in the footsteps of the Sooke Harbour House—an herb garden. The bar's tree-shaded porch just begs for you to wait there for your ship to come in. ■ *On the water, first left from ferry terminal; (604) 539-3388; PO Box 247, Galiano Island, BC V0N 1P0; $$$; MC, V; no checks.* &

THE GULF ISLANDS: SALT SPRING

Named for the unusually cold and briny springs on the north end of the island, Salt Spring is the largest and most populated of the Gulf chain, and its population is growing steadily. It's accessible by ferry from Tsawwassen (to Long Harbor, 2 hours); Crofton, near Duncan on Vancouver Island (to Vesuvius, 20 minutes); or Swartz Bay (32 kilometers from Victoria) on the Saanich Peninsula (to Fulford Harbor, 35 minutes). All roads lead to Ganges, as the natives are fond of saying. Ganges, the largest town on the island, has a colorful summer Saturday morning farmers market, several pleasant cafes, a condominium overlooking the harbor, and a flurry of retail development.

Good camping facilities are available at St. Mary Lake, the waterfront Ruckle Park, and Mouat Provincial Park on the southeastern tip of the island, where you'll find a spectacular mixture of virgin forest, rock and clamshell beach, and rugged headlands. Or drive Cranberry Road up to the top of **Mount Maxwell** for a panorama of the archipelago from Salt Spring to the U.S. mainland. For information, call the tourist bureau, (604) 537-5252.

RESTAURANTS

Piccolo's ★★ The best food in Ganges can be had at this cozy house restaurant right in the middle of things. The menu is European with a decided Scandinavian slant—sandwiches, salads, and pastas at lunch; seafood and other specialties for dinner. Someone in the kitchen really cares: the seafood on the fried combo platter is lightly breaded and greaseless and served with a spicy aioli, the shrimp pasta is delicate and topped with good-quality fontina cheese, the stuffed trout is light and subtly flavored. Don't miss dessert—Piccolo's coup de grace: particularly the homemade cheesecake, quietly flavored with cloudberries. Friendly service. ■ *At 2nd main intersection in town, near Thrifties; (604) 537-1844; Herford Rd, Ganges; $$; full bar; MC, V; no checks; breakfast, lunch, dinner every day.*

Vesuvius Inn ★ The big draws at this rebuilt version of a turn-of-the-century loggers' and fishermen's inn are the variety of brews and the spectacular view from the waterside porch of the ferry dock with Crofton in the distance. Also good at Vesuvius are the food—caesar salads (which are ubiquitous on Salt Spring), fish 'n' chips, burgers, pasta—and entertainment. A very casual place—order at the bar as you go in and find a good spot on the porch. ▪ *At the northwest point of the island; (604) 537-2312; Vesuvius Bay Rd, Ganges; $; full bar; MC, V; local checks only; lunch, dinner every day.* ⅍

LODGINGS

Hastings House ★★★★ Nestled among fruit trees, gardens, and rolling lawns that overlook a peaceful cove, Hastings House resort goes a long way toward satisfying the hideaway fantasies of most people. It stands in all its gentrified splendor, imbued with an almost formidable air of genteel hospitality. The accommodations consist of 12 suites in five revamped farm buildings, plus a recently renovated Cliff House. Each is individually furnished with down quilts, antiques, and thick carpets. Our favorites are the Hayloft, with its bay window seat, Franklin stove, and quaint folk art; and the Farmhouse, a charming stucco and half-timbered house with two suites—ideal for two couples. Although service here strikes some as just a little too *too* (new towels are supplied every time you leave your quarters; a personal note, thanking you for your stay, follows the visit), the guest gradually discovers that in spite of that, and the stiff tariffs ($290 to $420 in high season, which includes a morning wake-up coffee, breakfast, and afternoon tea), and the almost palpable air of formality, Hastings House is a remarkably warm place, thanks to a friendly staff.

Chef Lars Jorgenson, formerly of Vancouver's William Tell, offers a nightly $55 five-course table d'hôte dinner in the handsome Tudor dining room, beginning promptly at 6:30pm with cocktails on the lawn or in the parlor. A recent meal began with a creamy dariole of artichoke hearts on a chive and tomato salsa, followed by a potent Dungeness crab bisque sweetened with Cognac crème fraîche, and a wild greens salad rendered (slightly too) sweet by the counterpoint of caramelized and onion-stuffed pastry pouches. Choose your entrée from a list of five: perhaps a fascinating preparation of phyllo-wrapped Atlantic salmon in a black currant beurre blanc, or an herb- and garlic-encrusted game hen strewn with braised root vegetables. Dessert was a luscious Grand Marnier soufflé, poured over with sweet crème Anglaise. Both dinner and Sunday brunch are open to non-guests by reservation. ▪ *Just north of Ganges at 160 Upper Ganges Rd; (604) 537-2362; PO Box 1110, Ganges, Salt Spring Island, BC V0S 1E0; $$$; AE, MC, V; local checks only; dinner every day, brunch Sun.* ⅍

The Old Farmhouse ★★★ On this island boasting nearly 80 bed and breakfasts, the Old Farmhouse stands out. German-born hosts Gertie and Karl Fuss have turned their heritage farmhouse into an inn worthy of *House Beautiful*: four guest rooms, each with a private bath and a patio or balcony, are marvels of charming and elegant decoration. Brilliant whitewashed wainscoting, crisp floral wallpaper, stained-glass and leaded windows, French doors, polished pine floors, feather beds in starched duvets, a bouquet of fresh roses—it's all here, and scrupulously maintained by very professional hosts (who know everything about the island down to all the ferry times). Artful nooks and crannies abound in the public rooms as well, which, along with Gertie's collection of European crockery, make virtually every tableau an original refreshment to the eye. Outside, sun slants through the firs, madronas, and alders dotting the sloping meadow. A gazebo, a hammock, and a couple of porch swings abet the appearance and reality of near-perfect relaxation. There's even a canoe to take across the street to St. Mary Lake.

Coffee arrives at your threshold at 7:30am, followed by breakfast around the country dining room table at 9am. It's elegant and copious: a pretty presentation of fresh kiwi fruit and cream, a golden omelet soufflé folded in with blueberries and topped with powdered sugar, a platter of homemade cinnamon sticky buns and orange bread, fresh coffee, and whipped fruit juice. There's not a detail these hosts miss: they even supply doggie bags (so you can take the inevitable extras on with you for an afternoon picnic), then tell you where to have the picnic.
■ *4 kilometers north of Ganges; (604) 537-4113; RR 4, 1077 North End Rd, Salt Spring Island, BC V0S 1E0; $$$; MC, V; checks OK.*

The Beach House on Sunset Drive ★★ Not to be confused with the amiably dilapidated Beach House B&B on the south end of Salt Spring, this extraordinary property a couple of miles north of Vesuvius is in a league of its own. Jon De West, an affable, gregarious expatriate from the Vancouver rat race, and his wife, Maureen, a former instructor from the Cordon Bleu, were born to be B&B hosts. Coffee is delivered to each room in the morning. Maureen's four-course breakfasts, enjoyed around the big table in the view dining room, are legendary. The sprawling home lies right on the ocean, enjoying warm currents sweeping up from the south that heat the surf to bathtub temperature in spring and summer. Two large guest rooms are in a private wing of the main house, each with tastefully subtle decor, en suite facilities, eiderdown comforters, bathrobes, fresh flowers, fruit baskets, and decanters of port. A woodsy cottage is well kept, but best is the namesake Beach Cottage, a cozy refurbished boat house with a wraparound deck, kitchenette, bedroom, and breathtaking sunset vista ($175 a night). This one has honeymoon written all over it. ▪ *Up Sunset Dr from Vesuvius Bay; (604) 537-2879; 930 Sunset Dr, Salt Spring Island, RR #1, Ganges, BC V0S 1E0; $$$; MC, V; checks OK.* ⅃

Green Rose Farm and Guest House ★★ Hosts Ron Aird and Tom Hoff have restored this 1916 farmhouse on 17 acres of orchard, meadow, and woods, and the result is classic and inviting. The decor serves as welcome antidote to the chintz-and-Laura Ashley style of so many other B&Bs—here it's sort of farmhouse-nautical, surehandedly decorated with yachting accoutrements, painted pine floors, crisp white duvets on the beds, and handsome pinstriped wallpaper. One guest room has its own bath; two don't. The guests' living room has comfortable couches and a beautiful fireplace. Hoff, who attended culinary school, makes breakfast each morning. ▪ *Take Upper Ganges Rd, stay right until Robinson; (604) 537-9927; 346 Robinson Rd, Salt Spring Island, BC V0S 1E0; $$; MC, V; local checks only.*

Weston Lake Inn ★ The owners of this contemporary farmhouse just above Weston Lake, Susan Evans, Ted Harrison, and Wilson (their sheep dog), have become experts at fading into the background and letting their guests enjoy the comfortable space. Their touches are everywhere: in Harrison's petit-point embroideries, framed and hanging in the three guest rooms (all with their own baths), in Evans' excellent, hearty breakfasts (with vegetables from their organic garden), in the blooming results of their gardening efforts. Evans knows and loves her island and is a fount of local knowledge. Guests have access to a comfortable lounge with fireplace, library, TV, VCR (including a decent collection of cassettes), and the Jacuzzi. Open all year. ▪ *3.6 kilometers east of Fulford Harbour at 813 Beaver Point Rd; (604) 653-4311; C34 Beaver Point Rd, Fulford Harbour, BC V0S 1C0; $$; MC, V; checks OK.*

THE GULF ISLANDS: MAYNE

Rolling orchards, sheep farms, and warm rock-strewn beaches abound on this rustic 8-square-mile island. It's small enough for a day trip, but pretty enough for a lifetime. Hike out to the grassy point of the Indian Reservation; drop by the lighthouse; or stroll up to the top of Mayne's mountain for a view of the Strait of Georgia; and you'll begin to discover what Mayne's all about. By ferry the island's usually the second stop from Tsawwassen (1½ hours), and the fourth or second from Swartz Bay (1½ hours).

LODGINGS

Oceanwood Country Inn ★★★ Jonathan and Marilyn Chilvers are both innkeepers' innkeepers, and their magnificent property is worthy of the outstanding hospitality. Unobtrusively set on a cozy wooded cove with a tree-webbed view of Navy Channel and North Pender Island, the inn is right for its surroundings: big enough for all eight rooms to be booked without the sense that you'll be stumbling over your neighbors at breakfast, yet small enough that you're part of the group, especially at teatime. (Don't miss it: the cookies are buttery, and there are binoculars for eagle watching.) The best rooms are upstairs, especially the Rose Room with its marble-faced fireplace and a whirlpool bath with a view of the channel through French doors. The three rooms downstairs are slightly less private, as they open onto the terrace and the Jacuzzi. All have bathrooms. There's a meeting room attached to the garage, equipped with a screen, whiteboard, VCR, and flip chart, where conferences of up to 12 people can be held. The Chilverses are accustomed to meeting the needs of their guests; they seem to have thought of everything, down to a written list of nearby scenic walks. Breakfast is innovative yet hearty.

Equal energy is lavished on dinner, which is served to nonguests as well. Chef Chris Johnson changes the menu nightly, and generally serves it in four courses: for instance, a piquant garlic potato soup with a goat cheese-roast duck crouton, homemade herb fettuccine in a creamy parsley pesto, fresh seared tuna in a light aioli with crunchy green vegetables, a dessert tart of custard and stewed fruits in a rich hazelnut crust. Portions can be relentlessly large (who would complain?), but the wine list is carefully chosen and the dining room suitably intimate. Coffee (or something off the admirable list of ports and single-malt Scotches) by the fire in the library is the perfect finale. ■ *A 12-minute bike ride, 25-minute stroll, 3-minute drive, or 25-cent phone call from the island's ferry dock; (604) 539-5074; 630 Dinner Bay Rd, Mayne Island, BC V0N 2J0; $$$; full bar; MC, V; local checks only; dinner every day.*

Fernhill Lodge ★ The Crumblehulmes' eccentric taste permeates every corner, from Mary's vast collection of English pewter to the eclectic selection of books in the library to the eight guest rooms, each decorated in a period theme—Jacobean, 18th-century French, Victorian, Oriental, Canadiana, farmhouse. Most of the rooms are dark and a bit severe (steer clear of the garish Moroccan room), but guests are welcome to stroll through the herb garden, relax on the discreetly placed benches or gazebo along the hillside, or enjoy the wood-fired sauna under the trees. Brian Crumblehulme's passion is historical cookery. An unusual evening feast is prepared on prior notice (the first party to reserve gets to select one of five menus). The Crumblehulmes' hospitality is boundless—from loaning bikes to sharing a soothing cup of tea out on the patio. It's not on the water, but a good swimming beach is not too far. ■ *Left onto Village*

Bay Rd from the ferry terminal, go about 3.5 miles to Fernhill Rd; (604) 539-2544; C4 Fernhill Rd, Mayne Island, BC V0N 2J0; $$; MC, V; checks OK; dinner every day, brunch Sun.

THE GULF ISLANDS: NORTH AND SOUTH PENDER

Green, rural North and South Pender islands are separated by a canal and united by a bridge, from which you get lovely views of both Browning and Bedwell harbors. The ferry lands at the dock at Otter Bay on North Pender. South Pender is better for biking (fewer hills). You can rent kayaks at **Mouat Point Kayaks**; (604) 629-6767.

RESTAURANTS

The Restaurant at Bedwell Harbour ★★ The location of this South Pender Island dining room is stunning: perched over a perfect cove alongside a rocky outcropping, overlooking the marina and the sunset. Unfortunately, the Bedwell Harbour Resort of which this restaurant is a part is in what seems like an indefinite period of transition, from hotel to timeshare property/resort, so the accommodations aren't getting proper attention and aren't—yet, at least—fully recommended. Similarly, the waterside pub sports fine vistas but poor food. The dining room, on the other hand, deservedly enjoys the esteem of many Gulf Islanders. The cuisine borrows from French, featuring silken bisques and fine grilled fishes. Even in the off season (when meals are set-price tables d'hôte), attention is paid to the side dishes, and desserts are consistently exquisite. Service in the dining room is earnest and professional; hopefully a good sign of things to come when the resort is finished with its ambitious renovation. ■ *On the main street; (604) 629-3212; 9801 Spaulding Rd, South Pender Island; $$; full bar; AE, MC, V; no checks; breakfast Fri-Sun, dinner every day in summer (weekends only in winter).*

LODGINGS

Cliffside Inn-on-the-Sea ★★ Rarely does a place invoke such disparity of opinion. Some cringe at the dolled-up house and the rules to ensure privacy, while others swoon; however, no one disputes the landing. You're perched at the edge of a bluff beside a staircase leading down to a mile-long beach, with a sweeping view of the channel, the islands, and Mount Baker beyond. The emphasis here is on privacy: each of the four bedrooms has a private entrance, deck, and bath. Three face the ocean. The hot tub on the cliff-hanger deck with the 280-degree view can be reserved for private sessions well into the night (and if you're sitting anywhere near, you'll be asked to disappear). A set of steep steps leads to a private beach. Hostess Penny Tomlin will prepare gourmet dinners for guests, arrange boat excursions and the occasional island cookout. Breakfast served promptly at 9am in the solarium dining room (warning: late sleepers receive a wake up holler). Adults only, and smoking outside only. ■ *Follow signs to Hope Bay, government dock, turn on Clam Bay Rd to Armadale; (604) 629-6691; Armadale Rd, North Pender Island, BC V0N 2M0; $$$; MC, V; no checks.*

THE GULF ISLANDS: SATURNA

RESTAURANTS

Boot Cove Lodge and Restaurant ★★ In 1993, Claude Croteau took over as manager of Peter Jardine's lovely frame house, which sits high on a hill overlooking an inlet and an oyster farm. Gone are the days of the five- course and vegetarian-only meals. Croteau's menu changes so frequently they've dispensed with menus proper in favor of a large blackboard toted from table to table. Though an early visit in Croteau's reign found the kitchen somewhat disheveled (leaving hungry diners waiting only to find that there were no prawns left after all, or—hold on a minute—maybe there were), there's no doubt of a sure hand wielding magic in the form of, say, pan-fried goat cheese salad with a scallion vinaigrette, or an extraordinary blackened snapper with a delectable, not-too-rich Cajun cream sauce. Don't miss the in-season strawberries in Devonshire cream. The service is islandy, but the food is worldly. Reservations are a must. The bed-and-breakfast rooms upstairs are contemporary in feel. Work is being done to put in a games room downstairs, perhaps even a bike shop. There's a large fireplace (crackling warm when it's cold outside) in the oak-trimmed waiting room (which doubles as a living room for the inn's guests). ■ *Take your 1st right off the ferry onto Boot Cove Rd, then right on Payne Rd and follow to end; (604) 539-2254; 130 Payne Rd, Saturna Island, BC V0N 2Y0; $$; full bar; MC, V; no checks; dinner Fri-Tues.*

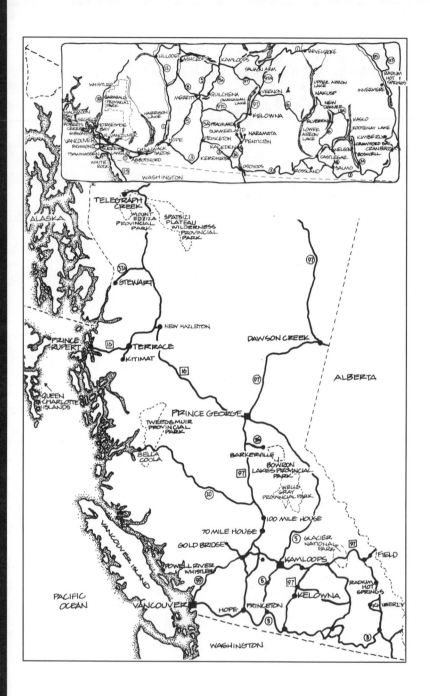

Mainland British Columbia

First, north from the U.S./Canada border (skipping Vancouver) along the Sunshine Coast to Powell River, then inland to Whistler, Lillooet, and Gold Bridge. North to Prince George, then west to Prince Rupert and the Queen Charlotte Islands. Then the eastward route out of Vancouver, through Harrison Hot Springs and Hope, turning northward at Manning Provincial Park, through Kamloops and Ashcroft. The Okanagan Valley at Osoyoos, then north along Lake Okanagan, east to the Rocky Mountains, turning south, then westward again along the southern rim of the province.

WHITE ROCK

RESTAURANTS

Giraffe ★★ This is that rarest of critters—a cozy, elegant neighborhood eatery. The three G's of California-style cooking (garlic, goat cheese, and grilling) are the tenets of Giraffe's tidy menu. A basket of crisp poppadums arrives promptly at the table, but nobody will rush you through luxurious appetizers of crunchy wonton skins filled with fresh crab and served with honey mustard, or a layered torta basilico of cream cheese, pesto, pine nuts, and sun-dried tomatoes. Lamb loin in a mustard herb sauce with caramelized onions is wonderful, as is a boneless chicken breast with mixed berries. Save room for the Graze, a dessert sampler that might include cheesecake, fruit, and berry sorbets, or a rich chocolate cake. And chef/owner Corinne Poole peeks out to ensure everyone is finishing what's on their plates. ■ *45 minutes from Vancouver, on Marine Dr across from the pier; (604) 538-6878; 15053 Marine Dr, White Rock; $$; full bar; MC, V; no checks; dinner every day.* &

THE SUNSHINE COAST

Inside the rain shadow of Vancouver Island, this aptly named area begins just west of Vancouver at Horseshoe Bay. The coast used to be—and still is—where Vancouverites vacation. But lately, as Vancouver expands in every direction, it is also where many of them are settling in an attempt to escape the madding crowds.

For the traveler, the crescent-shaped inlet of Howe Sound at Horseshoe Bay, flanked by green and snowy peaks, hints at the pleasures yet to come on the lower British Columbia coastline. Heading north, first on the ferry, then on Highway 101, you'll traverse lush wooded areas and rapidly growing small towns. Gibsons is home to a pioneer museum, but locals are eager to talk about more recent history: it was here that Canada's longest-running TV show, *The Beachcombers*, was filmed until 1990. Other highlights along Highway 101 include a local arts center in Sechelt and **Saltery Bay Provincial Park** near Lang Bay. Just north, the Earl's Cove-Saltery Bay ferry takes you to **Powell River**, the largest timber-and-fishing town on the coast. Highway 101 ends at the little fishing village of Lund. For ferry along the coast, call BC Ferries; (604) 921-7414.

HORSESHOE BAY

RESTAURANTS

Bay Moorings ★ This pretty pastel-colored view restaurant is a rarity in its genre: its food is generally a match for the scenery. The handsome proprietor, Gus Tsogas, serves consistently fine seafood (aromatic calamari, rich chowder) and Mediterranean specialties such as lasagne, plus pizza with a light spicy sauce and lots of topping choices. The preparations are careful, and the service is topnotch. They also have take-out available, but with such a dramatic ocean view, you won't want to leave. ■ *Across from the ferry terminal; (604) 921-8184; 6330 Bay St, Horseshoe Bay; $$; full bar; AE, MC, V; no checks; lunch, dinner every day.*

GIBSONS

RESTAURANTS

Ernie and Gwen's Drive-In This is a down-home picnic-table kind of place. If burgers and fries and "real milk" milk shakes are your thing, stop at Ernie and Gwen's after your trip on the

Langdale ferry. You can adorn your burger with multitudinous condiments. It all tastes real. (Off-season, it's not a sure bet that you'll find this place open.) ■ *In the middle of town; (604) 886-7813; Hwy 101, Gibsons; $; no alcohol; no credit cards; no checks; lunch, dinner every day.*

LODGINGS

Bonniebrook Lodge This simple yellow clapboard house on the water has been a guest house since it was built in 1922. Its combination of inn with campground and RV sites is not for everyone, but the new owners have been improving things recently. The four rooms (where there used to be six) are a bit more spacious and the views of the Strait of Georgia still lovely. If you prefer, there are a few campsites behind the lodge and on the water. Breakfast is served in Chez Phillipe restaurant (which is closed to non-guests off season). ■ *Outside Gibsons at Gower Point; (604) 886-2887; RR4, S10 C34, Gibsons, BC VON 1V0; $$; full bar; MC, V; no checks; breakfast for guests only, dinner every day in summer.*

ROBERTS CREEK

RESTAURANTS

The Creek House ★★ Here's a restaurant with continental cooking—by which we mean the continent of today, not the one enshrined in hotel cooking of 50 years ago. This restaurant is owned and operated by Yvan Citernesch (former owner and chef at Le Bistro in Vancouver). Situated in a house with a view of a tree-filled garden, the restaurant is decorated simply inside with white walls, light wood floors, flowers on the tables, and original contemporary art. On a given night, you may choose from 10 entrées that change seasonally: roasted duck, rack of lamb Provençal, or sautéed prawns. Fresh local seafood is usually offered too. Desserts include mango mousse. ■ *Beach Ave and Roberts Creek Rd; (604) 885-9321; 1041 Roberts Creek Rd, Roberts Creek; $$; full bar; MC, V; local checks only; dinner Wed–Sun.* &

LODGINGS

Country Cottage Bed and Breakfast ★ Philip and Loragene Gaulin's charming butterscotch farmhouse is surrounded by a cherry orchard and over 100 rosebushes. You stay in a one-bedroom cottage with an antique iron bed, a pull-out couch for kids, and a wood-burning stove. Or you can stay in the sunny Rose Room with your own bath and solarium and a view of the grazing sheep that Loragene raises for wool. In the morning, your uncommon, genial hostess will prepare you a breakfast from what's in season: garden-fresh asparagus crêpes with cheese and fresh fruit on our visit. Later on, join the Gaulins for

a full afternoon tea in the garden or the parlor. You're a pleasant five-minute stroll from a sandbar beach, and they have
bikes to borrow. The Gaulins' recent purchase of more land is
opening up all sorts of new opportunities here. No smokers, no
kids under 10. ■ *9 miles from the ferry off Hwy 101 at 1183
Roberts Creek Rd; (604) 885-7448; General Delivery, Roberts
Creek, BC V0N 2W0; $$; MC, V; checks OK.*

The Willows Inn ★ Just behind John and Donna Gibson's
lovely log house on a large wooded lot is this charming cedar
cottage. Newly planted vines ensure privacy in the cottage;
guests are invited onto the Gibsons' terrace for a late afternoon
glass of wine or pot of tea. The cottage has an L-shaped living-
room/bedroom area with cedar plank floors, skylights, a wood
stove, and rustic furnishings. Donna provides a muffin-and-fruit
breakfast. The beach (two blocks away) or the pretty country
road make good places for a morning stroll. No children under
12; no pets; no smoking inside. ■ *Beach Ave and Marlene Rd;
(604) 885-2452; 3440 Beach Ave, Roberts Creek, BC V0N
2W0; $$; no credit cards; local checks only.*

HALFMOON BAY

LODGINGS

Jolly Roger Inn ★ Changes of ownership don't seem to jostle
the Jolly Roger. This once seasonal resort (now open all year)
consists of a cluster of one- and two-bedroom dark brown town-
houses with fireplaces, kitchens, and decks; most have sweeping bay views. Boaters and fishermen find this spot enchanting:
good fishing, a first-rate marina, and pleasing accommodations.
■ *Hwy 101, 5 minutes from Halfmoon Bay at Secret Cove;
(604) 885-7184; Box 7 RR1, Halfmoon Bay, BC V0N 1Y0;
$$$; MC, V; checks OK; open weekends only Jan-Apr.* ᕱ

POWELL RIVER

The last town of any size on the Sunshine Coast gives a sense
of the industries that have predominated in this part of the
Northwest for more than a century: timber, fishing, and lime-
stone mining. The MacMillan Bloedel pulp-and-paper mill at
Powell River employs 1,900 people in the area and is one of only
two left on the coast (the other is at Port Mellon, near Gibsons).
Powell River is separated into the original mill town which sur-
rounds the plant; Westview, the newest residential area; down-
town and the ferry terminal; and Cranberry, surrounding Cran-
berry Lake.

The trail through **Willingdon Beach Park** is more of an
open-air forestry "museum" (old lumber industry equipment
placed throughout a wooded area above the beach). Across

from Powell River is **Texada Island**, the largest island in the Strait of Georgia and the Pacific Northwest's richest source of limestone.

Powell River also is western Canada's pre-eminent **scuba diving** center, and offers superb trout and salmon **sport fishing** as well. A ferry runs from Powell River to Little River near Comox on Vancouver Island; call (604) 485-2943 for schedule.

LODGINGS

Beach Gardens Resort Hotel ★ Sitting on a protected section of the Strait of Georgia, the Beach Gardens Resort is a mecca for scuba enthusiasts, who come for the near-tropical clarity of the water and the abundant marine life. Off-season, it's often filled with businesspeople who have come to see trade shows or attend training seminars and afterward to relax on the tennis courts or in the indoor swimming pool or fitness center. There's a marina to accommodate boaters, a decent dining room with reliable seafood entrées (try the warm seafood salad at dinner), and a locally popular neighborhood pub. The rooms are comfortable—nothing sensational, except the views of all that clear water. Less expensive cabins without views are popular with divers. Book far in advance for summer months. ■ *½ hour north of Saltery Bay ferry; (604) 485-6267; 7074 Westminster Ave, Powell River, BC V8A 1C5; $$; AE, DC, DIS, MC, V; checks OK. &*

▼

Whistler

▲

WHISTLER

Whistler

Whistler, nestled at the base of two mountains in British Columbia's Coast Range, has gained a reputation as a world-class ski destination—you'll hear plenty of Australian and European accents as well as Japanese and Cantonese spoken in the lift lines—and is recognized all over as a topflight place to ski. **Highway 99**, running north from Vancouver to Whistler, is an adventure in itself. The aptly named Sea to Sky Highway hugs fir-covered mountains that tumble sharply into island-filled Howe Sound. The grandeur and the views are breathtaking, and the curves of the road often demanding. The drive to Whistler from Vancouver takes approximately 2 hours, depending on road conditions and photo opportunities. As an alternative to driving, you can take buses or train (BC Rail) from Vancouver or fly via shuttle from Vancouver International Airport. For details, call Whistler Activity and Information Centre, (604) 932-2394.

The resort is actually made up of two main communities, **Whistler Village** and the **Blackcomb Benchlands**. Walking in the former is faintly reminiscent of wandering a European city, what with its sociable plazas, broad boulevards, and unexpected alleyways. A number of outlying clusters of condos and hotels (a little less atmospheric) add to the myriad of

I

accommodation options. Numerous shops tout everything from souvenir T-shirts to fur coats (one to check out is Gaauda Native Fine Art in Chateau Whistler, where knowledgeable gallery owner Gina Schubert, a Haida, will explain the art and jewelry in detail). The resort continues to grow in size as well as in reputation, and still more expansion is planned.

The **Whistler-Blackcomb** ski area is made up of two mountains and boasts some of the finest skiing in the Northwest (*Snow Country* voted it the top destination ski resort in North America in 1992). Blackcomb's newest high-speed quad, the Glacier Express, provides access to glacier skiing on *two* glaciers (a truly lunar experience), and a trip on three high-speed lifts (Wizard, Solar, then Seventh Heaven) can pop you onto the top of Blackcomb in just over half an hour. The two mountains now offer over 200 marked runs; the resort's Ski Esprit ski school offers individual and group lessons for adults. Kids age two and older can take a range of lessons or join Kids Kamp (at Blackcomb) or Ski Scamps (at Whistler); those 13 and up can join racing teams; (604) 932-3141 (Blackcomb), (604) 932-3434 (Whistler). Heli-skiing is available from several private outfits; 15 kilometers of cross-country ski trails begin just outside the Village and wind through the adjacent countryside (rentals available in the Village and Whistler Creek ski shops); 50 kilometers of groomed trails can be found 20 minutes to the south of Whistler; (604) 932-5128. Adventure activities include snow-boarding (rentals and lessons are available) and paragliding (lessons are available with or without skis), dogsledding, snowshoeing, snowmobiling, ice skating, and sleigh rides. There's even a restaurant *on* Blackcomb Mountain (Christine's on Rendezvous Ridge) for which reservations are a good idea. Call Whistler Activity and Information Centre, (604) 932-2394.

▼

Whistler

▲

Reservations far in advance are recommended at most of the lodgings in Whistler Village or the Blackcomb Benchlands. Call central reservations, (604) 932-4222; from Vancouver, dial (604) 685-3650; from the U.S. and Canada (except BC), (800) 944-7853. Many of the rooms in the area, as well as the condos, are owned by different management companies; the most high-profile management company (offering some of the resort's glitzier accommodations) is Whiski Jack Resorts, 4227 Village Stroll, (604) 932-6500, and Whistler Chalets, 4211 Sunshine Place, (604) 932-6699 or (800) 663-7711, can arrange for a group to stay in a deluxe log home. For a simpler, less expensive stay, ask about the hotels, pensions, and "budget" (a different meaning in Whistler) accommodations outside the village. Many lodgings now require 30 days' cancellation notice, with a 3-day minimum stay.

The resort has done a lot in recent years to develop **year-round recreation** and is definitely worth checking out even when there's no snow (though there is a relatively dead period in May). Besides summer skiing, hikers and bikers can take chair lifts to a network of alpine trails; mountain bikers can board their cycles onto Blackcomb's mountain express chairs to Seventh Heaven or take the gondola 3,800 feet above the Village for the ultimate mountain descent. Water sports abound at the five lakes in the valley surrounding the resort, all reachable from the resort by hiking, biking, or horseback riding along the Valley Trail. Summers are warm and ideal for fishing, swimming, board-sailing, canoeing, kayaking, sailing, or water-skiing. Golfers can try the scenic Arnold Palmer-designed Whistler Golf Club, recently rated as one of the best courses in the world by *Golf* magazine. There's a Robert Trent Jones Course at Chateau Whistler (open to the public), and a Jack Nicklaus-designed course slated for 1995 in the Emerald Lake area. Concerts are performed daily on the Village stage from June to September, and the resort hosts Labour Day, Canada's Birthday (July 1), and Octoberfest celebrations, as well as a country and blues festival (mid-June), a classical music fest (mid-August), and a jazz festival (mid-September).

RESTAURANTS

Rim Rock Cafe and Oyster Bar ★★★ This intimate cafe split into two rooms (smoking and non-, each with a stone fireplace) is housed in an unprepossessing hotel outside of the Village proper. Rolf Gunther's restaurant is remarkable proof that fresh seafood and wondrous cuisine are not anomalies in the mountains—presenting an exquisite and innovative menu. The freshest seafood appears on the specials sheet in all sorts of lovely incarnations, beginning (of course) with oysters. Even oyster purists slurp them down Rasputin-style (raw with vodka, crème fraîche, and caviar) or at least consider ordering Oysters from Hell (with a fiery salsa). And for the main event, you might have to chose between sea bass braised with scallops and porcini mushrooms and a melting, sweet-tart grilled ahi marinated in soy, sake, and mirrin. Great care is taken here with the rest of the menu as well. Salads and vegetables are never treated as a second thought. Service is top-drawer—knowledgeable without the airs, upbeat without being hip. White chocolate mousse pie with a dark chocolate crust and a raspberry sauce is an exercise in phenomenal excess. Reservations are a must in high season. ■ *Whistler Creek in the Highland Lodge; (604) 932-5565; 2101 Whistler Rd, Whistler; $$$; full bar; AE, MC, V; no checks; dinner every day.*

Val d'Isère ★★★ The younger sister to Vancouver's master of French cuisine, Le Crocodile, this restaurant escapes the usual twin banes of large-scale-resort dining—blandness and mediocrity—to maintain an intimate atmosphere and impeccably smooth, personable service. And best of all, the food is nearly as good as that at Le Crocodile—somewhat modified to accommodate the demands of its mountaintop location and its heavier flow of guests. We have no complaints about the place, especially their rendition of Le Crocodile's signature Onion Pie, a dense, smoky specialty. Reserve a window seat and try the medallions of salmon in basil butter sauce or the seasonal venison with morels in red wine—as tender as filet mignon. If you're not sure what to order, leave yourself in the capable hands of maîtres d'hôtel Michel Beranger or Hermel Rioux, or another waitperson. Desserts range from an extravagant chocolate orange torte capped with a white chocolate butterfly to a light, refreshing trio of blackcurrant, pineapple, and passion-fruit sorbets in a raspberry coulis. ■ *Upstairs in St. Andrews House; (604) 932-4666; 4433 Sundial Pl, Whistler; $$$; full bar; AE, DC, MC, V; no checks; dinner every day (Thurs-Tues off season).* &

Il Caminetto di Umberto ★★ The ubiquitous Umberto Menghi is at Whistler, too. Not surprisingly, this is a great place to go in the Village; few things can top fresh pasta and a bottle of red wine after a day of climbing up or schussing down mountains. This perennial favorite is also busy, the tables are too tightly packed together, and noise from the bar and cabaret interferes with table talk. Aim for the specials, such as the New York strip with mushroom sauce or the poached salmon with passion-fruit cream sauce. The less expensive Trattoria di Umberto in the Mountainside Lodge, (604) 932-5858, appeals to the more informal crowd for pasta and items from the rotisserie, and early samplings at Menghi's newest venture, Settebello, 2021 Karen Crescent, (604) 932-3000, suggest that things are up to par. ■ *Across from the Crystal Lodge; (604) 932-4442; Whistler; $$; full bar; AE, DC, MC, V; no checks; dinner every day.*

Sushi Village ★★ Sushi Village is a welcome reprieve from the boundless activity that Whistler offers. A civilized hush hovers over this refreshingly modest Japanese eatery, where the staff is knowledgeable and gracious. Consistently delicious sushi and sashimi plates are prepared by animated experts at the counter. It's straightforward and dependable, although the beer, as at most places in Whistler, is quite expensive. Reservations accepted only for parties of four or more. Tatami rooms available. ■ *2nd floor of the Westbrook Hotel; (604) 932-3330; Whistler; $$; full bar; AE, DC, MC, V; no checks; lunch, dinner Wed-Sun (weekends only, off season).*

Wildflower Cafe (Chateau Whistler Resort) ★★ Splashy Chateau Whistler's restaurant melds a big, formal space with folk-arty touches (a collection of birdhouses), and likewise combines a seriousness about food with personable service. Chef Bernard Casavant, formerly of the Four Seasons in Vancouver, uses local Northwest products—free-range chicken and lamb, wild salmon, and organic beef and produce—to create inspired dishes such as tartare of Pacific salmon with wonton wafers, or game bird stew of pheasant, duck, and quail with mushroom and rosemary dumplings. It's a tad dark at dinner, but in the shadows your taste buds will savor the seasonally oriented menu: wintry smoked duck and lentil soup with a touch of cilantro crème fraîche, or a warm spinach and mustard-green salad with an interesting texture counterpoint of fried glass noodles. The only problem you might encounter thus far is the *awkwardness* of some dishes: the aforementioned soup with bits of duck too large for the mouth and too difficult to cut with a spoon. All in all, however, the kitchen has an eye for lovely, distinctive ingredients and high standards. The Wildflower is a popular place for Sunday brunch, but it doesn't entirely escape the pitfalls of buffets—the meats can be dried and the coffee overbrewed. ■ *At the base of Blackcomb Mountain, in the Chateau Whistler; (604) 938-8000; 4599 Chateau Blvd, Whistler; $$$; full bar; AE, DC, MC, V; no checks; breakfast, lunch, dinner every day, brunch Sun.* ⅃

La Fiesta (Chateau Whistler Resort) ★ Festooned with piñatas and sombreros, the colorful La Fiesta is home to Whistler's finest fajita. The front page of the menu is a maze of appetizers and tapas ranging from marinated vegetables and garlic dip to oysters and caviar to enchiladas and burritos. Then take a breath and move on to the entrées. The most obvious choice is the fajitas, cooked and assembled by you on sizzling rocks brought to your table, certainly festive, especially in a group. There are also dishes that come to your table already cooked, such as fresh red snapper with a Spanish twist and a restrained (in flavor) paella. Chock-full of chorizo, prawns, chicken, mussels, and more, the paella easily serves two, particularly if those two have initiated their meal with some tapas. Unfortunately, saving room for dessert is next to impossible, except for that mango sorbet. ■ *On the 1st floor of the Chateau Whistler; (604) 938-2040; 4599 Chateau Blvd, Whistler; $$; full bar; AE, DC, DIS, MC, V; checks OK; dinner every day.*

LODGINGS

Chateau Whistler Resort ★★★ This is the place to see and be seen on Whistler—where else in Whistler will a valet park your ski gear? This Paul Bunyan-sized country mansion has 343 rooms (would Canadian Pacific construct anything small?). The lobby, appropriately termed the Great Hall, sets you amid a floor of giant slate slabs covered with oversize hooked rugs, walls decorated with huge hand-painted stencils of maple leaves, two mammoth limestone fireplaces, and a 40-foot-high beamed ceiling. The funky collection of folk-art birdhouses and weathered antique furnishings make the place comfortable and even cozy, especially in the Mallard Bar. The health spa is especially swank: a heated pool that flows both indoors and out, allowing swimmers to splash away under the chair lifts or soak in the Jacuzzi under the stars. Other services include a multilingual staff, baby-sitting, room service, and a dozen or so shops. The rooms themselves are a bit disappointing (if only because your expectations are set so high in the grand entrance); non-suite rooms are surprisingly small and undistinguished. Do it right and ask for a "ski-view" room. The casual, spirited La Fiesta makes for pleasant après-ski socializing, and the main dining event is the inventive Wildflower Cafe (see reviews for both in this section). ■ *At the base of Blackcomb Mountain; (604) 938-8000, or toll-free (800) 441-1414; 4599 Chateau Blvd, Whistler, BC V0N 1B0; $$$; full bar; AE, DC, DIS, MC, V; checks OK; breakfast, lunch, dinner every day, brunch Sun.* &

Brew Creek Lodge ★★ A quiet, welcome retreat a few kilometers south of Whistler. The lodge and two guest houses are decorated in a rustic style with post-and-beam timber frames, a huge stone fireplace, and nostalgic touches of Westernalia here and there. The lodge rooms with sumptuous beds covered with folksy spreads are spacious (room 1 is best, room 6 is over the kitchen). Still, Brew Creek is best suited for groups—a wedding party, a family reunion, or a corporate retreat—who reserve the entire place or at least a portion of it. Our favorite is the guest house (sleeps 12) with a tiny treehouse for lovers. The Brew House reminds one of something from Tolkien's *The Hobbit*. A separate conference room is built right over the trout-filled Brew Creek. Food is prepared with advance notice (and they're often catering dinner here); the breakfasts we've sampled have been satisfying, if a tad ordinary. Affable hosts Peter and Susan Vera are hard at work keeping the lodge a comfortable, attractive place to stay, and Cinders the cat is hard at work finding a warm lap in which to lie. ■ *Off Highway 99 just before Brandywine Park, south of Whistler Village; (604) 932-7210; 1 Brew Creek Rd, Whistler, BC V0N 1B1; $$$; MC, V; checks OK.*

Le Chamois ★★ The petite six-story hotel, though somewhat dwarfed by its gargantuan neighbor, the Chateau Whistler, has a sleek, refined air—much more inviting than most look-alike condos. Rooms are larger and more aesthetically pleasing than others we've seen. Light, airy, and clean, they feature simple European-style furnishings and smart color schemes against pine-wood furnishings. Single bedrooms are built to accommodate four people; each includes a living area with either a fold-out sofa bed or a Murphy bed (and every room has a view, though that of the mountain costs more). Studio rooms (with a Jacuzzi facing the mountain) are also available. During high season the hotel requires a minimum stay of five days. Unlike the other hotels we list, Le Chamois is a condo/hotel, meaning that all rooms are privately owned—so some have special touches. One of the three-bedroom corner suites is furnished with a piano. The compact kitchens stock all the utensils you need for quick meals: microwave, refrigerator, and all utensils, but no ovens. Downstairs, La Rua specializes in Mediterranean cuisine with a Spanish flair. There is also a small conference area, a very small fitness room with an outdoor pool, and a Jacuzzi. Children 12 and under stay free of charge. ▪ *At the base of Blackcomb Mountain at 4557 Blackcomb Way; (604) 932-8700; PO Box 1044, Whistler, BC V0N 1B0; $$$; AE, DC, MC, V; no checks.* &

Delta Mountain Inn ★ It may not be as grand as Chateau Whistler nor as chic as Le Chamois, but the Delta Mountain Inn, one of the oldest and largest hotels in the resort, offers nearly 300 rooms, restaurant and bar, exercise room, swimming pool, and dome-covered year-round tennis courts. It's a good spot for hosting business meetings, with a conference area that holds 250. The rooms are plain (though a nice teal color) and crowded with furniture; the better ones offer kitchen, fireplace, balcony, Jacuzzi, minibar, and view of the mountains; a snazzy restaurant, Evergreens, has some innovative items on its menu. Delta sits just 50 yards from Whistler's base lift. Dogs allowed. ▪ *Whistler Village at 4050 Whistler Way; (604) 932-1982, toll-free (800) 268-1133; PO Box 550, Whistler, BC V0N 1B0; $$$; AE, DC, MC, V; checks OK.*

Edelweiss Pension Inn ★ Regardless of how brisk, friendly, and accommodating the hosts are, you'll probably be awakened by the guests, who clomp about in their ski boots come morning. Still, Ursula and Jacques Morel's nonsmoking Bavarian-style guest house, run in a European fashion, is one of our favorites of its kind (there are many around Whistler). The eight rooms are simple and spotlessly clean, with down comforters and private baths. Extras include the shared sauna, Jacuzzi, and massage on request. Jacques (a former competitive skier) and Ursula cook ample breakfasts with an international flair (Norwegian style, for example, with eggs and British Columbia salmon) in their sunny breakfast room. Ask at least eight hours in advance, and your hosts will welcome you back from a day on the slopes or hiking trail with a raclette—a rich fonduelike treat made by wrapping melted cheese over ham, baby potatoes, bread, or vegetables—served with French or German wine and espresso drinks. If your legs are strong, Edelweiss is within walking distance of the Village; elsewise, hop the free bus (it's easier than parking in the Village). ▪ *1 mile north of Whistler Village in White Gold Estates at 7162 Nancy Greene Dr; (604) 932-3641; PO Box 850, Whistler, BC V0N 1B0; $$; AE, MC, V; checks OK.*

Haus Heidi ★ A short drive from Whistler Village, this eight-room pension is a refreshing change from the resort scene at the base of the mountain. Hosts Trudy and Jim Gruetzke will see that your stay is comfortable—a touch often lacking at the large resorts. The seven rooms have private baths, and guests have access to a Jacuzzi with a view of the mountains. One awakens to a marvelous breakfast of fruit, croissants, and omelets. ■ *Whistler Way at 7115 Nesters Rd; (604) 932-3113; PO Box 354, Whistler, BC V0N 1B0; $$; MC, V; no checks.*

Timberline Lodge ★ The enormous moose head that greets you in the lobby tells you this place has more of a sense of humor than the other big-name hotels. It's the kind of spot where you feel at home clomping into the lobby to warm your toes by the enormous fireplace. Timberline's 42 rooms are simple and rustic, with four-poster beds of rough-hewn wood—a nice change from the seemingly relentless mauve-and-taupe condo theme. Some rooms have fireplaces and others have balconies. A heated pool and Jacuzzi are also available. Timberline Lodge also boasts one of the hoppingest nightspots around; be sure to request a room away from Bill's if you plan to turn in early. ■ *Adjacent to Conference Center in Whistler Village at 4122 Village Green; (604) 932-5211 or toll-free (800) 663-5474; PO Box 996, Whistler, BC V0N 1B0; $$$; AE, MC, V; no checks.* &

LILLOOET

Two hours north of Whistler on a gravel road, you'll happen upon Lillooet—mile zero of the Cariboo Gold Rush Trail. The best thing about Lillooet is getting there. The **BC Rail** line between Lillooet and Vancouver is a vital link to the outside world for the loggers, miners, and farmers who live in remote areas of the Coastal Range. It's also one of the most scenic stretches in British Columbia, along pretty Howe Sound and into the jagged mountains. The route links Vancouver with Whistler, Lillooet, and Prince George; call BC Rail at (604) 984-5246.

FRASER RIVER

The **Fraser** and the **Thompson** rivers descend from Lillooet and Ashcroft, respectively, to converge in Lytton where they squeeze through the narrow walls of the 85-kilometer **Fraser River Canyon**. You can get a good sense of British Columbia's mightiest rivers from the many roadside pullouts. It's far more fun to pick a hot summer day, call a raft company, and buy some wet thrills. The Thompson River (Spences Bridge to Lytton) throws the most whitewater rapids. The biggest fleet on the river is Kumsheen Raft Adventures Ltd. (Main Street, Lytton; (604) 455-2296). Other companies include: Fraser River Raft Expeditions (PO Box 10, Yale, BC V0K 2S0; (604) 863-2336) and the River Rogues in Spences Bridge; (604) 452-2252.

Downriver the popular **Hell's Gate Airtram** (Boston Bar; (604) 867-9277) takes you across the boiling waters of the Fraser at the narrowest part of the gorge (from May to mid-October). The river turns sharply west and calms at **Hope**, 140 kilometers east of Vancouver.

GOLD BRIDGE

LODGINGS

Tyax Mountain Lake Resort ★ In the wilderness of the Chilcotin Range about a hundred miles north of Vancouver, floatplanes are seen dropping incoming guests off at Tyaughton Lake's dock and taking fishermen up to Trophy Lakes; a helicopter out back lifts thrill-seekers to enjoy heli-*anything* (heliskiing, heli-hiking, and even heli-fossilhunting). But it's not all a high-tech adventure: you can be just as happy canoeing, gold panning, ice skating, horseback riding. There are 28 suites (with beamed ceilings, balconies, and down-filled quilts) in the freshly hewn spruce log lodge. We prefer one of the large chalets (each with kitchen, loft, and a balcony overlooking Tyaughton Lake and the mountains)—especially for longer stays. Unless you're in a chalet, you take all your meals in the dining room, where the perfunctory food is overpriced. Other amenities include a sauna, a large Jacuzzi in the front lawn, a game room with a pingpong table, aerobics classes, and workout rooms. The only thing an active person might run out of in this paradise is energy (or money). ■ *If you're without a floatplane, take the train from Vancouver to Lillooet, the resort will pick you up; (604) 238-2221; General Delivery, Gold Bridge, BC V0K 1P0; $$$; AE, MC, V; checks OK.*

70 MILE HOUSE

LODGINGS

Flying U Guest Ranch ★ It's a working ranch, ideal for families who like to ride horses on their own. There are 25,000 acres to explore, and cattle to round up if you wish. Back at the lodge, you can stay in log cabins, canoe on the nearby lake, and you'll dine at the over-140-years-old main building. Movies, bonfires, hayrides, or square dancing often follow the meal. A saloon features a full bar and snacks. Rates are $100 per day or $550 per week per adult, all-inclusive (three meals a day, all you can chow). ■ *20 kilometers east of 70 Mile House on N Greenlake Rd; (604) 456-7717; Box 69, 70 Mile House, BC V0K 2K0; $$; AE, MC, V; checks OK.*

The facts in this book were correct at press time, but places close, chefs depart, hours change. It's best to call ahead.

100 MILE HOUSE

LODGINGS

  Best Western 108 Resort ★ At what seems like the edge of civilization (8 miles north of 100 Mile House, hence its name), a full-scale resort covers thousands of acres of rangeland. Recently purchased by Best Western, the guest rooms run between $90 and $115 depending on the season. There is horseback riding, a large pool, five tennis courts, and a topflight 18-hole golf course. In winter, the cross-country skiing is some of the best in the Northwest, with over 200 kilometers of well-maintained trails. The restaurant has a fine view of the golf course and two lakes, and a cheerful atmosphere, but the menu is limited to the expected steaks and seafood. ▪ *Hwy 97, 13 kilometers north of 100 Mile House; (604) 791-5211; C2 108 Mile Ranch, BC V0K 2V0; $$; AE, DC, DIS, MC, V; no checks.*

BARKERVILLE

Billy Barker found lots of gold here in 1862, whereupon the town became the largest city north of San Francisco; then it became a ghost town, and now it's a place revived for the tourist trade. It's not bad, really: restored old buildings and a general store full of 5-cent jawbreakers and lots of retro '60s (that's 1860s) goods. The whole place shuts down after the summer season (May to September).

Canoe trips. Six lakes form an amazingly regular rectangle in **Bowron Lake Park**, a scenic and challenging setting for a 120-kilometer canoe trip (with a number of portages in between). Plan on spending a week to 10 days. For outfitting, a couple of lodges offer canoe, paddle, and lifebelt rentals. Becker's Lodge also has campsites, cabins, and a dining room; contact the lodge at mobile phone N698 552, Wells YP, in winter (604) 492-2390; PO Box 129, Wells, BC V0K 2R0.

RESTAURANTS

Wake Up Jake's There's nothing about this old-time saloon that isn't 1870s authentic: they don't serve french fries (which hadn't been invented yet); they don't use processed anything. Instead, it's all real: soups, caribou stew, sourdough-bread sandwiches, potpies, steaks, flaky fruit pies, and even the specials—pheasant or perhaps cheese-and-onion pie—amid saloon decor. ▪ *In center of town; (604) 994-3259; Barkerville; $; beer and wine; MC, V; no checks; breakfast, lunch, dinner every day (May-Sept).*

Prices in the British Columbia chapter are given in Canadian dollars; distances are quoted in kilometers whenever possible.

PRINCE GEORGE

Prince George is the hub of north and central BC, and the jump-off point for brave souls heading up the Alaska Highway. The city sits between two mountain ranges on a dry plateau. Forestry is the main industry here, and loads of logging roads take hunters and fishermen back into remote and bountiful spots. The **Stellako River**, west of Prince George near Fraser Lake, is famous for its record trout. For recreational types, the **Cottonwood Island Nature Park**, along the Nechako River, has an extensive trail system suitable for hiking in the summer and cross-country skiing in the winter. Adjacent to the park is the **Prince George Railway Museum**. Two city galleries are of interest: **Prince George Art Gallery** features regional and national exhibits monthly; **Native Art Gallery** exhibits local native art and crafts.

Railroads. BC Rail will roll you through 462 miles of some of the most beautiful scenery in BC, from Vancouver to Prince George via Rail Canada in 13 hours; (604) 984-5246. Transfer to the passenger run to Prince Rupert, where ferries to the Queen Charlotte Islands, Vancouver Island, and Alaska depart regularly: (604) 669-1211 for ferries within BC; toll-free (800) 642-0066 for Alaska Marine Highway information.

RESTAURANTS

The Achillion Authentic Greek lunches and dinners can be found at Kostas Iliopulos' spot on Dominion Street. The combination plate is a good choice for two: you get pan-fried shrimp, beef shish kabobs, roast leg of lamb, potatoes, rice, and Greek salad or soup, all for $33. ■ *4th and Dominion; (604) 564-1166; 422 Dominion St, Prince George; $; full bar; AE, MC, V; local checks OK; lunch Mon-Sat, dinner every day.*

PRINCE RUPERT

Prince Rupert began as a dream. Founder Charles Melville Hays saw this island as the perfect terminus for rail as well as sea travel and trade. Unfortunately, on a trip back from Europe, where he was rustling up money to help finance his vision, he met with an untimely death aboard the *Titanic*. Seventy-five years later, a number of local folks rekindled Hays' dream. By the mid '80s Prince Rupert had two major export terminals and a booming economy. With this new-found prosperity have come culture and tourism. The **Museum of Northern British Columbia** has a fine collection of Northwest Coast Indian art: First Avenue E and McBride, (604) 624-3207.

Ferries. Prince Rupert is called the gateway to the north, but it's also a place where ferries can take you west (to the remote Queen Charlotte Islands—see listing) or south (through the Inside Passage to Vancouver Island—see Port Hardy). The Alaska ferry winds north through the panhandle to Skagway.

RESTAURANTS

Smile's Seafood Cafe ★ Since 1922, Smile's Cafe has been tucked unobtrusively among the fish-processing plants beside the railroad. Favorites still include the fresh Dungeness crab, halibut, and black cod; the french fries are a perfect nongreasy, brown-skinned complement to the fish. The service is small-town friendly. ■ *Follow 3rd Ave into George Hills Way; (604) 624-3072; 131 George Hills Way, Prince Rupert; $$; full bar; MC, V; no checks; breakfast, lunch, dinner every day.*

QUEEN CHARLOTTE ISLANDS

A microcosm of the British Columbia coast, the Galapagos of the Northwest, these sparsely populated, beautiful islands (150 in all) offer an escape to a rough-edged (and often rainy) paradise. There are countless beaches, streams, fishing holes, coves, and abandoned Indian villages to explore. Many unique subspecies of flora and fauna share these islands with the 6,000 residents.

The Haida Indians carve argillite—a rare black rock found only on the islands—into Northwest figurines.

Pacific Synergies offers sailing excursions in the area; (604) 932-3107. Or explore the island via kayak with the help of **Ecosummer**; (604) 669-7741.

Transportation. There are only 75 miles of paved roads in the Queen Charlotte Islands. Take the 6-to-8-hour ferry from Prince Rupert, fly in to the small airstrip on Moresby Island, or take a seaplane. Food and lodging are available, mainly on Graham Island, but most people who come camp. You can get tourist information through the local Chamber of Commerce, (604) 557-4600, or call Kallahin Travel Services (out of Queen Charlotte City) for island-related excursions, from a bus-tour package to a pick-up for you and your kayak; (604) 559-8455.

QUEEN CHARLOTTE ISLANDS: MASSET

LODGINGS

Copper Beech House ★★ The garden's a bit tangled, and so are all the memorabilia and rare collectibles inside this turn-of-the-century home. But come spring the garden smells wonderful and come morning so does breakfast. David Philips cans his summer fruits for year-round breakfasts and smokes his own seafood. Upstairs there are three guest rooms decorated with mission oak furniture: one has its own living room. But most would prefer to spend time at Philips' table (dinner for guests upon request). For on an island where fresh food is impossible to obtain, Mr. Philips' bounty might include fresh peaches from his tree, halibut from the local fishermen, and tomatoes from the garden. The unusual soup (a buttery peach and tomato) proves Philips is not limited, but challenged, by local ingredients. His culinary improvisations and unparalleled hospitality would be appreciated anywhere. In the Queen Charlottes, they're a godsend. ■ *Right by the fishing boat docks at Delkatlah and Collison; (604) 626-5441; 1590 Delkatlah, Masset, BC V0T 1M0; $; no credit cards; checks OK.*

QUEEN CHARLOTTE ISLANDS: QUEEN CHARLOTTE CITY

LODGINGS

Spruce Point Lodge What started as just a lawn and a shower offered to the occasional kayaker who needed a place to stay is now a cedar-clad building wrapped with a balcony on Skidegate Inlet that attracts families and couples alike—and still, most often, kayakers. There are seven clean rooms—each with a full bath, cable TV, and locally made pine furnishings. The reasonable price includes a continental breakfast and an occasional impromptu seafood barbecue. Mary Kellie and Nancy Hett's lawn is not available anymore, but kayakers and adventurers on a budget will appreciate the hostel rooms. There's use of the kitchen and laundry. Kayaks for rent. Pets and kids welcome. ■ *5.6 km west of ferry, left after Chevron station, then second left, at 609 6th Ave; (604) 559-8234; PO Box 735, Queen Charlotte City, BC V0T 1S0; $; MC, V; checks OK.*

▼

Chilliwack

▲

FORT LANGLEY

RESTAURANTS

Bedford House ★ A lovely place with a picturesque view of the Fraser River, this restored 1904 house is furnished with English antiques and has a pleasant, countrified elegance. The menu is rich with fancy continental cuisine: roast duckling with a fruit sauce, broiled salmon with hollandaise, or scallops and prawns served on puff pastry with a creamy champagne sauce. ■ *On the bank of the Fraser River in downtown Fort Langley; (604) 888-2333; 9272 Glover Rd, Fort Langley; $$; full bar; AE, MC, V; no checks; dinner every day, brunch Sun.*

CHILLIWACK

The name's not the only thing that's curious about this prosperous farming and dairy center: speakers set along the downtown portal blare easy-listening music, and antique cars seem plentiful. Local landmarks include an offbeat military museum at the **Canadian Forces Base**, open Sundays all year, midweek during the summer: (604) 858-1011; **Minter Gardens**, 10 large theme gardens, 14 kilometers east at the Highway 9 junction: (604) 794-7191; and **Bridal Falls Provincial Park**, 15 kilometers east on Highway 1.

RESTAURANTS

La Mansione Ristorante ★ There's a menu of mixed delights in this handsome mock-Tudor mansion with leaded-glass windows and a warm fireplace for winter evenings. (Beware the air conditioner in summer; sitting near it can easily ruin the meal.) We sampled a delicious seafood chowder, brimming with shrimp, crab, and clams. The veal pan-fried in butter, lemon juice, white wine, and capers was good and tangy. The dinner menu offers a wide variety of seafood dishes and pastas; other specialties include chateaubriand, rack of lamb, and veal scalloppine Sergio (the legacy of the former owner). This is a good place to sample wines by the glass; new owner Peter Graham carries an extensive selection. New banquet facilities for 45 are found on the second floor. ▪ *Near Williams St at Yale; (604) 792-8910; 46290 Yale Rd E, Chilliwack; $$; full bar; AE, DC, MC, V; no checks; lunch Mon-Fri, dinner every day.*

The New Yorker Steak House ★ This popular steak house in the center of town serves up enormous portions and consistently good quality. Charcoal-broiled Alberta grain-fed beefsteaks come in four different cuts and seven sizes, the most expensive being $13. Chilliwack residents swear by the mushrooms Neptune (baked with cream cheese, shrimp, and crabmeat) and the hefty seafood platter. For a lighter lunch, order the true Greek salad. The decor is BC casual, with the usual fringed cloth lampshades. ▪ *Near Ontario at Yale; (604) 795-7714; 45948 Yale Rd W, Chilliwack; $; full bar; AE, MC, V; no checks; lunch, dinner every day.* &

HARRISON HOT SPRINGS

Situated at the southern end of Harrison Lake, the town is a small, quiet row of low buildings facing the sandy beach and lagoon. The hot springs themselves are in a strangely enclosed temple with sulfur steam billowing out and an occasional Coke can strewn along the bottom of the pool. But don't be dismayed; the public soaking pool (which has cooled hot spring water pumped into it) is large and wonderfully warm (100 degrees average). In addition, there are sailboards and bikes to rent, hiking trails nearby, helicopters to ride, and a pub or two. In winter, skiers use Harrison as their spa after a day on the slopes at Hemlock Valley (a 40-minute drive).

RESTAURANTS

Black Forest ★ Bavarian food seems a staple in BC, and here's an authentic restaurant serving more than just schnitzels. The decor in this family place is perfect if you're a fan of goulash soup, schnitzel, and beef rouladen—sirloin stuffed with onions, pickles, mustard, and bacon, braised in red wine, and served with red cabbage and spaetzle. The place is popular, so stop by on your evening stroll and make a reservation. ■ *1 block west of Hwy 9 at Esplanade; (604) 796-9343; 180 Esplanade Ave, Harrison Hot Springs; $$; full bar; AE, MC, V; checks OK; dinner every day.* &

LODGINGS

The Harrison Hotel Located at the southern shore of long and beautiful Harrison Lake, this legendary hotel is really a better place to view than to visit. The first hotel was built here in 1885 to take advantage of the hot springs; it burned down, and the present "old" building dates back to 1926. Since then, the additions have changed the hotel into a sprawling mishmash of unrelated architecture. Grounds are quite lovely and spacious, with tennis courts and exercise circuit, but the best part about the place is definitely the hot spring water: two indoor pools (103 and 90 degrees) and one outdoor (90 degrees)—open only to hotel guests. A scenic golf course is 3 kilometers away. Staying here is expensive (there are extra charges for almost everything). Most of the rooms in the old wing still have 1950s decor. And since the hotel won't guarantee lake views, a safer bet is to book a room in the newer tower (on the east side). Our advice is to use the place for a short stay, arrive in time to enjoy the excellent pools and a poolside drink and then promenade down the street to eat. ■ *West end of Esplanade; (604) 796-2244; 100 Esplanade Ave, Harrison Hot Springs, BC V0M 1K0; $$$; AE, DC, DIS, MC, V; checks OK.* &

MANNING PARK

LODGINGS

Manning Park Motel Situated within the boundaries of this pretty provincial park, the simple lodge gives you easy access to both gentle and arduous hiking trails. With a short drive, you can be paddling a rented canoe on Lightning Lake or riding a horse through the surrounding country. Besides the 41 motel rooms, the low-key resort includes a restaurant, a coffee shop, cabins, and triplexes—all in the same plain, functional style. If you have 39 friends, however, book the Last Resort a few yards down the highway, a real old-fashioned '40s charmer that sleeps 40. In winter (two-day minimum then) the park turns into cross-country and downhill ski heaven: Gibsons Ski Area is just outside the back door. ■ *Just off Hwy 3 in Manning Provincial Park; (604) 840-8822; Manning Park, BC V0X 1R0; $$; MC, V; no checks.*

PRINCETON

RESTAURANTS

The Apple Tree Restaurant ★★ The big crabapple tree across from the Esso station marks the site of Douglas and Mary Rebagliati's excellent small restaurant in a house filled with greenery and fussy wallpaper. Expect such appetizers as escargots cooked in mushroom caps (an Okanagan favorite) and good, hearty, homemade soups (such as Slovak sausage and sauerkraut); hope for the deceptively simple oregano chicken, marinated in olive oil and herbs and broiled. Desserts receive just as much attention (the reputation of the Louisiana mud pie has spread to Vancouver). The patio in the back is pleasant come summer. Have an early supper here and make Osoyoos by nightfall. ■ *Vermilion at Dixie Lee; (604) 295-7745; 255 Vermilion Ave, Princeton; $; full bar; MC, V; local checks only; lunch Tues-Fri (Tues-Sat July-Sept), dinner Tues-Sun.* ♿

QUILCHENA

LODGINGS

Quilchena Hotel ★★ Remote Quilchena Hotel captures the ambience of southwestern BC's cattle country, and it attracts a motley assortment: moneyed urbanites in search of relaxation; cattle barons who come to buy livestock; gentlemanly seniors in search of the perfect golf course; and cowboys, Canada style (French accents belie their Texan appearance). It's a delightful stew, and meant to be that way: there are no phones or TVs in the 16 rooms; guests share bathrooms and dine together in the parlor. The rooms are decorated with the original iron bedposts and printed wallpaper. It's not elegant, but there's a worn comfort about the place, which was built in 1908 as a hotel for cattle ranchers traveling between Merritt and Kamloops. Guests often gather around the parlor's piano for an impromptu recital. Daytime finds you riding horses, playing tennis, golfing on the adjacent course, or searching the nearby fossil beds. For extended stays there's a three-bedroom ranch house on the grounds. There is lots of beef on the restaurant's menu; the old saloon and features appetizers and local wines. ■ *Take the 2nd Merritt exit off the Coquihalla Hwy; (604) 378-2611; Hwy 5A, Quilchena, BC V0E 2R0; $$; MC, V; checks OK (mid-April–mid-Oct only).*

MERRITT

LODGINGS

Corbett Lake Country Inn ★ French-trained owner and chef Peter McVey came originally from England to British Columbia on a fishing trip—and it must have been good. McVey's country inn caters to lovers of fly-fishing in the summer and cross-country skiers in the winter. There are three nondescript rooms in the lodge, but most guests choose to stay in one of the 10 simple cabins, each with its own kitchen. The three duplexes all have fireplaces and separate bedroom/living rooms. Aside from the outdoor activities, the food's the thing here. Dinner (by reservation only, guests and non-guests) is something different every night. McVey creates wonderful four-course evenings starting with soup (perhaps fresh mushroom), a salad (caesar, hot German, or cucumber), and continuing to an entrée which could be anything from loin of pork with Dijon mustard to beef Wellington with Yorkshire pudding. Corbett Lake holds plenty of fish, but an extra fee gains you the privilege of angling in two private lakes stocked by McVey himself. ▪ *16 kilometers south of Merritt on Hwy 5A; (604) 378-4334; Box 327, Merritt, BC V0K 2B0; no credit cards; checks OK; breakfast, lunch, dinner every day (closed Nov and March-May).*

KAMLOOPS

RESTAURANTS

Minos ★ Minos is a family-owned operation, with owner/chef Mike Frangiadakis' family living overhead. Wooden furniture and lively colored tablecloths help create a warm atmosphere. Service is exceptionally friendly, prompt, and well informed. We enjoy the chef's special, Mike's mezethes: bite-size pieces of chicken, pan-fried with mushrooms, onion, and wine, served with pita bread and tzatziki. Also good are the various souvlaki of lamb, chicken, and seafood. Minos' desserts are quite tasty; try a piece of honey-sweet baklava with a strong cup of Greek coffee. ▪ *1 kilometer north of Overlander Bridge; (604) 376-2010; 262 Tranquille Rd, Kamloops; $; beer and wine; AE, MC, V; no checks; lunch, dinner Mon-Sat.* ♿

LODGINGS

20 YEARS

Lac Le Jeune Resort ★ Well-equipped and pleasant, this lodge puts you right on the lake for fishing and at the edge of the wilderness for hiking. You can stay in the lodge, in a self-sufficient cabin (perfect for families), or in a chalet. The resort includes an indoor whirlpool and sauna, meeting rooms for up to 200, and a restaurant featuring breakfast, lunch, and an evening buffet. Adjacent is a downhill ski area; over 100 kilometers of cross-country skiing trails wind through the property. Boats and canoes are available for rent (the famous Kamloops trout are great to catch—and eat). Large tour groups tend to book the place en masse during the summer months, so reserve early, or take a chance on a last-minute cancellation. ▪ *Off Coquihalla Hwy, Lac Le Jeune, exit 29 km southwest of*

*Kamloops; (604) 372-2722; c/o 650 Victoria St, Kamloops,
BC V2C 2B4; $$; full bar; AE, DC, MC, V; checks OK; break-
fast, lunch, dinner every day.*

ASHCROFT

RESTAURANTS

Ashcroft Manor Teahouse ★ A beautiful, airy roadside tea-
room sits just behind the original Ashcroft Manor, which was
built in 1862 to accommodate travelers on their way to and from
the gold fields. For breakfast, new owners Bill and Stephanie
Agnew offer a fresh fruit platter with hot scones, eggs any way
you want, or huge fresh cinnamon rolls (a meal in themselves).
Lunch fare includes seafoods, salads, stir-fries, and fresh pasta
dishes; dinners range from T-bone steaks to red snapper poached
in orange sauce. Outdoor seating in summer under the flower-
ing trees. ■ *10 kilometers south of Cache Creek on Trans-Canada
Hwy; (604) 453-9983; Ashcroft; $; full bar; MC, V; local checks
only; breakfast, lunch, dinner every day (open March-Jan).* &

LODGINGS

Sundance Ranch ★★ Here's a dude ranch set in high plateau
country, with the Thompson River cutting a deep gorge just to
the west. Low-lying buildings of dark-stained wood contain
handsome pine-paneled rooms and public rooms. Children can
stay in their own wing or with their parents. The spare 20-per-
son family lodge is temporarily closed for repairs. The pool is
quite grand, and they've added a new tennis court, but the real
attraction is the corral, where 100 good horses await you for the
two daily rides, morning and late afternoon. It can get very hot
here during the day, but if the sun is not too brutal, the rides
will be simply wonderful. Over a dozen buffalo live in the adja-
cent fields. During the evening, the excellent meals are often
served on the barbecue patio, and rustic rooms set the scene
for drinks, parties, and games. You'll sleep well, breathing the
cool, sage-scented air. ■ *8 kilometers south of Ashcroft off High-
land Valley Rd; (604) 453-2422; Box 489, Ashcroft, BC V0K
1A0; $$; MC, V; checks OK.*

THE OKANAGAN VALLEY

The Canadian Okanagans, from Osoyoos at the border to Vernon to the north, are a summer playground. The valley is laden
with orchards, making it especially appealing in spring when
the fruit trees are in full bloom. The best time to pick up some
of the valley's bounty is mid-August through early September;
however, beginning as early as late June, the fruit starts ripening:
cherries (late June to mid-July), peaches (mid-July through September), pears (August through September), apricots (mid-July

through mid-August), plums (September), apples (August through October), and grapes (September through mid-October).

Nevertheless, **winemaking** is the hot ticket in the Okanagan. British Columbians have long taken inordinate pride in their wines—even when those mostly came from a few largish factories like Kelowna's **Calona**, on Richter Street, (604) 762-9144, and Penticton's **Cartier**, on Main Street, (604) 492-0621. However, ever since British Columbia authorized estate and smaller farmgate wineries, many excellent small wineries have popped up. Some of the best estate offerings come out of **Gray Monk**, 8 kilometers west of Winfield off Highway 97, (604) 766-3168; **Cedar Creek**, 14 kilometers south of Kelowna in the Mission, (604) 764-8866; **Sumac Ridge**, off Highway 97, just north of Summerland, (604) 494-0451; and **Hainle Vineyards** in Peachland, (604) 767-2525. A couple of farmgate vineyards to keep an eye on are **Quail's Gate Vineyards** in Westbank, (604) 769-4451, and **Wild Goose Vineyards** just south of Okanagan Falls, (604) 497-8919. Other notable wineries to visit: **Mission Hill**, south of Kelowna in Westbank off Boucherie Road, (604) 768-5125; **Gehringer Brothers**, 4 kilometers south of Oliver off Highway 97 on Road 8, (604) 498-3537; **Brights Wines**, between Oliver and Vaseaux Lake on Highway 97, (604) 498-4981; **Divino**, (604) 498-2784, and **Okanagan Vineyards**, (604) 498-6663, both 5 kilometers south of Oliver off Highway 97. Most offer tastings and seasonal tours; call ahead for times and dates.

Skiing is still the biggest hook the Okanagan swings. The local climate is a powdery medium between the chill of the Rockies and the slush of the Coast Range, and the slopes are distributed along the valley. **Silver Star**, east of Vernon, has full resort facilities; information: (604) 542-0224. **Last Mountain** is the nearest stop from Kelowna for day schussing, (604) 768-5189, but **Big White**, (604) 765-3101, to the east has many more runs (44, up to 1,850 vertical feet), full facilities, and even cross-country trails, and claims the greatest altitude of all the ski areas in the province. **Apex Alpine**, Penticton's full-facility resort known for its challenging terrain, has added a number of "family" runs to complement its harder stuff; (604) 292-8222. Southwest of Penticton on Highway 3A, the **Twin Lakes Golf Club** doubles as a cross-country course in winter; (604) 497-5359. There's more downhill at **Mount Baldy** west of Osoyoos, (604) 498-2262—one of the first mountains in the area to have snow.

OSOYOOS

Osoyoos bills itself as "the Spanish capital of Canada," but not because of any pioneer ethnic roots. In 1975 the city fathers realized they needed a gimmick, saw that the Bavarian motif had been preempted elsewhere, so decided to slap up some fake red-tile roofs and goofy matador billboards and "go Spanish." The climate is Canada's driest, with an average 10 inches of rain a year, and Osoyoos Lake is reportedly Canada's warmest freshwater lake.

A good short hike is up **Mount Kobau**, just west of Osoyoos off Kobau Road. Take the Kobau Lookout trail (2 kilometers) to the fire lookout or Testalinden Trail (5 kilometers) loop trail with views of the Similkameen Valley.

RESTAURANTS

Diamond Steak & Seafood House ★ Just about everyone in Osoyoos likes this casual steak, seafood, and pizza house on the main street of town. The decor carries off the town's ersatz Spanish theme better than most, with brick window arches and black leatherette chairs with shiny silver buttons. The pizzas are quite good, if you like crust that's crisp enough to snap, and the Greek salad is the best in town. No wonder—the owner is Greek. The wine list shows a collection of labels (literally) from several valley wineries, and there are refreshing Okanagan apple and pear ciders too. ■ *Main St near 89th; (604) 495-6223; Osoyoos; $$; full bar; MC, V; no checks; dinner every day (closed Feb).*

LODGINGS

Osoyoos

Inkaneep Down a steep winding road to a little peninsula in Osoyoos Lake is this unassuming resort—one of the first on the lake. The best thing about it is location: all 10 beach-level rooms face directly south (maximum sun) and open only feet away from the water's edge (the two dark cabins are north-facing). Families (some in their third generation of vacationing here) don't mind the fact that the accommodations are a bit campish because they really come for the sun. Don and Esme Hellyer book rooms by the week in the summer, love kids, and eschew loud boats and pets. ■ *3 kilometers north of Osoyoos off Hwy 97; (604) 495-6353; RR 2, Osoyoos, BC V0H 1V0; $; no credit cards; checks OK.*

KEREMEOS

LODGINGS

Cathedral Lakes Resort ★★ To say this resort is remote is more than an understatement. First you have to get to base camp, which is a 21-kilometer gravel-road journey off Highway 3 along the Ashnola River. Once you're there, a four-wheel-drive vehicle from the resort picks you up and takes you on a 1-hour 14.4-kilometer journey to the lodge. Needless to say, the resort is heavy on recreation (hiking, canoeing, fishing), light on modern conveniences. All rooms have views of the lakes and peaks that surround the resort. Choose a cabin (which can accommodate up to eight) or a room in the chalet or the lodge. Three big meals are served (box lunches available upon request). Make your reservations early, since the season is short and space is limited.

Located inside the Cathedral Lake Provincial Park, the entire area is a protected wildlife refuge and a unique geological region. At 6,000 to 8,000 feet, the air is cool and dry, the views of surrounding Cascade Mountains spectacular. Mount Baker, Mount Rainier, the Coast Range, and the Kootenays are all visible from Lakeview Mountain, a day hike from the lodge. Families will appreciate all this activity; smokers will not. ■ *Call ahead for directions; (604) 499-5848 (or cellular phone (604) 492-1606 off season); RR1, Cawston, BC V0X 1C0; $$; no credit cards; checks OK.*

KALEDEN

LODGINGS

Ponderosa Point Resort ★★ Ponderosa Point's compound of 26 individually owned rental cabins on a peninsula extending out into Skaha Lake is an ideal spot to take a thick book for three days in the off season or a week in the summer (minimum stays respectively). The most attractive units are the one- and two-bedroom Pan Abodes set on a ponderosa pine-covered bluff above the lake. There's a 600-foot sandy beach, boat rentals, tennis courts, a playground, and a big grassy central compound. The cabins, named after trees, are all individually furnished by the owners. They're not plush or contemporary, but they're universally comfortable and clean. Try Greasewood if there are two in your party—the furniture has a hand-hewn look that's perfect for the setting. ■ *319 Ponderosa Ave; (604) 497-5354; Box 106, Kaleden, BC V0H 1K0; $$$; no credit cards; local checks only.*

PENTICTON

Penticton takes full advantage of its dual lakefronts. The south end of town (with its go-cart tracks, amusement centers, miniature-golf courses, water slides, and RV parks) touches the north shore of Skaha Lake. The north end of town sidles along the southern tip of the 70-mile-long Lake Okanagan.

RESTAURANTS

Granny Bogner's ★★★ One of the province's best restaurants is also one of the most consistent. Regulars never tire of German-trained chef Hans Strobel's escargots and veal, and even when they think they'll venture farther down the menu, they end up ordering the same favored dishes again and again. Indeed, Strobel's capable of a lot more—meltingly tender sweetbreads, a fragrant goulash soup, and expertly herbed salmon. The menu remains admirable—poached halibut, duck in its own juices, beef fillet with béarnaise, excellent Russian eggs as a starter—and the preparations are consistently infused with creativity. Desserts remain outstanding, especially the fresh, lightly sweet strawberry tart.

Ambience is number one, with substantial old wooden chairs, cloth-covered tables well spaced throughout the rooms, and Oriental carpets and a brick fireplace to remind you that this was once a home. It's all just shy of precious, with fancy lace curtains and waitresses in floor-length paisley skirts. The bar with its comfy chintz chairs invites brandy and dessert. The wine list does a grand job of representing the best local estate wineries. ■ *2 blocks south of Main; (604) 493-2711; 302 Eckhardt Ave W, Penticton; $$$; full bar; AE, MC, V; checks OK; dinner Tues-Sat.*

Theo's ★★ The ever-popular Theo's sports a series of sun-dappled interior patios, roofed with heavy rough-sawn beams, floored with red tile, walled in white stucco. There's a two-sided fireplace to cozy up to in winter, healthy greenery, and lots of Greek memorabilia. The bar is hung with copper vessels and dried herbs. Patrons say Theo's cooks an excellent rabbit (from nearby Summerland) and swear by the octopus. We agree, but we wish the accompaniments (white rice, carrots, and overcooked potatoes) were a little more inspired and the taramasalata more authentic. That said, by all means go in the late afternoon for an aperitif and a plate of excellent fried squid, or late at night to eat moussaka. The belly dancer's only there on special occasions these days, as the place is usually too busy to bother. ■ *Near the corner of Main and Eckhardt; (604) 492-4019; 687 Main St, Penticton; $$; full bar; AE, DC, MC, V; no checks; lunch Mon-Sat, dinner every day.*

LODGINGS

Coast Lakeside Resort ★★ The Coast Lakeside (formerly the Delta Lakeside) is the flagship of the Lake Okanagan shore. This sprawling resort hotel is also the most expensive place in town but, since it's the only place with its own beachfront, it's hailed by locals, conventioneers, and tourists alike. There are 204 light, airy rooms with balconies: the north-facing rooms have lake views. There are outdoor tennis courts and an indoor pool that looks out to the lake beyond. The restaurants are better-than-average hotel restaurants. One of those, Peaches and Cream, makes a pleasant breakfast spot; the other, Ripples, features continental dishes plus a teppan table and such deliriously unusual (for the Okanagan) items as sake mushrooms and chicken yakitori. There's also the Lakeside Patio Grill and

Lounge. ■ *Main and Lakeshore; (604) 493-8221; 21 Lakeshore Dr W, Penticton, BC V2A 7M5; $$$; full bar; AE, DC, MC, V; checks OK; breakfast, lunch, dinner every day.* &

NARAMATA

RESTAURANTS

The Country Squire ★★★ Every meal becomes an event at this clubby old house. Dinner might take up to four hours; however long it is, the table's yours for the night—you can even take a walk in between courses if you'd like. Master of ceremonies is Ron Dyck, who owns and operates this shrine of Okanagan cookery with his wife, Patt. Some think the flourishes are simply too much; others like all of Ron's personal touches. The opening act takes place when you call for reservations, at which time you are asked to choose from among several seasonal entrées: stuffed loin of lamb with mint, béarnaise, and a touch of tarragon; pork fillet with green peppercorn sauce; fresh Dungeness crab cakes with basil; or the ever popular beef Wellington. Upon arrival you find a formal card detailing the courses to come: perhaps a coarse duck pâté surrounded with Cumberland sauce to begin; a soup; your entrée; a platter of well-selected cheeses and fruit; and dessert, such as the chocolate ginger pear, poached in sauvignon blanc. The food is good, if rococo, with only the occasional inexplicable lapse. The price is a flat $35—and Ron is at your side throughout the meal, decanting one of his 350 wines, flambéing the steak Diane, or carving the Wellington. He's also a splendid resource on local wines, many of which reside in his own deep cellar. ■ *On the waterfront, follow signs; (604) 496-5416; 3950 1st St, Naramata; $$; full bar; MC, V; local checks OK; dinner Wed-Sun.*

LODGINGS

Sandy Beach Lodge ★ Here is the archetypal summer-lodge-on-the-lake, where the same families have signed up for the same two weeks in the same cabin for as long as anyone can remember. The setting is just about perfect: a wide green lawn, breezy with stately pines and shady maples, sloping down to a quiet cove with a sandy beach perfect for horseshoes, croquet, or shuffleboard. And the nine new log duplexes (tastefully decorated and furnished) are a vast improvement over the old squat brown bungalows which they replaced. Request one of the five closest to the lake (they all have decks and outdoor barbecues). There are also five small rooms in the older, slightly dowdy, pine-log lodge (slated for a remodel and winterizing next year). Tennis courts, a small swimming pool, rental boats, and wooden lawn chairs provide ample diversions. During peak summer season, reservations may be necessary up to a

year in advance (and priority is given to returning guests).
▪ *Off Robson on Mill Rd; (604) 496-5765; Box 8, Naramata, BC V0H 1N0; $$; MC, V; no checks (open summer only until winterizing takes place).* ੬

SUMMERLAND

A theme town done in the same spirit as Osoyoos, only this time they chose Tudor. Old Summerland is down on the water, but most of the town's business now thrives up on the hill.

RESTAURANTS

Shaughnessy's Cove ★ Shaughnessy's strong suits are its dramatic view of Okanagan Lake (it's built as close to the water as the law allows) and its airy atmosphere. The restaurant is tiered into four levels, with two outdoor decks, 20-foot ceilings, an old oak bar, skylights, three fireplaces, and pleasant decor. The seasonal menu features fare from fish 'n' chips to chimichangas to a filling stew served in a hollowed-out loaf of bread. The caesars are so powerful, you'll also get a stick of Dentyne for later. Owners Ralph and Annette Oakes emphasize service and atmosphere: both are excellent. Watch for the new outdoor margarita bar and firepit for summer evenings. ▪ *Lakeshore Dr N in Old Summerland; (604) 494-1212; 12817 Lake Shore Dr, Summerland; $; full bar; AE, DC, DIS, MC, V; no checks; lunch, dinner every day.* ੬

PEACHLAND

RESTAURANTS

Chinese Laundry ★ True enough, the building once used to have a laundromat that doubled as a restaurant; however, the word is they did more laundry than dishes. But when Frank Jung opened his Cantonese and Sichuan restaurant here, he latched onto the name and, so to speak, the concept. The place is filled with laundry-related antiques (washing machines, sewing machines, and interesting pictures documenting Chinese and their role in the laundry business). At first people came to the family-owned Laundry because of its strange name; now they return for its good food. During the middle of the day you can get a hamburger, but after 4pm it's strictly Chinese. A popular place, especially on summer eves. There are now two other locations in Penticton and Kelowna, but we prefer the Peachland original. ▪ *Follow signs from Hwy 97 to Peachland, then signs to Chinese Laundry; (604) 767-2722; 5818 Beach Ave, Peachland; $; full bar; MC, V; no checks; lunch, dinner every day.* ੬ ▪ *On Front St in the Valley Motor Inn; (604) 492-2828; 123 Front St, Penticton* ▪ *At Cooper and Harvey; (604) 860-8777; 2090 Harvey St, Kelowna.*

KELOWNA

On the east side of Lake Okanagan, Kelowna is the largest and liveliest of the Okanagan cities, with some noisy nightlife, some culture (an art museum and summer theater), a growing range of continental and ethnic restaurants, a big regatta in July, and an interesting historical preserve at **Father Pandosy's Mission**, (604) 860-8369. It even has its own version of the Loch Ness monster: **Ogopogo**. Keep a lookout for him (or her) while supping on the gaily decked-out paddle wheeler *Fintry Queen* or touring aboard the *Okanagan Princess*.

Houseboating on 70-mile-long Lake Okanagan is a good three- to seven-day vacation alternative for the entire family—most houseboats sleep up to six ($2,100 per week). No previous boating experience is necessary—you'll get a "Captain's lesson" when you arrive; Bridge Bay Marina, (604) 769-4411.

RESTAURANTS

Papillon ★★ With the departure of social chef Jean Peeters (who spent more time in the dining room than in the kitchen), Willi Franz and René Haudenschild have expedited the service, stepped away from the strictly French menu, and added a number of pastas to keep up with the trend toward less expensive dining. You'll still find the standard French offerings such as moules à la marinière, escargots en croute, steak au poivre, and wild duck à l'orange—all presented with flair—alongside more Italian infusions such as fettuccine alfredo, gnocchi with a meat sauce, and tortellini primavera. The wine list includes a smattering of everything, from European to local. Decor is contemporary but comfortable. ▪ *Near the corner of Pandosy and Leon; (604) 763-3833; 375 Leon Ave, Kelowna; $$; full bar; AE, DC, MC, V; no checks; lunch Mon-Fri, dinner every day.* &

Vintage Room (Capri Hotel) ★★ Nobody really wants to like this elegant, pricey restaurant on the ground floor of the Capri Hotel. Maybe that's what makes the Vintage Room try so hard—and most often succeed. The service is impeccable, and the restaurant bends over backward to accommodate your whims. Only want a few appetizers, half-orders, or dessert? No problem—there's no pressure to order more. It's some of the most sophisticated food in the Okanagan with items such as a clear oxtail consommé, a watercress salad with a light Dijon-honey vinaigrette and tomato wedges with fresh basil. Vintage favorites include sweetbreads piccata or a spring salmon broiled with pesto and Pernod. Avoid the imported pastries and the runny chocolate mousse. The only other drawback is the tour groups that book here in summer. ▪ *Gordon and Harvey; (604) 860-6060, ext 229; 1171 Harvey Ave, Kelowna; $$; full bar; AE, DC, MC, V; checks OK; lunch Mon-Fri, dinner every day, brunch Sun.*

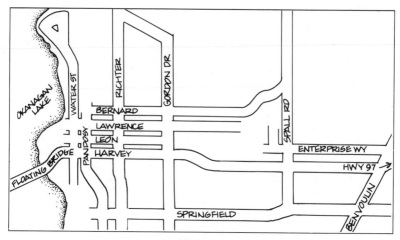

Kelowna

▼

Kelowna

———

Restaurants

▲

Talos Greek Restaurant ★ For 14 years now, Talos has been turning out superior Greek cuisine, and it just seems to be getting better. Favorites on the menu include horiatiki salad; very nice, creamy tzatziki with just enough garlic; and a dynamite souvlaki sandwich with thick slices of freshly grilled beef or lamb, stuffed into chewy pita bread. The last comes with a good Greek salad. All this takes place in a handsome, simple space, cool and pleasant, with checked tablecloths and lots of bare wood—like Greece, only better. Gallons of lemon juice go into the vegetables and grilled meats, and the prawns are reportedly excellent. ■ *Bernard and Water; (604) 763-1656; 1570 Water St, Kelowna; $$; full bar; AE, MC, V; no checks; lunch Thurs-Fri, dinner every day.*

LODGINGS

Hotel Eldorado ★★ Hands down, this is the best place to stay on Lake Okanagan—that is, if a boardwalk will do instead of a sandy beach. Originally located a few miles uplake, Eldorado Arms was built for a countess of Scottish descent in 1926. After its move to its current location in 1989, it caught fire and burned almost to the ground. Consequently, the rebuilt manse feels very new yet has the grandeur of a bygone era. Each of the 19 rooms (even the least expensive) has an antique armoire and a couch, most have balconies, and some have Jacuzzis. Best are the lakeside or corner rooms. The boardroom with a large patio is an excellent meeting place for 10 to 60 people. The round house nearby can hold up to 85 for banquets. There's not much of a lobby, as the restaurant and lounge take up most of the first floor. In the restaurant, we've sampled an excellent roasted breast of duck with peach brandy and pink peppercorns, accompanied by spaghetti squash, sweet peas, and roasted red potatoes, and preceded by a chunky tomato and gin soup. The wine selection is primarily British Columbian. Breakfast in the sun room is an extremely pleasant way to wake up. On summer afternoons you can have a hamburger on the Boardwalk. Rotary Beach is just a short walk away. ■ *Follow Pandosy (which becomes Lakeshore) for 6.4 kilometers south of the Okanagan Floating Bridge; (604) 763-7500; 500 Cook Rd, Kelowna, BC V1Y 9L5; $$$; full bar; AE, MC, V; no checks; breakfast, lunch Mon-Sat, dinner every day, brunch Sun.* &

Lake Okanagan Resort ★★ You reach the 300-acre resort via a beautiful, pine-clad winding road on the west side of Okanagan Lake. The place shows a little wear and tear, but the appointments were never first-cabin to begin with. Still, it's the best destination resort in the Okanagan. Now open year-round, it offers sailing, swimming, golf (9 holes), tennis (7 courts), and horseback riding to keep you busy. You can stay in a large condominium or a smaller chalet (both with wood-burning fireplaces), or any of four different inns. All rooms have kitchens and rent by the night. Since the resort is located on a very steep hillside, many of the rooms are a good climb or a steep descent away from the activities, but a resort shuttle makes quick job of it. The evening restaurant, Chateau, in the white art deco clubhouse serves fancy continental-resort fare such as wrapped and sauced veal and chateaubriand. The informal Fresco Cafe is open all day. A poolside lounge makes for an interesting social setting. ■ *2751 Westside Rd, 17 kilometers north of Kelowna; (604) 769-3511; 2751 Westside Rd, Kelowna, BC V1Y 8V2; $$$; full bar; AE, DC, DIS, MC, V; no checks; breakfast, lunch, dinner every day.* &

Capri Hotel All of the 185 rooms have seen an upgrade. The best still look out to the courtyard (with its outdoor hot tub and pool), but privacy is lacking on the ground floor. There are two dining options here, the informal Garden Cafe and the outstanding Vintage Room (see review in this section). For relaxation there's an outdoor hot tub and pool, saunas, and for nightlife, there's Angie's Pub or Cuzco's Lounge. ■ *Gordon and Harvey; (604) 860-6060; 1171 Harvey Ave, Kelowna, BC V1Y 6E8; $$$; AE, DC, MC, V; checks OK.* &

The Gables Country Inn & Tea House The Gables sits amid vineyards and open space, yet is only 10 minutes from downtown Kelowna. The expanded late-1800s house, filled with antiques, was remodeled with salvageable lumber and appointments from other old homes bidding adieu in the area. The four rooms are ornately decorated; the largest has a private balcony facing Lake Okanagan. Breakfast includes fresh fruit and hot-out-of-the-oven scones. ■ *Off Highway 97 south of Kelowna, turn east at Old McDonald's Farm to 2405 Bering Rd; (604) 768-4468; PO Box 1153, Kelowna, BC V1Y 7P8; $$; no credit cards; no checks.*

VERNON

RESTAURANTS

Intermezzo This musty green-colored restaurant looks as if it has been around for 20 years, and in fact it has been here for nearly 15. Chef Jim Grady's been cooking here since its beginnings, so you can count on consistency and big servings. If you don't feel like eating in a windowless room, take your hefty order of cheesy lasagne, fettuccine pesto, or perhaps even some barbecued pork ribs to go. ▪ *On 34th Ave near 32nd St; (604) 542-3853; 3206 34th Ave, Vernon; $$; full bar; AE, MC, V; checks OK; dinner every day, closed Sun off season.*

LODGINGS

Best Western Villager Motor Inn In terms of plush carpeting, contemporary accoutrements, and upkeep, this half-timbered-and-brick motel on the Highway 97 strip is the best in town. Of the 53 rooms, 24 open onto the inviting atrium pool and hot tub, but the regular rooms are quieter. ▪ *At the north end of town, directly across from Village Green Mall; (604) 549-2224; 5121 26th St, Vernon, BC V1T 8G4; $$; AE, DC, DIS, MC, V; no checks.* &

SALMON ARM

RESTAURANTS

Orchard House ★ A retired British colonel built this lovely house in 1903, planting an orchard and tulips on its surrounding 20 acres. Now it's a restaurant, serving seafood almost any way—baked, fried, poached—but the rack of lamb shipped from Australia is the starring item. Four rooms have been converted into dining areas: try to get into the glassed-in verandah with a view of Shuswap Lake, or the living room with its glowing fire. ▪ *22nd St NE; (604) 832-3434; 720 22nd NE, Salmon Arm; $$; full bar; MC, V; checks OK; lunch Mon-Sat, dinner every day.* &

SICAMOUS

Houseboating. You and your family can explore the 1,000 miles or so of the Shuswap Lake shoreline at the northern end of the Okanagan Valley on a houseboat—complete with everything from microwave oven to a water slide. Seven-day trips run you between $1,769 and $1,889 during peak season, not including gas (plan on $25 a day extra); **Waterway Houseboats**, (604) 836-2505.

All the places in this book are recommended; even "no stars" are worth knowing about.

REVELSTOKE

Heli-skiing. For the serious skier, Revelstoke serves as a base camp to some amazing runs in and around the Albert Icefields. The catch: you need a helicopter to get there. Selkirk Tangiers Helicopter Skiing Ltd., (604) 837-5378, boasts over 200 runs. For a few grand, Canadian Mountain Holidays will take you out, for a week at a time, to one of their fully staffed lodges in remote hideaways for some great skiing and hiking; (403) 762-4534.

RESTAURANTS

Black Forest Inn ★ Inside this A-frame you'll find a bit of Bavaria, with cute cuckoo clocks and German souvenirs cluttering every spare inch of space. Fondue Provençal, British Columbia salmon fillets, and a variety of beef tenderloins round out a rather extensive menu; we recommend one of the Bavarian dishes such as sauerbraten or schnitzel. Swiss-born chef Kurt Amsler's specialty is rainbow trout from a local hatchery; the servings grow larger as summer and trout progress. Try a glass of schnapps or a slice of Black Forest cake, made locally with cream and kirsch. ■ *5 kilometers west of Revelstoke on the Trans-Canada Hwy; (604) 837-3495; Trans-Canada West #1, Revelstoke; $$; full bar; AE, MC, V; local checks only; dinner Wed-Mon, lunch in summer (closed Nov).*

The 112 ★ Located in the Regent Inn downtown, the 112 is a unanimous favorite among locals. The masculine decor of dark cedar paneling, historical photographs of the Revelstoke region in the 19th century, and soft lighting blend well with the continental cuisine. Chef Peter Mueller specializes in veal dishes, but the cioppino and lamb Provençal also come with high recommendations. Most of the seafood is frozen except for the BC salmon. The wine list has been expanded to include some French and Australian labels but still emphasizes British Columbia's own vintners. A variety of after-dinner flaming coffees are good for show but little else. ■ *McKenzie and 1st; (604) 837-2107; 112 E 1st St, Revelstoke; $$; full bar; AE, MC; no checks; lunch, dinner Mon-Sat.*

FIELD

LODGINGS

Emerald Lake Lodge ★★★ In the middle of Yoho National Park, surrounded by the Kootenay Mountains and truly remarkable views, is the Emerald Lake Lodge. The geography is enough to lure you here, and the comfortably plush log lodge will keep you here. The owners (who gained their experience from running the Deer Lodge at Lake Louise) have brought in all the luxuries of a classy woodsy resort: numerous decks, three comfortable lounges with large stone fireplaces, a dining room, a billiards room (with a real English snooker table), a hot tub, sauna, and weight room. Stay in a suite (high season: superior $200, deluxe $240, executive $265); each has a deck, fireplace, and queen-size bed. The deluxe and executive rooms have "guaranteed" views (do you get your money back if you don't like it?) and minibars. Breakfast is well done and served buffet style. Dinners (a sort of mixture of California and Pacific Rim cuisines) are inventive.

The lake is too cold for swimming, so most people opt for horseback riding, fishing for trout, canoeing, or hiking (there's a nice trail around the lake). Come winter, there's access to nearby helicopter-skiing, or make the pilgrimage to Banff to cross-country ski out to hot springs. Smoking and children are allowed; but at least there aren't any TVs to distract you.
■ *8 kilometers north of the Trans-Canada Hwy in Yoho National Park; (604) 343-6321; PO Box 10, Field, BC V0A 1G0; $$$; AE, MC, V; checks OK.*

RADIUM HOT SPRINGS

Radium Hot Springs makes an ideal soaking stop at the base of the Kootenay mountain range. The hot springs, open to the public year-round, are equipped with two pools: one heated, the other cooler for more athletic swimming. If you didn't pack your bathing suit, don't worry; they'll rent you one for a buck. On Highway 93, 3 kilometers from Radium Junction, (604) 347-9485. Nearby you'll find golfing, camping, lodging, and tennis.

INVERMERE

RESTAURANTS

Strand's Old House ★★ Built in 1912 by pioneer Alexander Ritchie, this house has been converted to an idyllic setting for some of the finest dining in eastern British Columbia. Beyond the yard lined with beech trees are gardens with views to the mountains. Chef Tony Wood makes everything from scratch, right down to the mayonnaise served with the steamed artichokes, and prepares a different special each evening (around $15). Don't shy away from the elaborate leather-bound menu, though, which features page after page of outstanding appetizers and entrées. A cold, spicy avocado soup started our meal, followed by a well-prepared veal steak with a morel mushroom sauce, and an exceptional chicken Oscar, stuffed with crab and covered with a cream sauce. Regional wines and beers add gusto to occasional evenings of live music. A light menu (smaller portions of the regular fare) is offered after 9pm. Be sure to make reservations. ■ *In the middle of town; (604) 342-6344; 818 12th St, Invermere; $$; full bar; AE, MC, V; no checks; dinner every day (closed Nov).*

Panorama Resort ★ More than a resort, Panorama is its own village—a sprawling establishment in the Purcell Mountains that contains a seven-lift ski area, condos and a hotel (even kennels for your dog), lots of restaurants and nightspots, and outdoor recreation aplenty. Eight well-maintained tennis courts, horses, hiking trails, and river rafting on Toby Creek relieve the resort from dependence on the winter ski trade. But ski season is still the time to go. The snow is deep, white powder (World Cup competitions have been held here), and if nature doesn't dispense the white stuff, machines will. We recommend the condos rather than the hotel units: they're more expensive, but they all have kitchens. Wherever you stay, you're never more than 5 minutes' walk from the chair lifts. ■ *18 kilometers west of Invermere on Toby Creek Rd; (604) 342-6941; PO Box 7000, Invermere, BC V0A 1K0; $$; AE, MC, V; no checks.*

KIMBERLEY

Like many foundering mining towns in the early 1970s, Kimberley looked to tourism (and chose a Bavarian theme) as the panacea for a faltering economy. At 4,000 feet, Kimberley is (not surprisingly) the highest incorporated city in Canada. Views of the snow-capped Rocky Mountains are stunning, especially from the Kimberley Ski Resort, which has three chair lifts and a T-bar and over 30 downhill runs. There are 26 kilometers of Nordic runs, 3 kilometers of which are lit at night.

Kimberley

The town was named in 1896 by Col. William Ridpath and James Hogan of Spokane, after Kimberley, South Africa, because of a rich outcrop of minerals at the Sullivan Mine. Now owned by Cominco Ltd., Sullivan Mine is one of the largest lead, zinc, and silver mines in the world. It once employed 1,200; now half that many work there (the town's population is 6,700). The mountainside was initially mined as an open pit, and even though the pit was filled in, it remains as an ugly scar. Ore is now mined two miles deep into the mountain and carried by railcar to the Cominco smelter in Trail, BC. Gardeners shouldn't miss the teahouse, greenhouse, and immaculate gardens, once maintained by Cominco and now under the care of the city, on the grounds of the Kimberley District Hospital.

The Heritage Museum, 105 Spokane Street, (604) 427-7510, has an excellent display of the town's mining history and memorabilia, such as hockey equipment from the town team that won the World Senior Amateur Hockey Championships in 1937. For a good selection of regional books, try **Mountain High Book Store**, 232 Spokane Street, (604) 427-7014. Skiers and mountain-bike enthusiasts (roller bladers too) should check out **Rocky Mountain Sports**, 185 Deer Park Avenue, (604) 427-2838. Accordion music is played on loudspeakers on the bandstand at the center of the Bavarian Platz (the town's three-block walking street). For a quarter, a puppet pops out of the upper window of Canada's largest cuckoo clock and yodels. The Bauerhaus Restaurant on Gerry Sorenson Way (named for Kimberley's 1982 Olympic downhill gold-medal winner) has an outstanding view of the mountains; however, the well-reputed restaurant, dismantled in Austria and reconstructed here, is open only during ski season and for a few months in the summer; (604) 427-5133.

RESTAURANTS

Chef Bernard's Kitchen ★ Originally a fresh pasta eatery, Chef Bernard's has expanded its menu to include items such as pork tenderloins cooked in honey, walnuts, and cream; a variety of fondues; and a host of nightly specials which might include Florida alligator tail, Chilean trumpet fish, or British Columbia salmon. Nice tries; but the fresh pasta's the thing here. Try it with chicken fillets, raisins, coconut, pineapple, and curry, or with Italian sausage, tomatoes, and basil. The restaurant boasts an impressive German and Austrian wine list, alongside some of the better BC offerings. There's the fresh cream torte every day. ■ *On the Bavarian Platzl; (604) 427-4820; 170 Spokane St, Kimberley; $$; full bar; AE, DC, MC, V; checks OK; breakfast, lunch, dinner every day.*

The Snowdrift Cafe ★ The local hangout for the young sporting crowd, this small eatery located in a 100-year-old converted house boasts plenty of healthful foods—homemade whole-wheat bread and muffins, vegetarian chili and pizza, spinach and caesar salads. There's also the lasagne special with garlic bread and salad for those who need to carbo-load for vigorous skiing or cycling, and a variety of cheesecakes. The Hungarian mushroom soup, flavored with dill and loaded with mushrooms, comes with thick slices of the whole-wheat bread. Locals claim this is the best coffee in the Kootenay Mountains. ■ *On the Bavarian Platzl; (604) 427-2001; 110 Spokane St, Kimberley; $; beer, wine, and liqueurs; no credit cards; checks OK; lunch, dinner every day.*

LODGINGS

Kirkwood Inn/Inn West Five kilometers from Kimberley, adjacent to the ski and summer resort, is the Kirkwood Inn. There are hotel rooms, but opt for a condo instead. The condos have kitchens, fireplaces, access to laundry facilities and sauna, hot tub, and swimming pool (seasonal), and the balconies have views of the Rockies (through the trees in front of some). The trailhead of the Nordic ski-trail system is across the parking lot, and the ski lift at the downhill area is a block away. ■ *At the top of the hill at Kimberley Ski Resort; (604) 427-7616; PO Box 247, Kimberley, BC V1A 2Y6; $$$; AE, MC, V; checks OK.*

CRANBROOK

Cranbrook straddles the main highway north and hence has built several strip malls alongside the highway; however, the **Cranbrook Railway Museum**, Highway 3 and Baker Street, (604) 489-3918, takes visitors through a railroad yard of elegantly restored Canadian Pacific Railway TransCanada cars. After the tour, tea and scones are available in the dining car.

LODGINGS

Glen Flora Castle House This really is a castle, complete with turret. Built in 1909, it was restored to the original design by owners Paul and Bernice Sargent. Located in a quiet neighborhood adjacent to an elementary school and 5 minutes from downtown Cranbrook, the castle's grounds are landscaped in the formal English tradition. The hosts prefer nonsmokers for the two guest rooms, one with its own bath, one with a bath en suite. Continental breakfast is served. ■ *Turn onto Baker St from Hwy 3 and go south on 10th; (604) 426-7930; 324 10th Ave S, Cranbrook, BC V1C 2N6; $; no credit cards; checks OK.*

BOSWELL

LODGINGS

Destiny Bay Resort ★★ German-born Rold and Hanna Langerfel brought a bit of Europe to the little town of Boswell on Kootenay Lake. You stay in one of the five grass-roofed cabins or in one of the suites in the lodge. Tall pines shadow the lake view from the decks and the road is a tad too close for such a remote place. We don't might the absence of TVs, phones, or kitchens. The reasonably priced restaurant offers some of the best food for miles. On sunny days, the wraparound deck on the second floor is the spot—for seafood to schnitzels to herring salads, for the view, and for smokers. ■ *40 minutes from Creston on Hwy 3A; (604) 223-8455; Destiny Bay, Boswell, BC V0B 1A0; $$; beer and wine; MC, V; local checks only; breakfast, dinner every day (Apr-Nov).*

CRAWFORD BAY

The tiny community of Crawford Bay, accessible via an hour's ferry ride from Balfour (32 kilometers east of Nelson), happens to be the home of one of BC's finest golf courses, **Kokanee Springs Golf Course**; (604) 227-9226. Just up from the ferry dock is the **Last Chance Restaurant**, a local hangout with darn good sandwiches, (604) 227-9477.

*Did we lead you astray? Send us your gripe on the report form
at the back of this book.*

571

LODGINGS

Wedgwood Manor ★★ On 50 acres that tilt westward toward the Purcell Mountains, this lovely 1910 board-and-batten house has recently become one of the finest lodgings in southeastern British Columbia. Downstairs there's a dining room and a semiformal parlor with a fireplace (where afternoon tea is served). There are five rooms (all with baths en suite). The newest (and smallest) room is just off the parlor, but its wainscoting, leather-trimmed bookshelf, and fireplace make up for its lack of size and its central location. The four spacious upstairs rooms open onto a quiet, comfortable reading room; the Charles Darwin and Commander's rooms get most of the afternoon sun. In summer the large front porch is a very pleasant spot from which to gaze out over the big lawn and vegetable garden (from which many of Joan Huibert's breakfast ingredients come) to the Kokanee Glacier beyond. The owners have taken over the former servants' quarters next door, so the house is entirely yours, so to speak. ■ *East of Nelson on Hwy 3A, take Balfour ferry to Kootenay Bay and head south; (604) 227-9233; Box 135, 16002 Crawford Creek Rd, Crawford Bay, BC V0B 1E0; $$; MC, V; local checks only (open April-Oct only).*

NAKUSP

RESTAURANTS

Lord Minto ★ At almost any time of day, the Lord Minto is the busiest place in town. It's named after the SS *Lord Minto*, a paddle wheeler that used to haul supplies and passengers up and down Arrow Lake before the road went through. Owners Lorraine Kellock and Karen Hamling work just as hard, as they waitress, cashier, and cook. A great spot, especially for lunch. The juicy Greek burger on our last visit was piled high with feta, onions, lettuce, and tomato, with a side salad that was a meal in itself. Dinners extend to a vegetarian lasagne, salmon steak, and perhaps some stroganoff. Especially good after an afternoon at the hot springs just 8 miles up the road. ■ *5th Ave between Broadway and 1st; (604) 265-4033; Nakusp; $; full bar; AE, DC, MC, V; no checks; breakfast, lunch, dinner every day.*

ROSEBURY

RESTAURANTS

Wild Rose Cafe It's no problem finding the restaurant, just tough to find the town. Highway 6 used to run right through the middle of town, and now it's routed behind it. A small side loop takes you into the bustling town of almost 50 people. But it's not just townfolk who line up at this tiny Mexican cafe.

It's a pretty drive from Nelson, and for the past 10 summers, people have been dropping in for some of Andrea Wright's great Mexican food. Everything's homemade, right down to the beans. Sit out on the porch and enjoy the evening. ■ *In Rosebury, 3 miles north of New Denver; (604) 358-7744; Rosebury; $; full bar; MC, V; local checks only; dinner Wed-Sun (Fri-Sun winters).*

SILVERTON

LODGINGS

Silverton Resort ★ You'll be pleased with this little resort in the heart of the Hidden Valley. New owners Bill and Lorraine Landers took over these cabins on the shores of Slocan Lake in 1991. It's a great place if you like water play; bring your own or rent their canoes, windsurfer, or rowboat. There are a couple of mountain bikes available too. You stay in one of the five hemlock-log cabins—all spotlessly clean and simple and each named after a mythological hero. Some have sleeping lofts, all have kitchens and south-facing decks. They're all at the water's edge (though not far from the road either), but Thor 4 (situated just right) is our favorite. A lakefront resort backed by a glacier in the Valhalla Provincial Park: it's a fine spot to do absolutely nothing. ■ *On the lakeshore in Silverton; (604) 358-7157; Box 107, Lake Ave, Silverton, BC V0G 2B0; $$; MC, V; local checks only.*

Nelson

NELSON

Nestled in a valley on the shore of Kootenay Lake, Nelson sprang up with the silver and gold mining back in the late 1890s and has retained its Victorian character. Its main street has changed little in its 90-year history, which has drawn more than one filmmaker to use the downtown as a set. More than 350 heritage sites are listed in this picturesque city of about 9,000. An interesting pictorial exhibit of the region's history can be seen at the **Nelson Museum**, 402 Anderson Street, (604) 352-9813, which is open year-round. The mountains surrounding Nelson are a mecca for hikers; a popular destination is **Kokanee Glacier Provincial Park** 29 kilometers northeast of Nelson. Park maps available from the Ministry of Parks, RR 3, Nelson, BC V1L 5P6; (604) 825-4421. The town itself deserves at least an afternoon of browsing the fine art galleries and other interesting shops. Outdoors enthusiasts should stop in at **Snowpack**, 333 Baker Street, (604) 352-6411; for cards and stationery, head for **Through the Looking Glass**, 305 Baker Street, (604) 352-3913; **White Buffalo Gifts**, 636 Baker Street, (604) 352-6744, specializes in regionally made gifts; and for a large selection of used books, try **Packrat Annie's**, 411 Kootenay

Street, (604) 354-4722, where the **Vienna Cafe**, with a nice assortment of salads on the eclectic menu, shares the space.

Art. The art shows and theater brought into Nelson by the town's arts council are well selected. From theatrical productions to wildlife lectures to classical guitar performances to nationally known folk-rock groups, there's almost always something going on at the operatic-style **Capitol Theatre**, (604) 352-6363. From June through August the entire town turns into an art gallery, with artists' work exhibited in almost 20 shops, restaurants, and galleries. Maps of **Artwalk Gallery Tours** can be picked up at the Tourist Information Bureau at 225 Hall Street, (604) 352-3433, or contact Artwalk, Box 422, Nelson, BC V1L 5R2, (604) 352-2402. For a calendar of weekly events, pick up a free copy of the *Kootenay Weekly Express.*

Skiing. The small local ski area, **Whitewater**, provides some of the best (and most) powder in the lower Kootenays. There are only three chairs, with about 11 expert runs out of 22 total, and the summit chair is especially challenging; call (604) 354-4944 or (604) 352-7669 (24-hour snow report). Good **cross-country ski** trails begin at the base of Mount Ymir, where the road to Whitewater leaves the highway.

A scenic day trip through sleepy villages follows highways 31, 31A, and 6, then loops around to arrive back in Nelson. On the way, take the 2-hour (round-trip) Balfour ferry across Kootenay Lake to Crawford Bay. It's a pretty trip and happens to be the world's longest free ferry ride. Don't miss **Ainsworth Hot Springs**, (604) 229-4212, where for $5 you can explore caves of piping-hot (112 degrees), waist-deep water, or swim in the slightly cooled pool (open 365 days a year); or **Kaslo**, a town famed for its bakery—Rudolph's Pastries, 416 Front Street, (604) 353-2250.

RESTAURANTS

Fiddler's Green ★★ It's really best in the summer when you can dine in the garden. But regardless of the season, this is Nelson's favorite spot for a special occasion. Locals quibble over whether the food is really the best in town, but they agree unanimously that this old estate house has the best atmosphere. There are three intimate dining rooms, one larger area (if the season calls for inside dining, ask to sit next to the fireplace), and the only garden dining in Nelson. Don't be surprised if the food preparation is inconsistent. The focus is definitely not on the food—but sometimes, when you're seated next to the fireplace (or at Sunday brunch in the summer garden) and conversation flows, the stale bread comes and goes without your even noticing. ■ *On the north shore, 6 miles north of town; (604) 825-4466; Lower 6 Mile Rd, Nelson; $$; full bar; MC, V; local checks only; dinner every day, brunch Sun in summer (winter hours vary).*

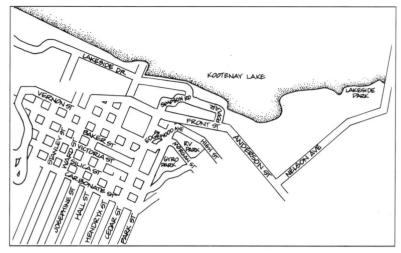

Nelson

Le Chatelet ★★ Unlike Fiddler's, this eatery (the name means "little castle," but it hardly resembles such) is spare in atmosphere but, according to locals, more particular about the food. Originally from the French Alps, chef/owner Eric Eriksen and his wife, Essylt have created a country French menu. People who dine often here know to stay with the turnovers (which resemble calzones and are baked in their huge, brick-lined, wood-burning oven). We sampled a crab, cheese, and tarragon turnover which was crispy on the outside and, in a whimsical touch, shaped like a crab. The salads are outstanding: fresh romaine lettuce topped with grated carrots, tomato wedges, and grated blue cheese (although they are available with a variety of other toppings). The wine list is primarily European and pricey; it would be bolstered by a sampling of regional wines. Essylt is attentive and always seems to know what you need. ■ *Along Lakeside Park; (604) 354-3911; 903 Nelson Ave, Nelson; $$; full bar; MC, V; checks OK; dinner Wed-Sun.* &

Main Street Diner ★ It used to be Milly's Fish & Chips, so owners Con Diamond and Linda Jamison decided to keep the famed—and still great—fish 'n' chips on what's now a predominantly Greek menu with a smattering of steak-and-seafood entrées to appeal to local appetites. You won't go wrong, however, ordering a cheeseburger and fries or a variation with an Athenian twist: a thick patty with tzatziki and feta. It's noisy at mealtimes, and no wonder: it's the most popular eatery in town, especially for families. ■ *At the north end of Baker; (604) 354-4848; 616 Baker St, Nelson; $; beer and wine; MC, V; local checks only; lunch, dinner Mon-Sat.* &

Nelson

Restaurants

LODGINGS

Willow Point Lodge ★★ Sue and Alan Dodsworth changed the name (it was formerly the Selkirk Lodge), redecorated, and now view landscaping as an ongoing project (Alan has plans to restore ponds and a stream in front of the lodge). You'll feel quite welcome in their large, rambling 1922 Victorian perched on a hill in the midst of 3½ acres. The living room's large stone fireplace adds to the welcome. There are six guest rooms, all restored with period furnishings, and two on the third floor have been combined into a suite. The Oak Room on the first floor has a big stone fireplace and sitting area, canopy bed, and private entrance. Three second-floor rooms, all of which are charming, have window seats looking east toward the Selkirk Mountains and Kootenay Lake; the spacious Green Room (our favorite) sports a large, private covered balcony. Breakfast is up whenever you are and always includes granola, homemade muffins, and perhaps waffles with Okanagan raspberry syrup. ■ *4 kilometers north of Nelson on Hwy 3A over Nelson Bridge at 2211 Taylor Dr; (604) 825-9411; RR 1, S-21, C-31, Nelson, BC V1L 5P4; $$; MC, V; local checks only.*

Emory House A quiet cottage at the north edge of downtown, the Emory House boasts a perfect location for those who want to explore Nelson on foot. Vancouver natives Michele Dupas and Colin Macrae, both with backgrounds in the tourism industry, moved to Nelson in 1993. Here they found the hardwood floors, woodwork, and built-in dining buffet beautifully preserved. The two guest rooms on the main floor are cozy, but New Denver looks out onto the lake and should be quieter than the street-facing Balfour room. Upstairs there are two slightly more private rooms. The home is adjacent to the Civic Centre and near downtown, so expect a little more noise than across the lake. ■ *At the north end of Vernon St in downtown Nelson; (604) 352-7007; 811 Vernon St, Nelson, BC V1L 4G3; $$; MC, V; local checks only.*

ROSSLAND

This 1890s Gold Rush town has been experiencing a second boom recently. This time the gold is not in Red Mountain, but on it. **Red Mountain Ski Area**, 3½ miles southwest of town, is one of the more challenging ski areas in British Columbia, with runs steep enough to keep even the most adventurous skiers alert, (604) 362-7700, toll-free (800) 663-0105, or (604) 362-5500 for snow conditions. There are over 40 kilometers of cross-country ski trails (about half are groomed); for information, call **Black Jack Cross-Country Ski Club**, (604) 362-5811.

In the summer, the colorful turn-of-the-century main street of tiny Rossland bustles with hikers bound for alpine lakes, mountain bikers en route to explore the numerous trails, or scenery-seeking visitors. A good place to get a good look at the town (and its surrounding scenery) is from the rooftop cafe of **Rockingham's**, 2061 Columbia Street, (604) 362-7373, with over 30 appetizers. **After the Gold Rush Espresso Bar and Book Store**, 2063 Washington Street, (604) 362-5333, with live Celtic music most Sunday nights, is a good place to linger over a latte and a good book.

Take a tour of the fascinating **Le Roi Gold Mine**, Canada's only hard-rock gold mine open to the public. It's not just another roadside attraction (open May through September); (604) 362-7722.

RESTAURANTS

Roundhouse Restaurant and Only Well Pub (Flying Steamshovel Inn) The inn named after the fellow who flew and crashed the first helicopter (dubbed the Flying Steamshovel by local miners) in North America is currently just a restaurant. You can sit in the formal Roundhouse or the boisterous Only Well pub. The atmosphere is minimal in the dining room, so we prefer the pub, where the pool tables, pull tabs, and loud conversation make for a sociable evening, and the menu from the Roundhouse is available in addition to lighter pub fare. The appetizers are only okay, so go directly to one of the favorite entrées such as the chicken curry (with fruit, coconut, and mango chutney) on coriander fettuccine. ■ *At the corner of Washington St and 2nd Ave, two blocks off Columbia Ave; (604) 362-5323; 2003 2nd Ave, Rossland; $$; full bar; MC, V; local checks only; lunch, dinner every day.*

Sunshine Cafe Virtually anybody will feel comfortable in Rossland's favorite little cafe. Sit in the front of the restaurant or walk past the kitchen to the back room. The food doesn't try to be fancy—just good, and there's lots of it. You'll do well to start with the Malaysian egg rolls (ground beef, coconut, and spices) dipped in a plum sauce and then go on to one of the Mexican dishes, the Budgie burger (boneless breast of chicken with ham and Swiss), or a simple entrée such as the curried chicken. Huevos rancheros are a favorite of the breakfast crowd. The staff is friendly, and if you happen to sit in the back room you may catch the kitchen staff being silly. No smoking. ■ *In the middle of town on the main street; (604) 362-7630; 2116 Columbia Ave, Rossland; $; beer and wine; MC, V; local checks only; breakfast, lunch, dinner every day.*

LODGINGS

Ram's Head Inn ★★ Dave and Doreen Butler's comfortable nonsmoking inn is the choice place to stay in this mountainous part of the province; it's just a few hundred yards' walk to the Red Mountain ski area. The nine guest rooms are homey, but the comfortable public room is best, with a lofty ceiling, a stone fireplace, and big windows looking out to the wooded backyard. Packages combine lift tickets with a bed and a full breakfast, making a ski weekend nicely affordable. Skiing here is surprisingly good—especially when the Butlers' hot tub and sauna are waiting. Young kids are quietly discouraged. ■ *Red Mountain Rd, 3.2 kilometers north of Rossland; (604) 362-9577; Box 636, Rossland, BC V0G 1Y0; $$; AE, MC, V; checks OK.*

Calendar of Events

JANUARY

Chinese New Year In January or February (depending on the lunar calendar) the International District greets the Chinese New Year with a fanfare of festivals and displays and a lively parade complete with lion dancers. ▪ *International District, Seattle, WA; (206) 623-5124.*

Great Northwest Chili Cook-off For 12 years now, the Chili Cook-off has benefited the Washington Park Zoo, raising funds for expansion and for the care of the animals. About 30 different chilis are sampled by no fewer than 2,500 visitors. ▪ *Memorial Park Coliseum, Portland, OR; (503) 226-1561.*

FEBRUARY

Chilly Hilly Bike Ride Held the third Sunday in February, this 28-mile family ride sponsored by the Cascade Bicycle Club has come to be recognized as the opening day of bike season. Up to 4,000 cyclists fill the morning ferries to Winslow. Don't expect the weather to be warm or the road to be flat. ▪ *Bainbridge Island, WA; (206) 522-BIKE.*

Fat Tuesday Seattle's own weeklong Mardi Gras celebration brings a colorful parade and the beat of Cajun, jazz, and R&B music to the streets and clubs of Pioneer Square. Nightclubs levy a joint cover charge, and proceeds from several events benefit Northwest Harvest, a local food bank. Held the week before Lent. ▪ *Pioneer Square, Seattle, WA; (206) 622-2563.*

Northwest Flower and Garden Show This enormous horticultural happening occupies almost 5 acres at the Convention Center throughout Presidents' Day weekend. Landscapers, nurseries, florists, and noncommercial gardeners outdo themselves with over 300 demonstration gardens and booths. Shuttle bus service is available from Northgate and Longacres. General admission is $8, evenings $6. ▪ *Washington State Convention and Trade Center, Seattle, WA; (206) 789-5333.*

Oregon Shakespeare Festival An unassuming little college town, set in lovely ranch country, just happens to house one of the oldest and largest regional theater companies in the country. Almost 100,000 visitors a year (from February to October) attend the festival and crowd into the three theaters. Lectures, backstage tours, and Renaissance music and dance are other attractions theatergoers enjoy. Last-minute tickets are rare in the summer, but not impossible. ▪ *Citywide, Ashland, OR; (503) 482-4331.*

Rain or Shine Dixieland Jazz Festival Every Presidents' Day weekend, rain or shine, Aberdeen hosts top Dixieland bands from up and down the West Coast. New bands take over every set. Multiple venues keep the town hoppin'. ▪ *Citywide, Aberdeen, WA; (206) 533-2910.*

24-Hour Ski Marathon Singles or teams of 6 to 12 skiers participate in this downhill ski marathon, with all proceeds going to help disabled children in the area. ■ *Grouse Mountain, BC; (604) 984-0661.*

Washington State Games What originated as the Washington Centennial Games is now the Washington State Games, a yearly event held in February (the summer games are in mid-July). The winter games feature downhill and cross-country skiing events; the summer games consist mostly of traditional Olympic sports. ■ *Call for location; (206) 453-1670.*

MARCH

Kandahar Ski Race Now in its 43rd year, this is possibly the last amateur-status, free-fall downhill race in existence. Anyone with the guts and a helmet can register. Generally held the first week in March. ■ *Forbidden Plateau Resort, Courtenay, BC; (604) 334-4744.*

Northwest Buddy Werner Ski Racing Championships An alpine ski event designed just for the younger members of your family. About 300 kids from 7 to 12 compete in the frosty event. Come out and watch Olympic hopefuls give it their all. Races are held in Washington, Oregon, or western Idaho. ■ *Call for location,(206) 392-4220.*

Oregon State Special Olympics Developmentally disabled athletes compete in ice skating and downhill and cross-country skiing just prior to the big international Special Olympics (usually held a few weeks later). Over 400 Olympians compete in the state meet. ■ *Mount Bachelor, Bend, OR; (503) 382-2442.*

Pacific Rim Whale Festival Migrating gray whales can be observed during March and April just off the shores of the Long Beach section of Pacific Rim National Park. Numerous charter boats and a seaplane company offer close-up looks at the pods. The actual festival, including dances and education programs, begins the last week in March. ■ *Tofino, BC; (604) 725-3414.*

Whale Migration From March to May, the gray whales return to Alaska from Baja California, where they winter and calve. Along the Washington and Oregon coasts are a number of excellent whale-watching spots; some towns, such as Westport, Washington, and Newport, Oregon, offer charters especially for whale-seekers. The return migration happens from October to December, a less favorable time for whale watching due to the weather. ■ *For information, call the chambers of commerce, Westport, WA, (206) 268-9422; or Newport, OR, (503) 265-8801.*

APRIL

Brant Festival The first annual Brant Festival, held in April 1991, celebrated the stopover of the brant (a species of geese) on their migration from Mexico to Canada. Staging areas provide fine opportunities to view the geese, once nearly extinct, as they feed. Wildlife art, photography exhibits, and carving competitions too. ▪ *Parksville, BC; (604) 248-4117.*

Cherry Festival This event has parades, cherry orchard tours, dances, a carnival, and golf and tennis tournaments. Held the second Sunday after Easter. ▪ *The Dalles, OR; (503) 296-2231.*

Daffodil Festival Grand Floral Parade The Daffodil Festival, a springtime tradition for over 60 years, celebrates the fields of gold in the Puyallup Valley. One of the largest floral parades in the nation visits downtown Tacoma, Puyallup, Sumner, and Orting—all in one day. ▪ *Tacoma, WA; (206) 627-6176.*

Hood River Blossom Festival The coordinators of this event assure us that any similarities between it and the one in The Dalles are purely coincidental. Altogether, there are 30 to 40 different things happening throughout the valley. Tours of the blossoming fruit orchards and wineries along a 40-mile loop are available. ▪ *Hood River Valley, OR; (800) 366-3530.*

International Wine Festival The largest and most prestigious wine event in Canada, the five-day festival attracted over 7,000 visitors in 1990, when 10 countries were represented by 113 different wineries and 370 wines. Events in this food and wine extravaganza include a Bacchanalia gala and complimentary palate cleansers; future festivals look equally promising. ▪ *Vancouver Trade and Convention Center, Vancouver, BC; (604) 873-3311.*

Seattle Mariners Baseball The crowd is predictably loyal—even to a team whose performance is not so predictable. Although the playing can be truly inspired, the outlook for the next few seasons isn't particularly bright. The season lasts from early April through the first week of October (game time is 7:05pm weeknights, 1:35pm on Saturdays and occasional weekdays). Bring your own peanuts (Kingdome food is too expensive and not too good) and prepare to get lively if you're sitting in the left-field stands. Tickets are cheap ($4.50 to $10.50). ▪ *Kingdome, Seattle, WA; (206) 628-3555.*

Skagit Valley Tulip Festival When the 1,500 acres of tulips burst into brilliant color in early April, Mount Vernon seizes the moment and entertains visitors with a street fair and the Taste of Skagit. Makes a nice—and flat—bicycle trip. ▪ *60 miles north of Seattle via I-5, Mount Vernon, WA; (206) 42-TULIP.*

TerrifVic Dixieland Jazz Festival Twenty Dixieland jazz bands from all over the world shake up the town for five days in April. Sixty dollars gets you an event badge good for every concert in every location. Shuttle service is available between participating hotels and the eight concert locations. ▪ *Victoria, BC; (604) 381-5277.*

Yakima Spring Barrel Tasting In late April, 20 wineries from Union Gap to Kiona hold special open houses to educate the public on the finer points of winemaking. Both owners and winemakers are on hand to explain the process, and wines from the barrel—some two or three years away from maturity—are available for tasting. Individual wineries add entertainment and food. ▪ *Various wineries, Yakima, WA; call for map, (509) 829-6027.*

Bloomsday Run Now the world's largest timed road race, Spokane's Bloomsday Run attracts thousands every year (over 50,000 runners) during the area's Lilac Festival, (509) 326-3339. Everyone who crosses the finish line gets an official Bloomsday T-shirt and his or her name in the city's major newspapers. Be sure to book hotel rooms well in advance (a year beforehand is advised). ■ *Spokane, WA; (509) 838-1579.*

International Children's Festival This popular event brings in children's performers from all over the world. Crafts, storytelling, puppet shows, and musical and theater performances entertain kids and their parents for six days in early May. ■ *Seattle Center, Seattle, WA; (206) 684-7346.*

National Western Art Show and Auction For nearly 20 years the three-day event has brought artists from all over the country to this college town off I-90. A hundred display rooms turned into mini-studios offer paintings and sculptures for sale. Three auctions are held as well, including one benefiting Elmview Industries for the community's developmentally disabled. ■ *Ellensburg, WA; (509) 962-2934.*

Northwest Folklife Festival The largest folkfest in the nation runs throughout Memorial Day weekend and brings many ethnic groups and their folk-art traditions (dance, music, crafts, and food) to stages throughout the Seattle Center. A must. ■ *Seattle Center, Seattle, WA; (206) 684-7300.*

Opening Day of Yachting Season Boat owners from all over the Northwest come to this festive ceremonial regatta, which officially kicks off the nautical summer. Arrive early to watch the world-class University of Washington rowing team race other nationally ranked teams through the Montlake Cut. Parade registration for watercraft is free. ■ *Lake Washington/Lake Union; Seattle Yacht Club, 1807 E Hamlin St, Seattle, WA; (206) 325-1000.*

Pole, Pedal, Paddle This grueling test of endurance is one of Central Oregon's most popular events. In '90, 3,500 people skied, biked, canoed, and ran in teams or alone past 35,000 cheering spectators. Usually the weekend after Mother's Day, the original small-town run is now a full-fledged two-day event complete with street fair and food. ■ *Mount Bachelor, Bend, OR; (503) 388-0002.*

Poulsbo Viking Fest In mid-May, Puget Sound's "Little Norway" celebrates Scandinavian independence with a weekend of folk dancing and live music, a carnival and parade, and a lutefisk-eating contest (definitely an acquired taste). ■ *Poulsbo, WA; (206) 779-4848.*

Rhododendron Festival This is the oldest festival in town, and it improves every year. Highlights of this two-week–long event include a Rover Run (dog and owner), beard contest (scruffiest, longest), adult tricycle race, keg put, carnival, senior citizen coronation and dance, and more. The "Grand Finale" is a classic parade; the "Anti-Climax Grand Finale" is the 12K Rhody Run. See all of the Rhododendron Queens' handprints in cement in downtown Port Townsend. ■ *Port Townsend, WA; (206) 385-2722.*

Sand Castle Day Oregon's original and most prestigious sand castle contest is 30 years old. Buckets, shovels, and squirt guns aid the 1,000-plus contestants in producing their transient creations. Upward of 15,000 spectators show up to view the masterpieces. ■ *Cannon Beach, OR; (503) 436-2623.*

Seattle International Film Festival Founded in 1976 by Darryl Macdonald and Dan Ireland, the 3½-week Seattle International Film Festival brings films for every taste—high art to slapstick—to Seattle theaters every May. Fans of the obscure will appreciate SIFF's archival treasures and independent films. Series tickets (full and partial) go on sale in January (Cinema Seattle, 801 E Pine Street, Seattle, WA 98122). ■ *Citywide, Seattle, WA; (206) 324-9996.*

Ski-to-Sea Festival A Bellingham civic festival over Memorial Day weekend that revolves around an 80-miles-plus, seven-event relay race that includes skiing, running, cycling, canoeing, and sailing. ■ *From Mount Baker to Marine Park, Bellingham, WA; (206) 734-1330.*

Slug Races In the Pacific Northwest, spring and slugs seem to go hand in hand. During Florence's Rhododendron Festival, the main attraction is the slug race. Watch the local gastropods slime their way toward victory. ■ *Old Town, Florence, OR; (503) 997-3128.*

Strawberry Festival The main attraction at this festive event is the world's largest strawberry shortcake (see the *Guinness Book of World Records*). Standing several feet tall and weighing a couple of tons, it's big enough for everyone to get a bite. Made with fresh strawberries, of course. ■ *Lebanon, OR; (503) 258-7164.*

Swiftsure Race Weekend Held every Memorial Day weekend, this event attracts boats from North America and foreign ports. Three races are held, the longest going west out the Strait of Juan de Fuca to the Pacific and back. Spectators can watch the vessels from Clover Point or Ogden Point. ■ *Victoria, BC; (604) 592-2441.*

Washington State Apple Blossom Festival When the apple trees burst into bloom in early May, Wenatchee hosts an 11-day festival (the oldest in the state) featuring arts, crafts, and plenty of food. ■ *Citywide, Wenatchee, WA; (800) 57-APPLE.*

JUNE

BC Lions Football Some people feel that a wider field and one fewer down than in American ball make Canadian football more exciting. Action is the name of the game in this eight-team league. The season lasts from late June to late November and culminates in the Grey Cup Game, the Canadian version of the Super Bowl. Regular game tickets cost around $25. ■ *BC Place Stadium, Vancouver, BC; (604) 280-4400.*

Britt Festival This musical extravaganza runs from mid-June through September in the hillside field where Peter Britt, a famous local photographer and horticulturist, used to have his home. A handsome shell has been constructed, and listeners sit on benches or loll on blankets under the stars. Programs run the gamut: classical, folk, country, jazz, musical theater, and dance. Season passes are available as well as tickets to individual events. ▪ *Jacksonville, OR; (503) 773-6077.*

Centrum Summer Arts Festival From June through September, one of the most successful cultural programs in Washington enlightens thousands with a multitude of workshops held by the nation's leading artists and musicians. For fiddlers, there's the Festival of American Fiddle Tunes. Jazz musicians can hone their skills at the Bud Shank Workshop or listen to the music at Jazz Port Townsend, one of the West Coast's foremost mainstream jazz festivals. Workshops are held at Fort Worden State Park; performances take place on the park grounds or at various locations around town. There are also a writers conference and theater performances. ▪ *Port Townsend, WA; (206) 385-3102.*

Chamber Music Northwest One of the finest summer festivals in the country, distinguished by the caliber of its performances, takes place in Portland at Reed College and Catlin Gabel School from late June through late July. ▪ *Portland, OR; (503) 223-3202.*

du Maurier Ltd. International Jazz Festival Still relatively new on the international music scene, the du Maurier has not disappointed jazz enthusiasts. Last year over 500 musicians from Africa, Japan, Europe, and North and South America appeared during the two-week festival, which presents the full spectrum of traditional and contemporary jazz. Happens over Canada Day weekend at the end of June or in early July. ▪ *Vancouver, BC; (604) 682-0706.*

Everett Giants Baseball This class-A minor-league affiliate of the San Francisco Giants plays real baseball on real grass in real sunshine from mid-June through August. In 1990, the 1,800-seat Everett Memorial Stadium was enlarged to 3,000 seats to accommodate the ever-growing number of fans. Tickets are only $4.50 for adults, $3.50 for kids 12 and under; reserved tickets are a little more. Call for season schedule. ▪ *Everett Memorial Stadium, Everett, WA; (206) 258-3673.*

Northwest Garlic Festival This two-day affair attracts about 20,000 people each year. A street fair, live music, and a garlic-peeling contest are just a few of the events that will keep you busy all day. A garlic-eating contest may keep your enemies at bay. ▪ *Ocean Park, WA; toll-free (800) 451-2542.*

Olympic Music Festival The Philadelphia String Quartet opens its season with one of the Puget Sound area's premier music festivals, held in a turn-of-the-century barn nestled on 40 acres of pastoral farmland on the Olympic Peninsula. Sit in the barn on hay bales ($16) or spread a picnic on the lawn ($8). The festival spans 10 weekends. Bring a blanket. ▪ *Quilcene, WA; (206) 527-8839.*

Rose Festival The Rose Festival is to auto racing what Seattle's Seafair is to boat racing. This 24-day celebration culminates in the CART 200, a race featuring Indianapolis 500–style cars. Don't forget to catch the parade and stop in at the festival center. ▪ *Citywide, Portland, OR; (503) 227-2681.*

Seattle-to-Portland Bicycle Ride There is a 10,000-rider limit for this 200-mile bike ride from Seattle to Portland sponsored by the Cascade Bicycle Club. Complete the course in one or two days (overnight facilities are provided at the halfway point). Registration is first come, first served, and in the past couple of years the limit has been reached. ■ *(206) 522-BIKE.*

Umpqua Valley Summer Arts Festival Over 100 booths, featuring every kind of art imaginable, sprout up in the park around the Art Center in Roseburg the last weekend in June. You'll find pottery, silk scarves, jewelry, teddy bears, quilts, folk art, porcelain, woven baskets, and stained-glass items (just to name a few). ■ *Roseburg, OR; (503) 672-2532.*

Washington Special Olympics In 1968 an act of Congress created the organization known today as Special Olympics. It has since grown to be the world's largest sports training and competition program for the mentally retarded. The June event is the biggest competition in Washington. ■ *Call for location, (206) 362-4949.*

JULY

Albany Dixieland Jazz Fest Bands from all over the country have participated in this music fest. A prepaid pass gets you into all performances. ■ *Albany, OR; (503) 928-0911.*

Bellevue Jazz Festival Top Northwest jazz artists entertain outdoors for three days, during the third weekend in July. Tickets are cheap (around $5) and one concert is free. ■ *Bellevue Downtown Park, WA; (206) 451-6887.*

Bite of Seattle A big chompfest that brings cheap nibbles from some 60 restaurants to Seattle Center on the third weekend in July. ■ *Seattle Center, Seattle, WA; (206) 232-2982.*

Chinatown International District Summer Festival This mid-July extravaganza celebrates the richness and diversity of Asian culture with dancing, music, and martial arts performances, food booths, and arts and crafts. A children's corner features puppetry, storytelling, and magic shows; various craft demonstrations (classical ikebana, a Japanese tea ceremony, basketry, calligraphy, and Hawaiian lei-making) take place in the cultural corner. ■ *Hing Hay Park, Seattle, WA; (206) 728-0123.*

Darrington Bluegrass Festival Every summer during the third weekend in July, bluegrass fans from all over the country turn their attention to the tiny town of Darrington, nestled in the Cascade foothills. Terrific foot-stomping, thigh-slapping bluegrass music is played outdoors by the country's best musicians. A convenient ticket package includes three nights of camping and three days of music: $60 for couples, $35 single. ■ *Darrington, WA; (206) 436-1177.*

Folk Music Festival What better way to international peace and understanding than through the universal language of music? Last year over 200 performers from 12 countries came together for three days. There is a bewildering array of ticket options: the most economical is to form a group of 15 or more to qualify for a discount; a pass for the weekend is about $65. Buy early—admission is limited. ▪ *Jericho Park, Vancouver, BC; (604) 879-2931.*

Fort Vancouver Fourth of July Fireworks The best fireworks in Oregon are across the Columbia River in Washington. Portlanders flock to the National Historic Site of Fort Vancouver for a day of activities and stage entertainment climaxing in the largest free aerial display west of the Mississippi. The bombardment lasts at least a full hour. ▪ *Vancouver, WA; (206) 694-2432.*

Fourth of July Fireworks Seattle's dueling fireworks. Cellular One's version rockets over Lake Union to the sound of the Seattle Symphony at Gas Works Park. Ivar's fireworks explode over Elliott Bay and are best viewed from Myrtle Edwards Park. A lucky few who think to make reservations for a late dinner at the Space Needle can view them both. The pyrotechnics start just after dark. ▪ *Seattle, WA; (206) 587-6500 (Ivar's); (206) 624-5700.*

Harrison Festival of the Arts During this nine-day event, over 35,000 people visit Harrison Hot Springs to celebrate the musical, visual, and performing arts of a different set of countries each year. Theater, lectures, workshops, and live entertainment give visitors many activities from which to choose. ▪ *Harrison Hot Springs, BC; (604) 796-3664.*

King County Fair The oldest county fair in the state is also its best, featuring five days of music by top country acts, a rodeo, 4-H and FFA exhibits, a loggers' show (remember ax-throwing contests?), crafts, and food. Begins the third Wednesday of July. ▪ *King County Fairgrounds, Enumclaw, WA; (206) 825-7777.*

McChord Air Show Come see the F-16s do their thing. Afterward watch military demonstrations—from an all-services attack demo to antique aircraft—and get your picture taken in the cockpit of a jet. In July or August; call for dates. ▪ *McChord Air Force Base, Tacoma, WA; (206) 984-5637.*

Pacific Northwest Scottish Highland Games Kilts are not the only thing you'll find here. Scottish piping, drumming, dancing, Parade of the Clans, and games are the major attractions, not to mention a chance to sample authentic Scottish food and drink. Seven dollars gets you in for the day. ▪ *King County Fairgrounds, Enumclaw, WA; (206) 522-2874.*

Renaissance Fair Local artists display their arts and crafts while the "jousters," knights in shining armor, rescue fair maidens during performances at various times during the day. Food and entertainment, too. ▪ *Riverside Park, Grants Pass, OR; (503) 474-7929.*

San Juan Island Dixieland Jazz Festival A three-day festival, $35 for all three days, sponsored by the San Juan Island Goodtime Classic Jazz Association, brings Dixieland fans out to enjoy the jazz of yesteryear, mid- to late July. ▪ *Friday Harbor, San Juan Island, WA; (206) 378-5509.*

Sand-Sations Sand Castle Contest Hundreds of children and children-at-heart flock to this annual event to build their sand castle masterpieces. With judging in all sorts of categories (teamwork, effort, intricacy, suitability to sand), there are prizes totaling $3,000. At least 10,000 people show up to watch the artists at work. ■ *Long Beach, WA; (206) 642-2400.*

Seafair Seattle's frenzied summer fête has been around since 1950 and—to the chagrin of many locals—isn't likely to go away. The hoopla begins on the third weekend of July with the milk-carton boat races at Green Lake and ends the first Sunday in August, when the hydroplanes tear up the waters of Lake Washington. Bright spots include a couple of triathlons, the Blue Angels air show, some excellent ethnic festivals (Bon Odori, late July; International District Festival, mid-July; Hispanic Seafair Festival, late July), and the Torchlight Parade (the Friday before the hydroplane races), which is a full-scale march in the downtown area and a kids' delight. Practically all Seafair events are free. ■ *Citywide, Seattle, WA; (206) 728-0123.*

Sweet Onion Festival Fort Walla Walla Park celebrates the sweetest onion around with the onion-slicing contest, the two-headed onion shot put, the onion hunt, the onion-dish recipe contest and cook-off, the onion-ring toss, and a weekend full of fun. ■ *Walla Walla, WA; (509) 525-0850.*

Vancouver International Comedy Festival Watch out, *Improv*, Vancouver has a 10-day shindig with international comedians that'll knock your socks off. Roving street entertainers and scheduled shows give you the most diverse forms of comedy. ■ *Granville Island, Vancouver, BC; (604) 683-0883.*

Vancouver Sea Festival This festival has everything from puppet shows and sand castle contests to a whole slew of sports demonstrations and competitions. ■ *English Bay, BC; (604) 684-3378.*

Victoria International Festival Artists from the Northwest gather at various Victoria venues to give classical music concerts, recitals, and ballet performances throughout the months of July and August. Ticket prices top out at $21 per performance. ■ *Victoria, BC; (604) 736-2119.*

Waterfront Blues Festival National blues artists such as Charlie Musselwhite play at this four-day benefit for the Oregon Food Bank. The shows are free, although sponsors accept donations of food and money. A big event: in 1992, 60,000 fans turned out. ■ *McCall Waterfront Park, Portland, OR; (503) 282-0555.*

Winthrop Rhythm and Blues Fest This late-July festival has attracted such national performers as Mick Taylor and John Mayall, as well as the best of the local bands. Now it has been expanded to three days, and events include a New Orleans–style street dance in the Old West streets of Winthrop and a full day of steamy blues under the blazing sun at Twin Lakes. A popular event with the Harley-Davidson crowd. ■ *Winthrop, WA; (509) 996-2111.*

AUGUST

The Bite, A Taste of Portland Eat to your heart's content and help Special Olympics at the same time. Thirty restaurants and 20 wineries offer scores of delectables while performers at different venues entertain you. ■ *McCall Waterfront Park, Portland, OR; (503) 248-0600.*

Camlann Medieval Faire Held on Saturdays and Sundays in late August and early September, this "faire" attracts thousands of people. Dancing, medieval food, performances, and a tournament of knights highlight the event. ■ *Carnation, WA; (206) 788-1353.*

Coombs Country Bluegrass Festival A three-day weekend of gospel, country, and bluegrass. Performers such as Rural Delivery or the Rocky Mountain Boys have been major attractions in the past. Tickets are sold for each day. Rough camping is available on a first come, first served basis. ■ *Coombs, BC; (604) 248-5142.*

Evergreen State Fair For 11 days, late August through Labor Day, the Monroe Fair features country music headliners, roping and riding, stock-car races, a lumberjack show, a carnival, and a chili cook-off. Great fun. ■ *Monroe, WA; (206) 794-7832.*

Filburg Festival A sophisticated arts and crafts show, this festival continues to grow in reputation as one of the region's finest juried shows. Woodwork, glass, pottery, and woven goods are just a few of the things on display. ■ *Comox, BC; (604) 334-3234.*

Fine Arts Show Residents of southern Vancouver Island display their paintings and sculptures in the largest juried art show and sale in BC. A $6 admission is good for the entire 10-day event. ■ *Sooke Region Museum, Sooke, BC; (604) 642-6351.*

Gig Harbor Jazz Festival The grassy natural amphitheater makes a great setting for a festival that draws national jazz artists. Boat owners can sail up to the site. ■ *Celebrations Meadow, Gig Harbor, WA; (206) 627-1504.*

International Airshow/Airshow Canada Want to see a Russian MIG up close or watch wing-walkers defy gravity? How about the aerobatics of the U.S. Thunderbirds and the Canadian Snowbirds? Abbotsford's International Airshow has it all and more. Airshow Canada is a trade show that happens in odd-numbered years. ■ *Abbotsford Airport, BC; (604) 852-8511.*

Mount Hood Festival of Jazz Definitely one of the premier festivals around, this weekend affair has featured such greats as Diane Schuur, Lou Rawls, and the Count Basie Band. Tickets are around $20 a day. ■ *Gresham, OR; (503) 666-3810.*

Omak Stampede and Suicide Run A hair-raising and controversial horse race: horses plunge down a 255-foot hill with a 120-foot vertical drop into the Okanogan River, which they race across to reach the arena (sometimes the horses break their legs). The stampede events last for three days; ticket prices range from $6 to $12. ■ *Stampede Grounds, Omak, WA; (509) 826-1002.*

Oregon State Fair It's everything a fair should be: food, games, rides, horse shows, and live entertainment. For 12 days the people of Salem go hog-wild. Ends on Labor Day. ■ *Salem, OR; (503) 378-3247.*

Seattle International Music Festival Previously known as the Santa Fe Chamber Music Festival, the SIMF (under new artistic director Dmitry Sitkovetsky) has plans to expand the format to include vocal and orchestral music as well as chamber music. The festival is held the last two weeks in August and will be based at University of Washington's Meany Hall and the Seattle Art Museum. ■ *Meany Theater, University of Washington; 622-1392.*

Washington State Games (summer) See February in this chapter. ■ *Call for location, (206) 682-4263.*

Washington State International Kite Festival On the last day of this colorful, high-flying week, the Festival of Kites attempts to break its own record for number of kites in the air. Every day there's a different event, from lighted kites to handcrafted kites to stunt fun and games. The glorious spectacle is free to watch, but flying your own will cost you $20. The entire Long Beach Peninsula is booked by January in anticipation, so plan (way) ahead. ■ *Long Beach; (206) 642-2400.*

Washington State Open Tennis Tournament The top players in Washington and the men's western pro circuit compete side by side during the first week in August at the exclusive Seattle Tennis Club. Tickets range from $1 to $5, and it's worth the admission just to stroll the idyllic grounds. Order tickets in advance. ■ *Seattle Tennis Club, Seattle, WA; (206) 324-3200.*

SEPTEMBER

Artquake Over Labor Day weekend, Portlanders let loose a grand celebration of the performing and fine arts. The Center for the Performing Arts is the hub of the festival, although there are events throughout the downtown area, especially in Pioneer Courthouse Square. There is no admission charge for many Artquake events; others ask a nominal entrance fee. ■ *Center for the Performing Arts and Park Blocks, Portland, OR; (503) 227-2787.*

Bumbershoot The largest multi-arts festival north of San Francisco is a splendid and eclectic celebration. Select craftspeople, writers, and 500 performing artists on 15 stages throughout Seattle Center entertain the hordes over the long Labor Day weekend. A $9 daily pass ($8 if you buy in advance) is all you need to stay thoroughly entertained. ■ *Seattle Center, Seattle, WA; (206) 682-4386.*

Ellensburg Rodeo The biggest rodeo in these parts brings riders in from far and wide for four days of Wild West events over Labor Day weekend. Admission to the big, colorful event is $8 to $15, depending on your seat. ■ *Ellensburg, WA; (509) 962-7831.*

Fall Kite Festival Lincolnites love to fly kites of all shapes and colors, and last year so did over 20,000 people who attended the festivities; these include a lighted show at night and a Japanese-style kite battle, which entails teams of five to 25 people trying to knock each other's kites out of the sky. Prizes are awarded in various categories. ■ *Lincoln City, OR; (800) 452-2151.*

Leavenworth Autumn Leaf Festival The last weekend of September is a grand time for a drive through the Cascade Mountains to Leavenworth, a mountain town gussied-up Tyrolean-style and home of this festival celebrating the glory of our deciduous trees. A parade, arts and crafts, and Bavarian music are all part of the festivities. Most events are free. ■ *Leavenworth, WA; (509) 548-5807.*

Pendleton Round-Up and Happy Canyon This four-day rodeo, complete with cowboys, bucking broncos, bulls, and clowns, is said to be one of the biggest in the country. Over 500 contestants and 50,000 spectators make it so. Admission ranges from $6 to $15. A carnival downtown keeps things hopping while the rodeo riders are recovering. ■ *Pendleton, OR; toll-free (800) 45-RODEO.*

Seattle Seahawks Football Chuck Knox's Seahawks may play conservative ball (and may have seen better seasons than the next few promise to be), but the fans' loyalty is steadfast. Consequently, it's nearly impossible to get tickets ($19 to $35), and Kingdome-area parking is a crunch, so take a free bus from downtown. The season starts in September (preseason games in August) and runs through December; games are usually Sundays at 1pm. Avoid scalpers. ■ *Kingdome, Seattle, WA; (206) 827-9766.*

Vancouver International Film Festival Similar to Seattle's (see May), this event at the end of September/beginning of October features over 150 films from 35 countries. Prices are about $7 per movie. Pick up your tickets at the Ridge Theatre by mid-September. ■ *Vancouver, BC; (604) 685-0260.*

Western Washington State Fair This 17-day extravaganza begins in early September. It's the rural fair you remember from your childhood, only bigger. Rodeo, music, barnyard animals, carnival rides, exhibits, and vast amounts of food (including the legendary scones and onion burgers) make for kid—and grown-up—heaven. ■ *Puyallup, WA; (206) 841-5045.*

OCTOBER

Children's Show A plethora of activities, such as workshops, fashion shows, and entertainment, geared toward kids from toddlers to preteens. A three-day kids' event ($6). ■ *Pacific National Exhibit, Showmart Building, Vancouver, BC; (604) 684-4616.*

International Festival of Films by Women Directors Despite its surge in popularity, this festival has retained its feel of intimacy. Films are shown in small theaters, and the directors usually make appearances for discussion afterward. There's no political agenda to this internationally recognized series, but provocative and challenging films by rising stars and established artists are guaranteed to make you think. ■ *Seattle Art Museum and other locations; (206) 323-4414.*

Issaquah Salmon Days Issaquah celebrates the return of the salmon the first weekend of October with a parade, food, crafts, music, dancing, and displays.

At the State Fish Hatchery you can get excellent views of the chinook and coho thrashing up the ladder. ■ *Issaquah, WA; (206) 392-0661.*

Portland Winterhawks Ice Hockey See tomorrow's NHL players today in the WHL (Western Hockey League). This developmental league grooms young hockey players for the big time (34 former Winterhawks have already made it). The 72-game season runs from October through March, with prices topping out at about $10.50. ■ *Memorial Coliseum, Portland, OR; (503) 238-6366.*

Salmon Festival When the salmon come home to spawn, the people of Gresham celebrate with an annual 8K run, a salmon bake, and arts and crafts. The name of the game here is environmental education. Old-growth and salmon-viewing walks (where you can see the fish spawning in the Sandy River Gorge) are conducted to teach the importance of our natural resources. ■ *Oxbow Park, Gresham, OR; (503) 248-5050.*

Vancouver Canucks Hockey A promising NHL team that is still working on making a name for itself, the Canucks host such teams as the Edmonton Oilers and the Calgary Flames. Season runs from October through April, and tickets are between $25 and $40. ■ *Pacific Coliseum, Vancouver, BC; (604) 280-4400.*

West Coast Oyster Shucking Championship and Seafood Festival On the first full weekend in October, Shelton holds this very serious oyster shucking competition (the winner goes on to compete in nationals) along with a wine-tasting and a seafood cook-off. ■ *Shelton; (206) 426-2021.*

NOVEMBER

Model Railroad Show A slew of different model train setups and clinics on how to make whistles, scenery, and train figures bring out the kid in all of us. Over Thanksgiving Day weekend; $6. ■ *Pacific Science Center, Seattle, WA; (206) 443-2001.*

Portland Trailblazers Basketball The Portland Trailblazers are not the most winning NBA team, but their home games are among the most exciting (and earsplitting). They've sold out every home game for the last 10 years! Tickets range from $10 to $50. ■ *Memorial Coliseum, Portland, OR; (503) 224-4400.*

Rainy Day Film Festival For eight years now, the folks at the museum have been showing films on the second Sunday of the month from November through April. Themes in the past have been nature and history, and featured artists have included Buster Keaton and Alfred Hitchcock. $3.50 per family. ■ *Douglas County Museum, Roseburg, OR; (503) 440-4507.*

Seattle SuperSonics Basketball From early November to late April, Seattle's home team tears up the court. In the past, the Sonics have played smart, competitive, and uneven basketball; they have a bright future, so grab tickets early ($7 to $42). Games are at 7pm. ■ *Seattle Center Coliseum, Seattle, WA; (206) 281-5850.*

Christmas Lighting Crafts, music, and food are part of the ceremony kicking off the Christmas season. Around 4:45pm (usually on the first and second Saturdays of the month) the Bavarian village square is officially lit up for the season. Evening concerts and sleigh rides are the only things that require money. ■ *Leavenworth, WA; (509) 548-5807.*

Community Hanukkah Celebration The arts and crafts, Hanukkah wares, games for children, and latke brunch are just the side attractions. The most significant thing about this event is the numbers—that is, the thousand or so people who come every year to the largest community Hanukkah celebration around. Everyone is welcome to take part in the *haimishe* (friendly) feeling the area's Jewish community creates when it gathers together for its Festival of Lights. You'll also find a vast selection of books on all aspects of Jewish life. The symbolic candle-lighting is quite moving. ■ *Stroum Jewish Community Center, 3801 E Mercer Way, Mercer Island, WA; (206) 232-7115.*

Eagle Watching (Qualicum Beach) Bald eagles converge on these rivers from December through February. The scavengers are best seen before noon, when they're hunting spawning salmon. Bring binoculars and wear rain gear. ■ *Big and Little Qualicum rivers near Nanaimo, BC; (604) 752-9532.*

Whale Watch Week For one week after Christmas (and then again in March), volunteers from the Science Center in Newport teach interested folks how to watch for gray whales and report their sightings from various stations along the coast. Volunteers assist approximately 11,000 people from all over the world. ■ *Newport, OR; (503) 867-0100.*

Index

Did you enjoy this book?

Sasquatch Books publishes high-quality books and guides related to the Pacific Northwest. Our books are available at bookstores and other retail outlets throughout the region. Here is a partial list of our current titles:

TRAVEL

Northern California Best Places
Restaurants, Lodgings, and Touring
Laura Hagar and Stephanie Irving

Seattle Best Places
A Discriminating Guide to Seattle's Restaurants, Lodgings, Shopping, Nightlife, Arts, Sights, and Outings
Stephanie Irving

Portland Best Places
A Discriminating Guide to Portland's Restaurants, Lodgings, Shopping, Nightlife, Arts, Sights, Outings, and Annual Events
Kim Carlson and Stephanie Irving

Northwest Cheap Sleeps
Lodgings for Under $50 and Hundreds of Travel Ideas for the Adventurous Road-Tripper in OR, WA, and B.C.
Stephanie Irving

Seattle Cheap Eats
300 Terrific Bargain Eateries
Kathryn Robinson and Stephanie Irving

Seattle Survival Guide
The Essential Handbook for City Living
Theresa Morrow

Back Roads of Washington
74 Trips on Washington's Scenic Byways
Earl Thollander

Back Roads of Oregon
82 Trips on Oregon's Scenic Byways
Earl Thollander

Atomic Marbles & Branding Irons
A Guide to Museums, Collections, and Roadside Curiosities in Washington and Oregon
Harriet Baskas and Adam Woog

REGIONAL INTEREST

Sexless Oysters and Self-Tipping Hats
100 Years of Invention in the Pacific Northwest
Adam Woog

West Coast Workboats
An Illustrated Guide to Work Vessels from Bristol Bay to San Diego
Archie Satterfield

Washington Homes
Buying, Selling, and Investing in Seattle and Statewide Real Estate
Jim Stacey

Mount St. Helens
The Eruption and Recovery of a Volcano
Rob Carson

FOOD AND COOKING

Pike Place Market Cookbook
Recipes, Anecdotes, and Personalities from Seattle's Renowned Public Market
Braiden Rex-Johnson

The Good Food Guide to Washington and Oregon
Discover the Finest, Freshest Foods Grown and Harvested in the Northwest
Edited by Lane Morgan

FIELD GUIDES

Field Guide to the Bald Eagle

Field Guide to the Gray Whale

Field Guide to the Grizzly Bear

Field Guide to the Humpback Whale

Field Guide to the Orca

Field Guide to the Pacific Salmon

Field Guide to the Sasquatch

For a complete catalog of Sasquatch books, or to inquire about ordering our books by phone or mail, please contact us at the address below.

SASQUATCH BOOKS
1008 Western Avenue, Suite 300 • Seattle, WA 98104
(206) 467-4300

Northwest Best Places
REPORT FORM

Based on my personal experience, I wish to nominate/confirm/disapprove for listing the following restaurant or place of lodging:

_____

_____

_____

_____

_____

(Please include address and telephone number of establishment, if convenient.)

REPORT:

(Please describe food, service, style, comfort, value, date of visit, and other aspects of your visit; continue on overleaf if necessary.)

_____

_____

_____

_____

_____

_____

_____

I am not concerned, directly or indirectly, with the management or ownership of this establishment.

Signed _____

Address _____

_____

Phone Number _____

Date _____

Send to: *Northwest Best Places*
1008 Western Avenue, Suite 300
Seattle, WA 98104

We Stand by Our Reviews

Sasquatch Books is proud of *Northwest Best Places*. Our editors and contributors take great pain and expense to see that all of the reviews are as accurate, up-to-date, and honest as possible. If we have misled you, please accept our apologies; however, if the 10th edition of *Northwest Best Places* has seriously disappointed you, Sasquatch Books would like to refund your purchase price. To receive your refund:

1) Tell us where you purchased your book and return the book to: Satisfaction Guaranteed, Sasquatch Books, 1008 Western Avenue, Suite 300, Seattle, WA 98104

2) Enclose the original receipt from the establishment in question, including date of visit.

3) Write a full explanation of your stay or meal and how *Northwest Best Places* misled you.

4) Include your name, address, and phone number.

Refund is only valid while the 1994–1995 edition of *Northwest Best Places* is in print. If the ownership has changed since publication, Sasquatch Books cannot be held responsible. Postage on the returned book is your responsibility. Please allow four weeks for processing.